Persuasion

Reception and Responsibility

TWELFTH EDITION

Persuasion

Reception and Responsibility

TWELFTH EDITION

CHARLES U. LARSON
Northern Illinois University, Emeritus

Australia • Brazil • Japan • Korea • Mexico • Singapore • Spain • United Kingdom • United States

WADSWORTH
CENGAGE Learning

Persuasion: Reception and Responsibility, Twelfth Edition

Charles U. Larson

Senior Publisher: Lyn Uhl

Executive Editor: Monica Eckman

Development Editor: Larry Goldberg

Assistant Editor: Kim Gengler

Editorial Assistant: Colin Solan

Media Editor: Jessica Badiner

Marketing Manager: Erin Mitchell

Marketing Communications Manager: Christine Dobberpuhl

Project Manager, Editorial Production: Michael Lepera

Art Director: Linda Helcher

Print Buyer: Betsy Donaghey

Permissions Editor: Bob Kauser

Production Service/Compositor: Integra Software Services Pvt. Ltd

Photo Manager: Dean Dauphinais

Photo Researchers: Martha Hall, Catherine Schnurr, Pre-PressPMG

Cover Designer: Rokusek Design

Cover Image: ©Shutterstock

For product information and technology assistance, contact us at **Cengage Learning Academic Resource Center, 1-800-423-0563**

For permission to use material from this text or product, submit all requests online at **www.cengage.com/permissions**.

Further permissions questions can be e-mailed to **permissionrequest@cengage.com**.

Library of Congress Control Number: 2008939488

ISBN-13: 978-0-495-56750-9

ISBN-10: 0-495-56750-7

Wadsworth
20 Channel Center Street
Boston, MA 02210
USA

Cengage Learning products are represented in Canada by Nelson Education, Ltd.

For your course and learning solutions, visit **www.cengage.com**.

Purchase any of our products at your local college store or at our preferred online store **www.ichapters.com**.

Printed in United States of America
2 3 4 5 6 7 12 11 10

For Mary, Without Whom...

Brief Contents

Contents

✳

Preface

My first persuasion teaching assignment was to a class of 50 college juniors and seniors back in 1968. They were expecting to have to give a series of persuasive speeches as had been done in semesters and years past. I simply felt that I couldn't assign persuasive speeches to such a large class. In the first place, it would have taken too long, and each of them would have gotten only a few opportunities to speak. Besides how many of us, I wondered, are asked to give a persuasive speech and how often? It seemed to me that as fast as the worlds of politics, government, media, and popular culture were changing that the persuasion most students would confront was not their own in a public speech but as receivers and from usually powerful others. They would spend far more time watching and listening to persuasion aimed at them and their fellow audience members. So instead of assigning a half dozen persuasive speeches and then having all 50 students listen to all 300 speeches, I decided that I would teach the course from the **perspective of the receiver**, the consumer of persuasion who was faced with thousands of persuasive appeals every day—some of which seemed benign, some even silly or fallacious, but others were malignant. At the time, many persuasive messages distorted or invented "facts," used fallacious reasoning, and paid little heed to ethics, and my students had never even considered such matters.

Finding an appropriate textbook to use in this course was my major teaching problem. Everything on the market at the time focused on training the producers of persuasion—public speakers of persuasion.

So I decided to write a book specifically for consumers in 1973. The result was the first edition of *Persuasion: Reception and Responsibility*. With the help of my friend and colleague Dick Johannesen and my editor, Becky Hayden, we discovered that there was a huge need among teachers of persuasion for a book aimed at the **consumption of persuasion**, and who felt the same as I did about when, how often, and with what consequences our students faced the confusing world of persuasion. During the first convention at which the book was displayed, the *New York Times* declared it "a runaway hit."

And what a history this book has seen since then. It has been a best seller since its earliest days and is now widely adopted around the country as well as internationally. And it was a wise decision to go "receiver-oriented" if you consider the enormity of just a few events that have happened since the book's inception—all of which had enormous impact on receivers of persuasion— much more than it did on producers of persuasion. In fact, when looking at the persuaders of yesteryear, it seems that they haven't grown very much in comparison to the receivers of persuasion. They seem to try the same time-worn strategies and tactics while their receivers have become increasingly skilled and skeptical. Consider just a few examples of the "then and now."

In 1973, cable television was just something most persons were "thinking of adopting" and not for the new programming available on it, but for better reception it promised. Now we have hundreds of channels—back then we had perhaps five if you counted educational programming. Aside from newspapers and magazines, there were only a few places where persuasion and propaganda could touch us. Today we have that many all-news channels alone. Now we have multiple all-talk television and radio demagogues who aren't a bit afraid of distorting the truth. Back then, AIDS was practically unknown, but since then it has infected and killed millions, and we still don't have a cure for a disease that could wipe out the populations of entire countries if not continents. Major fears were of being attacked by the Soviet Union with nuclear weapons, the seemingly unstoppable increasing power and abuse in government by the executive branch, and a rising discontent especially among the Muslim populations of the Middle East. Amazing isn't it that today we still remain fearful of what those weapons might do, but now in different hands, and we wonder about what that dissatisfaction and discontent in the Middle East might lead to. And since then we have seen what horrendous damage that kind of discontent can and did do if even on a "comparably limited scale." But now we also wonder and are fearful that certain unpredictable and smaller nations such as North Korea and Iran may soon obtain these weapons of mass destruction. Or worse yet, we fear what might happen if such weapons got into the hands of the discontented terrorist groups and cells around the world. In fact, fear of those weapons and those unpredictable potential enemies are precisely part of what got us stuck in that seemingly endless "Tar Baby" of a war in Iraq.

Ethics seemed to have gone out of style only to have recently restaged a remarkable comeback with deep-seated concerns in the arenas of politics, religion, international affairs, and other venues. We have been bamboozled into a wasteful and costly war, permitted our government to illegally spy on us, and allowed them to deal with us in many other questionable (and perhaps even unethical) ways. We have also seen what unethical lending practices have done to create crises in housing and credit. In 1973 it was unusual for students to qualify for a local checking account; today, just for the asking, they get a t-shirt and a credit card with a license to spend thousands. With the return in importance of ethical considerations in government, commerce, and everyday life, there has been an increasing level of doubt in the overall mass audience that is so essential in a democracy. This doubt extends to all types of persuasion—political, economic, religious, interpersonal, and international. Receivers no longer believe persuaders with the same level of naiveté they once did. And this makes the importance of training in responsible reception of persuasion even more essential. If each of us can feel that we are being more critical, more discerning, and more careful in processing the persuasion aimed at us, we can also be more open to the kinds of useful and beneficial persuasion that is essential to democratic institutions and to good government. So training in the responsible reception of persuasion seems more important than ever.

Other changes may have derailed us slightly as well. Once the Soviet Union dissolved, critics advised us and our editors to totally drop our chapter on propaganda, whose advice we heeded. It did seem like such an outdated concept that was only limited to wartime situations, and after the end of the Cold War in the early 1990s, it just seemed like extra baggage. But look what has happened in the few intervening decades. Beginning with 9/11 and even earlier, and becoming crystal clear with the advent of the war in Iraq that followed, suddenly propaganda seemed to be relevant again and emerging from almost every crook and cranny and in new and more sophisticated and frightening ways.

Additionally, today we are facing new and more complex problems that can mislead us and deter us from finding solutions to them, such as global warming, the aforementioned energy and credit crises, increasing suspicion and prejudice, fears about the global economy, and so forth. The problems actually were there all along, but critical receivers weren't paying much attention to them, and in many ways, like Topsy, they simply grew unnoticed. Taken together, these and other problems yet to be seen may deal a stunning blow to that global economy on which we all now depend and could send it into we know not what. You can be sure that propaganda will be present at every turn. All in all, the changes that have occurred across the years, those occurring more recently, and those yet to come make critical receivers more important to our way of life than ever.

The new millennium will also be one in which information is increasingly becoming the true source of influence. Those who control it will make the important decisions, probably in a world in which new nations will become as powerful or even more powerful than the United States and as a result will emerge as tomorrow's world opinion leaders. This will no longer be "The American Century" like the twentieth century. New leadership and power are emerging. For example, China and India have developed recently and amazingly quickly as contemporary modern states with powerful economies that were thought of as backward and nearly irrelevant not long ago. And "Old Europe" almost seems irrelevant to world affairs. Further, the dissatisfaction in the Muslim world could blossom into a worldwide mass movement. As a result of these and other problems which we face, we are returning to place heavy emphasis on the presence and changing face of propaganda in this edition. However, instead of referring to it in a chapter-length discussion going back to the beginnings of the twentieth century when modern propaganda emerged, as we did in earlier editions, we have employed our consideration of it in a series of student experiences woven throughout the 14 chapters of the book. Each of these will hopefully lead students to new experiences and insights into propaganda we are likely to face in

the near future. These experiences are highlighted in **propaganda boxes** in
each chapter and will be identified with a propaganda logo that looks
like this. When you see this logo, be alert that it has something to do
with propaganda and its tactics—first discussed in Chapters 1 and 2 and
later elsewhere. Using those discussions, analyze the examples in these
boxes and then consider the principles or patterns you discover in them later in
relation to uses of persuasive language, strategies, and tactics, especially in politics, ideology, government, campaigns, mass media, and advertising/marketing.

In terms of transformations in technology and how they have affected and
altered not only persuaders and persuadees, but the overall process of persuasion as well, the picture is very similar as we review past editions. One can
hardly keep up with the coming change, blasting at and past use with almost
numbing speed. Yes, "Persuasion Rocks!" and that rocking is starting to affect
our entire culture in ways we could never have predicted just a few years ago.
We now face a technological world in which not only is the process of receiving persuasion critically important, but also one in which the shoe has switched
to the other foot. We now need to learn to be responsible persuaders as well as
responsible receivers of persuasion, for in the new blogosphere, we all have the
potential to become influential persuaders who affect others through a variety
of technologies—e-mail, blogging, e-commerce, and as sources of persuasion
in a variety of other ways.

Technology especially has changed how we deal with language, and remember that in today's world of persuasion, only about two thirds of us are
literate enough to read menus, street signs, or simple directions, let alone newspapers, magazines, and books. This diversity makes it difficult to get a true random sample of public opinion from a survey or poll since up to one third of
respondents may not understand or be able to read the items. This also means
that one third of the population is extraordinarily vulnerable to the persuasion
they can only see and hear—technological and nonlinguistic forms. They—your
fellow citizenry—no longer depend on the written (and verifiable) word, as we
shall see, but on the technological "word" that you don't even have to learn to
translate. They won't be reading newspapers, magazines, or books. They will be
simply processing "screens" of information that may or may not be ethical, fac-
tual, or unbiased. Without responsible receivers to advise them or to lead them,
where will it all end? So remember that one third of your fellow citizenry probably won't be able to express their views either. They are likely to be the victims of history unless responsible receivers are able to educate them on the issues
of the day.

With the personal computer now as familiar to students as pencils were in
the classrooms of the past, those fellow citizens will be victims of nonverbal
signals, not words. Theirs will be a "point and click" world of persuasion.
And changes in terms of video resources have been improved and updated in
equally astounding and awesome ways. During the first few editions of the
book, instructors using it often relied heavily on references to ads, speeches,
discussions, political events, and other programming that they themselves had

videotaped—few commercial recordings were even available to be used as supplementary resources.

Now, of course, we all refer to and use DVDs, which have become equally more sophisticated and plentiful. They too might be the carriers of dangerous propaganda to that illiterate one third of the population who can rent them at will. And we have been referring to and using the Internet for decades now. Many of that one third will only be able to push the forward and backward arrows and to carefully, letter by letter, navigate to a Web site or more likely simply get there by clicking on a simple (perhaps propagandistic or misleading) image. There they may well meet clever, entertaining, and convincing persuaders. New terms that entered our vocabularies in recent editions play a part too. Imagine the persuasion that could be or is being sent or texted by cell phone, webcasts, blogs, podcasts, BlackBerry, e-mail, and the as yet infant worlds of digital video and audio, iPods, satellite radio, and many others. Let the receiver beware!

INSTRUCTIONAL FEATURES OF THIS EDITION

All these issues, problems, threats, changes, and trends, as well as others yet to come, have affected and will continue to affect recent and future persuasion. As a result, the need for critical consumers to be trained will continue more than ever. They must be prepared to use the **analytical tools** of this and previous editions to *deconstruct the persuasion blitz* we are now facing. The future persuasion and propaganda efforts are likely to be greater than ever. In the years since that first edition, my colleagues and students have helped me revise and update the book, pointing out issues, media, and technologies that needed to be addressed. And they have continued to enlighten me in the preparation of this twelfth edition of *Persuasion: Reception and Responsibility*. With their help we have included *many new learning tools* for both students and teachers alike such as the inclusion of **boldfaced key terms** in each chapter that can serve as signposts of your duties as responsible and critical receivers. (These key terms or concepts are also listed at the end of each chapter for easy reference.) Other instructional terms or those which relate to the organizational "lens" of the book—the Seven Faces of Persuasion—are *italicized*.

Probably the most major change in this edition is that, throughout the chapters, we return time and time again to what we call the **Seven Faces of Persuasion.** You will first hear of them in Chapter , and they will continue to ring out in the 13 chapters that follow. They are the touchstones of persuasion that we now face and that we are likely to face down the road. These are things that, while they may have been in existence while we prepared the eleventh and previous editions, did not seem to impact us as directly as they do today. These "faces" include the fact that we now face persuasion in a *24/7 networked world,* an *ethnically challenged world,* and a *media-saturated world* with no one able to process it all.

Additionally, other faces indicate that it is a *world of advocacy and propaganda*, a world that is *multicultural and diverse* and hence *prone to misunderstandings*, and a *deceptive world filled with scams* (like identify theft). It is also a world loaded with *doublespeak* and a *results-oriented world* looking only at the *bottom line*. These are all frightening thoughts, which is why we have also continued to include an **Application of Ethics** exercise at the end of each chapter to help train students to pay increasing attention to this topic in the future since *ethical issues* seem to be emerging more rapidly with each passing year. This requires that receivers *maintain increasing awareness* of ethical problems and prospects.

Also included are the new and sometimes interactive **propaganda boxes** that will help reacquaint both students and instructors with this growing pattern of propaganda mixed with advocacy in the world of the Seven Faces of Persuasion. We have also continued to insert **diversity boxes** to remind all of us how our culture is changing with the addition of many new ethnic groups, differing sexual preferences, religions, and so on, and the recognition of new life-styles and value systems. And with the increasing growth of media in which the

 receiver ceases to be a mere passive recipient of messages, we have also included **interactive media boxes** (identified by the logo shown) which will help both students and instructors to see these interactive innovations in a new light. (In addition, all boxes on any topic involving a Web search are identified by this logo.) Early evidence shows that by having receivers interact with the media via which they receive persuasive advocacy or propaganda actually increases the strength of the messages—be the messages ethical or unethical.

This edition also continues to provide the successful features of earlier editions—**updated examples** from the worlds of politics, economics, advertising, propaganda, ideology, and the Internet, as well as new reports on **recent theoretical developments**. Additionally, three critical developments have occurred that I believe will affect the world of persuasion enormously in just the next few years. These and other new developments and their implications have been woven throughout the 14 chapters. What are these developments? First, as noted above, our culture is becoming increasingly diverse and varied in terms of ethnicity, race, religion, sexual preference, education, and many other areas that have direct implications for the practice and teaching of persuasion from both the producer's and the consumer's perspective. Throughout this edition you will find **numerous examples, exercises, and explorations** into the implications of our increasingly diverse culture now and in the future.

As mentioned, our world has become astonishingly interactive, especially in terms of **new media**, and the newly diverse citizens are all able to use these media. The hundreds of new ways we have discovered to interact with one another also make each of us a journalist, editor, opinion expert, and artist; and each of us potentially has a huge audience for our persuasion if we do it well. So we must learn to be **interactively responsible and ethical** here as well. At the same time, new forms of interactivity have opened scores of new ways to appeal to us as consumers of persuasion. Some claim that we live in a "media

," but it is more accurate to say that we live in an **interactive age** where the old one-way, "hypodermic" model of persuasion is defunct.

Again, the book includes examples, recent theoretical developments, and exercises involving the **interactive media** in our lives and how they have and will continue to change the face of persuasion—especially for receivers or consumers of this essential form of human communication. These changes are also seen in our culture as it is facing a crisis in ethics. We saw the front edge of this crisis in the many recent corporate scandals and have witnessed an explosion of ethical lapses in all areas of our lives, including religion, politics, government, journalism, business practices, personal relations, the executive branch of government, and even foreign policy like the intentionally misleading information that led to our disastrous war in Iraq.

To address this crisis in ethics, Chapter 2 has been heavily revised and updated, and an **Application of Ethics** exercise or case study is now featured at the end of each chapter for individual or group exploration. In addition, ethical challenges and questions are raised throughout the text. Use all these features to test your understanding of each chapter, and to help students manage their roles as consumers of persuasion and understand their responsibilities as constant receivers of a myriad of messages.

ACKNOWLEDGMENTS

This edition would not have happened without the help of my colleagues and students at Northern Illinois—especially Richard L. Johannesen, who revised Chapter 2, and Joseph N. Scudder, who revised Chapters 3 and 4. Thanks also to the staff at Cengage Learning, beginning with Monica Eckman, executive editor; Larry Goldberg, development editor; Michael Lepera, senior content project manager; the many folks in the permissions, production, and marketing departments; and those colleagues who reviewed this edition and made wonderful suggestions. They were Richard Berleth, St. Francis College; Steve Depoe, University of Cincinnati; Randy Duncan, Henderson State University; Thomas N. Gardner, Westfield State College; Alex Wang, University of Connecticut; Valerie A. Goff Whitecap, University of Pittsburgh; and Lara Zwarun, University of Texas at Arlington.

And finally, I offer special thanks to the students and teachers who will use and hopefully profit from adopting, reading, and discussing the twelfth edition of *Persuasion: Reception and Responsibility*.

Charles U. Larson

PART I

✳

Theoretical Premises

Persuasion rocks. It rocks not only our individual worlds but the whole world around us. We carry it with us everyday to use as either the audience or receivers of persuasive messages or as the authors or sources of them. Persuasive devices hang on our belts or are stored in pockets, purses, and backpacks such as cell phones that are equipped with cameras, texting options, the means to listen to and/or view persuasion on the internet, and so on, or are available to us via mass media, the Internet and other interactive devices. Persuasion is disseminated not only by mass media like television, radio, and news publications but in more personal media like blogs authored by us or others, direct marketing appeals sent to us in the mail, e-mail, chat groups, and highly targeted appeals that surround us in our interactive media world. Persuasion both changes that world and re-presents ways that the same world changes us.

Persuasion is about choice. Thus, understanding persuasion better will help us make better choices and is essential to live in our ever-changing world where having to choose among alternatives, trivial and essential, is a constant. It is clear that persuasion can make the world a better place just as persuaders throughout history used it to make society a better place, but the phenomenon doesn't end there—there is a darker side. Persuasion can be used for much good and much evil.

We live in a period of human reconstruction in the United States and around the world—personally, interactively, locally, and globally. We face a different kind of enemy in the reality of the terrorist or the religious zealot—and theirs is a different kind of *influence* than we have previously considered very seriously in this country. Persuasion is also much larger than the United States or even the Western world—today persuasion is global. Perhaps, in the modern world, the more difficult task of societal reconstruction remains the restoration

1

of trust in our major institutions. How can we trust business leaders whose representatives used persuasion to cover up years of corporate deceit that ultimately cost employees their jobs and retirement funds and investors their fortunes? How do we trust religious figures when we learn of repeated revelations of sexual improprieties by priests, ministers, and others? How do we possibly trust political leaders when they have purposely led us into enormously costly and seemingly endless conflicts in Iraq and elsewhere in the world using falsified evidence, quarantining critical news reporting, obscuring or even hiding both sides of an issue, and using tainted testimony to serve personal goals or beliefs?

Another challenge to our understanding of persuasion involves the introduction and rapid adoption of new, high-impact technologies and interactive ones such as personal computers, the Internet, cell phones, texting, blogging, pod-casting, and the digitization of many older technologies like film and photography, both of which can now be easily distorted (even by the average user) for persuasive purposes. And we have the ongoing development of virtual realities of all sorts which allow us to experience, use, and manipulate many things never before possible, thus adding a whole new dimension to the persuasive process—artificial experience acting as the real thing and thus equaling evidence for making important decisions. Also, easy and instant global communication affects us as never before. Traditional ways of doing business, conducting national and international politics, business and religion, interacting with others, adopting popular culture, all face obsolescence with the globalization of virtually every aspect of human endeavor.

Underlying all of this change, however, is a constant. It is the overwhelming presence and enormous impact of persuasion as the most ubiqui-

tous of the many forms of personal influence. In fact, persuasion is now the great common denominator in the arenas of economics, politics, religion, business, and interpersonal relations. And today, persuasion has unprecedented potential as a tool for affecting our daily lives, as a means to many ends—both good and bad—and as a presence in every moment of our waking lives. The world we face rests on the power of persuasion.

We need to approach this profusion of persuasion in our everyday lives with an awareness that, at its core, persuasion is a *symbolic* act for both persuaders and receivers. We use symbols—usually words or images—in commercial interactions, interpersonal relations, family life, political endeavors, and international relations. Persuasion basically represents a democratic and humanistic attempt to influence others, instead of enslaving them. We want to convince them to take certain actions like purchasing, voting, or cooperating with one another—instead of forcing or coercing them to do so. For the most part, persuasion uses either logical or emotional means or a combination of both of them instead of force to accomplish desired ends. This logical or emotional persuasion seeks to give us "good reasons" for acting; and these good reasons are usually delivered to "receivers" via an appropriate medium, whether "one-to-one" interpersonal communication or "one-to-many" forms of communication, such as contemporary mass media. And the "good reasons" must be acceptable in terms of the norms and values of the target culture and society, be it local, national, or global. In my town, a company that slaughtered cattle for shipment to Europe to be used for human consumption, was protested against in many ways and at many times for engaging in cruelty to animals. They argued that these cattle were going to be destroyed anyway by euthanasia or abandonment and that their business made sense, especially since no American consumers of the meat were involved. Furthermore, the meat would otherwise go to waste, whereas European consumers favored it. The target culture's (American consumers) norms and values did not accept these "good reasons" and ultimately the company had to go out of business.

As you read this book, we hope that you change in important ways. We live in a world in which persuasive messages of various types continually compete for our attention, our beliefs, and our actions. Ironically, the exciting yet treacherous times in which we live depend heavily on successful persuasion for us as persuadees in our decision making. We spend far more time receiving persuasion and responding to persuasion than we usually do in sending it. We are predominantly in the role of the receiver, audience, or consumer of persuasive messages, though with the Internet the balance is shifting to sending in some ways. So the aim of this book and class is to make you a more critical and responsible consumer of persuasion while also alerting you to your role as an author or source of persuasive appeals.

In some ways, you are already a critical receiver, but you can improve your reception skills. You need to identify how critical a receiver you are at the outset. How easily are you persuaded? How does persuasion work on you? What tactics are most effective with you? With others? Which are least effective? How gullible are you? And most importantly what are the *ethical dimensions of the persuasion* we receive and that which we initiate. Is it ethical to cyber-bully someone by creating a false or pseudo Web site or damaging message about them just because we believe in free speech? Is it ethical for leaders to fabricate evidence to favor some issues simply because they believe their philosophy of government is right? Is it ethical to lie to save the

corporation and the jobs of its employees? Is it ethical to text the answers on an exam to a friend in the class or to photograph the exam with your cell phone camera so it can become part of fraternity test files?

Part I investigates these kinds of questions and others as it attempts to establish an ethically focused perspective for the persuasion you receive and initiate by examining some of the theories about persuasion and its primary tool—language—while keeping the question of ethics foremost in our minds. We begin by examining what we call **"The Seven Faces of Persuasion"** or seven characteristics of our contemporary interactive media world and how each impacts the process of persuasion in critical ways. These "faces" or characteristics will emerge and re-emerge in all the chapters that follow in one way or another. To assist you on your journey, you will find several instructional tools throughout all three parts of this book to help you understand the concepts, theories, real world applications, and ethical dimensions we will consider. First, a list of **Learning Goals** precedes each chapter. Second, you will find a list of **Key Terms** at the end of each chapter. To be a successful student of persuasion, you should be able to achieve the learning goals and identify and explain the key terms. To keep our eyes on the ethical issues hinted at in the preceding paragraphs, the book also has an interactive **Application of Ethics** exercise at the end of each chapter that you can role play either individually or as a class. Each chapter also contains one or more interactive boxes that direct you to become more aware of the increasing **cultural diversity** we face and the impact of the **interactive media** explosion we are facing. In fact, we have made certain to devote an informative "box" in each chapter devoted to these two topics—cultural diversity and interactive media—as well as at least one "box" devoted to **propaganda**, a kind of persuasion that has re-emerged powerfully since the terrorist attacks on 9/11/01 and with the "war on terrorism," which ultimately led our country into physical wars in both Iraq and Afghanistan with talk of carrying armed might into a confrontation in Iran. Look for these boxes and follow up on the sources they provide—they are important in training you to be a responsible receiver.

In Chapter 1, we examine how the Seven Faces of Persuasion dominate our lives and what persuasion, as a result, actually is—that, is how it differs from other forms of influence. Then we look at several definitions of persuasion with brief views of the kinds of theory they imply. These definitions and theories range from those rooted in ancient Greece to those derived from our contemporary diverse and interactivity-mediated world. Our discussion also focuses on a useful and easily applied model or tool for analysis of persuasion suggested by Hugh Rank, a scholar of persuasion, advertising, and propaganda, that grew out of his work with the National Council of Teachers of English (NCTE) and their concerns with the increase in "doublespeak"—the attempt to use words to confuse, mislead, and to miscommunicate. Here we will see the how "Seven Faces of Persuasion" can be identified at work in the real world.

In Chapter 2, Richard L. Johannesen discusses a variety of approaches to the ethical issues that arise whenever and wherever persuasion occurs—in the mass media, in interpersonal communication face-to-face, in propaganda, in interactive media, in blogs, in virtuality and a myriad other places. Keep in mind that these approaches and issues involve both persuaders and persuadees—senders and receivers.

In Joe Scudder's Chapter 3, we explore the traditional humanist (sometimes called "rhetorical") roots of persuasion. It is remarkable how many of the principles articulated long ago remain as good practice today and how they also change and are adapted. We also see the importance of understanding how persuasion is grounded in human experience and society even though that grounding may have existed long before mass media let alone before interactive and virtual media came on the scene. Scudder's Chapter 4 focuses on more contemporary or "social science" methods and theories of persuasion and what they have revealed to us about it. These more frequently do take into account the "Seven Faces of Persuasion" as well as the development of mass media, and only recently how they have begun to touch on changes happening around us—interactive media, the Internet, virtual reality, iPods, and blogging to name a few.

In Chapters 5 and 6, we examine human symbolic behavior, especially as it occurs in language—verbal and visual—which despite the many technological advances cited above, remains the primary symbolic raw material of persuasion. These theories also begin to look at the use of the critical characteristics of the seven faces of persuasion. Chapter 6 offers several alternative ways or tools receivers can use to analyze, interpret, decode, and critique persuasive language and imagery—verbal and visual. It is not important that you find one theory or approach that you prefer, but rather that you consider the most useful or insightful among the various alternatives presented here and elsewhere.

1

⁜

Persuasion in Today's Changing World

LEARNING GOALS

After reading this chapter, you should be able to:

1. Identify and explain "The Seven Faces of Persuasion" and point out examples.

2. Identify several definitions of persuasion (including the one used here) that have emerged across time and briefly explain the theoretical implications of each.

3. Identify, explain, and use the Internet and several interactive media.

4. Identify and explain instances of doublespeak, deception, and scamming in contemporary mass and interactive persuasion.

5. Recognize our increasing cultural diversity and make attempts to interact with persons who are culturally different from you.

6. Define advocacy and propaganda and give current examples of it in use in current events and issues.

7. Explain common ground and how it operates in interpersonal, public, mediated, and interactive media and understand how you use it in your varied persuasive encounters with others.

8. Explain the SMCR and ELM models of communication and their dynamics.

9. Identify persuasive messages that are processed in the central and peripheral information-processing channels.

10. Identify instances of Rank's intensifying and down playing strategies in persuasion targeted at you.

11. Develop your abilities to engage in self-protection using the Rank model.

We are engulfed in a sea of information. There is much more than we can ever hope to process let alone put to use in being persuaded or in persuading others. Much of it is useless, and we can safely ignore it, but the problem is that some of it is essential for our personal, national, and global existence. For example, it is probably critical that we understand the problems and promises of emerging hydrogen energy technology. We need to know the details in order to estimate global warming, the remaining supplies of other fuels, and the international political and economic implications. This essential information should influence us to make wise, rational, and educated decisions—some easy and some difficult. Several factors that can and do influence us are the environment, our social and cultural mores, interpersonal relations, persuasion, our access and ability to use the media of modern times, and other factors and/or people. Our focus here is on how persuasion as the central form of influence in our lives is used to prompt us to vote, to purchase, to believe, and to take action. We also live in the age of electronic and interactive media. Mass media have been with us for a long time—at least since the printing press—but in a highly media-rich and changing technological culture, persuasion gains new power. Consider but a few new media already noted that play important roles in our lives. How many hours of your days are devoted to sending and/or receiving communication via the Internet, cell phones, texting, camera or video phones, iPods, e-mail, pod-casting, blogs, virtual worlds and many others. All these make it easier for us as individuals to influence others by having our say for a change. For instance, enter the words "News Blogs" into a search engine and browse for a while. You will begin to realize how much, and how important you are as both a sender and a receiver of persuasive communication. A soldier fighting a war in a foreign land e-mails his family and friends or blogs about his experiences and what is *really* happening on a battle ground and his or her reality can spawn a mass movement to end the war or at least cause us to doubt our government's sanitized version. Or a person who witnessed an armed robbery describes the experience in her blog; thus, an ordinary person, becomes a "news reporter" in exciting and individual ways, and we receivers are faced with ethical decisions about how to behave in a similar situation, what to believe and pass on, how to determine how reliable she may be as an eyewitness, whether our biases regarding eye witness reports should enter in to our evaluation of the trial of the thief, and so on. All of these examples reflect in some way or another one or more of the **Seven Faces of Persuasion**. These "Faces" characterize the factors and processes involved in persuasion that are central to life in the twenty-first century, and each one can impact the numerous persuasive messages we encounter each day.

Another theme we'll also pursue throughout this book is the degree to which new **interactive media** (i.e., media in which the receiver is able to actively participate in the communication process) influence us (see Box 1.1). We have always had some of these like letters to the editor or public forums, direct marketing appeals, and more recently radio, television, or Internet "talk shows," all of which can persuade the public at large and individuals in particular. Recently, interactivity in media has ballooned and multiplied. As you probably know, you can now use the Internet to voice your opinion to thousands, give eyewitness testimony on problems, ask questions of characters in television series about their character, the ongoing plot, express your own hunches, make suggestions as to future

episodes, and engage in countless other interactive relationships via media. You can also use interactive media to get professional and amateur counseling on personal problems and on how to manufacture bombs and drugs, and you can use video gaming to test out alternate solutions to those and other problems large and small. While these media offer us the opportunity to participate in important decision-making processes like purchasing, voting, joining, participating, or donating (thus "democratizing" society) they also can "dehumanize" us because these media can and do track individual actions and results as never before (e.g., the number of "hits" on an Internet site and by whom, the level to which persons explore a Web site and, in some cases, what they do with the acquired information after accessing it, such as forwarding it). These "data sets" can and do turn us into mere statistics—ratings numbers for advertisers, public opinion numbers for politicians, and return-on-investment numbers for businesses (thus "un-democratizing" society). Earlier media could track results to a certain degree (e.g., the Neilson television or Arbitron radio ratings asked the audience to keep viewer or listener diaries), but increasingly sophisticated devices like the "People Meter" make data much more powerful using digital cameras to track your attention to programming and commercials. I recently heard of such a data set that tells the brand managers of certain products just how high they can raise brand prices without losing a critical volume of purchases that will most affect the bottom line or profit and how. In other words the data tells them just how much they can "gouge" us. Older methods like Neilson could be falsified, but with interactive media, the "footprints" of users are recorded by actual phone calls made to tailored 1-800 numbers or website and Web link selections, and the number and size of Web orders placed. This helps the marketer to determine which

One Web site called liveshot.com was recently developed by a Texas entrepreneur. It is an interactive hunt for big game—wild boar, antelope, deer, bear, and so on. It allows persons from remote locations to interact with a robotic telescope and rifle to locate and then target the game by using a mouse that allows the "hunter" to manipulate a real rifle mounted in a real blind located in Texas where the hunt takes place. The hunter visually inspects the hunting terrain, looking for targets using a webcam. When a target is found, the user manipulates (i.e., aims) the robotic rifle and squeezes its trigger. One of liveshot's first users was a quadriplegic man in Indiana who hadn't hunted in 17 years, and who did the aiming and shooting via a computer mouse operated by puffs of air he blew into a tube. By the way, he wore camouflage while "hunting." ("All Things Considered," 2005). This raises troubling ethical questions. Should he have had a hunting license? How could one tell if he was poaching or not? What other uses of this kind of interactivity can you imagine? What ethical questions do they bring up? By the way, such virtual hunt sites were later outlawed by several states. Why do you suppose they made them forbidden? Imagine the implications of this level of interactive media for various persuasive attempts and how such interactions will involve receivers. The possibilities are mind-boggling, and they're on the way or are already here in competitive sports (e.g., Fantasy Football is but one example), virtual shopping, dating and matching sites, virtual gambling, voting on line, and a host of other applications. For example, we have already witnessed stalking on the Internet, and in the United Kingdom sports fans can interactively tune in fan interviews and tune out the commentator's interpretations. They can even manipulate camera angles, volume, and more on an individual basis, thus determining their own individualized "version" of the soccer match. What might that ability do to sports broadcasting as we know it, especially in America?

advertised offer in the infomercial draws the most response, or which envelope in a direct mail offer gets the best return on investment, or via "spy ware." These new capabilities for interactive input and data harvesting (or perhaps data snooping) are but a few of the challenges facing receivers who are unknowingly giving parts of themselves away, and these interactive media are not limited to cell phone or Internet uses. They include video games (which research shows can increase violent behavior), touch-sensitive screens, being secretly observed and photographed as we shop by kiosks in malls, virtual reality, carefully tracked electronic financial transactions, and many more—all involve persuasion and perhaps even coercion to some degree.

Another powerful theme in our study of a persuasion world is the degree to which our culture reflects increasing cultural diversity. **Cultural diversity** (i.e., the increasing numbers of persons from other cultural backgrounds, races, ethnicities, sexual preferences, educational levels, political and religious beliefs, etc.) calls for us to make adjustments in all forms of communication, but especially in persuasion. Many times the communication results of cultural diversity are very positive. For example, in Gillette, Wyoming, the Prairie Winds organization regularly hosts a cultural festival with ethnic food, dancing, music, art and craft demonstrations, and attendees can participate in any of them (*News Record*, 2005). Unfortunately, sometimes the results of miscommunication across diverse cultures are tragic. For example, in 2004, a Hmong deer hunter in Wisconsin murdered five people because he misunderstood a persuasive attempt to convince him that the deer stand he was using belonged to someone else. He was found guilty of killing them and is now serving a life sentence without chance of parole.

Today, new immigrants to America face various appeals from their own culturally diverse backgrounds, and undoubtedly they will join, vote, believe in, and donate as their countrymen do. We are especially aware of differences emerging from cultures that embrace the Muslim religion. They involve things like the role and dress of women, beliefs about holy wars and about such controversial topics as revenge, the role of secular governments, and patterns in the marketplace. These kinds of changes can cause problems. For instance, French schools outlaw the wearing of a burka in school, and in 2007, swimsuit manufacturers tuned in to reach a new Muslim market segment by offering a model called a "Burkini." Such cultural differences can apply to existing subcultures as well (e.g., Latinos respond to persuasive appeals of their reference groups), and the same applies to Blacks, Asians, and Pacific Islanders, and so on. Consider a few of the many the decisions you make while pursuing your degree: to enlist in ROTC, to move out and rent your own place, your major, how you will use your time, whether to wear the school colors, to join the Young Democrats or Republicans, to pledge a fraternity or sorority, to vote for a certain candidate, or to join a cause. We all bring our own cultural values and psychological needs to these decisions and to others like them, and thus our decisions will be diverse. (*Note:* A box dealing with cultural diversity also occurs in each chapter in this book. Get involved with those by going to a search engine to do in-depth exploration of the various topics discussed throughout this book.)

A fourth overall theme to be pursued in this book is the increasing presence of various kinds of **propaganda/advocacy** in recent times. Advocacy or trying to promote a given belief or course of action is ubiquitous in our time. Wikipedia defines it as the act of "… arguing on behalf of a particular issue, idea, or person." (http://en.wikipedia.org/wiki/advocacy). **Propaganda** is a related word that we hear quite often. Wikipedia defines it as a set of messages designed to influence large numbers and warns that it is selective and that it "… presents facts selectively in order to… produce an emotional rather than a rational response to the information provided" (http://en.wikipedia.org/wiki/propagada). As you can see, the word propaganda carries a lot of negative baggage and seems to bring up images of a heavy-handed ministry of propaganda forcing ideas and beliefs down the throats of the citizenry. In today's world, most propagandists say they are using advocacy or are advocating for or against something—it seems less heavy handed. In fact some would even claim that advertising or branding is propaganda because it promotes the free market system, although its originators are probably really promoting a brand, not a belief set. For our purposes we will consider things like the fairly objective documentary film "An Inconvenient Truth" about global warming by former Vice President Al Gore and the responses of its critics as a kind of mid-level propaganda, compared to the more heavy-handed "Sicko" by Michael Moore, which focuses on the weaknesses in the American healthcare system. And at the most heavy-handed end of the scale might be the video and audio messages of Osama Bin Laden to his followers or the claims of the essentially powerless Iranian President Mahoud Ahmadinejad that the Holocaust never happened (Klein, 2007). And a few minutes of examining blogs related to almost any political or religious issue will show you propaganda at work in today's world at all of these levels. In the following chapter and others, you

FIGURE 1.1

Propaganda video and posters. Here are some examples of propaganda posters from the past. Examine them and then go to www.youtube.com/watch?tv=jabj7w-y8_w& mode. Notice the one-sidedness and heavy handedness of the both the videos and posters. Now go to any search engine, enter the words "propaganda posters" into the engine, and browse the posters from various eras and countries listed there. How do they differ? How are they similar? Also check out www.zone-h.org and enter the words "propaganda posters" in their search engine. Share your findings with the class.

SOURCE: *(left)* [LC-USZC4-13673]/Library of Congress Prints and Photographs Division; *(middle)* International Institute of Social History; *(right)* The Lilly Library, Indiana University.

will find a detailed definition of propaganda, current examples, and tools that are helpful in locating and analyzing it. You will also find interactive examples of propaganda in the various "propaganda boxes" that we include. Various examples of propaganda posters from different countries and eras are depicted in Figure 1.1. Let us now examine the "Seven Faces of Persuasion" that we shall encounter throughout our study of the topic and which greatly affect both senders and receivers of persuasive messages in contemporary times. Of course, these Seven Faces do not include each and every problem that persuadees will encounter, but we believe they rank among the most important ones and will refer to them repeatedly as we move along.

THE SEVEN FACES
OF PERSUASION
IN OUR CONTEMPORARY
WORLD

Persuasion in the 24/7 Networked World

As noted above, we live in an age in which more information is available than any person can hope to access and consider. Persuasion has changed a great deal since the days when one person could hope to reach only as many people as could assemble within reach of his or her voice even when using a megaphone, a handout, or later a loudspeaker. The arrival of the print medium permitted persuaders to reach many more people and allowed audiences, radio persuaders expanded this "one-to-many" model, but in a less permanent form, but the "new" electronic medium also brought us increasingly sophisticated persuasive techniques. It also brought to receivers new kinds of persuaders like the broadcast demagogue (e.g., Hitler, Huey Long, and later, Rush Limbaugh and others). Television extended the audience and brought us even more of these kinds of persuaders—ideological TV demagogues, religious rogues, corporate crooks and political pundits such as Bill O'Reilly and others. The Internet expanded things further breaking through previous "Iron Curtain" or "Bamboo Curtain" electronic jamming barricades. This made advocacy, propaganda, and other less extreme forms of persuasion global and available anytime and anywhere. And interactive media will probably continue to stretch the size of the audience of receivers and with its audience involvement, alter the nature of persuading as well as the experience of being persuaded. Virtually all candidates for political office now have interactive Web sites, including the candidates for Mayor in my small town of 12,000 residents. We also have become convinced that it is essential to own individual interactive media devices—each of which can expose us to more persuasion and advocacy—personal computers, home pages, the Internet, high-speed connectivity, cellular telephones complete with cameras, video, and texting that allow each of us to become news reporters and potential persuaders, advocates, or even propagandists.

Do these brief examples of emotional, knee-jerk forms of 24/7 global persuasion mean that we need to automatically reject all the persuasive appeals coming at us from advertisers, politicians, and others? Absolutely not—in fact, it's *essential* that we consider many of the persuasive appeals. Whether as individuals, families, corporations, or governments, we need to be persuaded to do our part on a number of fronts. Take, for example, the need to preserve and restore our environment while moving toward energy independence. This means we need to decide whether to support drilling for oil in unlikely places like Antarctica, whether we should allow firms that spew carbon

into the air to purchase carbon offsets from companies that do not, or whether our government should subsidize major oil companies to develop hydrogen energy. There are logical and emotional arguments on both sides. What are the potential costs, benefits, and alternatives? What are the dangers? Do such corporations have a good track record on the environment or on their good-faith efforts on behalf of consumers, employees, and investors? For these and other reasons, it is more important than ever to train ourselves to become critical receivers of persuasion in an interactive information age that is riddled with advocacy and propaganda. Providing this training is a central goal of this book and this class. As we move from chapter to chapter, you should be able to arm yourself with tools of analysis, perspectives, exercises, and examples that will allow you to become a truly critical receiver of persuasion. The size of that task is clear when we consider just a few of the reasons we need to become more selective receivers of persuasive messages.

Twenty years ago, Researcher Jamie Beckett (1989) reported in the *San Francisco Examiner* that the average U.S. adult is exposed to 255 advertisements every day. More recently, *Advertising Age* estimated that the average American sees, reads, or hears more than 5,000 persuasive advertising messages a day. Communications professor Arthur Asa Berger (2000) reported that the number was more like 15,000 (p. 81). The 5,000 figure is probably closest. These persuasive messages appear in many formats—print and electronic, verbal and visual, logical and emotional. Take the familiar television spot advertisement, with its artistic design, high-tech artistry, computer graphics, sophisticated special effects, computer animation, and digitally sweetened sound. Over 30 years ago, communications expert Neil Postman (1981) pointed out that these spots lead kids to perceive that every problem can be solved and that most can be solved by technology (p. 4). Ask anyone who has had a death in the family, gone bankrupt, experienced divorce, or faced another major crisis, if their problems can be so easily solved. How often are we affected by this comforting belief? Did we buy a product because we subconsciously felt that it might make us more attractive, help us land a job, or impress a teacher? As these ads become more and more sophisticated, they become shorter, so the receiver must confront more of them each day, and this requires us to be alert to our need to evaluate them more critically. Other media also contain influential persuasive messages—newspaper and magazine advertisements, print and electronic billboards and signs along the roadside, radio spots, clothing with product names, home pages, faxes, PR releases, blogs, and even signs in public restrooms. We find ourselves deluged with direct-marketing appeals such as catalogs, direct-mail offers, telemarketing, infomercials, Internet appeals, and more. And these persuasive appeals go beyond just building our brand awareness—they alter our perceptions. For example, recent research shows that persons who eat at Subway underestimate the calories in the meal and therefore, compensate with more snacks than Burger King lunch eaters, thus resulting in a higher caloric intake than if they had the Whopper to begin with (Ithaca, 2007). Massive global and always available databases and sophisticated data filing and retrieval systems now make it possible for persuaders to segment us into narrow groups that are vulnerable to highly tailored persuasion. These examples provide us with even more reasons to become critical receivers, carefully examining persuasive appeals aimed at us before taking action.

Persuasion and Its Ethical Challenges Today

At the same time that we face an anytime-anywhere world of advocacy, propaganda, and persuasion, we are also experiencing a crisis in personal and public ethics. In fact, two authors call us a "Pinocchio Nation" (Donaldson & Wamberg, 2001). The topic of ethics will be dealt with in depth by Dr. Johannesen in Chapter 2, but for now let's just consider how this crisis has developed to its present-day dimension. Lying goes back to Adam and Eve, and we have faced lying and unethical decision making by our government, our businesses, our religious institutions,

and by individuals throughout our history. There have always been duplicitous and deceitful advocates and propagandists in all of these institutions, but since the turn of the new millennium the dimensions of these problems mushroomed as seen in the book entitled *The Post-Truth Era* (Keyes, 2004). Just a few recent examples demonstrate this point:

1. World class corporations, accounting firms, and business leaders lied and cheated to help bilk thousands of law-abiding and trusting citizen employees, retirees and investors of not only their money but of their faith in the future and of business in general (Enron, Arthur Anderson).

2. World renowned religious spokespersons, television evangelists, everyday clergy, lawyers, counselors, and school teachers were unmasked as child molesters, unfaithful spouses, and/or financial greedy-guts throughout the 90s; and it continues on into the new century.

3. Our governments have clearly and repeatedly lied to us about the war in Iraq and the resulting use of governmentally-approved forms of torture (thus thumbing the country's nose at the global community). We have also seen numerous unethical if not illegal means of gaining and maintaining the highest political office and the use of these positions by such officials to line their own pockets as well as those of their friends at local, state, national, and global levels.

4. A number of studies show that individual honesty has deteriorated in recent times. Individuals in general seem to have much lower standards of honesty and ethical behavior whether in the honest filing of income taxes, academic honesty/cheating, plagiarism, marital fidelity, business dealings, marketplace transactions, and so forth (Philip Cook (1996), David Callahan (2004), Ralph Keys (2004)).

So, for many reasons, we need to train ourselves as critical receivers, if for no other reason than to deal

BOX 1.2   Becoming an Advertising Medium—Ethical or Unethical?

"Viral Marketing" is a new form of interactive persuasion that turns the audience into a persuasive advertising channel as each receiver spreads the message online like a (benign) virus resulting in an "epidemic" of interactive persuasion. The technique resembles a chain letter. First the advertiser places an attractive or entertaining and interactive message such as a game on the Web and begins to direct consumers to visit the Web site, which also contains a variety of advertising links from which to choose. One of these is "send this site to a friend." Others might include "Play the Yamaha Race for Profits" game. And the consumer does just that, because it is fun and easy to share things like games via the Internet. One such site at www.subservientchicken.com is sponsored by Burger King and plays on the old "Have it Your Way" slogan in promoting chicken offerings as opposed to the Whopper. The Web site features someone dressed in a chicken suit. The viewer can command the chicken to run, fly, hop, skip, and so on. There are several hundred actions programmed into the game, but if asked to perform a distasteful or obscene act, the "chicken" confronts the screen and shakes its finger at the "naughty" user. The technique persuades on at least two levels: the purchase of the product and the decision to forward the "fun" interactive site much as you might do with a chain letter. Can you think of other instances of persuasion in which this viral approach might be exploited? What about political campaigns? Religious appeals? Worthy causes? What are the ethical implications of participating in viral marketing (e.g., using "fun" media to hook consumers or urging them to spread the message)? Is it "Propaganda" in your mind?

with the "Post-Truth" globally unethical environment that we face on a daily basis (see Box 1.2).

Persuasion at Work in a Media-Saturated World

Ever since the first edition of this book, the impact of mass media has grown exponentially. Back then people worried about the effects of television (three channels plus Public/Educational TV) and radio on our culture. They had seen and heard about the media-inspired anti-war movement that effectively ended United States involvement in Vietnam and brought down a President of the United States while growing a huge "Alternate lifestyle" among the young (then younger than 30—they are now older than 60) in which drugs, free love, communes, and symbolic and physical protests were the lifeblood of the young (protest songs, marches, strikes, etc.). Television was the key culprit in increased violence, shorter attention caused by television programming for the young like "Sesame Street," a lack of common courtesy and civility, the death of civil responsibility and public life, the rise in drug use and free sex, public nudity, and a host of other societal ills. Since then the mass media of our everyday world has practically blasted that past out of relevant existence as already noted. New media—especially the internet and digital formats—have resulted in a whole new game of social "Monopoly." Nowadays, "The Boardwalk" is the Internet, Web sites, blogging, and new media devices, procedures, and related confounding changes that baffle us. That's where the action is and where the money is to be made. The very idea of infecting the computers of companies and other persons whom you don't even know with an intentional virus has a stench of ethical disgust that ought to eliminate one from receiving a "Get-Out-of-Jail-Free! card." Cellular phones that can photograph, videotape, text, and interact with instantaneous speed are surely more breathtaking than the B. & O. Railroad. They are in a way more frightening than the sci-fi *Brave New World* whose author Aldous Huxley, was mainlining LSD on his deathbed ("Hippie," The History Channel, 10/23/07). Recently, a British music Web site called "OINK" was having music downloaded from it before the music was actually released for purchase ("All Things Considered," 10/23/07), and Princeton Professor, Dr. Ed Felton predicts that within ten years "…we'll see a $100 device that fits in your pocket and holds all the music ever recorded" (Levy, 2007a). He also predicts that the digital book is presently a reality. It ("Kindle" is its official name) is about the size of a paperback and able to adjust font size for the reader while holding about 200 books at a time (Levy, 2007). Persuasion in such a world is certainly a new and potentially an exciting and dangerous phenomenon for both persuaders and receivers in the twenty-first century. Interact with media in Box 1.3.

Persuasion, Advocacy, and Propaganda

In addition to a 24/7 global world facing a crisis of ethics, and surrounded even engulfed by media, we are also entering an age of increasing advocacy and propaganda. Everywhere one looks, someone is advocating their own personal agenda or some affiliated group's agenda whether it be global warming, declaring war on Iran, increasing the capitol gains tax, feeding the poor, developing hydrogen energy, or the prevention of cruelty to plants by gardeners. At times this advocacy borders on the ridiculous and at times on heavy-handed propaganda. As noted earlier, the word "propaganda" carries loads of negative baggage. Advocacy doesn't seem nearly as sinister. However, it does share *some* of the five key characteristics of propaganda—things which set it off from other kinds of persuasion. Propaganda is delineated because it exhibits all of the following:

1. It is ideological or it carries and promotes a belief or system of attitudes that is dogmatic. That system is the one and only way to believe—no other system is acceptable.

2. It uses the mass media to deliberately spread its belief system in order to convince and recruit ever larger and larger groups of "true believers" who are frequently fanatical about the belief in system. In this way it becomes a mass movement.

3. It conceals one or more of the following:

    a. the source of the message (e.g., a political party, a religion, an economic system, etc.)

    b. the true goal of this source (e.g., attainment of power, discrimination of a minority, violence against a group or belief set, etc.).

    c. the other side of the issue or other perspectives from which to view the issue.

    d. the techniques being used to promote the message (e.g., subliminal cues, music, uniforms, "impromptu" marches or meetings, etc.).

    e. the result if the source reaches its goal (e.g., tyranny, secret surveillance of the citizenry, the abolishment of personal rights like habeas corpus, etc.).

4. It aims at uniformity of belief and behavior. In this way it is like mob psychology.

5. It usually circumvents the reasoning process and substitutes emotional argument and the hatred of stereotypes (e.g., Jews for the Nazis, Jihadists in contemporary times).

So one can advocate one side of an issue and still not do any (or only one or two) of these things, which characterize propaganda, and still be just advocacy. A person or set of persons can be in favor of drilling for oil on public lands and clearly identify who they are, what the other side claims, and the results of the action if adopted and not be judged as propaganda—it is not ideological in nature and still obtains a uniformity of thought among large numbers. True propaganda is dirty or unethical advocacy on behalf of an ideology using largely emotional argument that conceals in order to gather a mass movement, and we are seeing increasing amounts of it in recent times and are likely to see more in the future. The key for the critical persuadee or audience is to receive both honest advocacy and unethical propaganda and to distinguish between them. That will help us all to make better and wiser decisions when faced with important issues that will affect more than just us as individuals.

BOX 1.3 Interact with Propaganda

Log on to the Internet and enter the word "Propaganda" into the search engine. Go to the "Propaganda Techniques--Source Watch" option and explore some of the more contemporary uses of propaganda techniques like the U.S. government's publication of comic books targeted at the conflicts in the Middle East or the "Greenwashing" technique in which environmental issues are appropriated by corporate polluters for image building. Browse through a variety of key words/techniques links to learn more about the enormous number of new propaganda techniques are now being used (e.g., buzz words, Astroturf blogging or the creation of false blogs to make messages appear as if they came from grass roots organizations). Other examples include the "Echo Chamber" (in which bogus or conscripted news sources are paid or rewarded in some other way to re-utter issues in seemingly unbiased ways that actually mirror the politician, advocate, propagandist, corporation, etc.), Stealth-Marketing (in which low budget campaigns are waged to promote candidates and brands), Photographic Manipulation (where photo ops are created or existing photos are altered to make propagandistic points), and others. You will be amazed at the burgeoning propaganda existing that is just now coming to the attention of scholars and the public in general.

Persuasion in a Multicultural World

As can be seen in the crisis over immigration reform and various discriminatory actions against certain minorities, like Muslims, Blacks, Asians, and so on. we live in a world that is composed of many cultures, be they racial, religious, related to gender or sexual preference, nationality, modes of dress or grooming, and so on. Each of these cultures and subcultures has its own set of values and beliefs; and at the same time each has unique attitudes, beliefs, and values that they share with the culture as a whole. So we need to take into account not only those values that we share with others but also where we differ if we are to avoid tragedies like those previously noted about the Hmong hunter in Wisconsin. When that is the case, both persuading others and being persuaded by them becomes doubly complex. We have to say to ourselves (and perhaps unwittingly to others) that so and so is late because he or she is operating on the accepted values of their own subculture. Or we need to make sure that the action we suggest in our persuasion takes into account that some cultures place a higher value on males versus females when business decisions are being made, or that a proposed solution to problems had better contain an "escape hatch" so that those from another culture can engage in "face-saving" options because it is important in that culture not to lose face. And, of course, there are a multitude of other examples of the difficulties in both persuading and being persuaded in a multicultural world.

Persuasion as Protection in a Deceptive, Doublespeak, and Dangerous World

We have most likely had to live in a deceptive and dangerous world ever since Adam and Eve tried to lie their way out of eating the forbidden fruit. Ever since then, however, we have become increasingly more skillful and sophisticated in deceiving others in order to succeed in duping them. However, in all likelihood we have not become increasingly sophisticated in spotting and saying "No!" to the scam, the swindle, the political deception, the cheat, or the hoodwink at the same rate across the centuries as shown in Figure 1.2. ("You have won the foreign lottery." I was announced as the winner two times in the same day via e-mail.) How can someone believe that they have won a lottery that they haven't even entered? And how can they send

FIGURE 1.2 "He Is a Foreign Lottery Official and You Have Won!!!"
What techniques of the Seven Faces of Persuasion were used or ignored in this ad
warning others of a scam that often succeeds?
SOURCE: National Consumers League, Inc.

thousands of dollars in to an unknown address to "cover the charges" of so-called bookkeeping just because they receive a cashier's check for the prize money? Yet we read time after time that people (many of third world extraction—see "Persuasion in a Multicultural World") who appear to be relatively bright and educated are suckered by this relatively new scam. Not long ago a person I had greatly respected told me of remarkable "pills" that when put into your gas tank would coat the engine in lubricant and yield up to 20 percent better gas mileage, and that I could get in on the marketing of this miraculous invention "on the ground floor and for only a few hundred dollars." All of these cases and many others bear witness to the need to become critical and skeptical persuadees or receivers in the deceptive and dangerous world we face. And there are several kinds of deception that we face:

Doublespeak. This book preaches that your job as a receiver and as a sender is to engage in "**response-ability**," or your ability to wisely and critically respond to the persuasion you encounter and to make wise choices and ethical decisions when you both process and craft persuasion. Of course, it would have been good in past times for persuaders and audiences to have response-ability. If they had, many tyrants might not have risen to power, and wars might have been avoided. The National Council of Teachers of English (NCTE) recognized this need for people to engage their response-ability when it instituted its regular conferences on **doublespeak**, which it defined as deliberate miscommunication and which the *American Heritage Dictionary* defines as "evasive, ambiguous, high-flown language designed to deceive." NCTE conferences point out kinds of doublespeak that might be used by sources and interpreted by receivers, and also granted awards for the year's most outrageous examples. *Euphemism* is an example. It means "words to distort or soften reality" (www.damronplanet.com). In 2007, a U.S. Senator was accused of "cruising" for a homosexual encounter (a case of euphemism already) by reaching under the toilet stall in a public restroom at the Minneapolis Airport to establish contact with another potentially gay person. He denied doing this, saying that he merely reached under to retrieve a piece of dropped toilet paper and that he did his business from a "wide stance" meaning that he had made the initial signal of putting his foot into the territory of the next stall and tapping it. Chicken purveyors use euphemism when they claim that their frozen product is "deep-chilled, not frozen." In politics and business, "User fees" replaces "tax increases" or "price hikes," which are also examples of euphemism. Maybe we are faced with a new kind of "Euphemasia" in the early twenty-first century, so how can we as sources and receivers deal with this ubiquitous perversion of language? We shall see.

College students today are urged to take more core subjects and courses in computer technology. Parents tell them to reduce the volume of their audio systems to avoid hearing damage. The U.S. government tries to convince citizens to conserve energy by adopting energy efficient appliances, lightbulbs, or hybrid vehicles. Churches, schools, and community groups find it necessary to use sophisticated technologies (e.g., e-mail "care lists" or "canned" fundraising direct marketing campaigns) to gain or maintain membership and financial support. Meanwhile, marketers use new technologies to convince consumers that a given product such as a cell phone with camera/video cam will add excitement and new possibilities, relationships, and so forth to their lives. Students are urged to take more core subjects and courses in computer technology at college.

In a persuasion-riddled world such as ours, you would not need defensive training if all persuaders were open, ethical, and honest. Too many, however, try to persuade by using doublespeak, which comes in many guises. One way to protect ourselves is to become aware of these guises as they occur in propaganda, advertising, political discourse and elsewhere. You need to learn what the "half truth" technique of doublespeak is and how it works. As its name implies, it only tells half the story (and so resembles propaganda). An example might be our military telling the public that the United States is "making progress" in Iraq. What does that mean? Well, if we look at what has been brought out in Congressional inquiries, it means that "in some places and at some times, certain indices of progress have risen." But it doesn't mean progress as a whole was made or that the war is nearly over. In another example, immigrants to our country are urged to "assimilate" to the United States, but does that mean always? Everywhere? Regardless of conditions?

These are all half truths, We just noted several examples of the euphemism or the softened or distorted word as another type of doublespeak.

The "*bogus issue*" is another example of doublespeak from the Iraq War. It was claimed that we were getting into the war to find WMDs or weapons of mass destruction and also to dismantle terrorist training grounds. There were none to discover or dismantle. Both were bogus issues. The use of *jargon* is yet another kind of doublespeak. Because it is highly technical or specialized language, it confuses the receiver and as such is frequently seen in advertising, political rhetoric, and economic propaganda. In arguing for the dismantlement of Head Start (a program to bring disadvantage preschool children up to speed for kindergarten), President G. W. Bush advocated a "Leave No Child Behind" program of universal testing, which apparently forced teachers to focus on information for the national test items and not necessarily on concepts needed to truly understand the subject. The reason given for the change was "Management flexibility" (Rosen, 2003). Like all jargon, this term had very special meaning and thus misled and distorted the real reason (which was to cut education funding as a whole). If pressed for a true definition, the Bush camp would have probably said "To change things to our way." Consider the "peacekeeping" military missions engaged in around the world by our government in the recent past, or the term "ethnic cleansing," which actually referred to mass murder in several parts of the world, and the mass slaughter of thousands by using words that sounded almost antiseptic. Of course, there are hundreds of thousands of other examples with more appearing each day.

What can the average receiver do about doublespeak and related scams, swindles, and deception, and what should the average persuader/advertiser/blogger/and so on do to avoid engaging in it? The Doublespeak home page recommends asking the following questions about any piece of persuasion being received or planned:

1. Who is speaking to whom?
2. Under what conditions?
3. Under what circumstances?
4. With what intent?
5. With what results?

If you cannot answer *all* these questions with ease, or if you feel uncomfortable with the answers, or if you cannot determine any answer to them, you are probably dealing with doublespeak. You had better be prepared to delve deeper, or if you are sending the message, you'd better think about cleaning it up a bit.

Of course, doublespeak isn't confined to the world of politics. CEOs at Enron, AIG, WorldCom, and others used doublespeak to confuse and bilk investors and employees by convincing them that "liabilities" were "assets" and that "spending" meant "earning." As a result many lost hundreds of thousands of dollars and the CEOs went to jail. And you will find doublespeak elsewhere—in sales pitches, in your interpersonal persuasion with friends and relatives, in the classroom, at church, in politics, and economics—no area of interest is immune, so be on guard for what the words *really* mean.

Scams.   Another kind of deception in our dangerous world of persuasion is the **scam,** which again has been with us for ages—since the first person successfully cheated someone out of his birthright for something mundane. Today scams frequently involve the Internet and electronic housekeeping as happens with identity theft and corporate swindles. *Wikipedia* defines a scam as "A fraudulent business scheme—a swindle. To deprive by deceit" (www.thefreedictionary.com/scam).   The typical scam relies heavily on persuasion first in convincing the person to be scammed that the persuader or scammer is credible or believable as noted in Figure 1.2, and then in the steps taken to complete the scam. We will discuss credibility at length in several places later but sincerity, trustworthiness, and believability are good synonyms for now. In the next step, the scammer must persuade the target that the scheme is likely to succeed and yield rewards. (*Note:* Most such schemes promise some kind of payoff—usually money.) This is frequently done by using statistics and/or testimonials both of which we also discuss later. Then the scammer must persuade the person to make some kind of commitment—usually financial (see Figure 1.2). Other kinds of scams involve persuading a person to donate or pledge to a good cause such as a "walk" for the poor, like Habitat for Humanity, or on behalf of the cure of some disease like HIV (see www.lect law.com/files/cos68 for a "how to . . ." article). This kind of scam usually must also persuade the audience of the scammer's credibility and the reasonableness of the plan, and then to enact the commitment step. Interestingly, having a list of donors and amounts given or pledged (usually in advance) really helps get the bucks.

Identity Theft.   Yet another type of scam prevalent in our contemporary world is identity theft of which most of you are already aware. It is sometimes accomplished by "phishing" or representing oneself as a trustworthy financial institution in order to gain sensitive information that can be used to masquerade as someone else. Frequent targets are PayPal, eBay or online banking fronts. It involves persuading the target to give up key identity information because the fake bank says it needs the password or account number to verify its records. Another false front of the identity theft persuasion is needed for convincing the merchant to then take the false identity in payment for goods or services without asking for full identification. Again, credibility is key; once achieved, the rest of the pieces in the scam fall into place. Finally, another and far more dangerous kind of scam is the corporate or governmental scam or swindle. A few of these scams come to mind—Enron, the world's largest energy broker; WorldCom, the second largest long-distance company Adelphia, a major cable provider; and many others including Arthur Andersen, one of the 5 top accounting firms in the United States (forced into bankruptcy).

Self-Protection.   Government scams have been with us for a long time going back to the founding fathers and move on to the swindling of the Native Americans, Credit Mobilier, Teapot Dome, recent timber and oil swindles in this century, and the list

goes on. In both the corporate and the government swindle, step one—credibility of the source—is almost a given. After all, who wouldn't trust our government or most major corporations—look at all the regulations and oversight? The key persuasive step is similar to that in the individual scam, which is to convince the public—voters, investors, vendors or employees—that everything is being conducted honestly. That's the purpose of having oversight committees or regulators like the SEC. Of course, these can be rigged as we saw in the foreign policy swindle that got and kept us into Iraq. The commitment step is almost irrelevant in corporate or government scams because the public has already committed to the company, office holder, corporation by being employed by, investing in, or voting for the scammer. The critical thing to keep in mind regarding any of these deceptions from doublespeak to outright scams, is that **self-protection** is the only weapon the average person has with which to defend themselves. Again that's the magic bullet for combating these stings—to train you to be skeptical and responsible persuadees or audience members.

Persuasion in a Results-Demanded World

Efficacy.   More than ever before, our culture wants to see the results of its and our efforts, particularly if there's a group effort involved. Naturally, this has impact on how we receive and send persuasive messages. In fact some theorists maintain that persuasion that fails is not really persuasion at all, even if it follows all the rules and prescriptions. Because this kind of perspective implies that "The ends justify the means." there are huge ethical implications for both persuaders and persuadees (Callahan, 2004). As receivers, we need to recognize that the persuasive efforts aimed at us will be judged by how we respond to them—buying the brand, voting for the candidate, donating the money, signing the petition, demonstrating for or against the advocated policy, and so on. As persuaders we need to ask ourselves if we are willing to be judged and to judge ourselves and others and our efforts by such a results-oriented standard. Personally, I have failed numerous times in persuading others but was still satisfied by having articulated my position and made it known. It was on the record and could perhaps reinforce the morale of those on the "losing" side and even be used as evidence or opinion, in some future debate on the same issue(s). For me the results-oriented approach didn't work. The results-oriented standard has two criteria for success. The first is *Efficacy* or the "bottomline" of profits, votes, donations, signatures, bodies showing up to demonstrate, and so on.

Efficiency.   Efficiency is the second criterion in a results-oriented world. This really means a costs-Versus-resulting-benefits kind of dichotomy that judges results by comparing the efforts and various other investments (costs) made against the relative gains or recognition (benefits) achieved on the part of the audience. In other words, the costs of "Building the Brand" (a frequent goal of persuasion in advertising) cannot exceed the benefits of increased sales, attitude, or opinion changes regarding the brand. This kind of comparison ignores the fact that persuasion is often a cumulative process that achieves its ultimate goal(s) only in steps or stages. In fact, many advertising models such as the "Hierarchy of Effects" model claim that a series of stages are endemic in any advertising effort during the trip to ultimate success. So, as receivers we need to look at the overall efforts and results of the persuasive campaign or movement. As sources or persuaders, we need to plan our persuasion as if it is part of an ongoing campaign and not as if it is a single shot of persuasion leading to the desired outcome. For example, many persuaders worked for a change in immigration laws in the United States. Many of them failed as individual efforts, but ultimately the country was able to liberalize the steps need to become a legal alien worker and finally a citizen. Undoubtedly the final outcome could be labeled a success, while the individual efforts had to be called failures. If we go beyond this efficacy criterion, we might say that the outcome wasn't worth all the efforts, and hence the persuasion failed

the efficiency criterion. Both criteria are used at various times with differing persuasive efforts. Again the role of the persuadee or receiver is to be patient, skeptical, and critical until the final outcome is apparent. That is your task as we work through the various chapters that follow. Shortly we will investigate a handy model and tool that you can use to begin to become such an audience member, but first let's set the historical context for the study of persuasion and examine some of the theoretical foundations for its examination.

DEFINING PERSUASION: FROM ARISTOTLE TO ELABORATION LIKELIHOOD

Definitions of Persuasion

The ancient Greeks were among the first to systematize the use of persuasion, calling it "**rhetoric**." They studied it in their schools, applied it in their legal proceedings, and used it in the Senate to build the first democracies in their city-states. Aristotle was the primary information broker and theorist in ancient Greece, authoring more than 1,000 books and categorizing all of the types of knowledge in the known world of that time. He defined rhetoric as "the faculty of observing in any given case, the available means of persuasion." And, according to Aristotle, persuasion consists of artistic and inartistic proofs. The persuader controls **artistic proof**, such as the choice of evidence, the organization of the persuasion, style of delivery, and language choices. **Inartistic proof** includes things not controlled by the speaker, such as the occasion, the time allotted to the speaker, and the speaker's physical appearance. According to Aristotle, persuasion succeeds or fails based on three basic types of artistic and inartistic proof. First, persuasion depended on a source's credibility, or **ethos** much as it does today, which is why the testimonial is such an effective persuasive tactic. Second was the use of emotional appeals, or **pathos,** usually found in the kinds of colorful language and imagery used by the persuader or in the emotional level of evidence cited. Again we find this to be true in modern times—witness the language used in the 2008 persuasion of candidate Barack Obama or at the public's rejection of Michael Vick's characterizing dog-fighting as a "hobby" language that backfired given the emotional response to the activity. Finally, the idea of using logical or rational appeals, or **logos** in Aristotle's words was a persuasive tactic as well as the use of statistics on behalf or against a given policy of government or a brand or other issue. Of course most persuaders use a combination of all three of these tactics (Roberts, 1924), and we see all of them being used in both ethical and unethical persuasion occurring in our contemporary world. Aristotle also thought that persuasion is most effective when based on the **common ground**, or the shared beliefs, values, and interests between persuaders and persuadees that could be established by all of the tactics. This shared territory or common ground permits persuaders to make certain assumptions about the audience and its beliefs, such as assuming that using certain patterns or types of language, emotions and logic will persuade them.

Assuming these beliefs, persuaders use **enthymemes** defined as "a form of argument in which the first or major premise in the proof remains unstated by the persuader and, instead, is supplied by the audience." (Larson, 2007). Many of the chapters to follow explain broad examples of such commonly-held major premises. A familiar example is "All men are mortal; Socrates is a man; therefore Socrates is mortal." Today's persuaders need to identify common ground between them and the audience or those major premises probably held by the audience and which can be used in effective enthymemes (see Figure 1.3).

Roman students of persuasion added specific advice on what persuasive speaking ought to include. Cicero identified five elements of persuasive speaking: (1) inventing or discovering evidence and arguments, (2) organizing them, (3) styling them artistically, (4) memorizing them, and (5) delivering them skillfully. Both Aristotle's and Cicero's definitions focus on the sources of messages and on the persuader's skill and art in building a speech.

In the communication discipline, we consider these "rhetorical" approaches to the study of persuasion because they grew out of the rhetorical traditions of the Greeks and Romans. They are still applied in current research on persuasion and its effects.

Later students of persuasion reflected the changes that accompanied the emergence of electronic media and the social sciences following World War II. Over 50 years ago, communication scholars Winston Brembeck and William Howell (1952) broke new theoretical ground after WW II when they described persuasion as "the conscious attempt to modify thought and action by manipulating the motives of men toward predetermined ends" (p. 24). That had been what had happened to cause the war. In their definition, we see a notable shift from logic in persuasion toward a focus on the more "emotional" means of persuasion—those that stimulate the internal motives of the audience. Twenty years later they re-defined persuasion as "communication intended to influence choice" (p. 19) reflecting the interest on the idea of influence in the social sciences. Literary critic and language theorist, Kenneth Burke (1970) also defined persuasion in an intriguing way. His definition was an imaginative one. He said that persuasion was really the artful use of the "resources of ambiguity" usually revealed in an artistic, and frequently emotional format. Burke believed that if receivers feel they are being spoken to in their "own language" and hear references to their own beliefs and values, they will develop a sense of **identification** with the persuader, believing that the persuader is like them— a concept close to Aristotle's "common ground." In Burke's theory, when persuaders try to act, believe, and talk like the audience, they create a bond with listeners, who will identify with them and will follow their advice on issues. He also noted that such identification occurs most readily when wrapped in a drama, a story, or other kind of narration Burke, *A Grammar of Motives* (1970) and *A Rhetoric of Motives* (1970). We see this format in many if not most advertisements and in political, religious, economic, and other advocacy and propaganda, ethical and unethical. It has led to a set of communication and persuasive theories called "Narrative" theories

I've spent 40 years building a nest egg.

30 years paying off a mortgage.

20 years saving for college.

I've WORRIED enough.

Now I want to LIVE.

⩍Lincoln
Financial Group

At Lincoln Financial Group, we provide clear, understandable solutions to help you grow, manage and protect the work of a lifetime. *Clear solutions in a complex world.*
1-877-ASK-LINCOLN
www.lfg.com © 1996 Lincoln National Corporation SAM 05-0002

FIGURE 1.3 The Lincoln Financial Group establishes common ground in this advertisement between the company and any person of any race or ethnicity who is approaching retirement. Note the satisfied and happy looks on both of the faces and the healthy appearance of both persons (a non-verbal emotional appeal). This resonates with the desire to have a happy, healthy retirement and helps build the common ground. Note also the examples referred to in the ad copy—"40 years building," "30 years paying off," and "20 years saving," each of which would probably resonate with any potential retiree, and the idea that "Now I want to LIVE." (clearly both a logical and emotional appeal—they can occur at the same time). These words continue building common ground between the company and the potential customer.

SOURCE: Used by permission of the Lincoln Financial Group.

(see Fisher, 1987; Campbell, 1972, 1991). Taking our cues from Aristotle, Burke, and others, persuasion is defined here as "the process of **co-creation** by sources and receivers of a state of identification through the use of verbal and/or visual symbols." This definition implies that persuasion requires intellectual and emotional participation between both persuader and persuadee that leads to shared meaning and co-created identification. Communication professor and researcher Herbert Simons (1986) agrees and calls this result "co-active persuasion." Notice that, like our

definition, co-active persuasion is receiver-oriented and situational, relying on similarities between persuaders and persuadees and appeals to things acceptable to the persuadee, thus inducing action (p. 75). Because of the process of co-creation, all persuasion consists of **self-persuasion** to some degree. We rarely act in accordance with persuasion unless we participate or interact in the process logically and/or emotionally. The words "process," "co-created," and "identification" are central in this definition and draw on both Aristotle and Burke. Let us now examine a few of the well-known theories in persuasion that relate in one way or another to our definition.

The **Elaboration Likelihood Model** (ELM) is a theory that serves as an organizational model of persuasion and has resulted in significant changes in the way theorists view persuasion. It serves as a central model throughout this book. Social psychologists Richard Petty and John Cacioppo (1986) suggested the ELM as a cognitive model in which persuasion takes one of two routes. In the **central information processing route** the receiver consciously and directly focuses on the persuasive communication while mentally elaborating on the issues and actively seeking more information. This requires significant effort on the part of the receiver. The target of the persuasive message searches out the issues, supporting evidence, alternatives, respective costs and benefits, and other potential outcomes. It usually operates in making important decisions such as purchasing a new car, a new home, and so on. Here we probably read brochures, compare prices and interest rates, features, and benefits, or we go online to discover the dealer's/home owner's/other reputation and how the vehicle/house type/and so on is rated by various consumer publications. At other times, persuasion requires only a momentary period of concentration on an issue—a good price on Tide, whether to engage a lawn service, a good color of sweater on me, what channel to tune, and so on.

According to the ELM, this persuasion occurs in the **peripheral information processing route**. There, information may be processed almost instantly or just by the senses, without direct focusing on or researching of the decision. It is usually prompted by minor seemingly unimportant cues— a phrase of music that accompanies a television spot, a word or metaphor in a speech, or the color and shape of a package on the store shelf. We decide to buy Cracker Jacks at the ball park to get the "free" prize (though we know there has never been a good one in over 120 years) and because they are mentioned in the song "Take Me Out to the Ball Game" that is sung at the middle of the 7th inning. But we really don't think these cues through in any logical way—if we did we'd probably just settle for

singing the song. At any given moment, there are millions of pieces of such trivial or peripheral information available to us, but we consciously attend to only a few of them and process the rest in a kind of subconscious way where they lie dormant until a decision point on Cracker Jacks or whatever arises. The peripheral route resembles a sponge. We soak up persuasive information and may act on it, but more likely, we remain unaware, unconscious, and unfocused on it in any direct or effortful way until we need it to decide and then the sponge is squeezed. The peripheral route usually contains shortcuts for decision-making and mostly includes emotional not logical appeals. Instead of focusing on different variables in persuasion, the ELM focuses on the *processes* that go on during the overall act of persuasion. As noted above, it fits with one of the central ideas of this book—that we are bombarded by more information than we can possibly process in any given situation and hence must learn to focus on and study/elaborate on critical pieces of information and leave the others to less intensive study or unconscious "shortcuts"—what Cialdini (2001) calls the "Click, Whirr" response.

Because we focus or elaborate on some issues more than others, they are far more likely to affect our attitudes toward that/those issue(s) more than on peripherally processed issues that we unconsciously bypass or only consider briefly if at all. Therefore, more "powerful" persuasion occurs with more complete elaboration and vice versa with less focused or elaborated upon persuasion. However, in this book we maintain that even slightly elaborated on issues still make impressions on us, and because they are more emotional (and perhaps narrative), more unconscious and "subliminal," they can also affect our attitudes toward issues, though not as consciously or powerfully as those elaborated on in the central processing route where the attitudes that are formed last longer, predict behavior better, and combine to form attitude networks. At the same time and as noted earlier, attitudes formed in the peripheral routes are more likely to be prompted out of us by small, seemingly insignificant, cues such as those found in television advertisements. We really don't think about or elaborate on 30-second spots, but they probably affect our purchasing or voting behavior. We see a spot for Mr. Clean and don't really think of its logo (a muscular Genie) or the shape of its container (a wide-shouldered and narrow hipped bottle), but we pick up a bottle while shopping and perhaps thinking about our dirty car or floors. And in both routes a number of factors can affect our elaboration and the resulting attitudes. For example, if we have a certain health problem—say diabetes—we are far more likely to pay attention and to read fully the magazine or television advertisements about the problem that would usually be considered peripheral messages. That is why most major pharmaceutical companies recently began heavy television and print advertisements. The goal was to get you partially elaborating with them—you must read, view, and/or listen to them—and then to follow the advice of the ad to "Ask Your Doctor About It, and Get a Free Sample." Their traditional marketing strategy was to sample doctors with a load of "free samples" to give to patients (which patients always like—Free is always good). Did it work? Doctors tell us so and report that patients are now asking for free samples of drugs by names that they would have been unaware of previously. Would the industry have continued spending millions of media dollars on such ads if they didn't? Are the ads ethical? These are the kinds of questions critical receivers ask.

What are the methods receivers might employ to protect themselves in this confusing world of the Seven Faces of Persuasion? Let's examine a method for doing this by asking ourselves what criteria are needed for responsible persuasion to occur.

CRITERIA FOR RESPONSIBLE PERSUASION

How does cooperative and co-creative persuasion happen? These are two things that we value, and we should try to assure that they have the best chance of happening. What makes them work?

Although persuasion occurs under various circumstances, three conditions seem to increase the chances that responsible receivers will make wise and knowledgeable decisions.

First, responsible persuasion is most likely to occur if both parties have an equal opportunity to persuade and approximately equal access to the media of communication available. If one side imposes a gag rule on the proponents of the other side (as is the case in many international conflicts we are experiencing today) and the advocates of the other side have unlimited access to those media, then receivers will receive an unbalanced view of the issues. Unfortunately this happens all too often in our global world.

Second, in an ideal world, persuadees would reveal their agendas in advance to the audience. Again, this does not happen often in our global world. We were told, for example, that the agenda in invading Iraq was to remove a dictator and more importantly, destroy his WMDs or weapons of mass destruction—nuclear, deadly gases, and bacteriological weapons. It turns out that none of these existed in any operable form, and the real agenda was probably to advance a theory that the United States could "Democratize" the Middle East against its will or natural events and perhaps gain access to the oil of the region. If the true agenda had been known, receivers might have rejected the idea of invading Iraq and thousands of lives and trillions of dollars of national treasure—yours and mine—would not have been wasted.

In an ideal world, persuaders would also warn their audiences of any possible negative side effects of their advocated policies (e.g., loss of world prestige, higher gas prices, etc.), but unfortunately this does not always happen, which is why the third and final criteria is so very important. This essential element for responsible persuasion to occur is for critical receivers to test the assertions made by the persuaders, test their evidence against alternate sources, and withhold judgment until all of the facts are in. And even if the first two criteria—equal advocates and equal access to the media—are not operating, critical receivers can make the difference. In upcoming elections we are all likely to see negative

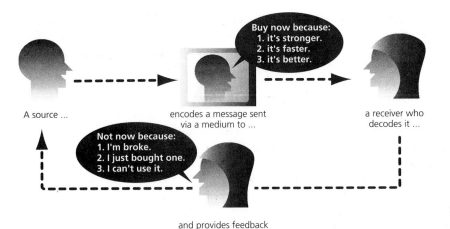

FIGURE 1.4 The SMCR model.

ads and false assertions by many candidates. We need to question them! As Kathleen Hall Jamieson (1992) observed almost two decades ago, "All forms of campaign discourse were becoming alike…ssertion was substituted for argument and attack for engagement." (p. 212). Today she thinks things have become worse—more assertion versus argument and more personal attack versus issue engagement. It is the job of the critical receivers—you and me—to insist on and carefully examine accurate sources, arguments and a clash of ideas instead of charges and countercharges. So let's keep that in mind as we examine how persuasion differs from other forms of influence.

Let us now look at how persuasion is different from other more and less powerful and more and less noticeable forms of influence.

THE SMCR MODEL OF PERSUASION

The simplest model of communication, and one of the oldest and most widely referenced, is Shannon and Weaver's (1949) **SMCR model** (see Figure 1.4). The model contains these essential elements:

- A source (S) (or persuader), who or which is the encoder of the message. The code can be verbal, nonverbal, visual, or musical, or in some other modality.

- A message (M), which is meant to convey the source's meaning through any of the codes.

- A channel (C), which carries the message and which might have distracting noise.

- A receiver (R) (or persuadee), who decodes the message, trying to sift out channel noise and adding his or her own interpretation.

Let's apply the model to a television ad for a brand of automobile. Suppose you tell a friend that the words used in a TV ad for the new Hummer emphasize how huge the car seems when it really isn't all that spacious—there's lots of wasted space, and its performance record stinks. In this case, you help your friend to make or not make a choice by explaining a source-related aspect of persuasion—in this case word choice—"HUMMER—Big Enough to Be A Virtual Party Car!" Then you alert your friend to the doublespeak in the ad—the claim to be "A Virtual Party Car!" You ask what the words "Virtual" and "Party Car" *really* mean and thus you focus your friend's attention on the message itself. You can also point out that skillful video editing and the use of special effects like zooming the car out on the screen or using the Mardi Gras as a background to make it seem huge and loads of fun. Here, you focus on the persuasive impact of the channel that conveys the persuasive information. Finally, you might ask your friend why he or she thinks the HUMMER (or any brand of car) will automatically result in fun times, a party atmosphere, and accompanying personal popularity. Here you focus your friend's attention on the receiver element of the model and what he or she (or you) bring to the communication.

Because persuasion is a process, being a critical receiver means being prepared for all four elements—the motives of the source (obvious or disguised), message elements (verbal and visual symbolic meanings), the channel or medium used to send the message (electronic, print, or interactive/interpersonal), and finally what the receiver brings to the source's argument(s). Try using several of these tools to determine a source's motives. For example, language choice often tips us off to the source's intent. The ideas that the source thinks are persuasive to the audience almost always appear expressed in the words, metaphors, and visuals used. Are they questions or exclamations? Are they short, punchy, and attention getting, or long and soothing? For instance, Schick introduced a "cosmetic" razor called the "Personal Touch." It is clear to whom the product was targeted and the language used in ads was a tip-off. What do the words "cosmetic," "personal," and "touch" tell you about Schick's view of its potential customer pool? Was it aiming at a "macho" man or at women? How might such receivers respond to the words? Do they suggest that Schick is giving them the special attention they've always deserved? The language used tells us that the brand is targeted to females, and the motive is to make them feel special when considering adoption of the product. Analyzing the source's message provides the receiver with two benefits. First, it alerts us to the persuasion being aimed at us. Second, it reveals things to us about the source that can help us when that source becomes the target of our own persuasion (e.g., when Schick wants to extend its brand to a new audience segment).

Other tools also help us to analyze the intent of the message—things like the sources beliefs about receivers' needs and emotions, the evidence contained in persuasive messages, and how it relates to the persuasive goal. Later, we will also consider the layout, graphics, and wording of ads. For example, consider an ad placed across the country by the International Fund for Animal Welfare (IFAW), opposing the harvest of baby seals in Canada—a highly emotional issue since the young seals are clubbed to death when they climb up on the ice floe to be nursed (see Figure 1.5). The copy in the ad reads:

> Do you really know what can go into a simple fish sandwich?.... Fish caught by Canadian Fishermen who also kill the baby seals. Your purchase of a McDonald's or Burger King Fish Sandwich could help buy the boats, hard wooden clubs, and guns used by the seal hunters as they turn from fishing to the cruelty of killing adult and baby seals.

The words such as "hard wooden clubs" and the image of the men battering the cute baby seal alert you to the underlying emotional persuasion being used. This should prompt one to investigate the facts more fully because emotional appeals are more likely to be biased, incomplete, propagandistic, or unethical. Research reveals that actually very few Canadian fishermen are also baby seal hunters; that clubbing the seals is actually the least painful means of the necessary harvesting of them; and that the furs of the seals are the object of the hunt not their flesh, which is not used in the fish sandwich as the visuals suggest. Furthermore, they are mammals, not fish. The connections are weak at best; notice the underlined weasel words—*some* Canadian fishermen also hunt seals and so *some* of the fish (not seals) they catch *could be* in a fish sandwich. It's a real stretch. Looking carefully at the message prompts you to get the other side of the story. It also alerts you to the kinds of effects that the print channel has on persuasion. A similar appeal using radio would probably fail because radio lacks the visual imagery needed (i.e., the fishwich, the baby seal, and the brutal clubbing). Imagine a TV ad documenting the harp seal slaughter. Would this

Do you really know what can go into a simple fish sandwich?

Fish caught by Canadian Fishermen who also kill the baby seals. Your purchase of a McDonald's or Burger King Fish Sandwich could help buy the boats, hard wooden clubs, and guns used by the seal hunters as they turn from fishing to the cruelty of killing adult and baby seals.

If you made a pledge today not to buy fish sandwiches from McDonald's or Burger King unless you were assured by the companies that no Canadian fish was used . . . your decision would save the seals. Canadian fishermen would have to stop sealing since they are totally dependent on their fish sales, with seal hunting a tiny sideline in comparison.

Canadian Globe and Mail of 13 March 1984, had this to say of IFAW's call for a worldwide boycott of Canadian fish: *". . . But what really has the officials spooked is the U.S. market. (There) The International Fund for*

Animal Welfare (IFAW), which spearheads the anti-sealing protest worldwide, has started pressing U.S. purchasers not to take Canadian fish. The U.S. market is worth $1-billion a year to Canadian fishermen and the fast-food business in the United States is about a fifth of that market. Canada fears that, if one U.S. fast-food chain caves in to the protestors, all will surrender."

Over 15,000 seals, mostly babies just 2-4 weeks old, have been clubbed or shot over the last 28 days . . . and yet the Canadian Minister of Fisheries says there is no baby seal hunt.

You have it in your hands to save the baby seals today.

Please write or telephone one or both of the companies listed below and seek an assurance that they will not purchase Canadian fish until the Canadian Government passes a law banning the seal hunt forever.

Mr Fred L Turner,
Chairman of the Board,
McDonald's Corporation,
McDonald's Plaza, Oak Brook, Illinois,
IL 60521
Tel: 312/887-3200

Mr J Jeffrey Campbell, Chairman,
Burger King Corporation,
7360 North Kendall Drive,
Miami,
Florida FL 33156
Tel: 305/596-7277

SAVE THE SEALS
NO TO CANADIAN FISH

To the International Fund for Animal Welfare
I'll put animals first . . . I'll do my part to help you fight the baby seal hunters.
Enclosed is my tax-exempt contribution to IFAW in the amount of:
☐ $10 ☐ $15 ☐ $25 ☐ $35 ☐ $50 ☐ $100 ☐ $500   Other $_____
We need hundreds of gifts this size to save the baby seals forever.

Name _____
(please print)
Address _____

_____
_____ Zip Code _____

International Fund for Animal Welfare
169 Main Street, Yarmouth Port,
Massachusetts 02675 U.S.A.
Our financial statement is available to contributors.

IFAW

Our boycott campaign needs your support. We cannot succeed without your funds, to carry our boycott to every community in America.
A copy of the last financial report filed with the Department of State may be obtained by writing to: N.Y. State Department of State, Office of Charities Registration, Albany, N.Y. 12231 or IFAW.

FIGURE 1.5 Ad encouraging people to boycott fish sandwiches to stop the killing of harp seals.
SOURCE: 1984 Historical IFAW Advertisement courtesy of the International Fund for Animal Welfare.

make the message more or less effective? TV makes us more vulnerable to certain types of messages, such as humorous ones, demonstrations, exaggerations, comparisons, and before/after appeals. Video and audio footage of the clubbing of the seals would certainly raise audience emotions. Is the ad "propaganda" per our definition?

Finally, the SMCR model suggests we need to look at ourselves to determine what kinds of motives, biases, and perspectives we bring to the persuasion. What fascinations, needs, and desires do we

add in the process of co-creation? How do we interact with the message and the medium used? Does our cultural heritage shade the meaning of the message? Do we inherently oppose the killing of innocent, harmless, helpless animals? Are we grossed out about the chance of eating them by mistake and so on? Persuaders including politicians, ideologues, advertisers, propagandists, other kinds of advocates, and even our coworkers, friends, and colleagues continuously seek discover our internal feelings and biases to develop persuasive tactics and strategies such as those noted here. Remember that *communication tactics* flow from *communication strategies*, which in turn flow from overall *communication goals*.

PERSUASION AND OTHER THEORIES OF INFLUENCE

The Theory of Reasoned Action

Another well-known theory in the study of persuasion is primarily passed on the central processing channel of the ELM. Communication researchers Fishbein and Azjen (1980) were dissatisfied with the inability of shifts in attitude to predict subsequent shifts in conscious and desired changes in behavior. Habitual, mindless, or scripted behavior is ruled out of this theory—it focuses on volitional behavior or those actions that you and I choose (on the basis of something) to enact or reject. A key concept in the theory is the *behavioral intention,* which is the result of individual Influences such as my or your feelings, attitudes, or predispositions and our cultural norms. Take for instance, my or your actions in regards to say practicing safe sex. Individually we may think it is a good practice for health reasons, to avoid unwanted pregnancy, and because we have been advised to do so by trusted sources like our physician, parents, or others. However, once we get to college we learn that practicing safe sex is not that cool or fun, and it is not the norm for our fellow classmates and friends. Now what do we do? Do we listen to the health warnings or do we follow the crowd? The theory predicts that our actions will flow from what we planned or intended to do beforehand (e.g., always carrying condoms when there is a chance that casual sex may occur). These *behavioral intentions* rest upon the strength of our beliefs about health risks involved and our evaluations of those beliefs, say the likelihood of encountering a partner who is infected with HIV, for example.

The other half of the behavioral intention rests upon cultural norms or patterns. If the persons in our fraternity think safe sex is laughable, that may change our initial intention to even carry condoms. The cultural norm also interacts with our motivation to comply. Would I rather feel secure against infection or pregnancy or do I want to feel accepted as part of the group? These factors then lead to a pre-behavior intention. I say that it can't hurt to be prepared—after all that's the Boy Scout motto, so I might as well carry condoms. In this case the personal rather than the cultural factors play the major role, and my ultimate action or behavior will probably be to carry condoms. The theory has been particularly predictive in issues involving health and safety (e.g., wearing seat belts, breast self-examinations, etc.) (Fishbein & Ajzen, 1991). The theory basically says that I use my reasoning abilities to balance my individual beliefs and values with those of my surrounding culture when taking voluntary action.

Narrative Theories

A final set of theories briefly examined here and elaborated on in later chapters are called *narrative theories*. Their basic premise is simple, and most would agree with it—human beings are instinctually the tellers of stories. Like the Ancient Mariner who stops the traveler to insist that he listen to the old man's tale of the curse of the albatross he killed while at sea, human beings, as sources of persuasion, are impelled to convince others of the rightness of our position(s) by recreating for them the story of how we came to believe as we do—"Let me tell you how…" As receivers, we are also more affected by, likely to remember longer, and are probably more likely to take action on persuasion if it is packaged in a story format. That is the basic premise for 95 percent of all television spot advertisements and probably a high percentage of most other persuasion we face on a daily basis. They tell us the tragic or comic story of the person whose company didn't have AFLAC insurance and who, as a result, lost everything or became a confused bumbler. It is also frequently the story behind most political candidacies. Obama Barack began his political race for the presidency in 2007 but preceded it with two books entitled *Dreams from My Father* and *The Audacity of Hope* (2006) in which he traced his roots and told how they led him to a political life and a belief that he could do something about today's political and public woes.

Public opinion at the time widely supported the invasion of Iraq in 2003, based largely on the story of a tyrant who repeatedly flaunted the United Nations and world opinion, used poison gas on his countrymen, committed other acts of genocide, and was developing nuclear weapons to use against the United States. The narrative played well for a time. In another example, many persons were convinced/persuaded to donate money to assist the victims of Hurricane Katrina and especially the citizens of New Orleans based on the story of how they had been displaced from their homes by faulty plans by the Army Corps of engineers, forgotten by FEMA and the federal government (which dovetailed with another narrative about the kind of President G. W. Bush was turning out to be) and discriminated on because of their race. And we could continue with hundreds of other examples where the power of the story worked both for persuaders and on persuadees. The point of these theories is to advise the use of the narrative, the dramatic, and the personal story in trying to persuade others and to caution receivers against being too willing to accept persuasion simply because it is packaged in a attractive story or narrative. As noted earlier we will encounter these theories in more depth as we move along. Now let us try to differentiate persuasion from other forms of influence because in the final analysis we want to learn about what gets us to do the things we do and believe the things we believe, both as individuals and as groups, governments, religions, and other social groups.

Most communication scholars agree that persuasion usually relies on communication that attempts to change another person in some way. Many suggest that the attempt must succeed to be considered persuasion, and most agree that persuasion requires participation by a sender and a receiver. Persuasion usually succeeds when it adapts to the receiver's world—the situation, the context, the culture and its norms, and the receivers'

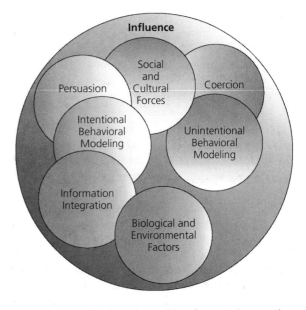

FIGURE 1.6 The relationship of persuasion to other forms of influence.

emotions and motivations. Figure 1.6 illustrates the relationships among various forms of influence that often confuse the new student of persuasion. The importance of each type of influence probably varies substantially from person to person and according to the context. The central point of this diagram is that many forces (including persuasion) bring change to our lives.

Those who study persuasion don't always distinguish among these forms of influence. In many discussions, "influence" and "persuasion" are interchangeable. We need to distinguish among several terms related to persuasion, including "influence," "coercion," "compliance-gaining," "acquiescence," "behavioral modeling," and "information integration." **Influence** refers to the the ways in which some kinds of things alter a person's attitude or behaviors. There are several ways that attitudes or behaviors may change. (See the best-selling *Influence: Science and Practice* by Robert B. Cialdini, 2001.) For example, many fans adopt the styles and/or behaviors of their pop idols. This represents influence through "behavior modeling." Similarly, many adults are embarrassed when their young child uses profanity in public—profanity that was overheard at home. This is also an outcome of behavioral modeling, though probably an unintended one. In contrast, most parents consciously try to model more positive behaviors for their children, hoping to "persuade" them to emulate those behaviors. Persuasion always entails some degree of choice. In contrast, **coercion,** another form of influence, always uses some level of force—physical or psychological—to gain compliance. A rather benign form is when peer pressure forces an individual to change attitudes or behaviors. Wikipedia defines it as "… compelling a person to behave in an involuntary way by use of threats, intimidation, or other form of pressure or force." Coercion also has levels. At one extreme it is being held at gunpoint. A slightly less direct use of force might be blackmail or threatening to harm another or deprive him in another way unless a ransom is paid. Peer pressure is a very mild but usually effective form of coercion—you really don't want to pierce your body or take drugs, but you submit to the pressure of conformity and go ahead and do.

Propaganda is also another form of influence—usually psychological versus logical—and, as we have already seen and shall continue to see throughout this book, it is frequently extremely effective—often changing entire cultures. It doesn't usually use direct or physical influence, but instead uses some level of psychological pushing that convinces us to believe, act, or act in accord with the sources' suggestions in some way. People weren't physically forced to oppose Al Qaeda, but after 9/11 and other terrorist acts, they felt compelled to label and oppose the enemy. Propaganda usually does that—it convinces us to label others as undesirable or hated and then to scapegoat them and take actions against them—imprisonment, death, discrimination, and so on. This was most dramatically seen in WW II Nazi Germany (see earlier examples of Nazi propaganda posters) and its occupied lands where children spied on parents, neighbors on neighbors, classmates on each other, and more, and where people enacted their own anti-Semitism often in horrific ways, which were whipped up by intense

propaganda. *Webster's Collegiate Dictionary* defines propaganda as "ideas, facts, or allegations spread deliberately to further or to damage an opposing cause." Notice the use of the words "deliberate," "spread," and "cause." The propagandist acts deliberately, not by chance and tries to extend his or her message as widely as possible—usually via some mass media and the message promotes or opposes some ideology. So most advertising, while deliberate, doesn't promote or oppose a cause but uses facts, ideas, or allegations to promote a *brand* or to oppose a competing brand. In some cases like advertising it is quite benign, but in other cases it can be malignant and psychologically coercive as was the case with Nazism or as is the case today with many Jihadist/terrorist messages.

Persuasion and coercion represent two ends of a continuum ranging from free choice to forced choice. Although terrorism uses coercion, the co-creation of states of identification between source and receiver doesn't often result, persuasion of a different sort can occur as an unexpected result. For example, acceptance of cultural diversity suffered after 9/11, and many people avoided air travel—especially if other passengers appeared to be of Middle Eastern extraction. In other words, events can be a form of influence, though not always in the hoped-for direction. Influence can also occur when a person chooses a certain action in return for some future concession, as frequently happens in political favor swapping: "You scratch my back and I'll scratch yours." In such a case, persuasion, as a kind of influence, occurred in making a political deal because some common ground was reached; but none of the people involved *really* changed their minds based on the merits of the actual issues. Information integration and analysis is yet another route to influence that doesn't involve real persuasion. For example, a retail manager may change his or her inventory management behavior after learning that quarterly sales in certain product categories (e.g., seasonal items) were up or down in the past quarter. Again, persuasion is not really involved, since neither co-creation, common ground, nor interactive communication occurred. And something overheard in a conversation, read in the newspaper, or seen on TV or the Internet may lead to changes in behavior; but this is not persuasion for the same reasons. Co-creation is central to our definition of persuasion. Persuasive contexts extend beyond public-speaking situations but all involve some kind of co-creation. For instance, most advocacy and related propaganda, protest marches, decision-making get-togethers, staff meetings, sales presentations, and mass media events all involve the co-creation of identification between persuaders and receivers. With all of these kinds of influence including persuasion, some of it is going to be unfair, untrustworthy, and even unethical. How can responsible influence (particularly persuasion-prompted influence) occur in today's confusing world? Let's examine an easy-to-use model that will help us, as receivers, to ensure that such persuasion can occur and that we can spot its opposite—irresponsible or unethical persuasion—when it occurs.

RANK'S MODEL OF PERSUASION—A FIRST MEANS OF SELF-PROTECTION

As noted in our discussion of doublespeak, the National Council of Teachers of English (NCTE) seeks ways to teach students to identify doublespeak and to become critical receivers of it and other kinds of persuasion. Researcher Hugh Rank (1976) offered a model for doing just that. He noted even back then that: "These kids are growing up in a propaganda blitz unparalleled in human history.... Schools should shift their emphasis in order to train the larger segment of our population in a new kind of literacy so that more citizens can recognize the more sophisticated techniques and patterns of persuasion" (p. 5). Think how much more challenging our Seven Faces of Persuasion world is today. Rank's easy-to-use, analytical tool is called the intensify/downplay model, and its goal is to help you to become more critical and analytical receivers. It defines and gives examples of four

major persuasive **strategies** and six associated **tactics** frequently used by persuaders which critical receivers can identify. Remember that a persuader's **goals** are implemented in the strategies she or he chooses, and these strategies are put in place using certain tactics. Rank maintains that persuaders employ these major strategies to achieve their goals. One of Rank's major *strategy* is to either **intensify** certain aspects of their product, cause, or candidate, or some aspect of the competition. Another of his strategies is to **downplay** certain aspects of their brand, cause, or candidate, or to downplay positive aspects of the competing brands, causes, ideologies, or candidates. Often, they do both. Figure 1.7 illustrates this model. Persuaders choose from *four strategies of action*. They can:

1. Intensify their own good points
2. Intensify the weak points of the opposition
3. Downplay their own weak points
4. Downplay the good points of the opposition.

Persuaders also use *tactics* such as **repetition, association,** and **composition** to intensify their own good points or the bad points of the opposition; they use the *tactics* of **omission, diversion,** and **confusion** to downplay their own bad points or the good points of the opposing brands, candidates, causes, or ideologies. Any one of these tactics can be used logically or emotionally and can employ interactive or more traditional media to accomplish the persuader's intentions. We have seen them in the powerful propaganda of the Nazis, and continue to see them in the propaganda surrounding the war on terrorism, the immigration issue, the war in Iraq, and other policy issues that continue to emerge as well as in more harmless persuasive attempts like advertisements, letters to the editor, and so forth.

Persuasive strategy, then, is an overall step-by-step program for reaching some goal. Strategy also dictates tactics or the specific kinds of arguments, evidence, or points the persuader makes. For example, politicians wants to persuade voters to support their candidacy (the goal), so they try to make the audience feel good about particular platform plans and their own character (the strategy of intensifying

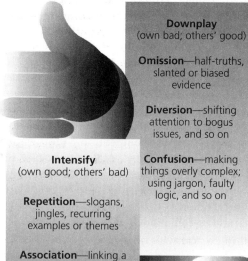

Downplay
(own bad; others' good)

Omission—half-truths,
slanted or biased
evidence

Diversion—shifting
attention to bogus
issues, and so on

Confusion—making
things overly complex;
using jargon, faulty
logic, and so on

Intensify
(own good; others' bad)

Repetition—slogans,
jingles, recurring
examples or themes

Association—linking a
positive or negative
valued idea to one's
persuasive advice

Composition—graphic
layout, design, typeface,
and so on

FIGURE 1.7   Rank's intensify/downplay schema.
SOURCE: Adapted by permission of Hugh Rank.

one's own good). Al Gore accomplished this by taking forthright stands on the issue of global warming and winning the Nobel prize for his documentary "An Inconvenient Truth." The documentary, associated public appearances, and noting what President Bush said about global warming not even existing were all tactics of the communication strategy to build a positive image for Gore.

Intensification

Persuaders either want to look good in the eyes of the audience—the voters, joiners, donors, or potential customers—or they want their opponents to look bad in the same eyes. Some tactics intensify the persuader's own good points ("He's always been on the right side of environmental and immigration issues"). Others intensify the bad points of the other guy, thus making the persuader look good by comparison ("He didn't tell us the truth on WMDs—so don't trust his opinions on Global Warming"). So the tactics of repetition, association, and composition are all effective in implementing the communication strategy of intensification of one's own good or the others' bad points.

Repetition.   One way to intensify good or bad points about a product, person, or candidate is to repeat them over and over again. That's why slogans, jingles, and logotypes work. For example, Energizer batteries "keep going and going" in TV spots, magazine ads, and even on their packages, have done so for decades and probably will continue to keep "working and working." We have repeatedly heard that the war in Iraq is central to the war on terrorism over and over again and from different sources; we repeatedly are warned against trans-fats in our diets; and we know that "At Ford; Quality is Job #1" by heart. All are examples of the power of repetition in persuading people—either intensifying one's own good or intensifying the opposition's bad points.

Association.   Another tactic for intensification is association, which operates in three steps. It (1) links a cause, brand, candidate, and so on (2) to something already liked or disliked (3) by the audience. Thus, the cause, brand, or candidate becomes identified with the thing liked or disliked and the favor or disfavor "rubs off" and hence is likewise liked or disliked.

Or consider that politicians know that we have fears about privacy, so they refer to secret surveillance by our government (i.e., without a warrant—something we would probably outlaw). Here association works the other way—something not liked (invasion of privacy) is associated with the politician or party to be defeated. In commerce, advertisers associate a certain kind of athletic shoe with a well-known professional athlete, everyday people who exercise, and with a person in a wheelchair as Nike did in one of their ads. Or NFL athletes regularly testify during televised games as to the good aspects of the United Way Fund appeal. These associations intensify the good aspects of the shoe and show that one needn't be an athlete to benefit from its features or promote the good cause to which the NFL is committed. Visual cues can also create association. That's why candidates are pictured in front of the Lincoln Memorial or the Capitol. Video footage also can intensify the good aspects of the United Way or other good causes and the bad aspects of world problems like poverty.

Composition.   The third and final tactic of intensification uses physical composition of the message to emphasize one's own good points or the other guy's bad points. This usually involves the use of nonverbal or visual means and takes several forms. Altering the makeup of the printed word (as in changing "U.S.A." to "U.$.A.") sends the message that the nation is only interested in money. Altering the composition of a candidate's publicity photo often manipulates meaning. A low camera angle makes the candidate look larger than life and tells us to look up to him or her. Altering the layout of an advertisement intensifies persuasive outcomes. For example, the upper-right and lower-left corners of a magazine page or a poster are considered fallow, or less likely to get full reader attention. The eye only glances at them momentarily, so guess where the tobacco industry usually puts the requisite health warning? A good example of composition being used is seen in Figure 1.8.

These cases also exemplify the use of the peripheral route of the ELM in persuasive appeals, and as a result we don't put much time, effort, or research into processing them. Furthermore, they also demonstrate the age of advocacy in which we live when a health clinic feels it must advertise that it is a "good citizen" in the community. Other of the principles we have discussed are also reflected here. What are they? What common ground has

been co-created? To give you an idea of how persuaders also use composition to compare and contrast, consider the following hypothetical TV spot against a candidate. To intensify the politician's bad points, an ad superimposes his or her image on a picture of a polluted river or a filthy harbor in the home district. To emphasize the negative identification and to encourage further emotional interaction with the spot, a muted version of "America the Beautiful" might accompany a voice-over talking about the incumbent's lack of social responsibility. The polluted river or harbor, the background, the music, and the voice-over combine to "compose" the ad's meaning. Another example of intensification is seen in most before/after ads that use composition to show us the good points about the brand that inevitably changes things for the better (e.g., whiter teeth, thinner bodies, happier babies). You can use Rank's intensification as a starting place in becoming a critical receiver by identifying the strategies and tactics used by persuaders in achieving their strategy of Intensification.

Downplaying

Sometimes persuaders want to avoid intensifying or calling attention to something because it undermines their persuasive goal. The government doesn't tell us over and over about the billions of dollars being spent by the Department of Defense (e.g., $171 for a hammer or $600 for a toilet seat), and it opposes other persuaders who do repeat those figures. Advertisers avoid advertising the good mileage results of the competing brand, and this strategy carries over to other kinds of persuasion as well. Downplaying can soften the persuader's own weak points while downplaying a competitor's strong points. The car manufacturer tells about their good styling but avoids telling us about the competition's superior safety. The politician, who knows he or she made a bad decision on a certain vote, tries to avoid mentioning it. Let's look at some tactics used in the strategy of downplaying: *omission, diversion,* and *confusion.*

FIGURE 1.8   This ad for Cleveland Clinic is another example of how composition persuades. Note Ryan's confident handwritten message—"After they control my seizures...."—the tear in the page and his scribbled over mistake the act of a young boy, making his determination to recover from epilepsy all the more moving. Now compare those elements of the ad with his wishes for a "totally awesome bicycle, a skateboard (with flames), a trampoline, and a big wrestling match with Dad," all of which will be fulfilled because of the quality care he will receive at Cleveland Clinic. Cleveland Clinic is world famous in its treatment of epilepsy and many other serious health problems of children and adults.

SOURCE: Courtesy of Cleveland Clinic.

Omission.   Some persuaders simply leave out critical information to avoid highlighting their own shortcomings or the competitor's strengths. For example, the government didn't tell us about the questionable "quality" of their intelligence on Weapons of Mass Destruction (WMD) in Iraq, that is, propaganda that conceals its source and its results by using omission. As a result, we went to war looking for something that apparently didn't exist, even after careful searching. Omission also occurs in many advertisements, for instance, in those for foods. Live photographs of some kinds of food are frequently unappetizing—lettuce wilts, ice melts, red meat color fades to gray, and so on. As a result, there is an occupation known as "food cosmetics" in which the expert uses a variety of techniques to make the food look better (e.g., photographs of salads look crisper if coated with hair spray, and photographs of floor tile adhesive look more appetizing than actual chocolate pud-

B O X 1.4   Cultural Diversity and Persuasion

 To become familiar with the many issues that are intertwined with our increasing diversity as a country, go to www.newsreel. org topics and explore the content and authors of various diversity-related documentary videos. Visit the video by Jean Kilbourne entitled "Killing Us Softly," which addresses the many ways in which advertising forces women to value attractiveness, sexuality, and gender stereotypes, thus making women and children vulnerable to violent abuse. Kilbourne claims that advertisers are the real pornographers of our times. Other interesting options include "The Politics of Love in Black and White," which explores the problems of interracial couples; and "Colorism," which investigates the caste system that operates in Black communities based on features, hair, and skin shade. Take a look at "Tough Guise," which focuses on the relationship between gender and violence. Other titles will interest and sensitize you to persuasion and diversity.

ding). The officials of a charitable organization omit telling that the administrative costs for dispersing the charitable donations exceed the actual donations themselves. And our propaganda-filled world also has examples of omitting the crucial information for making a logical or reasoned decisions like the one noted above. For instance, in the cattle slaughtering example mentioned above, advocates for its closure omitted telling the readers that since the closure of two similar plants in Texas, the number of horses found tied up in forest preserves or state and national to stave had sky-rocketed; and in the same debate opponents mentioning that with the closing of U.S. slaughter houses, thousands of the animals were sent to Mexican facilities where the animals were not disposed of in a humane way but were stabbed in the spinal cord. This kept them paralyzed and calm as well as "fresh" for slaughter.

Omission also means avoiding mention of the opponent's strengths. It is hard to imagine a toy manufacturer mentioning that kids love the competitor's doll or train set more than their own brand. Likewise it is rare that a politician would emphasize the opponent's honesty, hard work, and sincerity. And it would be foolish for a bank to note that other banks offer better rates. So the tactic of omission is a critical way to downplay either one's own flaws or the opposition's strengths.

Can you identify examples of omission from today's news reports?

Diversion.   Diversion consists of shifting attention away from an opponent's strengths or one's own shortcomings but this time not through omission but by using substitute issues to divert the receiver's scrutiny. Persuaders frequently use humor to shift attention. Making a joke of the competitor's image—("He's the Huck Finn of Community Leaders") diverts attention from the issues to the person (an example of what is called an *ad hominem* as we shall see later). In another advertising example, Headon over-the-counter headache "medicine" diverts attention from its bad points (e.g., time to take effect, messiness) by diverting our attention to its ease of application. Toyota doesn't mention that it is a foreign brand but instead focuses its ads on the U.S. factories that assemble the foreign-made parts. The polluting power company diverts attention from its use of high sulfur coal to its support of "Save the Species" programs. And the clever politician avoids mentioning his or her early support for the now unpopular war to their longtime support and promotion of universal health care. Diversion can also re-direct audience attention from the major issues of the debate to inconsequential ones and thus siphons valuable time away from discussion and interaction between the persuader and persuadee. This happened in the longtime debate over immigration. Instead of focusing the debate on the physical impossibility of transferring ten million illegal aliens back to their home countries, the office holder focused the debate on the effectiveness of putting a fence or wall along the Canadian and Mexican borders, thus diverting attention and downplaying the major difficulty in solving the complex issues involved in dealing with the large numbers of persons involved.

Confusion.   Another downplaying tactic creates confusion in the audience's mind. Using technical jargon that the receiver doesn't understand creates such confusion. For example, the Department of Defense has a jargonized term called BRAC. That's an acronym for "Base Realignment and Closure" a term sure to confuse. It actually means closing a base in one state and moving it to another, which naturally has good and bad results for both places; but the term confuses and camouflages the resulting effect the action will have on jobs, traffic, behavior problems, and so on. Another way to create confusion is by weaving an intricate and rambling argument that evades the real issues results in audience confusion.

Yet another device for confusing persuadees is the use of faulty logic. Consider the logic used in the following claim "Mr. Taco has delicious food— look at how clean its kitchen is!" The weak connection is apparent, but it will probably confuse some potential customers. It is what is called a "red herring" because it simply doesn't follow or isn't part of the school of thought of regular "herrings." Does cleanliness equal delicious tasting food? It may be that clean kitchens don't ever produce good tasting food. In 2008, the President wanted to build a ballistic missile shield in Poland to protect us from the possibility that Iran might attack us with as yet undeveloped nuclear weapons. The logic was that since they were working on nuclear capability, they could also

work on and get help with developing ballistic missile technology and could possibly use the weapons against the United States. How dumb! Look at the unlikely weasels here. In the first place, we have hundreds of nuclear weapons to turn on them in retaliation and that would totally destroy their country. Moreover, it would take them decades to get to a dangerous Level of military weaponry even with help from North Korea and others, especially since their economy is about the size of Finland's and their military expenditures are less than 1 percent of ours. And finally, what good would a shield be if it is located in Poland? Now consider a more insipid advertising claim that "She's Beautiful! She's Engaged! She Uses Earth Balsam Hand Creme!" It implies a "logical progression" that, because she used the hand cream, she became beautiful, and because of that, she met and won the man of her dreams.

A governmental example occurred when the White House declared in 2005 that it had adopted 37 of the 39 reforms recommended by the 9/11 commission, which was established to find out what caused the 9/11 terrorist attacks and resulting tragedy. Sounds like a very logical outcome doesn't it? The only problem was that one of the rejected recommendations was that the United States should comply with the Geneva Convention's standards on humane treatment of prisoners, which outlaw torture as a means of extracting information from captured terrorists. As a result many foreign governments now refuse to cooperate with the United States's "War on Terrorism" fearing that they will be labeled as also violating the international agreement. And there are other ways to confuse the persuadee as we shall see. Taken together with the other tactics of downplaying as well as those of intensification, we see that clever persuaders have many options when considering how to persuade gullible and uncritical audiences. So it is incumbent on us to train ourselves to be critical and skeptical receivers as we encounter the Seven Faces of Persuasion in today's world.

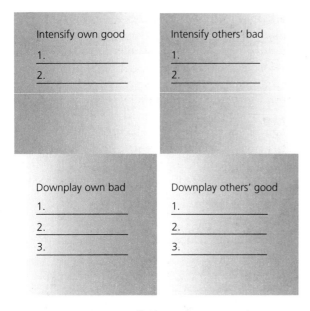

Intensify own good	Intensify others' bad
1. _____	1. _____
2. _____	2. _____

Downplay own bad	Downplay others' good
1. _____	1. _____
2. _____	2. _____
3. _____	3. _____

FIGURE 1.9   Intensify/downplay scorecard.
SOURCE: By permission of Hugh Rank.

A METHOD
OF SELF-PROTECTION

In his discussion of doublespeak, Rank (1976) offered some advice about how to detect the flaws of persuaders who use various tactics to intensify or downplay: "When they intensify, you downplay. When they downplay, you intensify." A way to follow Rank's advice systematically is to divide a sheet of paper into quarters, as shown in Figure 1.9, and then enter the kinds of downplaying and intensifying going on in the message(s). Simply seeing these items makes you more alert to the kind of manipulation going on. Try using the self-protection method on an advertisement or a political speech. When the ad or speech downplays something, you intensify its shortcomings. And when it intensifies something, you downplay the intensification. We will discuss a number of other tools of analysis as we proceed, but Rank's

intensify/downplay tool seems a useful general tool of analysis to employ when first faced with a persuasive blitz.

REVIEW AND CONCLUSION

If you now feel more alert to the possible ways persuaders manipulate you, congratulations! You're already on your way to becoming a more critical, doubting, and skeptical receiver. You now need to arm yourself with some tools of analysis that make for wise consumers. Rank's model is a good beginning, but there are more ways to tune our critical abilities And there is a bonus for learning them. Seeing what works in what circumstances, and with what kinds of people—yourself and others—helps you prepare to persuade others when encountering similar circumstances. Skillful consumers of messages learn to be more effective producers of messages. As we move ahead, apply the tools of persuasive analysis on your own and in the study questions at the end of each chapter. Use the diversity, propaganda, and interactive media boxes as well as the learning goals, key terms, and applications of ethics. Also, explore the Internet and research issues via a search engine. Examine the ways in which persuasion operates on the interpersonal level. Every day you make decisions in nonpublic settings. Your parents may try to persuade you to avoid certain occupational fields, to seek a summer job, or to put off a purchase. You need to decide to heed or reject your parents' career/major in college advice on the basis of your interpersonal communication with them. Rank's model helps here too. Identify what your parents intensify and downplay. Do the same thing with other interpersonal relationships—roommates, friends, colleagues, the government, your boss, advertisers, and others. Then try to spot the kinds of symbols that lead to or discourage identification. Critical analysis of interpersonal persuasion helps you to make informed decisions. People are persuaded daily in the public arena through advertisements, speeches, radio and TV programs, newspaper and magazine articles, and the Internet. But we also need to remember that, in addition to the world of the marketplace and political/ideological realms, persuasion also takes place in our personal lives and we need to become critical receivers in those venues as well.

KEY TERMS

After reading this chapter, you should be able to identify, explain, and give an example of the following key terms or concepts:

seven faces of persuasion

interactive media

cultural diversity

propaganda/advocacy

propaganda

response–ability

doublespeak

self-protection

rhetoric

artistic proof

inartistic proof

ethos

pathos

logos

common ground

enthymemes

identification

co-creation

self-persuasion

Elaboration Likelihood Model (ELM)

central information processing route

peripheral information processing route

influence

coercion

SMCR model

tactics

strategies

goals

intensify

downplay

repetition

association

composition

omission

diversion

confusion

APPLICATION OF ETHICS

The Ethics of Omission. A homeowner needs to sell his home but is hesitant to inform Realtors or prospective buyers that there has been a mold problem in the basement in the past and that it could become a toxic variety. Presently it only smells in damp weather and is soon removed by spraying bleach and washing down the basement. What should the homeowner do? (1) Spray the basement, list the house for sale, and not mention the mold problem. (2) Spray the basement and mention the problem and the present solution to both buyers and realtors. (3) Hire a toxic mold expert to find out if the mold really is likely to become toxic and discover what can be done about it if it is indeed toxic. (4) Don't spray the basement since the weather is now dry and simply list the house as "For Sale by Owner." What are the ethical problems in this case? How would you characterize each of the homeowner's options in terms of what has been discussed in this chapter?

QUESTIONS FOR FURTHER THOUGHT

1. If you or someone you know recently made a major purchase (e.g., an automobile, an MP3 player, iPhone, or a digital camera), identify the context in which persuasion occurred. Where did the persuasion take place? In the showroom? Through a television ad? Interpersonally, such as in discussing the purchase with a friend? What kinds of appeals were made? What characteristics were intensified? Downplayed? Was the persuasion emotional or logical, or both? What did you learn from the careful examination?

2. Much persuasion occurs in interpersonal contexts. Examine one of your interpersonal relationships, such as that between you and your parents, your roommate, a teammate, or a fellow member of an organization or church. Describe how, when, and where persuasion operated in the relationship. What characteristics about yourself have you intensified? Downplayed? What about the other person's intensification? Downplaying? Which tactics worked best? Repetition? Association? Omission?

3. Beginning with the definition of persuasion offered in this chapter, create your own model of persuasion that reflects all the important elements of the definition given here.

4. Identify three types of persuasion you recently processed, and analyze each according to the definition offered in this chapter and the ELM (e.g., an advertisement, a television talk show, a sermon, or an interpersonal relationship). What verbal and/or visual symbols were used? Did you interact with the message? What did the persuader intend? Which information processing route (peripheral or the central) operated for you? What created identification or common ground for you? What was intensified? Downplayed? Using which tactics? Repetition? Association? Composition? Omission? Confusion? Diversion?

5. Describe the tactics of intensification, and explain how they work. Give examples of their use on television, in print, on radio, by politicians, and by advertisers.

6. Enter the word "Propaganda" in a search engine and look at some historical and contemporary examples. How do they differ? What did the audience of the times (e.g., WW I or WW II) identifies with? How did the propaganda create common ground with the families of soldiers in each of the World Wars? How was it accomplished in the contemporary examples (e.g., the wars in Iraq or Afghanistan). Now do the same thing with the term "Advocacy."

7. Describe the tactics of downplaying and explain how they work. Give examples of their use on television, in print, on radio, by politicians, and by advertisers.

8. Identify a current "propaganda blitz" (e.g., the war on terrorism, the emigration issue, etc.) going on in the media coverage of an event or issue. Which route in the ELM was employed? Which (if any) of the five characteristics of propaganda (i.e., concealing source or results) is operating? Describe current examples of the strategies of intensification and downplaying that seem central in the "war on terrorism" propaganda. What tactics of intensification or downplaying are used regarding environmental issues? Are they ethical or unethical?

9. List some of the interactive media you use. How many of them came about in recent times—say since 2000? How many of them preceded the Internet?

10. Have you noticed the ways in which we are becoming a more diverse culture? How do they affect the persuasive process?

✳

 For online activities, go to the *Persuasion* book companion Web site at http://academic.cengage.com/communication/larson12.

2

✳

Perspectives on Ethics in Persuasion

RICHARD L. JOHANNESEN
Northern Illinois University

LEARNING GOALS

After reading this chapter, you should be able to:

1. Discuss the importance of ethical issues and standards in the persuasion process.

2. Recognize the complexity of making ethical judgments about persuasion.

3. Apply six ethical perspectives for judging persuasion.

4. Apply specific ethical criteria for assessing political communication and commercial advertising.

5. Recognize how moral exclusion functions in unethical persuasion to harm people of diverse cultures, religions, genders, and sexual orientations.

6. Recognize how interactive and cyberspace media pose significant ethical issues for persuasion.

7. Start developing your own workable and justifiable ethical framework or code of ethics for evaluating your persuasive choices of means and ends and those of other persuaders.

Students enrolled in persuasion courses frequently are preparing for careers in advertising, sales, law, journalism, business, or politics. But students interested in such careers may be surprised by the extremely negative perceptions people have of the ethics and honesty of persons in such professions. The 2006 Gallup Poll of perceived honesty and ethics of 23 professions ranked the following 11, in descending order, as lowest in perceived ethicality: journalists, state governors, business executives, lawyers, stockbrokers, senators, congressmen, insurance salesmen, HMO managers, advertising practitioners, and, at the bottom, car salesmen (retrieved 6-11-2007; http://www.gallup.com).

Evidence abounds that supports public concern over the decline of ethical behavior. A May 2007 Gallup Poll of citizen perceptions of moral values in the United States found that 83 percent of respondents rated the current state of moral values as only fair/poor and 81 percent thought the level of moral values was declining (retrieved 11-6-2007; http://www.gallup.com). The Gallup Poll editors note that "moral issues consistently appear in Gallup's monthly measurement of the most important problems facing the country," usually in the top 10 priorities citizens have for their elected representatives (retrieved 11-6-2007; http://www.gallup.com).

The Josephson Institute of Ethics conducted a 2006 national survey of over 33,000 high school students. The results show a puzzling contradiction. On the one hand, over 90 percent of those surveyed said that it is "important to me to be a person of good character," that "honesty and trust are essential in personal relationships," and that they are satisfied with their own "ethics and character." On the other hand, in stark contrast, 82 percent admitted that they had lied to a parent (57 percent two or more times) and 62 percent lied to a teacher (35 percent two or more times) about something significant in the past year. Sixty percent admitted they cheated during a test at school the past year, 35 percent two or more times (www.josephsoninstitute.org; released October 15, 2006). In his book, *The Cheating Culture*, David Callahan (2004) documents a "pattern of widespread cheating throughout U.S. society," observes that people "not only are cheating in more areas but also are feeling less guilty about it," and concludes that most of the cheating "is by people who, on the whole, view themselves as upstanding members of society" (pp. 12–14).

Imagine that you are an audience member listening to a speaker—call him Mr. Bronson. His aim is to persuade you to contribute money to the cancer research program of a major medical research center. Suppose that, with one exception, all the evidence, reasoning, and motivational appeals he employs are valid and above suspicion on any ethical grounds. However, at one point in his speech, Bronson knowingly uses a set of false statistics to scare you into believing that, during your lifetime, there is a much greater probability of you getting some form of cancer than is actually the case.

To help our analysis of the ethics of this hypothetical persuasive situation, consider these issues. If you, or society at large, view Bronson's persuasive goal as worthwhile, does the worth of that goal justify his use of false statistics as one means to achieve his end? Does the fact that he consciously chose to use false statistics make a difference in your evaluation? If he used the false statistics out of ignorance or a failure to check his sources, how might your ethical judgment be altered, if at all? Should Bronson be condemned as an unethical person or an unethical speaker, or, in this instance, for use of a specific unethical technique?

Carefully consider the standards you would employ to make your ethical judgment of Bronson. Are your standards purely pragmatic? (In other words, should Bronson avoid false statistics because he might get caught?) Are they societal in origin? (If he gets caught, his credibility as a representative would be weakened with this and future audiences, or his getting caught might weaken the credibility of other cancer society representatives.) Should he be criticized for violating an implied ethical agreement between you and him? (You might not expect a representative of a famous research institute to use questionable techniques, and so you would be especially vulnerable.) Finally, should his conscious use of false statistics be considered unethical because you are denied the accurate, relevant information you need to make an intelligent decision on an important public issue?

As receivers and senders of persuasion, we have the responsibility to uphold appropriate ethical standards for persuasion, to encourage freedom of inquiry and expression, and to promote public debate as crucial to democratic decision making. To achieve these goals, we must understand their complexity and recognize the difficulty of achieving them. One purpose of this chapter is to stimulate you to make reasoned choices among ethical options in developing your own positions or judgments.

Ethical issues focus on value judgments concerning degrees of right and wrong, virtue and vice, and ethical obligations in human conduct. Persuasion, as one type of human behavior, always contains potential ethical issues, for several reasons:

- In persuasion, one person, or a group of people, attempts to influence other people by altering their beliefs, attitudes, values, and actions.

- Persuasion requires us to make conscious choices among ends sought and rhetorical means used to achieve the ends.

- Persuasion necessarily involves a potential judge—any or all of the receivers, the persuader, or an independent observer.

As a receiver and sender of persuasion, you will evaluate the ethics of a persuasive instance based on the ethical standards you are using. You may even choose to ignore ethical judgment entirely. People often cite several justifications to avoid direct analysis and resolution of ethical issues in persuasion:

- Everyone knows the appeal or tactic is unethical, so there is nothing to talk about.

- Only success matters, so ethics are irrelevant to persuasion.

- Ethical judgments are matters of individual personal opinion, so there are no final answers.

However, potential ethical questions exist regardless of how they are answered. Whether you wish it or not, consumers of persuasion generally will judge your effort, formally or informally, in part by their own relevant ethical criteria. If for no other reason than the pragmatic motivation of enhancing your chance of success, you would do well to consider the ethical standards held by your audience. This chapter should increase your understanding of how the ethical "face" or dimension of persuasion relates to other faces of persuasion, such as our networked, interactive, media-saturated world, our multicultural world, and a world of doublespeak and propaganda.

Now we turn to the concept of ethical responsibility. What is it and what are some of its components?

ETHICAL RESPONSIBILITY
of Senders

Persuaders' ethical responsibilities can stem from statuses or positions they have earned or have been granted, from commitments (promises, pledges, agreements) they have made, or from the consequences (effects) of their communication for others. **Responsibility** includes the elements of fulfilling duties and obligations, of being accountable to other individuals and groups, of adhering to agreed-upon standards, and of being accountable to one's own conscience. But an essential element of responsible communication, for both sender and receiver, is the exercise of thoughtful and deliberate judgment. That is, the responsible communicator carefully analyzes claims, soundly assesses probable consequences, and conscientiously weighs relevant values. In a sense, a responsible communicator is "response-able." She or he exercises the ability to respond (is responsive) to the needs and communications of others in sensitive, thoughtful, fitting ways

(Freund, 1960; Niebuhr, 1963; Pennock, 1960; Pincoffs, 1975).

Whether persuaders seem intentionally and knowingly to use particular content or techniques is a factor that most of us consider in judging communication ethicality. If a dubious communication behavior seems to stem more from an accident, a slip of the tongue, or even ignorance, we may be less harsh in our ethical assessment. For most of us, it is the *intentional* use of ethically questionable tactics that merits the harshest condemnation.

On the other hand, we might contend that, in argumentative and persuasive situations, communicators have an ethical obligation to double-check the soundness of their evidence and reasoning before they present it to others; sloppy preparation is no excuse for ethical lapses. A similar view might be advanced concerning elected or appointed government officials. If they use obscure or jargon-laden language that clouds the accurate and clear representation of ideas, even if it is not intended to deceive or hide, they are ethically irresponsible. Such officials, according to this view, should be obligated to communicate clearly and accurately with citizens in fulfillment of their governmental duties. As a related question, we can ask whether sincerity of intent releases persuaders from their ethical responsibility to use fair means and effects. Could we say that if Adolf Hitler's fellow Germans had judged him to be sincere, they need not have assessed the ethics of his persuasion? In such cases, evaluations are probably best carried out by appraising sincerity and ethicality separately. For example, a persuader sincere in intent might use an unethical strategy.

American culture emphasizes dual concerns for maximizing the latitude of freedom of communication and for promoting responsible exercise of that freedom. In the United States we have a long history of First Amendment and Supreme Court protection of freedom of speech and press. At the same time, citizens generally expect that freedom to be used in ethically responsible ways. Often we may observe or experience a tension between communication freedom and responsibility, and we have to decide which one should take precedence in a particular situation.

The freedom versus responsibility tension might occur when we, as individuals, carry to an extreme the now traditional view that the best test of the soundness of our ideas is their ability to survive in the free and open public "marketplace" of ideas. We might take the mistaken view that, as individuals, we have no responsibility to test the ethicality of our persuasive techniques and goals before we present them. We incorrectly assume that the logical and ethical soundness of our ideas need only to be evaluated through their ability to survive in the marketplace in competition with other ideas and differing viewpoints. Such a view could lead each of us to ignore our ethical responsibilities as persuaders because, supposedly, the marketplace ultimately will render the necessary judgments. However, we must remember that while we do have First Amendment protection of our persuasion, each of us also has the responsibility to exercise that freedom in an ethical manner (adapted from Meiklejohn, 1948, pp. 73–74).

Questions about how far persuaders should go in adapting their message to particular audiences focus on a special type of ethical responsibility. We now examine this issue.

ADAPTATION TO THE AUDIENCE

What are the ethics of adapting to the audience? Most persuaders seek to secure some kind of response from receivers. To what degree is it ethical for them to alter their ideas and proposals to adapt to the needs, capacities, values, and expectations of their audience? To secure acceptance, some persuaders adapt to an audience to the extent of so changing their own ideas that the ideas are no longer really theirs. These persuaders merely say what the audience wants to hear, regardless of their own convictions. During the 2007–2008 Republican presidential primary campaign, for example, candidate Mitt Romney was criticized by opponents and the media for changing his views on significant issues depending on the audience he attempted to

persuade. One political cartoonist (Horsey, 2007) satirically depicted Romney as saying: "And on torture, immigration, and taxes, I'll adopt any viewpoint that'll get me elected. So you don't need to worry about my beliefs. I don't have any." In contrast, some persuaders go to the opposite extreme of making little or no adaptation to their audience. They do not take serious account of the nature of their audience, no matter whether that audience is much like them or whether it reflects cultural or religious diversity. To the audience, the speaker, writer, or advertisement seems unconnected to them or unconcerned about them.

Some degree of adaptation for specific audiences in language choice, evidence, value appeals, organization, and communication medium is a crucial part of successful and ethical persuasion. No absolute rule can be set down here. Persuaders must decide the ethical intermediate point between their own idea in its pure form and that idea modified to achieve maximum impact with the audience. The search is for an appropriate point between two undesirable extremes—the extreme of saying only what the audience desires and will approve and the extreme of complete lack of concern for and understanding of the audience. Both extremes are ethically irresponsible (Booth, 2004, pp. 50–54). In this era of heightened awareness of ethnic, racial, and religious diversity, persuaders face significant practical and ethical choices concerning the appropriate degree of audience adaptation.

A frequent ethical question facing persuaders is: Does the end justify the means? How should we answer that question? What are some guidelines for answering it?

THE ETHICS OF ENDS AND MEANS

In assessing the ethics of persuasion, does the end justify the means? Does the necessity of achieving a goal widely acknowledged as worthwhile justify the use of ethically questionable techniques? We must be aware that the persuasive means employed can have cumulative effects on receivers' thoughts and decision-making habits, apart from and in addition to the specific end that the communicator seeks. No matter what purpose they serve, the arguments, appeals, structure, and language we choose do shape the audience's values, thinking habits, language patterns, and level of trust.

To say that the ends do not *always* justify the means is different from saying that the ends never justify means. The persuader's goal probably is best considered as one of a number of potentially relevant ethical criteria from which we select the most appropriate standards. Under some circumstances, such as threats to physical survival, the goal of personal or national security may *temporarily* take precedence over other criteria. In general, however, we can best make mature ethical assessments by evaluating the ethics of persuasive techniques apart from the worth and morality of the persuader's specific goal. We can strive to judge the ethics of means and ends *separately*. In some cases, we may find ethical persuasive tactics employed to achieve an unethical goal; in other cases, unethical techniques may be used in the service of an entirely ethical goal.

Consider this report in the *Chicago Tribune* (April 12, 2000, sec. 1, p. 3):

> More than one-third of doctors surveyed nationwide admit deceiving insurance companies to help patients get the care they need. Their tactics include exaggerating the severity of an illness to help patients avoid being sent home early from the hospital, listing an inaccurate diagnosis on bills and reporting non-existent symptoms to secure insurance coverage.... More than one-quarter, 28.5 percent, said it is necessary to "game" the system to provide high-quality care.

Does the end of securing high-quality care for patients justify use of such deceptive communication tactics? Why or why not?

Although discussed in the context of journalistic ethics, the six questions suggested by Warren Bovee (1991) can serve as useful probes to determine the degree of ethicality of almost any means–ends relationship in persuasion (see Figure 2.1).

Here are the questions in paraphrased form:

1. Are the means truly unethical/morally evil or merely distasteful, unpopular, unwise, or ineffective?

2. Is the end truly good, or does it simply appear good to us because we desire it?

3. Is it probable that the ethically bad or suspect means actually will achieve the good end?

4. Is the same good achievable using other more ethical means if we are willing to be creative, patient, determined, and skillful?

5. Is the good end clearly and overwhelmingly better than the probable bad effects of the means used to attain it? Bad means require justification whereas good means do not.

6. Will the use of unethical means to achieve a good end withstand public scrutiny? Could the use of unethical means be justified to those most affected by them or to those most capable of impartially judging them?

Perhaps now we can better answer the question: In persuasion, does the end justify the means? Certainly we see more clearly some of the issues and options involved.

The ethics of persuasion are important both for persuaders and for receivers of persuasion. We turn now to special ethical responsibilities for audiences.

ETHICAL RESPONSIBILITIES OF RECEIVERS

What are your ethical responsibilities as a receiver of or respondent to persuasion? An answer to this question stems in part from the image we hold of the persuasion process. Receivers bear little responsibility if the persuader views them as passive and defenseless receptacles, as mindless blotters uncritically accepting ideas and arguments. If audience members actually behave as viewed by the persuader, then they have little or no responsibility to understand accurately and evaluate critically. In this

FIGURE 2.1

How might Bovee's questions apply for evaluating the justifications here?
SOURCE: CALVIN AND HOBBES © 1989 Watterson. Dist. By UNIVERSAL PRESS SYNDICATE. Reprinted with permission. All rights reserved.

view, they have minimal power of choice and almost automatically must agree with the persuader's arguments. In contrast, we can see persuasion as a transaction in which both persuaders and persuadees bear mutual responsibility to participate actively in the process. This image of persuadees as active participants suggests several responsibilities, perhaps best captured by two phrases: (1) reasoned skepticism and (2) appropriate feedback.

Reasoned skepticism includes a number of elements. It represents a balanced position between the undesirable extremes of being too open-minded or gullible, on the one hand, and being too closed-minded or dogmatic, on the other. You are not simply an unthinking blotter "soaking up" ideas and

arguments. Rather, you exercise your capacities actively to search for meaning, to analyze and synthesize, and to judge soundness and worth. You do something to and with the information you receive: You process, interpret, and evaluate it. Also, you inform yourself about issues being discussed, and you tolerate, and even seek out, divergent and controversial viewpoints, the better to assess what is being presented.

As a receiver of persuasion, you must realize that your accurate interpretation of a persuader's message may be hindered by attempts to impose your own ethical standards on the persuader. Your immediate, gut-level ethical judgments may cause you to distort the intended meaning. Only after reaching an understanding of the persuader's ideas can you reasonably evaluate the ethics of his or her persuasive strategies or purposes.

In this era of distrust of the truthfulness of public communication, reasoned skepticism also requires that you combat the automatic assumption that most public communication is untrustworthy. Just because a communication is of a certain type or comes from a certain source (e.g., a government official, political candidate, news media figure, or advertiser), it must not automatically, without evaluation, be rejected as tainted or untruthful. Clearly, you must always exercise caution in acceptance and care in evaluation, as emphasized throughout this book. Using the best evidence available, you arrive at your best judgment. However, to condemn a message as untruthful or unethical solely because it stems from a suspect source is a type of judgment that threatens the soundness of our decisions. If we reject a message, it must be after, not before, we evaluate it. Like a defendant in a courtroom, public communication must be presumed to be ethically innocent until it has been proved "guilty." However, when techniques of persuasion do weaken or undermine the confidence and trust necessary for intelligent, public decision making, we can condemn them as unethical.

As an active participant in the persuasion process, you need to provide appropriate feedback to persuaders. Otherwise, persuaders are denied the relevant and accurate information they need to make decisions. Your response, in most situations, should be an honest and accurate reflection of your true comprehension, beliefs, feelings, or judgment. It might be verbal or nonverbal, oral or written, immediate or delayed. A response of understanding, puzzlement, agreement, or disagreement could be reflected through your facial expressions, gestures, posture, inquiries, and statements during question-and-answer periods and through letters or e-mails to editors or advertisers. In some cases, because of your expertise on a subject, you may even have an obligation to respond and provide feedback while other receivers remain silent. You need to decide whether the degree and type of your feedback are appropriate for the subject, audience, and occasion of the persuasion. For instance, to interrupt with questions, or even to heckle, might be appropriate in a few situations but irresponsible in many others.

SOME ETHICAL PERSPECTIVES

We will briefly explain six major ethical perspectives as potential viewpoints for analyzing ethical issues in persuasion. As categories, these perspectives are not exhaustive, mutually exclusive, or given in any order of precedence. For a more extensive discussion, see Johannesen, Valde, and Whedbee (2008).

As a receiver of persuasion, you can use one or a combination of such perspectives to evaluate the ethicality of a persuader's use of language (such as metaphors and ambiguity) or of evidence and reasoning. You can also use them to assess the ethics of psychological techniques (such as appeals to needs and values) or the appeal to widely held cultural images and myths. The persuasive tactics of campaigns and social movements can also—indeed must—be subjected to ethical scrutiny.

Religious Perspectives

Religious perspectives on communication ethics are rooted in the basic assumptions a religion makes about the relationship of the divine/eternal to humans and the world, and vice versa. In light of such assumptions, various world religions emphasize values, guidelines, and rules for evaluating the ethics of persuasion. These are the moral guidelines and the "thou shalt nots" embodied in the ideology and sacred literature of various religions. For instance, the Bible warns against lying, slander, and bearing false witness. In the Buddhist religion, communication is a crucial dimension of ethical behavior and has equal prominence along with mind and body. The Buddha warned against four major categories of unethical communication: lying, duplicity, harsh speech, and idle speech. Contemporary Buddhists are urged: "If you have trouble knowing how to speak, try to imagine what the Buddha would say if he were in your situation" (Hsing, 1998, p. 24).

To explore the relation between religion and ethical persuasion, consider the following case. On two weekends in January 1987, evangelist Oral Roberts recounted on his nationally syndicated television program an encounter he had had with God the previous year. God told Roberts that he would not be allowed to live beyond March 1987 unless he raised $8 million to fund 69 scholarships for medical students at Oral Roberts University, to enable them to serve in medical clinics overseas. In an emotion-laden plea to his viewers, Roberts asked, "Will you help me extend my life?" Roberts' chief spokesperson, Jan Dargatz, defended Roberts' motives to reporters but conceded that his "methods have hit the fan." Dargatz said that Roberts sincerely believed, "from the very core of his being," that the fund drive was a "do-or-die effort." The Reverend John Wolf, senior minister of Tulsa's All Souls Unitarian Church, condemned the appeal as "emotional blackmail" and an "act of desperation" (Buursma, 1987). Another news report revealed that in 1986 Roberts had made a similar appeal. Roberts told a Dallas audience that his "life is on the line" and that God "would take me this year" if he did not raise necessary funds to finance "holy missionary teams." "Because if I don't do it," Roberts said, "I'm going to be gone before the year is out. I'll be with the Father. I know it as much as I'm standing here." Roberts failed to raise the necessary money (*Chicago Tribune*, Feb. 26, 1987).

To assess the ethicality of Roberts' appeals, you might bring to bear an ethic for Christian evangelism developed by Emory Griffin (1976). For example, to what degree could Roberts' persuasion be condemned as that of a "rhetorical rapist" who uses psychological coercion to force a commitment? Intense emotional appeals, such as to guilt, effectively remove the receiver's conscious choice. Or was Roberts' persuasion more that of a "rhetorical seducer" who uses deception, flattery, or irrelevant appeals to success, money, duty, patriotism, popularity, or comfort to entice an audience? What other ethical standards rooted in Christian doctrine or scripture might we use to evaluate Roberts' appeals, and how might those standards be applied?

Human Nature Perspectives

Human nature perspectives probe the essence of human nature by asking what makes us fundamentally human. They identify unique characteristics of human nature that distinguish us from so-called lower forms of life, characteristics that we can then use as standards for judging the ethics of persuasion. Among them are the capacity to reason, to create and use symbols, to achieve mutual appreciative understanding, and to make value judgments. The underlying assumption is that we should protect and nurture such uniquely human characteristics so that persons better can achieve their individual potential. We can assess the degree to which a persuader's appeals and techniques either foster or undermine the development of a fundamental human characteristic. Whatever the political, religious, or cultural context, a person would be assumed to possess certain uniquely human attributes worthy of promotion through communication. A technique that dehumanizes, that makes a person less than human, would be unethical.

In 1990 in Florida, a U.S. district court judge declared obscene the album *As Nasty As They Wanna Be* by the rap group 2 Live Crew. But in a local trial in Florida that same year, three members of the group were acquitted of obscenity charges for performing the songs. These incidents are part of a larger controversy concerning lyrics that explicitly refer to the sexual and physical abuse and debasement of women and that attack ethnic groups. For example, lyrics on the *Nasty* album vividly describe the bursting of vaginal walls, the forcing of women to have anal or oral sex or to lick feces, and such acts as urination, incest, and group sex. Similarly sexually violent lyrics can be found in songs by such individuals and groups as Judas Priest, Great White, Ice-T, and Guns n' Roses. And bigotry against immigrants, homosexuals, and African Americans surfaces in the Guns n' Roses song, "One in a Million."

Regardless of whether such lyrics are judged obscene or whether they are protected by the freedom-of-speech clause of the First Amendment, many would say that they should be condemned as unethical (Johannesen, 1997). Such lyrics treat women not as persons but as objects or body parts to be manipulated for the selfish satisfaction of males. Thus, they dehumanize, depersonalize, and trivialize women, they celebrate violence against them, and they reinforce inaccurate and unfair stereotypes of women, homosexuals, and ethnic groups. How do you believe a human nature perspective on communication ethics might be used to assess such lyrics?

Political Perspectives

The implicit or explicit values and procedures accepted as crucial to the health and growth of a particular political system are the focus of **political perspectives**. Once we have identified these essential values for a political system, we can use them to evaluate the ethics of persuasive means and ends within that system. The assumption is that public communication should foster achievement of these basic political values; persuasive techniques that retard, subvert, or circumvent the values should be condemned as unethical. Different political systems usually embody differing values leading to differing ethical judgments. Within the context of U.S. representative democracy, for example, various analysts pinpoint values and procedures they deem fundamental to the healthy functioning of our political system and, thus, values that can guide ethical scrutiny of persuasion therein. Such values and procedures include enhancement of citizens' capacity to reach rational decisions, access to channels of public communication and to relevant and accurate information about public issues, maximization of freedom of choice, tolerance of dissent, honesty in presenting motivations and consequences, and thoroughness and accuracy in presenting evidence and alternatives.

Hate speech is a broad label that includes communications that degrade, belittle, humiliate, or disrespect individuals and groups based on their race, ethnicity, nationality, religion, sex, or sexual orientation. Hate speech truly warrants our concern as an issue central to respect for diversity in our nation. In the late 1980s and early 1990s, the issue of hate speech on college and university campuses illustrated the tension between the right of freedom of speech and the ethically responsible exercise of that right. On one campus, eight Asian-American students were harassed for almost an hour by a group of football players, who called them "Oriental faggots." On another campus, white fraternity members harassed a black student by chanting, "coon," "nigger," and "porch monkey." On yet another campus, a white male freshman was charged under the school's speech code with racial harassment for calling five black female students "water buffaloes."

In response to hate speech incidents, many colleges and universities instituted speech codes to punish hateful and offensive public messages. Among the forms of expression punishable at various schools are these:

- The use of derogatory names, inappropriately directed laughter, inconsiderate jokes, and conspicuous exclusion of another person from conversation

- Language that stigmatizes or victimizes individuals or that creates an intimidating or offensive environment

- Face-to-face use of epithets, obscenities, and other forms of expression that by accepted community standards degrade, victimize, stigmatize, or pejoratively depict persons based on their personal, intellectual, or cultural diversity

- Extreme or outrageous acts or communications intended to harass, intimidate, or humiliate others on the basis of race, color, or national origin, thus causing them severe emotional distress.

 We call your attention to two Web sites that provide reliable information about hate groups that promote hate speech. Check the Hate Groups Map on the Southern Poverty Law Center Web site and surf its various links to see the nature and extent of such groups (www.splcenter.org/intel/map/hate.jsp). On the Anti-Defamation League Web site (www.adl.org) type in the search window: poisoning the Web. Then click on the table of contents to surf the various listings.

Whether hate speech is protected by the First Amendment and whether campus speech codes are constitutional, we should evaluate specific instances of hate speech for their degree of ethicality (Johannesen, 1997). We can use various ethical perspectives (such as human nature), but how might we use the values and procedures central to a U.S. democratic political perspective to judge hate speech?

Situational Perspectives

To make ethical judgments from a **situational perspective**, it is necessary to focus *regularly and primarily* on the elements of the specific persuasive situation at hand. Virtually all perspectives (those mentioned here and others) make some allowances, on occasion, for the modified application of ethical criteria in special circumstances. However, an extreme situational perspective routinely makes judgments only in light of *each different context*. This perspective minimizes criteria from broad political, human nature, religious, or other perspectives, and avoids absolute and universal standards (see Figure 2.2). Among the concrete contextual factors relevant to making a purely situational ethical evaluation are these:

- The role or function of the persuader for receivers
- Expectations held by receivers concerning such matters as appropriateness and reasonableness
- The degree of receivers' awareness of the persuader's techniques
- Goals and values held by receivers
- The degree of urgency for implementing the persuader's proposal
- Ethical standards for communication held by receivers.

From an extreme situational perspective, for instance, we might argue that an acknowledged

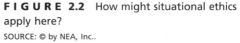
"It's exciting to be part of a firm that's on the cutting edge of 'MORAL FLEXIBILITY.'"

FIGURE 2.2   How might situational ethics apply here?
SOURCE: © by NEA, Inc..

leader in a time of clear crisis has a responsibility to rally support and thus could employ so-called emotional appeals that circumvent human processes of rational, reflective decision making. Or a persuader might ethically use techniques such as innuendo, guilt by association, and unfounded name-calling as long as the receivers both recognize and approve of those methods.

Legal Perspectives

From a **legal perspective**, illegal communication behavior also is unethical, but that which is not specifically illegal is ethical. In other words, legality and ethicality are synonymous. This approach certainly has the advantage of making ethical decisions simple: We need only measure commnication techniques against current laws and regulations to determine whether a technique is ethical. We might, for example, turn for ethical guidance to the regulations governing advertising set forth by the Federal Trade Commission (FTC) or the Federal Communications Commission (FCC). Or we might use Supreme Court or state legislative criteria defining obscenity, pornography, libel, or slander to judge whether a particular message is unethical on those grounds.

However, many people are uneasy with this legalistic approach to communication ethics. They contend that obviously there are some things that are legal but ethically dubious. And some social protesters for civil rights and against the Vietnam War during the 1960s and 1970s admitted that their actions were illegal but contended that they were justifiable on ethical and moral grounds. Persons holding such views reject the idea that ethicality and legality are synonymous, view ethicality as much broader than legality, and argue that not everything that is unethical should be made illegal.

To what degree, then, can or should we enforce ethical standards for communication through laws or regulations? What degrees of soundness might there be in two old but seemingly contrary sayings: "You can't legislate morality" and "There ought to be a law"? In the United States today, very few ethical standards for communication are codified in laws or regulations. As we have indicated, FCC or FTC regulations on the content of advertising, and laws and court decisions on obscenity and libel, represent the governmental approach. But such examples are rare compared with the large number of laws and court decisions specifying the boundaries of freedom of speech and press in our society. Rather, our society applies ethical standards for communication through the indirect avenues of group consensus, social pressure, persuasion, and formal-but-voluntary codes of ethics.

Controversies surrounding computer communication on the Internet and Web illustrate not only the tension between freedom and responsibility but also the pressures to apply legalistic approaches to ethics and to create formal codes of ethics. Should you be free to say or depict anything you want, without restriction, on the Internet or Web or in e-mail? What is your view on how ethical responsibility for computer communication on the Internet should be promoted? Through laws? Through institutional and professional codes of ethics?

University officials, perhaps on your campus, have debated whether to apply to the Internet and e-mail activities of students existing campus speech codes that prohibit hate speech and harassment, or whether to formulate special codes of computer communication ethics to guide student use. On your campus, what official policies (set how and by whom?) govern ethically responsible communication on the Internet and Web? How adequately and appropriately do these policies speak to specific issues of communication ethics? Do these policies actually seem to address matters of legality more than of ethicality?

Dialogical Perspectives

Dialogical perspectives emerge from current scholarship on the nature of communication as dialogue rather than as monologue. From such perspectives, the attitudes participants in a communication situation have toward each other are an index of the ethical level of that communication. Some attitudes are held to be more fully human, humane, and facilitative of personal self-fulfillment than others (see Johannesen, 1971; Johannesen, Valde, & Whedbee, 2008; Stewart & Zediker, 2000).

Communication as dialogue is characterized by such attitudes as honesty, concern for the welfare and improvement of others, trust, genuineness, open-mindedness, equality, mutual respect, empathy, humility, directness, lack of pretense, nonmanipulative intent, sincerity, encouragement of free expression, and acceptance of others as individuals with intrinsic worth regardless of differences of belief or behavior.

Communication as monologue, in contrast, is marked by such qualities as deception, superiority, exploitation, dogmatism, domination, insincerity, pretense, personal self-display, self-aggrandizement, judgmentalism that stifles free expression, coercion, possessiveness, condescension, self-defensiveness, and the view of others as objects to be manipulated. In the case of persuasion, then, we examine the persuader's techniques and presentation to determine the degree to which they reveal an ethical dialogical attitude or an unethical monological attitude toward receivers.

How might a dialogical ethical perspective apply to intimate interpersonal communication situations such as between friends, family members, lovers, and spouses? Or consider some of the popular interactive media such as e-mail, chat rooms, blogs, cell phone text messaging, and Microsoft Xbox. For example, blogs (short for Web logs) facilitate extensive participation between blogger and users. One 2005 estimate indicated that 8 million American adults have created their own blogs, almost 32 million indicate they read blogs, and over 14 million say they have responded to a blog. Blog activity has been compared to a conversation or a seminar (Primer, 2005, pp. 15–16). How might we apply ethical standards rooted in a dialogical perspective to communication via blogs or other such interactive media?

With knowledge of the preceding ethical perspectives (religious, human nature, political, situational, legal, dialogical), we can confront a variety of difficult issues relevant to ethical problems in persuasion. As receivers constantly bombarded with verbal and nonverbal persuasive messages, we continually face resolution of one or another of these fundamental issues. To further help us grapple with such issues, we next consider some traditional advice on ethics which most of us have heard at one time or another—The Golden Rule.

THE GOLDEN RULE
AND THE PLATINUM RULE

"Do unto others as you would have them do unto you." Most of us probably are familiar with this statement, which we have come to know as **The**

Golden Rule. Persons familiar with the Christian religious tradition may think the Golden Rule is unique to that religion. In the New Testament we find: "And as ye would that men should do to you, do ye also to them likewise" (Luke 6:31; also see Matthew 7:12). However, some version of the Golden Rule is found in the sacred literature of the major world religions, including Hinduism, Confucianism, Taoism, Zoroastrianism, and Jainism. For example, in Judaism: "What is hateful to you, do not to your fellow men." In Islam: "No one of you is a believer until he desires for his brother that which he desires for himself." In Buddhism: "Hurt not others in ways that you yourself would find hurtful" (Kane, 1994, p. 34; Samovar, Porter, & Stefani, 1998, p. 269).

One interpretation of the Golden Rule is that we should only do *specific actions* to others if we would allow them to do the same specific actions to us. Another interpretation would not require mutually specific actions but would require that the *ethical principles and standards* that we follow in relating to others are the same ethical principles we would expect others to follow in relating to us (Singer, 1963). Versions of the Golden Rule have been advocated not only by the major world religions but also by pagan philosophers. Thus a contemporary philosopher, Marcus Singer (1967), concludes: "The nearly universal acceptance of the Golden Rule and its promulgation by persons of considerable intelligence, though otherwise divergent outlooks, would therefore seem to provide some evidence for the claim that it is a fundamental ethical truth."

However, in the context of ethnic and religious diversity and of intercultural and multicultural communication, Milton Bennett argues that the Golden Rule best applies *within* a culture or group that has wide agreement on fundamental values, goals, institutions, and customs. In other words, the Golden Rule assumes that other people want to be treated in the same way we do. But this assumption is not automatically applicable in diverse intercultural and multicultural communication. Too often in such situations we may focus primarily or solely on our own values or preferences to the exclusion or minimization of values and preferences of others that differ from ours. As an alternative (or perhaps supplement) to the Golden Rule, Bennett (1979) offers **The Platinum Rule**: "Do unto others as they themselves would have done unto them."

Certainly the Platinum Rule forces us to take into serious account the values and preferences of others, especially others unlike us, perhaps through empathy for or imagining of their experiences and worldviews. But we need to be careful that we do not interpret the Platinum Rule as requiring us automatically and unquestioningly to do what others want us to do. In making our final decision about what and how to persuade, we should carefully weigh the ethical guidance embodied in both the Golden Rule and the Platinum Rule. Then we should decide which takes precedence in our particular situation.

ETHICS, PROPAGANDA, AND THE DEMAGOGUE

Is **propaganda** unethical? The answer depends upon how we define propaganda. A simplistic answer, sometimes resorted to in the heat of clash of opposing viewpoints, is to claim that my communication is persuasion but my opponent's/enemy's is propaganda.

Recall the definition (key characteristics) described in Chapter 1. (1) Propaganda is ideological—it promotes one and only one way to believe. (2) It employs various mass media to spread its belief system to ever larger masses of fanatical "true believers." (3) It conceals one or more of the message source, the true goal of the source, the other sides of the issue, the persuasive techniques being used, and the actual consequences of putting the belief system in action. (4) It aims as mass uniformity of belief and behavior. (5) It usually circumvents the reasoning process and relies heavily on irrelevant emotional appeals and hatred of stereotyped opponents. Thus the definition used in this book views propaganda as an unethical persuasion process.

In his book, *The Idea of Propaganda*, scholar of philosophy and communication Stanley Cunningham (2002, pp. 176–178) argues that propaganda is "an inherently unethical social phenomenon" because it undermines the significant values of truth and truthfulness, reasoning and knowledge, because it sidesteps voluntary choice and human agency, and because it "exploits and reinforces society's moral weakness." Because propaganda violates the normal communication expectations (implied ethical contracts) of trust, truthfulness, and understanding, it is best characterized as "counterfeit or pseudocommunication." He also describes the various "deep-structured constituents and enabling conditions" that mark propaganda.

Propaganda, contends Cunningham, is constituted by a "complex array" of deficiencies or shortcomings that undermine justified knowledge. We paraphrase and summarize those characteristics here. Propaganda plays on complexity and stimulates confusion; exploits expectations; poses as valid information and accepted knowledge; constructs belief systems of tenacious convictions that defy questioning; offers false or artificial assurances and certainties; distorts perceptions; disregards truth and truthfulness as values necessary for accurate knowledge and understanding; subverts "rationality, reasoning, and a healthy respect for rigor, evidence, and procedural safeguards"; promotes ignorance and passive acceptance of unexamined beliefs; and uses truths and information as mere instruments rather than as ethical ideals in themselves.

Today the label **demagogue** typically is used to render a negative ethical judgment of a persuader. Too often, however, the label remains only vaguely defined; the criteria being used to evaluate a person as a demagogue are unspecified. Consider the following hypothetical description of a politician: He is the perfect example of a demagogue, combining true-believer certainty, raw pursuit of power, blue-collar populism, chameleon-like adaptability, and blunt, sometimes crude, persuasive appeals (adapted from Lesher, 1972). Are each of the characteristics listed truly appropriate criteria for judging a demagogue? Why or why not? Are there any appropriate criteria omitted? Given the criteria listed, would you label this politician as a demagogue?

You now are invited to consider the following five characteristics (taken together) as possible appropriate guides to determining to what degree a persuader warrants the label demagogue (Johannesen, Valde, & Whedbee, 2008, pp. 114–115).

1. A demagogue wields popular or mass leadership over an extensive number of people.

2. A demagogue exerts primary influence through the medium of the spoken word—whether through direct public speaking to an audience or through speaking via radio, television, or on the Internet.

3. A demagogue relies heavily on propaganda defined in the negative sense of intentional use of suggestion, scapegoating, irrelevant emotional appeals, and pseudo-proof in order to bypass human rational decision-making processes.

4. A demagogue capitalizes on the availability of a major current social cause or problem.

5. A demagogue is hypocritical. The social cause serves as a mask or persuasive leverage point while the actual primary motive is selfish interest and personal gain.

Several cautions are in order when applying these guidelines. A persuader may reflect each of these characteristics to a greater or lesser degree and only in certain circumstances. A key determination would be whether the alleged demagogue shows a high degree of all the characterisitcs most of the time. A persuader might fulfill only several of these criteria (such as items 1, 2, and 4) and yet not be called a demagogue. Characteristics 3 and 5 seem to be central to a conception of a demagogue. How easily and accurately can we determine a persuader's actual motives? Should we limit the label demagogue solely to the political arena, or could it apply to religious figures, radio/TV show hosts, or Internet bloggers?

ETHICAL STANDARDS FOR POLITICAL PERSUASION

Directly or indirectly, we are daily exposed to political persuasion in varied forms. For example, the president appeals on national television for public support of a military campaign. A senator argues in Congress against ratification of a treaty. A government bureaucrat announces a new regulation and presents reasons to justify it. A federal official contends that information requested by a citizen action group cannot be revealed for national security reasons. A national, state, or local politician campaigns for election. A citizen protests a proposed property tax rate increase at a city council meeting. What ethical criteria should we apply to judge the many kinds of political persuasion?

During the latter half of the twentieth century, traditional American textbook discussions of the ethics of persuasion, rhetoric, and argument often included lists of standards for evaluating the ethicality of an instance of persuasion. Such criteria often are rooted, implicitly if not explicitly, in what we previously described as a political perspective for judging the ethics of persuasion. The criteria usually stem from a commitment to values and procedures deemed essential to the health and growth of our system of representative democracy.

Of all the ethical criteria for varied types and contexts of persuasion described in this chapter, the following 11 are the most generally applicable for you to use as a persuader and persuadee. Do not look on these standards as limited only to political persuasion. They can apply to a wide variety of persuasive efforts in which you engage or to which you are exposed. Consider adopting (and modifying) these standards as your own *starting point commitment* to ethical persuasion (also see Sellers, 2004; Baker & Martinson, 2001).

What follows is my synthesis and adaptation of a number of traditional lists of ethical criteria for persuasion (Johannesen, Valde, & Whedbee, 2008, pp. 28–29). Within the context of our own society, the following criteria are not necessarily the only or best ones possible; they are suggested as general guidelines rather than inflexible rules, and they may stimulate discussion on the complexity of judging the ethics of persuasion. Consider, for example, under what circumstances there might be justifiable exceptions to some of these criteria. Also bear in mind that one difficulty

---

B O X 2 . 1   **Evaluating Political Persuasion**

Read the book *The Lies of George W. Bush* by David Corn (2003). What ethical standards for judgment does Corn seem to employ? In what ways do you agree or disagree with Corn's ethical assessment of Bush's various efforts at persuasion?

In considering Corn's ethical criticisms, apply our previous discussion concerning *intention, sincerity, responsibility,* the political perspective, and suggested standards for political persuasion.

---

in applying these criteria in concrete situations stems from differing standards and meanings people may have for such terms as *distort, falsify, rational, reasonable, conceal, misrepresent, irrelevant,* and *deceive.*

1. Do not use false, fabricated, misrepresented, distorted, or irrelevant evidence to support arguments or claims.

2. Do not intentionally use specious, unsupported, or illogical reasoning.

3. Do not represent yourself as informed or as an "expert" on a subject when you are not.

4. Do not use irrelevant appeals to divert attention or scrutiny from the issue at hand. Among the appeals that commonly serve such a purpose are smear attacks on an opponent's character, appeals to hatred and bigotry, innuendo, and emotionally loaded terms that cause intense but unreflective positive or negative reactions.

5. Do not ask your audience to link your idea or proposal to emotion-laden values, motives, or goals to which it actually is not related.

6. Do not deceive your audience by concealing your real purpose or self-interest, the group you represent, or your position as an advocate of a viewpoint.

7. Do not distort, hide, or misrepresent the number, scope, intensity, or undesirable features of consequences or effects.

8. Do not use emotional appeals that lack a supporting basis of evidence or reasoning or that would not be accepted if the audience had

time and opportunity to examine the subject themselves.

9. Do not oversimplify complex, gradation-laden situations into simplistic two-valued, either/or, polar views or choices.

10. Do not pretend certainty where tentativeness and degrees of probability would be more accurate.

11. Do not advocate something in which you do not believe yourself.

During the 1980s, political analysts in the mass media often criticized President Ronald Reagan for misstating and misusing examples, statistics, and illustrative stories. They charged that he did this not just on rare occasions but with routine frequency in his news conferences, informal comments, and even speeches (Green & MacColl, 1987; Johannesen, 1985). The glaring misuse of facts and anecdotes in ethically suspect ways continues in national political discourse (Box 2.1).

ETHICAL STANDARDS FOR COMMERCIAL ADVERTISING

Consumers, academics, and advertisers themselves clearly do not agree on any one set of ethical standards as appropriate for assessing commercial advertising. Here we will simply survey some of the widely varied criteria that have been suggested. Among them you may find guidelines that will aid your own assessments.

Sometimes advertisers adopt what we previously called legal perspectives, in which ethicality is equated with legality. However, advertising executive Harold Williams (1974) observed:

> What is legal and what is ethical are not synonymous, and neither are what is legal and what is honest. We tend to resort to legality often as our guideline. This is in effect what happens often when we turn to the lawyers for confirmation that a course of action is an appropriate one.
>
> We must recognize that we are getting a legal opinion, but not necessarily an ethical or moral one. The public, the public advocates, and many of the legislative and administrative authorities recognize it even if we do not (pp. 285–288).

Typically, commercial advertising has been viewed as persuasion that argues a case or demonstrates a claim concerning the actual nature or merits of a product. This view is reflected in the formal codes of ethics of professional advertising associations, such as the American Advertising Federation. Many of the traditional ethical standards for truthfulness and rationality are applicable to such attempts at arguing the quality of a product. For instance, are the evidence and the reasoning supporting the claim clear, accurate, relevant, and sufficient in quantity? Are the emotional and motivational appeals directly relevant to the product?

The American Association of Advertising Agencies' code of ethics was revised in 1990. As you read the following standards, consider their level of adequacy, the degree to which they are relevant and appropriate today, the extent to which they are being followed by advertisers, and how they reflect truthfulness and rationality criteria. Association members agree to avoid intentionally producing advertising that contains the following:

- False or misleading statements or exaggerations, visual or verbal

- Testimonials that do not reflect the real choices of the individuals involved

- Price claims that are misleading

- Claims that are insufficiently supported or that distort the true meaning or practicable application of statements made by professional or scientific authority

- Statements, suggestions, or pictures offensive to public decency or to minority segments of the population.

What if ethical standards of truthfulness and rationality are irrelevant to most commercial advertising? What if the primary purpose of most ads is not to prove a claim? Then the ethical standards we apply may stem from whatever alternative view of the nature and purpose of advertising we do hold. Some advertisements function primarily to capture and sustain consumer attention, to announce a product, or to create consumer awareness of the name of a product. Many advertisements aim primarily at stimulating in consumers a positive or feel-good attitude about the product through use of metaphor, humor, fantasy, and fiction (Spence & Van Heekeren, 2005, pp. 41–53). What ethical criteria are most appropriate for such attention-getting or feel-good ads?

Consider advertiser Tony Schwartz's (1974) resonance theory of electronic media persuasion, which is discussed in detail in the chapter on modern media and persuasion. Schwartz argued that, because our conceptions of truth, honesty, and clarity are products of our print-oriented culture, they are appropriate in judging the content of printed messages. In contrast, he contended, the "question of truth is largely irrelevant when dealing with electronic media content" (p. 19). In assessing the ethics of advertising by means of electronic media, Schwartz said, the FTC should focus not on truth and clarity of content but on the effects of the advertisement on receivers. He lamented, however, that "we have no generally agreed-upon social values and/or rules that can be readily applied in judging whether the effects of electronic communication are beneficial, acceptable, or harmful" (p. 22).

What ethical evaluation of effects and consequences would you make of an advertisement for Fetish perfume in *Seventeen*, a magazine whose readers include several million young teenage girls? The ad shows an attractive female teenager looking seductively at the readers. The written portion of the ad says, "Apply generously to your neck so he can smell the scent as you shake your head 'no.'" Consider that this ad exists in a larger cultural context in which acquaintance rape is a societal problem, women and girls are clearly urged to say "No!" to unwanted sexual advances, and men and boys too often still believe that "no" really means "yes."

What harmful individual and societal consequences may stem from ads that negatively stereotype persons or groups on the basis of age (old and confused), sex (women as sex objects), or culture (backward)? Our frequent exposure to such ads may indeed influence the way we perceive and treat such stereotyped persons and the way the stereotyped persons view themselves and their own abilities (Spence & Van Heekeren, 2005, pp. 54–69). "Therefore, insofar as stereotyping in advertising degrades people as persons and harms their personal dignity by degrading the societal group to which they belong, stereotyping violates people's rights to freedom and well-being and hence is unethical" (p. 68).

Commercial advertisements sometimes can be criticized for containing ambiguous or vague elements. But concern about vagueness and ambiguity in persuasion is not limited to commercial advertising. Now we examine the more general ethical implications of ambiguity and vagueness.

THE ETHICS
OF INTENTIONAL AMBIGUITY
AND VAGUENESS

"Language that is of doubtful or uncertain meaning" might be a typical definition of ambiguous language. **Ambiguous** language is open to two or more legitimate interpretations. **Vague** language lacks definiteness, explicitness, or preciseness of meaning. Clear communication of intended meaning usually is one major aim of the ethical communicator, whether that person seeks to enhance receivers' understanding or to influence beliefs, attitudes, or actions. Textbooks on oral and written communication typically warn against ambiguity and vagueness; often, they take the position that intentional ambiguity is an unethical communication tactic. For example, later in this book, ambiguity is discussed as a functional device of style, as a stylistic technique that is often successful while ethically questionable.

Most people agree that intentional ambiguity is unethical in situations in which accurate instruction or transmission of precise information is the acknowledged purpose. Even in most so-called persuasive communication situations, intentional ambiguity is ethically suspect. However, in some situations, communicators may believe that the intentional creation of ambiguity or vagueness is necessary, accepted, expected as normal, and even ethically justified. Such might be the case, for example, in religious discourse, in some advertising, in labor-management bargaining, in political campaigning, or in international diplomatic negotiations.

We can itemize a number of specific purposes for which communicators might believe that intentional ambiguity is ethically justified: (1) to heighten receiver attention through puzzlement, (2) to allow flexibility in interpretation of legal concepts, (3) to allow for precise understanding and agreement on the primary issue by using ambiguity on secondary issues, (4) to promote maximum receiver psychological participation in the communication transaction by letting receivers create their own relevant meanings, and (5) to promote maximum latitude for revision of a position in later dealings with opponents or with constituents by avoiding being locked into a single absolute stance.

In political communication, whether from campaigners or government officials, several circumstances might justify intentional ambiguity. First, a president or presidential candidate often communicates to multiple audiences through a single message via a mass medium such as television or radio. Different parts of the message may appeal to specific audiences, and intentional ambiguity in some message elements avoids offending any of the audiences. Second, as political scientist Lewis Froman (1966) observed, a candidate "cannot take stands on specific issues because he doesn't know what the specific choices will be until he is faced with the necessity for concrete decision. Also, specific commitments would be too binding in a political process that depends upon negotiation and compromise" (p. 9). Third, groups of voters increasingly make decisions about whether to support or oppose a candidate on the basis of that candidate's stand on a single issue of paramount importance to those groups. The candidate's position on a variety of other public issues is often ignored or dismissed. "Single-issue politics" is the phrase frequently used to characterize this trend. A candidate may be intentionally ambiguous on one emotion-packed issue in order to get a fair hearing for his or her stands on many other issues.

During the 2004 presidential campaign, George W. Bush frequently charged his opponent, John Kerry, with "flip-flopping" on significant issues. That is, Bush claimed that Kerry often changed his position on issues and thus was inconsistent or ambiguous. Is it automatically unethical for a politician to change her or his position on an issue? Why or why not?

In some advertising, intentional ambiguity seems to be understood as such by consumers and even accepted by them. In your opinion, what might be some ethical issues in the TV ad for a popular beer, in which Sergio Garcia, a famous professional golfer, acts as a kind of secret agent? He sneaks into a plush party to meet a sultry, sexy-looking date.

SHE: "What took you so long?"

HE: "Tough drive."

HE: "How's your game?"

SHE (IN A SEXY VOICE): "Oh, there's nothing like a good up and down."

Nonverbal elements of commercial advertisements sometimes invite examination of their ethicality. But scrutiny of the ethics of nonverbal communication raises broader issues, which we now consider.

THE ETHICS OF NONVERBAL COMMUNICATION

Nonverbal factors play an important role in the persuasion process (Box 2.2). In a magazine advertisement, for example, the use of certain colors, pictures, layout patterns, and typefaces influences how the words in the advertisement are received. A later chapter provides examples of "nonverbal bias" in photo selection, camera angle and editing in news presentation. In *The Importance of Lying*, Arnold Ludwig (1965) underscored the ethical implications of some dimensions of nonverbal communication:

> Lies are not only found in verbal statements. When a person nods affirmatively in response to something he does not believe or when he feigns attention to a conversation he finds boring, he is equally guilty of lying.... A false shrug of the shoulders, the seductive batting of eyelashes, an eyewink, or a smile may all be employed as nonverbal forms of deception (p. 5).

Silence, too, may carry ethical implications. If to be responsible in fulfilling our role or position requires that we speak out on a subject, to remain silent may be judged unethical. But if the only way that we can successfully persuade others on a subject is to employ unethical communication techniques or appeals, the ethical course probably will be to remain silent.

Television coverage of the 9/11/01 terrorist attacks on the World Trade Center yielded many vivid pictures that were burned into our memories. An Associated Press photographer produced one especially emotional image—of a man plunging headfirst down the side of the still-standing North Tower. Although no captions identified the man, the photographer's telephoto lens was powerful enough that, in versions enhanced for clarity, the

BOX 2.2   Nonverbal Ethics in the Digital Age

To further explore ethical standards for nonverbal communication, you are urged to read several sources that are especially rich in extended case studies. Two books by Paul Martin Lester—*Photojournalism: An Ethical Approach* (1991) and *Visual Communication* (2003)—are good sources on the topic. Also thought-provoking is

Thomas H. Wheeler's, *Phototruth or Photofiction? Ethics and Media Imagery in the Digital Age* (2002). What standards do these authors suggest for judging the ethics of nonverbal communication? Apply some of the criteria to the 9/11 photo described below. What ethical judgments would you make and why?

man's face was recognizable to persons who knew him. With regard to ethics, this photo generated criticism of the media that used the photo and praise for the media not using it. On what ethical grounds might you condemn the use of the photo? On what ethical grounds might you justify its use? Consider the likely emotional trauma for persons who knew the man. Did the ends of selling papers or crystallizing the personal dimension of the attack justify using it as a means that intensified the grief and violated the privacy of family members and friends? How does the photo feed into the public's seemingly unlimited appetite for glimpses into the intimate details of the grief of others—a process that some scholars refer to as the "pornography of grief"? (Cooper, 2002; Singer, 2002.)

Persuaders sometimes use verbal and nonverbal communication to depict others, especially outsiders and enemies, as beyond the sphere where normal ethics apply. The nature and implications of such ethical exclusion are our next topic.

THE ETHICS
OF MORAL EXCLUSION

Moral exclusion, according to Susan Opotow (1990), "occurs when individuals or groups are perceived as outside the boundary in which moral values, rules, and considerations of fairness apply. Those who are morally excluded are perceived as nonentities, expendable, or undeserving; consequently, harming them appears acceptable, appropriate, or just." Persons morally excluded are

denied their rights, dignity, and autonomy. Opotow isolates for analysis and discussion over two dozen symptoms or manifestations of moral exclusion. For our purposes, a noteworthy fact is that many of them directly involve communication. Although all the symptoms she presents are significant for a full understanding of the mind-set of individuals engaged in moral exclusion, the following clearly involve persuasion:

- Showing the superiority of oneself or one's group by making unflattering comparisons to other individuals or groups

- Denigrating and disparaging others by characterizing them as lower life forms (vermin) or as inferior beings (barbarians, aliens)

- Denying that others possess humanity, dignity, or sensitivity, or have a right to compassion

- Redefining as an increasingly larger category that of "legitimate" victims

- Placing the blame for any harm on the victim

- Justifying harmful acts by claiming that the morally condemnable acts committed by "the enemy" are significantly worse

- Misrepresenting cruelty and harm by masking, sanitizing, and conferring respectability on them through the use of neutral, positive, technical, or euphemistic terms to describe them

- Justifying harmful behavior by claiming that it is widely accepted (everyone is doing it) or that it was isolated and uncharacteristic (it happened just this once)

B O X 2.3   Moral Exclusion in a Headline

The headline "An Eskimo Encounters Civilization—and Mankind" appeared in the Tempo section of the *Chicago Tribune* (May 29, 2000). Can you identify two ways in which the words in the headline reflect a process of moral exclusion? How do these words place people outside the categories where

human ethics normally apply? Hate speech, as discussed earlier in this chapter, and racist/sexist language, examined in the next section, also illustrate the process of moral exclusion. In what ways does hate speech embody the moral exclusion process?

An example may clarify how language choices function to achieve moral exclusion. The category of "vermin" includes parasitic insects such as fleas, lice, mosquitoes, bedbugs, and ticks that can infest human bodies. In Nazi Germany, Adolf Hitler's speeches and writings often referred to Jews as a type of parasite infesting the pure Aryan race (non-Jewish Caucasians or people of Nordic heritage) or as a type of disease attacking the German national body. The depiction of Jews as parasites or a disease served to place them outside the moral boundary where ethical standards apply to human treatment of other humans. Jews were classified or categorized as nonhumans. As parasites, they had to be exterminated; as a cancerous disease, they had to be cut out of the national body.

Another example of moral exclusion is the genocide (attempted extermination of an entire ethnic group) that occurred in the African nation of Rwanda in 1994. In about 100 days, some 800,000 people were slaughtered, most by being hacked to death with machetes. The ethnic Hutus in power organized soldiers and ordinary citizens to murder ethnic Tutsis (men, women, and children), many of whom had been friends and neighbors. While there are multiple causes or influences that led to the massacre, clearly the language of moral exclusion was a contributing factor. A lengthy government propaganda campaign using radio programs fostered in the minds of the Hutus a view of Tutsis as less than human, as prey "for hunting expeditions," and as "cockroaches" to be squashed. For horrifying yet routine examples of this process, we urge you to read Jean Hatzfeld, *Machete Season: The Killers in Rwanda Speak* (2005). To experience the hate-filled atmosphere at that time, rent the fact-based films *Hotel Rwanda* (2004) and *Beyond the Gates* (2005).

Even headlines we encounter daily in newspapers or magazines may reflect (perhaps unconsciously) the process of moral exclusion. Carefully consider the headline discussed in Box 2.3.

THE ETHICS OF RACIST/ SEXIST LANGUAGE

In *The Language of Oppression*, communication scholar Haig Bosmajian (1983) demonstrated how names, labels, definitions, and stereotypes traditionally have been used to degrade, dehumanize, and suppress Jews, Blacks, Native Americans, and women. Bosmajian's goal was to expose the "decadence in our language, the inhumane uses of language" that have been used "to justify the unjustifiable, to make palatable the unpalatable, to make reasonable the unreasonable, to make decent the indecent." Bosmajian reminded us: "Our identities, who and what we are, how others see us, are greatly affected by the names we are called and the words with which we are labeled. The names, labels, and phrases employed to 'identify' a people may in the end determine their survival" (pp. 5, 9).

"Every language reflects the prejudices of the society in which it evolved. Since English, through most of its history, evolved in a white, Anglo-Saxon, patriarchal society, no one should be surprised that its vocabulary and grammar frequently reflect attitudes that exclude or demean minorities and women" (Miller & Swift, 1981, pp. 2–3). Such is the fundamental position of Casey Miller and Kate Swift, authors of *The Handbook of Nonsexist Writing*. Conventional English usage, they argued, "often obscures the actions, the contributions, and sometimes the very presence of women" (p. 8). Because such language usage is misleading and inaccurate, it has ethical implications. "In this respect, continuing to use English in ways that have become misleading is no different from misusing data, whether the misuse is inadvertent or planned" (p. 8).

To what degree is the use of **racist/sexist language** unethical, and by what standards? At the least, racist/sexist terms place people in artificial and irrelevant categories. At worst, such terms intentionally demean and put down other people by embodying unfair negative value judgments of their traits, capacities, and accomplishments. What are the ethical implications, for instance, of calling a Jewish person a "kike," a Black person a "nigger" or "boy," an Italian person a "wop," an Asian person a "gook" or "slant-eye," or a thirty-year-old woman a "girl" or "chick"? Here is one possible answer:

> In the war in Southeast Asia, our military fostered a linguistic environment in which the Vietnamese people were called such names as slope, dink, slant, gook, and zip; those names made it much easier to despise, to fear, to kill them. When we call women in our own society by the names of gash, slut, dyke, bitch, or girl, we—men and women alike—have put ourselves in a position to demean and abuse them (Bailey, 1984, pp. 42–43).

From a political perspective, we might value access to the relevant and accurate information needed to make reasonable decisions on public issues. Racist/sexist language, however, by reinforcing stereotypes, conveys inaccurate depictions of people, fails to take serious account of them, or even makes them invisible for purposes of such decisions. Such language denies us access to necessary accurate information and thus is ethically suspect. From a human nature perspective, it is also ethically suspect because it dehumanizes individuals and groups by undermining and circumventing their uniquely human capacity for rational thought or for using symbols. From a dialogical perspective, racist/sexist language is ethically suspect because it reflects a superior, exploitative, inhumane attitude toward others, thus denying equal opportunity for self-fulfillment for some people.

A FEMINIST VIEW ON PERSUASION

Feminism is not a concept with a single, universally accepted definition. For our purposes, elements of definitions provided by Barbara Bate (1992) and Julia Wood (1994) are helpful. **Feminism** holds that both women and men are complete and important human beings and that societal barriers (typically constructed through language processes) have prevented women from being perceived and treated as of equal worth to men. Feminism implies a commitment to equality and respect for life. It rejects oppression and domination as undesirable values and accepts that difference need not be equated with inferiority or undesirability.

Sonja Foss and Cindy Griffin (1995) develop an "invitational rhetoric" rooted in the feminist assumptions that (1) relationships of equality are usually more desirable than ones of domination and elitism, (2) every human being has value because she or he is unique and is an integral part of the pattern of the universe, and (3) individuals have a right to self-determination concerning the conditions of their lives (they are expert about their lives).

Invitational rhetoric, say Foss and Griffin, invites "the audience to enter the rhetor's world and to see it as the rhetor does." The invitational rhetor "does not judge or denigrate others' perspectives but is open to and tries to appreciate and validate those perspectives, even if they differ dramatically from the rhetor's own." The goal is to establish a "nonhierarchical, nonjudgmental, non-adversarial framework" for the interaction and to develop a "relationship of equality, respect, and appreciation" with the audience. Invitational rhetors make no assumption that their "experiences or perspectives are superior to those of audience members and refuse to impose their perspectives on them." Although change is not the intent of invitational rhetoric, it might be a result. Change can occur in the "audience or rhetor or both as a result of new understandings and insights gained in the exchange of ideas."

In the process of invitational rhetoric, Foss and Griffin contend, the rhetor offers perspectives without advocating their support or seeking their acceptance. These individual perspectives are expressed "as carefully, completely, and passionately as possible" to invite their full consideration. In offering perspectives, "rhetors tell what they currently know or understand; they present their vision of the world and how it works for them." They also "communicate a willingness to call into question the beliefs they consider most inviolate and to relax a grip on these beliefs." Further, they strive to create the conditions of safety, value, and freedom in interactions with audience members. Safety implies "the creation of a feeling of security and freedom from danger for the audience," so that participants do not "fear rebuttal of or retribution for their most fundamental beliefs." Value involves acknowledging the intrinsic worth of audience members as human beings. In interaction, attitudes that are "distancing, depersonalizing, or paternalistic" are avoided, and "listeners do not interrupt, confront, or insert anything of their own as others tell of their experiences." Freedom includes the power to choose or decide, with no restrictions placed on the interaction. Thus, participants may introduce for consideration any and all matters; "no subject matter is off limits, and all presuppositions can be challenged." Finally, in invitational rhetoric, the "rhetor's ideas are not privileged over those of the audience." (Also see Gorsevski, 2004, pp. 75, 164.)

In concluding their explication of an invitational rhetoric, Foss and Griffin suggest that this rhetoric requires "a new scheme of ethics to fit interactional goals other than inducement of others to adherence to the rhetor's own beliefs." What might be some appropriate ethical guidelines for an invitational rhetoric? What ethical standards seem already to be implied by the dimensions or constituents of such a rhetoric?

A few scholars with a feminist viewpoint explore ethical issues concerning the Internet and cyberspace (e.g., Adam, 2005). Our next topic examines general issues of Internet ethics from several ethical viewpoints.

ETHICAL STANDARDS IN CYBERSPACE

What ethical standards should apply to communication in cyberspace—in the realm of the Internet, the Web, e-mail, blogs, and chat rooms? We can get guidance and suggestions from several sources (e.g., Berkman & Shumway, 2003; Cavalier, 2005; Hamelink, 2000; Johnson, 2001; Wolf, 2003). Some of the "Ten Commandments of Computer Ethics" formulated by the Computer Ethics Institute are particularly relevant. For example, "thou shalt not: Use a computer to harm other people; interfere with other people's computer work; snoop around in other people's computer files; use a computer to steal; use a computer to bear false witness against others; [or] plagiarize another person's intellectual output" (reprinted in Ermann, 1997, pp. 313–314).

In *The Weblog Handbook*, Rebecca Blood (2002, pp. 85–87, 114–121, 135–137) contends that "the weblog's greatest strength—its uncensored, unmediated, uncontrolled voice—is also its greatest weakness." Also she laments that there "has been almost no talk about ethics in the weblog universe." Blood thus is aware of the tension between freedom and responsibility in this form of Internet communication. At several points in her book, she suggests principles to highlight ethical responsibilities both for creators of and participants in the various types of blogs: (1) "Publish as fact only that which you believe to be true. If your

---

BOX 2.4   Ethical Implications of Cyberspace Metaphors

Some scholars argue that the dominant metaphors frequently used to describe the realm of cyberspace and the Internet actually function unethically to hinder Internet use by people who already are marginalized, neglected, and devalued by society (Adam, 2005, pp. 64, 114, 132–136; Gunkel, 2001; Kramer & Kramerae, 1997). Such metaphors for cyberspace as new world, frontier, anarchy, democracy, and community have been critiqued for their ethical implications. Consider the metaphor of cyberspace described as a community. In actuality, in what ways do cyberspace and the Internet primarily promote individualism, selfishness, intolerance of those not like us, and lack of trust through deception more than interdependence, concern and care for the less advantaged, and appreciation and tolerance of diversity within a sphere of common values and purposes? What might be some ethical issues related to metaphorically comparing the Internet to a superhighway?

---

statement is speculation, say so." (2) "If material exists online, link to it when you reference it…. Online readers deserve, as much as possible, access to all of the facts." (3) "Publicly correct any misinformation." If you discover that one of your links was inaccurate or one of your statements was untrue, say so and correct it. (4) "Write each entry as if it could not be changed; add to, but do not rewrite or delete any entry…. Changing or deleting destroys the integrity of the network." (5) Disclose any possible or actual conflict of interest so that audience trust is not undermined. (6) Clearly label biased or questionable sources, otherwise readers will lack necessary information to assess the merits of the source. (7) Respect other people's privacy. It is ethically questionable to repeat without permission someone's instant message, chat-room or real-life conversation, or e-mail. (8) Question someone's facts or arguments but don't personalize your attack by denouncing her or his stupidity or other personal characteristics. (9) Consider carefully the arguments and evidence presented by others and try to represent their positions fairly and accurately.

Advertising and marketing specialists increasingly capitalize on the interactive capacities of the Internet and of interactive television to create a two-way "conversation" between product and consumer. On the Internet, Java and Shockwave technologies facilitate interactive ads. Video on demand and personal video recorders (such as TiVo) afford opportunities for interactive television ads. But much of the contact, such as banner ads and pop-ups on the Internet, is not truly a conversation (Spence & Van Heekeren, 2005, pp. 96–107). "One-way unsolicited communications from advertisers to consumers, especially when they are conducted without the consumers' consent, are not 'interactive' and not 'conversations' even if the advertisers mislabel them as such. And insofar as they invade the consumers' privacy they are ethically unjustified" (p. 104).

How we conceptualize the Internet, what metaphors we use to describe cyberspace, actually may have ethical implications. Consider this issue as discussed in Box 2.4.

Standards, criteria, and guidelines are central to much of the earlier discussion in this chapter, and shortly we will present a framework of questions that can improve your ethical judgment. But now we discuss the often-neglected role of your formed ethical character in creating and evaluating persuasion.

ETHICS AND PERSONAL CHARACTER

Ethical persuasion is not simply a series of careful and reflective decisions, instance by instance, to persuade in ethically responsible ways. Deliberate application of ethical rules is sometimes impossible. Pressure for a decision can be so great or a deadline so near that there is insufficient time for careful deliberation. We might be unsure what ethical criteria are relevant or how they apply. The situation might seem so unusual that applicable criteria do not readily come to mind. In such times of crisis or uncertainty, our decisions concerning ethical persuasion stem less from deliberation than from our formed "character." Further, our ethical character influences what terms we use to describe a situation and whether we believe the situation contains ethical implications (Hauerwas, 1977; Johannesen, 1991; Klaidman & Beauchamp, 1987; Lebacqz, 1985).

Consider the nature of **moral character** as described by ethicists Richard DeGeorge and Karen Lebacqz. As human beings develop, according to DeGeorge (1999), they adopt patterns of actions and dispositions to act in certain ways.

> These dispositions, when viewed collectively, are sometimes called *character*. The character of a person is the sum of his or her virtues and vices. A person who habitually tends to act as he morally should has a good character. If he resists strong temptation, he has a strong character. If he habitually acts immorally, he has a morally bad character. If despite good intentions he frequently succumbs to temptation, he has a weak character. Because character is formed by conscious actions, in general people are morally responsible for their characters as well as for their individual actions (p. 123).

Lebacqz (1985) observes:

> … when we act, we not only do something, we also shape our own character. Our choices about what to do are also choices about whom to be. A single lie does not necessarily make us a liar; but a series of lies may. And so each choice about what to do is also a choice about whom to be—or, more accurately, whom to become (p. 83).

In Judeo-Christian or Western cultures, good moral character is usually associated with habitual embodiment of such virtues as courage, temperance, wisdom, justice, fairness, generosity, gentleness, patience, truthfulness, and trustworthiness. Other cultures may praise additional or different virtues that they believe constitute good ethical character. Instilled in us as habitual dispositions to act, these virtues guide the ethics of our communication behavior when careful or clear deliberation is not possible.

When we evaluate a person's ethical character in light of a specific action or persuasive technique, there are five issues or dimensions that may aid us in reaching a judgment. These issues may apply in varying degrees to a wide variety of persons, such as family, friends, coworkers, business leaders, leaders of volunteer or social organizations, or elected or appointed government officials. That is, these issues apply to anyone in whom we place our trust and whom we assume to have certain responsibilities in their roles.

First, we consider the *citizen-politician issue*. Should the ethical standards we expect of politicians be the same or higher than those for the average citizen? Why? Second, the *private-public dimension* warrants consideration. Is the behavior that is ethically at issue relevant to the duties or responsibilities the person has in the public realm? Or is the behavior purely a personal and private matter and not appropriate for public examination? Third for consideration is the *past-present dimension*. Should we be most concerned about recent behavior? Or should unethical behavior in the past also be of concern? How far past is past? Should we overlook a "youthful indiscretion" but worry more about unethical behavior of the mature person? Fourth, we must consider the *once-pattern issue*. Should we overlook a one-time unethical behavior ("we all make mistakes") while taking very seriously evidence of a pattern or habit of unethical behavior? What if the one-time mistake was intentional rather than unintentional? Is evidence of a pattern of unethical behavior a sign of a serious character flaw, such as poor judgment or hypocrisy? Fifth, the *dimension of trivial-serious* must be evaluated. Is the unethical behavior trivial and minor or is it serious and significant? Should we make allowances for minor ethical mistakes but not make allowances for major,

---

BOX 2.5   Ethics and Personal Character

The ethical character of President George W. Bush came under scrutiny during his two terms. For example, in *A Matter of Character*, journalist Ronald Kessler (2004) praised Bush's character for "vision, courage, patience, optimism, integrity, focus, discipline, determination, decisiveness, and devotion to America" (p. 290). In contrast, philosopher Peter Singer (2004) published *The President of Good and*

Evil: The Ethics of George W. Bush and condemned Bush's ethical character for dishonesty, inconsistency, weakness, and promise breaking. Read one of these books and evaluate the evidence and reasoning used to make the positive or negative judgment. Consider also how any of the five issues/dimensions just discussed have been used in making the judgments of ethical character.

---

serious, clearly harmful ethical errors? A careful consideration of these five issues/dimensions may help us reach clearer and more precise judgments about a person's ethical character (even our own) when that character is in question because of un-ethical persuasion. For an example, see Box 2.5.

Members of organizations frequently pattern their own communication behavior and ethical standards after those persons in leadership roles for the organization. The ethical or unethical behavior of leaders significantly influences the organization's ethical climate. A reasonable expectation by members would be that leaders should embody the standards presented in the organization's code of ethics. A leader with weak ethical character, however, may not embody those standards.

Consider the Enron Corporation scandal and collapse in the first years of this century. In July 2000, Kenneth Lay, the founder, chairman, CEO of Enron, sent all employees a 65-page code of ethics. Honesty, candor, and fairness were to mark the company's relations with its various stake-holders. Respect and integrity were basic values. Thus, "ruthlessness, callousness, and arrogance" were condemned, and open, honest, and sincere relationships were stressed. Kenneth Lay's signed introduction to the code emphasized that business must be conducted in a "moral and honest manner." He concluded by noting "Enron's reputation finally depends upon its people, you and me." How ironic, then, that in May 2006 Kenneth Lay was convicted in federal court of various charges that

involved lying and deception about Enron's profits and debts (for a copy of the code of ethics, see: www.THESMOKINGGUN.com).

IMPROVING ETHICAL JUDGMENT

One purpose of this book is to make you a more discerning receiver and consumer of communication by encouraging ethical judgments of communication that are specifically focused and carefully considered. In making judgments about the ethics of your own communication and the communication to which you are exposed, you should make specific rather than vague assessments, and thoughtful rather than reflexive, "gut-level" reactions.

The following framework of questions is offered as a means of making more systematic and firmly grounded judgments of communication ethics. Bear in mind philosopher Stephen Toulmin's (1950) observation that "moral reasoning is so complex, and has to cover such a variety of types of situations, that no one logical test … can be expected to meet every case" (p. 148). In underscoring the complexity of making ethical judgments, in *The Virtuous Journalist*, Klaidman and Beauchamp (1987) reject the "false premise that the world is a tidy place of truth and falsity, right and wrong, without the ragged edges

FIGURE 2.3 How might the guidelines for ethical judgment help to evaluate this situation?

SOURCE: © Phil Frank/www.farleycomicstrip.com.

of uncertainty and risk." Rather, they argue, "Making moral judgments and handling moral dilemmas require the balancing of often ill-defined competing claims, usually in untidy circumstances" (p. 20). How might you apply this framework of questions? See also Figure 2.3.

1. Can I specify exactly what ethical criteria, standards, or perspectives are being applied by me or by others? What is the concrete grounding of the ethical judgment?

2. Can I justify the reasonableness and relevancy of these standards for this particular case? Why are these the most appropriate ethical criteria among the potential ones? Why do these take priority (at least temporarily) over other relevant ones?

3. Can I indicate clearly in what respects the communication being evaluated succeeds or fails in measuring up to the standards? What judgment is justified in this case about the degree of ethicality? Is the most appropriate judgment a specifically targeted and narrowly focused one rather than a broad, generalized, and encompassing one?

4. In this case, to whom is ethical responsibility owed—to which individuals, groups, organizations, or professions? In what ways and to what extent? Which responsibilities take precedence over others? What is the communicator's responsibility to herself or himself and to society at large?

5. How do I feel about myself after this ethical choice? Can I continue to "live with myself" in good conscience? Would I want my parents or mate or best friend to know of this choice?

6. Can the ethicality of this communication be justified as a coherent reflection of the communicator's personal character? To what degree is the choice ethically "out of character"?

7. If called upon in public to justify the ethics of my communication, how adequately could I do so? What generally accepted reasons or rationale could I appropriately offer?

8. Are there precedents or similar previous cases to which I can turn for ethical guidance? Are there significant aspects of this instance that set it apart from all others?

9. How thoroughly have alternatives been explored before settling on this particular choice? Might this choice be less ethical than some of the workable but hastily rejected or ignored alternatives?

Remember that this framework for ethical judgment is not a set of inflexible and universal rules. You must adapt the questions to varied persuasive situations to determine which questions are most applicable. Also, this list may stimulate additional questions. The framework is a starting point, not the final word.

REVIEW AND CONCLUSION

The process of persuasion demands that you make choices about the methods and content you will use in influencing receivers to accept the alternative you advocate. These choices involve issues of desirability and of personal and societal good. What ethical standards will you use in making or judging these choices among techniques, contents, and purposes? What should be the ethical responsibility of a persuader in contemporary society? Obviously, answers to these questions have not been clearly or universally established. However, we must face the questions squarely. In this chapter, we explored some perspectives, issues, and examples useful in evaluating the ethics of persuasion. Our interest in the nature and effectiveness of persuasive techniques must not overshadow our concern for the ethical use of such techniques. We must examine not only how to but also whether to use persuasive techniques. The issue of "whether to" is both one of audience adaptation and one of ethics. We need to formulate meaningful ethical guidelines, not inflexible rules, for our own persuasive behavior and for use in evaluating the persuasion to which we are exposed.

KEY TERMS

After reading this chapter, you should be able to identify, explain, and give an example of the following key terms or concepts:

ethical issues	hate speech	The Platinum Rule	moral exclusion
responsibility	situational perspective	propaganda	racist/sexist language
religious perspectives	legal perspective	demagogue	feminism
human nature perspectives	dialogical perspective	ambiguous	invitational rhetoric
political perspectives	The Golden Rule	vague	moral character

APPLICATION OF ETHICS

Assume that you are employed in the public relations department of a large corporation. Your supervisor assigns you to present a series of speeches to community groups in a city where your company has just built a new production facility. In the speech prepared by your supervisor, you will describe the services and advantages of the plant that will benefit the community. But during a visit to the plant to familiarize yourself with its operation, you discover that the plant cannot actually deliver most of the services and advantages promised in the speech. Should you go ahead and present the speech as your supervisor prepared it? Should you refuse to give it at all? What changes might you in good conscience make in the speech? Should you make any changes with or without your supervisor's approval? What ethical standards might you use in making your decisions? Why? What additional ethical issues might confront you in this situation? (Adapted from McCammond, 2004.)

QUESTIONS FOR FURTHER THOUGHT

1. What ethical standards should be used to evaluate commercial advertising? Describe a current ad or ad campaign that you believe is unethical and justify your judgment.

2. The Web site of the Center for Media and Democracy presents evaluations of the public relations "spin" of both political and corporate communications (www.prwatch.org). Search the site for cases under such topic headings as ethics, rhetoric, or propaganda. What is your judgment of the ethics of a public relations example you select from this site?

3. How might a particular actual or hypothetical argument that a worthwhile goal (end) justifies use of unethical persuasive techniques (means) be viewed as an example of the Situational Perspective?

4. What current prominent person might warrant the label of demagogue? What is your justification?

5. What current example of public persuasion might illustrate the tension between freedom of communication and ethical responsibility? How?

6. How might cell phone text-messaging be used by a student (or by students) in unethical ways during an in-class written exam? Why do you consider these uses to be unethhical? (http://www.prwatch.org).

7. What ethical standards do you personally believe should guide communication on the Internet?

8. How does hate speech illustrate the process of moral exclusion?

For online activities, go to the *Persuasion* book companion Web site at http://academic.cengage.com/communication/larson12.

3

✳

Traditional, Artistic, and Humanistic Approaches to Persuasion

JOSEPH N. SCUDDER
Northern Illinois University

LEARNING GOALS

After reading this chapter, you should be able to:

1. Discuss the foundations in Aristotle's *Rhetoric* that guide contemporary persuasion and marketing.

2. Assess what Plato's dialogic approach adds to the practice of persuasion today.

3. Evaluate the merits of Quintilian's argument of the necessity of the good character of the persuader.

4. Explain Robert Scott's epistemic approach in relationship to Aristotle's and Plato's approaches.

5. Articulate how Burke's dramatistic approach differs from early approaches to persuasion.

6. Describe Fisher's reasons for developing his narrative approach and apply Fisher's criteria of coherence and fidelity to recent persuasive narratives.

7. Identify the objections to Fisher's narrative approach.

8. Discuss the controversy among feminist rhetorical scholars regarding the value of invitational rhetoric.

9. Differentiate between those who have power in a persuasive text and those who are absent or pushed to the margins.

10. Compare and contrast Truth and truth across all the approaches in this chapter.

The common phrase *it's mere rhetoric* irritates many serious scholars of persuasion. It implies that rhetoric contains little substance. This is not a new complaint. Plato warned in the *Gorgias* several centuries ago that speakers could sound impressive, but had little truth to convey. Unless you are an unusually motivated student, the classic writings of Plato and Aristotle probably have little natural appeal to you. Several years ago, I felt that way, too. I went to graduate school to study current, cutting-edge communication principles—not ancient classics. I struggled when assigned to read the entire volume of Aristotle's *Rhetoric* in one week. It took time for me to realize that Plato and Aristotle laid the foundation for much of what we study today. Persuasion still addresses many of the same basic human motivations they addressed: the promise of a better life, the security of our homes and lives, the joy of children, the love of family and friends, the desire for justice, and the respect of others.

Gaps, omissions, and blind spots, however, do exist in these early classics. They did not deal adequately with confronting powerful others—especially those in leadership positions involved in oppression. Nor did they address the multicultural face of persuasion. The absence of women as persuaders is rather remarkable from the perspective of contemporary standards. Thus, this chapter considers a wide range of persuasive approaches from the early traditional ones to more recent humanistic approaches exposing the exploitation of persons pushed to the margins of society.

✻ARISTOTLE'S *RHETORIC*

The formal study of persuasion has its early roots in ancient Greece where city-states valued the right of their citizens to speak on issues of the day. Greek philosophers like Aristotle tried to describe what happened when persuasion occurred. Much of what Aristotle said on the subject of persuasion has relevance today when his principles are adapted to fit contemporary society.

Aristotle was a remarkable person. Alexander the Great put Aristotle in charge of the educational

---

B O X 3.1 **Westboro Baptist Members' Use of Inappropriate Persuasive Attempts at Funerals Draws Fire**

Fred Felps and members of his congregation at Westboro Baptist Church provide evidence of the outrage that can occur when a group uses tactics inappropriate to the ceremonial context of the funeral. One of the more publicized controversial events was attendance at the funeral of actor Heath Ledger protesting his portrayal of a gay character in the movie *Brokeback Mountain*. A Fox News report quoted a Westboro Baptist church source as saying "Heath Ledger is now in Hell, and has begun serving his eternal sentence there."

Westboro Baptist Church has protested nationwide at over 30,000 funerals including those of American soldiers killed in the line of duty in Iraq. The group claims these deaths are the result of God's punishment for our nation's tolerance of homosexuality. These protests test the limits of the First Amendment right of free speech. Such protests would likely not exist without the persuasive face of the mass media. Here we see a case of propaganda that is manufactured through the complicity of the media. An emerging strategy is to block the visual presence of such protestors by having volunteers hold tall placards in front of the protestors while encouraging media outlets to ignore the protests that have nothing to do with the event.

---

system of Greece; in this position Aristotle developed schools using much that he had learned from Plato, his mentor. He established an ambitious program cataloguing everything known about the world at that time He used the findings of his researchers to write many books covering a variety of topics, including his *Rhetoric*, considered by many to be the single most important work on the study of persuasion. The next section summarizes key features from the *Rhetoric* that remain central to the practice of persuasion today.

Adaptation to Context and Purpose

Aristotle recognized that one approach to persuasion did not fit all situations. He proposed that a persuasive speaker must adapt to the context. In today's advertising and media markets, we talk about market segments and target audiences in a 24/7 media-saturated environment. Although mass media were not yet invented, Aristotle recognized **segmented audiences** long ago when he saw that it is important to customize the message strategies to the specific target. Three contexts dominated his thinking: (1) **forensic discourse** considered allegations of past wrongdoing in the legal arena; (2) **epideictic discourse** treated present situations that were often ceremonial focusing

on praise or blame; and (3) **deliberative discourse** dealt with future policy, with special attention to the legislative and political realms. Adaptation was not just to the place or setting but also to the purpose of the activity that would happen there. Each of these contexts imposes certain constraints or expectations about appropriate procedures and behavior. Legal procedures in U.S. courts are carefully prescribed. The legislatures at national and state levels not only have procedures that need to be followed for the conduct of business, but also have standards of behavior expected of its members. Ceremonies like weddings and funerals also have expectations that differ across cultures and contexts, but these expectations are very important to many communities of those involved. Funeral ceremonies do not typically get much attention unless high profile individuals are the focus. Recently, however, funerals have become a frequent site for protests (see Box 3.1). Rights of free speech come into conflict with a family's need to mourn in a dignified ceremony.

Aristotle's three types of discourse remain relevant today, though we pursue many other contexts and market segments with our persuasion. Entertainment and media play dominant roles in our society that had limited impact in Aristotle's world, and persuaders today are challenged to understand the similarities and differences between each new generation and its predecessors. For example, advertisers have paid premiums in the past to reach the coveted segment of 18-39-year-olds, but persuasive strategies are changing now to follow the next age cohort of 40-59, because those in the Baby Boom represent a large and lucrative market. The important point is that Aristotle recognized that successful persuaders match appropriate persuasive tactics to the context.

Audience Adaptation and a Common Universe of Ideas

Keep in mind that the world in Aristotle's time did not have the luxury of facts, statistics, research studies, and government reports that we have today. Speakers in that time had to create much of their proof from the world that existed around their audiences. Aristotle assumed that listeners would hold ideas in common. That is, certain types of stock appeals could be used to gain the attention of audience members. In Book I, Chapter 5, of the *Rhetoric* (pp. 37–38), Aristotle makes one of the earliest statements about the approach-avoidance tendencies of individuals. He proposed that speakers should promote things that bring happiness and speak against those that destroy or hamper happiness. Aristotle's popular appeals included having one's independence; achieving prosperity; enjoying maximum pleasure; securing one's property; maintaining good friendships; producing many children; enhancing one's beauty; attending to one's health; fostering one's athletic nature; and promoting one's fame, honor, and virtue. Most of these appeals remain effective today—especially appeals to a better life like the family fishing in Figure 3.1. Most elements of more modern needs approaches, such as Maslow's hierarchy of needs discussed later in this text, are found here. Aristotle clearly recognized that many of the things in this list are external and that others are internal. Tapping into common cultural values such as patriotism is commonly used, but many tire of draping every issue in the national flag. See Box 3.2 for an international example of using common cultural themes as persuasive devices.

In later parts of the *Rhetoric*, Aristotle provides examples of persuasive devices, such as maxims or

FIGURE 3.1 Aristotle's use of audience adaptation with appeals to the prospects for a better life and the joy of friends and family remains popular today.
SOURCE: Used by permission of Joseph N. Scudder.

sayings, with broad appeal to audiences. In Book II, Chapter 21, for instance, he introduces a maxim that is much like a common saying that Tony Soprano might use today: "Fool, who slayeth the father and leaveth his sons to avenge him" (p. 138). In advocating the use of maxims for listeners who love to hear universal truths in which they believe, Aristotle is advising the persuader to reinforce what the audience already knows. He says, "The orator has therefore to guess the subjects on which his hearers really hold views already, and what those views are, and then must express, as general truths, these same views on these same subjects" (p. 139). The point today is not that we need to learn the use of maxims, but that we must learn to adapt our messages to the world of our listeners. Adapting to the audience's views raises ethical issues that remain today (see Box 3.3).

Types of Proof

In the *Rhetoric*, Aristotle focused on what he called the artistic proofs or appeals that the persuader could create or manipulate. For example, persuaders create emotional moods by their choice of words and images and heighten the mood by varying their vocal tone, rate, and volume. Aristotle identified three major types of artistic proof—ethos, pathos, and

---

BOX 3.2 Pura Vida in Costa Rica: Drawing on Cultural Values and Dangers of Exploiting Them

Observant visitors to Costa Rica begin to see the phrase *pura vida* immediately upon arrival. The phrase is loosely translated as pure life. The phrase appears extensively at bus stops and elsewhere in an ad campaign for Imperial beer. The tourist industry promotes Costa Rica using the phrase in its promotional materials as well as on most tours that visitors take. There is an element of propaganda here. Costa Rica benefits from visitors who go home thinking of the country as *pura vida*. The phrase, however, is deeply embedded in the culture—it is not a creation of the advertising industry. Costa Ricans use it as a common greeting or farewell.

Costa Ricans using this phrase are not saying everything is actually good in Costa Rica. They often use it as their way to create more pleasant thoughts in a less than optimum situation. Some backlash, however, is

happening in the country because of the commercialization of the phrase. Many people do not want to see it in commercial advertising or on the shirts of tourists. This is a key point for those using campaigns with some element of propaganda. Many younger adults in San José embrace the term, while many of their older counterparts are less sanguine about its use except with those persons they know well. So, persuaders need to be sensitive to overusing common cultural understandings because negative sentiment toward the message may develop, and the message may be counterproductive. Crass commercialization of major holidays in the United States, such as Christmas, sometimes dilutes the impact persuaders make with their messages because many people believe the true sentiments of these holidays are lost in the overabundant advertising that pervades these occasions.

BOX 3.3 Effective Multicultural Audience Adaptation or Political Pandering?

On January 21, 2008, most presidential candidates made connections between themselves and Dr. Martin Luther King, Jr., on the national holiday named after him. This holiday presents an interesting opportunity to examine the progress of the multicultural face of persuasion as well as the work that remains to accomplish a truly multicultural society. It would probably have been a mistake not to acknowledge Dr. King on that day—particularly because candidates of both parties were campaigning in the South. On the other hand, such audience adaptation leads to cynicism by many persons that some of the candidates were not truly genuine about their commitment to Dr. King's goals of equality for persons of color. Thus, the occasion may produce expectations of what should be

said on that day, causing the audience to be suspicious of whether the speakers truly believe what they articulate at such times. It is often a double bind on such occasions. The candidate has to acknowledge the importance of the day and the expectations of what the audience wants to hear, but the candidate probably has more to lose than gain. The unresolved question is whether Aristotle was more concerned about *appearances* rather than substance. Thus, some see Aristotle's advice regarding the adaptation of messages as involving manipulation. Noted rhetorical scholar Kenneth Burke, however, defends the integrity of Aristotle's approach when it is modified to fit the special cultural conditions of the modern context to which the message is applied.

---

logos—which remain remarkably current in today's world. It should be noted that many scholars see all three of these types of proof as rational or cognitive appeals rather than three distinct ways to persuade an audience. Remember that there were fewer inartistic proofs, such as statistics and scientific evidence, in those times. It is useful to explore the types of proof more closely.

Ethos. Before the speaker actually makes a persuasive presentation, the audience holds an image of the persuader. Even if the persuader is totally unknown to the audience, members will draw certain conclusions based on what they see— body type, height, complexion, movements, clothing, grooming, and so on. If the audience already knows the speaker, he or she may have a reputation for being honest, experienced, and funny. Aristotle called this image or reputation of the speaker **ethos**. A contemporary example of the use of ethos appears on eBay, one of the most profitable electronic commerce sites on the Internet. One-line reports from individuals involved in past transactions form the basis of buyers' and sellers' reputations. Users of the site earn such reputations without even seeing others or having verbal interaction. The speaker in a television program might deliberately make eye contact with various audience members and with the television cameras because eye contact can be an important element in a person's believability. Trust and credibility are salient issues today in the wake of prominent scandals from Wall Street to the White House.

What establishes a person's reputation, however, often varies from person to person. Goodwill results for many toward Bill Gates, cofounder of Microsoft, and his wife when they learn that the Gates have donated over $20,000,000 to a charitable foundation that is one of the leaders in combating AIDS and other diseases in Africa. On the other hand, many computer professionals loathe Microsoft's business practices. Ethos involves many complex elements that are not always predictable. For example, former Speaker of the House Newt Gingrich was unfaithful to his wife even as he was criticizing President Clinton for being immoral. Gingrich was unable to sustain his political career after publication of the damaging information, but President Clinton survived impeachment. When a person's ethos is in question, it rarely happens without also creating an emotional reaction. This leads us to the next type of artistic proof.

Pathos.   **Pathos** describes emotions that come into play as appeals are made to the things people hold dear. Persuaders assess the emotional state of the audience and design artistic appeals aimed at those states. Sometimes pathos is evident in the delivery of the message. High levels of emotion have been common in the persuasive messages of prominent religious leaders of the past and present, such as Jonathon Edwards, Martin Luther King, Jr., Minister Louis Farrakhan, and Billy Graham. Yet the danger exists that listeners will perceive the prominent use of emotion as excessive. Howard Dean's bid to become the Democratic candidate for the presidential race in 2004 was severely hindered by his very emotional speech, deemed by some to be "over the top," given after his loss in the Iowa primary.

Pathos may involve the content of the appeal itself. Justice was one of the widely held virtues noted by Aristotle that often gives rise to emotions when it is violated. In a contemporary example, Wall Street reformers have intentionally attempted to provoke outrage toward illegal corporate actions that have cost thousands of people their jobs and caused thousands of others substantial financial losses. Emotions are easily provoked in those who suffered from the illegal actions taken by top-level executives at Enron, WorldCom, and Tyco. In the area of politics, both major political parties attempt to evoke fear of the future if the wrong people get elected. Advocacy groups for animal rights try to produce feelings of sadness or pity for suffering animals. It is clear that the frequent use of pathos continues in the content of appeals and in the way such appeals are delivered. Now we turn to the last of the three types of proof.

Logos.   Appeals to the intellect, or to the rational side of humans, are represented by the Greek word **logos**. Logos relies on the audience's ability to process evidence in logical ways and to arrive at some conclusion. The persuader must predict how the audience will do this; and thus, must assess their information-processing and conclusion-drawing patterns.

Aristotle and others in his time did not have the many types of scientific evidence that we have today to serve as the foundation for logical arguments. They frequently used a form of reasoning called an **enthymeme**. Aristotle describes it as following the form of what the study of logic today would call a **syllogism**, which we will study in depth in a later chapter. Syllogisms begin with a major premise such as:

Young children have not developed the ability to evaluate the merits of commercial messages on television.

This major premise is then associated with a minor premise:

Advertisers attempt to influence young children through many commercials or promotions.

This, in turn, leads to the conclusion:

Advertisers are being unethical when they attempt to persuade young children by directing messages whose worth the children cannot evaluate.

In Book II, Chapter 22, Aristotle also recommends that the persuader be an expert on the facts in order to use such reasoning effectively:

The first thing we have to remember is this. Whether our argument concerns public affairs or some other subject, we must know some, if not all, of the facts about the subject on which we are to speak and argue. Otherwise, we can have no materials out of which to construct arguments (p. 140).

Clearly, substance was important for Aristotle. Persuasion was not just a bag of tricks for pulling the wool over peoples' eyes. You can find logical appeals operating in your daily life. Politicians use events and examples to persuade you to believe a certain view or to vote in a certain way. Financial advisers use graphs and tables to persuade you that their investment options are superior to others. Often, college recruiters provide potential students and their parents with examples of jobs filled by recent graduates and their starting salaries, and information regarding the reasonable costs of their institutions, as well as potential sources of financial aid. In each case, the persuader is betting that you will process the information logically and predictably.

Yet the form of the argument may not appear to you to be exactly like the one in the example.

Consider a syllogism that Aristotle quotes: "Thou hast pity for thy sire, who has lost his sons: Hast none for Oeneus, whose brave son is dead?" (p. 145). Sometimes the language does not follow the format exactly. Let's consider this example again in contemporary language:

You have pity for a father whose sons have died (major premise).
The brave son of Oeneus is dead (minor premise).
You should have pity for Oeneus (conclusion).

So, enthymemes or syllogisms may leave out one of the premises or have parts in slightly different order. Nevertheless, the pattern of reasoning is there.

Places of Argument.   Contemporary market research attempts to identify consumers' major premises. With these in mind, marketers design products, packaging, and advertising that effectively develop *common ground* and hence the co-creation of persuasive meaning. Aristotle used the term **topoi** to refer to places or topics of argument that are a good way to establish common ground. Persuaders identify these "places" and try to determine whether they will work for a particular audience. Consider a few of these topics and identify where contemporary persuasion uses them.

- *Arguments as to degree, or "more or less"*: Will candidate A be more or less trustworthy than candidate B? Are less costly Lee jeans more or less durable than Levis?

- *Past fact*: Has an event really occurred? Did a person commit the alleged crime? This tactic is very important in the courts, where a prosecutor must prove that a crime occurred and that the accused committed that crime.

- *Future likelihood*: Is something likely to occur in the future? This argument focuses on probabilities. For example, colleges attempt to recruit students by arguing that the earnings of those with a college degree are substantially higher than the earnings of those without a college degree.

BOX 3.4   Metaphors and Sound Bites in Political Persuasion

In a media-saturated world, sound bites reign supreme. That is, media reports focus on short snippets rather than extended interviews with candidates. Metaphors make excellent sound bites because they can be captured in short segments, but provide interesting commentary. The 2008 presidential candidates used many metaphors to intensify the good about themselves. Senator Obama reiterated *change* about his own campaign. The term *underdog* was used frequently by many candidates to manage campaign expectations. After winning the New Hampshire primary, Senator Clinton *found her voice* and trumpeted her *experience*.

Candidates also used metaphors to intensify the bad of other candidates. Senator Clinton frequently used the term *young* to intensify Senator Obama's lack of experience. Several candidates used the term *Washington insider* against opponents such as John McCain. Republicans used terms such as *tax-and-spend liberal* to characterize their Democratic opponents, but fought for the label as the *true conservative*.

Yet Aristotle recognized that it was not simply the structure of the syllogism, but the language used within it, that was persuasive. His focus on language merits attention.

The Potency of Language

Aristotle recognized that carefully chosen language is part of a successful persuasive strategy. He promoted the use of emotional expression because it makes the audience share feelings with the speaker (Book III, Chapter 7). Yet emotional language has to be appropriate to the context and situation. Moreover, Aristotle understood that when the audience shares similar feelings about the topic, the speaker can use more emotionally charged language. He emphasized the importance of **metaphor** in conveying new ideas and facts through images of the familiar: "It is from the metaphor that we can best get hold of something fresh" (p. 186). However, not just any metaphor would do for Aristotle; rather, the metaphor needed to be so lively or active that it made those hearing it actually see things. Of course, metaphors can be overdone. Like any other form of language, the metaphor must be appropriate. Modern political discourse uses lots of metaphors. Rank's system discussed in Chapter 12 is a very good way to think about metaphors in political contests. Some metaphors are used to intensify a candidate's good characteristics and other metaphors are used to intensify the

opponent's weaknesses. Other metaphors downplay a candidate's weaknesses or an opponent's strengths. The Democratic primary campaigns in 2008 were particularly interesting because the leading candidates were very similar in many respects, but differentiated themselves with different metaphors (see Box 3.4).

Despite many possible contemporary applications Aristotle's *Rhetoric* provides for our practice of persuasion, there are some frequently noted limitations. A danger exists of making Aristotle's *Rhetoric* a cookie cutter. If Aristotle were alive, he would probably say that it is a starting point for instruction. Many serious scholars of persuasion such as Kenneth Burke take Aristotle very seriously as long as his principles are adapted to current situations and contexts.

Simply considering it a formulaic approach much like a cookbook clearly ignores much of what is happening in the persuasive situation. Simply thinking of evidence in terms of logos, pathos, and ethos is very simplistic. Things about some persuasive events that truly compel us by their passion, sincerity, and conviction become rather lifeless when dissected in terms of breaking them into logos, pathos, and ethos because the whole is greater than the sum of its parts. There are aspects of delivery and performance in some masterful persuasive messages such as the *I Have a Dream* speech, delivered by Dr. Martin Luther King, Jr., that have to be experienced. Such persuasive attempts are simply difficult to understand without hearing and seeing the message as it was delivered. So, we have to consider persuasion as a living event, but for instructional purposes we need to examine the component parts that fall short of comprising the overall experience.

In sum, Aristotle's principles of persuasion are remarkably contemporary and provide the foundation for modern persuasion research. Granted, there are portions that have little relevance today and that reflect values our society does not embrace. Yet, his principle of adapting the message to the context recognizes that changes in persuasive messages should occur as the context changes. Now we turn to alternative points of view.

PLATO'S DIALOGIC APPROACH

The contemporary practice of persuasion owes a large debt to Aristotle. It was presented first in this chapter because it continues to dominate the design of persuasive messages and campaigns. There are, however, other perspectives on how we come to know things that guide our decision processes. Frankly, Aristotle makes some people uncomfortable. The *Rhetoric* does not give as much consideration to establishing truth as Aristotle's mentor, Plato, did. It is difficult to know whether Aristotle made a conscious break with his mentor or whether the *Rhetoric* simply should be considered in a larger context. We could interpret Aristotle's opening line, "Rhetoric is the counterpart of dialectic," to mean that his advice in the *Rhetoric* needs to be considered in conjunction with the pursuit of truth through the use of dialectics. In other places he suggests that truth typically wins the argument when it is a fair contest among equally skilled persuaders. We simply cannot know which interpretation of Aristotle is more correct.

Surprisingly, many people have more trouble with Plato's approach to truth than with Aristotle's lack of attention to it. Plato believed that as humans we do not see absolute truth directly, but only glean indirect images, glimpses,

or shadows of the truth. Plato used **dialogue**, or the **dialectic method**, to pursue these truths. Dialogue is a form of discussion where the parties ask and respond to questions from the other parties involved. Plato frequently used dialogues in his writing that began with a question that defined the terms. The answers to the questions introduce the issues followed by a cross-examination from another party. In the end, some resolution results in changes, with each side of the issue demonstrating increased understanding of each position. Beyond an elitism that favored philosophers and excluded women, Plato's dialectic method promoted discovery and open public discourse. At least the value of open and public discourse was established in Greece, and dialogue began about important ideas like the practice of slavery, even though many of the issues were not ultimately resolved at that time.

Plato devoted a lot of attention to the concept of truth. In the *Gorgias*, he expressed little respect for rhetoric as it was commonly practiced because he viewed it as a skill used more to flatter, appease, disguise, or deceive than to discover truth and identify the important things in life. Plato presented the ideal speaker, in Socrates' dialogues with Phaedrus, as one who seeks the best interests of the listeners rather than advancing self-interests.

Plato clearly articulated that the facts of the situation do make a difference. Consider one dialogue between Socrates and Phaedrus. Socrates asked Phaedrus to assume that he had convinced Phaedrus to buy a horse and take it to war. Imagine that neither Socrates nor Phaedrus really knew what a horse looked like, though Socrates did know that Phaedrus believed a horse was a tame animal with long ears. Yet a donkey also has long ears and could be very functional in a war. So imagine that someone took that donkey to war instead of a horse, and the donkey performed well. Then imagine that after the war Socrates made a speech detailing the merits of the donkey, but instead called it a horse. Socrates pointed out that merely calling a donkey a horse does not make it a horse (Plato, 1937, p. 263). So, Plato did not believe that truth was relative. There were material facts that one simply could not ignore. Beyond the factuality of these mundane details, Plato's writings present a view of **Truth** that we sometimes call *big T truth*, in which absolute and certain truths exist, but are obscured from our direct view.

SCOTT'S EPISTEMIC APPROACH

Plato's perspectives remain very important to communication ethics and dialog as presented in Chapter 2. Rhetorician Robert L. Scott (1993) bemoans the dominance of the Aristotelian tradition: "In general what may be called 'Aristotelian instrumentalism' has dominated thinking about rhetoric and the teaching of it....I am suggesting that the dominant attitude…should be drastically altered" (p. 121). Scott objects to truth being presented as an objective package, as if it were a possession or commodity. He suggests that **truth** is never certain, whether in the realm of science or public affairs, but he differs from Plato here in that he advocates *truth with a small t*. For Scott, rhetoric is a process of constant discovery in which truth is seen as moments in "human, creative processes" (p. 133). This perspective is known as **epistemic** or as a way of coming to know about things.

Although truth can be stable at times, according to Scott it cannot be static in an ever-changing 24/7, multicultural world. Many discoveries come during our rhetorical encounters with others. These instances when we see something in a new way are often called *epiphanies* or *eureka moments*. Scott's perspective has many similarities to that of existential thinkers, who argue that truth is experienced in the lived moment and cannot be possessed forever. So, knowing is more than possessing facts.

Consider the game of golf. Would you invite a person who has studied the game, but never played it to give a presentation about the basics of golf? A person could read the official rules, watch the event on television, and rent some videos on playing better golf; but a person who plays the game experiences golf and knows it in a way beyond just

FIGURE 3.2 A successful persuasive transaction between a street vendor and an interested buyer requires complex interaction skills involving questions from the sellers and the buyers.

knowing facts. Yet, even the golf game of Tiger Woods changes as he constantly learns more about it through his experiences.

Seeing persuasion as a process of constant discovery is a key principle for students of persuasion to learn. Many persuasive situations are interactive with an exchange of many questions, like bartering with the street vendor shown in Figure 3.2. One quickly learns that the true price is not what is first quoted in many marketplaces of other countries. The true price emerges in the bargaining process. The price the next customer is charged may be higher or lower than you pay. One does not have to go to another country to experience this. Most prices at car dealerships are negotiable in the United States. Selling, whether it be fruit or automobiles, is not simply learning effective sales techniques and memorizing an effective sales script. Robert Scott's perspective clearly shows us why simply learning a set of tactics of persuasion is not enough. It seems as if this more personal approach to persuasion should have prevailed as the preferred method. Why, then, has Aristotle's influence on persuasion been greater?

Although that question cannot be answered with certainty, the 7 Faces described in the first chapter probably have a lot to do with it. Such interactive, personal approaches are not suited to many mass communication media such as television, radio, newspapers, and direct mail. Aristotle's methods can be adapted more readily to marketing and advertising, which are more efficient methods for reaching unseen consumers. Beyond the efficiency issue is the issue of certainty. It is much harder to explain or sell an approach that cannot speak with certainty. That is why sound bites are so important for the presentation of political candidates in the media. This does not mean, however, that we should ignore the lessons from Plato and Scott. Truth and trust are clearly in vogue in the aftermath of some of the biggest ethics scandals ever seen in corporate life. Moreover, the recent resignation of Elliot Spitzer is another of a series of political missteps that are making the character of the persuader a greater concern. Sound bites will not be sufficient means to promote trust. Yet, flaws in the moral integrity of those in the public are not new. We look at Quintilian's focus on character next.

QUINTILIAN'S FOCUS ON CHARACTER

Quintilian established a public school of rhetoric in Rome in the first century AD. Although there are many useful things for persuaders in his 12-volume work, *Institutio Oratoria,* he probably remains most noted for his focus on the character of the speaker.

Many parallels exist between the credibility of public figures in the first century and today. Corruption and illegal activity was a problem then as it is now. For persuaders, a central problem was believing what those in the public eye had to say. A

crisis of trust existed then about believing anything said by public figures just as it does today.

Quintilian was unusual in that he began his *Institutio Oratoria* by focusing on the character of the person rather than establishing the truth of the content. He opens the book with the following statement:

> Let the orator whom I propose to form, then, be such a one as is characterized by the definition of Marcus Cato, a good man skilled in speaking. But the requisite which Cato has placed first in this definition— that an orator should be a good man—is naturally of more estimation and importance than the other. It is important that an orator should be good because, should the power of speaking be a support to evil, nothing would be more pernicious than eloquence alike to public concerns and private.

Although the logic of Quintilian's argument for the importance of character probably suffers because of all the exceptions he covers such as a lawyer providing a defense for a guilty individual, it is important from the standpoint that he acknowledged the character problem was present for believing persuaders in that early period. Just as in the days of the Roman Empire, establishing believability is a critical burden of the persuader today. Professional sports seems to be particularly plagued with credibility crises (see Box 3.5).

BURKE'S DRAMATISTIC
Later on APPROACH

Kenneth Burke, whom we noted earlier in Chapter 1 and will revisit later, is considered to be the most influential rhetorical scholar of the modern era. He continues to wield major impact upon communication scholarship even though he was a literary scholar and critic. Burke's perspective on persuasion has probably influenced the perspective of this book more than any other. His approach was important

---

BOX 3.5   Believability in the Sports Steroid and Doping Controversies

 The persuasive face of an effects-oriented, bottom-line world is clearly seen in the substance-abuse scandals of the sports world. The steroid crisis in professional baseball came to a critical point with the release of the Mitchell report in December 2007. Although home-run leader Barry Bonds had received the most scrutiny of any major league baseball player in recent months regarding steroid use because of his breaking of Hank Aaron's home-run mark, pitcher Roger Clemens became the focus after being named in the Mitchell Report as one of the professional players that an informant implicated in the scandal. Clemens admits that he was injected with B12 shots, but denies he intentionally used steroids. He appeared on *60 Minutes* to defend his reputation.

The stripping of the Tour de France title from Floyd Landis and the conviction of Olympic standout Marion Jones for perjury regarding the use of illegal substances are other examples of high profile sporting figures accused of using performance-enhancing substances. Lance Armstrong continues under a cloud of suspicion for the use of performance-enhancing techniques, even though no credible evidence has ever been produced against him beyond hearsay evidence. Several questions are prominent for persuaders regarding players named in reports without legal bearing such as the Mitchell Report. First, what are legitimate sources of evidence appropriate for such documents? Second, what persuasive tactics could be used to protect one's reputation for a person accused unjustly? Is it impossible for an unjustly accused player to prove the negative that he or she is really innocent?

See the Mitchell Report: http://mlb.mlb.com/mlb/news/mitchell/report.jsp.

---

to the definition of persuasion in Chapter 12 and will be referenced in future chapters as well. Most of this section considers his book *The Rhetoric of Motives.*

A prolific writer with extraordinary breadth, his **dramatistic** approach cannot be neatly captured in a short statement. His perspective clearly emphasizes the performance aspect of persuasion as opposed to the scientific orientation presented in the next chapter. In other words, the art of persuasion is at its best in his writings. In one of the better articles regarding Burke's work, Marie Hochmuth Nichols maintains that Burke draws upon his study of motivation by using key terms from drama. Perhaps the most prominent of these terms are labeled the **pentad.** The pentad includes: the *act* or the description of what takes place, the *scene* providing the background or context of the act, the *agent* or the person who performs the act, the agency or the means or instruments of accomplishing the act, and the *purpose.* Burke proposed that combinations of the elements of the pentad commonly occur with one being a primary and the other being a secondary motivation.

One should guard against only considering Burke's pentad as a tool to break a situation into its component parts. A key factor for Burke is the dynamic of the interaction of the parts. Significantly influenced by the alienation and destruction of World War II, Burke focuses on healing the divisions among people. The term *identification* that was a focus of the definition of persuasion presented in Chapter 12 of this text clearly focuses on establishing those things that are common among us. Beyond the immediate task of persuasion in his discussion of identification and the *autonomous,* Burke took care to place a persuasive act in its larger context and its impact on the community. In this discussion, it is very clear that Burke just does not see persuasion as a set of tools to accomplish an end. That is, the component parts clearly do not comprise the whole.

Interestingly, Burke draws much from Aristotle, but suggests his principles need a makeover to be more relevant to current cultural contexts. Burke suggests that readers often fail to see that Aristotle was often highly dramatistic in his context. A key element, often lost in the consideration of other persuasive approaches, is that persuasion is a performance. Persuasion cannot be separated from actually doing it. There is a clear experiential element in his approach. Like a theatric play, the play can be performed many times, but a shift in situation and attitudes of the audience changes the effectiveness of the play.

His emphasis on identification makes the dramatistic approach not just experiential, but also relational. His dramatistic approach suggests to those who study persuasion that much of what is important in persuasion is found in relationships among the actors and the actual enactment or use of persuasion. These are intangible elements that are often missed in the analysis of persuasive events. Consider what dramatic elements that appear in the story of Professor Randy Paush in Box 3.5 might be missed when using an Aristotelian approach to analyze it. The next perspective approaches the narrative with some similarities to Burke, but is cast in terms quite different from Burke.

FISHER'S NARRATIVE APPROACH

Communication theorist Walter Fisher (1978) shook up the dominant assumptions in the communication discipline by suggesting that humans are "as much valuing as they are reasoning animals" (p. 376). Fisher (1984, 1987) challenged the dominance of the **rational world paradigm**, which assumes people are essentially rational individuals basing their decisions on the quality of arguments and evidence. In his narrative theory, Fisher (1978, 1984, 1987) proposed instead that we can better understand behavior using the story, drama, or narrative as an analytical device, and then casting the persuasive event in narrative terms. At the core of this perspective is the belief that the drama or story is the most powerful and pervasive metaphor that humans can use to persuade and explain events. Fisher (1984) described the **narrative paradigm** as a synthesis of argumentative and aesthetic themes, challenging the notion that rhetorical (persuasive) human communication must be argumentative in form and evaluated by standards of formal logic; thus, the narrative paradigm subsumes rather than denies the rational world paradigm.

So what was it that bothered Fisher so much that he decided to take on many in the established tradition? Part of Fisher's mission appeared to be to change the trend in scholarship that was increasingly focusing on the elite rather than the common. Fisher was frustrated with the way attention had shifted to technical argument that excluded most people; in his view, it was elitist. In this respect, Fisher differs from Plato. Fisher wanted to return to the rationality of everyday argument where consideration is given to the narratives of all members of the community—not just to the specialized few. Those skilled in technical aspects of argument often use such skills to reveal the deceptive face of persuasion. Lawyers may use technical arguments from legal statutes to prevent clients from being convicted, but such technicalities do not persuade many familiar with the situation that the accused is actually innocent. Fisher's narrative approach gets more to the core of what constitutes believability.

A second motivation was his desire for a more vital communication field that returned to the roots of human experience—a very existential idea. The story became such a recognized focus of Fisher's argument that those new to the study of his narrative paradigm often overlook his focus on the human experience as the generative force behind the narratives. It bothered Fisher that traditional approaches to communication often lost the soul and conviction of the human experience by dissecting the text with systems of formal logic and argument. The difference is like that between studying the human body in anatomy class by dissecting cadavers and studying it by examining living people—both approaches have value, but one misses the lived experience.

Fisher proposed that narratives succeed or fail depending on whether they have coherence and fidelity. **Coherence** refers to the way the story hangs together and thus has meaning or impact. **Fidelity** relates to whether it rings true with the hearer's experience. With a coherent story, almost everyone understands its premises or the points it tries to make. The story is told artistically, and it is believable.

BOX 3.6   Randy Pausch's Last Lecture: Really Achieving Your Childhood Dreams

One of the most moving contemporary examples of a persuasive narrative to inspire people to action was given by Professor Randy Pausch at Carnegie Mellon University on September 18, 2007. To view this lecture, go to http://www.cmu.edu/randyslecture/. If the link does not work, search on Google for Randy Pausch.

Professor Pausch was diagnosed with pancreatic cancer in September 2006 and given only a short time to live. Although he claims that his first objective was to record these comments for his children, the lecture clearly attempts to inspire others to a different way of thinking about life. Consider whether this video is better analyzed as a dramatistic event as Burke would suggest or with Fisher's narrative approach. The fidelity of Fisher's narrative approach clearly comes through in this lecture where Randy Pausch talks about his experience of achieving his childhood dreams through the many relationships he has had. The combination of humor, passion, irreverence, emotion, and real-life tragedy make it a real-life tragedy for this gifted man and his family. It is nearly impossible to watch this event without being affected personally by it. Consider whether you can truly ever say again that it was merely rhetoric after watching this lecture. Professor Pausch died on July 24, 2008.

Coherence relies on the degree to which the story is consistent. Consistency means that the story is logically organized or told. In other words, we generally don't know the outcome of the story or the fate of the characters until the story is complete (i.e., it has a beginning, middle, and end in the most traditional cases). In consistent narratives, the characters have good reasons for doing what they do, and the impact of the situation or setting of the story also makes sense.

Fidelity in a narrative is similar to coherence but focuses more on whether the story seems realistic and is the kind of thing that really happens. It presents a rationale or *logic of good reasons* (Fisher, 1987) for the setting, plot, characters, and outcome of the narrative. Fisher presented several benchmarks of narratives demonstrating good fidelity. First, they deal with human values that seem appropriate for the point or moral of the story and for the actions taken by the characters. Next, the values seem to lead to positive outcomes for the characters and are in synch with our own experiences. Finally, the values form a vision for our future. Persuasive narratives cut across a broad expanse of human behavior. They appeal to our native imagination and feelings. Consider how fidelity is conveyed in Randy Pausch's last lecture (see Box 3.6).

Narratives can also form communities of identification that together lead to a common worldview. Because of this, they have been a central part of most if not all ideological movements throughout history. For example, America's founding fathers promoted a narrative of freedom and an inherent set of human rights that continues to be important for our expected conduct today.

Although many welcomed the discussion opened by the narrative paradigm, Fisher met resistance from those who had built careers on the rational world paradigm. For example, Barbara Warnick (1987) challenged Fisher's criteria as being so context-dependent that listeners would need extensive knowledge of the situation before attempting to understand a narrative. In her opinion, Fisher's standards allow so much room for interpretation that they leave the theory open to the inconsistencies of personal judgment. Others such as Rowland (1989) were not convinced that narrative encompasses as much of the communication domain as Fisher maintained.

Much territory in the narrative paradigm remains unexplored regarding bridges across differing cultures, but negotiating our different cultural narratives seems to be a good starting place to understand our differences. Whether or not the narrative paradigm is the single dominant organizing paradigm in the way communication operates is questionable, but Fisher did articulate a descriptive approach to persuasion that better captures the human experience of the average person than the more technical approach that appears to have become elitist in its assumptions. Despite the imperfections of the narrative paradigm, narratives are one of the most powerful persuasive tactics available. At times, good stories counter many facts. Fisher's narrative theory helps us understand this. The key point here is that you should never underestimate the value of a good story that resonates with its hearers.

POWER-ORIENTED PERSPECTIVES

Themes challenging the authority and power of the dominant culture run through the final group of perspectives covered in this chapter. These approaches allow us to look at a persuasive situation from the position of groups that are not in power. Such approaches naturally address the multicultural face of persuasion and the voices that have often been silenced such as women and the poor.

This group of theories has great utility in constructing defensive strategies against the abuse of power, and applications are clearly demonstrated in many social movements (see Andrews, 1980; Bowers & Ochs, 1971). These perspectives also offer reasons why some persuasive campaigns have failed with groups that are not in the majority. Understanding this point of view is also important as we are moving toward a global economy and global view of the environment. Understanding the dissatisfaction with past colonial practices can help persuaders in a global context prepare better adapted persuasive tactics to meet resistance.

Many people do not understand attacks on traditional perspectives of persuasion. These perspectives seem to function in our daily lives. After all, many of the forms of persuasion we use today have been in use for centuries. Various groups perceive, however, that the dominant culture ignores or silences them. These perspectives usually articulate some variation of the argument that traditional forms of persuasion have been the tools of the powerful to maintain control over those

without power. It is evident that former colonial powers have profited from taking natural resources and used cheap or slave labor for their own benefit from third world countries to the detriment of third world countries.

Superficially, there is little question that the foundations of persuasion were established among the privileged class. Aristotle was a member of the privileged class and encouraged the use of wealth. In Book I, he says wealth comprised "plenty of coined money and territory; the ownership of numerous, large, and beautiful estates; also the ownership of numerous and beautiful implements, live stock, and slaves. All these kinds of property are our own, are secure, gentlemanly, and useful" (p. 39). A lifestyle such as Aristotle describes is out of the reach of most in society—and it was in his day as well. Part of the critique of traditional persuasion is that people (or groups) of privilege cannot meaningfully engage those who have been pushed to the margins of society. The argument is that most of the elite cannot really understand what it is like to live in poverty or to suffer the humiliation that the disadvantaged feel. The poor are invisible to many of us. Many communities have enacted legislation to keep hustlers away from central shopping districts where consumers would rather not be reminded of the unpleasantness of poverty. Despite the substantial progress resulting from civil rights legislation, it is very difficult, if not impossible, for those who are white to fully understand the constant assaults on the dignity of persons of color, for whom advantage is usually assumed to be due to preference given because of their skin color rather than their competence. Similarly, white males in positions of power find it hard to identify with the struggle of women for respect of their intelligence and competence. We now turn to several perspectives that challenge the dominant culture.

The Women's Movement

Although activism waned after the Vietnam conflict ended, it hardly disappeared. The women's movement has been very critical of the dominant culture

---

B O X 3.7   Culture Clash of Genders in the Salesroom

Consider a real event that happened to one of our neighbors. She has been in the workforce for twenty years and, by all accounts, she is very competent at her job. She is married and is raising two sons, and she is no stranger to managing financial assets. One day she visited a local car dealership to buy a van to replace the family's old one. She found the salesperson to be very condescending. He did not want to negotiate price with her and suggested that her husband stop by to talk. This condescending attitude led her to purchase a vehicle from another dealership. How should females who get no respect from car salespersons address this lack of respect?

---

that has suppressed women. **Feminist criticism** represents one part of the women's movement that attempts to better the lot of women. Feminist scholar Sonja Foss (1996) argues that "feminist criticism has its roots in a social and political movement, the feminist or women's liberation movement, aimed at improving conditions for women" (p. 165). So, feminist theory fits well with the prior discussion of social movements. The term *feminist* does not have one single meaning, but Foss suggests that the different varieties of feminism do share a commitment to end sexist oppression and to change the existing power relations between women and men.

[A central issue for feminist theory is that traditional considerations of rhetoric and persuasion have focused on the discourse of males and been dominated by male perspectives] Feminists clearly articulate that history is "his story" and not "her story." Feminist theory questions the exclusion of the consideration of women and the issue of whether women have approached communication situations differently. Important questions are raised about how women are represented—particularly through language, but increasingly through other forms of imagery in mass media. Although feminist scholars do not all agree on the causes of and the remedies for oppression, many American feminists approach the issue as one of emancipation or liberation from male oppression, with a goal of obtaining the power necessary for women to create their own reality. Feminist scholar Karen Foss and her colleagues (1999) suggest that feminists also generally agree women's experiences are different from men's, due

to differences in socialization and biology. Foss et al. claim that feminists' values of self-determination, affirmation, mutuality, care, and holism are part of a world that is superior to the traditional culture dominated by male values. Finally, says Foss, women's perspectives are not incorporated in our culture, which means that the culture has silenced women.

Sonya Foss and Cindy Griffin (1995) attack traditional notions of persuasion and propose an **invitational rhetoric** that promotes understanding rather than change. Invitational rhetoric resembles Plato's dialogical approach and is clearly not Aristotelian. It also bears a strong resemblance to Scott's proposal that rhetoric is epistemic. There are feminist activists such as rhetorical scholar Karlyn Kohrs Campbell, however, who reject the assumptions of invitational rhetoric. As a veteran of years of struggle for female equality, Campbell does not believe that simply inviting oppressors to change gets real change to happen. Whether or not such feminist values can ever become the dominant values of society, it is important to hear some of the points being made about traditional practices of persuasion.

Males in sales positions can often be very condescending to women, assuming that women know very little about items like cars and computers (see Box 3.7). Such insensitive persuasive tactics make little sense because women drive the consumer economy through their purchases much more than do men. On the bright side, we are seeing increasing use of gender-free or gender-equitable language, especially with pronouns—some organizations are getting the message. For example, many

---

B O X 3.8 **Media Portrayals of Multicultural Inclusiveness and Correspondence to Reality**

In today's increasingly diverse society, it is desirable for most organizations to have a diverse and multicultural membership that, at a minimum, reflects the diversity of their immediate environment. Attracting potential employees and potential students to the organization from underrepresented groups, however, can be a difficult task. Frequently, organizations use various media campaigns for outreach and promotion that portray a much higher percentage of diversity than is actually represented at the institution. My university's Web site often uses pictures that display a higher percentage of women, international students, and other persons of color than are represented by our actual student population. Do you think it is an ethical problem to portray an organization as more diverse than it really is so that those who are underrepresented are persuaded to become a part of that organization? Alternatively, are such portrayals simply positive indicators signaling a more inclusive climate for persons of all backgrounds?

---

see the financial potential of professional women and are directing advertising toward them. Those crafting persuasive messages for women must be attuned to all the possible meanings being sent. Organizational scholar Gail Fairhurst and consultant Robert Sarr's (1996) work on framing demonstrates how our communication can change to be more friendly to women. It is quite possible that future research will more clearly define a style of communication that women prefer. It is already evident that a chauvinistic style is not a wise choice for attempting to persuade women. Bringing about change through understanding does have one very clear implication: Understanding requires a lot of listening. Whether they fully embrace the feminist approach to change or not, persuaders can learn the valuable lesson that change begins with *listening* rather than *telling*.

Advertising has a mixed record in terms of fostering a more progressive view of women and minorities in general. Even attempts to be more inclusive are sometimes controversial and we can question the appropriateness of many media messages (see Box 3.8). Questionable persuasive practices in the media may be fostering poor ideals for girls and women. The book *Deadly Persuasion: Why Women and Girls Must Fight the Addictive Power of Advertising*, by author and filmmaker Jean Kilbourne (2001), details the problematic influence of advertising on the development of the female image. Kilbourne calls into question many of the poor habits of our culture and the ways in which

the media reinforce them. For example, she observes that mostly thin models are used in TV ads. Although some merchandisers have begun using models with more realistic body types to promote their clothing and underwear, considerable consumer sentiment exists for portrayals of images of what they want to be rather than what they are. Some consumers want some degree of illusion to escape the harsh realities of the real world. Thus, the persuasive face of the bottom line or effectiveness emerges again. Tactics that sell typically get used.

The Environmental Movement

Environmentalists are, perhaps, being taken more seriously now than ever. When Al Gore was Vice-President of the United States, his environmental message did not gain much traction with the public. More serious attention has been paid to environmental advocacy since the release of his 2006 documentary *Inconvenient Truth* that led to him winning an Academy Award and the Nobel Peace Prize. His work was widely embraced by the scientific community. More controversial propositions from the environmental movement are that countries like the United States and other major industrial countries such as Japan and Germany use a far greater percentage of the world's natural resources than their populations merit. Moreover, environmental critics claim industrialized nations are causing far greater impact on global warming per citizen than nonindustrialized nations, who have, are, or will experience the severe consequences of natural disasters linked to global warming. Considerable skepticism and opposition, however, exists for these propositions from some scientists as well as many business and political leaders. Substantial debate continues whether human intervention can make a difference and what corrective actions are needed immediately. Interestingly, much of the persuasive case relies on scientific evidence for the environmentalists with heavy use of visual and graphic evidence from the polar ice caps and melting glaciers.

not bad by itself

The Marxist Critique

A major feature of **Marxist theory** is a focus on the inequitable economic system. This theory challenges the effectiveness face of persuasion. Some of those in the feminist and environment movements adopt some form of Marxist ideology. Marxist theorists address the issue of economic power as it exists in capitalistic countries such as the United States, Japan, and Germany. They believe that those who control the means of production (the bourgeoisie, or power elite) also control and determine the nature of society. Such elite circles were as prominent in Plato and Aristotle's time as they have been in U.S. society.

not good for my

[The major economic motive in capitalism is profit.] The bottom line is the essence of the effectiveness face of persuasion. Profit is naturally tied to the production and consumption of goods and services. The elite achieve production and profit by exploiting the abilities of the workers (the proletariat), dominating and oppressing them in a variety of ways. For example, the workers are enticed to produce so they can earn wages, which then permits them to purchase the essentials (and later the non-essentials) of life. This produce-earn-purchase cycle creates a never-ending and ever-increasing necessity to work in order to produce and, in turn, earn wages in order to buy products.

not into persuasion anymore

How does this all relate to our study of persuasion? Much of persuasion discussed in this book has ties to capitalism in terms of buying and selling. So, some see persuasive tactics as naturally biased toward maintaining the economic well being of the elite. Other connections should also be fairly obvious. Because political power is needed to maintain economic power, the power elite must find members willing to run for political office and support their campaigns with money, volunteers, and other things necessary for political persuasion. Marxist critics [note how the profit motive and its resulting cycle of consumption are instilled in the citizenry through subtle forms of persuasion.] Belief in the value of earning money begins in childhood (e.g., having a lemonade stand and taking out the garbage to earn an allowance) as well as with immigrants who see the United States as the land of economic opportunity. As consumers and family members, we should be attuned to [the persuasive push to obtain material goods supporting this type of culture and how it can erode other values that are more important to us.] The focus on earning money continues throughout adulthood (getting a well-paid job, accumulating wages to purchase a home, furnishing a home to a certain standard, etc.) and is constantly reinforced in the media. Those in power, however, largely control the economic system. Workers and citizens sometimes can exercise their own persuasive power through nonviolent protest marches (see Figure 3.3).

Bad persuasion

Radical Movements

Although we will give social movements additional attention later in the book, we should here ask a key question: whether moving from verbal to physical confrontation is ever justifiable[Physical confrontation means crossing the line from persuasion to coercion.] Currently, the debate continues over the ethics of physical confrontation. It is difficult to bring about change in large corporations when lax government regulations support many environmentally unsound practices. Violence and protests are two of the few avenues of influence available to groups with few economic resources and little political clout to bring about change in problematic actions of large organizations. So, groups of radical environmentalists such as Earth First! drive spikes into trees, knowing that loggers may be

F I G U R E 3.3 Argentinean government workers exercise their power by protesting their low wages in a nonviolent protest march on the capitol.

seriously injured when their chainsaws hit the spikes. Cut brake lines appeared on corporate vehicles of a seafood company that was not conforming to environmentally sound policies. Radicals set fire to the Two Elks Lodge in Vail to protest the actions of a company they believed to be environmentally unsound.

The question of whether intimidation, harassment, force, and violence are justifiable has no easy answer. The difficulty of addressing it is reflected in the different philosophies embodied by Dr. Martin Luther King, Jr., and Malcolm X. Dr. King promoted nonviolence as the means for change, whereas Malcolm X advocated armed self-defense and revenge against the Klan and other white terrorists. It is easy to understand Malcolm X's point about not taking abuse from white people anymore when we consider that over four thousand black people were lynched in the South in the decades following Reconstruction (see Burns, 1990). These violent tactics draw attention to serious issues. Although they are forms of influence, they are not persuasion.

REVIEW AND CONCLUSION

Aristotle's *Rhetoric* created the dominant pattern of persuasion that held for centuries, but alternative models in the tradition of Plato view persuasion in a different way. Traditional forms of persuasion have many limitations, including the impression that those using them often do so in manipulative ways. Quintilian introduced a corrective element by insisting that personal character is the center of socially redeeming discourse. Credibility crises in professional sports illustrate the importance of character as an issue in the media. Alternatives to the traditional approaches include processes of discovery in which the best interests of all parties are identified. Burke, who introduced the dramatistic approach, sees persuasion in a larger performance context. Narratives represent an alternative way of seeing the world—the persuasive nature of a good story and true personal experience such as the last lecture of Randy Pausch should not be underestimated. Power also plays an important role in persuasion. For example, in social movements, persuasion is used by those who have less power in society to address those who have more power. Critical theory represents another way of thinking about the abuse of power in society. Overall, the message of these latter perspectives is that greater attention must be paid to situations in persuasion studies in which the interests of some groups are ignored by more powerful others.

KEY TERMS

After reading this chapter, you should be able to identify, explain, and give an example of the following key terms or concepts:

segmented audiences	enthymeme	epistemic	fidelity
forensic discourse	syllogism	pentad	feminist criticism
epideictic discourse	topoi	dramatistic	invitational rhetoric
deliberative discourse	metaphor	rational world paradigm	Marxist theory
ethos	dialogue	narrative paradigm	
pathos	dialectic method	coherence	
logos	Truth/truth		

APPLICATION OF ETHICS

Assume a major tobacco company is recruiting you to work in its advertising unit. Realizing that public perception of its products is becoming more hostile, the company wants you to create an advertising campaign that you believe violates no ethical boundaries, effectively promotes tobacco products, but improves relations with the public at the same time. Discuss which perspectives in this chapter you could use to create an ethical campaign that meets these criteria. Is such a campaign possible?

QUESTIONS FOR FURTHER THOUGHT

1. What would your reaction be to the Westboro Baptist Church if they were protesting at a funeral of one of your friends?

2. For today's generation in college, which of the three dimensions of credibility makes the most difference to you for evaluating someone as a parent? A professor? A boss?

3. How would you define the character of a good person if you think Quintilian has a point about the character of the speaker?

4. What examples of hate speech as described in Chapter 2 are found in the violations of sanctity of the funerals such as that of Heath Ledger by members of the Westboro Baptist Church?

5. What are Walter Fisher's big issues with communication approaches in the Aristotelian tradition? How does his approach solve or fail to solve these issues?

6. Is there more to analyzing a narrative than assessing coherence and fidelity in Randy Pausch's last lecture? Might not this lecture be better analyzed by Burke's dramatistic approach than by Fisher's?

7. Was the burning of Two Elks Lodge at Vail by radical environmentalists justified as a means to convince others of the environmental tragedies that are created by ski resorts? When is violence justified in a protest? Why?

8. Was the violence used in the American Revolution to break away from England ethically justifiable?

9. What is your overall impression of feminists? In your world, is feminism a good or a bad thing? In your experience, when are the opinions of women typically ignored?

✳

 For online activities, go to the *Persuasion* book companion Web site at http://academic.cengage.com/communication/larson12.

4

＊

Social Scientific Approaches to Persuasion

JOSEPH N. SCUDDER
Northern Illinois University

LEARNING GOALS

After reading this chapter, you should be able to:

1. Describe the major theories and approaches used by social scientists to study contemporary persuasion.

2. Compare and contrast the dominant dual-process models: the elaboration likelihood model and the heuristic-systematic model.

3. Show what the expectancy-value theories, the theory of reasoned action, and the theory of planned behavior do that the dual-process theories do not accomplish.

4. Evaluate whether Zajonc's mere exposure principle poses a fundamental problem to the major cognitive approaches.

5. Explain the connection of the memory and the activation of attitudes to persuasion.

6. Indicate why efficacy may be more important than the actual fear generated through fear-inducing tactics.

7. Illustrate how the use of anchors through tactics such as decoy effects may make political candidates appear more or less favorable.

8. Discuss why compliance gaining and persuasion are not the same thing and what contemporary compliance-gaining studies do that gives a more informed view of influence practices.

Social scientific approaches to persuasion emerged only recently compared to the foundations of persuasion discussed in Chapter 3. They study persuasion using modern empirical methods. The term **empirical** refers to the practice of validating knowledge by experience or observation. Most empirical studies of persuasion use statistical methods to analyze experimental results, surveys of persuasive behaviors, or actual behaviors. Increasingly, persuasive studies also use qualitative approaches such as interviews, observations, and thematic analysis.

Changing attitudes and behaviors are typically the focus of empirical studies of persuasion. For the purposes of this chapter, attitudes are the positive, neutral, or negative evaluations a person holds of objects, activities, people, or institutions. This chapter uses current understanding of attitude change as a lens to examine the early unfolding of social scientific study of persuasion up to its most recent empirical developments. This is not intended to be a complete history of empirical studies of persuasion. Rather, the intent is to show how many of the early issues studied by persuasion researchers still are reflected in more current process-oriented theories of persuasion and how our understandings of earlier findings have changed. First, we turn to the dominant framework in persuasion research today.

DUAL-PROCESS THEORIES

According to social psychologists Shelley Chaiken and Yaacov Trope (1999), **dual-process theories** propose two qualitatively different modes of information processing that operate in making judgments and decisions. The first is a "fast, associative, information processing mode based on low-effort heuristics," and the second is a "slow, rule-based information processing mode based on high-effort systematic reasoning" (p. ix). The second route is similar to traditional understandings of persuasion we considered in Chapter 3. Dual-process theories, however, challenge the dominant rational world paradigm we met in Chapter 3, which assumed that people primarily reasoned their way to persuasion through careful consideration of arguments and evidence. Moreover, they moved persuasion to a more dynamic process orientation.

We consider the two dual-process theories that command the most attention: (1) the elaboration likelihood model and (2) the heuristic-systematic model. We will also consider a third mental process often discussed in conjunction with dual-process theories—the automatic activation of attitudes.

The Elaboration Likelihood Model (ELM)

We saw in Chapter 1 that social psychologists Richard Petty and John Cacioppo (1986) articulated a dual-process theory they called the **elaboration likelihood model (ELM)**. The ELM revitalized researchers' interest in persuasion. Elaboration in the ELM refers to the conscious scrutiny we use in making an evaluative judgment and requires both the motivation and the ability to process information. They place elaboration on a continuum whose ends are two different routes of information processing. [The **central route** forms the high end of the continuum. It is information processing that occurs "as a result of a person's careful and thoughtful considerations of the true merits of the information present] (p. 3). It is a slower, deliberative, high-effort mode of information processing that uses systematic reasoning. When persons use the central route, it is clear that they are consciously engaged in thinking. Petty and Wegener (1999) maintain not only that the greater amount of thinking is done at the high end, but also that elaboration at the high end uses a kind of thinking that adds something beyond the original information. People are making the best-reasoned judgments they can make based on their scrutiny of the information available.

Even though you possess exceptional ability to process information, that ability goes to waste if you are not motivated to process the information. This motivation may, however, happen in different ways for different people. Demonstrating relevance and importance are two key factors of motivation to centrally process a persuasive message. In other words, a persuader must be able to answer the question, *why should my target audience pay attention to this message?* Beyond importance and relevance, Petty and Cacioppo proposed that another component

of cognitive motivation to process information is a general trait that some persons enjoy thinking and others do not. They called this trait the **need for cognition (NFC)**. It ranges from one extreme where persons enjoy thinking to the other where others wish to avoid cognitive effort. So, some people naturally like to think and analyze across situations, whereas others prefer not to expend any more energy thinking than is necessary.

At the low end of the elaboration continuum, people use the [**peripheral route** of information processing, requiring much less cognitive effort and sometimes surveying less information than in the central route] The peripheral route may also rely on simple classical conditioning, or the use of mental shortcuts or rules of thumb. It often occurs as the result of some simple cue in the persuasion context, such as an attractive or handsome source such as Angelina Jolie or Brad Pitt promoting their movie.]

Persuasive messages bombard us constantly through the peripheral route, such as the brand names displayed on shoes or clothing or the sponsorship acknowledgments at events we attend. The constant reinforcement of these brands often happens without our conscious awareness; we take the information in like a sponge soaking up water. For example, find the repeated cue in the picture of a street café in Figure 4.1 that typically would be processed by the peripheral route. I call this the *sneaky route* to persuasion because brands and other messages often are stored in our memory outside our conscious awareness. In a recent persuasion class I asked if anyone had seen the first political commercial for an election more than two years away. One student said she had seen it, but had not paid attention to it. I asked her what she remembered. She recalled every important aspect of the commercial's message—even though she had not been carefully thinking about it. It is often harder to actively resist this type of persuasion because the tactics are not always obvious—especially to children.

Buying a computer is a complex decision. We might compare memory capacity, processor speed, software, warranty, service, size, monitor

FIGURE 4.1 Find the persuasive cue in this picture of a street café that would typically be processed by the peripheral route proposed in the ELM.

about computers for a recommendation, giving their price range and the typical ways they use computers. Relying on the recommendation of others we trust or an expert requires only a small amount of central processing.

In contrast, brand preferences and our habits often lead us to process information peripherally. For instance, when asked at a fast-food restaurant what you want to drink, you may respond automatically, "Diet Coke." You do not evaluate all the choices carefully or even ask what they are. Strong brand preferences reduce the central processing necessary.

The ELM, however, does not provide much help in determining which people will rely heavily on brands and which make purchase decisions based on price (see Box 4.1). A sale price of $3.99 for a case of Diet Pepsi may lead a person with a preference for Diet Coke to change brands that week. Others may select generic diet colas because they use a different decision rule like "get the most volume for the least money." Sometimes other factors such as a strict budget, organizational regulations, or our insurance plans may influence the brands we buy.

Peripheral processing covers a large range of behaviors. For example, the speech rate of individuals influences the way we perceive them, with some evidence suggesting that we prefer rates as fast as or faster than our own. The use of physically and socially attractive persons in advertising also reflects an appeal to peripheral processes. Sometimes, appeals to peripheral processes are more useful in drawing our attention to the message than in altering our perception of its content.

Petty and Cacioppo's ELM rests on the assumption that people are motivated to process information because they want to hold correct attitudes, or at least those perceived as being correct in light of social comparisons and norms. Petty and Cacioppo also believe that various factors can affect the direction and number of individuals' attitudes and enhance or reduce argument strength. For instance, if an attractive or highly credible source opposes flag burning, that factor could increase or decrease the weight you might give to the Supreme Court's decision that flag burning is legal. The ELM

type, and other factors such as whether to buy a laptop or a less portable tower. Our thinking processes will include reasoning, scrutiny of evidence, price comparisons, and an evaluation of our computing needs, to name a few. This information will be centrally processed. Many people, however, simply do not have the ability or the motivation to evaluate which computer is best for their needs. They may call a friend or relative who knows a lot

---

B O X 4.1   Brand Influences

What influences your choice of brands or labels? Think about purchases you made or influenced in the past month. Did you choose brand names or generic products? Do you have a brand preference for any of the following items: toothpaste, shampoo, pizza, car, gas, computer, soda, athletic shoes, clothing shops, hamburger, French fries, or ketchup? If you do have preferences, where did they originate for you?

---

also suggests that as people increase scrutiny through the central processing route, peripheral cues have less impact, and vice versa. This controversial proposition represents a marked difference from our other dual-process model, the heuristic-systematic model.

The Heuristic-Systematic Model (HSM)

Similarities are apparent between the ELM and the **heuristic-systematic model**, or **HSM** (Chaiken, Giner-Sorolla, & Chen, 1996). The HSM proposes a **systematic processing route** that represents a comprehensive treatment of judgment-related information. It is a slow, high-effort reasoning process bearing strong resemblance to the central processing route in the ELM. The other route, the **heuristic processing route**, is a fast, low-effort process that relies on the activation of judgmental rules or heuristics. Heuristics are mental rules of thumb that are not the most accurate procedure, but often very useful to deal with common situations; they are adaptive strategies that help us reduce the time it takes to make decisions. For example, to calculate the distance around a circle we often multiply the diameter of the circle by 3 to get a rough estimate instead of a more precise value for π of 3.14159. The HSM proposes the sufficiency principle whereby people attempt to strike a balance between minimizing cognitive effort and satisfying their goals.

We use heuristics daily. Instead of trying to remember the exact rules of right-of-way when two people come to a stop sign at the same time, many people simply wave the other person through the stop sign to avoid having to think too much. Some heuristics can be very misleading, like the saying that moss only grows on the north side of a tree—this simply is not true. A much better heuristic if you are lost in a forest is the fact that the sun rises in the east and sets in the west, but even this is not much help when you are lost and it is cloudy or dark.

In the HSM, systematic processing and heuristic processing operate independently and may occur simultaneously. This is probably the largest difference between the ELM and the HSM. In the ELM, there is an inverse relationship between the use of the central and the peripheral routes—as one rises, the other falls. In the HSM, we assume that people could make systematic use of some evidence at the same time they are using heuristics for other information. For example, you could make the judgment using systematic processes that a member of your work group made a good argument for doing a project a certain way, while at the same time you were making a judgment using heuristic processes about the attractiveness of that group member.

The impact of receiving too much persuasive information has not received much empirical study. It is clear, however, that people respond differently to large amounts of information. Some prefer a restaurant menu with only three choices to one that has ten pages of options. According to the ELM, the motivation of an individual to process the information is a key factor. Overloading central or systematic information processes should result in a shift to peripheral or heuristic processing. Traditional advice for creating persuasive presentations recommends the use of supporting visuals to assist understanding. After all, isn't redundancy better? We simply cannot make the blanket assertion that the use of visual aids with persuasive messages is

B O X 4.2   Graphics May Detract from the Message

Conventional wisdom suggests that a picture is worth a thousand words, but psychologists Kurt Frey and Alice Eagly (1993) provide evidence that even vivid elements in the persuasive messages may reduce the message's effectiveness when they result in low scrutiny of the message. We know from other research on split attention effects that misplaced graphics may direct attention away from the main point of the message. In your experience, when do graphics aid understanding and when do they distract audiences from the point of the message?

B O X 4.3   Triggers That Activate Us

Think about the checkout aisles of supermarkets and the items placed there. What have you purchased in checkout aisles? What triggers do they activate for you? Why do these checkout displays frustrate parents bringing children to the market? What are some markets doing to respond to complaints resulting from this marketing practice?

always a recommended practice. Images in multimedia presentations may require so much attention to process that they detract from the message content rather than enhance it (see Box 4.2). Some backlash is occurring against the use of PowerPoint© because viewers may pay so much attention to writing and recording the information on the slides that they do not, or cannot, process what the information means at the same time. It may be that information overload is the reason behind the tendency some researchers have found for visual cues to override what a person is saying. Clearly, more research is needed regarding the processing of visual forms of persuasive messages and whether they enhance or detract from the oral or written persuasion that accompanies them. Simpler may be better.

The Automatic Activation of Attitudes

Psychologist Russell Fazio (1989) believes attitudes can be triggered automatically, without deliberation. This perspective has important applications in persuasive messages intended to overcome resistance to change. For example, it allows us to understand why it is difficult to change our attitudes about our addictions, health practices, and use of stereotypes.

The automatic activation perspective treats the mind as a place where a massive amount of information is stored. As in a library, some of this information is easy to access. Most pieces are connected by pathways to other pieces of information, and accessing one piece may activate others connected to it. Connections vary in strength, and those we make regularly will typically be more accessible in our memories than those we access rarely, just as places we travel frequently become easier to find.

The difficulty of changing problematic parts of our lives, like a smoking habit, is that it often requires changing many of these connections. Establishing new behaviors means creating new pathways in our minds for accessing positive attitudes and behaviors that we learn to prefer to the old ones. This does not happen overnight. Understanding this process is very important in resisting persuasive attempts that automatically trigger certain processes for us. Controlling impulse buying requires understanding our triggers (see Box 4.3).

B O X 4.4   Credibility May Be Centrally Processed: The Case of Ward Churchill

Ward Churchill's remarks about the United States deserving the 9/11 attacks generated a lot of controversy. Many called for his firing from the University of Colorado. Is the fact that Professor Churchill is a Cherokee and *was* chairman of the department of ethnic studies at University of Colorado more likely to be a central or peripheral processing issue? His ethnic heritage as a member of one of the most abused Native American peoples certainly provides a different perspective that draws attention as does his position at a prestigious university. This is certainly a case where credibility of the speaker is not simply a peripheral cue for those who read his entire remarks. A search of the Web will reveal many materials for and against the actions of the university to not fire him.

VARIABLE-ANALYTIC APPROACHES TO PERSUASION

Now that we have explored the general dual-process models that form the general framework of much of contemporary persuasion research, we return to the early years of empirical persuasion research to establish some of the long-standing specific principles of persuasion that remain important in our contemporary world. During World War II, psychologist Carl Hovland established a program of research investigating the relationship of communication to attitudes. His work carried over to one of the most extensive programs of persuasive research ever conducted, which is now known as the Yale Communication and Attitude Change Program.

Hovland considered the main persuasion variables through a number of studies focused on single issues—much like the approach used in the natural sciences (see Hovland, 1957); thus, one label for his work is the **variable-analytic approach**. The Yale group assumed that people would change their attitudes if provided with sufficient reinforcement in support of the change. In other words, people need motivation to process information that will change their existing attitudes and the actions that flow from them.

Source Effects

The Yale studies particularly focused on the source's credibility or believability and the source's attrac-

tiveness to the receiver. In terms of today's dual-processing framework, source credibility usually influences attitude change through the peripheral or heuristic route, but central processing of a person's credibility could occur when a controversy erupts. For example, many people have centrally processed the credibility of controversial professor Ward Churchill (see Box 4.4).

Research in the 1960s proposed several dimensions of credibility, but expertise, trustworthiness, and attractiveness continue to be the most widely investigated. The Yale researchers conducted credibility studies in which the same message was attributed to persuaders having various kinds of reputations. A message about smoking and lung cancer, for example, was attributed either to a college sophomore or to a doctor from the surgeon general's office. Not surprisingly, greater attitude change occurred when the audience believed the message was coming from the doctor as opposed to the student. A critical point found in these studies is that the effect of speaker credibility may decline over time if the content of the message becomes separated from the source in the hearers' memory. This is a particular problem with messages we hear only once.

Hovland and his colleagues called the decaying link between message and speaker's credibility the **sleeper effect**. It can work to a speaker's disadvantage when his or her credibility is initially high, because it means that high credibility can be lost over time. However, the sleeper effect may work to the speaker's advantage when initial credibility is medium or low but very strong arguments are offered, because people may remember the strong arguments and forget about the credibility factor. Although subsequent research on the sleeper effect has yielded mixed outcomes at times, it generally provides support for the idea. The meta-analysis of the sleeper effect by Kumkale and Albarracin (2004) found that persuasion did increase over time for persons initially exposed to a less-credible source when the quality of the message arguments were initially judged as strong. Thus, years of research tend to support the original formulation of the sleeper effect by the Yale researchers (see also Allen & Stiff, 1998). Consistent with the more contemporary ELM, persuasion was stronger when recipients of the persuasive messages had the ability and motivation to scrutinize the message. This issue of the motivation of the listeners is one of many places where the ELM refines our understanding of past research without questioning the foundations of the original concept. Many questions remain about how it works. For instance, research is not conclusive as to whether information is even stored in memory when the credibility of the speaker is very low or the relevance of the information is low.

A review of five decades of credibility research (see Pornpitakpan, 2004) supports the conclusion from the Yale studies that high-credibility sources are generally more persuasive than low-credibility sources. High-credibility sources often enhance the impact of high-quality evidence. Yet, the review notes a reduction or reversal of the impact of high-credibility in some conditions. For example, high-credibility sources appear to be less effective where motivation to process the message carefully is low. Notice that the motivation of the receiver again becomes a qualifying factor of the general finding. Another consideration is the position currently held by the target audience. High-credibility sources may be more important to use in situations where the message is advocating substantial changes from positions currently held than when attempting to get only minor changes from current positions. High-credibility sources have also been found to be more persuasive when using threats or presenting negative opinions.

A trustworthy source for one group may not carry the same weight with another group. In some contexts expertise is a better route to establish credibility, but it must appear certain and have little ambiguity. One of my family members who was experiencing back pain received conflicting recommendations from two surgeons with extensive expertise in back surgery. In this case, there was great ambiguity, it was not clear which expert had the best recommendation, and the advice from both surgeons was discounted. The two conflicting experts negated the influence of each other. The person turned to people she trusted for advice.

Another important factor in determining the credibility of a source is the degree to which the source is similar to us. Using similarity in persuasive appeals is usually attempting to appeal to peripheral processes rather than making it an explicit focus. Many organizations use visual appeals to provide evidence that other people like them are part of their organization. Examine Figure 4.2 to see how the Southern Company effectively uses this tactic.

Building unwarranted trust is a common, but unethical appeal to similarity that operates through peripheral rather than central processing. Frauds often occur when persons pose as group members or enlist the help of actual group members. Such tactics are called **affinity scams** because they exploit the trust and friendship existing in groups whose members have much in common. In a Ponzi (pyramid) scheme new investor money is used to pay off earlier investors, who may make a very good return on their money and so unwittingly convince other potential investors that it is a good deal. One scam bilked $2.5 million from a group of 100 Texas senior citizens who were asked to switch safe retirement savings to securities promising a higher investment return. Consumers from close-knit groups or communities must be especially wary of deals proposed just because several of their trusted associates participate. Offers that look too good to be true deserve more examination in the central route of processing.

The Yale studies also considered whether the height of a source leads to more or less attitude change, how the rate of delivery affects persuasion,

Anthony James
President and CEO
Savannah Electric

**HE'S SEEN A LOT OF CHANGES,
BUT ONE THING HAS REMAINED THE SAME.**

In 1978, Anthony James began his career with Southern Company, the South's premier energy provider, as a Safety and Health Supervisor for Georgia Power. Today, he is the President and CEO of Savannah Electric. A lot has changed over the years, but Anthony can tell you one thing hasn't — Southern Company's commitment to our customers, employees and the region we serve. This dedication has helped us become one of FORTUNE® Magazine's 2002 Most Admired Companies. We will always embrace change, but Southern Company's commitment to you will remain the same. To learn more, visit us at **southerncompany.com.** | NYSE>SO

SOUTHERN COMPANY
Energy to Serve Your World™

Alabama Power   Georgia Power   Gulf Power   Mississippi Power   Savannah Electric

FIGURE 4.2 Although this Southern Company ad explicitly emphasizes to investors how it is changing to meet today's values while also maintaining its traditional values, it is probably saying something else implicitly.

SOURCE: Photography by Ernest Washinton/EW Productions.

and when eye contact produces desired effects. Taller persuaders were rated more believable and more trustworthy than shorter ones. Standards of attraction clearly vary by culture, gender, and sometimes by generation. The general assumption is that attraction is routinely processed in the peripheral or heuristic routes, but it may be centrally processed when explicit focus is placed on it (see Box 4.5).

Attractiveness goes beyond physical characteristics. Have you ever heard someone remark that a person is "beautiful, but too high-maintenance for my tastes"? For many, attractiveness includes prestige, social standing, and influence. The **Pelz effect** suggests that people like to be associated with those who have power and influence at high levels because it enhances their self-esteem to be associated with these people. Attractiveness also describes whether one's social style is friendly, open, and approachable.

What are some other attractiveness factors? Persuaders delivering their messages in halting or introverted ways tend to exert less effect on attitudes than those who deliver their speech in smooth and extroverted ways. Gender influences acceptance as well. Although results are mixed, attractive same-sex persuaders are often rated as less credible than attractive persuaders of the opposite sex.

Message Effects

The Yale studies considered the impacts of several message effects on persuasion, not all of which were new to researchers.

Primacy-Recency Effects. One of the oldest findings of persuasion research, presented by psychologist F. H. Lund in 1925, claimed that the most important piece of evidence should come first. We call this the **primacy effect**. The **recency effect**, that is, information most recently presented, also has been found to have significant impact. Whether the primacy or the recency effect is more effective has received substantial attention. Hovland (1957) reported that the primacy-recency issue is not so straightforward. They found the first speaker did not necessarily have an advantage over the second speaker. However, the primacy of negative information has an important role in impression formation—it is particularly difficult to overcome negative information presented first.

The time frame is important in predicting whether primacy or recency effects prevail. It appears that recency effects often decay over the longer term but may be relevant in short-term situations. Research within the ELM framework suggests that listener motivation plays a large role in the processing of information and in determining the impact of primacy-recency effects. The order of the content appears to make little difference to those with high motivation to process who carefully scrutinize messages, but recency effects appear to play a greater role than primacy effects for persons less motivated (see Petty, Wegener, & Fabrigar, 1997). Again, notice that listener motivation is an important factor in the primacy-recency debate.

Message Bias and Two-Sided Arguments. Sometimes persuaders must address people who hold views that are neutral or may be contrary to their own. Should the persuader present one side or two sides of an issue? We call this aspect of persuasion, where only one side or all sides of an issue are considered, **message-sidedness**. Hovland (1957) suggested that it may be wise to first introduce the negative arguments people are already considering. Such tactics launch a preemptive strike against unfavorable information that persuaders expect the hearers may already possess. In the dual-processing framework, using two-sided arguments encourages listeners to centrally process information. Consider United Airline's ad campaign strategy dealing with its filing for bankruptcy. The campaign attempted to establish that travelers need not fear flying with United and it promoted the company's new beginning. The ad engages readers to process this information centrally rather than peripherally. It gets the lingering issue of the airline's bankruptcy out in the open.

Allen's (1998) meta-analysis of message-sidedness considered 70 studies involving over 10,000 people. It indicated that two-sided messages are more effective than one-sided messages when they refute the opposition's arguments. Even those holding similar values are likely to benefit from two-sided messages. Such messages inoculate those whose belief systems are not yet mature by forewarning them of the dangers out there. They may also generate more support against the opposition, much like a pep rally. However, it is not enough merely to mention the positions of the other side; the persuader must refute those positions. Biased information processing suggests that the need to use two-sided messages depends largely on the goals and motivation of the persuader.

Biased information processing occurs when decision-makers favor a certain position and interpret the world in light of that position. They are not giving objective or fair consideration to all possibilities. For example, an employee who has worked for Ford Motor Company for 25 years may be so loyal to Ford that she or he would never think of buying a vehicle from a competitor. Other people come from families who have been Democrats or Republicans for generations and will tend to evaluate persuasive political messages from the biases of those long-standing traditions. Some biased processing occurs because people have a lot more facts and information stored in their memories for activation of one side of an issue than others (see Petty & Wegner, 1999). If you prefer an Apple computer and have used it for years, you probably have a lot more knowledge of Apple computers than of its competitors. You can probably articulate far more features of the Apple system and why you would be most comfortable buying another Apple computer. The same would be true if you have been a loyal user of Microsoft Windows. So, long-standing ties with products, services, and institutions often lead us to have substantially more information about them. When the quality of information accessible in our memories is very lopsided, objective processing is less likely unless we recognize and correct this deficiency.

According to psychologist Shelley Chaiken and her associates (1996), objective and biased processing originate from different motives. The HSM distinguishes among accuracy, defense, and impression motives. Two-sided messages are appropriate when the goal is to present an accurate assessment such as when making a hiring recommendation from a pool of several qualified candidates. One-sided messages, however, are perfectly fine in persuasive situations where a person is defending a position or trying to maintain an image with important others. For instance, one-sided messages are fine at a political rally that people have paid $1000 per plate to attend—those are not people who have to be convinced to support the candidate. Similarly, Petty and Cacioppo (1979) propose that biased processing is likely when the issue at hand is relevant to the target of the message and that person holds a vested interest; but objective processing is more likely when relevance is high, but the person has no vested interest in the outcome or little knowledge about the topic. Consequently, persons with large investments in a company are more likely to favor that company's products. They often do not try to do a fair comparison with the products of the competition. This biased-processing tendency is a critical problem with many boards of directors at large corporations. Biased processing appears to be more common when persuasive messages contain ambiguous information or arguments of mixed quality rather than clearly strong or weak arguments (see Petty & Wegener, 1999).

Inoculation. Inoculation is probably the foremost strategy for helping others resist persuasion. In the persuasive context, **inoculation** is the practice of warning people of potentially damaging information or persuasive attempts that will probably happen in the future. This is typically done by giving them a weakened version of the threats and dangers in arguments, practices, or behaviors they will encounter in the future. Michael Pfau (see Pfau et al., 2001) highlights the robust nature of inoculation and demonstrates the multiple and surprising ways of accomplishing it across contexts. Increasingly, political campaigns use it to warn their supporters that attempts will be coming from opponents to turn them to "the dark side." Inoculation provides a heuristic strategy to get people to ignore persuasive attempts from the opposition without careful processing of those messages, rather like throwing away junk mail unread.

The Influence of Mood and Affect on Biased Processing. It is fairly common for persons taking their first persuasion class during the holiday season to ask whether holiday music and holiday decorations that attempt to put people in a happy mood are an effective strategy for store sales. Although such holiday features appear to bring more shoppers to major urban centers known for such displays, such as New York City and Chicago, the exact impact of mood on specific purchases is less clear. A review of several studies of mood and its impact on the processing of information by psychologists Herbert Bless and Norbert Schwarz (1999) indicates wide agreement for the proposition that people will pay more direct attention to specific information when they are in a neutral mood or are sad. Generally, anger does not encourage objective processing. In contrast, positive moods or happy moods appear to encourage less careful analysis and greater reliance on heuristic processes or stereotypes. Thus, positive or happy moods increase the likelihood of biased rather than objective processing of information. Bless and Schwarz argue that these differences in processing may be due to the increased motivation to process information in negative situations where systematic processes are required to handle problematic situations. They suggest that persons in good moods have little motivation to expend the energy to systematically process information unless other goals require it. Moreover, they suggest that the less-efficient processing we may do when in a positive mood results from using past experiences and ways of coping with the world. Others, such as psychologists Mackie and Worth (1989), however, maintain that being in a good mood limits information processing capacity because it activates a large amount of positive material in our limited processing capacity; and thus, it is an information capacity issue. The general conclusion is that we make greater use of heuristics and stereotyping in positive moods and

do more scrutiny of specific information under neutral or sad moods. Yet, several exceptions to these general conclusions have emerged (see DeSteno et al., 2004; Nabi, 2002; Mitchell et al., 2001; Petty & Wegener, 1999; Pfau et al., 2001; Wegener, Petty, & Smith, 1995).

Fear and Drive Reduction

Inducing **fear** continues to be one of the most studied tactics in persuasion research. Hovland, Janis, and Kelley laid the foundation in 1953 by proposing that the use of fear would increase the likelihood of persuasion, because compliance reduces emotional tension. The drive-reduction model is a more specialized version of the **pleasure-pain principle**—that is, people are attracted to rewarding situations and seek to eliminate uncomfortable conditions. Janis (1967) summarized the use of fear appeals and the drive-reduction model:

> Whenever fear or any other unpleasant emotion is strongly aroused, whether by verbal warning or by a direct encounter with signs of danger, the person becomes motivated to ward off the painful emotional state and his efforts in this direction will persist until the distressing cues are avoided in one way or another. Thus, if the distressing threat cues do not rapidly disappear as a result of environmental changes, the emotionally aroused person is expected to try to escape from them, either physically or psychologically (pp. 169–170).

Hovland and his associates suggested that the fear appeal is effective only if it is sufficiently intense to create a drive state that recipients believe can be effectively countered by the recommended action. This perception that the threat can be handled is now called **efficacy**. If the negative outcome seems insubstantial to the receiver, then its effectiveness is likely to be negligible. Likewise, if the credibility of the person issuing the threat or warning is low, less compliance occurs.

Controversy remains over whether using more fear is better. In the most famous fear appeal study of all time, Janis and Feshbach (1953) studied fear appeals in a dental hygiene context. They found that too much fear arousal can be less effective than more moderate fear arousal. Janis (1967) attributed these effects to an inverted U-shaped curve measuring reaction to fear appeals. That is, high levels of fear (the top of the inverted U-curve) lead to defensive avoidance, but low levels of fear are not enough to induce attitude change. Thus, Janis maintained that using moderate levels of fear produces optimal results.

The superiority of moderate fear appeals has not received support from two meta-analyses by communication researchers. Paul Mongeau (1998) reviewed 28 fear appeal studies involving over 15,000 individuals. He found significant and consistent links between the use of fear appeals and attitude change; that is, more fear is more effective than less fear. Kim Witte and Mike Allen (2000) qualified Mongeau's conclusions, proposing that strong fear appeals coupled with high-efficacy messages produce the greatest behavioral change. Perhaps even more important is their conclusion that strong fear appeals with low-efficacy messages lead to **defensive avoidance** where people try to avoid, ignore, or minimize the issue if they cannot do anything about it. These results suggest that efficacy and perception of substantial fear are central to whether fear appeals succeed or fail; strong fear messages alone are not enough. Witte (1992) provides a clear articulation of these processes in her extended parallel process model (EPPM) of fear appeals.

Witte's (1992) EPPM builds on the findings and limitations of Leventhal's (1970) parallel response model and Rogers' (1975) protection motivation theory. Witte's EPPM proposes that fear appeals invoke two processes: threat appraisal and perceived coping appraisal. The first process assesses the danger presented by the threat and how urgent it is to attend to it. So, if a park ranger sees a rattlesnake ahead on the path while conducting a nature walk, she might choose to take another path or go ahead of the group and encourage the snake to go elsewhere with her walking stick. The ranger's action removes the actual danger. The second process of fear control happens when the threat is judged to be real, but it is perceived that the remedies will not be totally effective. For example, it can be a terrifying experience to be caught out on a large body of water in a sailboat during a thunderstorm producing lots of lightning when you cannot return to shore fast enough to avoid it. The tall mast on the boat makes it an attractive target. After you do all you can do to secure the boat and take as much cover as possible, coping with the fear is all you can do. Ineffective fear control in a serious situation leads to the production of anxiety and stress.

Recent research by psychologist David Roskos-Ewoldsen and his research team (2004), however, failed to support the EPPM and the conclusions of Witte and Allen (2000). They studied fear appeals in an attitude accessibility framework (see the earlier discussion of Fazio, 1989) that examines how easy it is to access information stored in our brains that fear appeals generated. They studied fear-inducing messages regarding breast cancer and messages advocating the efficacy of self-breast exams. Their results indicate that high-efficacy messages ("you can do something about the problem") produced greater accessibility to attitudes stored in the brains about the adaptive behavior (doing the exam), but high fear-inducing messages appeared to decrease the accessibility of attitudes toward the threat itself. In other words, you could make the information regarding the effectiveness of doing breast cancer self-exams more prominent and focused without creating greater perceptions of the high danger of breast cancer itself. This finding revives the debate about whether producing more fear is better to change attitudes. More research is necessary to determine whether these results are limited to certain contexts or more generally challenge the conclusions of Witte's EPPM.

Why so much attention to fear appeals? Fear appeals are one of the most common persuasive devices encountered by consumers today. In a class lecture at our university, a product manager at a telecommunications giant acknowledged that one of the firm's most common sales techniques is to use fear, uncertainty, and doubt—also known as

N

B O X 4.6   Mixed Perceptions of the Effectiveness of Using Scare Tactics

Think about campaigns using fear to reduce the use of illegal drugs, deaths from drunk driving, and infections from HIV/AIDS. Some schools show videos of the tragic consequences of mixing alcohol with driving. Others show the consequences of unwanted teen pregnancy resulting from unprotected sex. Abstinence programs such as DARE attempt to gain commitments of students to not use drugs. The goals of many of these programs are motivated by good intentions, but there is no room for discussion or true two-way dialogue about the issues with many proponents of theses approaches. Thus, many of these well intentioned programs are propaganda. This does not mean that such propaganda is all bad, but advocates of such approaches usually are not open to changing their minds. Mixed opinions exist of the effectiveness of using scare tactics. Has persuasion using fear appeals led to change in your behavior or of anyone you know?

FUD (see FUD-counter, 2001). The origin of the term is attributed to Gene Amdahl, who claimed that salespeople at IBM tried to instill fear, uncertainty, and doubt in the minds of potential customers who were considering Amdahl computer products. Using FUD tactics also may be a component of propaganda campaigns where appeals are made to people to support various causes such as saying no to drugs or smoking (see Box 4.6). Such causes have good intentions, but some programs appear more like indoctrination rather than discussion of the issues behind these problematic behaviors. Clearly, FUD tactics will not disappear any time soon, but the ethics of using them, especially in messages directed to senior citizens, need more debate.

Anchor Effects

The book *Social Judgment* (Sherif & Hovland, 1961), the final volume of the Yale Studies in Attitude and Communication, marked the end of an era, along with Hovland's death that year. **Social judgment theory** focuses on how we form reference points, or what Sherif and Hovland called "anchors." The **anchor** is an internal reference point with which we compare other persons, issues, products, and so on that we encounter. Every issue has an anchor at any given time. Research compares the consumer's original anchor to an anchor established later by a persuasive communication.

Perhaps the most important contribution of social judgment theory is the idea that the anchor really represents a range of positions rather than one single point. Thus, "the individual's stand on a social issue is conceived as a range or a **latitude of acceptance**" (pp. 128–129). The anchor is a range of positions acceptable to persuadees, including the most acceptable one. Yet it also includes the **latitude of rejection**, which is the range of positions that persuadees find objectionable, including the most objectionable one. Moreover, research indicates that highly ego-involved individuals have very narrow latitudes of acceptance and very broad latitudes of rejection, so that the likelihood of changing the minds of highly ego-involved people is very small. The best chance of persuasion is a message advocating a position within the hearer's latitude of acceptance and only a small distance away from the position he or she holds. One of persuaders' more important tasks is determining whether various groups of people have firmly set anchors on positions that relate to the issue at hand.

An important question is how these anchors are established. Although anchors come into our lives in many ways, the people around us in our early childhood experiences provide some of the early anchors in our lives through patterns of behavior labeled *norms*. It is common for younger siblings to desire what their older siblings have at the family table. Most of us still find special foods from our childhood comforting in times of distress like macaroni and cheese or ice cream. Perhaps these foods remind of secure and safe times with our family. As

---

BOX 4.7 Decoy Effects in Politics

 An interview with Washington Post columnist Shankar Vedantam on National Public Radio aired examining the **decoy effect** in political races discussed how a third-place candidate may impact the choice of the number one candidate. He suggests perceptions of characteristics of Democratic candidate John Edwards in the race had impact on perceptions of the frontrunners Obama and Clinton in the race. He maintains that characteristics of a third option can either improve the image of certain front-running candidates or detract from them. In essence, the third candidate provides an anchor against which to judge the number one and two candidates. http://www.npr.org/templates/story/story.php?storyId=9585221.

---

we mature, it is natural to want things our peers have or to do things our peers do to fit into the culture.

Anchors, however, may be manufactured by persuaders. A common anchor is the *Manufacturer's Suggested Retail Price (MSRP)* which is also known as the full retail price. Most customers rarely pay full retail price for many items. The MSRP is usually the upper anchor or limit a customer should pay, but in many cases it is an artificially high number to make the actual price being charged appear more reasonable. Many manufacturers create a line of very high-end products that are very expensive, a range of mid-level products of very good quality, and a low-end line of products that provide significantly less benefits or are inferior to the mid-range products. The central intent of many manufacturers is to sell a high volume of the mid-level products with a few upper-level customers being a welcome bonus. Auto manufacturers often limit sales of their base models to less than 2 percent of total sales and customers may have long waiting times for a base model to become available. Even though it is difficult in many cases to actually see a base model on the lot of an automobile dealer, the base model does serve as a point of comparison for additional features a customer gets in a mid-range or high-end model. General Motors (GM) perfected this anchoring strategy by creating divisions catering to differing price-points of customers with Chevrolet division being the anchor for its basic customer and the Cadillac division serving as its upper-end anchor as its definition of luxury. The company's goal was to elevate customers to higher quality lines as their ability to spend more on a vehicle became a possibility. All strategic development of anchors, however, has not been in the retail or corporate environment. Many have suggested that some political candidates for major offices serve an anchor function labeled the **decoy effect** that makes certain major candidates look better (see Box 4.7). It remains unclear the degree to which candidates with little chance of winning are encouraged to enter political races to make other candidates look better, but the social comparison process happens whether the process has been intentionally manipulated or not.

ALTERNATIVES TO DUAL-PROCESS MODELS

The theories and models that follow are alternative approaches to persuasion that do not neatly fit within a dual-processing framework. There are scholars who suggest that some of these perspectives account for changes in attitudes and behaviors better than dual-process models under certain conditions. We begin by discussing balance and consistency theories that have been very popular approaches to persuasion and attitude change over the past 50 years.

Disruption by Shock Tactics

A more recent marketing tactic often intended to create dissonance is the use of messages intended to shock as a means of cutting through the clutter of the information glut. Companies such as Benetton, Abercrombie & Fitch, and Calvin Klein have come under attack for using these tactics. Advertisers and framers of campaigns widely use attempts to shock, but empirical study of these messages has been limited.

Messages intended to shock are part of the more general class of messages intended to assault the human senses or to offend sensibilities. Whereas fear appeals seek to avert future negative consequences, shock appeals are persuasive tactics that assault the senses or intentionally offend us in some way. Some fear appeals also fall in the shock category. Shock tactics typically evoke dissonance by violating our sense of appropriateness. People for the Ethical Treatment of Animals (PETA) uses shock tactics regularly to call attention to the abuse of animal rights. Their persuasive campaigns have, at times, used very graphic images; but sometimes they use pointed statements that show how major institutions violate standards of human decency, as in one campaign where they state "IAMS tortures animals." Although using these tactics has been controversial, PETA has had several successes in getting major corporations to change their problematic animal care practices such as their campaign against fur (see Figure 4.3).

In academic research, Nabi (1998) is one of the few communication researchers to consider such messages that are not primarily focused on fear. In her consideration of disgust-eliciting messages she found that the impact of disgust could enhance or inhibit attitude change.

Although several advertising campaigns have intended to shock to promote their products, only limited empirical evidence of its impact exists. Dahl, Frankenberger, and Manchanda (2003) note the widespread use of shock appeals in public health campaigns promoting awareness of breast cancer, AIDS, domestic violence, seat belt safety, and alcohol abuse. They studied the effectiveness of shock advertising for HIV/Aids prevention. Their study suggests that offending the audience often means breaching "norms for decency, good taste, aesthetic propriety, and/or personal moral standards" (p. 269). Their results confirmed that norm violations "heightened awareness of shocking advertising content"

(p. 275). Their results also indicated that the shock condition produced greater recall than the information and fear conditions. So, the violation of norms that we hold can produce dissonance that draws attention to activities violating norms.

It appears that shock appeals actually attract younger audiences because they violate traditional norms and establish individualism. Although the reasons vary, using dissonance-producing tactics such as messages intended to shock may help gain attention for a persuasive message as well as encourage cognitive processes such as message elaboration and message retention, but many ethical issues remain to be resolved. On the other hand, those using graphic images to dislodge people from their comfortable positions on important issues suggest a simple dissonance reduction strategy for those who are disgusted or repulsed—change the channel or turn the page; and, many of us do so to avoid the unpleasantness.

Accessibility and Activation of Attitudes

Some of the most recent advances in persuasion recognize the importance of the site where persuasion takes place, the mental processes of the brain. Although we are likely to see great advances over the next decade in our understanding of persuasion and brain functioning, precise understanding of the connections between persuasion and centers of the brains are not well understood at this time. Nevertheless, several research programs have studied processes related to persuasion that clearly involve the importance of storage of information in memory, accessing that memory, and modifying stored attitudes in the memory. We have already discussed Fazio's line of attitude accessibility research, but at least two other notable developments are important to understand how persuasion works.

Mere Exposure and the Primacy of Affect. Psychologist Robert Zajonc's (1968) **mere exposure** hypothesis is quite simple: Repeated exposure to a stimulus results in more favorable evaluation of that stimulus. In other words, the more we are exposed

HERE'S
THE REST
OF YOUR
FUR
COAT.

Shirley Manson for

peta2

FOR FREE STICKERS AND DVDS,
VISIT PETA2.COM

FIGURE 4.3
Describe the reactions you experience when viewing this persuasive message by musician, actress, and model Shirley Manson on behalf of PETA. Which routes do you believe process the different parts of this message?

SOURCE: Reprinted by permission of PETA.

to something, the more we are likely to be favorable toward it. In a classic study, Zajonc asked participants to pronounce a series of Turkish nonsense words. In varying the frequency of times of pronouncing each word, he found that more frequently pronounced words received more favorable evaluation. He re-

ported the same pattern for different photographs of men and for Chinese-like characters. Favorability increased substantially up to about ten exposures and continued to increase at slower rates until reaching 25 repetitions. Other studies of mere exposure suggest a point of diminishing returns whereby more repetitions yield no benefit and sometimes become counterproductive, with people getting bored with overexposure.

Psychologist Robert Bornstein's (1989) meta-analysis of over 200 studies indicated that the mere exposure phenomenon appeared reliably across many different types of stimuli and objects. Moreover, Bornstein found that the mere exposure effect tended to be larger when stimuli occurred in a subliminal manner—too quickly to be consciously recognized. The very interesting finding in this analysis is that rapid exposure below the level of consciousness had greater impact than some stimuli that were consciously recognized. Given that there is much skepticism over subliminal advertising and its effectiveness, this line of research demonstrates that at least subliminal effects can be effective. Recent studies of priming behavior confirm that attitudes change in response to visual materials presented below the level of conscious awareness.

There is little doubt that mere exposure makes information very accessible simply through repetition, but there is much disagreement as to *why* it occurs. Zajonc frequently used the mere exposure findings to argue against the primacy of cognition—that is, to argue against the idea that everything—especially emotion—begins with explicit cognitive thought processes. He instead argued that affect needed no prior cognitive preferences for activation. Although Zajonc's contentions about the primacy of affect were not widely embraced when cognitive psychology was dominant, perspectives are emerging that incorporate arguments from both sides. Psychologist Icek Ajzen (2001) suggests that a multicomponent view of attitudes is becoming more popular among attitude researchers; that is, more researchers see the importance of considering the roles both affect and cognitions play in changing attitudes. Affect may be a more important influence on the development of some attitudes, and cognition in the formation of others. Some evidence suggests that we rely more on our feelings when our feelings and our beliefs do not agree (see Lavine et al., 1998). The evidence clearly supports the mere exposure principle, but there are obvious exceptions where repeated exposure may have the opposite effect, such as at my home, where the same satellite company keeps calling us even though we are on the national "do not call" registry.

Today's mass media regularly use mere exposure. Its application to politics is especially worth noting. Psychologists Joseph Grush, Kevin McKeough, and Robert Ahlering (1978) examined political campaigns for political newcomers and low-visibility offices. They found a significant connection between increasing the exposure of unfamiliar candidates through greater campaign spending, and winning the election. Although it is frustrating to those who want voters to base their decisions on the issues, the use of short commercials with sound bites makes sense for candidates unfamiliar to the masses.

Expectancy-Value Models.   Given that the mere exposure principle and expectancy-values approaches disagree fundamentally on whether affect or cognition is more important in attitude formation, you may be surprised that expectancy-value models heavily depend on attitude accessibility. Icek Ajzen (2001), a major proponent of expectancy-value models, clearly articulates that "the expectancy-value model assumes an object's evaluative meaning arises spontaneously, without conscious effort" (p. 32). **Expectancy-value models** are built on the foundation that changes in behavior result from a rational process of assessing personal beliefs and attitudes in conjunction with the normative beliefs of important persons around us.

Persuasion researchers have had difficulty in consistently finding significant **attitude-behavior relationships**. That is, researchers have frequently found low or no relationship between attitudes and behavioral change resulting from persuasive messages. For example, many smokers report that smoking is bad for their health and that it may eventually kill them, but if you ask them whether they intend to stop, they may say no or maybe in the future. So our attitudes may be negative toward the dangers that behaviors pose, but our attitudes toward the solutions to avert the dangers are negative, neutral, or so weakly positive that we do not start a program to change our behavior. In the **theory of reasoned action (TRA)**, psychologists Martin Fishbein and Icek Ajzen (1981) suggest that attitudes have been defined so generally that it is no surprise there are mixed results for finding the attitude-behavior

attitude ≠ behavior

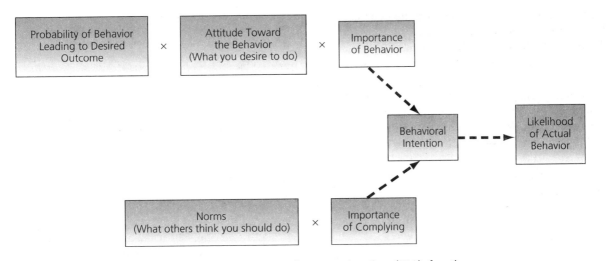

FIGURE 4.4 The Fishbein and Ajzen theory of reasoned action (TRA) for the prediction of intentions and behavior.

recycling example not only your opinion but your effort to engage into this behavior.

relationship (see Figure 4.4). Instead, they propose that our **behavioral intentions** toward *changing* our behavior are the most important predictor of actually changing behavior, not our attitudes toward the behavior itself. In research attempting to convince people to recycle, Fishbein and Ajzen asked people to rate their intentions to actually engage in recycling and indicate how important that activity was to them, instead of asking them to rate their attitude toward recycling in general. They criticize past attitude research for not measuring specifically enough and for measuring the wrong predictors. Behavioral intentions are clearly the central feature that distinguishes this approach from all other attitude research. Many other parts of the TRA appear also in other perspectives.

As the model in Figure 4.4 indicates, the behavioral intention is a product of two assessments: (1) a person's attitude toward a behavior and its importance to him or her and (2) the normative influence on an individual and its importance to the individual. **Normative influence** is a person's belief that important individuals or groups think it is advisable to perform or not perform certain behaviors (see Box 4.8). What we commonly call peer pressure is a form of normative influence. Normative pressure may simply be the desire to

please one individual. For instance, a person in my family started flossing her teeth regularly because she did not want her dental hygienist again to tell her she was not doing a good job of flossing. Weight Watchers also uses normative pressures in its weight loss programs. Participants do not want the scale to go up instead of down at their weekly weigh in. In many cases, some combination of influences makes the difference. For example, many people are motivated to stop smoking or to lose weight for their own health, but also because they want to live long enough to be here to support their children and to see their grandchildren.

The same principles generally apply to an intention *not* to perform a certain behavior. It follows that, in testing the effects of a certain advertising or public relations campaign, we should test behavioral intentions, not broader attitudes. This means asking consumers, "Do you intend to try the new brand?" instead of, "How positively or negatively do you feel about the new brand?" The act of saying, "Yes, I intend to try the brand," is a symbolic commitment to actually purchase the brand.

Ajzen proposed modifications to TRA in his **theory of planned behavior (TPB)** (see Ajzen, 1991, 2001). He added a third factor, **perceived behavioral control**. The original TRA worked

---

BOX 4.8   Impact of Normative Influence and Peer Pressure

Frequently, peer pressure is mentioned in persuasive campaigns that attempt to reduce the extremely high death rate of adolescent males in automobile accidents. Have you ever been persuaded to do something because of normative influence or peer pressure that you would not have chosen to do on your own? Have you ever purchased a particular item of clothing resulting from peer influence? What kinds of normative pressures do family members often exert on other family members in college? When do you think normative pressure is a positive or functional force, and when do you think it is a negative or dysfunctional influence? Have you ever had normative influence used to pressure you into doing something that you are really glad you did it after it was over?

---

well in conditions where individuals perceived a strong personal sense of control over their behaviors, but it became apparent after several studies that in many situations people felt little control. This addition of perceived control better articulated whether people really expected that a particular outcome would happen if they tried. So, you may resist your doctor's recommendation to lose weight if you have tried many diets, but never have been able to control your love of regular soda, your tendency toward binge eating, your nervous eating when you are not hungry, and your disdain for vegetables.

Overall, TRA and TRB have been strong predictors of changes in behavior (see Armitage & Christian, 2003; Ajzen, 2001). They have had broad application in health care and have had good success in predicting condom use, safe-sex behaviors, use of illegal substances, adherence to taking prescribed medications, the wearing of safety helmets, use of dental floss, and physical activity. No other theoretical perspective on persuasion and attitude change compares to the successful predictions of behavior of these two expectancy-value approaches. Of all the persuasive approaches to behavioral change, expectancy-value models appear to have the clear edge in predicting behavior, but they are far from perfect. Two large challenges remain in order to refine these approaches: (1) a better procedure for recognizing and incorporating the most relevant personal beliefs and (2) improved ways to identify and measure relevant normative influences.

Related to these models are **norms-based approaches** to behavioral change. Many persuasive campaigns use norms to demonstrate that indivi-

duals selecting the recommended behavior are in the majority. One such campaign to fight alcohol abuse is used at our university to show that the majority of students do not participate in binge drinking. Another normative approach being used at our university shows that females do succeed at calculus and actually receive higher grades than their male peers. The label *norms-based approach* is misleading because concrete facts and information are typically key components of such appeals.

Questions arise about the success of norms-based programs because it is often modest. As is often the case when the effectiveness of persuasive campaigns is assessed, success is in the eye of the beholder. Programs such as DARE and abstinence-based campaigns to reduce early sexual activity have advocates who look at the results and see success while critics look at the same numbers and see program failures. Some critics suggest that sensation-seeking individuals may find attempts to create fear or negative stereotypes about performing a problematic behavior to be motivation to try it (see Box 4.9).

↯PERSPECTIVES ON COMPLIANCE GAINING

Compliance gaining considers how one person can get another to do something. It is closely related to persuasion, but they are not synonymous. Unfortunately, many people assume that all compliance tactics are a subset of persuasion. Certainly,

B O X 4.9 Effectiveness of Abstinence Approaches

Have you ever attended a norms-based program such as DARE, an abstinence-based sexual education program, or a *Say No* or similar program to combat use of drugs, alcohol, or smoking? From your experience, are such programs effective? What percentage of persons attending these programs would have to actively participate for you to consider them to be effective? Such programs may deter problematic behaviors for some participants through fear tactics such as having a person in a wheelchair talk to high-school students about his car accident after drinking alcohol that left him unable to walk and left his girlfriend dead. Others, however, with sensation-seeking tendencies may find the danger revealed in this type of presentation to be appealing.

compliance-gaining tactics are forms of influence. Some, such as making a request of an individual, fit within the realm of persuasion, but other tactics, such as threats, sometimes fail to respect a receiver's freedom to choose and are more coercive than persuasive. We usually study compliance gaining in the interpersonal context. Gerald Marwell and David Schmitt (1967) first focused on the ways people seek to gain the compliance of others, but communication per se was not part of their agenda (see Dillard, 1990, pp. 3–5). Interestingly, they believed that compliance-gaining appeals could be made from a common set of behaviors—much like the Aristotelian idea of topoi we considered in Chapter 3. They generated a set of 16 compliance-gaining strategies, clustered into groups of positive and negative strategies. Generating an exhaustive list of compliance-gaining strategies is difficult. Kellermann and Cole (1994) detail over 60 types of compliance-gaining messages that were identified across numerous studies, but this list is far from complete (see Kipnis, Schmidt, & Wilkinson, 1980; Rule, Bisanz, & Kohn, 1985; Wiseman & Schenk-Hamlin, 1981).

This initial phase of compliance-gaining research has been widely criticized for lacking any theoretical base, but it did identify two important dynamics. One is the situational nature of compliance gaining, as revealed in the classic study by communication researchers Gerald Miller et al. (1977) that brought compliance gaining to the attention of communication researchers. In this study, people reported using different Marwell and Schmitt compliance-gaining strategies in differ-

ent interpersonal situations. This suggests that when planning influence messages, the persuader should ask, "What special considerations need to be made for this particular situation?"

A related dynamic is the matching of appropriate tactics to the intended goals. Communication researchers Michael Cody, Daniel Canary, and Sandi Smith (1987) reported that college students use different tactics when they believe others have some obligation, such as a landlord making repairs, than when they are asking favors of friends.

Most who still engage in compliance-gaining research have found solid theoretical bases for their research. Cognitive compliance-gaining goals are a current focus of communication researchers (see Wilson, 2002). The consideration of multiple goals is one of the most important lessons from this recent research. So, the persuader may need to consider a multilevel strategy instead of assuming that there is only one objective. Some consideration has been given to tactics following prior unsuccessful attempts (see Cody, Canary, & Smith, 1987). Compliance-gaining attempts appear to move from positive tactics to more negative ones as more resistance is encountered. In many of these episodes, making simple, direct requests is the preferred approach. Using reasoning to make basic arguments is another popular approach. Yet the situation, the goals, and the power relationship all play a role in choosing the most effective strategy.

One of the limitations of compliance-gaining research is that it usually focuses on short-term results

BOX 4.10 Fighting Fairly

What persuasive strategies do you think are acceptable when you are having a dispute with a significant other such as a spouse, partner, or good friend? Have you ever held a grudge against a person for using an unfair compliance-gaining tactic against you? What tactics would be considered fighting fairly versus fighting dirty?

while many business relationships are the result of long-term efforts. Still, a unifying framework has not emerged to clarify whether it is best to classify compliance-gaining tactics by the message's form, the message's goals, or the message's impact experienced by the receiver. Theoretical underpinnings for compliance-gaining studies are emerging—particularly from communication researchers. In his book *Seeking and Resisting Compliance*, Steven Wilson (2002) focuses on how people produce and resist compliance-gaining behaviors rather than just responding to them. An important new focus in this work is the understanding of a concept called **face threats**. Face threats are basically attacks on the receiver's image. We need to understand what persuasive approaches might actually make the situation worse instead of improving it. Sometimes we dig a deeper hole for ourselves when trying to repair a relationship than we were in before we attempted to improve the situation.

Understanding Kathy Kellermann's (2004) goal-directed approach to gaining compliance helps us understand that some compliance-gaining behaviors are more likely to threaten the message receiver's image. This more complex examination of compliance gaining involves both the consideration of the message framer's goals as well as concerns of the receiver to maintain a positive identity and image. In complex negotiations where conflicting opinions can be very heated, it is very important for all sides to maintain a positive image. It is not a desirable situation for persons to feel embarrassed to be seen by others who are important to them or to feel uncomfortable around those important others. Moreover, most of those involved in negotiations want to be able to return to the negotiating table retaining respect from the other negotiators present. The perception of fighting fairly is important—

raising irrelevant, sensitive issues that are not germane to the present issue is considered inappropriate in most cases (see Box 4.10). So, instead of thinking of compliance gaining as a competitive situation where people win and lose, true winning strategies often provide more stable solutions where the images of all concerned are strengthened rather than diminished. Such solutions do not have to be revisited often because of dissatisfied parties. These face-saving strategies will typically build more positive intimate relationships with significant others and within families as well. This more recent emphasis in compliance gaining is very consistent with the idea of co-creation established in Chapter 1.

not what we are going for

Although resistance strategies have been put forth to address the receiver's side of compliance gaining, little research has explicitly considered power relations and perceived control in the compliance-gaining situation. Another difficulty for compliance gaining from a persuasion perspective is that behavioral compliance often reflects mere acquiescence, without the development of mutual understanding. For example, all except one of the major airlines are facing major difficulties in trying to stem their economic losses. Management is fighting for survival and employees are trying to salvage a decent pension and take much smaller pay cuts than management is asking. Even though many agreements are being reached, compliance does not appear to contribute to a positive work climate. Management negotiators are using many heavy-handed compliance-gaining tactics such as threats to gain these new agreements. Polarizing compliance-gaining tactics also failed the National Hockey League in the 2004–2005 season when management locked out NHL players for the entire season (see Box 4.11).

B O X 4.11   Impact of NHL Owners Compliance Gaining in 2004 Lockout

Although the NHL owners and players reached an agreement to play hockey again in 2005, the players are not pleased with the outcomes after losing a whole season of play. The owners have achieved much of what they wanted, but the agreement provides very few changes that benefit the players. What arguments can be made that the persuasive attempts by the owners were successful and what arguments can be made that their persuasive attempts were unsuccessful? What arguments can be made that the owners were using coercive tactics rather than persuasive ones when they scuttled the 2004–2005 season?

Current compliance-gaining research as yet provides little direction for those placed in such a difficult position. Compliance-gaining research has not focused on short-term versus long-term attitudes that result from the tactics used during such difficult economic conditions where people's livelihoods are at risk. It is important to keep in mind in any dispute that the parties usually have to live together after the negotiations end. Thus, it is important to note that the outcome of a compliance-gaining attempt may achieve acquiescence and accomplish the immediate objective, but may create unfortunate long-term consequences that make long-term relationships a lot less pleasant and satisfying.

REVIEW AND CONCLUSION

There is little question that the ELM has been the superhero in the last two decades of persuasion research. Still, no single theory addresses every persuasive situation. Some, such as the ELM and HSM, address larger (macro) issues regarding overall approaches to persuasion while others address very specific (micro) persuasive situations at the tactical level, such as approaches intended to arouse fear or shock. Often we need multiple perspectives to explain fully different parts of a persuasive situation. One of my objectives of this chapter was to emphasize that the most appropriate persuasive tactics for a given situation depend heavily upon the motivation of the audience to listen and analyze carefully. The use of more statistics and evidence is unlikely to be effective when the audience is not listening. Thus, attempting to beat people into submission until they start listening is probably not the best first line of action. Another of my objectives was to make it clear that much attitude change and persuasion takes place through peripheral or heuristic processes so that as consumers of persuasion you will become more aware of what often is happening below your conscious awareness. Despite the many persuasive trends found over a number of years, it is also important to recognize that such findings are fallible. Although research findings typically represent a greater likelihood that specific persuasive strategies or tactics will produce predictable reactions, there are often important factors like the motivation of the audience to listen and daily events that create some unpredictability in every persuasive situation.

Although others may disagree, I award the title of the most effective predictor of behavioral change to the expectancy-values approaches by Martin Fishbein and Icek Ajzen. No other approach has been as widely adopted in persuasive campaigns—particularly those that are health related. The importance of affect in the persuasive situation is gaining more respect from researchers but still needs better integration in the mainstream approaches. These theories in this chapter are representative, but not a complete consideration of the persuasion literature. We will revisit many of these perspectives throughout the remainder of the book.

KEY TERMS

After reading this chapter, you should be able to identify, explain, and give an example of the following key terms or concepts:

empirical

dual-process theory

elaboration likelihood model (ELM)

central route

need for cognition (NFC)

peripheral route

heuristic-systematic model (HSM)

systematic processing route

heuristic processing route

variable-analytic approach

sleeper effect

affinity scams

Pelz effect

primacy effect

recency effect

message-sidedness

biased information processing

inoculation

fear

pleasure-pain principle

efficacy

defensive avoidance

FUD

social judgment theory

anchor

latitude of acceptance

latitude of rejection

decoy effect

mere exposure

expectancy-value models

attitude-behavior relationships

theory of reasoned action (TRA)

behavioral intentions

normative influence

theory of planned behavior (TPB)

perceived behavioral control

norms-based approaches

compliance gaining

face threats

APPLICATION OF ETHICS

The use of decoy effects suggests that political parties may benefit by having weak candidates to make leading candidates appear stronger. When would the deliberate encouragement of the entry of weak candidates into a political race be ethical or unethical? Is it fair to compare this practice to a student hired to fail a course to set the curve lower?

QUESTIONS FOR FURTHER THOUGHT

1. An ethical issue raised by the ELM is determining when children develop the ability to centrally process persuasion at a level that allows them to make informed choices. In what situations should parents allow their children to make their own choices about purchases like cereal, toys, and clothing?

2. Discuss why females and males might process the issue of keeping abortions legal in the United States differently.

3. Given that attractiveness has proven to be a valuable factor in persuasion, what can people do in persuasive situations to make up for the fact that they are not among the beautiful people in this world?

4. Put yourself into the role of the parent of a teenager who has just obtained his or her license. What inoculation strategy might you use to try to persuade your teenager not to drink and drive?

5. Do you believe norms-based approaches can work to combat undesirable behaviors in young people? Why or why not?

6. Parking policies on campus are often hot button issues on many college campuses. Is it realistic to approach compliance with parking regulations from a persuasive rather than coercive approach? That is, could parking be regulated on campuses without the threat of fines? Does a $100 fine for parking in a handicapped space induce greater compliance?

✳

 For online activities, go to the *Persuasion* book companion Web site at http://academic.cengage.com/communication/larson12.

5

✳

The Making, Use, and Misuse of Symbols

LEARNING GOALS

After reading this chapter, you should be able to:

1. Identify significant human developments that were made possible via language.

2. Identify several unique facts about the English language.

3. Explain and give examples of eloquence.

4. Explain why language is symbolic action.

5. Give examples of the use and misuse of linguistic symbols.

6. Discuss Langer's theory about language use.

7. Discuss the general semanticists and their theories and goals.

8. Demonstrate how an emotion laden sentence can be defused using the extensional devices suggested by the semanticists.

9. Discuss Burke's notions of identification, substances, and the role of language as a cause of guilt.

10. Explain semiotics and its use of terms such as text, code, signifiers, and signifieds.

Author, language columnist, and critic Richard Lederer (1991) observes:

> The boundary between human and animal—between the most primitive savage and the highest ape—is the language line. The birth of language is the dawn of humanity; in our beginning was the word. We have always been endowed with language because before we had words, we were not human beings. [Words] tell us that we must never take for granted the miracle of language (p. 3).

Throughout history, the uniquely human ability to create **symbols** made possible all our major cultural advances, and this is more true than ever in the current age of the Seven Faces of Persuasion. Each face is expressed either in auditory, verbal, or visual ways, and we as persuaders need to recognize these symbols for what they are and what they do to us in order to accomplish persuasive results. Symbols can be many things, such as words, pictures, art works, music, and others. The dictionary definition reads "Something that represents something else by association, resemblance or convention" (*American Heritage Dictionary*, 2005). The most widely used type of symbol is probably language, and we all use it on a regular basis. As a result, we tend to overlook its importance in persuasion and elsewhere. Since words stand for or represent things, ideas, feelings, and so on, we tend to react to words as if they actually are the things they only represent. Take name-calling for example; if someone calls me a dumb Swede, I am likely to at least examine carefully some of my less than intelligent decisions and actions. In its most malignant uses, such name-calling can prove fatal. Witness the Missouri teenager who committed suicide in 2007 because of names she was called online on her MySpace account, and the name caller was not a real person—but the parent(s) of a former friend. And they had not committed a crime, though they had induced someone else's death. Symbols and language are powerful stuff as history has repeated time and time again. The ability to use symbols for communication enabled humans to live very differently—they could form tribes, enact rituals, trade with one another, and persuade. Communication facilitated the specialization of labor, the recording of history, and allowed humans to create culture, but the use of visual and verbal symbols to communicate also allowed humans to engage in less-constructive behaviors such as lying, teasing, breaking promises, scolding, demeaning, propagandizing and the cyber-bullying in the case noted above to name a few.

And with the development of writing and print, people found that promises, treaties, and legal contracts could be both made and broken, and laws could be used for evil as well as good. The title of the book *Deeds Done in Words* (Campbell & Jamieson, 1990) indicates that language serves as a frequent surrogate for action—consider the cyber-killer parents in the suicide case where the words stood for, prompted, and resulted in action. Researcher and professor Neil Postman (1992) maintains that language is an "invisible technology" or a kind of machine that can "give direction to our thoughts, generate new ideas, venerate old ones, expose facts or hide them" (p. 127). And this universal technology is closely linked to the Seven Faces of Persuasion. Language theorist Kenneth Burke (1966) said it best when he noted that humans are "symbol making, symbol using, and symbol misusing" creatures. This ability to use symbols—whether words, pictures, music, or art—lies at the heart of persuasion. As a result, receivers must carefully analyze the verbal, auditory, and visual symbols being used or misused by persuaders. We need to ask whether the symbols prompt logical or emotional meanings, how they strengthen or weaken any or all of the Seven Faces of Persuasion and if they are centrally or peripherally processed in the Elaboration Likelihood Model (ELM) mentioned repeatedly earlier. For instance, imagine a TV advertisement for a brand of beer. It probably uses verbal, visual, and musical or lyrical (auditory) symbols. Visually, the screen displays a group of youthful males and females drinking bottles of Michelob and having fun while watching a football game and maybe hoping to meet an important someone. Musically we hear the Michelob jingle. Verbally the voiceover tells us that we should treasure and seek out the "Michelob Moments" that almost guarantee fun and perhaps a future sexual relationship. Together, these various kinds of symbols show that people who drink Michelob enjoy a certain lifestyle, are happy-go-lucky, sexually motivated, and models to be emulated.

In addition, persuaders frequently use artistic metaphors (which are a kind of symbol, such as the "Marlboro Man") to emphasize their points in dramatic ways, which can either intensify or downplay the points being made. For example, two recent books on the right to privacy issue use metaphors in their titles: *No Place to Hide* by Robert O'Harrow (2005) and Daniel Solove's *The Digital Person* (2005). Both titles imply in their metaphors that we face two dangers—a loss of privacy and that we are becoming mere ciphers or digits—both topics we discussed at length in relation to the 7 Faces, ethics, propaganda, the ELM, and the humanistic as well as the social science theories related to the process of persuasion. Recent research on persuasive metaphors shows that their use increases persuader credibility, and that they operate best when their theme is reiterated throughout the persuasive message, especially if used initially and in the conclusion (Sopory & Dillard, 2002). This is especially so if the metaphors are universal or archetypal—ones that can be understood over time and across cultures—

the light and dark family where light is generally associated with positive, good, knowledge, and uplifting emotions or ideas, while dark is generally associated with mysterious, unknown, potentially dangerous and maybe evil things. By examining various metaphors and other symbols used in persuasion, we accomplish several things:

1. We discover the persuader's pattern of use or misuse of symbols.
2. We discover the persuader's stylistic preferences and what they reveal about his or her motives and how they can intensify or downplay.
3. Knowing these things, we can anticipate the kinds of messages likely to come from this source in the future and be prepared for them.

One reason we can infer so much is that the making of symbols is a highly ego-involving and creative act. When we make a symbol, we own it—it belongs to us, has our stamp of ownership on it—and it reveals a good deal about us, how we think and respond to events and issues and it reveals our motives. The same thing happens when others try to persuade us. They make symbols (usually language) and metaphors, and as a result they "own" their creations, and through their choice of symbols reveal things about themselves. For example, what could we infer about a persuader—say an editorial cartoonist—who continually used dark metaphors, referred to conspiracies working against us, and chose visual symbols that involved predatory creatures like sharks or wolves? We might well conclude that the cartoonist was paranoid, felt him- or herself to be in the minority on public opinion, and was distrustful of others. So you see, critical receivers need to know something about symbols, particularly linguistic symbols, and how to read them for clues regarding the persuader's motives.

Let's look a little deeper into the enormous power that lies in the English language and how it rules the multicultural, interactive, 24/7 networked world saturated with advocacy, propaganda, constantly changing media, increasing ethical challenges, and doublespeak. And in regard to the ELM, we know from history that language cues, metaphors, and what we call eloquence have often acted as the powerful emotional cues that are processed in the peripheral channel and which prompt our action in significant, if unconscious, ways. We will examine several examples of these in the following discussion but first let's look at the English language itself. After all, it is the dominant linguistic force in the world today, accounting for overwhelming percentages of language used in scientific knowledge, research journals, diplomacy, international trade and travel, and in the vast majority of existing and likely to be produced computer files. If a person is without English, flipping burgers is one's likely future occupation, as we shall see.

THE POWER
OF THE ENGLISH LANGUAGE

In his book *The Miracle of Language*, now nearly 20 years old, Lederer (1991) also offers many observations about the power of the English language (the common denominator for most persuasion we process and much that is sent around the world today) that warn us not to take language symbols for granted. His advice is even more poignant than ever given the burgeoning presence of the Seven Faces of Persuasion in contemporary culture and the many changes we have seen in communication technologies since he first noted his observations. Consider just a few of them:

1. Of almost 3,000 languages in existence today, only 10 are the native language of more than 100 million people, and English ranks second in the list only behind Chinese. It is the first language of 45 countries, and its second-language users outnumber its native users making it a truly global tongue (pp. 19–20).

2. English is used in most of the world's books, newspapers, magazines, two thirds of all scientific publications, and 80 percent of all stored computer texts are in English (p. 20).

3. English has one of the richest vocabularies—615,000 words in the *Oxford English Dictionary*—not including slang or the many new technical terms that come into play on almost a daily basis—the iPhone, blogs, and so on. Compare that with the 100,000 words in French, the 130,000 in Russian, or the185,000 in German. It is also an economic language requiring far fewer words to translate Mark's gospel than any other language. The same goes for the rest of the Bible as well as many other important documents; translators prefer using it above any other language.

4. English is now the international language of science, business, politics, diplomacy, literature, tourism, pop culture, and air travel. Japanese pilots flying Japanese airliners over Japanese air space must communicate with Japanese flight controllers using English, not their native Japanese, and the same is true of the airspace over every other country in the world (p. 30).

5. Nonnative speakers report that English is the easiest second language to learn (p. 28). Lederer also demonstrates the power of a permanent aspect of the English language—its syntax. He asks students to arrange five words—*Lithuanian, five, scholars, Shakespearean,* and *old* in proper order to make syntactical sense. Everyone comes up with the same order—"five old Lithuanian Shakespearean scholars." The adjective strings begins with the most specific and runs to the least. There are Shakespearean scholars in countries other than Lithuania just as there other kinds of scholars.

In spoken English, try to determine the difference between "no notion" and "known ocean," or between "buys ink" and "buys zinc," or between "meteorologist" and "meaty urologist," or between "cat's skills," "cats' kills," and "Catskills," or between "tax" and "tacks." Figure 5.1 demonstrates

BOX 5.1   Interactive English

Go to www.englishforum.com/interactive/ and explore the many interesting and fun ways interactive media can help you improve your use of the English language. One of the many activities at the site is the daily display of a new idiom. If you don't know what an idiom is, consider this one: "As different as chalk from cheese." What do you suppose it means? At the site there is a daily famous quote and a chat group where you can leave or receive a message about the use of English. You can trade English language lessons with students from other countries. For example, Oman will trade lessons in Arabic with you. You can leave your term papers or other texts there for free critiques. Try to solve the word puzzles and learn new slang words. The site also lists good English schools in eight countries and offers students budget travel hints. And there is even an online wizard who can read your mind. You will learn much about the English language there, and you may want to invent your own words as Shakespeare did (see Figure 5.1).

these differences in a humorous way. This last example resulted in a humorous student blooper. The student wrote, "The American Revolution came about because the British put tacks in their tea." So, as persuadees, we must consider whether the persuasion is coming to us in written or spoken language or via visual symbols—the channel plays an important part in our development of meaning and deciding how to react to it as seen in Box 5.1.

LANGUAGE, ELOQUENCE, AND SYMBOLIC ACTION

Eloquent persuasion always seems unique, fresh, exciting, and somehow emotional. It strikes us as capturing the moment, and it may even prophesy the future. As seen from Figure 5.1, the talented wordsmith can invent such eloquence or he or she might borrow it. Take the speech made by Martin Luther King, Jr., on the night before he was assassinated where he said that God had allowed him "to go up to the mountain top," and that he had "seen the Promised Land," but that he doubted that he would get there with his followers. He concluded, "But, I am happy tonight! I'm not fearing any man! Mine eyes have seen the glory of the coming of the Lord!" Although the words were not wholly original (they were drawn from the Old Testament and Julia Ward Howe's "Battle Hymn of the Republic"), his use of them was prophetic, emotional, and processed in the peripheral channel.

Today we find many groups using and misusing linguistic symbols in dramatic ways on buttons, badges, or bumper stickers—many of them emotion laden and hence peripherally processed. Consider a few: "Think Globally; Act Locally," "Guns don't Kill; People Do," or "Da Bears." Others use license plates as a medium to make symbolic declarations about themselves and the times: IM N RN, REV BOB, BMW BFD, 3MTA3 (hint—use a mirror), I M SX C, MR X TC, 3NON (read upside down), XME OUT, TACKY, GWS WAR, IMVAIN2, DON H1, DZ BLND, IH8 MYX, 400 GPA, CRE 8TIV, and so on (see Box 5.2).

Each of these messages symbolically makes a revealing statement about its user. Researchers note that persons displaying bumper stickers or wearing T-shirts with product, cause, or candidate labels imprinted on them will buy the products, donate, or vote for the candidate, cause, or brand they are promoting far more often than those who don't display the words. Making the symbolic statement equates with action in their minds, and their words become deeds or substitutes for action. As Burke (1966) observed, "Language is symbolic action," and we often act out what we speak.

Language can also be misused. The deaths of Afghani and Iraqi civilians were labeled "collateral damage," in operations Rolling Thunder

F I G U R E 5.1   Other words coined by Shakespeare include *amazement, bump, clangor, dwindle, fitful, majestic, obscene, pious, road, flibbertygibbet, slugabeat,* and *useless.* Can you invent some words of your own?

SOURCE: Word for Word by Michael Atchinson. Reprinted with Permission.

B O X 5.2   Interact with Vanity Plates

Go to www.chaos,umd.edu/ and read about the series of 154 actually issued California license plates that tell the entire story of Oedipus Rex.

Report back to class. While you're at the site, explore some of the very funny vanity plates imagined or real—enjoy.

---

and Enduring Freedom (both names also examples of euphemisms in doublespeak), while "surgical air strikes" made the enormous damage sound neat and clean. Market researchers decided to use the words "recipe for success," for example, to assure working women who use Crisco that they are indeed "cooks" and not merely "microwavers" who thaw and reheat meals. A great pair of words—"Budget Gourmet"—describes an inexpensive, okay, prepackaged meal, but not really one of gourmet quality.

Another reason language requires careful analysis is that it tells us a lot about the persuader's motives and reveals much through its particular verbal and visual symbols.

Consider the demeaning and dehumanizing language used by anti-Semitic persuaders in past (and perhaps in present) examples of propaganda in referring to Jews and other minorities. Words such as vermin, sludge, garbage, lice, sewage, insects, and bloodsuckers were frequently used. What do we do with such creatures? We EXTERMINATE them. The recent influx of immigrants from the Middle East spawned similar linguistic venom: camel jockey, dot head, pak head or Q-tip, all of which demean and dehumanize others. We need to remember that "ethnic cleansing" still occurs, and that language serves as the major weapon for dehumanizing others and worse. In less-dramatic settings, words create emotional responses and devalue people.

What do the words "lady doctor" imply? That the doctor is not as good as a male physician? That the doctor is in the business only for the fun or sport of it? Why does "lady" convey so much meaning and evoke emotional responses? Communication scholar Dan Hahn (1998) points out how language depicts males as sexual aggressors and females as stalked prey or passive entities. Consider a few examples in which the language

FIGURE 5.2 As this cartoon demonstrates, language used in its spoken form can be quite different from its use in its written form.

SOURCE: Reprinted by permission of Aaron Johnson.

of seduction becomes the language of stalking: the male is described as "a real animal" or unable to "keep his paws off her," while the female is "a real dish," or "a real piece of meat" to be "turned on" or "cranked." Recently we have become sensitized to the use (and misuse) of Native American references in athletics—the Braves, the Redskins, the Chiefs, the Fighting Illini, and the Seminoles. And as Figure 5.2 demonstrates, confusion can frequently arise from similarities and differences between the spoken word as it sounds and as it might be interpreted in its written form.

The world of marketing provides many examples of the persuasive power in language choice. Brand names often reveal manufacturers' attitudes toward customers. For instance, Oster Corporation markets a "food crafter" instead of a "food chopper," which tells us that Oster takes a gourmet approach. (Chopping sounds like work. Crafting? Now, that's art.) One can easily sense the emotional flavor of these words and why they are processed almost unconsciously via the peripheral channel of the ELM. They certainly reflect Doublespeak and the Efficacy Face of persuasion. Smoking certain brands of cigarettes can also make a gender statement—Eves and Virginia Slims are for her not for him; he's better off with Marlboro or Camels.

LANGER'S APPROACH
TO LANGUAGE USE

To become truly responsible receivers of persuasion, we need to identify the uses and misuses of symbols, especially in the language used by politicians, advertisers, employers, and other persuaders. A useful approach to the study of language is based on the work of philosopher and language pioneer Suzanne K. Langer (1957). She recognized the power of language symbols, and like Lederer and others, she believed that the ability to create powerful symbols distinguishes humans from nonhumans. Language lets us talk and think about feelings, events, and objects even when the actual feelings, events, or objects are not physically present. Langer associates two concepts with this capacity—signs and symbols. Signs indicate the presence of an event, feeling, or object. For instance, thunder signals lightning and usually rain. My dog goes into a panic at the sound of thunder—lightning struck close to her as a pup, so she tries to hide from it. If she could process symbols, I might talk to her about thunder and explain the futility of trying to hide from it. Only the comforting tone of my voice (another sign) seems to calm her down. We know that the red traffic light at an intersection signals potentially dangerous cross traffic. Guide dogs recognize the red light by its location on the top of the traffic signal (they are colorblind) and even learn to stop the person they are leading, but you cannot teach them to recognize the symbolic link between the red light and the words "cross traffic"—a much more complex connection. As Langer (1957) put it, "Symbols are not proxy of their objects, but are vehicles for the conception of objects" (p. 60). Because of our ability to use symbols, you and I understand the presence of danger by such things as the color red, the word "danger," or the skull and crossbones on a bottle.

B O X 5.3   Brand Names: Discursive or Presentational?

Developing brand names entails more effort than you would think. It is no accident that Snuggle—a fabric softener—has a teddy bear as its logo. When you see Snuggle on the shelf, you probably do not think of actually "snuggling" up with a good book and a cup of coffee, but you might put a package of it in your shopping cart and feel good about having done so. There is no string of words to be followed when you look at the brand, its logo, or its packaging. The brand's name is a presentational symbol. Observe the brand on your next shopping

trip. Now consider this metaphoric brand name— Thera-Flu—a cold medicine meant to be taken as a hot drink before you go to bed. There is no evidence (other than 24/7 media-saturated examples) that the brand works any better than any other nighttime cold medicine having similar ingredients. However, the brand is threatening sales of NyQuil, the first over-the-counter nighttime cold medicine on the market. Why? Perhaps there is a presentational (or metaphorical) media explanation (Feig, 1997).

Using symbols seems to be a basic human need. Even persons unable to write, hear, or speak make symbols using visual signs, hand motions, and other symbolic means. Some symbols have a common meaning upon which most people agree. Langer called such symbols **concepts**, in contrast to **conceptions**, which she used to refer to any particular individual's unique meanings for the concept. All human communication and hence persuasion relies on concepts and conceptions. So, naturally, the possibility of misunderstanding always presents itself. How might the activities in Box 5.3 reflect map and territory differences?

Langer also introduced three terms to be used when discussing meaning: "signification," "denotation," and "connotation." **Signification** means a sign that accompanies the thing being considered. So the skull and crossbones on a bottle signifies "Danger—Poison!" **Denotation** refers to the common and shared meaning we all have for any concept—we all have similar meanings for the concept of "profit" versus loss, unless some scoundrel CEO redefines his or her definitions of the terms. **Connotation** refers to my or your private, metaphorical, emotional (and perhaps propagandistic) meaning for any concept such as "profit" which for me means revenue that exceeds overall costs but which for the crooked CEO may mean "…the amount of money he or she can skim from overall revenue without it showing up on a financial statement." The denotation of the word would be

the dictionary definition of the word "profit" as "the amount of return on an investment after all expenses have been deducted" (*American Heritage Dictionary*, 1985).

The connotation of the word is my or your personal and individual conception of danger. For example, because of my Minnesota background, I find blizzards to be dangerous; but someone from Florida might not, and the obverse would be true for my connotation for the word "hurricane." And of course, we are increasingly facing culturally diverse connotations for words and concepts. For example, China thinks of itself as extraordinarily egalitarian. However, professor and marketing consultant Barry Feig (1997) reports that a flourishing trade exists there for counterfeit labels for high-priced and high-status brands of bicycles. Chinese workers remove their low-end labels and substitute the high-status ones. Few persons in China own autos, but most have bicycles, and most of them are quite ordinary—almost generic. The fake labels are symbols that communicate status (connotation) in a society where status differences supposedly don't exist (denotation). Langer also maintained that meaning is either "discursive" or "presentational." **Discursive symbols** are usually made up of sequential, smaller bits of meaning that unfold across time to yield ultimate meaning. They are like advocacy or propaganda which occurs step-by-step. Musically, this would be equivalent to movements in a symphony. In a drama it would be the unfolding of a plot. For our purposes, discursive symbols usually occur in the form of language and the development of meaning in a sentence, paragraph, chapter, and so on. **Presentational meaning**, on the other hand, occurs all at once and the message is experienced in its entirety at one time, such as when one looks at a painting, architecture, or a statue, or experiences a ritual or an emotional gasp of approval to eloquent language use. In this way it resembles a metaphor which is recognized all at once and is best fit for a media-saturated dramatic world. Thus, some of the "meaning" in any advertisement is discursive (the slogans, jingles, plot, and ad copy), while some is presentational (the graphic layout, logos, fonts, and photos or pictures). Similarly, some of the meaning in a political campaign occurs discursively (the speeches, press releases, and interviews), while some is presentational (the way the candidate looks, his or her image, the candidate's artful use of language, and/or the pictorial and music in spot ads). That's why politicians employ the services of speech writers and image consultants to get you processing their advocacy/propaganda in both the peripheral and the central information processing channels of the ELM and repeatedly in a 24/7 networked world. Box 5.3 illustrates the differences. And both kinds of meaning can occur simultaneously or discreetly in persuasion that is impacted upon by any or several of the other Seven Faces of Persuasion.

GENERAL SEMANTICS AND LANGUAGE USE

Beginning with his landmark work *Science and Sanity* by Count Alfred Korzybski (1947), language scholars known as general **semanticists** began a careful and systematic study of the use of language and meaning. Korzybski had been an intelligence interrogator questioning prisoners for intelligence about the enemy. He specialized in de-briefing spies and double or triple spies, so it is not surprising that he became fascinated with language use and its true meanings. Apparently with the de-briefing of Al Quaeda suspects, the difficulties with determin-

ing true meaning from tricky language choices is still with us, even with the use of water-boarding and other forms of torture, which most experts agree is ineffective at getting to the "truth" of a situation. Korzybski and his colleagues intended to devise tools for improving the understanding of human communication and to encourage careful and precise uses of language and when they were occurring. Most of these scholars were from academic departments of English or psychology. Their theory grew out of the difficulty in determining what double spies really meant when they communicated something. The semanticists wanted to train people to be very specific in sending and receiving words, to avoid the communication pitfalls such as stereotyping, over-generalization, euphemism, and others that had led to the rise of demagogues like Hitler and Stalin in many countries prior to WW II. For instance, the general semanticists believed people needed to learn to be aware that the language appeals made by most persuaders/advocates and propagandists were only **maps** or inner perceptions of places, persons, or things and not true **territories** or realities. A map is what exists in my or your head, but a territory is what physically exists in the real world as we shall see later in an extended metaphorical example and in future chapters. For example, you might have an image of a certain place, experience, or event. That image is only a map, which probably flows from our media-saturated, 24/7 world of advocacy and propaganda. That place, experience, or event may not really or accurately resemble your map of it at all. In fact, if you were to visit the place or experience the event, you might not even recognize it. With the advent of such interactive media as virtual reality, Internet gaming and dating, the home shopping network, and telemarketing, receivers face an increased blurring of map and territory. This of course can lead to Internet deception like "phishing," which is the gathering of personal (financial) information or other scams and swindles. As a result, we need to heed the advice of the semanticists more than ever because much of the interactive world is virtual—remember, interactive messages are only maps, not territories, even though we confront them 24/7 in a media-swamped and multicultural world. Considering them otherwise is bound to lead to misunderstandings and worse.

Take the case of stereotyping. Stereotypes are supposedly unreliable. No member of a class or group is exactly like any other member. To counter the miscommunication that can result from stereotyping all Muslims in the same way, for instance, we need to heed Korzybski's reminder that "the map is not the territory." In other words, our internal conceptions of other persons, ethnic groups, and ideas will differ widely from the actual persons, groups, things, and ideas. Korzybski and his colleagues recognized the difference between an event, object, or experience and any individual's conception of it. In their scheme, the word "map" equates to Langer's "conception," and the word "territory" equates to "objective reality" or close to Langer's "concept." Our faulty maps get expressed through the language we create to convey them, and they usually miscommunicate in some way. For the general semanticists, the real problems occur when people act as if their maps accurately describe the territory, thus turning the map into the territory. Following the bombing of the World Trade Center, many persons refused to fly on airplanes if persons of Middle Eastern abstraction were on board. In a way these stereotypes serve as maps or metaphors for certain special classes of people.

Korzybski believed that we all carry thousands of such maps or connotative metaphors around in our heads that represent nonexistent, incorrect, or false territories. We probably refer to them via the peripheral channel and react emotionally, not logically, to such persons or events. To demonstrate this concept for yourself, write down the name of a food you have never eaten, a place you have never been, and an experience you have never had. These words serve as maps for unknown territories. You probably think that fried brains would feel slimy and gooshy in your mouth. In reality, they have the texture of well-scrambled eggs and are frequently scrambled together with eggs. From that reality, we have invented the concept of having "fried" one's brains on drugs. What about your map for skydiving or for being a rock star? What about your maps for various ethnic groups? What about your map for places that you have only visited via the Internet? What about some occupation you are considering for your major?

In most cases, your maps will be very different from the territories as they really exist. Our mental, visual, and word maps present a real problem in communication, and especially in persuasion. Just as persuaders must discover the common ground of ideas so they can persuade us, they also must identify the maps we carry around in our heads. Then they must either play on those maps (using our misperceptions to their advantage) or try to get us to correct our faulty maps as Figure 5.3 illustrates. Only then can they persuade us to buy, vote, join, or change our behavior. Our faulty maps are frequently expressed through language and often by using metaphors.

We create and use words to communicate and to build our maps, and then we often behave in accordance with what might be very faulty perceptions. We react to these words as if they are true representations of the territories we imagine. The semanticists called this a **signal response**, which is equivalent to my dog trying to hide from lightning whenever she experiences the sign or signal of thunder. Signal responses are emotionally triggered reactions to symbolic acts (including language use), and these responses play out usually in the peripheral channel of the ELM as if the act were actually being committed. In a recent example of the signal response, an official in the Washington, DC city council and aide to the then African-American mayor was removed from the council because he used the word "niggardly." Now, the dictionary definition of the word is "unwilling to give, spend, or share ... stingy, scanty, or meager" (*American Heritage Dictionary*, 1985). But because the word sounds similar to a racial epithet—the "N" word—it prompted a signal response among members of the council, even after a definition of the word was given. The semanticists were accurate about the power of the signal response (National Public Radio, 1999), and the signal response is a reflection of our 24/7 networked and media-saturated world at work to make us less

FIGURE 5.3 It is clear that Bob doesn't understand the map/territory distinction.
SOURCE: Used with permission of Al Ochsner.

critical receivers. Signal responses are also a prime objective of the propagandist.

The semanticists also wanted to train senders and receivers to be continually alert to the difference between signals and symbols so that they would not be misunderstood by receivers. In other words, they wanted to train not only responsible and ethical receivers but such senders as well. Semanticists also try to isolate and specify meaning in concrete terms. Let's examine a fairly inflammatory sentence that might be used by either an insensitive sender or an anti-student propagandist and then try to defuse it using the techniques of the semanticists and of responsible receivers. Suppose the sender tells you, "Your generation of college students is addicted to technology, irresponsible to others, and as a result is antisocial, self-centered, and selfish." Your response will probably be negative because of the connotations of some of the words used "selfish" and "addicted" for sure, and maybe "irresponsible" as well. Semanticists would advise us to use what they call **extensional devices**, or techniques for neutralizing or defusing the emotional connotations that often accompany words by adding information that makes my meaning clear to you and others. One extensional device in my language use would be to identify the specific college students I have in mind. Semanticists call this **indexing**. In this case, the statement would change to something like,

"Your generation of college students, who have everything paid for by their parents, is addicted to technology, selfish, and irresponsible to others." That would calm some of you because it means that you aren't irresponsible to everyone, but to certain special others and you aren't irresponsible in all ways—only those referred to in a special ways as indicated by the quotation marks. You probably know fellow students who have everything paid for, including lots of extras that you don't get. But the sender still would not be as clear as possible, according to the semanticists. They would further urge him or her to use an extensional device called **dating**, or letting you know the time frame of my judgment about college students. Using dating, they might say something like, "College students who were in high school during G. W. Bush's terms of office and who have everything paid for by their parents are...." That might cool you down a little more because now there is only that special set of college students enrolled from 2000 to 2009, and that's not you; but there might still be some dissatisfaction with the statement. Here is where the extensional device semanticists call **etc.** comes into play. This device is meant to indicate that we can never tell the whole story about any person, event, place, or thing. Using this device, senders might say, "Generation X college students who were in high school during G. W. Bush's terms of office and who have everything

---

B O X 5.4   Is the USA Too Pro-Israel—Our Propaganda?

Go to www.ifamericansonlyknew. org and enter the word "Mujohid1" in the search engine and learn about how our country discriminates against persons of Middle Eastern countries and propagandizes about the neglect while ignoring the other side of the story—how Israel behaves toward those countries—from various world experts including a U.S. congressman, *Newsweek* and *Time* journalists, former *ambassadors* to these countries, former government officials, and others.

---

paid for by their parents are…, among other things." Now conservatism, selfishness, and laziness aren't their only attributes. For example, they also might be "societally concerned about environmental issues," "worried about honesty," or any of a number of other positive attributes.

Finally, the semanticists would advise using an extensional device called **quotation marks**, which is a way to indicate that the sender is using those flag words in a particular way—their own way, which isn't necessarily your own way. For example, their use of the word "selfish" might relate to the students' unwillingness to help other students succeed in class. Or it could relate to their unwillingness to volunteer in the community or to do any of a number of other things that wouldn't necessarily match your meaning for the word "selfish." The sender's sentence might now read, "Generation X college students who were in high school during G. W. Bush's terms of office and who have everything paid for by their parents are addicted to technology 'selfish' and 'irresponsible' to others, among other things." Now you would probably probe for my meanings for the emotional words, or you might even agree with the sentence. How does Box 5.4 help you understand the extensional devices and the ideas of the semanticists?

Using extensional devices in decoding persuasion helps us make sure the maps in our heads more closely resemble the territory to which we refer. Persuaders need to design specific, concrete extensional messages, especially when using emotionally charged words or abstract words for which there can be many meanings. More important, persuadees need to consider whether they are be-

ing appealed to via the map or the territory. Abstract words such as "power," "democracy," "freedom," "morals," and "truth" are particularly vulnerable to misunderstanding and are probably best communicated using a familiar metaphor. Unethical persuaders and propagandists often intentionally use abstract or emotionally charged language to achieve their purposes. It is our task to remember the map/territory distinction and to use extensional devices as we attend to symbols. We must remember that receivers also have "response-ability."

BURKE'S APPROACH TO LANGUAGE USE

Perhaps no language theorist or critic wrote as many treatises in as wide a variety of fields or with as broad a knowledge of human symbolic behavior as Kenneth Burke whom we first met in Chapter 1 and who is associated with many narrative theories, which we have now encountered several times. He focused on language as it is used to persuade people to action, and defined persuasion as "the use of language as a symbolic means of inducing cooperation in beings that by nature respond to symbols" (Burke, 1970, Grammar, p. 43). This active cooperation is induced by what he termed **identification**, a concept similar to Aristotle's "common ground" and our use of "co-creation," as noted in Chapter 1 and which frequently results in a media-saturated world. According to Burke, identification develops through the linguistic

---

B O X 5.5   Language and Cultural Diversity

Did you know that only four countries in all of Latin America have populations greater than the Latino population of the United States, which is now about 22.5 million? Or did you know that there are more Asians in the United States than there are in Cambodia, Laos, Hong Kong, or Singapore? Or did you know that at some point in this century, Latinos will outnumber non-Latinos? These are just a few of the many facts mentioned by Nido R. Qubein. He is an internationally known consultant, award-winning speaker, president of High Point University, and he sits on the boards of several Fortune 500 companies and is chairman of a national

public relations firm, Business Life Inc., and CEO of the Great Harvest Bread Company. He came to the United States as a teenager, with no contacts, no English language skills, and less than $50 to his name. He travels the globe and urges his audiences to remember that "people from different backgrounds send and receive messages through cultural filters" and that the same words, facial expressions, and gestures have different meanings depending on one's cultural heritage. You may want to access his home page at www.nidoqubein.com/index. There you can listen to him speak, get samples of his video and audio tapes, and get free articles written by him.

---

sharing of what he called **sub-stances**. He divided the word into its prefix *sub*, meaning "beneath," and *stances*, which refers to "grounding" or "places." In other words, identification rests on the beliefs, values, experiences, and views of the self that we share with others or with our groundings or our first principles. Burke noted that these sub-stances or "places" emerge in the words we use to define things, persons, and issues. Critical receivers of persuasion need to pay particular attention to the words, images, and metaphors that persuaders use to create (or undermine) identification. Our self-concepts are made up of various kinds of symbolic and real possessions, including physical things (clothing, cars, books), experiential things (work, activities, recreations), and philosophical possessions (beliefs, attitudes, values) which we acquire (frequently as a result of media). Identification with others develops to the degree that we symbolically share these possessions. In other words, we identify with persons who articulate a similar view of life, who enjoy the same kinds of activities, have similar physical possessions, lifestyles, beliefs, attitudes, and so on. If we identify with persuaders, we naturally tend to believe what they say and probably follow their advice. Thus, the job of persuaders is to call attention to those sub-stances or basic beliefs and experiences that they share with receivers, so poli-

ticians will try to remind us that they are like us ("of the people") and advertisers will depict brand users as like their target market. The receivers' job, in turn, is to critically examine these sub-stances to see whether they truly are shared values and beliefs or whether the persuader merely makes them appear to be shared. In other words, persuadees need to decode persuaders' messages for their authenticity, and determine whether the messages reflect or resonate with persuaders' real beliefs and values or are merely convenient metaphorical concoctions. Frequently these artistic creations rely on the persuader's skill with language. Let's explore the concept of substance further.

To Burke, most persuasive attempts to describe our "essential parts," and his description is always revealing. All words have emotional shadings and reveal the feelings, attitudes, values, and judgments of the user. For example, take the word "manipulate." It carries a lot of potentially negative meanings, although its denotation is quite benign. Wikipedia defines it as social influence involved with changing people's minds—not too terrible? Yet some of its links for the words include "abuse, puppeteer, propaganda, mind control, fraud, and brainwashing" not too harmless, eh? Check out the words "emotional manipulation" in any search engine and you will discover how terribly harmful

---

B O X 5.6   Is Persuasion Bad? Exploring Changing People with Language

"If you give people a gun, they will kill someone." What's wrong with this conditional premise? (Hint: See Chapter 8 on logical premises.) Is it true about teaching people to persuade with clever language? Go to www. changingminds.org and explore the caveat and other links located there to learn about this quandary.

---

manipulation can be. Examining persuasive language not only can tell us about ourselves but it can also tell us things about the persuaders who solicit our interest, support, and commitment (see Box 5.6).

Burke further suggested that symbolic activities like the use of language inevitably cause people to have feelings of guilt. From the beginning, language automatically led to rule making and moralizing. Because we all break the rules or don't measure up to moral standards at some time, we experience some degree of guilt. Burke argued that all human cultures exhibit patterns that help explain guilt, and the development of language in each of us is foremost. For example, the word "puppy" is clearly not an actual puppy, so language that names what something is inherently leads to the idea of what something is not—**the negative**. The negative then leads to sets of "thou shall nots," whether supernatural, parental, spousal, or societal. Inevitably, we fail to obey some of these negatives and again experience shame and guilt. "No" is one of the first things we learn as children, and we realize that it means we just displeased someone. We hear "No, no, no," over and over, and then we begin to use it ourselves. It gives us power, and we go about testing the extent of that power during the "terrible twos" and, in fact, throughout life. So some language can induce feelings of guilt in the audience which becomes a powerful motivator. For example, persons who have been abused frequently feel guilt for such things as being raped or beaten. Why? Probably because the word "SHAME" or some variant (e.g., ashamed, mortified, humiliated, sorry, disgrace, embarrassed, etc.) is being used to describe them/us or their/our behavior. Probably, we first hear of shame from our parents who tell us that we should feel it when we do something that displeases

them. This powerful word can then be tied to other issues like the feelings we might have at being tricked or fooled by terrorists, politicians, or a friend/lover. Whenever we hear persuasion that uses some of these variants, we need to listen carefully because someone is probably laying blame on us and it is probably unjustified, and further, it probably describes what the persuader him or herself feels in regard to the issue.

The second behavioral pattern that contributes to guilt relies on the principle of hierarchy, or "pecking order." It happens in all societies and groups, and it leads to either jealousy of others or to competition. We rarely (perhaps never) reach the top of the pecking order, and we feel guilty about that as well. A third source of guilt is our innate need to achieve perfection. Unfortunately, we all fall short of our goals and then feel inadequate and ashamed for not doing our best. This shame makes us feel guilty about not living up to our own or others' expectations. The persuader tells us that we could have done better if only we had really tried instead of only giving a half-hearted effort. That's what the United States was given for its failures in Vietnam and Iraq. How do we rid ourselves of this shame and resulting guilt? In most religions, guilt is purged symbolically—we offer up a sacrifice or engage in self-inflicted suffering, penance, and so on. In everyday life we may offer up a scapegoat, laying the blame on him/her/ or it/them. The real reason we lost those wars was because American will was weak or because "liberals" weren't committed enough or because our armed forces were unprepared. But the handiest and most flexible, creative, artistic, and universal means to whip guilt is through language. We usually try to get rid of guilt by talking about it—in prayer, to ourselves, to a counselor or authority figure, or to someone with whom we identify. Consider how frequently persuaders offer us symbolic ways to alleviate our guilt. The parents who feel guilty about being absentee, can take their family on a week's vacation to Disney World. The imperfect child tries to do better at school by using the Internet and spending more time studying and doing extra credit assignments. The weak-willed nation can purge the national guilt by following the new tough and demanding leader as Germans did with Hitler a century ago and which Americans have done repeatedly in this century.

In summary, persuasion via identification works because we all share sub-stances and because we all experience guilt. In processing persuasion, try to recognize that persuaders create identification by referring to shared sub-stances—preferred beliefs, lifestyles, and values. They motivate us by appealing to our internal and inevitable feelings of inadequacy, shame, or guilt. Examine the language and images in advertisements, sermons, political appeals, and other messages, reminding yourself of the strategies being used to create identification and also feelings of imperfection, shame, and guilt.

THE SEMIOTIC APPROACH TO LANGUAGE USE

Semiotics is another field concerned with the generation and conveyance of meaning. (See Figure 5.4.) A number of scholars are associated with this "science" of meaning. These semiologists apply the tools of linguistics to a wide variety of texts—verbal and nonverbal. Almost anything can be a text that has one or more meanings—semioticians talk about the "meaning" of a doctor's office, a meal, a TV program, a circus, or any other verbal or nonverbal symbolic event. They also try to describe the underlying meaning in any of these which they call the "subtext" of any symbolic act. For example, what is the subtext for "America's Next Top Model?" Some things are obvious. The importance of being slim and beautiful is clear, but what about

the probable ethnicity of the next top model? It used to be Caucasian. What is their body type? It seems to me like they need to visit an "All You Can Eat" buffet for their morning, noon, and evening meals and load their plates. What are their family values? Their political leanings? Who knows (because they don't follow politics?) These and others may be there in the program, but probably not so clearly.

According to semiotic theory, all texts convey meaning through **signs** or **signifiers**. A signifier in a restaurant could be the presence or absence of a hostess. It signifies that either we are to wait to be shown to our seat or that we can select our own in the case of the absent hostess. **Signifieds** are the things (events, rules, etc.) to which the signifiers refer. These signifiers interact with one another in meaningful and sophisticated, but not obvious, relationships, or sign systems, which make up the "language," or "code," of the text. What are the signifiers in America's Next Top Model? Probably the styles of clothing, the body shapes of the contestants, the sponsors of the program, and so on. In all likelihood the signs flow from our 24/7, media-saturated, advocacy- or propaganda-filled world, and efficacy-oriented world and also reflect a multicultural world and value system.

These codes (and others like them from any text—celebrity behavior, sports, films, political events) can be inferred from the text's signs, codes, and signifiers. For example, consider your classroom as a text having its own signifiers and signifieds—some linguistic and some visual, some logical and some emotional. The room usually has an institutional "meaning" signified by the type of walls, lighting, boards, and so on. Blackboards and plaster walls usually signify that the building is an old one. Green or white boards and cinder block walls signify a newer building. The kinds of student desks (with or without arms), the arrangement of the room (e.g., desks in rows vs. groups), and the physical objects (an overhead vs. a video projector) are all signifiers that tell us about what to expect when entering this "text." There may be a clock on the wall, signifying that time is important here, and it may be in view of the students or only

FIGURE 5.4

Bob doesn't get the meaning of the word "euphemize."

SOURCE: Used with permission of Al Ochsner.

to someone facing the back of the room (usually the teacher). Consider several of the codes embedded in various texts. For example, a simple code is the use of black and white hats in old cowboy movies to indicate the good guys and the bad guys. Pages being blown off a calendar in a movie signify the passage of time. What meanings are conveyed by drinking out of mugs as opposed to Styrofoam cups or fine china? Each type of cup is a signifier, and each coffee drinker, consciously or unconsciously, is communicating a different message, yet words aren't necessarily involved.

In a semiotic approach to the study of meaning, we try to read each message from several perspectives: (1) the words that are or are not spoken, (2) the context in or from which they are spoken, the actions that are or are not taken, are or are not approved of, and so on, and (3) the other signifiers in the message—visuals, colors, tone of voice, music, background settings, furnishings, and so on. More and more marketing and advertising research is being conducted from a semiological approach, according to Curt Suplee (1987) of the *Washington Post* when he notes that "When advertising is great advertising, it fastens on the myths, signs, and symbols of our common experience and becomes, quite literally, a benefit of the product.... As a result of great advertising, food tastes better, clothes feel snugger, cars ride smoother. The stuff of semiotics becomes the magic of advertising."

Semiotics also can help us understand where a persuader is coming from and what his or her agenda might be. What is the semiotic meaning of the following letter sent to the chair of my department?

Dear Professor Jones,

I am interested in directives as to how one may proficiency out of the speech requirement. Having been advised to seek counsel from you *specifically*—I sincerely hope you will not be displeased with my enthusiasm by asking this indulgence. There is a basis for my pursuing this inquisition as I am an adept speaker with substantiating merits. I will be overburdened with more difficult courses this fall—at least they will be concomitant with my educational objectives in the fields of Fine Arts and Languages. It would be a ludicrous exercise in futility to be mired in an unfecund speech course when I have already distinguished myself in that arena. I maintained an *A* average in an elite *advanced* speech course in High School. I am quite noted for my bursts of oratory and my verbal dexterity in the public "reality"— quite a different platform than the pseudo realism of the college environs. There is a small matter of age—I shall be twenty-two

B O X   5.7   An Interactive Short Course on Semiotics

Go to www.uvm.edu~tstreeter/semiotics, if you want to get an "A" on an extra credit paper in this course and enjoy an interestingly illustrated short course on the terms and methods of semiotics that show us a lot about advertising.

Use the lessons and terms you learn there to create a well-written semiological analysis of some type of advertising such as fashion, beer, sports, home furnishings, or cosmetics. Be sure to follow the entire short course through all of the "continue" links.

this fall. I am four years older than the average college freshman. I am afraid that I would dissipate with boredom, if confined with a bunch of teenagers. Surely you can advise something that would be a more palatable alternative?

Yours sincerely,

P.S. Please do not misconstrue this *inquiry* as the enterprise of an arrogant student, but one who will be so immersed in serious intellectual pursuits that the *speech* requirement will be too nonsensical and burdensome.

If ever a student needed to learn about communication, it was this individual. But what does the language usage here tell you about the writer of the letter? She (yes, it's a female author) uses 64-dollar words—perhaps a code for insecurity—but she seems unsure about her choice of words, as shown by her putting words into quotation marks, which indicates that she has her own special meaning for them. She also uses italics to signify that this word has special meaning and importance. She also misuses some words. For example, she says that she is pursuing an *inquisition* when she means an *inquiry*. An inquisition is a tribunal for suppressing religious heresy. She says she has *substantiating merits* when she probably means that she has *substantial reasons* for being excused from the course. She seems uncertain about what she means as she italicizes, capitalizes and puts words in quotes as if they have a special meaning for her. These and other signifiers add up to the semiotic meaning of the letter, which is that the author is insecure and hopes to impress the recipient of the letter.

So the study of semiotics and its tools, terms, and methods is another tool of language that can help alert us as receivers to the persuasion that is targeted at us and others (see Box 5.7). Like the earlier theories discussed above, it can also be used to craft the language we use in trying to persuade others in this world dominated by at least Seven Faces of Persuasion.

Let us now take a brief look at one of the most powerful and artful of all language devices used in persuasion—the metaphor.

LANGUAGE, METAPHORS, AND MEANING

Most language theorists agree that of all the figures of speech, the **metaphor** is the most powerful, most persuasive and most likely to require truly artistic language creativity. The Merriam-Webster online dictionary defines metaphor as "…a word or phrase literally denoting one kind of object or idea is used in place of another to suggest a likeness…(as in drowning in money)." Literary critic I. A. Richards long ago distinguished between two key parts of any metaphor—the **tenor** (or subject of the metaphor) and the **vehicle** or the means of embodiment or transmission of meaning (from the Latin "vehere" or "to carry"). Since then, many other language theorists and critics have used his system. For example, take the experience of drowning in the metaphor cited above. It serves as the vehicle for tenor or subject/idea of having an overwhelming abundance of money. Another way to put it is that the tenor is equal to the vehicle. In the words of the semanticist they are map and territory. In a way, a metaphor is a small sentence. In the example above it states that "An over-abundance of money is as fearsome as drowning." So the metaphor creates a new image or concept by tying the familiar or the subject (tenor) to a less familiar image (vehicle) and herein lies its creativity, its persuasiveness, and in semiotic terms, its code(s) or subtext(s).

A good and persuasive metaphor is one in which the vehicle can be readily and repeatedly "mapped" back to the tenor, and preferably on several dimensions. In the example above, the vehicle (drowning) maps back to the tenor (an overabundance of money) in several ways. First the sensation of drowning is related to being surrounded by the threat or water. Another dimension of drowning is feeling helpless to escape the threat. Third, drowning is probably a lonely experience where one feels that only he or she can remedy the situation. Finally, experiencing drowning or near drowning probably feels like one is pursued by the water. Now, can we determine if any or all of these dimensions "maps" back to the tenor (an overabundance of money)? If we are to believe the stories of persons who say they are cursed by too much money, these dimensions of feeling surrounded by the overabundance; helpless to divest oneself from it; cursed or pursued by it and reliant only on the self to escape the curse, then indeed the vehicle "maps" back to the tenor quite well and there are several such maps. (See www.changingminds.org/techniques/language to explore metaphor for further illumination.) Clearly most of us haven't experienced near drowning, so while the repeated mapping is good, a broad familiarity with the vehicle doesn't exist. That's why the most effective and persuasive metaphors are broadly familiar to the audience as well as being repeatedly "mapped" to the tenor and on several dimensions.

In their broadest level of familiarity, metaphors can be what is called "archetypal," which means they have universal and cross cultural themes. Many persons, at different times in history and faced with differing circumstances, can relate to and are familiar with these themes. Some examples are the dark/light, hot/cold, quest/journey, sailing/navigating, water/fertility, seedtime/harvest, and the life/death families to mention only a few. You can see

that these experiences are shared by large numbers of persons from diverse backgrounds and cultures. In other words, they have broad familiarity or applicability. As a result, they provide ideal places in which to design or create persuasive metaphors and an important place to see how they might be effective in persuading you and others. (See www.voxcommunications.com/ccc/speechterms for further explanation and definitions of a number of other speech terms related to eloquence and persuasiveness.) Let's identify one of many archetypal families that could be put to use in persuasion. Remember that the key to determining the persuasiveness of metaphors is to identify and isolate the tenor(s) and vehicle(s), then to see how broadly familiar they are to the audience(s), and finally to see how many ways the vehicle(s) "map" back to the tenor(s). For example, take the seedtime/harvest family and its relation to our election cycles wherein the spring primary season leads to the autumnal general election. Spring is a time of testing candidates so they can be "winnowed" or thinned out to the two (or more if there are independents) "best" presidential and vice presidential candidates for the general election in November. A primary candidate might use this invented metaphor.

It is now spring, and we are testing the seeds of our platform so that we will reap a full harvest and the best fruits of our labors. Some seeds will fall by the wayside to be consumed by the birds of the air and the beasts of the field. Others fall on parched land and will wither and die. Some fall among brambles and will be choked with cares and pleasures. Happily, some will fall on good ground and take root and will yield the accomplishments of this administration and the first fruits of the "New Democracy," which is the theme of the Larson administration—let us bring the harvest in!

The applicability of this metaphor (that the election process is both seedtime and harvest) is clearly broad and understood by persons of many backgrounds, cultures, and times. And to an American audience also familiar with biblical references, it rings of the parable of the sower and his seed from the New Testament. Does the vehicle (planting and harvest) connect in people's minds with the tenor (the election process)? Anyone who has planted a garden (and many who have only experienced that act vicariously) will map back to the reference to spring as planting time and will also map to the fact that not all sowed seeds (or tested ideas as in "seeds of thought") will develop to be fully productive and ultimately harvested. So here are at least three "map/territory" connections. Another "map" from the vehicle (planting/harvest) to the tenor (elections) is the seed that is either eaten (or stolen by the other candidates) or disregarded (ignored by the electorate). Yet another "map" flowing from the vehicle is the seed that is overshadowed by other problems (cares and pleasures of the day). And finally the seed that takes root on good ground (ideas that are favored by the electorate and the press) maps back to tenor to become the best (or the first fruits) accomplishments leading to a "New Democracy" or the campaign theme followed by the action metaphor of bringing in the harvest. In other words this should be a highly effective and widely accepted metaphor for the election campaign—one that will be clearly understood and widely resonated with by the voter especially in our 24/7, widely-networked, media-saturated, and multicultural world of advocacy.

What are some of the other archetypal metaphors which we might encounter as responsible receivers and how can we analyze them as well as the other uses of language discussed above? In Chapter 6 we will explore some of them and devise specific tools of analysis that have been developed from the theories and concepts discussed here.

REVIEW AND CONCLUSION

By now, you probably have deeper appreciation for human symbol making, use, and misuse, and for the power of language as a tool of persuasion—especially the English language. You might realize how much meaning you can uncover when you critically analyze the symbols used in persuasion. It takes time and effort to decode discursive and presentational persuasion, to locate the meanings being used to create a state of identification, to determine the difference between the map and the territory, and to learn the many semantic and semiotic codes operating in various kinds of texts as well as the powerful effects of metaphors. To become a responsible persuadee, you need tools to assist you in analyzing the many persuasive messages and language techniques targeted at you. Chapter 6 focuses on some tools for doing this.

KEY TERMS

After reading this chapter, you should be able to identify, explain, and give an example of the following key terms or concepts:

symbols	presentational meaning	dating	signs
concepts	semanticists	etc.	signifiers
conceptions	maps	quotation marks	signifieds
signification	territories	identification	metaphor
denotation	signal response	sub-stances	tenor
connotation	extensional devices	the negative	vehicle
discursive symbols	indexing	semiotics	

APPLICATION OF ETHICS

Here is the situation: An interpreter arrives a few minutes before a court of law is called to order. He wants to speak to the defendant, who is a non-English speaker, to determine if using Spanish instead of English will be acceptable. The defendant lets the interpreter know that Spanish is a second language for him (his first language is an indigenous dialect), but that he understands the interpreter and proceeding in Spanish is acceptable. The interpreter has three options: (1) Tell the judge of the situation and that Spanish interpretation is acceptable to the defendant. (2) Say nothing and proceed with the interpretation in Spanish since the defendant has said it is okay with him. (3) Inform the defendant's attorney and let him decide how to proceed. Which option seems most ethical to you? Does the interpreter have any ethical obligation to inform the Judge? Is he ethically obliged to say anything?

QUESTIONS FOR FURTHER THOUGHT

1. Why is symbol making such a powerful human activity? Give several examples of how symbols create high involvement in people. Are symbols logical or emotional? Are they processed centrally or peripherally?

2. What is meant by Burke's phrase "symbol misusing"? Give some examples of the misuse of symbols.

3. Why is the English language so powerful?

4. Why is a red stoplight a sign to a leader dog, and how is that "meaning" different from the words "red stoplight" or "dangerous cross-traffic"?

5. What did Suzanne Langer mean when she said that symbols are the "vehicles for the conception of objects"?

6. What is the difference between signification, denotation, and connotation?

7. What is the difference between a presentational and a discursive symbol?

8. What is the difference between a map and a territory, according to the general semanticists? Give an example of one of your food maps. One of your geographic maps? One of your experience maps?

9. Was Bill Clinton's meaning for "sexual relations" (with Monica Lewinsky) an ethical use of language? Why or why not?

10. What is a signal response? Give several examples.

11. What are the extensional devices recommended by general semanticists? What purpose do these devices serve? Give examples.

12. What did Kenneth Burke mean by "identification"? By "sub-stance"? By the "need for hierarchy"? By "guilt"? How do these concepts explain why language is so important in persuasion and in living life?

13. What is the difference between a signifier and a signified? What is a code? Give examples of simple codes from the worlds of sports, politics, and/or advertising.

14. What is a metaphor and why is it likely to be persuasive?

15. What is the tenor in a metaphor? What is the vehicle? What is "mapping" back?

16. Is it ethical for advertisers to use guilt to get us to buy? Why or why not? Give some examples.

 For online activities, go to the *Persuasion* book companion Web site at http://academic.cengage.com/communication/larson12.

6

✳

Tools for Analyzing Language and Other Persuasive Symbols

LEARNING GOALS

After reading this chapter, you should be able to:

1. Identify the three dimensions of language focused on in this chapter and give examples of each that you have found or invented.

2. Discuss the powers of symbolic expression in persuasion.

3. Give examples of tools of analysis for each of the dimensions of language.

4. Explain the pentad and give examples of each term in contemporary persuasion.

5. Explain and give examples of god, devil, and charismatic terms in contemporary persuasion.

6. Explain and give examples of archetypal metaphors being used in contemporary persuasion.

7. Explain the difference between the pragmatic and unifying styles and give examples of each from contemporary persuasion.

8. Explain and identify metaphors, archetypal metaphors, the tenor and vehicle, and "mapping" of the various vehicles to their tenor.

9. Explain semiotics and discuss how texts and codes work.

N ow that you have some perspective on the making, use, and misuse of symbols and an appreciation for the power of language (and the English language in particular), let's consider several ways to analyze both verbal and nonverbal persuasive symbols. Such analysis helps us to reject misguided, fallacious, and deceptive messages. We mentioned several recent examples such the nonexistent "WMDs" in Iraq, the lies of CEOs and corrupt practices of their corporations who bankrupted their companies while getting rich in the process, and the official rejection or global warming by the highest officials in the land until it was almost too late. All of these used persuasive language, and we'll face many more examples in the future, so receivers need to learn about language use and to use tools of language analysis that can uncover deceptive persuasion. In more modern terms, receivers need to acquire the tools of deconstruction in order to uncover potentially misleading and harmful persuasion.

The cube in Figure 6.1 represents three of the many dimensions of language. They are (1) the **semantic dimension** (the meanings for a word), (2) the **func-tional dimension** (the jobs that words can do, such as naming), and (3) the **thematic dimension** (the feel and texture of words like "swoosh"). Following our consideration of these dimensions, you will find a discussion of several tools useful in analyzing each dimension and several example analyses. Notice that the cube consists of many smaller cubes, each representing a word or set of words having its own unique semantic, functional, and thematic dimensions. Now consider this line of ad copy: "Sudden Tan from Coppertone Tans on Touch for a Tan That Lasts for Days." On the functional dimension, the words "Sudden Tan" name a product. Semantically, much more is suggested. The word "sudden" describes an almost instantaneous tan, and, indeed, the product dyes skin "tan" on contact. The ad's headline—"Got a Minute? Get a Tan"—is superimposed over before-and-after photos of an attractive blonde who has presumably been dyed tan. On a thematic level, the words do even more. The word "sudden" sounds and feels like the word "sun," so the brand name sounds like the word "suntan" and notice the repetition of the consonant sounds of "s" and "t" which are central to the word "suntan," which is the benefit promised by the brand.

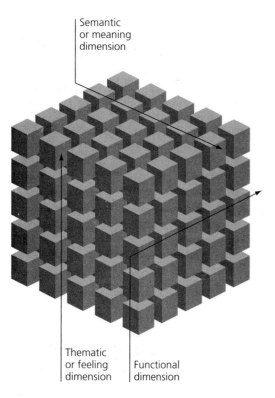

Semantic
or meaning
dimension

Thematic
or feeling
dimension

Functional
dimension

F I G U R E   6.1 This figure shows three of the many dimensions of language that are at work when persuadees decode or deconstruct the many persuasive messages of our 24/7 and media-saturated world.

Consider these examples of thematic language use.

- The "Kero-Sun" heater burns kerosene and warms your house like the sun.

- Have a "Soup-erb Supper" with a package of Hamburger Helper's beef-vegetable soup.

- Try My Mom's Meatloaf mix—Meat Loaf that Tastes Like Home.

- Presto named its popcorn popper "The Big Poppa," which sounds like popcorn being popped.

- Satin Cigarettes are so Smooth and Silky.

Each example demonstrates one or more of the three dimensions of language depicted in the cube

above—the functional dimension, the semantic dimension, and the thematic dimension. Let us explore these dimensions more fully.

THE FUNCTIONAL DIMENSION: WHAT DO THE WORDS DO?

Words can do many things. They can motivate action, identify causes and effects, and lay or deflect blame. During a trial in which an abortionist and the woman who had the abortion faced charges of manslaughter, language functioned in several ways. The defense referred to attempts to abort the fetus early in the pregnancy (months before the trial), saying, "After two unsuccessful attempts…." The prosecutor used active verbs and pronouns, saying, "They tried twice… they were unsuccessful." This language helped to lay blame on the woman and the doctor. In one case, the function of the words blunted the accusation because the unsuccessful attempts weren't anyone's fault. In the other, it focused blame on both the woman and the doctor, which was the prosecution's aim.

The functional dimension also has powerful potential to simply shift our focus (Andrews, 1984). Take, for example, the function of defining, which can "frame" or set the perspective for the persuasive appeal. As communication scholar Dan Hahn (1998) observes, "Definitions are like blinders on a horse: They focus attention on some aspects while blinding us to others" (p. 53). For example, consider the quarantining of trade to a country to stop shipping into and out of its ports such as we did in the past and probably will do in the future. You could call such an action a "blockade," which (in the eyes of the world) is considered an act of war. Now, call the actions "sanctions." That's what the United States did when it outlawed trade by American companies with Iran, Iraq, and North Korea, portraying these nations as part of an "axis of evil" that had sinister worldwide motives. These word choices (i.e., "sanctions" and "axis of evil") served at least three functions. First, they signaled the three nations, and others that objected to the sanctions, that the United States wasn't necessarily interested in all-out war (though we ultimately did invade Iraq with unsuccessful and even damaging results). Second, they gave a justification for the resulting hardships being endured by the populace of the three countries. Finally, they vilified the three nations as "outlaws" in the world community. So the words served several functions—reassuring world fears, placing and deflecting blame, and the building of a negative image for the three nations. In another example, Hahn points out the meanings associated with the label "middle class." For some, the term means those earning between $20,000 and $70,000 per year (pp. 61–62). To others it means a lifestyle that includes a house, two late model cars, and membership in the local YMCA. And for others it would include membership in a golf club, a summer cottage, and a winter cruise. So an important dimension of persuasive language is the functions, tasks, or jobs that the words perform.

Communication researcher Robert Cialdini (2001) observes that some language functions to compensate for our personal feelings of insecurity or low self-worth. He notes that "the persistent name dropper" is a classic example (p. 173); name droppers bolster their own self-esteem by knowing important personalities. So bolstering is another function of words. Sometimes, words create fear that can be very persuasive. Consider how the United States responded to the fear appeals associated with terrorism—it formed an entirely new cabinet level agency to fight terror, implemented cooperation between intelligence agencies formerly independent, allocated funds to very small towns where terrorism is not likely, and so forth. In another successful example, a "Got Milk?" ad claimed, "One in five osteoporosis victims is male. Luckily, fat free milk has the calcium bones need to beat it." The words create fear in the male reader who uses this new knowledge to change his behavior. So naming potential problems interacts with the reader and prompts fear and a motivation to take action—drink more milk.

Cialdini (2001) identifies several other functions that language can perform. These include the function of creating deference or blind obedience to authority (p. 182). Cialdini says that the use of titles can also function to convey authority (p. 188). Today, we hire an "administrative assistant" not a "secretary," and the new name functions to build the employee's self-worth. Another function Cialdini identifies is the power of language to create "the scarcity effect" (p. 205). Consider the words "Price Good Only While Supplies Last!" or "Act Now! Only a Few Left." These phrases function to convince the persuadee that the product is in short supply. This creates "a sense of urgency" and prompts the prospect to take action. So language has a functional dimension which refers to the number of the jobs or functions language can perform while persuasion is going on, and it has a second dimension dealing the meaning(s) of words.

THE SEMANTIC DIMENSION: WHAT DO THE WORDS MEAN?

The semantic dimension explains the various shades of meaning given to language. For example, in the abortion case discussed earlier, the defense won a ruling that censored the use of the terms "baby boy" and "human being," and allowed only the word "fetus" to be used by the prosecution. What a difference. We react very differently to the word "fetus" than we do to "baby boy." Or take the example of a person saying, "I'm really anxious to visit you again." What they really mean is that they are "eager" to see you and won't experience a bit of anxiety over the visit. Clearly, choosing words with the proper semantic meanings can be critical to the interactive co-creation of persuasive meaning in a multicultural world, especially where misunderstandings are all too frequent.

Word choice also provides clues about the source's underlying intentions. It is not surprising that words like "questionable business practices" would raise suspicions in the audience even though they do not function to lay blame. If a persuader says, "I'm responsible" versus "I'm culpable" versus "I'm guilty," receivers are going to have very different levels of response. So the words a persuader chooses can make a huge difference. Word choice also provides clues about the source's underlying intentions. It is not surprising that words like "questionable business practices" and "insider trading" convey different meanings than the words used by industry critics, which include terms like "looting" the company's pension fund, "destroying employee security," "auditing flimflams," and "corporate sharks drawn in a feeding frenzy by the smell of blood."

The impeachment trial of Bill Clinton produced many examples of carefully chosen language characterizing Clinton with terms such as "perjurious," "willfully corrupted," and "betrayed." They encourage certain kinds of co-created persuasive meanings. For example, receivers could infer from these words that Clinton was a habitual liar who didn't even respect the office he held or the oath of office to which he swore (Democracy Project, 1999). All of these examples used persuasive language, and we'll face many more examples in the future, so receivers need to learn about language use and how to uncover deceptive persuasion. When we talk about the meanings words have we need to remember the words of Humpty Dumpty from *Alice in Wonderland*. Like many persuades, he held that "When I use a word, it means just what I choose it to mean—neither more nor less." So when persuaders choose to use certain words in our 24/7 doublespeak world, receivers need to examine them carefully, not only for what they do (their functional dimension) but for their various shades of meaning (their semantic dimension) because to the persuaders they mean just what they choose them to mean—"neither more nor less." As a result they reveal much about the persuader and his or her beliefs and intentions. We will look at several tools to get at the both the functional and semantic dimensions of the language used in persuasion a bit later, but for now, let us turn to the thematic dimension of language to discover how words can convey not only meanings but feelings and sensations, sometimes via one of the five senses.

THE THEMATIC DIMENSION, HOW DO THE WORDS FEEL?

In addition to having functional and semantic meanings, some words also have a feeling, a texture, or a theme to them. You almost physically sense them. Onomatopoeic words sound like their meaning. For example, listen to the feel of "shush," "whir," "rustle," "buzz," "hum," "ding," or "boom." Somewhat less obvious thematic examples rely on **assonance**, or the repetition of vowels or vowel sounds—for example, "the low moans of our own soldiers rolled across the battlefield like the groans of the doomed." Or Hoover vacuum's "It beats; it sweeps; it cleans." **Alliteration** is similar except that it relies on the repetition of consonants, as in the familiar motto of the recycling movement "Reuse, reduce, recycle;" or brand names like Banana Boat or Calvin Klein; or ad slogans like "Renting is Better than Buying at Blockbuster." Both alliteration and assonance are favorite tools of advertising. They're fun to hear and repeat. By carefully considering the functional, semantic, and thematic dimensions of any persuasive message, we exercise our response-ability as receivers. Even if our interpretation of a message doesn't match the persuader's, the analytic process we apply to persuasive messages helps ensure the responsible reception of persuasion.

METAPHORS, ARCHETYPES AND THEIR MEANINGS

Sometimes, figures of speech can also produce a texture or theme at the same time they perform a function and carry a meaning. For example, the use of powerful metaphors creates thematic meaning or texture. According to communication researcher Michael Osborn (1967), wartime British Prime Minister Winston Churchill, repeatedly used what Osborn termed archetypal (universal) metaphors of "light" to characterize the British military and citizenry and "dark" ones for the enemy. In a speech during WW II, he said,

If we stand up to him (Hitler), all Europe may be free and the life of the world may move forward into broad, sunlit uplands. But if we fail, then the whole world, including the United States, including all that we have known and cared for, will sink into the abyss of a new Dark Age made more sinister, and perhaps protracted, by the lights of perverted science.... Good night then: sleep to gather strength for the morning. For the morning will come. Brightly will it shine on the brave and the true, kindly upon all who suffer for the cause, glorious upon the tombs of heroes. Thus will shine the dawn (pp. 115–126).

Archetypal metaphors usually refer to common substances or events like light and dark, birth and death, and rite of passage, and frequently are associated with the sacred or profane. Some familiar ones include references to fire, water, and blood. President George W. Bush repeatedly used the fire metaphor to characterize the rise of democracy in the Middle East and elsewhere in the world where freedom's "flames need to be fanned." Opponents of the invasion into Iraq declared that it would take a long time to "wash the blood" from America's hands. So metaphoric language can carry a lot of persuasive cargo.

As we noted in Chapter 5, the study of metaphor is extensive and revealing. Recall that every metaphor has at least two parts—the tenor or subject/idea of the metaphor and the vehicle or the means of transmitting or expressing the new concept or meaning of the tenor/idea. In that way the metaphor is like a sentence that basically says, "Idea X is similar to Vehicle Y in several ways." In the Bush example above the sentence reads something like "Fledgling democracies are like a spark that heeds to carefully urged along in order to develop into a full fire that is self sufficient." Recall also that metaphors are artful and hence persuasive to the degree that their vehicle "maps" back to the tenor in ways to which the audience can relate and respond. In

other words, the truly persuasive metaphor seems "just right" for the occasion—it couldn't be said any better. So persuadees need to pay attention to the metaphorical strategies being used by persuaders as well as the functional, semantic, and thematic ones.

THE POWER OF SYMBOLIC EXPRESSION

Symbolic expression affects emotions and/or the intellect, but it sometimes has actual physical effects. For example, the kinds of symbols people use and respond to can affect their health. People who use expressions such as "I can't stomach it," "I'm fed up," or "It's been eating away at me now for a year" are more likely to have more stomach ulcers than do others (*Chicago Daily News*, 1972). Symbolic days like birthdays have dramatic effects. In nursing homes, more persons die during the two months after birthdays than during the two months before (Lewis & Lewis, 1972). Thomas Jefferson and John Adams both died on the Fourth of July, a date of tremendous significance for both of them (Koenig, 1972). Some people die soon after the death of a loved one—and sometimes from the same disease. Symbolic sympathy pains can become real (Koenig, 1972). According to Seigel, the words we say to ourselves can also cure disease and even stop hemorrhaging (1989).

Burke (1960) makes an argument that language is symbolic action, and that may be an explanation of why words have almost magical possibilities. We know that words are central to most religious beliefs (e.g., see John 1:1, and Genesis where God speaks with each act of creation) and words are usually spoken at and central to sacramental enactments (i.e., marriage or the burial of the dead) in most if not all religions. Words are also important in law (e.g., the defendant must plead "guilty" or "not guilty" unless handicapped, and the verdict and sentence must also be spoken). Not only do symbols deeply affect individuals, but they also serve as a kind of psychological cement for holding a society or culture together. Traditionally, a sacred hoop representing the four seasons of the earth and the four directions from which weather might come served as the central life metaphor for the Lakota Indians. The hoop's crossed thongs symbolized the sacred tree of life and the crossroads of life. A Lakota holy man named Black Elk (1971) explained the symbolic power of the circle for his people:

> You have noticed that everything an Indian does is in a circle, and that is because the Power of the World always works in circles, and everything tries to be round. In the old days when we were a strong and happy people, all our power came to us from the sacred hoop of the nation and so long as the hoop was unbroken the people flourished....
> Everything the Power of the World does is done in a circle.... Even the seasons form a great circle in their changing and always come back again to where they were. The life of a man is a circle from childhood to childhood and so it is in everything where power moves. Our tipis were round like the nests of birds and these were always set in a circle, the nation's hoop, a nest of many nests where the Great Spirit meant for us to hatch our children (p. 134).

Black Elk believed that his tribe had lost all its power or "medicine" when forced out of traditional round tepees and into square reservation houses. What symbols serve as the cultural cement for our way of life: the flag, the Constitution, the home, competition, and sports? What are the symbols that unite our diverse cultural segments? What might someone of Chinese heritage use for cultural cement? References to wisdom and age occur frequently in Chinese literature from the past to the present. What about persons of Indian extraction? Moslems? Hindus? Buddhists? Eastern Europeans?

A good place to find the central symbols of our culture is in the language used in advertisements if the particular culture advertises. In marketing advertisement services, particularly to new emigrants from other cultures, I have found that in some cases, they have no concept of what an advertisement is or why a business should use one. That makes sense at least in countries of the former Soviet Union. When all goods are in short supply, there is no need for a merchant to advertise that his business has some in supply. I recall seeing a huge truckload of bananas drive up to a street market in Leipzig, East Germany and watching it sell out in less than 5 minutes. The string shopping bags that people used to take the fruit away were called a "perhaps" meaning to be used just in case something, it didn't matter what, became available and for sale.

This is obviously very different from the case in American culture. Here, goods are in strong supply, so we must advertise other reasons (other than "availability") to prompt consumers to buy. As a result, most ads promise a benefit to the consumer, elaborate on it, provide proof, and give a call to action—usually purchase. Benefits must reflect our wants and needs. Elaboration and proof for taking action, such as purchasing, probably reflect our need for knowledge. And we are an action-based society, as we shall see when we discuss cultural premises. To be short and concise, the ads and slogans "distill" or simplify complex ideas. This boiling down of meaning is called **synecdoche**, and politicians frequently use it. They know that concise words and phrases often become part of the evening news, thus acting as unpaid advertisements. The words also suggest a common denominator between persuader and persuadee. In an ad in *Newsweek*, the AARP used the slogan "Let's Not Stick Our Kids with the Bill!" referring to its opposition to proposed changes to the Social Security system. The phrase unified members and nonmembers of the organization to object to the proposed changes.

Political rhetoric also reflects our cultural values. Two important words used by politicians are "freedom" and "equality." As columnist David Broder (1984) noted, "Words are important symbols, and ... 'freedom' and 'equality' have defined the twin guideposts of American Democracy" (p. 41). The words have the thematic qualities to stir patriotic emotions. However, they are not rated the same by all persons. As Broder notes, "Socialists rank both words high, while persons with fascist tendencies rank both low; communists rank 'equality' high but 'freedom' low, and conservatives rate 'freedom' high but 'equality' low" (p. 41). Considerable power in linguistic symbols resides in their functional, semantic, and thematic dimensions. Not only do words reveal motives, but they also affect our self-image and express cultural ideals. Let's examine tools for analyzing these dimensions of language in persuasion.

TOOLS FOR ANALYZING PERSUASIVE SYMBOLS

Becoming aware of the three dimensions of language, metaphors, and nonverbal symbols helps us to become responsible receivers of persuasion. We also need to become increasingly aware of the interactive world of film, architecture, and other forms as explored in Box 6.1. We can use various tools for the analysis of persuasion to focus our critical eyes and ears on more specific aspects of language symbols. Let us now explore some of them.

Tools for the Functional Dimension

Two tools for analyzing the functional dimension of language symbols in persuasion are language critic Richard Weaver's grammatical categories (especially regarding sentence and word types) and the effects of word order or syntax in sentences.

Weaver's Grammatical Categories. Language theorist and pioneer Richard Weaver (1953) suggested that the type of sentence preferred by an individual offers clues as to that person's worldview (the way the person uses information and comes to conclusions). Weaver discussed some persuaders' preference for simple sentences, compound sentences, or complex sentences.

Simple sentences express a single complete thought or point and must contain one subject or noun and one action word or verb and an object ("He hit the ball"). Persuaders who prefer simple sentences don't see the world as a very complex place. Such a person "sees the world as a conglomerate of things…[and] seeks to present certain things as eminent against a background of matter uniform or flat" (p. 120). The simple sentence sets the subject off from the verb and object. There is a clear foreground and background in simple sentences, and they highlight cause and effect.

Compound sentences consist of two or more simple sentences joined by a conjunction such as "and" or "but." Weaver observed that the compound sentence sets things either in balance ("He ran, and he ran fast") or in opposition ("He ran, but she walked"). The compound sentence expresses either resolved or unresolved tension. According to Weaver, it "conveys that completeness and symmetry which the world ought to have" (p. 127). Persuaders using compound sentences see the world in terms of opposites or similarities. When you encounter compound sentences, try to identify the tension and the symmetry (or lack of it) in them.

Complex sentences also contain two or more distinct components, but not all the components stand alone as complete simple or compound sentences. Some of the elements in the sentences rely on another element in the sentence to be fully understood. Once, in speaking about word choice, Mark Twain used a complex sentence: "Whenever we come upon one of these intensely right words in a book or a newspaper, the resulting effect is physical as well as spiritual and electrically prompt" (Lederer, 1991, p. 128). The first portion of Twain's sentence ("Whenever…newspaper") could not stand alone; it is dependent on the last half of the sentence ("the resulting…prompt"), which could stand alone. The complex sentence features an intricate world with multiple causes and effects at the same time—dependency and independency or completeness and incompleteness. Weaver (1953) said it "is the utterance of a reflective mind" that tries "to express some sort of hierarchy" (p. 121). Persuaders who use complex sentences often express basic principles and relationships, with the independent clauses more important than dependent ones, as in this description by an ex-Olympic athlete:

> But after having represented the United States in five Olympic track and field teams from 1980 to 1991, I certainly have a feel for what the next class of Olympians is doing now. … if you are lucky enough to make it, there is the singular drama of Olympic competition (Lewis, 1999, p. 56).

Weaver (1953) also had some observations about types of words. For example, people react to **nouns** (which are defined as the name of a person, place, or thing) as if they were the things they name. Nouns "express things whose being is completed, not … in process, or whose being depends upon some other being" (p. 128). A persuader's noun use can reveal clues to his or her perceptions of things. When persuaders reduce persons to the level of things or objects by name calling, they do so for a reason—to deal with the people as objects, not as subjects or human beings.

According to Weaver, **adjectives** function to add to the noun, to make it special. The dictionary defines adjectives as "words that modify nouns … by limiting, qualifying or specifying" (*American Heritage Dictionary*, 1985). For example, "the little blue Ford hybrid with the Alabama plates" limits, qualifies, and specifies which vehicle we mean. For Weaver, adjectives were "question begging," and showed uncertainty. If you must modify a noun, you're uncertain about it in the first place. To Weaver the only certain adjectives are dialectical (good and bad, hot and cold, light and dark). Examining a persuader's adjective use can reveal his or her uncertainty and what they see in opposition to what.

Adverbs, to Weaver, are words of judgment. The dictionary defines adverbs as "words that modify verbs, adjectives, or other adverbs" (*American Heritage Dictionary*, 1985). Adverbs represent a community judgment that helps us to agree with what the persuader thinks we believe. For example, adverbs such as "surely," "certainly," and "probably" suggest agreement. When persuaders say, "Surely we all know that thus-and-such is so," they imply that the audience agrees with them. Such adverbs encourage interactive co-creation.

Syntax or Word Order.   In addition to using word or sentence types to analyze persuaders' messages, we can look at the syntax used. **Syntax** is defined as "the pattern or structure of the word order in sentences or phrases." How can that have a persuasive effect? Word order can either alert or divert the reader/listener. Consider the difference between these two sentences:

> "Before bombing the terrorist headquarters, we made sure the target was the right one."

> "We were sure the target was the right one before bombing the terrorist headquarters."

In the first sentence, the dependent element occurs at the beginning of the sentence ("Before …") and alerts the reader/listener to the conditions needed before taking action. The independent element expresses the main point of the sentence. In the second sentence, the action comes first, and the dependent element focuses the attention of the listener/reader on the justification for the action.

Some persuaders place emotional or surprising words at the beginning of a sentence to reduce the impact of what follows. The audience focuses on the evidence because of the emotionality of the claim. For example, the speaker might say, "There is no greater hypocrite than the animal rights advocate who opposes the use of animals in research labs during the day and then goes home and has beef, pork, or chicken for dinner!" The readers/listeners know beforehand that the claim is about hypocrisy, and they focus on the reasons for the claim. The sentence is dramatic and creates a puzzle—"There is no greater hypocrite than whom?" we ask ourselves.

The other side of the coin is the speaker who diverts attention from the evidence by hiding the claim at the end of the sentence. This makes the audience wonder where all this evidence is leading. The speaker says, "The animal rights advocate who opposes the use of rats in the research lab and then goes home to eat beef, pork, or chicken is the kind of hypocrite we don't need in this country!" The drama of the sentence is reduced, and the power of the evidence diminished because the audience wonders about the speaker's destination.

Communication scholar L. H. Hosman (2002) notes that language variations affect one of three elements of the persuasion process: "judgment of speaker, message comprehension and recall, or attitude toward the message" (p. 372), and that these effects are crucial in information processing. This, of course, brings us back to the Elaboration Likelihood Model (ELM), and the old debate over the comparative effectiveness of emotional appeals (peripheral processing) and logical ones (central processing). Hosman also reports that active sentence structure influences perceived believability, clarity, appeal, and attractiveness in print advertisements in different ways than does passive sentence structure. "The nature of a sentence's grammatical construction or of a narrative's construction has important persuasive consequences" (p. 374). Sentence structure and word choice can reveal the persuader's motives and act as indicators of information-processing channels being used in the ELM.

Tools for the Semantic Dimension

While the functional dimension carries important verbal and nonverbal meanings, the semantic dimension of co-created interactive meaning carries the bulk of persuasion in most messages.

Strategic Uses of Ambiguity.   Some think it unethical for persuaders to communicate in intentionally ambiguous ways, but they quite often do just that. They try to be unclear, vague, and general to allow for the broadest possible degree of common ground, identification, and co-creation of meaning. During the 2008 primary election season for the nomination of a President, almost every candidate's slogan on both the GOP and the Democratic sides involved the word "change" (e.g., "Change We've Been Waiting For," "Our Time For Change," "Change That We're Ready For," and "Change We Can Believe In."). Obviously, they all didn't mean the same thing by that word. They used this exciting but ambiguous word because they wanted each receiver to fill in his or her own private meanings or connotations for the word, thus "owning" the concept of change. This strategy results in the maximum number of interpretations and thus creates the largest potential audience for the persuader's brands, candidates, or causes. It also pleases as many and offends as few persons as possible. Receivers need to identify intentional ambiguity being used in persuasive messages and then analyze the persuader's reason(s) for using the ambiguous term(s).

Persuaders use several methods other than using ambiguous words to create strategic ambiguity. One is to choose words that can be interpreted in many (often contradictory) ways. A politician may support "responsibility in taxation and the cost of educating our youngsters." Those who think teachers are underpaid might hear this as a call for increasing funding for education. Those who hold the opposite view could as easily interpret the statement as meaning that education spending needs to be cut. The key word that increases ambiguity is "responsibility." The speaker or writer does not say what cause he or she favors. Another ambiguous word is "astronomical," as in

"The budgetary implications of the war in Iraq are astronomical." Does this mean millions or billions or hundreds of billions of dollars? Depending on one's position, several meanings might result.

Another way to create strategic ambiguity is to use phrases like "noted authorities on the subject seem to concur that...," which appear to lend support and credibility to the persuader's point. Another way is to refer to several topics at once and imply that they are parallel or equivalent. "Truth" and "justice" are examples. The persuader might say that his program will provide justice for all because it is based on truth when, in fact, injustice can flow from truth as well as false thinking. Of course the most fertile field for the use of persuasive ambiguity is advertising. This is especially so because most ads include both words and pictures and can thus imply multiple meanings through each or both of these media. The simplist use of ad ambiguity is the testimonial. We see a picture of a celebrity—say a professional athlete wearing a certain brand of athletic shoe, and we are supposed to conclude that the shoe made the athlete's success. Why aren't there any ads showing the celebrity and a certain brand other of sports equipment—shoulder pads, hockey stick, athletic supporter? Obviously, there is a much smaller general audience for shoulder pads than for athletic shoes, and there are fewer obvious differences between brands. Communication scholar E. M. Eisenberg (1984) held that strategic uses of ambiguity can also help get agreement on things like mission statements and at the same time allow individuals to interpret the statements as the persuader hopes.

In some cultures ambiguity is considered offensive. There, listeners want to "cut to the chase" and stop wasting time. Persuadees in other cultures (such as Japan) value talking around the point and establishing a relationship before talking business. Still others want to mull things over and look at the issue from several perspectives.

Persuaders also create ambiguity when they juxtapose or combine words, phrases, and or visuals in startling ways that present issues in a new light. For example, the term "born again" is persuasive to many people. It suggests that the person's earlier religious beliefs were weak, and that their conversion

caused the person to be spiritually re-created. Some born again politicians labeled themselves the "Moral Majority," thus creating persuasive intentional ambiguity. The term was ambiguous because the group wasn't a majority but a minority, yet it had great persuasive appeal as media preachers created what political researchers Dan Nimmo and James Combs (1984) called "the Electronic Church." Another highly ambiguous term is "Moral Decay." It reminds us of "tooth decay," which nobody likes. In the area of advertising, visual and verbal juxtapositions can create ambiguious meanings that permit receivers to co-create and achieve persuader goals in both efficacious and efficient ways, thus demonstrating another face of our 24/7, media-saturated world.

How can we defend ourselves against ambiguous persuasion, both visual and verbal? Paul Messaris (1997), communication researcher, scholar, and director of the Visual Communication Laboratory at the Annenberg School of Communication at the University of Pennsylvania has some advice. First, he advises recognizing that the visual image is meant to be a print for a previously real physical image and that there are connections between the two—real and co-created. In this case the original was the presence of two face cards—the queen of diamonds and the jack of spades. Prior to the image we see in the magazine, they were real, separate, and without character—simple face cards in a simple deck on the playing table. But the new image transforms them as Messaris says will happen. The new image gives them life that excites the viewer. They become man and woman, seducer and seduced, lovers-to-be sometime in the future—in a new image we cannot see. The transformation happens in one place only—the Paris Casino in Las Vegas where similar transformations await us all. That's the visual persuasion that we experience as we turn the page. In the twinkling of an eye, sex rules the day there. "Most people do not actively seek out exposure to advertising" (Messaris, p. 5), so unless something is done, we quickly slip past ads like Paris and the Queen and Jack liaison. As a result, advertisers must continually find new ways to attract and hold, however briefly, our attention, and that is what the Paris ad does. Messaris points out that "... one of the surest ways of attracting the viewer's

---

B O X 6.2   Semantics, Propaganda, and Diversity

Go to www.anxietyculture.com/propagan.htm. There you will find a detailed discussion loaded with examples and explanations of how language is used as a tactic for producing three kinds of propaganda: Hypnotic Propaganda, Semantic Propaganda, and Cognitive Propaganda. Hypnotic propaganda attempts to mesmerize the audience by avoiding any highly emotional terms or words so that the reader or listener must add his/her own interpretation—an interpretation that has been carefully pre-programmed by their culture. Semantic

Propaganda relies on deletions, generalizations and distortions in order to make the audience believe the map is the territory. Cognitive Propaganda relies on language that leads to highly emotional reactions such as fear, hate, anger, and so on, some of which appeals in far different ways to diverse cultures. Additionally, the article discusses propagandistic language strategies for each type. If you are required to write a paper in this class, here is an excellent place to start including excellent examples, clear organization, and commonsense discussion of the propaganda topic as well as related references.

---

attention is to violate reality" (p. 5), which is precisely what the Paris ad does with the addition of the seduction theme.

We could devote an entire chapter to visual persuasion and indeed many of the examples and discussions throughout this book call your attention to the impact of visual images, but suffice it to say that truly critical receivers don't just "flip the page" when encountering persuasion of any kind; instead, they remember that we live in an advocacy/propaganda riddled world that is filled with persuasive deceptions that are results oriented, ethics be damned, ubiquitous, and always present. Instead of being oblivious to this kind of persuasion we need to take that second look and try to mind read the persuader's purposes and tactics. They are trying to guide us into a world of strategic ambiguity as Burke calls it. The semanticists advise using increasing specificity about and concrete elaborations on any ambiguous terms by using extensional devices to clarify meaning. Semioticians go further and advise us to seek meanings in persuasive "texts" by digging into various verbal and nonverbal "codes" and signifiers in the text. Doing this helps determine the real thing being "signified," not the reality being violated. Keep in mind that it is your response–ability that will protect yourself from the unethical persuader in our 24/7 media-saturated world.

Make no mistake about it, advertisers will use semiotics, reality violation, semantic trickery, and

any other strategy to devise global marketing and advertising strategies (Domzal & Kernan, 1993) and we need to discover and then continually apply tools of analysis to the persuasion we encounter. For example, examining the denotations and connotations of persuasive symbols also helps us study the semantic dimension of language. Other tools address the semantic dimension of language. Among the more useful tools addressing the semantic dimension of language is the dramatistic approach suggested by Kenneth Burke which we will now explore. Note how it helps reveal things about propaganda as shown in Box 6.2.

Burke's Dramatism.   In addition to his ideas on language discussed in Chapters 1 and 5, Burke offered students of persuasion a theory and a tool for analyzing the semantic dimension of language. He called his theory **dramatism**, and his tool of analysis the **pentad**. Dramatism maintains that the basic model used by humans to explain various situations is the narrative story or drama. Burke (1960) thought of the drama as "a philosophy of language" capable of describing and analyzing a wide variety of human symbolic acts such as language use. He focused on the differences between action (which is motivated) and motion (which is not motivated). Basic bodily functions, such as sweating or digestion, are unmotivated nonsymbolic acts. Action requires motivation, and the ability to use language

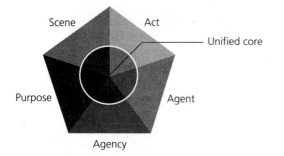

FIGURE 6.2 The five elements of dramatism ultimately affect one another, and each emerges from a common unified core—the drama itself.

symbolically is surely such a motivated act. We bring the action into being, and language use is the tools we use, thus a kind of symbolic action—it is motivated. Burke believed that we choose words because of their dramatic potential and that different individuals find certain elements in the drama more potent than others do though all terms begin and terminate from the same source as seen in Figure 6.2. Those who favor epic dramas differ from those who favor psychological ones. Burke's model, the dramatistic pentad, as its name implies, has five central elements which one might favor and which work together in balance or imbalance to give life to the drama: scene, act, agent, agency, and purpose (see Figure 6.2).

Scene includes physical location, the situation, time in history or time in life, social place, occasion, and other elements. The scene could be something like "Campaign 2008," "the Oval Office," a Web site, NYC on the day the terrorists killed 3,000, or "The Oprah Winfrey Show." Any of them can be ripe scenes for a drama. Scenically oriented persons feel the scene should be a "fit container" for the action, or that heroic actions occur in heroic settings and vice versa. That's why foul deeds in film are usually conducted in dark and sinister settings with proper music accompaniment. Scenic persons also believe that changes in the scene will cause other changes—if the scene for assassination of a powerful Muslim political leader is a Holy Mosque, the mean-

ing of the act will be far different than if it were done on a military base or in an open-air market. Time, as an element in the scene, would also be important—if it were time for the twice daily prayers to Mecca for example versus a state banquet or a wedding. If the scene was "family" they would be unlikely to approve of nonfamily characters in that scene—witness, for example, reactions to Brittany Spears arriving late and perhaps intoxicated or under the influence of drugs when the scene was a hearing for her getting custody of her children. The Clinton-Lewinsky sex scandal was distasteful less because it happened but more because the Oval Office of the White House was the container for the act. That's where Ms. Lewinsky and the then President performed oral sex—certainly not a fitting scene for sexual dalliance. The Lincoln Memorial was a "fit" scene for Martin Luther King's historic, "I Have a Dream" speech. The setting helped make the speech memorable. And the scene of Barack Obama's unexpected win in the Iowa caucuses (a rural, Midwestern, almost 100 percent white, farm state) made the victory of an urban, Black, Chicago, lawmaker all the more dramatic and exciting for his supporters and surprising for the rest of the audience.

Act refers to any motivated or purposeful action that occurs within the scene. How likely or dramatic is the movement of the Queen of Diamonds to the side of the Jack of Spades on a gaming table? In persuasive messages, the verb is the best indicator of the act. After all, verbs are defined as words that describe acts or actions, so looking at the verb is the best place to start applying the term act to your analysis. The words and actions taken by a person, and their appropriateness for the scene, ultimately affect outcomes. This kind of balance/imbalance between Act and Scene happens in all kinds of persuasive contexts—advertisements, films, speeches or sermons, public documents, news stories, and so on, and again they affect our interpretation of the actions. Why, for instance, did the 9/11 terrorists pick the twin trade towers in New York and the Pentagon in Washington, DC to use as targets for their acts? Why use passenger airplanes? What if they had picked the Sears Tower in Chicago and the Denver Mint? What if they had used tourist buses as the vehicles to carry the bombs? How would the "persuasion" of their action have been different? So the Act must "fit" the scene, and if it doesn't, the meaning of the act shifts.

Agent is Burke's term for the person or group of persons who take action in the scene, and again the balance or imbalance between them and the Acts they perform and the Scenes in which they perform them affects their persuasive meanings. If the assassination at the Mosque is done by a street beggar, its meaning is far different than if the assassin had been a rival member of the leader's own party. What if the NBA official who was caught gambling on games he officiated had been Black instead of white? What if he had a family with mob connections? How would the meaning of his action have changed? Agents are the actors or characters who make things happen (the police officer, the corrupt politician, the terrorist, Brittany Spears, etc.), and they too must "fit" or be in balance with the action and the scene for a certain persuasive message to result. If not, a very different interpretation will emerge and the results will be altered dramatically.

Such balanced or unbalanced matches of Agents with Acts and Scenes occur frequently in advertisements as well. For example, examine Figure 6.3. You will see that there is a clear focus on the Agent and nearly every other element in the Pentad is missing. But why include the bottle of Secret Obsession on which she is carefully balanced? It is clearly the Agency through which she can express herself to others using at least the sense of smell that will be processed by others in their peripheral channel and thus passed by almost unconsciously, but with enhanced effect of her attractiveness. In this sense (using Burke's terms), it is a balanced Agent–Agency ratio. And remember that all sorts of factors such as hatred, instinct, greed, or jealousy sometimes motivate agents and these too can alter meanings. Countries and organizations (e.g., UN peacekeeping forces, the NRA, Al Quaeda, or pro-choice groups) can also act as Agents and can alter meaning. If the 9/11 attacks had been perpetrated by militia organizations within the USA, there would not be war on terror but on militarist groups. After all, that's what occurred following the attack on the McMurrah Federal Building in Oklahoma City a few years prior to the 9/11 tragedies—it killed almost

FIGURE 6.3 This ad for Calvin Klein's Secret Obsession clearly focuses on the Agent and her obsession with the brand or the Agency in getting others to notice her via the peripheral sense of smell.

SOURCE: Image Courtesy of The Advertising Archives.

a thousand innocent persons and the deed was done with a bomb (though it should be noted that officials began looking for persons of Middle Eastern abstraction immediately following that attack—why?). Agent-oriented persuaders believe that strong, honest, committed, and well-intended individuals determine the outcome of important events and even of history as was the case of the fourth airliner that was taken over by the passengers and crew. What would have been the interpretation if they had failed and the hijackers had hit the White House or the Congress? On the other hand, Agent-oriented persons believe that unthinking, deceitful, or dishonest agents cause bad outcomes. Was NFL star quarterback Michael Vick simply no good and that's why he loved dog fighting and gambling?

And was that sufficient to imprison him and dismiss him from play, thus ruining his star-potential career which was worth millions to him? If he hadn't been a celebrity would he have received the same punishment? How different was his acts from the several CEOs who lied and cheated regarding the financial health of their companies in order to line their own pockets? After all, their actions bankrupted their companies, their companies' retirement plans, and the retirement future of thousands of employees. Again, the elements of the pentad must fit or the meaning is altered.

Agency is the tool, method, or means used by persuaders to accomplish their ends. Some auto companies now focus on development of the fuel cell and hydrogen energy as the agencies to solve our dependence on fossil fuels. In Shakespeare's *Hamlet*, the Prince uses the play within a play as the Agency to establish his uncle's guilt. Calvin Klein uses nudity and prepubescent females as agencies to draw attention to Obsession "Night for Men" cologne. Wheaties uses pictures of famous athletes on its packages to promote the brand as "the Breakfast of Champions." Communication strategies can also act as agencies (such as intensifying one's own good points or others' bad ones or a politician focusing on his or her humble beginnings). Certain diplomatic agencies like boycotts or walking out of a conference or sanctioning a country can act as agencies and can result in historical outcomes such as war. There is some reason to believe that the sanctioning of Japan prior to WW II was one cause of the attack on Pearl Harbor, for example. Recently some groups have proposed boycotting gasoline from companies that import oil from countries that gouge the United States (e.g., Shell, Exxon, Amoco) or that oppose us like certain countries in the Middle East and to favor companies that purchase their oil from South American countries (e.g., Marathon, Conoco, Sinclair). The boycott was proposed using an e-mail chain letter format to spread the word. The chain letter and the boycott were both agencies used to promote the supposed purpose of the action which was to reduce gas prices.

Purpose is the reason an agent acts in a given scene using a particular agency. The persuader's true purpose can be more or less apparent in the persuasion. The U.S. Army's old persuasive and successful recruiting slogan, "Be All That You Can Be," suggested that the purpose for enlisting was improving your skills to maximize your potential, a likely reason for volunteering in the post-draft era. Its later slogan, "Join the Army of One," suggests a different purpose for enlisting—make an individual difference and develop your skills. More recently it advertises "Army. Army Strong," which seems to involve the Agent-Purpose pairing of terms of the pentad wherein the Agent joins to become strong as the Purpose. When the amount of aid sent by the Bush administration to victims of a disastrous Indonesian tsunami was low compared to that sent by much smaller countries, critics in this country and abroad interpreted the action as meaning that the administration was less interested in helping others than in saving money. The administration was embarrassed by the criticism and later upped its donation—the Purpose of the criticism. What is the purpose in promoting the use of Botox and Lasik eye surgery? What was the purpose in 2008 in centering the themes of almost every candidate for nomination on the key term "change" regardless of which party they were in? What is your purpose in choosing Facebook over MySpace? Why engage in blogging? Why purchase an SUV? All of these decisions involve the Agent-Purpose pair of terms from the pentad.

These five elements can also help develop a persuasive strategy in various interpersonal relationships. For example, suppose you were trying to get a friend to accompany you and others on a wilderness canoe trip. Your friend is a total amateur at canoeing and so is understandably somewhat reluctant about going, especially so far from civilization. You might emphasize the Scenes that your friend will see—the undisturbed nature and its environment, the vastness of the undisturbed and uninhabited wilderness lakes and streams, the thrills of going through rapids, or the quietness of the trip across satin smooth lakes at sunrise.

An alternative strategy would be to focus on the Act, describing the kinds of terrain you will be crossing on portages, the interactions between other canoeists around the campfire in the evening or the fun of stipping for an afternoon swim and diving off huge rock outcrops or boulders into crystal clear waters.

You might choose to focus on the Agents who will accompany you on the trip—describing the musicians with their harmonicas and guitars singing an endless repertoire of hilarious songs and telling uproarious jokes and stories. If you chose to feature Agency, you might mention the new ultra-light Kevlar canoes that slide through the waters like a smooth sleek creature, that can be portaged with minimal effort, and that afford you the chance to cast lures into previously never fished ideal spots for huge bass.

Finally, you could feature Purpose by telling your friend how in 10 short days they will develop marvelous new skills, muscles, and stamina. Or you might focus on the memories and stories of the trip that will remain in your friend's mind—the meals more delicious in the wild than they cold ever be back home, the immensity of the nighttime sky and its stars and borealis, the thrills of near accidents, the big fish that got away, and the multitude of wildlife that visited your campsites and beachfronts.

Burke compared them in pairs, or "ratios," to identify a persuader's "key" term. For example, the Scene can be compared with each of the other terms one at a time, and we can determine which term seems most important or favored by the persuader through a process of elimination. For instance, if Scene supersedes Act, Agent, and Agency but not Purpose, we can then infer that Purpose is a good candidate for the persuader's probable key term. But then Purpose must be compared to Act, Agent, and Agency to see if it supersedes those terms of the pentad. The end result of this process of residues will most likely focus in on the persuader's key term and will help to predict future persuasion coming from them, thus preparing you as a receiver to critically receive their messages.

There are ten possible such ratios or pairs of terms. In *Hamlet*, for example, the dramatic tension

created in the Scene-Act ratio comes from the fact that Hamlet's mother has married his uncle (the Act) during the period of mourning (part of the Scene) for Hamlet's father, the king, who has died mysteriously. His uncle inherits the throne and marries Hamlet's mother less than one month after the funeral (also part of the Scene). Clearly the Scene was tainted by the Act. In fact, to the young Prince it might seem as if were almost orchestrated by his mother and uncle/stepfather. Disturbed by this imbalance, Hamlet curses his mother, and says to his friend Horatio, "She married. O, most wicked speed, to post with such dexterity to incestuous sheets!" He seems to consider her Act as being motivated by an illicit Purpose—to commit adultery with her brother-in-law. Later, Hamlet asks Horatio whether he came to court for the funeral or the wedding, and expresses his anger and perhaps his suspicions in these bitter words: "Thrift, thrift, Horatio! The funeral baked meats did coldly furnish the marriage tables."

We also frequently see the persuasive power of the Scene-Act ratio in advertisements. Scene can also interact with the other elements of the pentad. In the Scene-Agent ratio, balance or imbalance again can indicate potent persuasion or high drama—comedy, tragedy, or melodrama. In Hitchcock's classic film, *Psycho*, viewers see a Scene-Agent imbalance when Anthony Perkins tells Janet Leigh that he has "stuffed" all the animal specimens in the motel office. Then we see him spy on her through a secret peephole in the eye of one of the specimens. This is not the behavior of a normal motel owner. It makes the audience uneasy. This uneasiness implies the strong possibility of danger. The tension caused by the scene-agent imbalance is increased when we hear Perkins and his "mother" (whom he also "stuffed") arguing at the Victorian house near the motel (see Figure 6.4). We want to warn Leigh to go to another motel or at least to "lock the bathroom door." Hitchcock uses Scene-Agent tension throughout the rest of the film to keeps the audience on the edge of their seats. It usually arises because we, the audience, infer the imbalance between the Scene (a run down motel) and the Act that is going to happen—murder by a "mummy" Mommy.

FIGURE 6.4 The imbalance in the Scene-Act ratio in Hitchcock's film classic, *Psycho*, heightens dramatic tension.
SOURCE: Used with permission of Doug Walker.

Any of the other ten possible pairs of elements of the pentad (Act-Purpose, Act-Agency, Scene-Purpose, Scene-Agency, and so forth) might be examined to discover a persuader's key term or element. Burke believed that a persuader's key term infuses every aspect of life—home, family, job, political choices, and philosophy of life. Identifying a persuader's key terms or elements alerts us to the motives of and reasons for the persuasion and helps us predict future persuasive appeals. As you encounter persuasion, try to listen for the key term being used.

Tools for the Thematic Dimension

We've seen that the thematic dimension of language is that quality in certain words or sets of words that gives them a texture or "feel." While the words do have a variety of semantic meanings and syntactical functions, their most important persuasive aspect is their ability to set a mood, a feeling, or a tone or theme for the persuasion. For example, Abraham Lincoln set the theme for his famous Gettysburg Address with these words: "Fourscore and seven years ago our forefathers brought forth on this continent a new nation, conceived in liberty and dedicated to the proposition that all men are created equal." How far less stirring the speech would have been if he had said, "Eighty-seven years ago the signers of the Declaration of Independence started a new country designed to assure us of freedom and equality." The two sentences have equivalent semantic and functional meanings, but the obvious difference between them lies in their texture. We also noted how the repetition of consonants (alliteration) or vowels (assonance) carries thematic meaning. The advertisements for Satin cigarettes, for

example, used alliteration to create a thematic meaning for the brand—"Smooth. Silky. Satin. Cigarettes." Or consider the slogan for Lexus: "The Relentless Pursuit of Perfection." It sounds unstoppable.

Sometimes parallel sentence structure communicates a thematic meaning. For example, consider the no-nonsense theme in the parallel sentences in an ad promoting MTV to advertisers. The copy accompanies a picture of a male in his twenties in an easy chair holding a TV remote, and reads,

> If this guy doesn't know about you, you're toast. He's an opinion leader. He watches MTV. Which means he knows a lot more than just what CDs to buy and what movies to see. He knows what clothes to wear, and what credit card to buy them with. And he's no loner. He heads up a pack. What he eats, his friends eat. What he wears, they wear. What he likes, they like. And what's he never heard of … well … you get the idea. MTV. A darn good way to influence the MTV Generation (*Advertising Age*, 1993, p. S-3).

Thematic meaning also can come from the use of metaphors or onomatopoeia which we covered earlier in Chapter 5. Let's turn now to several other tools for discovering the thematic meaning in persuasive messages including finding metaphorical themes; noting the use of **sensory language**; looking for god, devil, and charismatic terms; identifying the pragmatic and unifying styles; and use of semiotics to determine the thematic meanings of nonverbal symbols or "signifiers."

Metaphorical Style. Persuaders set the mood for persuadees by repeatedly using certain sounds, figures of speech, and images. Recent research on the effects of metaphors shows that using them increases the credibility of the persuader because they make the persuader seem more dynamic and interesting. This is especially so when the source uses only a single metaphor instead of multiple ones (Sopory & Dillard, 2002). Dan Hahn (1998) applies another archetypal metaphor—that of water as a dangerous image. Notice the positivism and the negativity of the underlined water images:

> Due to *foggy thinking* the tide has been *running against freedom* and we are *sinking* in a *swampland of collectivism*. Therefore, despite the detractors who say *don't rock the boat*, the campaign we launch here will *set the tide running* again in the cause of freedom. The *past will be submerged*, and we will travel *democracy's ocean highway* where freedom will accompany *the rising tide of prosperity* (p. 115).

Hahn reminds us of other associations we have with the water metaphor. It is life giving and is also the basic element from which life emerged (p. 115). Other archetypal metaphors include references to wind and windstorms, blood and blood bonds, the locomotive as representative of the economy, and the boxing ring or the horse race as stand-ins for any of life's contests and struggles. Roads and maps also serve as metaphors for planning (e.g., "the roadmap to peace" in the Middle East). Metaphors also help in **framing** the issue or topic to give the audience a way of seeing things. For example, imagine a persuader trying to inform the audience about the AIDS crisis in Africa, where grandparents are now raising most children due to the premature deaths of the parents. A good metaphor might be warfare, with the persuader saying, "We're in the early stages of the battle here with the veterans of past battles having to fight to the bitter end. It's not going to end with a single decisive weapon." The audience sees the fight against the disease is likely to be a long one with no real miracle cures. We will look at some tools for the analysis of metaphors a bit further on. Suffice it to say, they can do a lot of the persuasive work in advertising, politics, interpersonal relations and elsewhere.

Sensory Language. Courtroom communication expert Stephanie L. Swanson (1981) maintained that most effective lawyers rely on words relating to one or more of the five senses: sight, sound, touch, smell, and taste. She speculated that jurors respond to the particular sensory information channel they prefer. How could a persuader use these preferences? Suppose an attorney asks three witnesses to describe an automobile accident. The witness preferring the auditory channel might say something like, "I was walking down Oak Street, when I heard the screech of brakes, and then a sickening sound of crashing glass and metal, and someone screamed." The witness who prefers the visual channel might say, "I saw this blue Beamer coming around the corner practically on two wheels. Then he hit the brakes, and it looked like the car slid sideways toward me. Then I saw his front end make a mess of the little GEO." The witness who prefers the kinesthetic channel might say, "I had this feeling that something was about to happen, and when it did I felt frightened and helpless, and I cringed as the cars crumpled up like scrap paper." Swanson advised attorneys to "listen closely to the sensory language used by your clients ... try to respond in kind—matching the sensory language of the other person" (p. 211). She suggested attending to the kinds of words used by individuals during the juror selection process—then "tailor your language to your listeners' primary sensory channel. You can 'paint a picture' for a visual person, 'orchestrate the testimony' for an auditory person, and 'touch the heart' of the kinesthetic individual. Using sensory language lets the jurors feel that your discourse is directed toward them individually" (p. 211). The use of sensory language acts like an interactive medium, and it increases the likelihood for the co-creation of meaning. Thus, in trying to identify a persuader's use of the thematic dimension of language, explore the sensory language used in the persuasion.

God, Devil, and Charismatic Terms. Another thematic or textural element of style in persuasion is the development of families of terms. Persuaders like to divide the world into tidy categories that prompt co-created meanings. Richard Weaver (1953) held that one of these category sets is made up of **god terms** and **devil terms.** These terms can be seen in action in Figure 6.5. Although terms or labels make up only parts of propositions, they often link with other terms or labels to shape a message or a

FIGURE 6.5   It is clear that giving parking tickets is a god term for the evil queen, but getting a parking ticket from any of her helper dwarfs is a devil term for her.

SOURCE: Used with permission of Al Ochsner.

persuasive argument. Weaver defined a god term as an expression "about which all other expressions are ranked as subordinate and serving dominations and powers … its force imparts to the others their lesser degree of force" (p. 211). Persuaders repeatedly refer to such terms and even fashion their **visual persuasion** in accord with the god term. Weaver saw a god term as an unchallenged word (or phrase) demanding sacrifice or obedience. He used three terms as examples of god terms: "progress," "fact," and "science." Progress still persuades, but is hampered by negative associations—pollution, for example. Science lost some of its credibility in recent times also, due to negative associations such as nuclear power or genetic engineering. Change was such a god term in the Campaign of 2008 and was usually in the largest font on signs, direct mail appeals, or background materials at televised news conferences, and others.

Devil terms are just the opposite. They are "terms of repulsion" and express negative values. As Weaver put it, "They generate a peculiar force of repudiation" (pp. 210–215). Today's god and devil terms include the *environment, green, the family, security, terrorism, deficit spending, politically correct, technology, change, ditto-heads, surfing the Web, budget surplus, consumer debt, foreclosure, diversity*, and many others emerge daily. God and devil terms can vary in a diverse culture. For example, Western culture

places considerable value on the term "forgiveness," considering it the correct response when one is wronged. Middle Eastern cultures believe "forgiveness" is a devil term—the sissy's way out. For them, the god term when wronged is "revenge" as their history for thousands of years has shown and will probably continue to show. Such god and devil terms alert you to potential persuasive appeals aimed at you or that you might choose to use in your own persuasion.

As we move further into the new millennium, other god and devil terms are emerging. Some of the more recent god terms include *family/family values, low fat, rule of law, green vehicles, air security, financial security, education, phased retirement, weight loss, nutrition, fuel cell, hybrid car, bio-energy*, and *debt free*. Try to discover others as you search for the thematic dimensions of words or terms used in advertising or political and ideological statements.

Weaver said that the connotations of certain negative terms can sometimes be reversed, making the terms neutral or even positive. Take, for example, the expression "wasted" or "getting wasted." Its use during the 1970s referred to killing Viet Cong or others perceived to be the enemy. Later, it referred to getting drunk or "stoned." Today, "wasted" has recovered its original meaning of "squandered" and refers to such topics as the squandering of corporate trust, thrown away energy, and lost credibility among others; and the term is referred to in reference to current political and economic issues as in "Bush wasted his 'political capital' after the 2004 election." or "Arthur Anderson wasted its longtime credibility when it verified the corporate book keeping practices of Enron. As a result the firm went bankrupt." Or "The war in Iraq has wasted our grandchildren's inheritance."

Weaver described another kind of term which he called the charismatic term and defined as "terms of considerable potency whose referents it is virtually impossible to discover. Their meaning seems inexplicable unless we accept the hypothesis that their content proceeds out of a popular will that they shall mean something" (p. 48). His examples are the words "freedom" and "democracy," which have no apparent concrete referent but still seem to have great potency and serve as god terms for U.S. foreign policy. As noted earlier, the god term "Change" was powerful in the 2008 election and may well become a charismatic term for facing the future problems of global warming, the credit crisis, depletion of the productivity of our land and seas, the oil crisis, and others.

The terms "budget surplus" and "fanning the flames of freedom" became charismatic recently, and most agreed that a "budget surplus" was great after decades of "budget deficits" (a devil term). Initially nearly everyone agreed on the wisdom of "saving Social Security" but later the term lost its power. An older candidate for a charismatic term is "recycling." With the growing awareness of declining natural resources, the concept of recycling applied to a host of things, such as paper, plastic, aluminum, glass. "Patriot" and "patriotic" recently became **charismatic terms**, but they were devil terms during the Vietnam era.

Pragmatic and Unifying Styles.   Persuaders tend to rely on one of two persuasive styles—pragmatic or unifying. Pragmatic persuaders want to convince neutral or opposition listeners. They want to change minds instead of reinforcing existing beliefs. Politicians speaking at a news conference rather than at a rally of their supporters tend to favor the **pragmatic style**. Unifying persuaders use a different style because they want to motivate people who already believe what

they're going to say; they just reinforce beliefs to whip up enthusiasm, dedication, or encouragement. Thus, when Rush Limbaugh, Howard Stern, Bill O'Reilly, Chris Matthews, and others speak to their respective television and radio audiences, they use the tactics of the unifying speaker—their audiences already believe them. The problems for pragmatic persuaders are clear—they must change opinion before expecting action. **Unifying style** persuaders can be much more idealistic, emotional, and use less objective claims and data than the pragmatic persuader.

What stylistic devices typify these extremes? The unifying persuader can focus on the "then-and-there"—on the past or future—when things were ideal or when they might become ideal. Because the audience fills in the blanks, abstract language choice works well for unifying persuaders, and their language frequently is poetic, emotional, and filled with imagery that excites the imagination. Although there is little that is intellectually stimulating or requires logical examination, lots of emotional and stirring things emerge. The unifying persuader is a sounding board for the audience and provides them with the gist of the message but not the details. The audience participates with unifying persuaders in the co-creation of the message. In fact, audiences sometimes participate actively by yelling encouragement to unifying persuaders or by repeating phrases to underscore their words—"Right on." "Amen, brother." "Tell it like it is." "Hill—oh—ree!" or "Huck—aaah—bee!"

Pragmatic persuaders, because they need to win the audience, avoid appealing to abstract ideals or emotions. They use concrete words, and focus on facts instead of undisputed images and issues. They avoid depicting an ideal situation in "then-and-there" terms. Rather, they focus on real aspects of immediate problems of the "here-and-now"—things that seem realistic, pressing, and not idealistic. Pragmatic persuaders orient their message to the present instead of the future, and tend to focus on facts, problems, solutions, and statistics instead of imagery about an idealistic future or past. Their messages pass through the central information-processing route of the ELM instead of the peripheral route, as is the case for unifying persuasion. Consider these words of a pragmatic persuader describing his feelings about a fairly emotional but realistic hobby—skydiving:

> When I stand in the door of an airplane in flight, I alone am responsible for the decision to jump. If the winds, clouds or any other conditions are unfavorable, I have the option of riding down in the plane—something I have done on several occasions. Neither the pilot nor the drop zone operator forces me to jump if I choose not to. Once a skydiver exits the plane there's no going back. One person and one person only has the responsibility of deploying the parachute ... and executing a safe landing.... Skydiving is not a preprogrammed carnival thrill ride with simulated risk.... While the trend in American society is to find someone else to blame for your own mistakes; that is not the way it is in skydiving. To suggest otherwise indicates total misunderstanding of the sport on the part of your reporters (Kallend, 2002, p. 8).

The language is concrete and prosaic, the references are here and now, and the persuader is trying to change the audiences' mind instead of uniting them. The pragmatic and unifying styles depend on the needs of the audience and the demands of the occasion, not on the needs of the speaker.

TOOLS FOR
ANALYZING METAPHORS

We have mentioned the power of the metaphor several times already and have briefly explained how they work in a variety of stages in the persuasive process—attracting attention, providing emotional arguments, retaining messages and prompting action to mention a few. Let us now explore a few ways the average receiver can analyze and process them. Recall that a metaphor is like a sentence in which a familiar thing, emotion, experience, and so on, is made clear by comparing it to a less familiar thing, emotion, experience, and so on. A simple example would be "the wings of time" in which

time (unfamiliar) flies by as if on "wings." Our early example compared being overly wealthy to drowning as in "Paris Hilton's problem was that she was drowning in money and that's why she couldn't get enough of anything for all her trying." It was as though she was trapped by riches and tried to spend her way out of the trap, hoping to be disciplined. Interestingly, her billionaire father solved this problem for both Paris and her sister by writing his will so that they each got "only" $5 million on his death with the rest going to charity. In this case "too much money" was the tenor of the metaphor or the thing to be clarified and "drowning" was the "vehicle" or the unlike thing that was meant to clarify the tenor.

So the first thing receivers should do when analyzing the metaphors used in any persuasive message is to identify the tenor and the vehicle, and then ask oneself if they are appropriate—do they work together in any meaningful and persuasive ways? The slightly different metaphor "the wings of space" is far less meaningful than "the wings of time" since space doesn't disappear so fast or unnoticed as does time. Some might argue that space does disappear almost instantaneously when it is traversed electronically and thus "the wings of space" do make sense. But to the average persuadee, they would only make that kind of sense when accompanied by some sort of explanation of electronic message travel that precedes or followed the near-flawed new metaphor.

Recall that we also mentioned "mapping" of metaphors back in Chapter 5. The next step in analyzing metaphors in persuasion is to identify as many ways that the vehicle "maps" back to the tenor. Aside from the electronic space travel mentioned above, the metaphor "the wings of time" make little sense—and even then some explanation of the metaphor would probably be needed, so there is but a single mapping that is plausible, and that one is weak. But for "the wings of time" there are several mappings such as the way time in our lives seems to fly by; time spent at the computer seems to evaporate; the time of history zips past and people say "it seems like just yesterday that they blew up the twin towers," "I don't know where time goes to," and "time is fleeting." So there are several "maps" proving the

---

B O X 6.3   Visual Metaphors, Movies, and Music for FREE!

 In researching visual metaphors I found the following site for visual metaphors in photography, graphics, and many other media. Its address is http://knowgramming. com. There I also ran across a bargain spot for downloading current movies and music for FREE. It is www.dvxcrawler.com/now. A one-time $12 membership charge is assessed. The same site also has links to many other metaphoric related sites. Try it; you'll like it.

---

credibility of the metaphor and its resonance with most persons.

Another tool for the analysis of metaphors and their persuasiveness is the Metaphor Checker (www. knowgramming.com/metaphor_checker). It posits that you can ask three essential questions of a particular figure of speech thought to be a metaphor and holds that if the three questions can all be answered in the affirmative, then you have a metaphor. Positive answers also give a strong indication of the power of the metaphor. The three questions are:

1. Is the statement figurative instead of literal? For example, the statement "Love is a flower" is clearly figurative since love is not a flower versus the statement "Love is a feeling," which is literal, so it is not a metaphor.

2. Is it an equation? Are its two parts being made equal? Again take the statements "Love is a flower" and "Love is a feeling." In this case the answers are yes for both statements, but "Love is a feeling" did not get an affirmative for question 1, so it is not a metaphor.

3. Can it be expanded figuratively? In the two statements again, "Love is a flower" can be expanded—love is a red, red rose; love is a fragrant bloom; love is a fast fading blossom; and so on. All are figurative expansions of the original. In the case of "Love is a feeling" any expansion will be literal, not figurative such as "love is an emotion" or "love is a physical response."

In addition metaphors, unlike similes, imply an exact similarity not an approximate one and as a result similes always have the words "like" or "as" in them (e.g., "My love is like a red, red rose" or "My vacation was as short as a dream" as opposed to "My vacation was a dream"). Finally, metaphors are not idiomatic or untranslatable (e.g., "Nuts!" or "Nuts to you!" are untranslatable). In fact, the German Army High Command could not comprehend General McAuliffe's response of "Nuts!" or interpret it as a highly negative response to their demand that he surrender his army during the Battle of the Bulge in WW II).

Metaphors can also be visual (Larson, 1982). In a way, the ad for Paris casino is a powerful metaphor that says "Paris is Seductive." The same is true of many other advertisements, television programs, music, and movies. Identify the tenor and vehicles in them, and you're on your way! This is especially true with interactive media as seen in Box 6.3.

Metaphors can function in other ways as well. For example, following the 9/11/01 attacks (Zhang, 2007), President Bush's use of metaphor included such images as an "Axis of Evil," "Second Front," and "Old Europe"—all meant to foreshadow his dominating metaphor "War on Terror." He continued to prop up his war metaphor in his April 2004 news conference—only the third prime time one held since his inauguration. His approval rating had sunk from 71 percent to 49 percent by that time (though it would ultimately drop to 28 percent) and repair was needed (Benoit, 2006). He used similar war metaphors but no apologies. He might have done this since metaphors for apologies (another of their functions) are readily available (e.g., "I really blew it," "I'm groveling before you," "Now I owe you," "I wish I'd paid more attention," "If I had it to do all over again"). Metaphors are also available for the function of taking credit (e.g., "You owe me on his one," "It was nothing…" "You don't need to repay me for that—it was nothing," "I've brought you this far"). And metaphors exist for practically any issue or event—in fact enter the word "metaphor" and any issue or event into a search engine, and you'll find lots of examples.

We briefly discussed archetypal metaphors in Chapter 5, recognizing that they were cross-cultural, not time bound, easy to relate to, and widely applicable. Our example there was Osborn's discussion of the "light/dark" family of metaphors as they occurred in a speech by Winston Churchill. We also used the planting and harvest archetypal family to craft a pretty effective campaign message. Other archetypal families include the bound/free metaphor, water (as we also in Chapter 5), the spreading, consuming, or epidemic metaphor (e.g., disease or trouble such as cancer metaphors, fire metaphors), and the predator metaphor (e.g., the corporate shark, devouring the marketplace).

SEMIOTICS, SIGNIFIERS, SUBTEXTS, CODES AND DECONSTRUCTION

We referred to the field of **semiotics** earlier as a way to study meaning. Its most important contemporary theorist is Umberto Eco. He proposed that the process of "signification" (or the giving of meaning to a "sign") has four elements: (1) the objects or conditions that exist in the world (e.g., a busy intersection); (2) the signs available to represent these objects or conditions (e.g., a traffic light and warning sign stating "Warning—Busy Traffic Ahead"); (3) the set of choices among signs, or the repertoire of responses available for use (e.g., one can choose to obey the green and red traffic lights, to disobey them or to proceed on yellow keeping the warning sign in mind); and (4) the set of rules of correspondence that we use to encode and decode the signs we make and interpret when we communicate (e.g., almost every driver—there are some dunderheads—understands warning signs and the meaning of the three colored lights in a traffic light).

This final characteristic most directly relates to the goal of this course—the discovery of the various **codes** or sets of rules used by persuaders and understood by persuadees in the process of co-creation. We know that when a stage manager lowers the lights and asks us to turn off our cell phones and pagers, and to unwrap our candies, then the event is about to begin; this is an example of a code. We participate in our own persuasion by "agreeing with" the code(s) the persuaders use. We become critical consumers of persuasion by continually striving to uncover and reveal these codes and then to evaluate them (Eco, 1979). For example, do I need to unwrap opened lemon drops when they are in a metal box in my shirt pocket? Can I just put my cell phone on vibrate so I know when an important call comes in?

We find more subtle examples of codes in some advertisements. For example, consider the ad for Bostonian shoes in Figure 6.6. What codes operate in this ad? Some seem obvious, but others are more subtle. In fact, some codes found in the ad embed themselves within other codes. The most obvious code is that the ad tries to sell the product, although the kind of product is not so clear. But after some consideration, we discover that the product is men's shoes. Another less obvious code is that the product is an upscale one, as indicated by the composition and copy of the ad and the price of the shoes—$105. The ad is understated, with little actual ad copy. Finally, the illustration is distinctively "fine art" in its composition. Within these codes, we find a more subtle code that is only implied and never directly stated. This code signifies the lifestyle that goes with the product. The shoes merely serve as an emblem of that lifestyle. What do we see in this photograph? Clearly, it is the "morning after" a satisfying night of lovemaking—perhaps in a fine hotel (notice the coffee cups and pastries on the bed, the negligee on the well-rumpled bedding, the indentations on both pillows). The lifestyle includes a fine home (notice the expensive furniture and the framed photographs on the nightstand in the upper left corner). This lifestyle includes expensive accessories such as the Rolex watch and the Mont Blanc pen on the dresser. The stylish suspenders, the theater ticket stubs

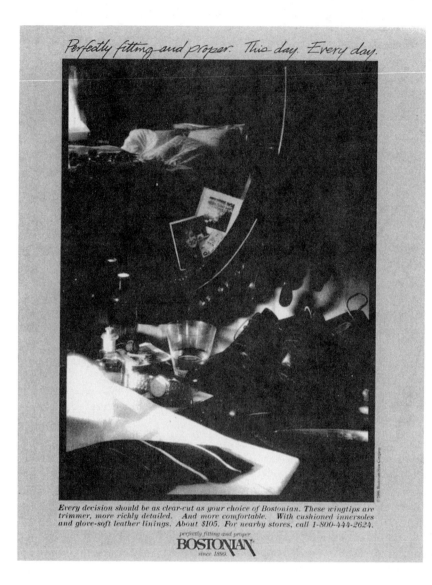

Perfectly fitting and proper. This day. Every day.

Every decision should be as clear-cut as your choice of Bostonian. These wingtips are trimmer, more richly detailed. And more comfortable. With cushioned innersoles and glove-soft leather linings. About $105. For nearby stores, call 1-800-444-2624.

perfectly fitting and proper

BOSTONIAN
since 1899.

FIGURE 6.6 What messages are implied by the "code" of physical objects in this ad (theater tickets, rumpled bedclothes, articles of clothing that seem to have been hurriedly discarded, an empty cocktail glass, etc.)?

SOURCE: Reprinted by permission of the Bostonian Shoe Company/Copyright Clarks.

slipped into the frame of the mirror, and the picture of a beautiful wife under the tickets signify a lifestyle that values the arts, stylishness, beauty, and physical attractiveness (note the snapshot of the man, bare-chested and muscular). Clearly, this ad carries a lot of meanings, "signified" by the verbal and nonverbal symbols being used (or perhaps misused). Its persuasive message must be decoded and then co-created based on agreed upon and shared semiotic codes. The signifiers, or collection of objects in the room, probably trigger emotional values that the audience holds dear. It is not propaganda, but borders on advocacy and is surely an example of our 24/7, media-saturated world, and the success depicted indicates that the wearer of Boston shoes is a winner in a results-oriented world.

B O X   6.4   Semiotics and the Culture of Circuses

Semiotician Paul Buissac (1976) offered some fascinating examples of codes in his semiotic analysis of circus acts, illustrating this idea of an easily discernible code understood by "children of all ages" around the world.

> Wild animal, tightrope, and trapeze acts never occur back-to-back in the circus ... they are always interspersed with clown acts, small animal acts, magic acts, or the like. If a daring act is canceled, the entire order of acts needs to be altered because of audience expectations, tension reduction, and the need to communicate that the world is alternately serious and comedic.... Death-defying acts also have a code—usually a five-step sequence. First, there is the introduction of the act by the ringmaster (a godlike figure able to control not only the dangers but the chaos of the circus). This introduction, with its music, lights, and revelation of dazzling and daring costumes, is followed by the "warm-up," in which minor qualifying tests occur: The animal trainer, dressed as a big-game hunter, gets all the animals to their proper positions; the trapeze artist, with his beautiful assistants, can easily swing out and switch trapeze bars in mid-air; the tightrope walker dances across the rope with ease. Then come the major tests or tricks: getting the tiger to dance with the lion, double trapeze switches, and walking the wire blindfolded. Having passed these tests, the circus performer then attempts the 'glorifying,' or 'death-defying,' test. It is always accompanied by the ringmaster's request for absolute silence and, ironically, by the band breaking the critical silence with a nerve-tingling drum roll. Then comes the feat itself: The animal tamer puts his head into the lion's mouth; the trapeze artist holds up a pair of beautiful assistants with his teeth, demonstrating his amazing strength; and the blindfolded tightrope walker puts a passenger on his shoulders and rides a bicycle backward across the high wire. Frequently, there is a close call: An unruly tiger tries to interfere with the "head-in-the-mouth" trick, there is a near miss on the trapeze or a stumble on the high wire, and so on. Once the glorifying test is passed, the ringmaster calls for applause as the act exits and then returns for a curtain call. This sequence is a 'code' we all understand (n.p.).

Suppose the circus tent caught fire. What would be the appropriate code for the ringmaster to use in order to reduce panic?

Although analyses like this are fun and intrigue us, they are difficult to carry out without some kind of systematic methodology. The fields of theoretic (e.g., reading Eco or Pierce) and applied semiotics (e.g., advertising and image/political consulting) expanded rapidly in recent times and are used in political campaigns, advertising, public relations, religion, and elsewhere. As receivers we need a simplified way to pin down their uses (or misuses) of symbols, and the following brief discussion of the semiotic approach to language and meaning gives us yet another tool for discovering the important first premises emerging from language preferences and the images molded from them. By the way, most of these meanings are processed in the peripheral channel of the ELM and we are only dimly aware of them unless we pause and do a deeper analysis. Consider the detailed meaning described by Buissac concerning a familiar and seeming meaningless act of entertainment—the circus in Box 6.4. From a semiotic point of view, it contains signifiers, codes, and subtexts, and can be deconstructed to arrive at an entirely new meaning other than an act of entertainment for "children of all ages."

TUNING YOUR EARS
FOR LANGUAGE CUES

Consumers of persuasion need to become vigilant when processing and responding to persuasive messages in our ethically challenged world of advocacy

---

BOX 6.5   Diversity and Semiotics

Semiotics and cultural diversity are a particularly hot topic just now, and many Web sites will pop up when by you enter the words into any search engine. If you want to try a favorite of mine go to www.aptalaska.net/~ron/ FOOD%2005/glob/irrealis.htm, which is the Web site for Globalization Theory. Sample the links found there (e.g.,

modality irealis depicts a variety of global images and contradictions such as the superimposition of Chairman Mao's face on the U.S. Capital building) and discover how many things apply to semiotics. You might also enter the words "semiotics" and "cultural studies" in any search engine and discover more.

---

and propaganda. In the course of this vigilance, one of the most important things persuaders can do is tune their ears to language for various clues to style and motives—to the codes of deceptive, sometimes multicultural, and results-oriented world of persuasion. Using some of the tools described in this chapter helps. Applying the study questions at the end of this and other chapters also helps. There are at least three specific strategies you might use to make yourself more critical of style and to "decode" persuaders:

1. *Role-play the persuader.* Assume that you are the persuader. Or assume that you are a persuader from a different cultural background (see Box 6.5). Now, you shape the persuasion he or she presents in your own personal style. For example, if you are supposed to favor high salaries for professional football players, frame a pragmatic message for half-hearted believers, those who are neutral, or others who are only moderately opposed. Would you mention the shortness of most players' careers? After all, they receive a relatively low overall salary if calculated across across a lifetime, especially when compared with team owners or even CEOs of medium-sized corporations. You might compare ball players to professional entertainers, who also make several million dollars per year for relatively little actual work time. Be sure to include job requirements such as training camps, weekly practices, body building, and so on. If your audience were the players' union, you might bypass the numbers and use highly emotional and abstract language

to motivate them—create images of club owners as rich bloodsuckers who use up the best years of an athlete's life and then dismisses them to the trash heap of history with inadequate health insurance for the injuries they may have had during their on-the-field careers. You would probably use then-and-there language, and refer to concrete statistics and examples that favor the Agent, not the Agency, and to the new goals or the Purpose of the group. And you might want to use emotional metaphors of broken-down race horses being sold off to secondary careers where they suffer endlessly. Doing this role-playing can alert you to the original persuader's true purposes and to their favored tactics as well. At the very least, you will be on your way to becoming a highly trained and critical receiver.

2. *Restate a persuasive message in various ways.* Ask yourself, "What other ways could I say this?" Try to determine how these alternatives change the intent and effects of the message. Try using the parts of Burke's pentad. For example, take the following slogan for Grand Marnier Liqueur—"There Are Still Places on Earth Where Grand Marnier Isn't Offered After Dinner." The words appear on a photo of a deserted island. The appeal is scenic. An agent-oriented version of this slogan claims that, "People of Taste Offer Grand Marnier." A purpose-oriented version might read, "Want to Finish the Conference? Offer Grand Marnier." An agency-oriented version might say,

"Grand Marnier—From a Triple-Sec Recipe." The act-oriented message emphasizes action by saying, "Make a Move—Offer Grand Marnier." And appropriate settings or visual persuasion that would serve as the backdrops for the ads instead of the deserted island.

3. *Attend to language features in discourse.* Don't allow yourself to passively buy into any persuasive advice without a thorough inspection of the tactics being used. Instead, get into the habit of looking at each message's style. Analyze messages on billboards, in TV commercials, the language used by your parents when they try to persuade you, the wording on product packages, or in the phrases used in discussions between you and friends, enemies, or salespersons. Start listening not only to ideas but to word strategies, pentadic focus, the visual and verbal metaphors, and so on. In other words examine the packaging of those ideas. Focusing on these features gives you an intriguing pastime, and helps develop an ear for stylistic tip-offs.

Communication scholar Arthur Asa Berger (2005) offers a methodology for doing semiotic analysis, and he provides a fairly simple checklist. First, he advises us to consider the persuasion aimed at us as "texts" to be read, and then to start looking for clues. He has a checklist of questions to ask when trying to read persuasive texts:

1. Isolate and analyze the important signs in the text.
   a. What are the important signifiers?
   b. What do they signify?
   c. Is there a system that unifies them?
   d. What codes can be found (e.g., symbols of status, colors, or music)?
   e. Are ideological or sociological issues being addressed?
   f. How are they conveyed or hinted at?

2. Identify the central structure, theme, or model of the text.
   a. What forces are in opposition?
   b. What forces are teamed with each other?

   c. Do the oppositions or teams have psychological or sociological meanings? What are they?

3. Identify the narrative structure of the text (i.e., if a "story" is being told, what are its elements?).
   a. How does the sequential arrangement of events affect the meaning? What changes in meaning would result if they were altered?
   b. Are there any "formulaic" aspects to the text (e.g., hard work leads to success, justice prevails, or honesty gets its reward)?

4. Determine whether the medium being used affects the text, and how.
   a. How are shots, camera angles, editing, dissolves, and so on used?
   b. How are lighting, color, music, sound, special effects, and so on used?
   c. How do paper quality, typefaces, graphics, colors, and so on contribute?
   d. How do the speaker's words, gestures, and facial expressions affect meaning?

5. Specify how the application of semiotic theory alters the original meaning ascribed to the text.

REVIEW AND CONCLUSION

Responsible receivers of persuasion relate to the language and images persuaders choose. They gain insight by looking at the semantic connotations of the words being used. They look at word order, or syntax, and at the frequency of various parts of speech. The degree of ambiguity used by the persuader is often revealing, as in the dramatistic analysis suggested by Burke. The motifs and verbal and visual metaphors chosen by persuaders often reveal motives. Persuadees also need to look at the god, devil, and charismatic terms used, as well as the choice of pragmatic versus unifying styles. Finally, try to apply the semiotic approach to the interpretation of persuasive messages to uncover their codes and signifiers as is done in the caption to Figure 6.7. All these

WHAT DO YOU CALL A WOMAN WHO'S MADE IT TO THE TOP?

Ms.

She's a better prospect than ever. Because we've turned the old *Ms* upside down to reflect how women are living today. And you're going to love the results.

The new *Ms* is witty and bold, with a large size format that's full of surprises. Whether it's money, politics, business, technology, clothing trends, humor, or late breaking news — if it's up-to-the-minute, it's part of the new *Ms*

So if you want to reach the top women consumers in America, reach for the phone. And call Linda Lucht, Advertising Director. *Ms. Magazine*, One Times Square, New York, N.Y. 10036. Tel (212) 704-8581.

The new Ms. As impressive as the woman who reads it.

FIGURE 6.7

Using the semiotic approach in Berger's checklist, uncover the meaning of this ad. Note that the woman has "lost" items from her pockets—a passport, the keys to an Audi, credit cards, a picture of herself drawn by her child, jewelry, aspirin, a champagne cork, a $100 bill, and other signs. What do they signify? How old is this woman? Is she sentimental? Busy?

SOURCE: Reprinted by permission of Ms. Magazine, ©1992.

critical devices improve with role-playing, restating, and developing awareness of the words, styles, and ideas used in co-created speech, TV ads, films, polit-ical slogans, social movements, package designs, visual print advertisements, public relations appeals, and other acts of persuasion.

KEY TERMS

After reading this chapter, you should be able to identify, explain, and give an example of the following key terms or concepts:

semantic dimension	complex sentences	act	devil terms
functional dimension	nouns	agent	visual persuasion
thematic dimension	adjectives	agency	charismatic terms
assonance	adverbs	purpose	pragmatic style
alliteration	syntax	sensory language	unifying style
synecdoche	dramatism	metaphorical style	semiotics
simple sentences	pentad	framing	codes
compound sentences	scene	god terms	

APPLICATION OF ETHICS

Considering Richard L. Johannesen's description of ethical standards in Chapter 2, do you consider the strategic use of ambiguity ethical, unethical, or dependent on the persuader's goal and the ultimate outcome? What if ambiguity convinces you to make an unwise purchase decision? What if government reports are ambiguous about the sources of intelligence used to justify the use of U.S. troops? What if they claim this is to protect their sources or to protect national security? What if optimistic but incomplete research about possible cures for a disease gives the individual sufferer a reason to hope?

What might be some ethical standards for the strategic uses of ambiguity? Support your proposed standards and apply them to sample cases like those in the preceding paragraph to demonstrate how well they might work. What shortcomings, if any, did you discover in your proposal?

QUESTIONS FOR FURTHER THOUGHT

1. Transcribe the lyrics of a popular song. Now analyze them according to the functional tools presented in this chapter. Is there a preference for a certain word type? A certain sentence structure? Is the message ambiguous or concrete? Is it propagandistic? What metaphors are used? Explain.

2. Describe several semantic tools. What do you think is the pentadic perspective of the present President of the United States? Of your instructor?

3. Describe the tools for a thematic or textural analysis of language, and use them to analyze the persuasion occurring in a recent political campaign. What do these analyses tell you about the candidate? Try the same thing with a recent advertising or P.R. campaign.

4. What god terms work for your parents? What about their devil terms? Shape a request for something from your parents expressed in their god terms. What god terms motivate the user of the interactive medium being sold on www.livehunt.com where you can hunt big game via a computer?

5. How do unifying persuaders differ from pragmatic ones? Find examples of each type of

persuader in your class, in persuasive attempts of the past, or in defenders and opponents of some issue in your community. What differences exist between these two types? Which style seems more or less likely to carry unethical persuasive appeals? Describe the differences between semantics and semiotics. Which seems more objective? When might it be appropriate to use each approach? Do you use semantics and semiotics to both analyze and create persuasive messages and, if so, how?

6. What is the difference between a text and a symbol? What is the difference between a signifier and the signified? What kinds of things might be considered a text? What could act as a code?

7. If language use serves as a medium of communication, describe its interactivity. How is it used when delivered via interactive media? Describe some cultural differences in symbolic language use within subcultures.

✳

 For online activities, go to the *Persuasion* book companion Web site at http://academic.cengage.com/communication/larson12.

✳

Identifying Persuasive First Premises

[U]nderlying all means of analytically processing the symbols of persuasion are the ancient Aristotelian concept of the **enthymeme** and his triad of **Ethos, Pathos**, and **Logos.** The enthymeme serves as the analytical metaphor or organizational device for Part II. Part II is a search for the types of **Major Premises** that work in enthymemes. We identify those major premises that most audiences believe and those that audiences can be convinced of to prompt action or change.

Pathos The first category of major premise is studied in Chapter 7. It is called the process (or psychological and emotional) premise. Process premises rely on psychological factors—such as physical needs and psychological yearnings—that operate in nearly all persuadees. Persuaders tie their product, candidate, or idea to these process premises, which are then used as the major premises in enthymematic arguments that have wide appeal. In terms of the Elaboration Likelihood Model (ELM), most process or emotional premises are dealt with in the peripheral information-processing path and we find them reflecting many if not all of the Seven Faces of Persuasion.

Chapter 8 covers a second category of major premises called logical or content premises. *Logos* Their persuasiveness lies in the audience's belief in the truth or validity of the argument—be it simple advocacy or more devious propaganda—and they get processed in the central channel of the ELM. You have probably noticed that there is considerable similarity between process premises and content premises. Process premises rely on psychological or emotional needs, whereas content premises rely on logical or rational patterns like the belief in a results-oriented world, so we believe persuasion that emphasizes efficacy and efficiency without a second thought. We learn these patterns of inference beginning in early childhood, and they are reinforced throughout our lives. For instance, suppose we tell two-year-old children that if they continue to cry they will have to take a "time-out" or go without television or a particular toy. What we really are using is "if … then" reasoning, or the rational pattern that actions have consequences. And of course there are a multitude of other patterns. Once again they reflect one or more of our Seven Faces of Persuasion. These are typically processed in the central route of the ELM.

Chapter 9 examines cultural premises that rely on patterns of behavior or beliefs taught to us by our increasingly multicultural society. They resemble articles of faith for audiences and really are the shared values that typify any culture. For example, Americans learn that when faced with a problem they must seek a solution to it, perhaps by establishing a task force or swallowing a pill. This seems so obvious that we are dumbstruck to discover that people from some other cultures prefer simply to accept the inevitable when faced with a problem. Problem solving is a culturally transmitted pattern for us. Knowing that, persuaders motivate us to take actions by portraying the actions as solutions.

Clever persuaders can create problems and then sell us a cure. Cultural premises consist of the myths and values our society holds dear, and they are probably processed in the peripheral information-processing route of the ELM, and again reflect our Seven Faces of Persuasion but especially the challenging face of a multicultural world in which misunderstandings dominate the shared and unshared values of various elements in our many faceted culture. They too are probably processed in the peripheral channel of the ELM.

Chapter 10 explores nonverbal premises, which are sometimes more potent than sophisticated verbal premises. Often, nonverbal premises contribute to the ultimate success or failure of persuasion. These premises are usually processed almost unconsciously following the peripheral path of the ELM, and they can vary widely depending on one's culture or subculture. Thus they represent the cultural premises discussed in Chapter 9.

As you read Part II, think of yourself as searching for major premises that you and an audience hold in common. Identifying these major premise types helps you to become a more skillful persuader, but also—and more important—a better and more critical consumer of persuasion.

7

✳

Psychological or Process Premises: The Tools of Motivation and Emotion

LEARNING GOALS

After reading this chapter, you should be able to:

1. Identify, explain, and give examples of Packard's hidden needs. Give current examples.

2. Identify, explain, and give examples of Feig's hot buttons. How do they operate in your life?

3. Identify, explain, and give examples of several positive and negative emotions. Which are most powerful for you?

4. Explain the difference between attitudes, opinions, behavioral intentions, and behavior.

5. Explain and give examples of each of the levels in Maslow's pyramid of needs. Who do you know who seems to be self-actualizing?

6. Explain and give examples of cognitive dissonance. Where is it operating in your life?

7. Explain and give examples of consonance. Where is it operating in your life?

8. Discuss the ethics of appealing to the emotions, needs, and attitudes held by persuadees.

This chapter examines what are commonly called appeals to the emotions or the will. We will look at four kinds of emotional appeals:

1. Appeals to deeply held needs, physical or psychological

2. Appeals to positive and negative emotions

3. Appeals to attitudes and opinions

4. Appeals to psychological states of balance or consonance and imbalance or dissonance.

Some persuasion theorists distinguish between logical and emotional appeals, arguing that they represent opposite ends of a continuum and that the "better" appeals are the logical ones. This explanation assumes that persuasive appeals are either one thing or another and that the two types of appeals operate separately and independently. It is easy for us to think that both "rational" and "emotional" persuasion occur all at once or as a result of some key phrases, statistics, a sensational speech, the known qualities of the persuader, or other factors. While some persuasion does occur this way it is rare, and far more often true persuasion occurs over time, step-by-step, and incrementally.

In recent times, we've seen that most persuasion depends in part on self-persuasion, usually occurs incrementally or bit-by-bit, and often includes many kinds of communication. Few even were aware of Global Warming a decade ago. Then a few persons began to hear of it and we began to hear of some of its symptoms—decreased size of polar ice caps, species threats, and so on. Probably the most impactful piece of the picture was Al Gore's film "An Inconvenient Truth" for which he won the Oscar and a Nobel prize. Thereafter, further evidence, the declaration by the United Nations that there was global warming and finally even the recognition of Global Warming (but not its causes) by former doubters such as President Bush, various political groups, Ann Coulter, and other conservative media personalities made the issue finally real for many doubters via this incremental process. One "emotional" appeal might have served to capture receivers' attention. A series of "logical" arguments might then have reinforced the first appeal and led to the final decision, belief, and/or behavior. Such changes are part and parcel of a 24/7, media-saturated world of advocacy and propaganda. In fact, both sides of the issue accuse the other of propagandizing in unethical ways, and so the persuasion process on Global Warming continues. The point is that no conclusion has or will be reached in a single moment or as the result of a single persuasive appeal (unless it might result from a global catastrophe). No, these conclusions are far more likely to be incremental and ongoing and will probably never result in 100 percent agreement on the issue. In all likelihood, they will involve the processing of information in both the Central and the Peripheral routes and will involve several of the Seven Faces of Persuasion discussed in Chapter 1.

In a far less dramatic and more "normal" example that demonstrates both the points about the ELM and the 7 Faces, an organization called Volunteers in America asks you to donate your car to them because the money earned from selling the car helps place neglected and abused children in safe and nurturing homes. Is the appeal emotional or logical? Well, it has elements of both. The emotional appeal is about helping kids get better treatment in a good environment. Helping others makes most of us feel good about ourselves. But there are some logical reasons for donating your car. For instance, you can get a tax deduction for the donation (something you need), and you don't even have to take the car to them or get the car in running order—the organization has free pick-up within 48 hours and they repair it before sale. The real question is not whether this is a logical or emotional appeal, but whether you process the message centrally or peripherally. In this case, the peripheral route processes—the "feeling good" part—and the central route processes—the tax break, the 48-hour pick-up, and the repair—are the emotional and logical parts of the persuasion respectively.

In this chapter, we are going to examine several emotional appeals or major premises that tap into the psychological or emotional processes operating in the peripheral route of the ELM for each of us. These appeals rely on (1) human needs, (2) human emotions, (3) attitudes, and (4) the psychic comfort or discomfort that normal people always feel over the decisions they make. We call these appeals **process or emotional premises** or appeals because they target psychological and emotional processes that operate in most people. When we call them premises, we are referring to their uses as major premises in enthymemes. When we refer to them as appeals, we are talking about how they operate in the persuasive worlds of politics, advertising, public or interpersonal persuasion, and so on. It is probably okay to think of the words *process, premises,* and *appeals* as nearly synonymous. All are subtypes of persuasion that get at our psychological processes rather than our logical or reasoning abilities. For example, most of us have fear-based emotions that cause psychological tension, and we eagerly take action to relieve this tension. So, advertisers work to generate fears about our grooming, potential for success, and acceptance/approval by others, and then they offer us products that supposedly relieve those fears and tensions. Consider the mouthwash Listerine. Initially, it was used as a powerful surgical antiseptic, a floor cleaner, and a cure for gonorrhea. It wasn't until the 1920s that it was marketed as a cure for halitosis—an obscure word for bad breath (Levitt & Dubner, 2005). A headline in one of its early ads read, "Got halitosis? Listerine mouthwash makes your breath kissing sweet."

Psychological appeals or process premises also operate in business, marketing, advertising, sales promotions, politics, interpersonal communication, and ideological persuasion where a variety of fears might be developed—fear of losing one's job, fear of going bankrupt, fear of voting for a candidate who will mess up and so on. Then the persuader offers us a "cure" for the fear—unemployment insurance, stricter business accounting practices, or their candidate.

Process or emotional premises operate when we buy a product because of brand loyalty, brand name, a memorable slogan, a catchy jingle, or even packaging. Recall the Snuggle fabric softener example from Chapter 5? The brand name was cuddly, as was its logo of a stuffed teddy bear, and these were the elements that appealed to the prospect's emotions and desires to be psychologically and physically comforted. Process premises also operate in more serious situations than the right fabric softener such as enactment of homeland security laws, appeals from prison reform candidates to reduce subsequent crimes being committed against us, from advocates for a candidate they claim to be reliable, or from advertisers trying to convince us to make major purchase decisions for a new car or home. Emotional premises appear in everyday interpersonal persuasion between neighbors, spouses, parents and children, siblings, lovers, bosses, and employees.

The first such premise we will examine is the appeal to real or imagined needs that we might have as individuals or as groups. In some cases (such as physical needs for the basics of human existence), the needs really do exist and we will die if they are not met. In other cases (such as being considered masculine or feminine or being thought of as competent and ethical), we won't die if the need is not met; but we won't feel content either, so psychological or imagined needs can be motivating and persuasive as well.

NEEDS: THE FIRST PROCESS PREMISE

Each of us has our own set of individual needs. As noted some of them are critical—we can't live without things like food, water, clothing, and shelter. Others are not critical—we can get along without approval from others. And not everyone's needs have the same priority. I might need group approval while you might need symbols of success. Diverse

cultural roots can also influence the priority of our needs, but most needs resemble those of lots of other people, so various theories of motivation apply to the general population. Many appeals focus on needs, which when satisfied lead to our overall sense of well-being (e.g., success on the job, being liked, or having religious faith). Without the satisfaction of these needs (or some substitute), we feel frustrated, anxious, afraid, even angry, and tension results. We infer these needs from patterns of behavior that presumably satisfied and happy people exhibit. Because other people seem concerned about being successful, we quickly infer a need for the physical symbols of success like a Jaguar, a summer place, a large home, a happy family, or a feeling of religious salvation. Persuasion in today's changing world usually focuses on promoting or selling symbolic ways to meet people's physiological and emotional needs. Some products, such as self-improvement courses, really can help individuals make a better impression on the boss, but what people buy, vote for, or support doesn't usually have such direct effects. They drive a BMW and enjoy what they believe to be the admiring looks they get from other drivers. Our support for a candidate may relate to a need for approval from others or a need for self-esteem—the candidate's supporters are our friends or neighbors, and they appreciate our support. And we feel good about ourselves because our support for the good candidate just might "make a difference." Or we might feel good if we exhibit the traits of good children, parents, or responsible persons of a certain religious faith, or maybe just of being a good citizen.

If the persuader relying on the needs process premise analyzes audience needs or emotions incorrectly, persuasion sometimes boomerangs. For example, an advertiser, assuming that travelers needed and wanted tough luggage, produced an expensive TV spot in which the luggage was handled roughly while being loaded onto an airplane and then accidentally falling out of an accidentally open door on the plane in flight, plummeting down 30,000 feet, landing on some rocks, and bouncing into the air. When the luggage was opened, the camera showed the undamaged contents. The ad seemed persuasive.

However, sales of the brand plummeted following its initial test airing. Why? Focus group interviews revealed that most if not all people have some level of fear that their flight might crash, and they resented the idea that their luggage would survive when they wouldn't. So the emotions of fear and resentment serve as powerful motivators to encourage or deter purchase, as might emotions like anger, jealousy, hatred, joy, or love. Sometimes brand preferences are based on such non-logical factors. I avoided automatic transmissions for years because my father said they weren't as good in snow and ice. Persons of the Jewish faith avoided purchasing and product by the Ford Motor Company because old Henry Ford supported an anti-Semitic organization that claimed there was a worldwide Jewish conspiracy to monopolize the financial industry. My spouse only uses Downey because she thinks its odor pleases me when I can't smell it and really don't sniff my clean laundry that much.

To discover why consumers respond as they do, advertisers, political candidates, and others use **motivation research** to zero in on our needs. Motivation Research or M.R. is based on the social sciences and the study of marketing rather than on our traditional political, ideological, or rhetorical traditions, and it grew rapidly after World War II. In his best-selling book *The Hidden Persuaders* (1964), Vance Packard, author and advertising theorist, reported that a majority of the hundred largest ad firms in the country used psychoanalytic motivation research to discover deep-seated psychological needs and responses. Other persuaders such as public relations executives and fund-raisers also turned to psychological theories to discover receivers' motives, emotions, or needs, and then they tied products, candidates, and causes to those motives and needs. Packard held that much motivation research

...seeks to learn what motivations or **hidden needs** influence people in making choices. It employs techniques designed to reach the subconscious mind because preferences generally are determined by factors of which the individual is not usually

Not Right now

aware. In most buying situations the consumer acts emotionally and compulsively, unconsciously reacting to images which they subconsciously associate with the product (p. 5).

One expert and critic said, "The cosmetic manufacturers are not selling lanolin; they are selling hope....We no longer buy oranges, we buy vitality. We do not buy just an auto; we buy prestige" (p. 5). Packard says that motivation researchers assume three things about people: (1) they don't always know what they want when making a purchase; (2) you can't rely on what they say they like or dislike; and (3) they don't usually act logically when they buy, vote, or join. *(use sheet of Packard)*

Motivation research reflects the symbolist tradition in psychology rather than the experimental tradition. By that I mean the tradition that symbols are just as or more important than real things to most people. Advertising and marketing researchers use focus group interviews, surveys, psychological tests, and so on, to get consumers to describe the fears, pleasures, or fantasies they associate with brands and ads. Other researchers ask people to complete sentences or do word associations about the brand. Though initiated to the marketing industry over 75 years ago, this trend continues just in more sophisticated forms using more technologically advanced techniques (e.g., the galvanic skin response, MRIs), and recent research about consumer behavior confirms many of the claims made by Packard so long ago. This kind of motivational research is still with us but now uses sophisticated techniques that take cultural diversity into account and use demographic, socio-graphic, and psychographic techniques as well as interactive media to involve the receiver. They know for example that the subscribers to MySpace agree less well educated than users of FaceBook, less interested in upscale sports (e.g., golf, squash, or polo), equipment, and fashion than FaceBook subscribers who avoid less sophisticated activities (e.g., fishing, bowling, or gardening), and if they join the armed forces, they will be enlisted persons rather than officers. N.Y.U. professor Neil Postman (Freedman, 1988) long ago observed that

---

B O X 7.1   Consumer Insight—Getting Into Your Head

A Chicago-based nationwide marketing company, Claritas, used psychographics and lifestyle data to develop its PRIZM system. PRIZM is a marketing tool that identifies more than 60 market segments across the United States with names that reflect the inner psychological needs of the consumers in each. Take, for example, the segment called "Pickups and Gun Racks." Persons in "Pickups and Gun Racks" tend to live in manufactured housing or mobile homes and are heavy users of generic or house brands of sweetened soda pop. If they purchase lingerie, it tends to be from Frederick's of Hollywood. Their most recent financial transaction is the purchase of a lottery ticket. They obviously have different needs from those of the people in the segment "Town and Gowns" (you may be living there right now), and these needs, in turn, differ from those of the people in the segment "Red, White, and Blue Collar." For persons in "Town and Gown," the most frequent financial transaction is the use of an ATM. If they purchase lingerie, it is frequently at a department store or Victoria's Secret, and most of them live in houses, apartments, dorms, or fraternity and sorority houses. PRIZM is a popular tool among many consumer marketing firms.

"Advertisers,… desperate to keep you tuned to their pitches, (are) trying some new tricks. Many of these commercials have more impact on the subconscious level" (p. 5).

Ad agencies often enlist psychologists and neurophysiologists to produce the desired effects (Freedman, 1988). For example, Amherst Incorporated developed a research instrument called the Motivation and Attitude Profile (MAP) and used it to market goods, services, and politicians. Amherst's creative director describes the idea behind MAP this way: "People are driven by their emotions—it's not about fact or logic. Increasingly, the only button you press is an emotional one. You find out what their needs are and you discover how to reflect those needs" (Booth, 1999, p. 32). Products as varied as Haagen-Daz ice cream, Volkswagen, and life insurance rely on psychographics, which is a research technique that identifies the psychological reasons for purchase behavior. Whether we call it motivational research, lifestyle research, hidden persuaders, or psychographics, using the process amounts to the same basic idea—finding hidden or obvious needs and developing the products and ads to fulfill those needs. See Box 7.1.

Packard's "Compelling Needs"

One approach to the needs premise was Packard's "**compelling needs**," which were based on his observations on the rapidly evolving advertising industry of the motivation research era. He claimed that these needs were so powerful that they *compelled* people to buy, and he identified eight such compelling needs that advertisers used to sell products. We still see them in use today, although with far more sophistication than Packard described— digital images, morphing, special effects, color psychology, and other techniques all of which allow today's marketers to design ads promising that the product, brand, or service will provide real or symbolic fulfillment of these compelling needs (e.g., Nutri-System, Air Jordan's, the Hummer, and Viagra to mention a few).

Marketing consultant Barry Feig (1997) discussing such process premises notes that advertisers are looking for the **hot buttons** that will motivate people and prompt purchase behavior. Feig defined hot buttons as verbal or visual appeals that cause receivers to become emotionally involved with a product or brand rather than responding rationally to product/ brand reality. For example, he claims that new car purchases frequently result from the test drive and the new car smell, not from any hard research into performance, which though readily available is often ignored or simply overlooked. The purchaser becomes emotionally involved with the feel, smell, sounds, and styling of the new car and puts aside other factors like mileage, warranty, auto magazine ratings, or *Consumer's Reports*. Some clever persuader

FIGURE 7.1 This ad plays on our inherent feelings of insecurity, especially in an age of identity theft and other means used to defraud people.

SOURCE: Used by permission of Sanford Corp.

found a way to package that new car odor in an aerosol spray that can be used to sell used cars more effectively on the same emotional bases also. Feig's own work in the 1990s verified nearly all of Packard's hidden needs occurring in today's advertising, and he also found other needs not noted by Packard that still get at our hot buttons via process premises. Let us now examine a few of Packard's emotional needs. He called them "compelling needs," and they are even more effective in today's world with its Seven Faces of Persuasion.

The Need for Emotional Security. Packard's first compelling need was for **emotional security**, which is defined as feelings of anxiety about the future and feelings of insecurity about our personal welfare and safety in the near future as well in the more distant one, as seen in Figure 7.1. These feelings emerge whenever our world becomes unpredictable, and we then try to dispel the unpredictability in symbolic ways. Today, we are seeing this kind of insecurity in persons who fear the loss of their jobs, foreclosure on their homes, Global Warming, the Jihadist movement, new emerging and competing economies like China and India, and the skyrocketing costs of energy. Originally, Packard attributed this need for emotional security to the Great Depression, but we can fast-forward to the emotional fears of today's citizenry and can predict their longevity into tomorrow's citizenry. Let's look back a bit and see what it was Packard originally identified as that day's causes for emotional insecurity.

Following WW II, people desperately wanted to avoid the insecurity of unemployment, the inability to make ends meet, the fear of nuclear war, and so on. Unlike more recent times, when people had employment, they saved regularly and tried to stock up on life's essentials by buying home freezers to preserve food for the possibly uncertain future. They didn't go into much consumer debt. Credit or debit cards didn't exist. Persons I knew refused to have checking accounts to avoid impulse spending and because they still had a distrust of the banking industry that went back to the foreclosures and bank failures of the 1930s. We may be witnessing a similar situation today with bank failures due to the mortgage meltdown. The need still operates, but for somewhat different reasons. Terrorism seems unstoppable and is certainly unpredictable. Identity theft is mushrooming, making everyone feel insecure. AIDS threatens the economic future of the continent of Africa and elsewhere, and dangerous pollution fouls our environment hourly as it contributes to global warming, which may cause global flooding that will destroy large parts of many countries. The world economy seems precariously balanced. If oil prices continue to escalate, the stock market might crash, resulting in another Great Depression. With mergers, downsizing, and outsourcing, job security now concerns many people, and literacy rates have dropped to less than 70 percent from earlier highs over 90 percent, making it hard for many people to get any job other than flipping burgers.

No wonder we search for substitute symbols of security. Deodorants promise us secure social relationships. Self-improvement courses promise better job security. Retirement planning programs offer financial security for an uncertain future. These products and services act as minor premises in the process premise driven enthymemes mentioned in previous chapters that have as a major first premise the belief that "security is good." Even in interpersonal relationships, the need for security causes people to search for commitment. At first, "living together" seemed to be a liberating lifestyle, but this is now questioned by some because there is no security without commitment. Author Stephanie Staal (2001) points out that the divorce rate of those who live together before marriage is 50 percent higher than the rate for those who did not. We all face unpredictable change, and that makes us vulnerable to persuasion that promises some symbol of security—a good investment program, membership in respected social groups, safety derived from security systems, owning a weapon, or interpersonal confidence stemming from trusting and reliable relationships. Feig (1997) equates this need for security with a universal hot button he calls the "desire for control." This need for security or control varies within our culture. For example, in some subcultures—perhaps yours or that of your parents—security is put off until tomorrow in favor of gratification today.

The Need for Reassurance of Worth.   We live in a highly competitive and impersonal world in which we often feel like mere cogs or numbers in some database. Packard noted that people need to feel valued for what they do whether it is at a factory, a desk, a classroom, or a day-care center. Homemakers, blue-collar workers, sales persons, service workers, managers, and others need to feel that they are accomplishing something of value and are appreciated by others for the work they do either voluntarily or out of necessity or commitment. Packard called this the need for **reassurance of worth**, which is defined as a feeling that we are valued by others. This need forms the basis of many persuasive appeals, from ads promising to make us better parents, spouses, or friends to appeals for volunteers in good causes. An old but interesting study asked managers and workers to rate ten factors in job satisfaction. Managers rated wages, fringe benefits, and working conditions at the top, but workers placed them at the bottom. They rated "appreciation for work done" at the top, followed by "my boss listens to me," and "fellow workers."

Feig (1997) verified the existence of the reassurance of worth need, saying, "Consumers need to feel good about themselves and fulfill their self-images—it's a basic human need" (p. 14).

Based on hundreds of interviews, sociologist Robert Bellah and colleagues (1985) concluded that most contemporary Americans see themselves in a race for material goods, prestige, power, and influence. They separate themselves from others and find self-worth in material things. Ethics author Kathleen Sibley (1997) noted the feelings of distrust felt by many employees when they learned of a company policy of monitoring employee e-mail.

When we feel less and less important as individuals, we become vulnerable targets for persuasion that promises reassurance of worth. Reassurance of worth has its cultural implications also. Schiffman and Kanuk (1997) observed that Asian-Americans are very brand loyal, but especially so when the brand lets it be known that they are welcome and that their patronage is appreciated by offering preferred customer cards, premiums, and so on. Other ethnic subcultures value bargaining, and still others value quality over price.

The Need for Ego Gratification.   Packard found that many consumers not only needed to be reassured of their basic worth, but they also needed **ego gratification**, which he defined as feelings of self-importance and having one's ego stroked. In a widely run ad targeted at the traveling business woman—showing the woman in a Courtyard hotel room by Marriott—the ad focuses on the woman getting all the extras from Marriott, including Internet access, fine furnishings, and even a cup of coffee served in a china cup instead of a Styrofoam one. Marriott also emphasizes that they cater to female business travelers and especially to those from different ethnic groups, thus reinforcing the growing importance of females and ethnic diversity in the workplace. Earlier ads by Marriott usually showed white male executives as customers who get all these extras.

Satisfaction of the need for ego gratification comes from a variety of sources—friends, coworkers, neighbors, parents, groups, institutions, and ourselves. Feig (1997) called this need the "I'm better

than you" hot button, and emphasized that consumers display the possessions that build their egos and meet this need. Persuaders often target groups whose members feel that they have been put down for some time, such as teachers, police officers, firefighters, and postal or social workers. After 9/11, the media brought many of these groups into a well-deserved public spotlight. They got ego gratification from being featured on TV, in newspapers and on the covers of news weeklies. Such groups can also now get special rates on their mortgages, grants in aid to help them buy homes, and other benefits showing national appreciation for public service.

Persuaders frequently sell products, ideas, and candidates by targeting an out-group's ego needs in personal ways that appeal to self-perception. Take family values, for example. From the late 1960s until the late 1980s the traditional family was out of style. Communal living was popular, as was living together. Those who remained committed to the ideal of the traditional family felt like outcasts. From the 1990s to the present, persuasive "pro-family" appeals succeeded in presidential campaigns, religious appeals, public relations, and the marketing of products promising a restoration of family values. Feig (1997) called this need the "family values" hot button, and noted that marketers sell a vision of the family as we all wish it would be. Similarly, politicians know how to stroke the egos of appropriate groups of targeted potential voters. In the 2008 primaries, for instance, Arkansas Governor Mike Huckabee repeatedly emphasized his conservative social values and that he rejected the theory of evolution. Not surprising then that he won all of the religious southern states in the "Super-Tuesday" primaries. Mitt Romney emphasized his experience in the business world, and Hillary Clinton emphasized her longtime belief in universal health coverage. All of them were making the "I'm like you" point as is seen in Figure 7.2 where the milk drinkers' egos are stroked. Earlier, one Republican female candidate for governor used ego gratification with two widely differing audiences, making the same point on similarity with the audience but nonverbally. For a GOP women's luncheon she arrived by limousine, wearing a

Make ours doubles.

My sister and I hate to lose-nutrients, that is.
So we drink milk. It has 9 essential nutrients active bodies need.
You might say it's the only thing we serve.

got milk?

FIGURE 7.2 The Fluid Milk Promotion Board strokes the ego of average citizens by making them feel special, hinting that they are sophisticated, and suggesting that they can avoid health problems by drinking three glasses of milk a day.

SOURCE: Image courtesy of The Advertising Archives.

conservative dress and scarf, and ate chicken salad for lunch. Afterward, she changed her clothes to a black leather jacket, boots, gloves, and pants, and then drove a Harley to the Young Republicans club at a nearby college. She got rave reviews at both events (National Public Radio, 2002).

The Need for Creative Outlets. In our modern technocracy, few products can be identified with a single artisan. This was not always the case. For example, until the Industrial Revolution craftsmen such as cabinetmakers created a piece of furniture from beginning to end—it was their unique product. The same applied to blacksmiths, silversmiths, and other craftsmen. They all could point with pride to their product. That is not often the case today, which is why we feel a need for **creative outlets**. Packard saw this need being met by offering substitute creative activities that would replace the creations previously produced by individuals. They felt less and less creative in many ways, and they needed to find ways to express their own unique creativity. Packard said persuaders targeted this need for creative outlets by promoting products and brands related to hobbies, crafts, and social activities. Today more than half the population works in the service and information industries, where most important products are intangible and not really very creative. There is no actual creation of anything, and more work is now being accomplished through technologies such as robots. People still need to demonstrate their own creativity—a need that Feig (1997) identified as the "excitement of discovery" hot button—so they engage in gardening, gourmet cooking, home decorating, collecting and restoring antiques, art, or music. Take a look at the articles included in almost any women's homemaking magazine, and you'll find several ideas for meeting the need for creative outlets.

The Need for Love Objects. Packard noted that people whose children have grown up often feel a need for **love objects**. These "empty-nesters" feel lonely and unneeded when the last kid goes off to college, gets a job, or gets married. Empty-nesters fill their love needs in various ways such as doing volunteer work, devoting more time to their jobs or hobbies, or becoming a big brother or sister or a foster grandparent. Persuaders target these empty-nesters in a variety of ways. For instance, many older persons get pets to serve as substitute love objects. They coddle them, spoil them, and even dress them up. The pet food industry targets "gourmet" lines to such persons who bring home Premium Cuts, Tender Vittles, Beefn Gravy, Tuna Surprise, or Chicken Spectacular. The food sounds and even looks like something a human might consume. Feig (1997) calls this the "revaluing" hot button, and he predicts a major increase in products that attempt to fill this need as the baby boomers approach retirement and an empty nest (see Figure 7.3).

FIGURE 7.3 This cartoon is based on a true incident. A wounded goose was taken in and nursed to health by an assistant to NIU's president, who was single and nearing retirement.

SOURCE: Used by permission of Al Ochsner.

The Need for a Sense of Power or Strength. More than members of other cultures, most U.S. citizens seek emblems of potency or a **sense of power or strength** in symbolic ways. Packard defined this as the need for a personal extension of one's *perceived* power or strength rather than true power or strength. The bigger the car or outboard motor, the better. Snowmobiles, ATVs, jet skis, Hummers, SUVs, and Harley Davidson motorcycles sell because they give the user this sense of power. Whether the brand is a double-triggered chain saw or a Hummer, an increased perception of power is the central issue. Stanley Tools sells "heavy duty" tools, not wimpy, "light duty" hammers and wrenches. Similarly, Americans seem to elect politicians who do macho things. In fact, any major candidate for the presidency must demonstrate physical strength in some way. And as males approach midlife, they often engage in macho activities like bungee jumping or bodybuilding.

The Need for Roots. One of the predominant features of modern society is mobility. Individuals employed by any large firm will probably have to move several times during their careers, and most persons have three or more careers during their lifetime. In the decade following graduation from college, the average graduate moves a dozen times, usually crossing state lines at least once. Few persons remain at "home" for their entire lives. As a result, most persons feel a **need for roots**, symbolic or real. The need for roots is defined as feelings of homesickness and a yearning for family-centered activities. When individuals move away from home, especially if it is some distance, there are some pieces of home that they can take along with them. Brand loyalty, which develops most strongly between the ages of 18 and 24, is a reminder of home; and recent college graduates have one of the highest levels of brand loyalty, which is why my university agreed to give Pepsi exclusive "pouring rights" on campus. Only Pepsi products (e.g., Mountain Dew, Lipton Tea, or Fruitopia) can be sold or served on campus. All materials used to serve the brands (cups, straws, napkins, etc.) must have the Pepsi logo imprinted on them. Pepsi gave over $8 million to the scholarship fund for this right, knowing that brand loyalty would develop.

The need for roots and the sense of brand loyalty also helps explain *line extensions* or the development of new products based on old and familiar brands. We feel more at home buying the new Quaker Oats Squares or granola treats than another brand because of the familiar, friendly, and old-fashioned face of the Quaker Man promising "An honest taste from an honest face." He serves as an emblem of our tradition, our need for an "old-fashioned" hearty breakfast, and our need for a sense of roots. The nice thing about brand names is that they are portable—we can take them to a new home anywhere. The Lane Furniture Company appealed to the need for roots and emotional ties to home by offering newlyweds a Lane cedar chest to "take part of home" with them when they marry. We've already noted the appeal politicians make to family values. The trend toward increasingly mobile and fragmented lives is likely to continue. As a result, the need for roots remains an important motivator, and advertisers, politicians, and ideologues continue to use it in their persuasive appeals to us. Feig (1997) equates this need with his "family values" hot button and notes, "Quality time with families is still of utmost importance to Americans." Schiffman and Kanuk observe that in some subcultures (such as Asian-American and Latino) family and roots stretch across several generations. In this regard, The *New York Times* noted the trend of taking generations of family on road trips (Feig, 1997).

The Need for Immortality. None of us wants to believe in our own mortality. The fear of growing old and dying clearly drives the healthy-living industry, which promotes such things as good nutrition, stress reduction, exercise, and a healthy lifestyle. Packard suggested that this need for immortality grew out of the need to maintain influence or control over the lives of family members. The breadwinner is made to feel that by purchasing life insurance, he or she obtains life after death in the form of continuing financial security that will help the kids go to college even if he or she isn't there (see Figure 7.4). Other products make similar appeals to the fear of death. For instance, Promise margarine will keep you healthy longer because "Promise is at the heart of eating right." And Nivea's Visage face cream will make your skin "firmer, healthier, and younger" for only pennies a day. As the ad executive noted in an earlier quote, we aren't buying lanolin, we are buying hope—hope for a little more immortality. This need for immortality seems particularly relevant in our modern technocracy. The much-talked-about "midlife crisis" is an example. This occurs when people realize that "time marches on," that they have probably passed the halfway

point in their lives, or when they confront some other major life event such as the death of a parent. So many try to start over and get divorced, quit or lose their job, buy a sports car, run off with someone half their age, and speed away in the sports car, determined to make a new life as a ski bum, thus underscoring their indestructible youth. They want to be young again, or at least to enjoy some of the experiences they missed along the way. Frequently, they engage in dangerous activities such as skydiving, whitewater rafting, wilderness thrills, or hot air ballooning.

There are many other persuasive appeals that succeed because they are somehow tied to the desire for immortality (Lafavore, 1995). Feig (1997) calls this the "self-nurturance and the ability to stay ageless and immortal" hot button, and noted that older persons are more willing to spend money on things that make them feel better about themselves than they are on some of the essentials of life.

We now turn to perhaps one of the most well known models of human needs that was first described more than 50 years ago, and it is still going strong (Rowan, 1998). For a recent update about this relevance go to www.reinventingyourself.com/authors/maslow.

Maslow's Hierarchy of Needs

Abraham Maslow (1954), a well-known psychologist and pioneer in the discipline, long ago offered a simple starting point for examining people's needs. His theories about the power of human needs are judged by many to be as relevant for persuasion today as they were when he first described them. In fact, many have been adapted to management training, humanistic psychology, education, and so forth. Nancy Austin (2002), a California management consultant, maintains that, though the theory may be over a half-century old, "for modern managers looking to pump up performance, it still has zing." Robert Zemke (1998), the senior editor of the journal *Training*, notes, "It's ironic that this '50s psychologist with no head for business played such a central role in the development of the psychology of management and the thoughts of modern managers." In 1998, Maslow's daughter published a revision of his

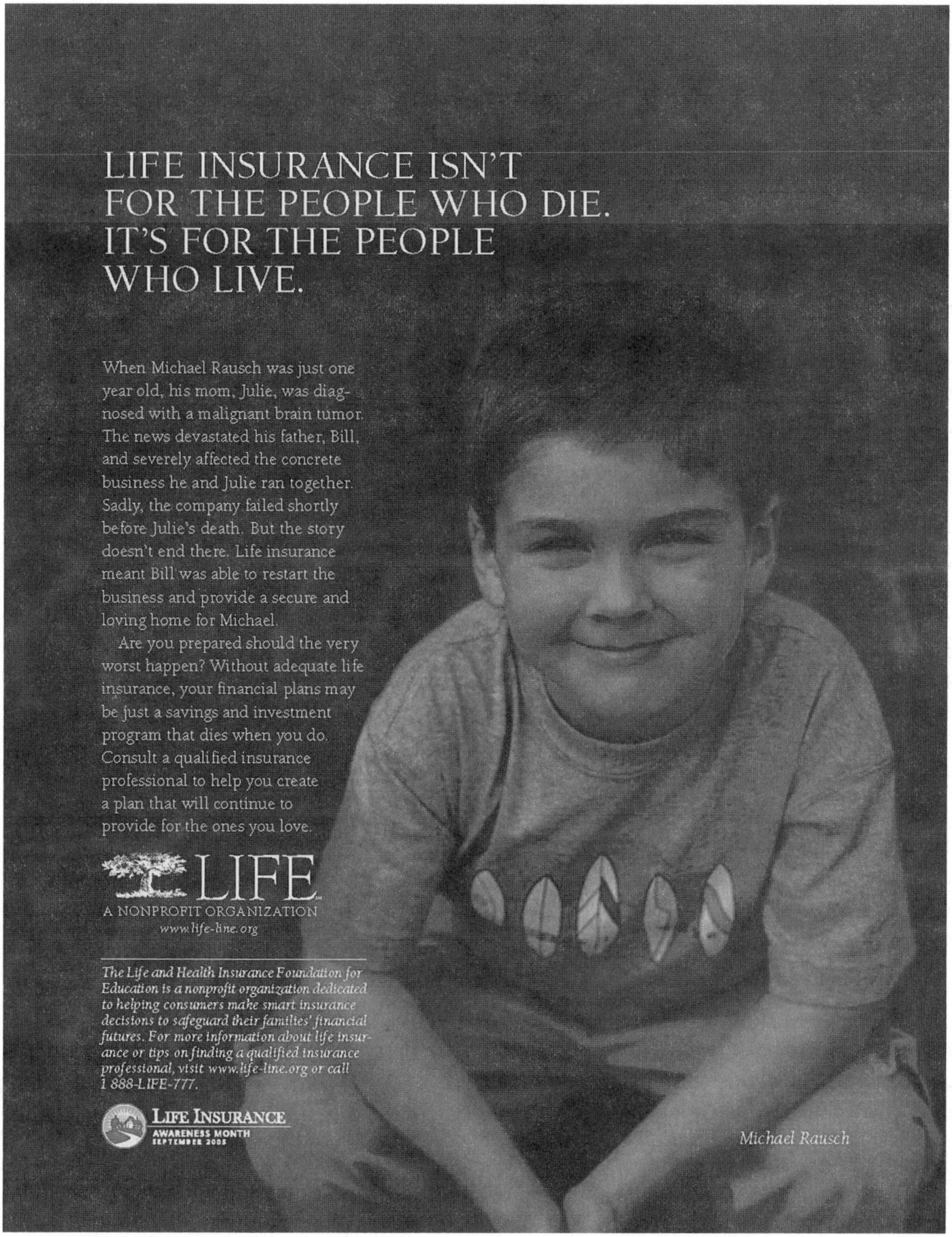

FIGURE 7.4 This ad appeals to the need for immortality by assuring readers that even if they are no longer there, they will still be able to influence the lives of their survivors.

SOURCE: Reprinted with permission of the LIFE Foundation.

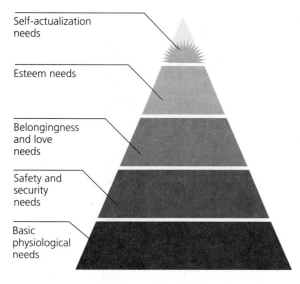

Self-actualization needs

Esteem needs

Belongingness and love needs

Safety and security needs

Basic physiological needs

F I G U R E 7.5   Maslow's hierarchy of needs.

work, entitled *Maslow on Management*, which was greeted with rave reviews (Rowan, 1998). And Schiffman and Kanuk (1997) say that in spite of its age, "Maslow's hierarchy is a useful tool in understanding consumer motivations and is readily adaptable to marketing strategy" (p. 100). Some of Feig's (1997) hot buttons equate to Maslow's need levels.

Despite its vintage, Maslow's hierarchy still has much to teach us about all Seven Faces of Persuasion. Maslow theorized that people have various kinds of needs that emerge, subside, and then reemerge. In his hierarchy of needs, the lower levels of the hierarchy represent the strongest needs and the higher levels the weaker ones (see Figure 7.5). Maslow did not believe that higher needs are superior to lower needs—rather, they are less likely to emerge until the stronger lower needs have been met. The base of the pyramid represents universal needs or beliefs about which there is unanimous agreement. As we move up the pyramid, we find needs or beliefs on which there may not be unanimous agreement and on which individuals place varying degrees of value. As a result, there is an upward dynamic in Maslow's hierarchy, which means that as powerful needs are met, less potent ones emerge. Maslow called this upward dynamic

prepotency. In other words, weaker needs (such as the need for self-respect) emerge only after stronger needs (like food or shelter) have been filled. Don't try to persuade a dehydrated person to dress up before having a drink of water. The need to slake our thirst is prepotent; and until it is fulfilled, we ignore other needs. As time passes, the earlier needs also reemerge again. For example, the needs for food or water emerge and then recede as we eat or drink, but they reemerge at a later time.

Basic Needs.   The bottom level of Maslow's pyramid contains the strongest needs we have—our **basic needs**, which he defined as the physiological things required to sustain life—regular access to air, food, water, shelter, sleep, and so on. Until these needs have been met, we don't usually concern ourselves with higher needs. However, basic needs can motivate behavior. For example, the person who is starving can be motivated to do all sorts of unusual things to secure food, ranging from stealing it to eating insects. And we know that the need for air can cause drowning victims to panic and drown not only themselves but also their would-be rescuers. Shelter as another basic need is necessary and motivating enough to motivate persons to take drastic and apparently illogical action such as burying themselves in a snow bank in below zero weather, and the need for air was demonstrated by the pyramidal piles of corpses left in the Nazi death camp gas chambers. The least poisonous air was at the ceiling because the gas—Zyklon-B was heavier than air.

Security Needs.   The second level of Maslow's pyramid is the **need for security**, which he defined as the ability to continue to fill the basic needs of life. We can look at these needs in several ways. If we fear losing our jobs, we have a strong need to obtain income security; and we try to find a more secure job, or we save money for hard times. During the recent mortgage meltdown, many feared losing their homes and sold their houses at drastically deflated prices, even when they weren't in real danger of foreclosure. Even if we have job security, we still might feel insecure about maintaining our personal safety because of the rising crime rates in our neighborhood. We might take drastic action to ward off criminals by keeping a gun on the nightstand or perhaps by moving to a gated community. Even when we feel secure in our community, we still might feel insecure because of world politics. We fear that our country is vulnerable to terrorists, who may manage to soon acquire nuclear and biological or chemical weapons. Or we fear that our leaders are considering unwise military actions against some country. Those not technically trained for the computer age have a realistic fear of being out-of-date and soon out of a job. Political analysts explained several recent election results as related to fears of economic displacement. In the interpersonal realm, we have a need for "social security," or the continuing acceptance by others. In other words, the need for security emerges and re-emerges as various threats to our security become evident (see Figure 7.6).

Today, insecurity, like change, is one of the few predictable things in life. Eight of every ten jobs being filled by tomorrow's college grads don't even exist today. It's almost impossible for you to prepare for the future because the rate and pace of change is accelerating so quickly. Computer technology now becomes obsolete in less than a year. No one can keep up with all the new (and frequently essential) information about jobs, health, communities, and a host of other personal and social issues. This need is similar to Feig's (1997) "desire to control" hot button. Feig says this need explains home-based businesses because in them you can become own boss and avoid layoffs.

Belongingness and Affiliation Needs. Once our security needs have been met, we become aware of needs on the third level of the pyramid—**belongingness or affiliation needs**, which are defined as the need to interact with others and to identify with some group. A number of options are open to us to meet our need for association. Usually, individuals go beyond the family and workplace and become members of groups with which they want to affiliate, such as service groups, places of worship, the PTA, bowling

BREAST CANCER BEGINS EVEN SMALLER THAN THIS. THAT'S WHY YOU NEED A YEARLY MAMMOGRAM, ESPECIALLY AS YOU GET OLDER. MAMMOGRAMS CAN DETECT LUMPS TOO SMALL FOR YOU TO FEEL AND EARLY DETECTION MAY SAVE YOUR LIFE, SO CALL 1-800-ACS 2345.

GET A MAMMOGRAM.
EARLY DETECTION IS THE BEST PROTECTION.

A Public Service of This Publication — AMERICAN CANCER SOCIETY

FIGURE 7.6 The need for security is the appeal used in this ad from the American Cancer Society.

SOURCE: Reprinted by permission of the American Cancer Society.

leagues, or golf and health clubs. Generally, we limit the number of groups we join, and we are active members in only a few. Feig (1997) identified the "need for belonging" as another of his hot buttons and noted that "Americans are the 'joiningest' people in the world." He advises doubters to examine the number of membership cards in their wallets if they don't think this is so (p. 29). The flip side of belonging and affiliation needs is the recent trend toward isolation that has been hastened by the personal computer and the Internet where one can be isolated for hours at a time—even days for true addicts. A number of people and organizations are concerned about the tendency of people to cocoon or isolate themselves. In his article "Bowling Alone" (1995) and his follow-up book, *Bowling Alone: The Collapse and Revival of American Community* (2000), Robert Putnam observed that more and more persons join what he calls checkbook groups such as the Citizen's Utility Board, the Sierra Club, or the American Association of Retired Persons. Belonging only requires that you write a check, because the groups rarely if ever meet. Membership is down in civic and fraternal groups like the Lions, Elks, and Moose Clubs, and fewer people bowl in leagues, preferring to "bowl alone."

Like physiological and security needs, the need to belong often interacts with other needs and continues to reemerge throughout our lives. Also, what fulfills our belonging needs differs at various points in our lives and will probably change across time. It may be important to belong to a fraternity or sorority when we are in college, but after graduation, these affiliations fade and are replaced by job-related associations or other social activities. Later, when we have families, other affiliations tend to be more important to us, and we join community groups and a church or other religious organization. In this context, a recent trend is the emergence of "mega-churches" like the Mariners Church of Newport Beach, California. This church offers programming for various market segments—grief therapy, Gen X activities, and seminars on a variety of topics like twelve-step recovery, divorce dynamics, and the parenting of adolescents—all served up with cappuccino and scones. The need to belong

will always be with us because humans by nature are social beings.

Love and Esteem Needs.   Once we satisfy our affiliation or belonging needs, we feel the emergence of needs in the fourth level of Maslow's model, which he called **love and esteem needs**, defined as the need to be valued by the members of the groups with which we affiliate—our families, fellow workers, friends, church congregation, and neighbors. Once we are part of a group, we want to feel that the group values us as a member and as an individual. We are happy when our families understand and admire the things we do. In her recent book *My Life So Far*, Jane Fonda quotes Oprah Winfrey as naming this need the "Please Disease" (2005) and describes it as a lifelong and unending desire to do things that will please our parent(s) and bring us love or esteem. The esteem need is also a reemerging one. That is, when we find that we are needed, loved, and esteemed by our family, our need for esteem does not fade away—instead, its focus shifts, and we now want to feel needed by our co-workers, our boss, and our friends.

Many product appeals offer a kind of symbolic substitute for esteem. For example, as Figure 7.7 shows, the kids will hold Mom in high esteem if she uses a certain brand of gas grill.

At various times, a person's esteem seems rooted in conspicuous consumption for purposes of display. At other times (e.g., wartime), conspicuous consumption borders on being unpatriotic. However, important events and life experiences can change the way people satisfy esteem needs. For instance, recent political, financial, and religious scandals have shaken people's faith in traditional institutions and their leadership's ability to show esteem. What kind of esteem for employees and stockholders does the crooked CEO have? Schiffman and Kanuk (1997) note that the Asian-American subculture is highly motivated by esteem needs and therefore they are strivers, particularly in terms of education. People realize that working in community can help them meet their esteem needs. In fact, "community" has become a kind of god term.

THE GRILLER: MARATHON MOM

No time to waste, right? So a gas grill has to perform quickly, easily. Enter MasterFlame². It's built with your schedule in mind: easy push button ignition, sturdy shelves for extra work space, a cooking system that virtually eliminates uneven heat, and multi-level cooking to prepare the main course and side dishes at one time. Give it a try... you'll find you've made a delicious dinner for your family and it wasn't a chore at all. In fact, it's our guess you'll find you even had fun.

To locate Char-Broil MasterFlame² gas grills, and find out about a free gift with purchase, just call

1-800-477-0118

THE GRILL: MASTERFLAME²™ FROM **Char-Broil**

FIGURE 7.7

Esteem needs are the key appeal in this ad claiming a Char-Broil gas grill allows the mother to whip up a great meal for her kids, and she feels good about that.

SOURCE: Reprinted by permission of Char-Broil.

Self-Actualization Needs. Maslow put **self-actualization needs** at the top of his pyramid (thereby implying that they rarely emerge). He defined self-actualization as the achievement of one's full potential or capability. At first, Maslow believed that individuals could live up to their potential only when all four of the lower needs had been met. It is hard for young people on the way up to think about self-actualization, just as it is difficult to meet love or esteem needs if individuals don't belong to some group that can offer love or esteem. But in reality, self-actualization is an integral part of everyone's life. In fact later in life Maslow said another need—the need to help others find self-actualization—emerged in some persons. Feig (1997) labeled this need "the desire to be the best you can be" hot button, and he identifies several examples, including the pride we all had as children when we brought home our gold-starred papers from school—they were proof of self-actualization. Poor Cardinal Sicola in Figure 7.8 won't get to self-actualize because of his name.

Maslow later came to see self-actualization as occurring through what he called "peak experiences" in life. These events allowed individuals to enjoy and learn about themselves, or experience something they had only dreamed of previously. Thus, the person who ventures into the wilderness and learns to be self-reliant and not to fear isolation enjoys a peak, or self-actualizing, experience. When people take their first job after high school or college and discover that they have abilities that are of value, they probably experience a degree of self-actualization.

F I G U R E 7.8 The humor here is based on Cardinal Sicola's inability to self-actualize.

Cultural trends also affect the ways in which we seek to satisfy our self-actualization needs. Social critic T. J. Jackson Lears (1983) noted that the search for ways of identifying ourselves and our potential came about when the United States shifted from being a culture of production to a culture of consumption; that is, in moving from a secure farm existence to an unsettling urban isolation, we experienced a loss of traditional values and chaotic changes in our lifestyles. The result, Lears claimed, was the search for a "therapeutic ethos" or an identity that would let us be at ease with ourselves—that would permit us to self-actualize. To a large extent, this therapeutic ethos offers inner harmony, reduced feelings of emptiness, and hope for self-realization through patterns of consumption. As you are exposed to various persuasive events, whether public or interpersonal, try applying Maslow's model to them, and see whether it sheds light on the needs that people feel and that may motivate their actions and persuade them. You may want to experiment with persuading another person using several levels of Maslow's model. If the person doesn't seem motivated by appeals to security, try appealing to basic or belongingness needs.

Uses of the Needs Process Premise

In our search for the first premises that serve as springboards for persuasion in enthymemes, human needs demonstrate one area of our vulnerability to persuasion. Whether we identify them using Packard's compelling needs, Maslow's hierarchy, Feig's hot buttons, or some other model, we all experience strongly felt needs that require some sort of satisfaction. Persuaders frequently tie minor premises to these powerful needs and allow audiences to complete the enthymematic argument by drawing the conclusion. As persuadees, we must consider the persuasive requests made of us from the perspective of our own needs. And as persuaders, we should examine the current needs of those we wish to influence. If we do that, we are more likely to succeed and to do our audience a service by giving them a way to satisfy their needs.

It is important, however, to be ethical in appealing to audience needs, especially in an ethically challenged world. As persuadees we need to ask, "Is this appeal really to my true needs ethical or not?" thus practicing our response-ability, and we need to ask the same questions when we take on the role of persuader. A good way to train yourself to evaluate appeals from this critical perspective—as persuadee or persuader—is to restate persuasive messages, such as TV commercials or political appeals, from the perspective of the Packard, Maslow, Feig, or other need models. As first premises on which persuasion can be built, psychological and physiological needs are powerful motivators, and they are frequently used in our world of advocacy and propaganda. See Box 7.2.

B O X 7.2   Interactive Marketing and Human Needs

Go to www.everybodysinteractive.com and discover how marketing experts are delving into human needs using interactive media. The home page you will discover there will show you how marketers use interactive media to appeal to human needs and emotions. Explore the various options, including how the Watson Communication Group plans and executes advertising strategies for various clients such as Levi Straus, Microsoft, cosmetic dentists, skin care specialists, and others. You will see how human needs and emotions are being tapped by persuaders of all sorts.

B O X 7.3   Disney, Emotions, and Propaganda

Go to www.youtube.com/watch?v=nvp3zAPraF4 and watch an 8-minute video "Reason and Emotion" on wartime propaganda. Emotion is personalized as a caveman and a naughty and sexy young girl. Why? Reason is personalized as a nerdy fellow with big eyeglasses and as a spinster school teacher. Why? If you wish you can also view several WW II animated cartoons or parts thereof from Disney. Now enter the words "Institute for Propaganda Analysis" and review the seven techniques of propaganda introduced by the discussed Institute beginning with the link entitled "Name Calling." Try to determine which of their techniques, as well as the needs and emotions discussed in this chapter, are being played upon in the initial Disney film and the optional clips from the other cartoons.

EMOTIONS: THE SECOND PROCESS PREMISE

Another kind of psychological or process premise relates to our emotions (see Box 7.3). Appeals to our emotions are the second of four such process premises including needs. What does it mean when, in the midst of a discussion, someone says, "You're just being too emotional about this?" It may mean that they have noticed a physical change in your behavior. Perhaps your voice changes in timbre or volume, your face gets red, you begin to show a nervous tic, or your eyes reveal anger. Or they might be responding to the fact that you have started rattling off statistics, sounding like a courtroom attorney. Borchers (2005) refers to these two symptoms of being emotional as demonstrating the physiological and the cognitive dimensions of emotion. In the *physiological dimension* you feel a change in the way your body is responding to the situation. You feel your voice change in timbre, your face flush, and your change in facial expression. With the *cognitive dimension* of emotions, the changes in you are not physical responses—they are perceptual changes in the way you think about a person, an issue, or a situation. These cognitive changes are usually expressed verbally. We are probably born with the physiological dimension of emotions hardwired into our brains. However, we must *learn* the cognitive dimension and how to express what emotions we are feeling. We learn these things from experiences, parents, authority figures, friends, or role models whom we observe in films, on television, or elsewhere. In both the physiological and the cognitive dimension, there are cultural variations (Porter & Samovar, 1998), particularly when our emotions are publicly displayed. We can see this in ethnic stereotypes of the emotional, gesticulating Italian or the authority-driven German. You probably have learned that the British are very polite even when expressing anger whereas other ethnicities might be outright rude.

In both the physiological and the cognitive dimension, we are dealing with models for understanding and reacting to our feelings and beliefs. Nabi (2002) maintains that emotions have five basic components: (1) cognitive evaluation of a situation, meaning that we are aware and have thought over the situation; (2) physiological arousal, or a change in bodily functions, such as an adrenalin rush; (3) motor expression, or what we physically do about the situation; (4) motivational intentions or readiness, or what we are prepared to do and plan to do and why; and (5) a feeling state in the subject, such as when you feel happy or disappointed (p. 290). You have learned to "bite your tongue" or to "count to ten" when feeling the emotion of anger, either from experience or more likely from parents or authority figures. Let's examine a few emotions that most persons feel or respond to in some way and see how persuaders use them to move us to action.

Fear

Fear is one of the most familiar emotions that we experience. Initially, you learned to be afraid when you did something wrong and angered someone else—usually a parent—and were punished for the behavior. As time passed, you learned that other situations and events can also lead to negative outcomes, and you became fearful of a number of things such as disease, injury, loss of property, or personal embarrassment to name a few. Nabi (2002) says that fear includes a threat to our physical or psychological self that is out of our control, and that it can change attitudes (pp. 291–292).

Appeals to the emotion of fear have been one of the most researched issues in persuasion, but the conclusions of the research are often contradictory. Sometimes the fear appeal works powerfully, but at other times it boomerangs, especially if it is too strong to stomach, inappropriate for you in your situation, or simply is unbelievable. Politicians have used fear appeals in negative television advertisements in campaign after campaign, and 2008 will probably not be any different. In the 2004 presidential campaign, President Bush implied that a vote for his opponent would lead to a loss of national security. Fear appeals

are also common in marketing communication. For example, the insurance industry tells us to be afraid of financial loss. We are told that we need insurance for everything from floods to identity theft, the need for long-term medical care, or national disasters like Hurricane Katrina in 2005, which made New Orleans essentially uninhabitable and resulted in billions of dollars in insurance claims. Personal grooming ads emphasize the possible loss in prestige that comes from teeth that aren't white enough, underarm odor, or poor taste in choice of clothing. And cause-related persuasion frequently uses fear appeals in campaigns advocating family values, safe sex, and national security. In most uses of fear appeals, the persuader must first convince persuadees of the probability of the threat before offering a means (usually a product or practice) of avoiding it and then demonstrating that the proposed solution will work. As receivers of fear appeals, you need to carefully examine the probability of the threat, the difficulty of taking the proposed actions to dodge the threat, and the evidence that these actions will prevent the problem.

Guilt

As we observed elsewhere, guilt is a powerful motivator in persuading others to vote, purchase, donate, or join. Guilt usually comes from a realization that we have violated some rule or code of conduct but can reduce the guilt by atonement or punishment. Borchers (2005) defines guilt as "a psychological feeling of discomfort that arises when order is violated" (p. 195). Guilt frequently arises out of some kind of interpersonal situation—we have wronged our parents, children, spouse, friends, or the community, and we must set things right. For example, the politician claims that we have underfunded education, and many poor kids are left behind, doomed to failure. We can atone for the mistake by having nationwide competence tests, eliminating tenure for teachers, and getting actively involved in our children's learning. If we missed an appointment, we can send flowers or an "I'm sorry" card. If we have engaged in unsafe sex, thus endangering our partner, we can notify that partner and vow to engage in preventive actions in the future. The best way

THINK HOW MUCH YOUR KIDS COULD DO IN LIFE. NOW THINK HOW DOING POT COULD STOP THEM.

Reliable evidence shows that marijuana today is more than twice as powerful on average as it was 20 years ago. It contains twice the concentration of THC, the chemical that affects the brain. Pot can turn your hopes and dreams for your kids into a nightmare of lost opportunities.

It can start with messing up in school. Kids who regularly smoke marijuana can develop symptoms of what psychologists call an "amotivational syndrome," which in plain English means:

- *decreased energy and ambition*
- *shortened attention span*
- *lack of judgment*
- *high distractibility*
- *impaired ability to communicate and relate to others*

And pot can cause a whole lot more problems than just doing badly in school. But the good news is that kids whose parents get involved with them are far less likely to do drugs.

So lay down a few laws for your kids. And the sooner the better, because the average age when teens first try marijuana is under 14 years old. To learn more, call 1-800-788-2800 or come to the web site.

PARENTS.
THE ANTI-DRUG.
`theantidrug.com`

OFFICE OF NATIONAL DRUG CONTROL POLICY/PARTNERSHIP FOR A DRUG-FREE AMERICA®

FIGURE 7.9

This ad by the Partnership for a Drug Free America uses the avoidance of future guilt to persuade.

SOURCE: Reprinted with permission of The Partnership for a Drug Free America.

to prevent drug usage by teens is for parents to ask where the teen is going, who will be there, when they expect to come home, and whether adults will be present. That advice is part of a cause-related campaign sponsored by the Partnership for a Drug Free America and is about avoiding guilt in the future. Its slogan is "Parents: The Anti-Drug" and its ads emphasize the guilt a parent can feel if their child becomes a drug user. Nabi (2002) notes that the causes of guilt vary greatly across religions and cultures. In some cultures, losing face is about the worst thing a person can do. In others, dishonoring one's elders is the big guilt button. Receivers need to recognize guilt appeals for what they are and then determine what they need to do to reduce their own

sense of guilt and try to avoid guilt if possible as seen in Figure 7.9.

Anger

We usually become angry when things don't go our way. When we face some obstacle that keeps us from reaching our goal or that harms us or loved ones, we become frustrated; and we want to strike out at those who make things difficult for us. Anger is also very powerful. Nabi (2002) noted that while anger generates high levels of energy, it sometimes leads to constructive problem solving and often prompts careful analysis of messages (p. 293). Take the sentence "What did he mean by saying that I was naïve?" You might get angry over being called naïve, but you seek to get down to the actual meaning of the accusation, which is usually a constructive use of your anger.

We see appeals to anger in politics and cause-related persuasion—advocacy or propaganda—and in some types of marketing and advertising. A significant proportion of the population was fearful and angry enough following 9/11 that in 2003 that they supported President Bush's call to go to war in Iraq. The justification for the action was that Iraq had caused the disaster because it harbored terrorists and had hidden Weapons of Mass Destructions (WMDs), and we wanted to strike back to remove the problem and punish the country for the tragic attacks. In hindsight, we clearly needed more careful analysis of the situation and the facts by critical receivers. The "striking back" was enormously costly in human and national wealth plunging us into the longest war in our history and the largest deficits in history in our national budget, not to mention and pain and costs of the deaths and injuries suffered by the troops. Many of these costs will continue for decades (e.g., physical or psychological injuries). Furthermore, the invasion didn't result in fewer terrorist attacks, but, in fact, it may have led to an increase in the number of suicide bombers (including women and children) in Iraq and elsewhere and may have been used to recruit new members of terrorist organizations. Employees, stockholders, and retirees in the late 1990s became angry with CEOs who looted their company's resources and pension funds. Some of them went on a crusade to reform the Securities and Exchange Commission, and they succeeded. They used cause-related persuasion to recruit supporters and donors by appealing to the anger felt by those who were cheated by the crooked CEOs. In my state, an organization called the Citizen's Utility Board (CUB) regularly gets donations by appealing to the anger felt by consumers when utility rates are arbitrarily raised. On an intrapersonal level, some persons are angry with the way they look, even if it's their own fault. A "Fatties" organization is now bringing suit against food manufacturers for not disclosing ingredient information that might lead overweight individuals to avoid the products (see Figure 7.10). We have also recently seen persons in

middle age go to orthodontists to have braces put on their crooked teeth. Perhaps they were angry with their parents, who didn't take care of the problem earlier in adolescence; but now they are willing to pay for the improvement themselves. So anger frequently serves as a motivator in persuasion. Other negative emotions include envy, hatred, and disgust (Nabi, 2002).

Pride

On a more positive note, persuaders appeal to pride to enact legislation, sell products, and prompt joining an organization or donating to a particular candidate or good cause. A feeling of pride usually includes taking credit for some positive outcome in our lives. As a result, people become expressive about their accomplishments and may make announcements about the good deeds. Sometimes this causes resentment in those who haven't achieved as much, so persuaders need to be careful about using appeals to pride. And cultural differences affect the emotion of pride. Nabi (2002) reports that collectivist cultures (such as China's) "respond more favorably to pride-based appeals" (p. 296) than do cultures that are more individualistically based (such as the United States). We can find pride appeals in many persuasive contexts. Politicians tout the accomplishments of their administrations or programs. Cause-based pride appeals are intended to make the potential donors feel proud about making a donation to the good cause, and frequently use testimonials from persons helped by the good cause. And of course many products promise to make consumers feel proud when they use the brand to improve their appearance. For example, Neutrogena Skin Clearing Tint uses a pride appeal when the ads urge consumers to "Rethink makeup … now, don't cover up. Clear up." The ads give the brand credibility by using the words "Dermatologist Recommended" together with the pictures of two young females who are presumed to use the product and who appear not to have acne or blemishes.

Happiness and Joy

Happiness and joy are obviously similar. Happiness is associated with a mood, and joy indicates a posi-

Obesity:

"~~Epidemic~~"

"~~Problem~~"

"~~Threat~~"

"~~Issue~~"

"Hype"

Americans have been force-fed a steady diet of obesity myths by the "food police," trial lawyers, and even our own government.

Learn the truth about obesity at:

ConsumerFreedom.com

The Center for Consumer Freedom is a nonprofit organization dedicated to protecting consumer choices and promoting common sense.

FIGURE 7.10

This ad by the Center for Consumer Freedom builds on the anger that overweight persons have felt throughout their lives.

SOURCE: Used with permission of The Center for Consumer Freedom.

tive emotional response to such happy events. For our purposes they are synonyms. Happy persons are positive about their future, confident, sharing, and trusting, and they seem to attract other persons (Nabi, 2002). We can all think of persuasive happiness appeals made by advertisers who link use of their brand with happy outcomes and satisfied consumers. Estee Lauder's *Pleasures* and *Pleasures for Men* ran a three-page fold-out ad in the May 2005 issue of *Cosmopolitan*. It had no copy aside from the name of the brand. Instead it showed nine pictures, seven of which focused on the members of a young family. The other two pictures were of cherry blossoms and a puppy. The implied conclusion was for consumers to "Use the brand and be as happy as these folks." Politicians promise better, happier, sharing, and more trusting times if we enact their policies on the economy, health care, the environment, education, and other issues. Cause-related advertising usually implies that support for a cause such as *Save the Children* or *Gun Ownership Rights* will bring the joiner or donor a sense of well-being, self-respect, and happiness instead of a sense of guilt for ignoring the issue. Nabi (2002) also says that appeals to happiness frequently use humor in advertising because of its ability to distract audience attention and cause laughter (p. 296). Other positive emotions that persuaders can invoke include relief, hope, compassion, and many others.

ATTITUDES: THE THIRD PROCESS PREMISE

In Chapter 4 we looked at how researchers use a variety of theories to explain attitudes. One unifying element among these theories is that attitudes can and do serve as the unstated major premises in persuasive enthymemes. We also noted that attitudes act as predispositions to behavior, so holding an attitude or a set of attitudes makes us ready to take action. However, while attitudes are sometimes excellent predictors of behavior, at other times they are not. Psychologists Martin Fishbein and Icek Ajzen (1975) now believe that a better predictor of behavior is what they call the *intention to behave*. When the person tells you how he or she intends to act, the person is prone to act that way. By articulating their intentions, they have already acted symbolically.

The initial series of studies into the effects of attitude were conducted by researcher Carl Hovland and over 30 of his colleagues at Yale in the 1950s and 60s (e.g., Hovland et al., 1953) They identified a series of stages through which information must pass in order to effect persuasion. Stage 1 was *Attention* (for if no one paid attention to the information, it could not

persuade). Stage 2 was *Comprehension* (for if no one could understand the information, it could not persuade—not necessarily true for information passed through the peripheral channel of the ELM). Stage 3 was *Retention* (for if no one remembered the information it could not persuade—again not so in peripherally processed information as in the ELM). The final stage was *Action* (for if you did not act on the suggested behavior, persuasion did not occur—again not true in the peripheral channel and not true in many other circumstances like when the persuasion goal is simply to make people aware). So while quite incomplete, the Yale studies and the Yale Stage Model did initiate an ongoing series of studies conducted elsewhere and by different researchers that persists up until today, some of which produced significantly predictive results (such as the fear appeal studies), and they led to more and more sophisticated definitions of attitudes. (See Box 7.4.)

For example, psychologists Alice H. Egley and Shelley Chaiken (1993) define an attitude as "a psychological tendency that is expressed by evaluating a particular entity with some degree of favor or disfavor" (p. 1). The important word here is "tendency," by which they mean "an internal state that lasts for at least a short time" (p. 2). Since the attitude is internal (in our heads), we must infer it by using "evaluative responses." Evaluative responses include expressing "approval or disapproval, favor or disfavor, liking or disliking, approach or avoidance, attraction or aversion, or similar reactions" (p. 3). Researchers into consumer behavior identified a social function served by attitudes. For instance, they asked whether family, friends, authority figures, or celebrity figures affect our attitudes toward a brand, candidate, or ideology. They concluded that socially significant persons do influence our attitudes (Schiffman & Kanuk, 1997), and note that mass media exposure correlates highly with the formation of consumer attitudes (pp. 260–262). Advertising researcher Shavitt (1990) maintained that attitudes serve both social and utilitarian functions. In researching audience reactions to advertisements, he found that the social functions of attitudes in the ads tell us what persons responding to the ads were like and in all likelihood what

---

B O X 7.4   The Stage Model and Superbowl Ads

 Go to any search engine and enter the words "superbowl ads." Select from any of the links there and carefully examine several of these spots from different years; | Try to determine if they get attention, can be remembered, and/or are accepted or acted upon. Does the stage model help you as a receiver in analyzing these multimillion dollar ads?

---

sorts of appeals would prompt them to action. For example, the ad might claim that discriminating people prefer high-fiber diets to high-fat, low-carb Atkins' Diets that only temporarily take off pounds. If we want to be a discriminating and slimmer person, we adopt the eating habits of other discriminating and slim persons.

Utilitarian functions of attitudes stress the features and benefits of the product. An ad might claim that the Honda Prius gets up to 60 miles per gallon, and it is extremely quiet in the electrically powered mode. Two utilitarian elements operate here—mileage and quietness. This also fits with elements of the ELM model. For example, psychologists De Bono and Harnish (1988), Petty and Wegener (1998), and others found that for high self-monitoring individuals (e.g., those who were usually very aware of why they were responding to an ad), an attractive source of persuasion usually triggers elaborate processing of the message. For low self-monitoring individuals (e.g., those who were barely aware of even responding to the ad), elaborate processing is more likely to occur only if an expert rather than an attractive source conveys the message. This makes sense. If you are a high self-monitoring person, you do not want to blunder simply because a celebrity recommends the product. That makes you seem impulsive in the eyes of others. So, you do serious investigation of the product in the central processing route. Low self-monitoring persons respect expertise more than advice from a celebrity, and they avoid looking foolish by relying on the recommendation of the expert.

We usually find attitude objects in the persuader's requests for action or offers of products, ideas, candidates, beliefs, and so on. For example, recently many Americans started flying the flag and displaying patriotic bumper stickers, yard signs, and other emblems with slogans like "United We Stand" or "These Colors Won't Run." These displays are in response to political persuasion emphasizing the value of patriotism. These attitude objects serve a social function because they announce the person's attitudes. This, in turn, causes alignment or identification with others who feel the same way and helps to foster interpersonal relations and influence. The attitude object of the flag, bumper sticker, or sign serves as part of the appeal; and we follow suit if we want to identify with them. The obverse is also true: If we want to distance ourselves from jingoistic patriotism, we won't follow the requested action and may even display a "Get Out of Iraq!" sign in our yard. This reduces the possibility of forming interpersonal relationships with super-patriots.

So, attitudes have an important social function since they can either foster or discourage social networking. Nelson (2001) notes that the social function of attitudes in organizations (especially businesses) can make or break the organization. And according to Schrader (1999), the social function of interpersonal influence is largely dependent on the goal complexity of appeals. In other words, if the persuader's advice is too complicated, we judge his or her attempts to influence us as unworkable, incompetent, or inappropriate. As a result, the social function of attitudes often affects persuasive outcomes.

Attitudes, Beliefs, and Opinions

As noted in Chapter 4, Rokeach (1968) pointed out that individual beliefs range from primitive and strongly held to those based on authority and not as strongly held. These belief sets cluster and form **attitudes** which fall into two categories: (1) attitudes toward objects or issues and (2) attitudes toward situations. Both predispose us to action, but they also might confuse us when they conflict with one another. For example, when parents protest the presence of a student with AIDS in their children's school, attitudes toward the object (the infected student) and toward the situation (the possibility of infecting my own children) can either conflict or converge. When the two attitudes conflict, the parents sympathize with the victim; but they don't want their child infected.

Opinions resemble beliefs but are far more fickle; as opinion polls demonstrate—opinions can change overnight. We have opinions about politicians, what they say in campaigns, and their actions taken after assuming office. These opinions change, especially if the politician blunders, loses to Congress on an issue, or supports a corrupt friend. Usually, the politician's errors lead to low voter ratings and sometimes rejection at the polls. But opinions are fickle and unpredictable. For example, during Bill Clinton's impeachment trial, his ratings in the polls actually went to an all-time high in spite of the sordid sex scandal. Why? Rokeach's theory helps explain the riddle. People had a highly negative attitude toward Clinton's sexual dalliance (attitude toward object). But they had highly positive feelings about other issues like the economy, low unemployment, budget surpluses, and a bullish stock market (attitude toward situation). These opinions conflicted with their feelings about the scandal, and the economy won out. A similar scenario played out for President George W. Bush on his plan to institute private investment accounts as part of the Social Security system. After he campaigned for the change in over half of the states, his ratings on the issue plummeted in the public opinion polls.

Social psychologist Zimbardo and his colleagues (1976, 1991) note that attitudes are "either mental readiness or implicit predispositions that exert some general and consistent influence on a fairly large class of evaluative responses" (p. 20). A school of advertising research known by the acronym DAGMAR suggests that ad agencies ought to *D*efine *A*dvertising *G*oals for *M*easured *A*dvertising *R*esults (Colley, 1961). In other words, establishing positive attitudes toward a brand serves as the goal of advertising, not instant purchase behavior. The idea is that if consumers have an improved image of a product, they will probably buy it sometime in the future. Therefore, if the marketer can change their attitudes, purchase eventually follows. Unfortunately, this attitude-behavior link sometimes flip-flops, perhaps because of intervening variables that also affect purchase behavior such as time of day, attractiveness of the offer, a store display, price, or background music. Even in experiments with these causes filtered out, attitude and behavior do not consistently link.

The Functions of Attitudes

Attitudes can have several functions. For example, they have a cognitive or knowledge function because we aren't born with attitudes but must learn them. Consider our attitudes about being environmentally responsible. How did they come about? Probably we first learned about air and water pollution and the dangers that they bring. Then we learned about recycling and what it can achieve. Then we learned that endangered species may act as early warnings about what might ultimately happen to humans. Only after learning all of these things do we finally form an overall attitude toward environmental responsibility. Likewise, some advertisements also persuade by teaching. A mutual fund company advertises that it is "no load" and goes on to explain what that means—customers don't have to pay commissions when they make investments. Persuadees learn the value of this and form a positive attitude toward that company, and they decide to use the company when they make investments. The same learning operates in political or cause-related campaigns. For example, since the March of Dimes no longer supports polio research (the disease has been nearly eradicated), it must teach potential donors that now it supports research into premature births—the leading cause of infant mortality. The receiver learns about the organization and its purposes and only then forms an attitude toward it and ultimately decides whether or not to send a donation.

Attitudes also function to influence our emotions and feelings, and thus they have what has been termed an *affective function* or an emotional outcome. For instance, our attitudes about the development of hydrogen fuels affect how we feel about this new source of energy. If we equate hydrogen energy with the hydrogen bomb, we experience fear and may actively oppose its production. Some ads target the affective dimension, or emotions. For example, how did *The Sopranos* affect viewers' attitudes and emotions toward mob figures? Chris Seay, a Christian minister, worried about his wife's response when he rushed home from church activities to watch the nudity and profanity-filled fourth season. He ultimately convinced her that the show was about "faith, forgiveness and family values." That nifty bit of persuasion got him out of his affective dilemma (Pinsky, 2002).

Finally, attitudes have a behavioral function in that they prepare us to take certain actions. Because we hold certain attitudes toward air and water pollution, we may choose to recycle, to not buy a gas guzzler, or only use biodegradable detergents. The behavioral function of attitudes affects what we do about these issues. Some ads aim at changing attitudes in order to prompt behavior change. Two goals of advertising are to create traffic in a store and to get consumers to try a brand. The advertiser offers huge discounts or special events such as the visit of a celebrity to create traffic. They may send a free sample or offer an attractive rebate with a purchase. Few people reject anything that is free or cheaper, so they give the brand a try. The marketer's hope is that visiting the store will prompt impulse purchases or that satisfaction with the performance of the brand will lead to brand loyalty and future purchases.

Attitudes and Intention

As we noted earlier, the work of Fishbein and Ajzen (1975) added the concept of **behavioral intention** to the research on attitude and behavior change. Here, a fairly consistent set of results emerges.

Attitude change usually precedes what people say they intend to do. As noted above, when people articulate what they intend to do, they have already acted symbolically. Nonverbally, when the person clips or saves a coupon, he or she has already "bought" the brand. Likewise, the person who displays a bumper sticker in favor of a certain candidate will show up at the polls to vote for that candidate on election day. Knowing this, politicians urge people to display bumper stickers, buttons, and yard signs to guarantee their votes rather than trying to persuade others who may be undecided.

Attitudes and Interpersonal Communication/Persuasion

There are several other dimensions of attitude change and the subsequent behavior puzzle. One of these is the degree to which attitudes function as tools of interpersonal communication or persuasion, or both. In other words, do expressions of attitudes have more to do with fitting ourselves into a comfortable position with others than they do with our ultimate behavior? Eiser (1987), a critic of attitude research puts it this way: "One of the main shortcomings of many attitude theories is their emphasis on individualistic, intra-psychic factors to the relative neglect of the social and communicative context within which attitudes are acquired and expressed" (p. 2). In other words, we overtly express attitudes in order to get along with and identify with others.

Attitudes and Information Processing

The focus on human information processing in the ELM, which serves as a unifying model throughout this book, also relates to behavioral intentions. We can't look at attitudes and behavior without also looking at how audiences process such persuasive information. One of the first questions to ask is whether the audience even comprehends the message. In the central path, they usually do comprehend the message and may even research it. In the peripheral path, they probably don't. For example, "cents off" coupons as persuasive information fit with several memory networks in our minds, such as whether we already use the brand, how often, and whether the coupons are valuable enough to justify clipping them. Peripheral cues may prompt behavior. For example, people will clip more coupons if there is a dotted line around the coupon and clip even more if there is a little scissors on the dotted line. And there are diversity issues to be concerned with in deciding whether or not to offer coupons. For example, Latinos tend not to clip coupons because they associate them with food stamps, a social stigma in their subculture. So if an advertiser is targeting Latinos, that advertiser should not use coupons but may want to emphasize the warranty or quality instead.

Research into how information is stored in our Long-Term Memory (LTM) is fairly recent, and most researchers agree that information is usually stored in networks and in the form of key words, symbols, and relationships. A good organizing device for LTM is to make one's persuasion episodic in nature, probably due to the power of the narrative or story form. For example, we all have been late for an appointment and find ourselves stuck behind the slowest driver on the road, who also misses all the green stoplights. Imagine a television commercial to promote Compoz, an over-the-counter treatment for settling people's nerves. This episode could act as a script for the commercial. The ad opens with the character realizing that he or she has nearly missed a doctor's appointment. We see them rush out to the car, get in, and speed off, only to get behind the slowpoke. They glance nervously at the clock and begin having a silent "conversation" with the slow driver. They are about to commit road rage, but instead they take a Compoz tablet. The ad closes with the slow driver turning at the next intersection and the product's slogan, "For those nerve-racking occasions try Compoz." At the behavior stage of the ELM (voting, buying, joining, or donating), the critical episode is retrieved from LTM and provides persuadees with good "reasons" for taking action.

The ELM model has prompted a multitude of research insights into the process of persuasion since its introduction. Researchers S. Booth-Butterfield and J. Welbourne (2002) suggest that the model "has been instrumental in integrating the literature on source,

message, receiver and context effects in persuasion and has also been a springboard for new research in this domain" (p. 155). Although people want to have "correct" attitudes, the degree to which they will elaborate on an issue varies from individuals and situations; but the following patterns remain clear.

1. A number of variables affect attitude change and can act as persuasive arguments, peripheral cues, or attitudinal positions.

2. When motivation or ability to elaborate decreases, peripheral cues become more important and carry the persuasive load. For example, persons who are uninterested in the implications of diversity will rely on stereotyping.

3. Conversely, as motivation or ability to elaborate on a claim increases, peripheral cues lose impact. For example, if our new boss is ethnically different from us, we devalue stereotypes.

4. The persuader affects consumers' motivation by encouraging or discouraging careful examination of the argument or claim. The persuader says, "April 15 is only a week away, so bone up on the new tax laws," instead of saying, "At your income level, you might as well use the short tax form 1040EZ and file online."

5. Issues and arguments flowing from the central processing path persist, predict actual behavior best, and seem resistant to competing persuasion. Persuasion using process premises is likely to follow the peripheral path, whereas persuasion using reasoned premises is likely to be processed in the central route. Petty and Cacioppo's (1986) chart in Figure 7.11 depicts various options and routes.

Notice that the various options in the ELM depend on whether you have the motivation to process a persuasive message. You must want to investigate a given product, candidate, or cause or the elaboration process is short-circuited. If they are motivated to process an offer, appeal, or claim, persuadees must also possess the ability to complete the processing. Thereafter, the nature of the attitude change depends on which path is followed. If the

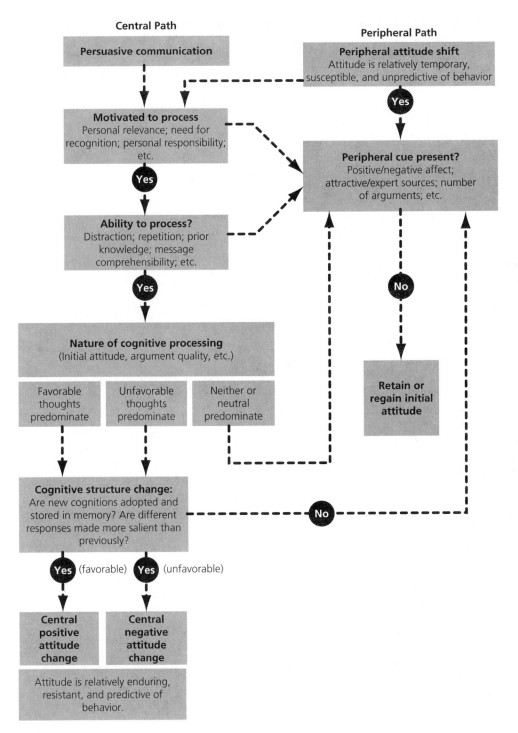

FIGURE 7.11 Decision flow in Petty and Cacioppo's elaboration likelihood model.

B O X 7.5   Ten Lenses and the Diversity Channel

In his book entitled *The Ten Lenses: Your Guide to Living and Working in a Multicultural World* (2001), Mark A. Williams, author and founder of The Diversity Channel (a diversity training company), discusses how human emotions vary in organizations and institutions. He describes and explains ten "lenses" or perceptual filters through which most of us view our diverse world. There are the *Assimilationists* who believe that all diversities should behave like regular Americans, and then there are the *Cultural Centrists* who believe that we must not tamper with the diversity of others. The *Meritocrats* believe that if you work hard enough and pull yourself up by your bootstraps, you will achieve your goals regardless of your race, ethnicity, or other aspects of diversity. The *Victim/Caretakers* believe that bias will forever hold down persons of diverse origins. The *Colorblind* believe in ignoring cultural differences and seeking the true value of any individual whose diversity

differs from the majority. The *Elitists* believe that it is their destiny and their right to be superior to others of varying diversities. The *Integrationists* believe that the best way to break down biases and stereotypes is to merge persons of various diversities in the workplace and elsewhere. The *Multiculturalists* want to celebrate our diversity—the more diversity we have, the better things will be for everyone. *Seclusionists* want to distance and protect themselves and their families from persons of diverse cultures. And *Transcendentists* believe that race, gender, and ethnicity reflect our unified humanity. Where do you fit? Speculate on how these lenses might apply to human needs, emotions, and attitudes. How do you look at persons of other races, nationalities, genders, sexual preference, or ethnicities? If you want to explore Williams's work further, pick up his book and take his Ten Lenses Survey or go online to www.thediversity channel.com and explore its home page options.

---

peripheral path is used, the attitude change will be weak, short-lived, and less likely to yield behavior. If the central processing path is used, attitude change will be potent, long-lived, and likely to lead to behavior.

Each path has its strengths and weaknesses. Most researchers agree that attitudes have something to do with behavior, that attitudes can be altered by persuasion, and that the suggested behavior usually follows a change in attitude. What does all this mean to us as persuadees who live in a world concerned with diversity and ethics? What can we do to uncover persuaders' intentions toward and beliefs about the diverse audiences? Being aware of attitudes helps us to pinpoint what persuaders think of us and others. Identifying the attitudes that persuaders assume we have makes us more critical receivers, and so we judge persuasive attempts as ethical or unethical. We also become conscious of our attitudes, and as a result, we anticipate how persuaders use them to get us to follow their advice. However, few situations involve a single attitude. Most situations involve several attitudes, which leads to a need for consistency among those attitudes. (See Box 7.5.)

CONSISTENCY: THE ~~FOURTH~~ *third* PROCESS PREMISE

We looked at balance theory in Chapter 4. It posits that we feel comfortable when the world lives up to (or operates consistently with) our perceptions or our predictions of it. By **consistency** we mean that our expectations about future events, the behaviors of other persons, and so on, ought to live up to or be consistent with what we expect. When that is not the case we feel what we earlier called "imbalance" or psychic discomfort and will tend to doubt the expected relationship and evidence related to it. Further, when this consistency doesn't happen, we try to change either ourselves or our interpretations of events to bring about a balanced state. As a result, persuaders offer a strategy or means (usually a product, service, or action) to return to balance and psychological comfort. If you want to change attitudes toward health care, for instance, then try to create imbalance in health care users. You might say, "With an HMO, you can't go to the best surgeon."

We all seek out psychological equilibrium, so as receivers we need to identify what puts us into states of imbalance or inconsistency, thus making us vulnerable to persuasion. If psychological equilibrium is our goal, we need to feel comfortable and look for persuasion that reinforces attitudes. As Eiser (1987) pointed out, defining the "existing frame of reference" is a critical factor in predicting attitude shifts. Once we identify the receiver's current frame of reference, we create the kind of inconsistency that prompts psychological uneasiness, which leads to attitude change.

Cognitive Dissonance Theory

A problem with balance theory is that it doesn't relate to the degree of difference between the two people or the two instances judged. Instead it looks at the kinds of differences—positive or negative—that exist in the comparisons of persons or instances. In other words, the theory accounts for *qualitative* differences between judgments but it doesn't deal with *quantitative* differences. That may seem like a minor problem, but major differences might exist between persons or concepts regarding controversial topics such as abortion, school prayer, or patriotism, so it's important to determine how far persons and their issue positions are from one another on a topic. Leon Festinger's cognitive dissonance theory (1962) addressed this problem of quantitative and qualitative differences between persons and ideas.

Unlike balance theory, **cognitive dissonance theory** predicts that when we experience psychological tension, or dissonance, we try to reduce it in some way instead of totally resolving the tension. Tension reduction has a quantitative dimension. We can change our attitudes a little, a moderate amount, a lot, or not at all. The tension caused by dissonance grows out of our psychological belief system, whereas balance theory relies more on logical inconsistencies. Festinger defined dissonance as a feeling resulting from the existence of two nonfitting or contrasting pieces of knowledge about the world. As in balance theory, there are times when things fit or go together and times when they do not. For Festinger, the opposite of dissonance, or

"consonance," exists when two pieces of information do fit together, and hence reinforce one another. Some persons change dissonant cognitions by moving their beliefs closer to one another. Others rationalize the problem away or discredit the source of the information. Others reduce dissonance by selective perception, selective retention, or selective exposure—they choose not to receive or perceive the dissonance, they forget about it, or they choose not to be exposed to conflicting information.

Recently, dissonance theory helped explain the new sense of uneasiness affecting sexually active individuals who have multiple partners. Most of us know that the main causes of infection by the AIDS virus are unsafe sex practices, the sharing of needles among drug users, and sometimes from blood transfusions or accidental exposure to the blood of AIDS carriers. What can sexually active people do to reduce the uneasiness or dissonance they feel regarding their own sexually activity? They can:

1. Devalue their beliefs about the most effective methods of birth control and use condoms

2. Devalue AIDS information, telling themselves that this is just a scare tactic to cut down on the promiscuity of the younger generation

3. Selectively perceive the information and choose to believe that *their* sex partners don't have the AIDS virus

4. Try to forget the information about AIDS through the process of selective retention

5. Try to rationalize the problem away by believing that a cure for AIDS is just around the corner

6. Become celibate or have fewer partners

7. Do more than one of these things.

Although Festinger mainly dealt with the notion of dissonance, it seems clear that we seek its opposite, consonance, to reinforce our existing attitudes. We listen to the candidates of our choice and avoid listening to their opponents. Conservatives read conservative newspapers, and liberal people read liberal ones. We seek information that confirms our position and reinforces our beliefs. Several actions build consonance in this way. We can:

1. Revalue our initial beliefs, making them stronger
2. Revalue the source of the information input by giving it more credibility than it deserves
3. Perceive the information as stronger than it actually is
4. Remember the most positive parts of the information and highlight them
5. Seek out even more supporting information
6. Do several of these things.

Creating consonance strengthens and reinforces attitudes, increases credibility, and probably induces action. Persuaders probably use consonance at least as frequently as dissonance. They often want to reinforce people's opinions, attitudes, beliefs, or behavior.

In many cases, dissonance theory oversimplifies the human situation. Recently, researchers in communication, psychology, and sociology have looked at a variety of other factors that affect feelings of dissonance. Wood (2000) points out that social factors play a role in reducing dissonance. People want to fit in with significant reference groups and engage in normative behavior to do so. Internal states determine the outcome of persuasion as much as do the source's skill at designing the dissonance or consonance producing messages.

Sources of Dissonance

What causes you to feel imbalance or dissonance? Some factors are unique to you, but many of them are similar for large groups of people. These more universal factors are useful for persuaders because they are potent first premises in enthymemes. Descriptions of a few common ones follow.

Loss of Group Prestige.   This relates to the pride felt by members of a well-respected reference group, profession, or organization that has fallen on bad times and no longer is as highly respected. For instance,

Martha Stewart was highly respected by many people who identified with her because they felt that they also had her class and good taste. They wanted to emulate her, to try her recipes, and to have a flower garden like hers. One of her fans said, "We put a copy of Martha Stewart's *Living* magazine on a coffee table. It's the prettiest thing in the living room." Another said, "We want a little of what she's got—a scant teaspoon in Marthaspeak—of her taste and talent" (Rowell, 2002, p. 16). After she suffered a financial scandal and served jail time, her sheen dimmed a bit. A former fan observed, "There's nothing in her magazine that even hints at her virtue" (Rowell, 2002, p. 16). Ultimately, however, Martha regained some of her previous sheen. The loss of group prestige affects small and large groups alike—from a sorority to an entire profession such as lawyers, or a region of the country such as the East Coast.

Economic Loss.   When we feel that our economic value is in danger of being reduced, we experience dissonance. We deal with the obvious dissonance of losing a job in a number of ways. After the dot-com bubble burst, many displaced workers chose to take early retirement, others returned to school or accepted jobs with much lower salaries, and others started their own businesses.

Loss of Personal Prestige.   Ads promoting hair restorers or weight reduction plans play on one's loss of personal prestige resulting from physical appearance. Being passed over for a promotion at work also leads to a loss of personal prestige. Other fears relating to loss of prestige include the loss of youth, the loss of health, and the lost of self-respect.

Uncertainty of Prediction.   Whenever we move, change schools, take a new job, or break up with a spouse or significant other, we feel uncomfortable because we can no longer predict probable outcomes. Products that promise to protect us from some negative circumstance (illness, job loss, financial difficulties) use the inability to predict as a "hook" to persuade us.

Sources of Consonance

On the other side of the coin, some appeals give receivers a sense of consonance, and reinforce beliefs, attitudes, or behaviors and activate receivers.

Reassurance of Security. Today, police stations, airports, courthouses, schools, and other public buildings are protected with metal detectors and even armed guards. We want to feel secure in public places, and these preventatives provide that sense of security. Promises of job security are powerful persuaders for persons making career choices, and IRA and Keogh accounts offer retirement security.

Demonstration of Predictability. Consonance happens when the world operates in predictable ways. Manufacturers rely on the appeal to predictability by offering guarantees or warranties. And everyone likes to know what to expect at work, at home, in the community, and so on.

The Use of Rewards. Rewards or positive reinforcements increase feelings of consonance and the probability that a behavior will be repeated. Persuaders often use positive and complimentary statements to reinforce behavior. In his best-selling book *How to Win Friends and Influence People*, Dale Carnegie (1952) advised his readers to "try to figure out the other man's good points ... and people will cherish your words and treasure them and repeat them over a lifetime" (p. 38). Carnegie put his finger on ways to make audiences feel good about themselves. This is still good advice for persuading audiences or influencing people. Successful supervisors seem adept at giving rewards rather than offering criticisms.

REVIEW AND CONCLUSION

We are searching for various kinds of unstated and widely held major premises that can serve in persuasive enthymemes. One of these kinds of major premises is the process or emotional premise, which appeals to our needs, emotions, attitudes, and the psychological processes of dissonance and consonance operating daily in each of us. We can see needs and wants operating in Maslow's hierarchy of needs, Packard's compelling human needs, and Feig's hot buttons. Although some of these models have been around for a long time, they still have applicability for us as their many rejuvenations demonstrate.

A second kind of process premise involves our emotions. Persuaders target our emotional states and get at us through such things as fear, guilt, and anger or by appeals to more positive emotions such as happiness, joy, or pride. A third kind of process premise involves attitudes, beliefs, and opinions. If persuaders change our attitudes about fuel efficiency, they predispose us to buy fuel-efficient autos, furnaces, and water heaters. If persuaders want us to continue voting for a certain party, they reinforce our existing beliefs and attitudes about that party. Both of these persuasive types can be used with either attitudes toward objects and issues or attitudes toward situations. It may be important for persuaders to reinforce or change our behavioral intentions. Attitudes also impact important and not so important purchase, voting, joining, or donating decisions, as depicted in the ELM.

The fourth kind of process premise is the human desire for psychological consonance, in which we seek a world where our predictions are verified, and in which people we like approve of the same things we do. If we feel a lack of balance, or dissonance, we actively seek ways to bring our world into congruity by reducing psychological tensions. If we perceive balance or consonance to exist, we experience a sense of ease and can be easily motivated to continue to act as we have been. Persuaders try to create dissonance if they want us to change our behavior, and they create consonance if they want us to maintain our behavior. Process premises are important in the ways we persuade others and the ways in which we are persuaded.

KEY TERMS

After reading this chapter, you should be able to identify, explain, and give an example of the following key terms or concepts:

process or emotional premises	reassurance of worth	prepotency	attitudes
motivation research	ego gratification	basic needs	opinions
hidden needs	creative outlets	need for security	behavioral intention
compelling needs	love objects	belongingness or affiliation needs	consistency
hot buttons	sense of power or strength	love and esteem needs	cognitive dissonance theory
emotional security	need for roots	self-actualization needs	

APPLICATION OF ETHICS

It is finals week at a state university. A professor of communication gets an e-mail from a student in one of his classes in which the student expresses a fear of failing the final exam. The two previous exams were so difficult that she was only able to get low "D" grades on them, and since the final counts double, she is in danger of failing the class. She tells the professor that she is already on probation and will be dismissed if she fails the class. Her parents have already given her an ultimatum—"get off probation or support yourself through the remaining two years of schooling!" By chance, the professor runs into the student in the library and tells her that he is not about to cater to stu-dents who don't study enough and chides her for even sending the e-mail. She denies having sent the message and says that she suspects someone has stolen her pass-word and sent a forgery to embarrass her. The professor convinces the manager of the university e-mail system to track down the source of the message, and indeed it had not been sent from the student's computer but from the male teaching assistant for the class. The pro-fessor suspects that the teaching assistant wants to use the e-mail to sexually harass the female student. There are emotional issues involved. Has the teaching assistant used a fear appeal? Is that ethical, given the professor's suspicions? What should the professor do?

QUESTIONS FOR FURTHER THOUGHT

1. What is a process premise? Explain.
2. What is the difference between an attitude and a need? Give examples.
3. What did Maslow mean when he called his hierarchy of needs "prepotent"?
4. Which needs described by Packard are the most ego involving or personal in nature?
5. What is an example of the need for emotional security?
6. What is an example of how advertisers use the need for ego gratification?
7. What is an example of the need for a sense of power?
8. What emotions are being used when persuaders alert us to the possibility of job loss or identity theft?
9. What emotions are being used when a persuader tells us that we have been cheated by an auto repair shop?
10. What are three functions of an attitude?

11. What is the difference between an attitude and an opinion?

12. What is the difference between a behavior and a behavioral intention?

13. According to the ELM, which decision path will be used when purchasing ice cream?

14. According to the ELM, what happens if the audience isn't motivated to vote?

15. According to the ELM, what happens to a decision if the audience can't respond?

16. Using the elaboration likelihood model in Figure 7.11, explain the flow of information regarding a current issue.

17. What are some sources of dissonance?

18. What are some sources of consonance?

19. What ethical standards should we apply when using process or emotional appeals?

 For online activities, go to the *Persuasion* book companion Web site at http://academic.cengage.com/communication/larson12.

8

✳

✳Content or Logical Premises in Persuasion

LEARNING GOALS

After reading this chapter, you should be able to:

1. Give everyday examples such as ads or speeches that rely on logical versus emotional appeals.

2. Find everyday examples of each of the types of evidence discussed.

3. Explain the difference between the two types of analogy and when they might be appropriate.

4. Find everyday examples of the three types of syllogisms and explain them to the class.

5. Explain the three major elements and the three substantiating elements in the Toulmin model.

6. Identify examples of logical fallacies in ads, newspaper editorials, and letters to the editor in a news weekly like *Time* or *Newsweek*.

7. Identify logical fallacies used in sensational publications like *The National Enquirer*—our nation's largest circulation "newspaper."

8. Explain the various types of reasoning (e.g., reasoning from symptoms).

9. Explain how the Seven Faces of Persuasion relate to Content/Logical Premises.

Chapter 7 looked at premises based on psychological processes or emotions. Another type of premise frequently operating in enthymemes is based on people's ability to think logically or rationally. The elaboration likelihood model (ELM) suggests that this kind of persuasion uses the central information-processing route and entails considerable analysis and intellectual activity. The Advocacy face of persuasion relies heavily on this kind of premise while the Propaganda face tends to rely on the process or emotional premise discussed in Chapter 7. Premises relying on logical and analytical abilities are called **content premises** because they do not rely on psychological processes and/or emotions as process premises do. Many content premises such as "causes have effects" are perceived as valid and true by large segments of the audience almost automatically on first glance, so persuaders can use them as major premises in enthymemes. Some persuasion theorists call these premises **arguments** or propositions while marketers might call them brand benefits or offers. In fact, argumentation scholars and professors Lunsford and Ruszkiewicz (2004) claim that everything is an argument, including stained glass

windows, the Presidential seal, and most bumper stickers. Aristotle defined an argument as a statement that is supported by some kind of proof. The dictionary defines it as "a discussion in which disagreement is expressed for some point" (*American Heritage Dictionary*, 1985). Most theorists agree that argument contains a controversial claim (i.e., there are at least two sides), which should be debatable and be able to be supported by evidence (Lunsford & Ruszkiewicz, 2004). They make the case that an argument seeks to discover the truth in order to win conviction, while persuasion seeks to apply the known truth in order to prompt others to action. Whatever the label—premise, argument, proposition, offer, or claim—this chapter looks at persuasion that uses the receiver's logical, reasoning, rational, and intellectual abilities and which is therefore processed through the central route of the ELM.

Of course it is also persuasion that reflects one or more of the Seven Faces of Persuasion discussed in Chapter 1 as it is part and parcel of our 24/7, media-saturated, ethically-challenged, multicultural, and Advocacy/Propaganda world. For example, suppose I want to persuade you to support a system of regional national presidential primary elections to select presidential nominees instead of the present mixture of caucuses, winner take all primaries, super delegates, and proportional delegate primaries. What would you consider good and sufficient reasons for supporting the idea? For some persons, there aren't any good (let alone sufficient) reasons for such a policy, so there would be no way to persuade those folks. For others, the policy seems so sensible on the face of it that you don't need to persuade them either. But what about those who neither approve nor disapprove—the undecided members of the audience? They require more information, evidence, discussion, and debate before taking a side. In other words, they are asking for good and sufficient reasons for supporting the proposition. You might tell them about past elections when the truly popular person was not nominated because of super delegate influence or because of proportional versus "winner take all" primaries. And you might point out that such instances have led to subsequent election problems. The success or failure of any of these arguments, claims, or propositions relies on beliefs already held by the audience. They already believe that tax revenues are needed and that criminal elements in any activity are undesirable. Those widely held beliefs serve as major or minor premises in persuasive enthymemes, and all of them are subject to the various distortions we have discussed thus far.

We have all encountered and learned logical patterns from our earliest years. Most of us believe, for example, that causes have predictable effects. When certain things occur, other things invariably follow. Problems have causes, but their removal resolves the problems. Infants learn quickly that crying brings parental relief of various kinds of discomfort—hunger, thirst, wetness, and so on. Crying becomes the cause, and relief is the welcomed effect. This pattern of rational and intellectual reasoning is called **cause-effect reasoning**. Huglen and Clark (2004) define it as "linking some cause and effect to prove their exis-

tence" (p. 23). This makes sense, because if you have no effect(s), there obviously would be no cause, and vice versa. The two have to exist together. For instance, a certain baseball team's pitching staff had experienced many training camp injuries. A logical effect of this cause would be that the team ends the season with a poor record. It's not necessary to convince anyone that injuries lead to losses. You just need to list the various injuries and rely on the cause-effect premise already at work in the audience's mind. The end of the season results may not be a losing record, but, as this example shows, the cause-effect pattern is a potent first premise in a persuasive enthymeme. Politicians and government officials, the courts, businesses, and advertisers all use cause-effect reasoning. Content premises persuade because they rely on widely held patterns of logical reasoning. Our goal in this chapter is to identify some of these patterns. Recognizing them will make you a more critical receiver.

Bad question. What is content proof. Better

WHAT IS PROOF?

Basically, content or logical premises consist of two elements—proof and reasoning. **Proof** is defined as enough evidence connected through reasoning to lead the majority of typical receivers to take or believe the persuader's advice. For example, one claim given to justify going to war in Iraq was that Iraq had chemical, biological, and nuclear weapons, and that these were a threat to stability in the region. What evidence would be needed to prove this claim? For some, satellite photos of supposed weapons sites sufficed. For others, physical evidence was needed—they wanted to see the actual weapons. Others required the actual weapons and evidence that Iraq intended to use them. In hindsight, we learned that there were no Weapons of Mass Destruction (WMD) but that there was an intention on the part of Iraqi leadership to develop such weapons. Therefore, the case for invasion would not have been as strong as it first seemed so maybe support for that policy would not have been so strong. This example tells us that "proof" varies from person to person and from situation to situation. For example, in 2008, the administration claimed that cutting certain taxes and sending almost everyone a rebate of some other taxes would spur economic growth (the effect) and thus avoid a recession. Their evidence convinced some people but not others. When the economy did not improve after the tax cuts and rebates, many of the believers in the actions were disappointed and blamed the government for doing too little too late. Other economists argued that cuts in the estate tax, taxes on dividends, and capitol gains would spur growth in the economy; the taxes were cut (the cause), but growth didn't follow (the effect) so the actions were judged to be faulty.

Most contemporary theorists agree that proof is composed of two facets: **reasoning** and **evidence**. The dictionary definition of reasoning is "the use of reason especially to form conclusions, inferences, or judgments." Evidence is defined as "the data on which a conclusion or judgment may be based; something that furnishes proof" (*American Heritage Dictionary*, 1985). In the proper mix, these two elements lead persuadees to adopt or believe in the changes a persuader advocates. There are several ways to look at evidence and reasoning. First, by examining how persuaders operate, we can infer their motives and discover what they are up to. For example, suppose I want to persuade you that an unrequested kiss on the lips between a male and a female was NOT a cause for a charge of sexual harassment. In terms of finding proof, Lunsford and Ruszkiewicz advise asking four questions: (1) Did something happen? (2) What is its nature? (3) What is its quality? and (4) What action should be taken? In this case there was an unrequested kiss on the lips, witnesses observed it, and the female objected to it. Usually, unwanted kisses on the lips are considered harassment. In this case the answer to the third question—What is its quality?—provided the proof because both participants were six years old. "Most people don't consider six year olds as sexually culpable" (pp. 16–17).

Another way to look at evidence and reasoning is to investigate how specific the evidence is in re-

lation to the reasoning it supports or the conclusion that most persons draw. Before the advent of electronic media, modern advertising, and contemporary propaganda, audiences were accustomed to receiving very specific and verifiable evidence. For example, if a person gave testimony to prove a point, it was critical to tell the audience why that person qualified to give the testimony. Audiences were also suspicious of some kinds of evidence such as analogies. Today, however, we accept the testimony of professional athletes when they endorse an investment plan even though they don't qualify as experts on finance. And we frequently do accept visual or other nonverbal analogies as evidence, such as animated automobile tires depicted as having tigers' claws to grip the road better than other brands.

Other kinds of premises and evidence convince us through the central information-processing channel that a certain brand is superior. For example, if a neutral rating agency such as "Good Housekeeping Seal of Approval" gives its imprimatur to a brand, that may constitute proof to some persons. Politicians offer us evidence in support of a policy. Brands give us various kinds of proof—testimonials, test results, past history, and so forth to prove that their features and benefits are worth buying. Economists and financial advisors give us reasons for investing in certain things (e.g., the likelihood that future energy prices will increase so invest in bio-fuels). And parents supply what they think are good reasons for not living with someone of the opposite gender prior to being married. Underlying these examples is the pattern of "enough evidence with reasoning results in proof."

TYPES OF EVIDENCE

Evidence varies in persuasive power depending on the context in which it is used. In some situations, for instance, statistics have a powerful effect while in other situations, pictorial evidence persuades; and in yet others, vicarious or retold experience convinces us. Experiential evidence relies on the assumption that people learn about and act on information gained indirectly, and this is why stories about the experiences of others are so persuasive. Advertisers use testimonials from both ordinary people and celebrities to endorse products, assuming that consumers vicariously absorb the experiences and buy the product. Demonstrations can also logically persuade us, as so many TV direct marketing ads for food preparation devices shows. But even when we do not learn from or become swayed by the experiences of others, our own experience is usually enough to cause us to change. The Lakota were aware of this. As a Lakota baby crawled close to the campfire, no one pulled it away with shouts of, "Hot! Stay away, baby! Hot!" as we would do in our culture. Instead, they watched the baby's progress very closely and allowed the baby to reach into the fire and touch a hot coal, burning itself mildly. They then quickly pulled the baby away and treated the burn. The experience persuaded the child to be careful with fire.

Suppose a professor explains to you his or her very stringent attendance policy for a television production class, but you take the policy with a grain of salt and fail the class, necessitating taking it over. You hear the same lecture on attendance on the first day of the class the next semester. If experience persuades, you won't miss a class. Or, remember your first auto accident and what you did, who you called, and so on? Chances are that you took away several lessons that you will use in your next accident (don't worry, you will have one).

There are three broad forms of evidence: (1) **direct experience**, (2) **dramatic or vicarious experience**, and (3) **rationally processed evidence**. The first two usually are processed via the peripheral information-processing route of the ELM without much forethought, whereas rationally processed evidence usually follows the central information-processing route. Direct experience demonstrates the major premise that actions have consequences. Dramatic evidence relies on the human tendency to structure our lives in narrative or story form. Rational evidence relies on our innate ability to reason using logic and evidence. In previous chapters, we looked at some theorists who pres-

ent the case for dramatic evidence convincingly. Burke (1985), for example, discusses the power of dramatic or narrative evidence. Let us briefly examine these three broad categories of evidence in more depth.

Direct Experience

Direct experience is probably the most powerful kind of proof or evidence that there is and usually remains a part of one's memory for one's lifetime, being referred to repeatedly as a way to make a point or determine one's own actions. As I write these words, the television news channels are reporting on the tragic events of yesterday, Valentine's Day 2008. On our campus a former graduate student walked into a lecture hall with a 12-gauge shotgun and three pistols and opened fire, shooting 54 times, injuring 21, and killing 6 students before killing himself. The students who were in that class will never forget that event and may always feel uncomfortable in lecture-hall-type situations. Public responses to the event ranged from conclusions pro and con regarding gun control, to gated campuses, to arming volunteer student security forces, to inviting Jesus into one's life. Most direct experience is far more mundane and leads to far less extreme responses. For example, most parents of more than one child tell of their one kid who always had to learn the hard way by experiencing the "actions have consequences" principle. Most of us learn the power of this principle after only a few experiences, but some seem never to catch on. Probably each of us has been in an auto accident, and as a result we have learned to call the police, family, and insurance agent, in that order. You also learned that even a minor accident can take up an inordinate amount of time, paperwork, and effort. You can probably identify some direct experiences in your life that provided a powerful form of evidence for you, but even if you have no direct experience with a violent massacre such as we had yesterday, you can be persuaded by other related forms of proof or evidence such as dramatic or vicarious experience related to you by others or via the media.

🎋 Dramatic or Vicarious Experience

All of us have learned or been persuaded by hearing about the experiences of others—that is, by vicarious experience. There are a variety of types of vicarious experience, most of them dramatic in nature. Very frequently, advocates or propagandists use dramatic experience to capture your attention. Hearing a story or narrative that relates to you or your life in some way is likely to get your attention, so such persuaders either relate real experiences that they or others have had or the create fictional ones.

🎋 **Narratives.** A good way to use dramatic evidence is through the narrative or the story of an event recounted to you by others or enacted in some way (e.g., a documentary, media news report, sermon). People have always been fascinated by stories, including myths, legends, and ballads, handed down in oral/aural cultures and are often persuaded by them. Literacy brought other forms of the narrative (plays, poetry, novels, and short stories). Technology has brought us still other forms such as movies, cartoons, video games, documentaries, talk shows, and broadcasts of athletic events—all having roots in storytelling. Evidence that is dramatic invites our vicarious involvement as it attempts to persuade us to a course of action. It relies on the human ability to project ourselves into the situation described by the persuader and to co-create proof. The results are powerful and long lasting though probably not as impactful as the direct experience of witnessing a stranger aiming and shooting a shotgun at you.

In his book *People of the Lie: The Hope for Healing Human Evil*, noted author and psychotherapist M. Scott Peck (1983) related "The Case of Bobby and His Parents." The narrative began with Bobby, who had been admitted to the hospital emergency room the night before for depression. The admitting physician's notes read as follows:

> Bobby's older brother Stuart, 16, committed suicide this past June, shooting himself in the head with his .22 caliber rifle. Bobby initially seemed to handle his sibling's death rather well. But from the beginning of school in September, his academic performance has been poor. Once a "B" student, he is now failing all his courses. By Thanksgiving he had become obviously depressed. His parents, who seem very concerned, tried to talk to him, but he has become more and more uncommunicative, particularly since Christmas. Although there is no previous record of antisocial behavior, yesterday Bobby stole a car by himself and crashed it (he had never driven before), and was apprehended by the police. ... Because of his age, he was released into his parents' custody, and they were advised to seek immediate psychiatric evaluation for him (p. 48).

Peck went on to observe that, although Bobby appeared to be a typical fifteen-year-old, he stared at the floor and kept picking at several small sores on the back of his hand. When Peck asked Bobby if he felt nervous being in the hospital, he got no answer—"Bobby was really digging into that sore. Inwardly I winced at the damage he was doing to his flesh" (note how little details lend drama and crediblility to the narrative). After reassuring Bobby that the hospital was a safe place to be, Peck tried to draw Bobby out in conversation, but nothing seemed to work. Peck got "No reaction. Except that maybe he dug a little deeper into one of the sores on his forearm." Bobby admitted that he had hurt his parents by stealing the car; he said he knew that he had hurt them because they yelled at him. When asked what they yelled at him about, he replied, "I don't know." "Bobby was feverishly picking at his sores now and ... I felt it would be best if I steered my questions to more neutral subjects" (p. 50). They discussed the family pet, who Bobby took care of but didn't play with because she was his father's dog. Peck then turned the conversation to Christmas, asking what sorts of gifts Bobby had gotten.

> BOBBY: Nothing much.
>
> PECK: Your parents must have given you something.
> What did they give you?

BOBBY: A gun.

PECK: A gun?

BOBBY: Yes.

PECK: What kind of a gun?

BOBBY: A twenty-two.

PECK: A twenty-two pistol.

BOBBY: No, a twenty-two rifle.

PECK: I understand that it was with a twenty-two rifle that your brother killed himself.

BOBBY: Yes.

PECK: Was that what you asked for, for Christmas?

BOBBY: No.

PECK: What did you ask for?

BOBBY: A tennis racket.

PECK: But you got the gun instead?

BOBBY: Yes.

PECK: How did you feel, getting the same kind of gun that your brother had?

BOBBY: It wasn't the same kind of gun.

PECK: (I began to feel better. Maybe I was just confused.) I'm sorry, I thought they were the same kind of gun.

BOBBY: It wasn't the same kind of gun—It was the same gun.

PECK: You mean it was your brother's gun? (I wanted to go home very badly now.) You mean your parents gave you your brother's gun for Christmas—the one he shot himself with?

BOBBY: Yes.

PECK: How did it make you feel getting your brother's gun for Christmas?

BOBBY: I don't know.

PECK: (I almost regretted the question: How could he know? How could he answer such a thing?) No, I don't expect you could know (p. 52).

Peck then brought the parents in for counseling. However, they seemed unable to realize what message they had sent their remaining son by giving

him his brother's suicide weapon. Bobby continued therapy until he was sent to live with a favorite aunt.

When I first read this dramatic example, I literally gasped as I learned about the Christmas gift, and I was totally dumbstruck to learn that it was the gun. When I read this dialogue aloud in class, I always hear gasps from around the room. Although the story was emotionally charged, we would be hard put to call it "illogical." In fact, it is probably totally logical to conclude that the parents' behavior was harmful, perhaps even evil. If the evidence is dramatic enough or emotional enough, persuadees will not ask for more.

Most great preachers, orators, and politicians are also great storytellers. They use the narrative to capture the audience's attention and to draw them into the topic. This effect is reinforced with other evidence, and more narratives might be worked in to keep the audience interested. Chances are, you have heard speeches or sermons in which the narrative was skillfully used. Such speeches seem to have the most impact and to be remembered the longest. As a professor of mine once said, "The narrative will carry more persuasive freight than any other form of evidence."

Testimony. Testimony of a person who has seen, heard, and experienced events also is persuasive. The persuader might read aloud an eyewitness account or simply recount his or her personal experience. If the issue is unemployment, receivers might be swayed by hearing from people who are out of work. The humiliation of waiting in line for an unemployment check, the embarrassment of accepting government surplus foodstuffs, and other experiences of the unemployed will probably have dramatic persuasive power. As receivers, we vicariously live through what the witness experienced when we hear direct testimony. Although eyewitness testimony is potent, studies have shown that it is often unreliable and even incorrect (Loftus, 1980). In many cases, as has been documented, persons have been wrongfully imprisoned on the basis of eyewitness testimony

THE INVESTIGATION

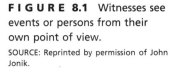

FIGURE 8.1 Witnesses see events or persons from their own point of view.

SOURCE: Reprinted by permission of John Jonik.

(Loftus, 1984). As Figure 8.1 illustrates, witnesses often see and hear what they want to see and hear, and give testimony from their idiosyncratic points of view.

As receivers, we need to carefully examine the testimony used to persuade us. We need to ask questions like these: Was the witness in a position to see what is claimed? Could the witness be mistaken in any way? Does the witness have a bias that might cloud his or her testimony? Might the witness have a motive for giving the testimony? Is the witness being paid for giving the testimony? What might he or she have to gain from testifying? Has the 24/7 media-saturated world colored the testimony? Is it advocacy, propaganda, or something else? And we should remember that there are several other kinds of narrative proof or evidence that can persuade such as anecdotes, jokes, demonstrations, quotes, and so forth.

Anecdotes. Anecdotes are short narratives that make a point in a hurry—maybe in only a sentence or two. For example, there is the anecdote of the optimist who was asked to describe his philosophy: "That's simple. I'm nostalgic about the future." Anecdotes are often funny and are frequently hypothetical, so they are quite different from actual testimony. The key thing about anecdotes is that, unlike testimony, we rarely take them as truth. Instead, we tend to process anecdotes as if they are the exclamation points of persuasion—the core of an obvious truth. Consider the anecdote about Abraham Lincoln being asked why he had pardoned a Union deserter during the Civil War—he quipped, "I thought he could do us more good above the ground than under it" (Moore, 1909).

Participation and Demonstration. There are several other ways in which persuaders can dramatize evidence. At an antismoking presentation, for instance, audiovisual materials can show cancerous lung tissue. Smokers can participate by exhaling cigarette smoke through a clean white tissue and observing the nicotine stains left behind. Sometimes persuaders dramatize a point by using visual aids to demonstrate the problem and solution. The demonstrations that form the core of most direct marketing on television (e.g., kitchen devices, exercise equipment, weight loss formulas) also use participation in that the viewer is asked to visualize him- or herself using the device and is repeatedly urged to call the 1-800 number to place an order that is usually sweetened with some "extra" bonus for acting "Now." The viewer sees the greaseless grill, the guaranteed bass bait, or the shapely persons using the Bowflex, and imagines what it would be like to use the product, and then he or she takes direct action by phoning and placing the order. The direct marketing industry is able to fine-tune its persuasive demonstrations using these immediate response behaviors and to test various bonus gifts against one another, selecting the most effective one for prompting purchase behaviors.

Rationally Processed Evidence

Not all evidence is dramatic. Sometimes evidence appeals to our logical processes in nondramatic and intellectually oriented and rational ways. For instance, newspaper editorials frequently use evidence that appeals to readers' logical processes, as do other persuasive messages such as legal argument, political discourse, and some advertising. Look at Figure 8.2. The Campbell Soup Company knows that persons concerned with health and nutrition are aware of the need to increase the amount of fiber in their diet. Most of the literature on this subject has recommended eating high-fiber foods such as whole wheat bread and bran cereals. Campbell's offers similar benefits. You can get fiber by eating Manhandler soups such as Bean with Bacon or Split Pea with Ham.

As you can see from these examples, the appeal to logical processes often relies on a reasoning pattern such as "the past is a guide to the future" or "the benefit far exceeds the cost." What are some other logical patterns that persuaders often use? They often emerge in the types of reasoning involved in the commercial, legal, financial, and political persuasion, and advocacy/propaganda, all of which reflect a results-oriented culture such as ours where the "bottom" line is what *really* counts.

TYPES OF REASONING

Recall our definition of proof as "enough evidence connected with reasoning to lead an audience to believe or act on a persuader's advice." We now explore the second step in the process of logical persuasion which is the connecting of pieces of evidence using some kind of logical reasoning. Several patterns of reasoning seem to be deeply ingrained in our culture and often differ from those of the many other cultures coexisting in our world of persuasion. When people violate these accepted deep structures of such logical reasoning, they are often labeled "off the wall" or "out in left field." Perhaps the student classroom shooter referred to earlier acted on Valentine's Day because he had been jilted

MADE OF THE FINEST FIBER

If you're like most people who eat right, you probably give high fiber high priority.

And like most people, when you think of fiber, you probably automatically think of bran cereals.

Well, there's another good source of dietary fiber you should know about. Delicious Campbell's Bean with Bacon Soup.

In fact, Campbell's has four soups that are high in fiber.

And you can see from the chart that follows exactly how each one measures up to bran cereals.

So now when you think of fiber, you don't have to think about

FIBER IN A SUGGESTED SERVING			
CAMPBELL'S SOUP		BRAN CEREALS	
Bean with Bacon	9g	100% Brans	11g
Split Pea with Ham	6g	40% Brans	6g
Green Pea	5g	Raisin Brans	5g
Low Sodium Green Pea	7g	Others	5-10g
This comparison includes soluble and insoluble fiber			

having it just at breakfast.

Instead, you can do your body good any time during the day. With a hot, hearty bowl of one of these Campbell's Soups.

You just might feel better for it—right to the very fiber of your being.

CAMPBELL'S SOUP IS GOOD FOOD

Campbell's has a full line of low sodium soups for those people who are on a salt-restricted diet or have a concern about sodium.

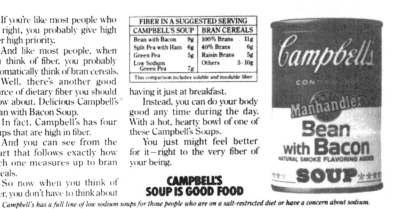

F I G U R E 8.2 This appeals to our logic. What rational argument does it present?

SOURCE: Used by permission of the Campbell Soup Company.

by a female student in the class and thought that shooting at her and her fellow classmates was justified. At this point we may never know, but while not "sane," there is a line of reasoning there. Or perhaps he was angry at the lecture hall since he had often attended classes there. There is obviously much less of an insane line of plausible reasoning there. Sometimes a logical deep structure is violated, and tragedy or humor results. Sometimes, such violations make a potential persuader sound like a lunatic. What follows is a more mundane example of such reasoning in a letter to the editor of a local newspaper which discussed alternatives for removing nuisance deer from public parks in the area (Scott, 1989). The author pointed out what it had cost for other alternatives used to remove such deer from other parks (e.g., trapping them, using trained sharpshooters to kill them, chemically induced birth control) and he pointed out the advantages and logic to opening the areas to controlled hunting—as well as to the taxes hunters pay on ammunition and guns—and how removal costs were cut at another park by allowing controlled hunting at the park. So far, so good. He begins with what appears to be an inductive line of argument using **effect-to-cause reasoning**, which is defined as citing a set of effects and then concluding by identifying their cause. We anticipate that he is about to claim something like, "Therefore, hunters are positive persons and deserve to hunt in a highly controlled environment to reduce the numbers of nuisance deer in the park." But what does the author conclude? Take a look.

> If you were an animal, would you prefer to live ten years free, even if you died a slow death, or would you want to live it penned up, sleeping in your own manure? I think most Americans would want to be free. That's also the way God wanted it. That's why he said it is a good thing to be a hunter. For Jesus Christ is alive and well, but Bambi never was (n.p.).

The conclusion is wacky. It seems unrelated to the evidence. Remember that we are looking for content premises—logical patterns that serve as the first premises in enthymemes. The deeply ingrained logical preferences serve in this way. We believe and act on what we perceive to be logical arguments backed by good and sufficient evidence and well presented to us. Fishbein and Ajzen's (1975, 1980) Theory of Reasoned Action (TRA) is one such deeply ingrained logical structure. The theory predicts that actions are the effects of behavioral intentions. Behavioral intentions, in turn, are the results of people's attitudes on issues and on the social norms that they hold in high esteem and which they use as guides to action. For example, if we were trying to persuade people to stop buying SUVs and to consider purchasing one of the new hybrid automobiles, we might compare the hybrid's performance with the poor mileage of most SUVs,

note that four-wheel drive isn't really necessary for most people's needs, and back that up with a quote: "Critics claim that 95% of SUVs never venture off road" (Lunsford & Ruszkiewicz, p. 28). This might change peoples' attitude toward SUVs. Then we could point out that the hybrid owners are opinion leaders, tend to be better educated, to have better jobs, to earn more, and to be more socially conscious. According to TRA, if our audience believes that these traits are ones to be emulated, then the shift in attitudes toward SUVs and the audience's changing respect for hybrid users will lead to a behavioral intention—the audience will consider buying a hybrid instead of an SUV or perhaps a compromise option of a hybrid SUV. Communication scholar S. Sutton (1998) points out, however, that intentions are subject to change over time and are provisional in nature. Several researchers have found the predictive power of behavioral intentions to be either weak or negative as more and more time passes. Let us now turn to some other traditional forms of reasoning.

Cause-to-Effect Reasoning

We've already seen that **cause-to-effect reasoning** is powerful in our culture, and even our language depends on it. For example, we rarely say, "The ball was thrown, and the window was broken." Instead, we put the cause out front and let it "create" the effect. We say, "Johnny threw the ball and broke the window, and his parents punished him severely." This active-voice sentence tells us that Johnny caused the ball to fly through the air, resulting in the broken window, which in turn resulted in the punishment. It gives us much more information: It tells us who did what and with what effect.

Persuaders frequently use cause-to-effect reasoning to identify events, trends, or facts that have resulted in certain effects. They tell us that if a cause is present we can expect certain effects to follow. If the effects are bad and we want to do something about them, we usually try to remove the cause. For instance, we are using too much carbon-based fuel and the result or effect is increased global warm-

BOX 8.1   Interactive Reasoning in Wonderland

 Go to www.cut-the-knot.org/LewisCarroll and explore the many logic games, conference announcements, interactive activities, and more. Lewis Carroll is of course most famous for his children's stories, such as *Through the Looking Glass* and *Alice in Wonderland*, and his poetry, such as "Jabberwocky." However, few realize that he was a professional logician and that he worked with many elements of logic, reasoning, and fallacy throughout his fiction. A great example of illogical reasoning occurs when the Queen of Hearts insists that she must sentence Alice before, not after, the verdict. And the Cheshire cat is a whole different case.

ing and further destruction of the environment, resulting in potentially dangerous climate changes. Or, if you are carrying too much credit card debt, some suggest that you should get rid of all but one of your credit cards to avoid the resulting effects of poor credit and possible bankruptcy. This argument assumes that cutting up all but one credit card (cause) will reduce your ability to accumulate consumer debt (effect). This effect then becomes a new cause resulting in positive effects like good credit ratings. Both examples make sense, and that is why cause-to-effect has such persuasive power.

There are three kinds of causal reasoning: (1) A cause is identified, and you seek out its effects; (2) An effect is identified, and you try to trace it back to its cause; and (3) As we have seen above, a series of cause-effect relationships lead to a final effect (Lunsford & Ruszkiewicz, p. 207). Advertising frequently uses the first strategy, as in an ad for a cellulite-reducing complex. It identifies the cause—a weak skin support system—and its undesirable effect—ugly cellulite in body cells. Regular use of the product strengthens the skin support system, thus removing the cause and its effects. In the second strategy, the effect is identified. We look at the effect—global warming—and try to identify its possible causes (e.g., carbon dioxide from the burning of fossil fuels, the greenhouse effect). Or take the case of food poisoning. Only those who ate the dishes that contained mayonnaise became ill. Conclusion? They probably were ill from salmonella, a kind of food poisoning that occurs when mayonnaise is not properly refrigerated. In the third strategy, we trace a series of cause-and-effect relationships—the persuader says sulfur dioxide emissions from power plants cause acid rain, which in turn causes hydro-plant life to die, which in turn reduces plankton, which in turn causes stunted fish populations. Conclusion? Stop using high sulfur energy sources because there are multiple negative effects. In law courts, establishing a motive for the crime is sometimes seen as the same thing as identifying its cause. We speculated about a romantic cause or motive for the student deaths on my campus yesterday. But the fact that the shooter had stopped taking his medication might have been the best cause for his tragic behavior. So here can be varying causes for a given effect. There may be twisted kinds of reasoning (see Interactive Box 8.1).

Effect-to-Cause Reasoning

Another type of reasoning that is less frequently used (and sometimes flawed) is called effect-to-cause reasoning. Mistaken sources of food poisoning, for example, are sometimes identified this way. In another example, many auto accidents are attributed to the driver using a cell phone while driving. There is a problem here with the possibility of an intervening cause due to whom the driver is talking to, or what the topic of the conversation is, or what the traffic conditions were at the time of the call. Suppose that further investigation shows that in a high percentage of these accidents the drivers were arguing with their spouses about family matters. Is the cell phone the cause of the accidents, or is the discussion of family problems the intervening cause?

FIGURE 8.3 What is the figurative analogy here?

SOURCE: Reprinted by permission of Aaron Johnson.

Reasoning from Symptoms

Persuaders sometimes identify a series of symptoms or signs and then try to conclude something from them. For example, politicians cite how much worse things are now than they were when their opponent took office. Unemployment is up, and the stock and bond markets have been ravaged, and foreclosure rates on family homes are skyrocketing. Additionally, recent polls show that people have lost faith in their ability to control their own destinies and fear losing their jobs. The hope is that the voters will blame the incumbent for all of these the troubles even though he or she is totally unrelated to any of these symptoms. In a results-oriented world of advocacy/propaganda with multicultural sets of values, this line of reasoning may be extremely persuasive. Many advertisements present receivers with a set of symptoms that indicate there is a real or potential problem for them. Receivers have lost their job, can't pay the bills, are faced with foreclosure, and therefore need to contact a financial advisor. Interpersonal persuasion is frequently laced with **reasoning from symptoms**, especially when laying blame.

Criteria-to-Application Reasoning

Sometimes persuaders establish a reasonable set of criteria for purchasing a product, voting for a candidate, or supporting a cause and then offer their product, candidate, or cause as one that fits these criteria. For example, when a credit card company makes an offer to you, you probably have several criteria in mind that the card must meet before you

will take the offer. There must be no annual fee. There must be free balance transfers and an introductory rate of 0.0 percent and a reasonable rate thereafter. The initial 0.0 percent must hold for at least a year, and the company must give you frequent traveler points on any airlines plus discounts on other travel services. These are your criteria for accepting the offer and unless the card meets your criteria, you apply these criteria and reject the offer. Remember the student who cut classes and flunked because of his absences, only to have to retake the class and maintain perfect attendance, thus earning a passing grade? Reasoning from criteria to application persuaded him.

Reasoning from Analogy or by Comparison

Sometimes persuaders use figurative or real analogies as their logical reason for some conclusion. In this form of reasoning, the persuader analyzes and describes an issue, and an analogy is made comparing this issue with an example of a similar one or a figurative one. In a real-case analogy on the war in Iraq, opponents to the war compared it to the war in Vietnam because in both cases we were losing by fighting an indigent population that was very different from us culturally, both sets of terrain were not conducive to traditional warfare, and we did not have United Nations cooperation. The conclusion was that we should not invade Iraq. In the figurative analogy, comparisons are done through a figure of speech, usually a simile or a metaphor. Returning to the Iraq War, some opponents compared the war to walking through heavy mud with the next step gaining little ground and further exhausting one's physical strength while the progress made by one's footprints is quickly wiped away as the mud flows back to result in the initial situation. Therefore, either don't go into the war or get out before you exhaust your physical and financial resources. Or consider the following figurative analogy: "War is like a boxing match in which the opponents are evenly matched and there's no referee. Rarely does anyone throw a single knockout punch. It's slugging it out in round after round until you get the other guy on the ropes, and his managers admit defeat."

We frequently see argument by comparison in real analogies in advertising, with competing products compared in realistic terms of cost, effectiveness, safety, and so on. For instance, the big battle over the light beer market largely relies on reasoning from comparison, with one brand claiming fewer calories and better taste than others. The same thing is seen in ads for low-tar and low-nicotine cigarettes. And the Energizer rabbit uses comparison to make the point that the Energizer brand is much longer lasting than, say, Duracell, by using the figurative analogy of the mechanical rabbit, one of the most effective and long-lived figurative analogies.

Deductive Reasoning

A familiar form of appeal to logic is **deductive reasoning**, which is reasoning from the general to the specific. For example, in a legislative body a persuader might support a bill or a motion by saying something like, "The legislation before us is desperately needed to prevent the state budget from going into a deficit situation," and then providing the specifics that support or "prove" the conclusion. An editorial might begin, "Sycamore needs to pass this school bond referendum to save its extracurricular sports, its music and art programs, its newspaper, and its drama program," and then go on to describe the details. One of the problems with the deductive approach is that receivers who feel negatively about the persuader's general point

may quickly lose interest, not pay attention to the specifics that are at the heart of the issue, and simply dismiss the entire argument or tune-out.

Inductive Reasoning

Inductive reasoning gets the specifics out on the table before bringing up the generalized conclusion. For example, in the school bond case, the persuader might begin this way: "Many of you know that it costs over $60,000 just to run the athletic program. The budget for the marching band is over $12,000 for travel, instruction, and uniforms. I was surprised to learn that it cost over $2,000 just to pay the royalties for the spring musical. We have cut and cut until there is nothing left to cut. The last referendum increase was 14 years ago—inflation has risen over 200 percent since then. Unless we pass the referendum, the district now faces elimination of these valuable extracurricular programs." With the specific evidence apparent, the generalization flows logically from it.

MISUSES OF REASONING AND EVIDENCE

Of course, logical persuasion is vulnerable to intentional or unintentional misuse of either evidence or reasoning, or both. Let's look at some examples of the misuse of reasoning and evidence so that we can spot it when it occurs.

Statistics

One of the mainstays of logical persuasion is the use of **statistics**. We tend to believe statistics without questioning them simply because they seem specific and well researched. But we ought to ask several questions when statistical evidence is offered. First, "Is the sample from which the statistics are drawn a representative one?" In other words, is the sample selected in a way that might bias the results? Or is it a reliable representation of the larger population? We might want to know how the sample was

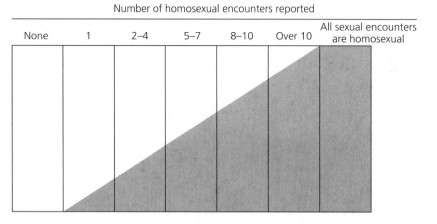

Number of homosexual encounters reported

None	1	2–4	5–7	8–10	Over 10	All sexual encounters are homosexual

FIGURE 8.4

P This graph is misleading because it implies that half the population is homosexual when the statistics being represented are much lower than that.

selected. Perhaps the researchers took names from the phone directory. But not everyone has a telephone number listed, some people have several, and others only use cell phones for which there is no directory. Perhaps the subjects were approached at a shopping mall versus on campus and given a survey there. But, again, mall shoppers might not be representative of the campus population at large. Maybe the subjects were intercepted in front of the student union late in the evening. Would we find any different results if we interviewed them early in the morning rather than in the evening when most students are studying? These and other questions should be asked of any statistical proof used by the persuader. Another misuse of statistical evidence is the use of a single instance as an example of all instances. Thus, we hear of an enormously wealthy person who pays no taxes and are led to believe that other enormously wealthy persons pay no taxes. Or we read of a hammer costing $50 when purchased by the Department of Defense. Still another misuse of statistics is biased sampling, which occurs when a nonrepresentative portion of the population is sampled. Responses from a sample drawn from subscribers to *Newsweek* will be very different from one drawn from subscribers to *Horticulture* or *The Organic Gardener*.

The mode of presentation can also misrepresent statistics. For example, the graph in Figure 8.4 was used to demonstrate the degree to which homosexuality exists in the general population. The shaded portion indicates persons who have had at least one homosexual encounter; the unshaded portion of the graph indicates heterosexual persons. The graph suggests that the proportion of the population that is homosexual is at least 50 percent when actual research indicates that it is far smaller—around 2 percent (Guttmacher, 1993). Clearly, the graph visually misrepresents the actual case and distorts the meaning of the statistics. What the graph fails to provide is information about the size of the sample in each segment.

Testimony

One problem with the use of testimonials is that the person testifying might not be providing accurate information. In fact, eyewitness testimony is frequently erroneous. In the Valentine's Day killings, students in the lecture hall at the time differed on the color of the killer's hat when his entire outfit was clearly black. Also, seemingly insignificant shifts in wording can lead witnesses to certain answers. Most of the time, we don't have the opportunity to cross-examine the person giving the testimonial. Instead, when we see or hear a person endorsing a product, a candidate, or an organization, we are forced to make up our minds right away about whether the person is qualified to give the testimonial. When testimonials are used to persuade, we need to ask whether the person giving the testimonial is an authority on the subject, and if so, how reliable he or she is. Was the person close enough to have witnessed what he or she is testifying about? Is it possible that the person giving the testimonial is biased, and if so, in what direction? For example, in Chicago, a violinist was recently awarded nearly $30 million from METRA, the commuter train conglomerate. Her $500,000 violin got caught in the train doors, and when she tried to save it her leg was torn off. She testified at the trial, offering "dramatic detailed testimony ... as she painfully recalled for jurors the winter day in 1995 when she became pinned against the doors of a commuter train and was dragged more than 360 feet before she fell under its wheels" (Deardorf & Finan, 1999, p. 1). Could her testimony have been biased? How much of it was used to build sympathy and thus boost the size of the award? How well could you remember what happened if you were in that situation? Was she partially responsible for putting herself at risk? These and other questions are the kinds of issues to be raised when the testimonial is being offered as evidence.

As persuadees, we need to be alert to the ways in which testimonials can be distorted or misused. We know that in many cases the testimonial is being given only because the sponsor has paid the person to give it. So, the next time you see a sports personality endorsing a product, don't assume that he or she uses it on a daily basis. By law, they only have to have tried it one time. And try to determine the degree of authority the person has about the product.

✗ COMMON FALLACIES USED IN PERSUASION

Merriam-Webster's Collegiate Dictionary defines **fallacy** as "deceptive appearance ... a false or mistaken idea ... an often plausible argument using false or invalid inference." It is this last definition that concerns us here: believable arguments or premises that are based on invalid reasoning. Keep in mind that a logical fallacy is not necessarily false, but its process of inference is invalid. In spite of the fact that these fallacies have been identified for centuries, they still pop up frequently in advertisements, political persuasion, interpersonal persuasion, and other arenas. Briefly, here are some of the common fallacies we encounter almost daily.

↪ Post Hoc, Ergo Propter Hoc

Post hoc, ergo propter hoc, commonly called **the "post hoc" fallacy**, derives from the Latin meaning "after this, therefore because of this." As the translation implies, because one event follows another, the first event is assumed to be the cause of the second. One sometimes sees this in the world of sports where the acquisition of a new player or coach is seen as the cause for a winning or losing season for the team. Views on history sometimes argue that a particular event or organization is the cause for subsequent results (e.g., the birth control pill came before the decline in morals and was therefore the cause of the decline). We constantly run into this fallacy in the world of advertising. After using the diet pill, Jane lost 40 pounds. Maybe she just got more exercise. Citizens might charge that the reason the school system is out of money is that the superintendent and school board wasted all the money from the referendum eight years ago on unneeded frills, but it is not necessarily so.

↙ Ad Hominem

The Latin term **ad hominem**, meaning "to or at the person," refers to any attack against an individual instead of against her or his position on the issues. The purpose is to lead the audience to take certain actions simply because of an alleged character quirk or other flaw in the person presenting the opposite viewpoint. The cartoons in Figure 8.5 are good examples of the ad hominem argument being used against your author when he was the faculty president of the policy-making body on our college campus. "Mudslinging" in politics is a frequent platform for the ad hominem. This tactic is not usually used in advertising because products, not people, are being promoted. However, it is frequently

FIGURE 8.5

These cartoons use the ad hominem fallacy. They are aimed at the person, not the issue.

SOURCE: Reprinted by permission of Kevin Craver.

used in ideological persuasion such as in the abortion debate where the argument is aimed at the abortionist, not the law. Whenever attacks are made on a person's character instead of on his or her stand on issues, be aware that the ad hominem fallacy is probably at work. If persuaders have nothing to debate, they frequently resort to attacking the personality of the opponent.

🗡 Ad Populum

As its name implies, the **ad populum** fallacy relies on whatever happens to be popular at that time. It is aimed at or to the populace or public opinion. In fact, public figures frequently attack the polls or claim them as proof positive for supporting or opposing public policy. There are many historical examples of ad populum arguments—some important, some tragic, and some trivial. For example, consider just a few popular notions that justified themselves using the logic of the ad populum: Prohibition (which was evidence for loose living), the baby boom (which was blamed for all the faults of the "boomer" generation from birth on until old age), rock 'n' roll (which caused juvenile delinquency and free sex), and the suburbs of the 1950s and later (which caused global warming by commuters driving so much). Appeals using the ad populum also abound in the worlds of fashion and popular culture—for example, wearing one's baseball cap backward or askance, getting one's body pierced, tattoos, and short skirts (which encouraged fornication). Encouragement to "follow the crowd" clues us in to the ad populum fallacy in operation.

🗡 The Undistributed Middle

doesn't make sense.

The fallacy of the **undistributed middle** can be defined as "inferring that because an individual, group, or philosophy shares some aspects or attributes with another, it shares all other aspects or attributes." It occurs in most cases of what we call "guilt by association"—for example, ["Gut Malloy is a member of Tappa Kanna Bru fraternity, and fraternity boys are heavy drinkers, so he must be a heavy drinker, too."] Common sense tells us that there is something missing here. The heart of the fallacy is in the phrase "fraternity boys are heavy drinkers," which is used to suggest that all fraternity members share all attributes beyond group membership. In other words, the argument assumes that heavy drinking is equally distributed among all members of fraternities when some are moderate drinkers or don't drink at all (Jensen, 1981). Of course, this example is trivial, but persuaders use the undistributed middle principle to sway opinion and alter behavior in significant ways. For example, because someone serves on the school board, many critics assume that the person must favor all the board's decisions. This example appeared in a small-town newspaper recently:

> Consider these facts: The Japanese eat very little fat and suffer fewer heart attacks than the British or the Americans. On the other hand, the French eat a lot of fat and suffer fewer heart attacks than the British or the Americans. The Italians drink excessive amounts of red wine and also suffer fewer heart attacks than the British or Americans. Therefore eat and drink what you like. It's speaking English that kills you (*Consider the Facts*, 2002, p. 10).

This fallacy also underlies any appeal suggesting that using a certain popular brand will make us like others who use it.

🗡 The Straw Man

The **straw man fallacy** sets up a weak, or "straw man," case that can be easily defeated. The persuader represents this case as the position of the other side in the debate, and then brings out key evidence and reasoning to defeat the bogus case, along with the opposition or opposing candidate. Political persuasion is riddled with this tactic. For instance, candidate A might charge that candidate B's position on defense spending is reliance on conventional weapons. This is an easy position to demolish. Candidate A promptly shows how wrong the straw man position is by presenting impressive statistics and examples to the contrary. In the world of advertising, we occasionally see, read, or hear a straw man case. A good example is the TV ad in which the announcer says something like, "Some think this Chevy pickup truck can't climb this tough mountain carrying a Dodge pickup on its back." Then we see the Chevy climb the mountain with the Dodge on its back. Of course, if the Chevy couldn't do the job, they would never have aired the ad. Most comparative advertising depends on the straw man fallacy. In the cola and burger wars, for instance, the opposition is often set up as a straw man waiting to be overcome by the advertiser's brand. The straw man fallacy is also commonly used in ideological arguments. Antiabortion advocates frequently argue that abortion is an inhumane form of birth control and should thus be outlawed. However, pro-choice advocates have never recommended abortion as a means of birth control—that claim is a straw man argument that will naturally be demolished by pro-life advocates.

Other Common Fallacies

Another type of fallacious reasoning uses partial or distorted facts (such as telling only one side of the story or quoting out of context) or specious reasoning. My Dean once explained the reason for me not receiving a raise for promotion to full professor by comparing me to other full professors with lesser records by saying "Yes, Charles, but you are younger than them and can work longer." Other fallacies include substituting ridicule or humor for argument (such as depicting the opposition candidate as "a slow-dancing bureaucrat"), using prejudices or stereotypes, appealing to tradition, begging the question or evading the issue ("National health care is nothing less than socialism!"), using a non sequitur (a thought that doesn't logically follow from the preceding one), or creating a false dilemma ("either outlaw deficit spending or declare the country bankrupt") (Kahane, 1992; Thompson, 1971).

LOGICAL SYLLOGISMS

A form of logical argument that goes back to the ancients is called the syllogism. **Syllogisms** are forms of reasoning with three parts: a major premise, a minor premise, and a conclusion. They typify content premise persuasion and can be of three types: conditional syllogisms, disjunctive syllogisms, and categorical syllogisms.

Conditional Syllogisms

Conditional syllogisms are defined as arguments using "If/Then" reasoning. Like other syllogisms, they have a major premise, a minor premise, and a conclusion. The major premise states a logical relationship that is presumed to exist in the world and that receivers are to accept. The minor premise states the existence of one element in the relationship, and the conclusion is then drawn between the relationship and the existence of one element in it. Here is a conditional syllogism in classical form:

> If the U.S. government can't control terrorism with the present laws, then we need to give it new laws that are tough enough to stop terrorism (major premise).
>
> The World Trade Center bombings and the events of 9/11 are proof that the government can't control terrorism with the present laws (minor premise).
>
> Therefore, we need to give the government tougher laws to stop terrorism (conclusion).

The first element, or the "If" part in the major premise, is called the antecedent, and the second element is called the consequent. Affirming the antecedent, which we did in the minor premise by referring to the attacks, we can draw a valid conclusion that tougher laws are needed. Note that the syllogism is valid, but the premises are not necessarily true. **Validity** refers to how well the syllogism conforms to the general rules of reasoning, and not to the true or false nature of the premises. The other valid way of affirming a part of the conditional syllogism is to deny the existence of the element in the major premise. Using the same example, we could state, "Since 9/11, there have been no major terrorist acts in the United States (minor premise). Therefore, there is no need for new laws (conclusion)."

Advertisers frequently make perfectly valid arguments using false premises. A good example is this statement on a package of Trilene fishing line: "If you are seeking a world record, you should use one of the pound tests coded in the chart at right." You can detect the "if … then … " format in the sentence. We all know that using the right line—Trilene—won't assure anyone of a world record fish, but receivers tend to accept it as logical and buy the line. There are two valid ways to draw a conclusion in a conditional syllogism. First, we can affirm the "if" part of the major premise and accept the "then" part of the major premise. For example, if we affirm the first portion of the premise ("If you are seeking...") we can affirm the second half about using Trilene line. The other valid combination begins by stating something about the first part of the initial premise. For example, we might say, "Smaller fish taste better," and then reject the advice on using Trilene line. A related but invalid procedure is to deny the antecedent and conclude that the consequent has also been denied. In the Trilene example we might state, "You don't want a lunker," and conclude that therefore you shouldn't use Trilene. The fallacy becomes apparent immediately—you might still want to use Trilene for another reason—perhaps because of its warranty.

In a related but also invalid procedure, suppose in the terrorism example we had denied the consequent in the minor premise by saying, "We have not given enough tough new powers to the U.S. government," and then concluded, "Therefore, the U.S. government will not be able to control terrorism." The fallacy is less apparent but is still there—the lack of tough laws doesn't necessarily indicate an inability to control terrorism. Again, there could be intervening causes. Although invalid, this form of syllogism is frequently used in advertisements. For instance, a romance is "saved" by a certain mouthwash or shampoo. Be alert to this trap. Persuaders can use a logically valid syllogism to camouflage untrue premises. Ask yourself whether the premises are true and whether the argument is valid. The conditional syllogism is similar to the cause-effect linkage described earlier.

Disjunctive Syllogisms

The **disjunctive syllogism** uses an "Either/Or" format. Consider this major premise of a disjunctive syllogism: "Either we reduce the deficit or we increase taxes." The premise is usually accompanied by some proof or evidence in the minor premise, and the conclusion is then drawn. For example, a school board threatens, "Either we vote to increase property taxes or you lose all extracurricular activities." The voters would provide the minor premise of the syllogism through their votes—if they vote to increase taxes, the board denies the need to eliminate the activities. A second valid conclusion comes about if the voters vote down the tax increase and the board eliminates the activities. This strategy works if the issue is clear-cut.

However, few situations have a clear "either/or" dichotomy, even in extreme cases such as the Terry Scheivo case in 2005. She had been in a comatose state for several years, and her husband wanted to remove her feeding and water tubes, but her parents objected and the issue went into the courts. Ultimately, the U.S. Congress voted on the right to life aspects of the case. The central issue revolved around the disjunctive syllogism "Either she is alive or she is dead." The real question should have been "Will she ever recover?" This argument would still exemplify a disjunctive syllogism—either she will recover or she will not—but the controversy would not have been as extreme. Strict either/or logic cannot take into account other belief systems or more than two alternatives in a situation. Examine persuasion framed in the either/or mode to search for other alternatives or belief systems under which the disjunctive model will not work.

Categorical Syllogisms

Categorical syllogisms deal with parts and wholes, or sets and subsets, of events in which the major and minor premises both involve membership or nonmembership in one of two categories. The conclusion relates the clusters of both premises into a new finding or result, as shown in the following classic categorical syllogism:

All men are included in the class of mortal beings (major premise).

Socrates is included in the class of men (minor premise).

Therefore, Socrates is a mortal being (conclusion).

Although this example is frequently used to demonstrate the categorical syllogism, it is not one that you will find many opportunities to use. Its format, however, is frequently seen, read, or heard in various kinds of persuasion. Take, for example, the U.S. Marines' recruiting slogan: "We're looking for a few good men." The implied categorical syllogism is as follows:

All U.S. Marines are included in the class of good men (major premise).

You are a good man (minor premise).

Therefore, you should become a Marine (conclusion).

Because you are a member of one category, it is assumed that you must or should be a member of another.

When you really think about it, human beings often do much of their everyday reasoning via categorical thinking. For example, consider what we all do when we first meet a person, or encounter a new event, or sense the presence of a certain logical system in the way things work, or decide how you will act in certain situations. You and I probably try to compare and then group, these unfamiliar persons, events, systems of logic, or potential plans of action into categories that we have learned from past experiences. In the case of new persons: He's an athlete or a nerd, or a hale hearty and well-met jokester, or a griper and a pain in the sitter while she's a blabbermouth, a demure and shy girl, an organizer-librarian type, or a party girl. In the case of events, the new one calls for certain actions because it is a formal parliamentary procedure-type one versus a casual mixer "meet-and-be-met" type, or it is a combative event in which you can practically feel the tension and combat just beneath the surface event versus a "pitch in and get the job done" type of event. In terms of systems of logic, we quickly categorize the system into highly authoritarian, laissez faire, autocratic, or democratic system of thinking and as a result we should act accordingly—submissive to authority and the "chain of command" or free to do what you feel like doing versus acting like a "yes sir" subservient-type person. Mostly we infer categories into which to fit these person's, events, ways of thinking, or appropriate actions. At the base of these inferences are categorical syllogistic patterns described long ago and which seem to have remained valid across the centuries.

IBM used this technique when it ran a two-page public relations ad that features two pairs of baby booties, one pink and one blue, and the question "Guess which one will grow up to be the engineer?" The question implies a cultural gender stereotype—women are poor at math and science. One underlying premise concerns engineers. It is "Persons encouraged to excel in math and science are likely to become engineers" (major premise). The next step is "Males are encouraged to excel in math and science" (minor premise). Thus we infer that "Males are likely to become engineers" (conclusion). On another level, the ad creates good public relations by implying that "Good companies encourage women to excel" (major premise); "IBM encourages women to excel" (minor premise); "IBM is therefore a good company" (conclusion). Although the first syllogism is valid (and probably true as well), the second is invalid. IBM uses the illusion of a valid syllogism to make its case that good companies encourage women to excel, but simply doing that does not necessarily guarantee that a company is "good." And in our 24/7, media-saturated and multicultural world of advocacy/propaganda such syllogisms can make great differences, so responsible receivers will carefully consider all of the premises leading to a conclusion. For other examples of such cultural biases see Box 8.2, where nonverbal patterns and different ways of considering time and space are part of the cultural stereotype involved in the syllogism.

This tendency to use categorical reasoning usually serves us well and allows for a great deal of

---

B O X 8.2   Fallacies as a Tool of Propaganda—The Illusion of Logic

 Propagandists wish their prospective converts in the audience to believe that they are converting to the cause for "good and sufficient reasons." The key word here is "reasons," which naturally leads to the reasoning process. One way to make their arguments appear to be logical is by creating the illusion of logical reasoning through the use of fallacies such as the few discussed above. Go to http://www.nizkor.org/features/fallacies/where you will find a list of links to over 40 separate fallacies that can be used in propaganda including those discussed above but going well beyond with such fascinating fallacies as "Appeal to Spite," "Burden of Proof," "Appeal to Novelty," and "Slippery Slope" all accompanied by clear and concise definitions and good examples. Another good site that could provide you with a multitude of good term paper topics with links to excellent sources and examples is http://www.publiceye.org/media/logic96.html and each topic is loaded with links, resources, and examples and again would be an excellent starting point for a paper on propaganda, logical fallacies, or logic.

---

flexibility as we encounter many new people and events, but occasionally a miscue or faulty conclusion using categorical reasoning can lead people, groups, and even nations to make disastrous, even tragically flawed decisions. For example, ever since the 9/11/01 terrorist attacks on NYC and Washington, DC, U.S. foreign policy has operated on the categorical premise that democracy is the best weapon against terrorism. If we can just democratize the rest of the world, terrorism will cease to be used to influence national issues. Unfortunately, the facts don't seem to justify this premise. In fact, they seem to prove the opposite—authoritarian and autocratic militaristic regimes seem to be the best preventative against terrorism. Across a decade, India had over 400 terrorist incidents while China had only 18; Russia saw an increase in terrorism once the old Soviet system collapsed in 1990; and the shining star of democracy—the United States has had more terrorism than Cuba, North Korea, or many other autocratic regimes. Why did we draw the conclusion that democracy was best? Because we've been propagandized to believe that? Partly. It is more likely we came to that conclusion/premise based on categories developed from our past experience in world events where other nations sought to emulate us and our system of government in dealing with national issues other than terrorism, and therein likes the potential flaw in categorical thinking—our familiar logical flaw—Gut Malloy or the problem of the

undistributed middle. Events aren't necessarily shared by both (or all) categories under consideration. So our watchword when dealing with categorical (and other) syllogistic reasoning is to avoid placing too much faith in any logical system no matter how venerable and seemingly attractive, but to continue to be critical and skeptical receivers of persuasion.

THE TOULMIN FORMAT

Most of us do not encounter persuasion that is overtly syllogistic—conditional, disjunctive, or categorical. Instead, the syllogism often is just the underlying and basic structure in persuasive arguments. British philosopher Stephen Toulmin (1964) developed a model that identifies the kinds of logical persuasion we encounter in everyday events. According to Toulmin, any argument aimed at our logical reasoning processes is divided into three basic parts: the claim, the data, and the warrant.

Basic Elements

The **claim** is the proposition or premise that the persuader hopes will be believed, adopted, or followed by the audience. But claims usually need to be supported by **data**, the second part of the model, which is more simply stated as "evidence.

B O X 8.3   The Logic of Cultural Transformation

In his book *Communication and Cultural Transformation: Cultural Diversity, Globalization and Cultural Convergence*, Stephan Dahl (2000) draws a distinction between "high culture" (the opera or symphony, art museums, live theatre) and mass or popular culture (MTV, sports events, newspapers), which emerged in the mid-nineteenth century. He argues that it is popular culture that really is affected by diversity issues. Some of the diversity issues he lists include social groupings, language, nonverbal communication, values, concepts of time and space, perception, and national character. For example, he maintains that in Western culture time is thought of as linear, while in Eastern cultures time is thought of as being circular in nature. Or take our nonverbal signal for "A-Okay," which is the thumb and forefinger forming the letter O. In other cultures or subcultures, the same signal has sexual implications. What kinds of differences in persuasive meaning might follow from these ways of viewing time and space? Various nonverbal gestures? Which of his other diversity issues can you see operating in your everyday life? You may want to view a copy of Dahl's book and other of his publications at www. stephweb.com/capstone/1.htm.

Data give the receivers plausible reasons for following the advice of the claim. The **warrant** is the reasoning that demonstrates that the data do indeed support the claim; it explains the relationship between them. These three elements become clear as we examine persuasion at work in our everyday affairs—deciding which brand to choose, which policy to adopt, whom to believe or reject, which path to follow to satisfy our goals and desires (without costing us or others too much). Most of these decisions are benign and not very momentous, but the overall process of persuasion seems to follow a series of very rational and economical steps. For example, if there is reason to believe that receivers will accept the claim on its face, there is no need for the persuader to continue. However, if the persuader expects receivers to doubt the claim, then data must be presented. If the data are anticipated to be strong and hence likely to be accepted, thus agreeing with the claim, again there is no need to proceed further. However, if the persuader anticipates some doubt about the claim now supported by data, then it will be necessary to present a warrant that explains the reasoning by which the data support the claim. This pattern of moving the logical argument from claim to data to warrant, and the resulting three kinds of responses (agree, disagree, and uncertain), are typical of almost every reasoned argument in the everyday marketplace of ideas. Figure 8.6 uses the claim that the United States must become a "globo-cop" to show how the flow of argument goes in the **Toulmin system**. Trace the stages of argument in the figure.

Substantiating Elements

Toulmin's system has a number of secondary terms. For example, a claim may be modified by a qualifier—usually a simple word or phrase such as "In most cases" or "Probably" or "It is likely that." Conceding that the claim is not necessarily universal qualifies or limits the claim. In our globo-cop example, the persuader might alter the claim to state, "In most cases, the United States should become an international peacekeeper in world crises." **Qualifiers** limit the claim, thus allowing for the possibility that this is not a simple case of the either/or argument. Another minor term in the model is the **reservation**, defined as a statement that specifies the conditions under which the warrant is valid. The reservation features words like "unless" or "only if there is a reason to believe that." In the globo-cop case, suppose the warrant stated, "Except in the case of revolutions, the United States is the only remaining superpower capable of establishing and maintaining world stability." Another reservation is expressed with the word "Unless," in which case the warrant might state, "Unless the United States is not the only remaining superpower capable of establishing and maintaining world stability…."

Claim: The United States should become an international peacekeeper using military intervention and other assistance in world crises.

    Option 1. Accept the persuader's claim, and the United States becomes globo-cop.

    Option 2. Reject the persuader's claim and rely on other means of solving global crises.

    Option 3. Request evidence to support the claim.

Data: Past crises have escalated into full-scale warfare and its resulting loss of life and property (Vietnam, Kuwait, Somalia).

    Option 1. Accept the claim now supported by the data and work to institute global police power for the United States.

    Option 2. Reject the claim as unsupported by the data—work to keep the United States out of international conflicts.

    Option 3. Request an explanation of how and why the data support the claim.

Warrant: The United States is the only remaining superpower capable of maintaining stability in a world that would otherwise lapse into total war, suffering, death, disease, and so on.

    Option 1. Accept the claim now supported by the data and explained by the warrant.

    Option 2. Reject the claim as unsupported by the data and the warrant.

    Option 3. Ask the persuader to refine the claim, back up the data, or provide for possible exceptions in the warrant.

FIGURE 8.6 Toulmin's basic elements of an argument, applied to the example of U.S. intervention in world crises.

Both persuaders and persuadees often overlook the use of the reservation to cite circumstances in which the claim should not be accepted. They assume that both parties begin from the same point, from the same frame of reference. We must begin at the same point or make allowances (such as reservations) to make real progress in any persuasive transaction. Coupled with the qualifier, the reservation allows for great flexibility in persuasion because both encourage dialogue; both provide the persuadee with an opportunity to object or agree to part but not all of the persuasion.

Advertisers are clever with the use of qualifiers. For example, the label on Cascade dishwasher detergent says that it will make your dishes, not spotless, but "virtually spotless." Who can say whether one spot or three spots or twelve qualifies as being "virtually spotless"? Thus, we need to be aware of two problems connected with qualifiers and reservations: (1) their absence, which can lock us into one course of action or belief; and (2) the use of vague qualifiers, which allows persuaders to wriggle out of any commitment to a product, action, person, or idea. Persuaders may still try to interpret the qualifiers to their advantage, but it is more difficult when more details are given. The final element in Toulmin's system for showing the tactics of argument is the **backing** for the warrant, which is information that establishes the credibility of the reasoning or connection between data and claim.

We can now see that the tactics of persuasion are not usually simple syllogisms. Instead, persuaders make claims that persuadees can respond to by (1) accepting them outright, (2) rejecting them outright, or (3) asking for proof. Persuaders then can provide data, which receivers can accept, reject, or question. If the persuadee continues to request more proof, the persuader ultimately must provide the warrant, or reason, for linking the proof to the request. Given enough time, three other elements may enter into the persuasive appeal: the qualifier, the reservation, and the backing. What matters is that persuadees be aware, critical, and systematic as they are exposed to persuasion. Toulmin's system provides us with a simple tool that operates well with many kinds of persuasion.

REVIEW AND CONCLUSION

Mistake

Content or logical premises don't rely on the internal states of persuadees, as do process or emotional premises. Instead, they rely more on universally agreed upon norms or rules. Evidence tends to be either dramatically oriented, intellectually oriented, or experiential/participative in nature. Users of dramatic evidence lead persuadees to a "logical" conclusion by creating a dramatic scene and then inviting the audience to join in the drama. Persuadees thus "prove" the validity of the premise to themselves. Users of intellectually oriented evidence lead their persuadees to "logical" conclusions by presenting them with a set of data in support of a certain claim or content premise. The persuadees provide the connection between these data and the claim in the form of a warrant. And experiential or participative evidence may prove to be the most persuasive because of persuadees' personal involvement with the evidence and its sometimes interactive nature. All three types of evidence rely on self-persuasion on the part of the persuadee, and all

three kinds of evidence appear prominently in our 24/7, media-saturated and advocacy/propagandistic, and results-oriented multicultural world. Also, persuadees participate in some way in their own persuasion, whether the evidence is intellectual, dramatic, or experiential/participative. When we engage in self-persuasion, even if it runs counter to our own beliefs, the effect of the participation is powerful.

The traditional syllogism usually forms the skeletal structure of arguments or content premises. Within this structure, the tactics or particular arguments or premises are represented by claims supported by data. Claims and data are linked through warrants.

Finally, of the types of evidence available to the persuader, several seem more important than others. Most important, probably, are those that support the three major linkages: cause-effect, symptoms, and comparisons. Also, evidence that provides a perspective for the audience is probably more effective than evidence that does not. We focused on two particularly effective methods of providing this perspective: the use of analogy, which provides a comparative perspective; and the use of narrative, which has the same ability to provide a perspective within a dramatic frame of reference. Both are also "artistic" in the sense that neither merely presents information; rather, both depict evidence in dramatic or visual formats. In sum, we are most effectively persuaded by experiences—real, vicarious, or imagined. Successful persuaders try to shape content premises—their linkages, claims, data, and warrants—in terms of the audience's experience. If persuaders invite audiences to participate in drawing conclusions, audiences will share in their own persuasion.

KEY TERMS

After reading this chapter, you should be able to identify, explain, and give an example of the following key terms or concepts:

content premises	proof	direct experience	rationally processed evidence
arguments	reasoning	dramatic or vicarious experience	
cause-effect reasoning	evidence		narratives

participation and demonstration	reasoning from analogy or by comparison	ad populum	claim
effect-to-cause reasoning	deductive reasoning	undistributed middle	data
cause-to-effect reasoning	inductive reasoning	straw man fallacy	warrant
reasoning from symptoms	statistics	syllogisms	Toulmin system
criteria-to-application reasoning	fallacy	conditional syllogisms	qualifier
	the "post hoc" fallacy	validity	reservation
	ad hominem	disjunctive syllogisms	backing
		categorical syllogisms	

APPLICATION OF ETHICS

Two logical opposites in decision making are (1) conflict of interests and (2) compatibility of interests. In conflicts of interest, a person in a position to have inside information might be able to influence decisions so that she or he might personally benefit, as in the case of most corporate scandals. When compatibility of interests exists, persons with an inside position and information make decisions that benefit both themselves and all others with the same interests. For example, a company is having production problems that may lead to layoffs. The CEO decides to bring in efficiency experts to analyze the problem. They do so and cut costs, returning the company to profitability, and removing the layoff option. Apply both of the options to the following example: A CEO at a major automobile corporation sees the prices for energy rising at increasing rates and a resulting drop in sales of SUVs. The executive has several choices. One is to provide incentives for buying SUVs (e.g., "Now you can buy an SUV at employee discount rates). Another option is to develop hybrid models, which will result in higher costs of the vehicles because of the research and development needed. Still another option is to "cook the books," which will jack up the stock value, at which point the CEO can sell off his stock at a profit. Which option should the CEO choose?

QUESTIONS FOR FURTHER THOUGHT

1. What are the three types of syllogisms discussed in this chapter? Give examples of each from advertisements, political speeches, or some other source of persuasion.

2. Define proof. What constitutes adequate proof for you? Does it change from issue to issue? If so, in what ways?

3. Review some magazine commentary concerning a particular issue, and attempt to identify the data offered. What kinds of evidence are they? Are they dramatic? If so, in what ways? If not, are they persuasive? Why or why not? What is the underlying syllogistic structure inherent in the discussions of the issue?

4. What is the difference between intellectually oriented evidence and emotionally oriented evidence? Give examples and explain how they differ.

5. Give examples from your own experience of (a) opinion, (b) attitudes, (c) beliefs, and (d) values that affect behavior. Give examples that do not affect behavior. How do they differ?

6. Why was "The Case of Bobby and His Parents" so persuasive? Was logic involved?

Was the example an illogical one to prove the point Peck wanted to make?

7. What is the difference between a figurative and a literal analogy? Which is being used when a political campaign is compared to a horse race?

8. What are some of the ways in which statistics can be misused? Give examples.

9. What are some of the ways in which testimony can be misused? Give examples.

10. What is a post hoc fallacy? Give an example.

11. What is an ad hominem fallacy? Give an example.

12. How has the ad hominem been used in recent elections?

13. What are some contemporary examples of the ad populum being used in advertising?

14. How does the undistributed middle fallacy operate? Give examples.

15. How does the straw man fallacy operate? Give examples.

16. What is the false dilemma fallacy? How does it operate? Give examples.

17. How does the ELM help to explain the differences between content and process premises?

18. How do content premises reflect our Seven Faces of Persuasion?

✳

  For online activities, go to the *Persuasion* book companion Web site at http://academic.cengage.com/communication/larson12.

9

✳

Cultural Premises in Persuasion

LEARNING GOALS

After reading this chapter, you should be able to:

1. Identify and explain what cultural patterns are.

2. Recognize how you are affected by cultural training and societal pressures.

3. Recognize in persuasive messages the cultural myths of the wisdom of the rustic, the possibility of success, the coming of a messiah, conspiracy, the value of challenge, and the myth of the eternal return.

4. Identify, explain, and give examples of Reich's cultural parables in advertisements, editorials, or political speeches.

5. Identify messages that appeal to the myths of the man's man and the woman's woman.

6. Discuss image and charisma as cultural premises and explain their three central elements.

7. Identify Redding and Steele's core American values, giving contemporary examples of each.

8. Relate the values, myths and cultural patterns discussed here to how persuasion seems to operate in

Face 5—Our Multicultural World of Shared Values of the Seven Faces of Persuasion. We are all prisoners of our own culture, and as a result, we often overlook patterns of behavior that influence us and by which we are persuaded, and yet a major face of persuasion discussed in Chapter 1 and continuing on through Chapter 8 is the fifth of that list—our "multicultural world of shared values" that typifies persuasion today. Anyone who has visited another culture (even a similar or related culture) immediately becomes aware of significant differences between our patterns of behavior and language, and those of the foreign culture. Not only are values, languages, and customs different, but hundreds of little things are also different, such as bus passengers lining up in orderly fashion in England, whereas Americans usually crowd around the bus door. In the United States, skiers line up in orderly fashion to wait their turn to use the lift in the United States, but in France, locals walk over others' skis to get ahead in the line. In a more significant example of cultural differences, one third of the world's people eat using knife, fork, and spoon; another third eat with chopsticks; and the rest use their fingers.

I visited several formerly communist countries in Eastern Europe in the 1990s following the fall of the Soviet Union, and quickly understood the immense difference between hard currency and soft currency. Hard currency has real worth, but soft currency is widely overvalued, so people don't want to accept it. The hotel I stayed at in Prague refused to accept soft Czech currency but was more than willing to accept hard currencies like the U.S. dollar or the German Mark and more recently the euro. It has been that way for so many years that it has become a cultural habit in Czechoslovakia to trade currency on the black market even though trading at above the official rates has been outlawed there for more than 50 years. I was told the best exchange rate in Czechoslovakia could be gotten from any priest. That's something that would never occur to someone from America.

In Eastern European countries at that time, most people carried a net shopping bag just in case they found something available to buy. In fact, the slang term for such a shopping bag was a "perhaps." People at that time didn't buy something because they needed it, but because it was available. Usually store

---

BOX 9.1   People of the Deer

Consider the following instance of cultural patterning. Suppose you are a member of a tribe whose sole food supply is caribou. When the animals make their fall migration south, the tribe kills enough to supply it with food until spring, when the animals migrate north to follow their food supply. The custom is to kill and preserve these deer in a period of a week or two. You have just finished the fall hunt, only to discover that you face a severe winter without having killed enough caribou to last until the spring migration north. Death is certain without sufficient supplies of protein and fat. You attend a council of elders called by the chief to address the crisis and to solicit input and ideas. What would you do? For many years, students in my persuasion classes have brainstormed solutions to this problem and come up with the following suggestions, usually in this approximate order:

- Follow the deer and kill more of them, thus increasing the supply.
- Seek an alternative food supply—we can eat berries or fish or birds.
- Send a band of the young and healthy to get help.

- Ration food to make it last longer.
- Eat all the parts of the caribou—skin, horns, everything—to increase the supply.
- Send some of the people away to another place where food is more plentiful and thus decrease demand.
- Kill some members of the tribe to decrease demand.
- Kill the most useless persons—the old first, and the very young next to decrease demand.
- Resort to cannibalism; let's eat those we kill.

The most practical solutions emerge first, and then the ideas become increasingly desperate. The actual tribe does nothing. They eat the food at their regular rates, knowing that it will not last through the winter. Then they sit and wait for death. They accept the situation, whereas Americans try to find solutions for all problems, even though some are probably insoluble. In all the years of using this example, not a single one of my students has suggested doing nothing. Do you think it is good to be solution oriented? Why or why not?

---

shelves were nearly empty of any goods, and as a result hoarding was common—an idea that would rarely cross an American's mind, and carrying one's own cloth or net shopping bag indicates a societal awareness of potential global climate change.

Although many aspects of any given culture are relatively permanent (e.g., ways of doing business, religious patterns and dress, national pride as can be seen from the example of "People of the Deer" in Box 9.1), cultures are also subject to constant change. In the United States and elsewhere, for example, the constant influx of different ethnic groups and minorities is reflected in the culture in a variety of ways; and diversity and multiculturalism are apparent everywhere. For instance, in our supermarkets the shelves are always loaded, which astounds many foreigners from Eastern Europe. In

addition, you will usually find ingredients for foreign dishes that weren't available just a decade ago. So increasing diversity is changing our shopping options. Many schools have sought the help of translators and interpreters to assist them in communicating with the immigrant parents of their newest students. In such small things we can see the continual changes in U.S. culture.

CULTURAL PATTERNS

Cultural patterns are defined as the "socially transmitted values, beliefs, institutions, behavioral patterns, and all other products and thought patterns of a society" (*American Heritage Dictionary*, 1985). These are instilled in us from early childhood through our language, the myths and the tales we hear, and our observations of the behavior of those around us. These become cultural patterns, or the activities, beliefs, and values that typify a culture. Women in Muslim countries have a cultural pattern of dress which obscures all but the upper face and covers the head, whereas American women go to great lengths to decorate and call attention to their faces, shape, and hair. In Japan professional "packers" stuff as many persons as possible into their subways, while in American subways there is always room for a street entertainer to try to earn some money. Most persons from the United States would view sardine packing as unacceptable, and Japanese wouldn't allow the entertainer to have enough room to display his or her talents. Cultural training or patterning is the basis for some of the widely held premises we have discussed in earlier chapters.

These cultural preferences, myths, and values which we embrace can all serve as major premises in enthymemes. Persuasion that builds on cultural premises occurs at a low level of awareness and is usually processed in the peripheral information-processing channel of the ELM. Thus, we often react subconsciously to various stimuli based on our cultural training. Robert Cialdini (2001) calls these reactions fixed action patterns or shortcuts, which are automatic and instantaneous. Cialdini observes that "you and I exist in an extraordinarily complicated environment, easily the most rapidly moving and complex that has ever existed on this planet. To deal with it, we need shortcuts.... As the stimuli saturating our lives continue to grow more intricate and variable, we will have to depend increasingly on our shortcuts to handle them all" (p. 7). And cultural patterning and cultural premises are just such shortcuts to being persuaded.

A major cultural pattern for most Americans is the value of individualism. We like the idea of pulling ourselves up by the bootstraps. There is a flip side to this individualism, as Robert Bellah and his associates (1985) pointed out in *Habits of the Heart: Individualism and Commitment in American Life.* Bellah and his colleagues did in-depth interviews with more than 200 Americans from various walks of life, and described the core American values and

beliefs as "habits of the heart." Key among them was the value of the individual. Bellah and his co-authors point out:

> The central problem of our book concerned the American individualism that Tocqueville described with a mixture of admiration and anxiety. It seems to us it is individualism and not equality, as Tocqueville thought, that has marched inexorably throughout our history. We are concerned that this individualism may have grown cancerous (p. viii).

What they meant by "cancerous" is that until very recently, individualism equaled me-ism, with emphasis on the individual and not the community, thus drawing people into themselves and forgetting others. Many other observers have echoed this theme. Recall that the initial student responses to the dilemma of too few caribou are positive and action oriented, reflecting the good side of the American value of individualism. The middle responses are more reflective of a sense of community and cooperation, but the last three reflect the bad or cancerous side of American individualism. Perhaps in difficult times, we are returning more to the idea of the individual in community, but how do we identify these patterns of cultural values? Where do they come from? How do persuaders appeal to them? To see how these premises relate to persuasion in general, we look first at how we get them—through cultural training and societal pressure. Then we look at two kinds of cultural premises: (1) **cultural images and myths**, which are defined as real or imagined narratives that illustrate a society's values, and (2) our value system, which is defined as the hierarchical network of beliefs and values that typify a culture. Bear in mind that a value is an idea of the good or the desirable that we use as a standard for judging people's actions or motivations. Examples of American values are honesty, justice, beauty, efficiency, safety, and progress. Because our value system is a major source of persuasive leverage, you may be interested in discovering how persuaders link proposals and arguments to such values. Cultural training forms the core of our values, which then become rules for governing ourselves. Persuaders appeal to and believe these premises and expect their audiences to do so too.

CULTURAL IMAGES AND MYTHS

Every culture has its own myths and heroic figures that do things valued by the culture, and many of these myths are borrowed from other cultures, particularly European cultures. An ancient example that Greek society developed centuries ago was a series of myths surrounding the sin of pride. The hero of their tragedies was almost always guilty of this sin and wore purple to indicate his or her hubris. We have similar beliefs. You know that the overly proud student won't be elected or chosen as team captain. The more humble person will be picked. What are some of the myths or legends or images underlying American culture and society, and how do persuaders use them? Can these images be changed, and if so, how? Are they being changed at present, and if so, how? Stereotypes and proverbs are indicators of cultural myths. Let us consider a few.

The Wisdom of the Rustic

One of the legends in American lore that has great persuasive appeal is **the wisdom of the rustic**. No matter how devious the opposition, the simple commonsense wisdom of the backwoods hero or heroine wins out. Numerous folktales rely on this rustic image, including the Daniel Boone tales and many Abraham Lincoln stories about his humble beginnings and meager education. We believe in humble beginnings, and we believe that difficulty teaches even the most uneducated to be wise and worldly. Thus, politicians throughout American history have emphasized their humble origins. For example, Ronald Reagan emphasized his humble origin in Dixon, Illinois, and Bill Clinton let it be known that he was born in a small house in the tiny

town of Hope, Arkansas. Neither President Bush (father or son) emphasized that they came from privileged origins. If the politician cannot claim humble beginnings, he or she finds some substitute, usually hardship or suffering such as being a P.O.W. or suffering from some disability. In campaign 2008 several candidates referred to their humble beginnings (e.g., Barack Obama referred to the fact that he was multiracial and that his father had left the family, Mike Huckabee (whose name even suggests the rustic image) referred to his humble Arkansas backwoods roots, and John McCain referred to his years as a P.O.W. to indicate his humility). Others who came from better circumstances skipped discussing this issue (e.g., Hillary Clinton and Mitt Romney) and instead emphasized experience or accomplishments.

Products are frequently marketed using a rustic as the spokesperson. Wilfred Brimley, for instance, served as a rustic when he endorsed the value of good old-fashioned Quaker Oats and was a spokesperson for AARP, and the smiling Quaker man on the package reinforces the rustic image. Nothing could be more rustic conveying common sense about basic survival issues than a caveman—right? Well Geico Insurance must think so since they use him as their spokesperson giving advice on a fairly complex product like insurance. In fact, his rustic nature even led to a regular television series. It failed, but the wisdom of the rustic myth upon which it was based is with us today. Even as we value the simple, commonsense rustic, our culture tends to devalue the intellectual or the educated. Persuaders often use this reverse side of our faith in the wisdom of the rustic: The intellectual or egghead is the brunt of jokes, and the rustic wins out over the smart guy.

The Possibility of Success

The **possibility of success** myth is easily seen in the numerous television series where desperate housewives, wimpy lawyers, ugly Betty, and bumbling home repair figures achieve their individual goals of success by the end of each episode. These all reflect the power of our hopes for the American dream of success. It was probably most powerfully introduced to our culture in the numerous novels on the topic written mainly for boys, in the early twentieth century by Horatio Alger with titles like *Ragged Dick, Tattered Tom*, and *Pluck and Luck*. The protagonist of these novels was invariably a young man who, through hard work, sincerity, honesty, law-abiding behavior, and faith in the future, was able to make good. He might even rise to the top and own his own company, have a beautiful wife, live a fine life, and be able to do good for others. The possibility of success myth appealed to immigrants, the poor, and the downtrodden, and it still does today. They passed it on to their children, and today's immigrants still do today, admonishing their children to work hard to achieve success. The myth has been generalized to include women and minorities, and has great appeal for new groups of immigrants. These new immigrants, particularly those from Third World countries, often share living quarters to save money or go into business for themselves, and all members are expected to help provide for the family. The myth of possible success is as alive today as it was when immigrants came mainly from Europe. Again, this myth was observed by Tocqueville (1965):

> No Americans are devoid of a yearning desire to rise....All are constantly seeking to acquire property, power, and reputation....What chiefly diverts the men of democracies from lofty ambition is not the scantiness of their fortunes, but the vehemence of the exertions they daily make to improve them....The same observation is applicable to the sons of such men...their parents were humble; they have grown up amidst feelings and notions which they cannot afterwards easily get rid of... (pp. 156–158).

You may recognize your grandparents in this description if they or their parents emigrated to the United States. You may also see yourself in it at times. Isn't that why you are in college? You want to be as successful as your parents and grandparents or preferably exceed their levels of achievement.

Naturally, we are receptive to persuasion that promises the possibility of success. Self-help programs and products and services are marketed promising success for the entire family. Politicians promise a bright future for voters who support a commonsense approach to problems. Whether it is a pyramid marketing scheme, the lottery, or a weight-loss club, the carrot is always the same—try and you will succeed.

The Coming of a Messiah

A cultural myth related to the possibility of success myth is the **coming of a messiah**. Whenever our society is approaching disaster or is already in a terrible mess—economic, religious, or political—or we are in a period of great uncertainty and pessimism or when things are chaotic, confusing, and frightening, we believe someone or something will save us. We want to be rescued from the chaos and danger by some great leader who projects a sense of confidence and who can turn things around or about a new technology that will solve our problems (e.g., the fuel cell or coal gasification). Many past leaders filled this role. For example, Abraham Lincoln emerged from semi-obscurity to save the Union. Franklin Roosevelt used his patrician education and background to lead the common people of United States out of the Great Depression and to victory in WW II. Ronald Reagan delivered us from 18 percent interest rates and unbelievable inflation. And George W. Bush was depicted as the leader who would help us win the war on terrorism. Products can also be messiahs of a sort. Ethanol or the low energy lightbulb are both such products in that they both are depicted by some as ways to free us from foreign energy. Policies are also frequently put forward as messiahs to save us from vexing problems. Carbon dioxide caps for corporations are seen as such messiahs and there are other inanimate things and policies which are seen as messiahs to save us from problems. The future will no doubt bring us other problems, and you can rest assured that there will be someone or something that/who will emerge in the role of a messiah.

What makes us so receptive to the messianic? First, we are action-oriented, as we noted earlier as one of our Seven Faces of Persuasion. We live in a results-oriented world of persuasion in which efficacy and efficiency is what really counts, we decide by looking at the bottom line, and we want our saviors to be doers not just idealistic dreamers. Second, we want their solutions to be simple and practical. So as a persuadee, be aware of the advocates/propagandists who promise a messianic figure, policy, product or idea to solve the problems we face. These appeals can come at you from persons, products, organizations, and so forth; and they will always be attractive and easy to believe in, which is what makes them so potentially persuasive—and treacherous.

☿ The Presence of Conspiracy

Another cultural premise is the belief that when we face enormous, almost overwhelming problems, the only plausible explanation is that a powerful and conspiratorial group must be behind them. This pattern is called the **paranoid style** and is defined as using conspiracies as explanations for otherwise unanswerable dilemmas (Hofstadter, 1963). Probably the best examples are the various conspiracy theories concerning the assassination of J.F.K. by conspiracies hatched in a variety of possible places depending on who is making the argument (e.g., the mob or the C.I.A.). Many other conspiracy arguments have recurred throughout our recent history such as those about the Masons and Knights Templar, conspiracies that lent credence to the recent novel and film *The DaVinci Code* or Papal Conspiracy theories. Most recently, the conspiracy argument was used to explain the 9/11 bombing and the Jihadist terrorism of our times. Some people believe that Muslim groups are presently conspiring to overthrow governments in the Middle East and build nuclear weapons. Some feel that the Iranian government is already in the hands of international conspirators including radical fundamentalist Muslim leaders and Russian coconspirators. A conspiracy theory regarding terrorism apparently prompted the Bush administration to illegally wiretap phone calls to American citizens without obtaining a warrant, even when such warrants are granted as a matter of course. This in turn led to a conspiracy theory about the administration's disregard of constitutional rights.

When it comes to persuasive communication, and if Hofstadter is right, we can expect to hear conspiracy offered as an explanation for problems any time three factors are operating for the audience members:

1. They have something of value to lose—power, property, or privilege.

2. They feel in danger of losing this power or property, or they have already lost some of it.

3. They see themselves as helpless to prevent the loss.

It is easy to see how belief in a conspiracy could give rise to a messiah as well. Only a messiah can defeat evil conspirators and save us. One of the dangers of this myth is that it invites mass hysteria and the rise of charismatic leaders, who seem to be heroes but who may be just the opposite.

The Value of Challenge

The myth of **the value of challenge** is fairly simple and parallels tribal tests of strength and character. It suggests that a kind of wisdom can be gained only through rigorous testing and suffering, and that some rite of passage or initiation gives us power, character, and knowledge. You are probably now going through such a test in attending college. People say that going to college is more a test of endurance than training for a specific job. By graduating, you show that you can meet a challenge and handle it, that you have matured, and that you have learned how to learn. Job training comes after that. The challenges that are offered by persuaders are myriad. Boot camp offers another example of belief in the value of overcoming difficulty and meeting challenges. The Outward Bound program rests on the value of challenge myth. It says the most problematic children will be restored to good behavior if they get through a mountain-climbing expedition, a rafting trip down the

Colorado River, or a wilderness canoe trip. Even corporate America believes in this concept and often sends its executives on such Outward Bound types of experiences to shape them up and build unity. Brands also offer you something like "The Chevy Challenge," and many ideological groups challenge you to step up and join. In the world of the Seven Faces of Persuasion, challenges are promoted by both advocates and propagandists.

Political persuaders frequently offer voters a dramatic challenge to be met by their election. For instance, John Kennedy said that with his election a torch had been passed to a new generation and that the light from the torch would "light the world." George W. Bush promised to rise to the challenge to win the war on terrorism and return security to America, and the candidates for the 2008 elections all promised changes that were really challenges to be met—in fact "Change" was a key word to almost all of the candidate's campaigns. Product appeals frequently present consumers with a challenge. "Use the Soloflex machine regularly and lose 20 pounds in 30 days!" and "Get your MBA at Olivet College by attending one Saturday a month!"—both rely on the value of challenge. The value of challenge suggests that suffering could be good, or that nothing was ever accomplished without pain. Second, the myth suggests that suffering begets maturity, humility, and wisdom. Individuals learn and grow as they meet challenges and surmount them. Finally, all great leaders became so because they were tested and found equal to the challenge. Thus, defeats and failures are both just tests that prepare you for the future. As you begin to catalog the persuasion aimed at you, you will find the value of challenge used frequently, whether for products, candidates, or ideologies (see Figure 9.1).

The Eternal Return

Mercia Eliade (1971), a French professor of history and cultural myth, identified a historical myth persistent not only in Western culture but in other cultures as well. He called it **the myth of the eternal return**, and defined it as a rejection of concrete historical time or things as they actually happened, and substitutes a return to an interpretation of history as we wish it might have been accompanied by a yearning for and reenactment of a "periodical return to the mythical time of the beginning of things, to the 'Great Time.'" American culture embraces this myth, perhaps because our beginnings are so recent. As you are aware, America was conceived as a "second Eden," a chance to start anew with no historical baggage to clutter up its purpose. This was a key element in Barack Obama's campaign in 2008. Many immigrants of the past and present want this chance to start over at a time when things were perfect and harmonious, when events could be shaped or molded as they were meant to be. This time of creation is usually associated with a specific geographical center where things are assumed to have begun. In the United States, this center is probably Philadelphia where the Continental Congress signed the Declaration of Independence and where the Liberty Bell is housed. Another potential symbolic center is Washington, DC, where our great historical documents are enshrined in the National Archives. At the creation there were great heroes (George Washington, Benjamin Franklin, Paul Revere, John Hancock, and others) and there were villains (King George, the colonial governors, Redcoats, and Tories). After suffering indignities, the heroes enacted some critical feat that was redemptive, and it released them and the people from their former enslavement and permitted them to create the "Great Time" or the "Golden Age." The Boston Tea Party is a familiar example.

Included in the myth is the notion that society has lost sight of its archetypal beginning and must find its way back if we are to rid ourselves of the corruption and confusion that have developed since then. We often accomplish this through reenactments of the original feat in a ritual, usually held at the center where everything began. The presidential campaign of 2008 exemplified this repeatedly, especially in the personages of its newcomers—Barack Obama and Mike Huckabee—both of whom promised a return to a time and things as they were originally envisioned by the Founding Fathers. This periodic return to the origins of our beliefs reestablishes our values for us and redeems

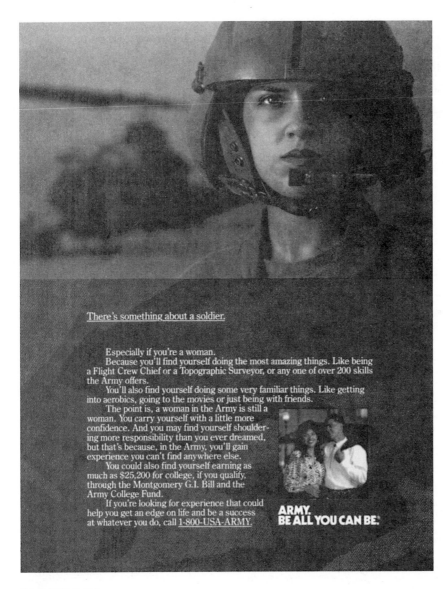

There's something about a soldier.

Especially if you're a woman.
Because you'll find yourself doing the most amazing things. Like being a Flight Crew Chief or a Topographic Surveyor, or any one of over 200 skills the Army offers.
You'll also find yourself doing some very familiar things. Like getting into aerobics, going to the movies or just being with friends.
The point is, a woman in the Army is still a woman. You carry yourself with a little more confidence. And you may find yourself shouldering more responsibility than you ever dreamed, but that's because, in the Army, you'll gain experience you can't find anywhere else.
You could also find yourself earning as much as $25,200 for college, if you qualify, through the Montgomery G.I. Bill and the Army College Fund.
If you're looking for experience that could help you get an edge on life and be a success at whatever you do, call 1-800-USA-ARMY.

ARMY.
BE ALL YOU CAN BE.

FIGURE 9.1

The U.S. Army's older "Be All You Can Be" campaign exemplified the persuasiveness of the value of challenge myth. The most recent campaign—"Join the Army of One"—is especially challenging for women in this advertisement. The newer slogan is "Army Strong," which also hints at challenges for women.

SOURCE: Army photograph courtesy of U.S. Government, as represented by the Secretary of the Army.

the culture. The ritual freezes us in a mystical time that has power to transform us. As Eliade noted, "Time, too, like space is neither homogeneous nor continuous. On the one hand there are the intervals of a sacred time, the time of festivals and on the other hand there is profane time, ordinary

This is as good a place as any to start perfecting a waterproof boot.

It was cold. It was wet. And losing your life was as easy as falling off a log.

Among early loggers in the Northwest, the boot that earned the highest praise—"Skookum tough"—was the one made by W.B. Danner. All leather, it had caulked soles to give "river pigs" a grip on shifting logs. A pair weighed about 6 lbs.

Nowadays Danner makes boots for every kind of outdoorsman. We use the same full-grain 5½ oz. leather but we chrome tan it to repel water and reduce weight (to about 3½ lbs.).

For the inside we invented the Gore-Tex™ bootie. Water cannot penetrate its 9 billion pores per square inch, but perspiration can evaporate to the outside. The boots are guaranteed waterproof.

We use Thinsulate® Thermal Insulation. One forest ranger said the insulation was so good he couldn't tell his boots were on fire. He asked for one of our uninsulated models.

In any case, with a cushioned insole, neoprene and EVA midsoles, and Vibram® outsole, your feet are well protected from the primary source of cold, the ground.

For even lighter weight, we use Cordura® nylon in our fabric and leather boots. Originally used as tire cord, it has ten times the scuff resistance of leather, and can bring the weight of a boot down

to 24 oz. So there's a lot that's new in a Danner boot.

But it still takes 72 square feet of material to make a pair. And it still involves 250 separate operations, most of them by hand (we're about the only manufacturer that bothers with double lasting).

If you'd like a boot that's good enough to go back for resoling, we should be your bootmaker.

We got our feet wet a long time ago.

Danner

Call us for a free brochure or the name of your nearest Danner retailer. 1-800-345-0430.

Gore-Tex is a trademark of W.L. Gore & Assoc., Inc. Thinsulate® is a registered trademark of 3M. Cordura® is a registered trademark of Dupont.

CORDURA® GORE-TEX™ Thinsulate

FIGURE 9.2 This ad by Danner boots appeals to the myth of the eternal return with its reference to a "Golden Age" when men were men and their boots stood the test of time.

SOURCE: Reprinted by permission of Danner Shoe Manufacturing Co.

temporal duration" (Beane & Doty, 1975, p. 33). We believe in and talk about the cyclical nature of things in the two types of time. For example, when we say, "What goes around comes around," or "History repeats itself." we really mean, "This will come back to haunt you," or "What ye sow, so shall ye reap." We have a reverence for certain sacred times like historical holidays, ritualistic meals such as Thanksgiving or Passover, and national rites such as the Inaugural Address, the Oath of Office, or the State of the Union Address. The ad for Danner boots in Figure 9.2 demonstrates this appeal of the Myth of the Eternal Return.

Commercial persuaders are aware of the importance of sacred time. They have invented special sales on historical holidays—a "Hatchet Days Sale" on Washington's birthday, an "Independence Day Sale" on the Fourth of July, and, in recent years, a "Super Bowl Sale" in mid-January. And every four years, the Olympics provides numerous instances of sacred time being celebrated. At the same time, we disdain persons who waste time, who are just passing the time, or who are "couch potatoes" living through profane time. Recessions are profane times, as are losing seasons for athletic teams. Politicians are skilled at challenging us to return to an earlier time to reestablish and renew ourselves. Not only is this apparent in their speeches, but also in the inaugural ceremonies themselves, which are acts of renewal that promise to return us to the untainted past.

In ideological campaigns and mass movements, the return-and-renewal theme is also persistent. Martin Luther King, Jr., used it in his "I Have a Dream" speech. We hear strains of the myth but referring to profane times in the pro-life, antiabortion movement. One pro-life leader said, "People are going to look back on this era the way they look back on Nazi Germany. They'll say 'Thank God there were a few sane people'" ("America's Abortion Dilemma," 1985, p. 21). This profane time was echoed by a "moral majority" leader who said of abortion, "This criminal activity…sets us back to the Stone Age" (p. 22).

Even in product ads we can detect appeals to the new beginnings or to the return and renewal myth. NEC Corporation says, "The new information age is built on the merging of computers and communication…you deserve no less. NEC, the way it will be." Mercedes-Benz reminds us, "This Year, as for Ninety-nine Years, the Automobiles of Mercedes-Benz are Like no Other Cars in the World." This myth of the eternal return is a powerful tool that persuaders use in a variety of circumstances. It is reflected in a set of cultural myths or parables described next.

REICH'S CULTURAL PARABLES

In his book *Tales of a New America*, Robert Reich (1987) contends that the future appears chaotic for a variety of reasons: rapidly advancing technology,

rising expectations for prosperity throughout the world, and general confusion about where we are headed as a nation, what is happening to human values, the environment, and the dangers of global warming. Reich and his Harvard colleagues have identified what they call basic cultural parables for the United States. These parables convey lessons about the how and why of life through metaphor, (that) may be a basic human trait, a universal characteristic of our intermittently rational, deeply emotional, and meaning-seeking species. In America the vehicles of public myth include the biographies of famous citizens, popular fiction, films, and music, and feature stories about people who do good things. They anchor our political understandings. What gives them force is their capacity to make sense of, and bring coherence to, common experience. The lessons ring true, even if the illustration is fanciful (p. 7). Reich's work often echoes what has been emphasized earlier in our study of persuasion: Human beings are fascinated with and driven by the power of the dramatic.

Reich's parables are manifest in the following story about a man named George, the son of immigrant parents who worked hard to provide a good home for his family and a good community for his friends and neighbors. He did well in school and worked long hours as a young man to bring home a few dollars for the family. He was good in sports although he didn't have much time to participate. He never picked a fight, but on one occasion he did step in to stop the town bully and banker's son, Albert Wade, from beating up on the smallest kid in class. He let Albert have the first swing and then decked him with a single punch. George went off to fight in Europe in World War II and saved his squad by single-handedly destroying a machine gun nest, but he was too humble to wear or display the medal he received for bravery. After the war, he returned to his hometown, married his childhood sweetheart, and built a successful construction business. He gave his spare time to good causes and lived modestly. George kept to himself until his old nemesis, Albert Wade, inherited his father's bank and began to squander the depositors' savings by making shady loans to his buddies and buying himself into the office of mayor. The only person to stand up and challenge the corrupt election was George. Then Wade's bank refused to loan any money on houses built by George. In a showdown town meeting, one of Wade's corrupt councilmen finally broke down under George's accusatory gaze and spilled the beans on Wade, who ended up in jail while George went back to his modest life. It is the American morality play, according to Reich. This brief story has been told over and over again in many versions, including Horatio Alger novels, and biographies of famous Americans. It contains Reich's basic cultural parables that have remained current for generations. We see it every Christmas in the classic "*It's a Wonderful Life*" with Jimmy Stewart as its George. As you read about this and other parables, look for the similarities between them and the following cultural myths.

The Mob at the Gates

The basic idea in this parable is that America stands alone as the last, best hope for a good, moral, and affluent life in a world filled with perilous possibilities and awesome problems. This parable creates an "us versus them" mentality or mind-set. The **mob at the gates** may be drug traffickers, illegal aliens, terrorists, Jihadists, the pro-choice movement, or it may be environmental polluters, the militia movement, or foreign or slave labor that can provide goods at lower prices than American companies charge. The mob may also be the greedy corporate executives who exploit workers through insider trading, outrageous salaries and perks, outright cheating, and moving their companies offshore. The mob may be secular humanists, minorities, tree-huggers, and do-gooders. Those who see themselves as heroes may defy the mob at the gates on some issue, such as foreign competition, global warming alarmists, or tax and spend politicians; but on other issues, the mob may be acceptable for one side but not for the other. For instance, most liberals see illegal aliens as less threatening than conservatives do.

Reich (1987) cites several persuasive events of central importance to our nation that rested on the mob at the gates parable. One is the "rotten apple" metaphor. Several rotten leaders or countries can ruin the "whole barrel" of free nations. The rotten apples at the top of corporate America have ruined the trust and confidence so essential for a healthy and growing economy. We also have seen this myth applied to George W. Bush's condemnation of "rogue nations" that he said formed an "axis of evil" that condoned, supported, and even trained terrorists. Note how the language used frames the issues for us. "Rogue" nations don't play by the "rules," defined by Bush as American ways of behaving; and the "axis of evil" is reminiscent of the German, Italian, and Japanese "Axis" of World War II, thus equating those nations with fascist tyrannies. Interestingly, a few years after Bush's speech, our invasion of one of these rogue nations resulted in thousands of deaths and wounds and an enormously enlarged national debt, all accompanied with a growth in the recruitment of terrorists by Al Quaida and others—the very thing the invasion was sure to eliminate. So the mob at the gates may not be the real cause of our problems. Nonetheless, this parable has attractive appeal and allows us to easily lay blame.

Advertisers base many of their ads for products on this parable. Millions of germs are lying in wait to infect you, but if you use Listerine mouthwash, you'll knock them for a loop. Hordes of mosquitoes will ruin your picnic unless you are vigilant enough to spray the area with long-lasting Raid insect fog. The mob myth is a natural for ideological campaigns as well. For example, the secular humanists are supposedly tainting America's moral fiber, so it is absolutely essential to join the Born Again group. And, of course, politicians use the image in a variety of ways: The mob may be the other party, the homeless, or tax-and-spend politicians. Not to worry—the "good guys" will save the day.

The Triumphant Individual

The **triumphant individual** parable has as its subject the humble person who works hard, takes risks but has faith in him- or herself, and eventually reaches or even exceeds goals of fame, honor, and financial success. It is the story of the self-made man or woman who demonstrates what hard work and determination, combined with a gutsy approach to problems and a spunky style, can do. Usually, the individual is a loner (sometimes even a maverick) who is willing to challenge the establishment and try to do something on a shoestring. A modern example is Bill Gates, the inventor of Microsoft, and now a major philanthropist donating more than $20 million to worthy causes. Another is Steven Jobs, who invented the Apple computer and built the Apple empire, beginning in his garage. Both Gates and Jobs were self-reliant and hardworking, and they believed in themselves. Another example from the fairly recent past is Lee Iacocca, the maverick at Ford who bucked the odds and the office politics, and finally persuaded the company to bring out its most successful product ever—the Mustang. He took over the nearly bankrupt Chrysler Corporation and turned the company around, paying off a $1.2-billion government bailout loan early; innovating with front wheel drive, the minivan, airbags, customer rebates, a 70,000-mile warranty, and a return of the convertible—all affordable for the common man.

The triumphant individual myth strikes the same chord as several cultural myths mentioned earlier, such as the wisdom of the rustic. We frequently see the triumphant individual in a variety of persuasive arenas. In politics, self-made men or women are the ones to put your money on. They made it this far on guts and a belief in themselves, and as a result, they will come out winners on election day as well. A good example is Senator John McCain who was tortured as a P.O.W. during the Vietnam War refusing to be freed before his comrades, and who was finally returned to his home state of Arizona where he triumphed and became a senator, and later became the Republican nominee for President after overcoming enormous odds in the 2008 primaries. Triumphant individuals are attractive because our culture is fond of cheering on an underdog: Companies that are willing to take risks on new technologies, small teams who get into the final four, fringe religions that attract large congregations after finding the right preacher, and new products that overcome the competition. Sometimes these triumphant individuals become spokespersons for certain brands, ideological causes, or political interests.

The Benevolent Community

The myth or parable of **the benevolent community** reflects the essential goodness of people and their willingness to help out the other guy in time of need. A magazine story once portrayed this myth in action. A small dying town in Greensburg, Kansas was struck by a tornado that demolished several homes, businesses, and nearby farms. But the men and women of surrounding communities joined forces and within weeks had nearly rebuilt all that had been destroyed. It was all done in environmentally sound ways—better insulation, sounder foundations, etc. thus justifying its name. During devastating floods and storms, students, neighbors, and others volunteer to fill sand bags, build levies, and help out the victims. And the hurricane-ravaged Gulf states received billions of dollars in relief from donations by ordinary citizens of the "benevolent community."

Though recent events have soured our trust in CEOs, corporate America regularly enhances its image after various disasters by advertising that it has donated money and products to the victims, and thus the corporation becomes part of the benevolent community. The U.S. Marines are a part of the benevolent community with their annual Toys for Tots campaign around the holidays. We find this cultural parable recurring throughout our history in struggles like abolition, women's suffrage, the civil rights movement, past and current anti-war movements, and pro-life or pro-choice demonstrations. As Reich notes, "The story celebrates America's tradition of civic improvement, philanthropy, and local boosterism" (p. 10). Persuaders will continue to use the lesson of this parable to market products, candidates, and ideologies.

Rot at the Top

The **rot at the top** parable or myth has conspiratorial aspects and revolves around a number of sub-themes such as corruption, a lack of morals or ethics, decadence, greed, and the malevolence of persons in high places. Like the **presence of conspiracy** myth, it allows us to lay blame easily and always seems to follow a cyclical pattern, which Reich calls "cycles of righteous fulmination." First, we trust the elite, but then we find them lacking in trust or goodwill, and finally, we end up unseating them and "throwing the rascals out!" Almost every Presidential administration leads to scandals as it nears its end—feathering the financial nests of its friends, losing moral direction, lying about important issues or events, and so on. Reich traces the myth to the Founding Fathers' sensitivity to the abuse of power experienced under King George and his colonial governors. Abuses of power by elites who buy their positions of power with money and favors (as did Albert Wade) or who have been corrupted by power always exist. Our history features numerous and varied types of rot at the top, but Reich believes that the myth usually has one of two main targets: political corruption or economic exploitation. Politically, we have seen it in Teapot Dome in the 1920s (the damages of which continue on even today as seen in the film "There Will be Blood"). We saw it in Watergate during the 1970s with the scandal reaching to the highest levels of government, in Bill Clinton's sex scandals in the 1990s, the fiscal scandals in corporate America, and the financial scandals associated with military cost overruns and over-charging in Iraq in the new millenium. We often hear that big business has exploited the common man, and we still see Wall Street scandals based on insider trading by "stock market jackals" and "corporate barracudas." All of these are examples of rot at the top. The lesson of this myth is simple: Power corrupts; privilege perverts. Writer Michael Parenti (1994) identifies several other myths that are fairly self-explanatory. "You can't fight city hall," "Our leaders know best," "You can't legislate morality," and "All politicians are the same" (pp. 2–13) are all examples. Communication scholar D. Hahn (1998) identified several other political myths, such as the myth of progress, the myth of youth, and the myth of love and openness (pp. 128–129).

In all Reich's cultural parables provide fertile ground for persuaders whether they be politicians,

idealogues, business interests, or religious leaders. As a receiver, you should be armed against such appeals and as you encounter them, examine them carefully. Try to see if there are flaws in the plot, weaknesses in its heroes, deception in its outcomes, and so on.

🔏 THE MAN'S MAN AND THE WOMAN'S WOMAN

Another popular cultural myth for many Americans is that for a male to be a success, he must be a macho **man's man**. Schools, family, and television tell children that important males are those who do macho things: compete in manly activities, use colognes with names like "Iron," get involved in sports, talk tough, own guns, and drive SUVs. They never show their emotions, and they die with their boots on. In contrast, the ideal **woman's woman** is soft-spoken, kind, and nurturing but also practical and competent. She may work, but she is also the perfect wife and mother and is always immaculately groomed. However, she may also be vain, rarely has meaningful thoughts, and never wastes time talking about serious things.

These myths, of course, affect the way we treat our children, valuing certain things they do and devaluing others. Until recently, it was unfeminine for females to engage in any sport except tennis, golf, gymnastics, figure skating, boxing, or swimming. Today they are cheered on in basketball, lacrosse, field hockey, and many other sports. On the other side of the coin, it was not masculine for males to take up gourmet cooking, needlepoint, or flower gardening (vegetables were okay). Further, males weren't very nurturing or emotional, and they talked about big things like jobs, the economy, cars, and sports.

However, this myth of the distinctions between the sexes is obviously changing beyond the arena of competitive sports. Female executives are now featured in ads for business hotels, and female pilots are shown using deodorant, and we see female champs at poker and billiards—two activities that used to be reserved for men only.

At the same time, men are now expected to contribute their fair share of housework, and they can be affectionate to their wives and children, not just their bird dogs. Old myths do not die easily, however, and we still see many examples of the stereotypical macho man and the perfectly feminine woman. Beer ads feature retired athletes engaged in a man's world, bragging to one another over beers or testifying to the effectiveness of potency and erection enhancers. One look at any magazine shows ads pitching their products at people who buy into these images of men and women.

Although gender-bound and stereotypical representations of men and women are changing, these images still have persuasive power and are still used to advertise products and promote ideas. Despite reductions in gender differences in job and political candidacy and in gender-related language use, the old stereotypes are still potent persuaders. The major change in attitude towards gender-related issues has occurred in young, college-educated, upper-middle-class, nonminority populations. But the far greater proportion of our population still seems to buy into the man's man and woman's woman myths. We still see ads for SUVs, assault weapons, and chain saws, and we continue to see ads for Victoria's Secret, *Elle* magazine, and many beauty products. All of these examples still promote gender stereotypes. Count the number of women's features or ads in a single issue of a magazine like *Elle* or *Marie Claire*. Consider a few of the following feature titles from the cover of a single issue of *Cosmopolitan*: "Super Sensual Sex—Touch Him Tricks," "A Man's Body Craves Certain Strokes, Caresses and Pressure. Here's Your Hands-On Guide," or "28 Romantic Rituals to Do With Your Man," or "Try This Simple Trick and Get What You Want." They all promote gender stereotypes and the woman's woman is not only good at work and home, but she is also skilled at lovemaking. They are just a few appeals to the woman's woman myth we encounter every day. Persuaders will adapt as Americans shift their values regarding gender and other human characteristics, such as age, single parenthood, and economic status,

but their persuasion will reflect the premises that the audience believes. Persuasion is more often a reflection of a culture's values than a shaper of them (see Figures 9.3 and 9.4).

IMAGE AS A CULTURAL PREMISE

Sometimes persuaders are successful because of their **image or charisma**. Somehow they seem to have a special presence, and they command the public's attention. We believe them because their presentations are convincing and dynamic, or because they have a reputation for being truthful or knowledgeable. Barack Obama seemed to have this kind of charisma during the 2008 primary campaigns. As we noted earlier, Aristotle called this kind of credibility ethos, or ethical proof. More recently, researchers have worked at identifying exactly what causes or creates high ethos in some persons and low ethos in others. In other cultures, the elderly are revered even if they are not articulate, and the most effective leaders are not necessarily the most articulate—though being articulate always seems to help. One research technique to measure the effectiveness or presence of such charisma is to have audiences rate speakers on a variety of scales that have sets of opposing adjectives at either end. For example, the scales may have words like "fast/slow." On one end of the scale is the number 1 and on the other end is the number 5. Other word pairs include strong/weak, hot/cool, or active/inactive. Researchers see where the ratings cluster and infer that those items with positive loadings are important to credibility, image, charisma, or ethos. The choices tend to cluster around the three traits or dimensions of source credibility: expertise, trustworthiness or sincerity, and dynamism or charisma. Together, they accounted for more persuasive success than all the rest of the dimensions. For example, the dynamism ratings were associated with words like "active," "fast," "hot," and "strong." Let us explore these dimensions of source credibility more fully.

FIGURE 9.3

Here are examples of the myth of the "man's man" done tongue in cheek.

SOURCE: *Making It,* copyright 1988 Keith Robinson. All rights reserved. Reprinted by permission of Making It Productions.

FIGURE 9.4 The myth of the man's man has always revolved around sexual potency, as can be seen in this Big Stinky cartoon.
SOURCE: Reprinted by permission of Nick Jeffrey.

Expertise

The **expertise** dimension of source credibility means that highly credible sources are perceived as having knowledge and especially experience regarding the topic they address and therefore are credible. Hillary Clinton expressed this in 2008. This makes sense because we tend to put more store in ideas and advice that come from experts than in those that come from nonexperts. To whom would you go for advice on gourmet cooking—Emeril or the cook at the local cafe? The clustering of words such as "competent," "experienced," and "professional" related to the expertise dimension and have been verified by experiments in which a variety of groups listened to the same audio tape of a speaker giving the same speech. The speaker was introduced to some of the groups as the surgeon general while to others the speaker was introduced as a college senior. The listeners found the "expert" much more credible than the nonexpert. This same kind of respect and credibility applies to a person's media literacy as seen in Box 9.2. When President Bush said that a person could look for maps on "The Google" during a 2007 CNBC news interview, he betrayed his lack of media literacy by putting the word "the" in front of "Google" and thus embarrassed himself and members of his staff and probably lost some credibility as well. Many advertisements use expert testimony from doctors, financial advisors, and scientists because they are deemed to be credible, and consumers feel that they can rely on these experts' advice. Over 35 years ago, researchers reported that three believability factors emerging from audience-generated words describing credible sources were safety, qualification, and dynamism (Berlo, Lemmert, & Davis, 1969). Qualification is similar to expertise. This dimension seems to be one of the more stable factors in determining whether we believe someone.

Trustworthiness or Sincerity

Another dimension that recurs in studies of image, credibility, or charisma is **trustworthiness** or sincerity. Early persuasion researchers at Yale first identified this factor in their attitude studies, concluding that the credibility of any source is tied to "trust and confidence" (Hovland, Janis, & Kelley, 1953). This dimension emerged in numerous other studies over the years, and has sometimes been called "safety" or "personal integrity" (Baudhin &

Davis, 1972). An interesting indicator of trustworthiness occurs in situations in which a biased source testifies against his or her own self-interest or bias. This may give us a clue to what is really involved in the trust dimension. Psychology researchers Herbert Kelman and Carl Hovland (1953) wanted to know who would be believed in the following situation: A message promoting the need for stiffer penalties for juvenile delinquents that was attributed in one case to a juvenile court judge and in another case to a reformed drug-pushing juvenile delinquent. The audience believed the judge because of his expertise in dealing with juvenile cases, but their belief in the delinquent came from their trust that his sincere testimony was obviously against the speaker's image. Trust or sincerity requires us to analyze speakers' motives or hidden agendas. The etymology of the word sincerity gives us some insights. It comes from the Latin *sincerus*, which literally means "without wax." This referred to a practice of unethical pillar carvers, who used wax to cover up blemishes in an otherwise perfect pillar that had been ruined by the carver's mistakes. Only after decades of weathering did the wax fall out and reveal the deception. So a sincere person was without wax or not camouflaged.

Audiences believe speakers who are sincere and trustworthy. These speakers maintain good eye contact, don't shift back and forth on their feet, and lack a tremor in their voices. Or audiences judge sincerity from speakers' reputations—offices they have held, accomplishments, and what others say about them. Trustworthiness has been repeatedly demonstrated in research studies as a key component of credibility. Although its effects vary from situation to situation, receivers believe persons they trust, whether because of their reputation, delivery, or motivation.

Dynamism

A final dimension of credibility that has been demonstrated through experimental research is not as easy to define or even describe. This factor has been labeled **dynamism**, ~~charisma~~, or **image** by various researchers. It is the degree to which the audience admires and identifies with the source's attractiveness, power, forcefulness, and energy. The following word pairs have been used in the testing referred to above searching for the dynamism factor: "aggressive/meek," "emphatic/hesitant," "frank/reserved," "bold/passive," "energetic/tired," and "fast/slow." The ratings clustered around the first word in each pair. Dynamism equates with charisma, and although it is influenced by a speaker's attractiveness, unattractive persons can be charismatic or dynamic. Dynamic speakers don't necessarily move about or wave their arms to give off dynamism cues. They simply seem to take up a lot of psychological space. They enter a room and people expect them to be in charge. Their voices seem to be assured and confident. They are eloquent and sometimes border on being poetic. They seem to know just what to say in tough or even tragic moments, and the audience lingers on their words. Dynamic persuaders populate important occasions and crisis events across American history. Researchers have investigated other dimensions of source credibility. A tall speaker, for example, is generally more likely to be believed than a short one. Timid or shy and reserved persons are likely to have low credibility, whereas authoritative and self-assured ones have high credibility. Bossy and egotistical persuaders lose credibility, whereas pleasant and warm persuaders do not. These and many other dimensions of source credibility interact and affect the three fundamental dimensions of credibility—trust/sincerity, expertise, and dynamism/potency.

These elements of source credibility are not shared by all cultures. In cultures in which the baksheesh (bribe) is the order of the day, people actually are admired for being untrustworthy. The popularity of haggling over prices in bazaars is based on insincerity, not sincerity. So credibility has cultural differences, too.

✘ THE AMERICAN VALUE SYSTEM

The myths and parables we have examined are actually fantasy forms of deep and enduring values held by most Americans. They are expressed in myths in order to simplify them. For example, Americans have a belief or value that all persons are to be treated equally and that in the eyes of the law, they are equal. This value has been debated for more than two centuries in the context of such issues as slavery, women's suffrage, civil rights, desegregation, and affirmative action. It is acted out or dramatized in the possibility of success myth. We see the myth portrayed in print and TV ads. For example, a recent print ad for the DuPont Chemical Company featured a man who was still able to play basketball even though he had lost both legs in Vietnam. This was thanks to DuPont, who sold the raw materials for making the artificial limbs that enable the man to succeed in the world of amateur sports (see Figure 9.5).

One of the early speech communication studies that explored American core values was conducted by Edward Steele and W. Charles Redding (1962). They looked at the communication used in several prior presidential election campaigns and tried to extract core and secondary values. Their work has been replicated numerous times since then with very similar outcomes, suggesting that these core American values have great durability

and persistence. They seem to be the core values appealed to in the rhetoric of our most recent Presidential campaign, which testifies to the validity of the original research that identified them. These values are frequently articulated by the media as the values that relate to various social issues (Kosicki, 2002). You will be able to see them if you look around. The following are descriptions of the core values observed by Steele and Redding and since verified by other communication researchers.

✘ Puritan and Pioneer Morality

The **Puritan and pioneer morality** value is our tendency to cast the world into categories of right and wrong, good and evil, ethical and unethical, and so forth. Although we tend to think of this value as outdated, it has merely been reworded. Persons on the political right and left frequently make judgments based on it. The advocates and foes of marijuana laws and of legal abortion both call on moral values such as just/unjust, right/wrong, and moral/immoral to make their cases. The injustice of terrorism, whether perpetrated against us or against others, is viewed as morally inexcusable, and the resulting loss of innocent lives leads Americans and others to see it as having major moral dimensions. The decision by the Bush administration in 2004 not to fund new stem cell research was viewed by both sides as a morality issue. For those who favored the research, Bush's decision was bad because stem cell research might have provided cures for many diseases like diabetes and cancer. For those on the other side there was the good of not harming embryos that hypothetically could become living persons.

We saw John McCain become a Presidential nominee in 2008, in part because of his stand on the morality of abortion. Other politicians argued over the morality of invading Iraq and its resulting human and material costs and depicted their stands as highly moral.

✘ The Value of the Individual

This value ranks the rights and welfare of the individual above those of the government or other

For Bill Demby, the difference means getting another shot.

When Bill Demby was in Vietnam, he used to dream of coming home and playing a little basketball with the guys.

A dream that all but died when he lost both his legs to a Viet Cong rocket.

But then, a group of researchers discovered that a remarkable DuPont plastic could help make artificial limbs that were more resilient, more flexible, more like life itself.

Thanks to these efforts, Bill Demby is back. And some say, he hasn't lost a step.

At DuPont, we make the things that make a difference.

Better things for better living.

FIGURE 9.5

 This ad enhances DuPont's ethos by implying that the company is responsible for Bill Demby's "getting another shot" at an active life.

SOURCE: DuPont Company photograph. Used by permission of DuPont.

groups. It is encapsulated in many of our historical documents—the Declaration of Independence, the Constitution, the Emancipation Proclamation, and others. All politicians claim to be interested in the **value of the individual**, and our laws ensure and protect individual rights over all others. Further, each person has the right to succeed or fail on his or her own. Although no one is an island, no one is tied to the will of the majority either. This value was called into question by our government following the 9/11 attacks. The right to privacy was repeatedly violated by our government as it unlawfully jailed individuals, wiretapped their phone conversations, and suspended the writ of habeas corpus, and the governmentally subordination of appointments to the judicial bench. We have yet to see the results of these offences, but they will be a kind of testimony to the continuing validity of this long-standing cultural value. In the more mundane world of advertising, most products are marketed with the individual in mind. Cosmetics, according to this value, are also made "especially for you," and Burger King lets you "Have It Your Way." And if the bottom line is the measure, it seems that attention to the individual consumer pays off for most businesses and most of them find that it is profitable to trumpet their interest in the value of the individual throughout their advertising of the brand. In politics and government the real power of a democracy lies within each individual as we hear politician after politician testify to in election after election. It meshes with the parable of the triumphant individual. In the Presidential campaign of 2008, candidate John McCain profited in many ways from being literally on the bottom during the primaries, having to carry his own luggage and to fly commercial airlines when his funds ran out, and yet winning the nomination in the end. And most good causes target both the individual recipient of aid and especially the individual donor as individuals who are "making a difference" without whom the cause could not advance. In a multicultural and media-saturated world where the bottom line cause is what counts, it is essential for government, religion, business, and human charity to depend on the value of the individual. And that makes for good persuasion.

Achievement and Success

Achievement and success entails the accumulation of education, power, status, wealth, and property by triumphant individuals from any and all of the multicultural parts of our society. It is the successes and achievements of individuals that make up the history and myths/parables of our times at whatever point in our history one looks. During the anti-Vietnam War years, many young Americans rejected these values, favoring communal living and refusing to dress up for job interviews. That phase soon faded with most of the participants becoming normal, achievement-oriented, and hopefully successful individuals. Many of those same young people are now the upwardly mobile, achievement-oriented, and graying muppies (mature urban professionals). Many of these former renegades now evaluate others by the symbols or emblems of success they own—whether a BMW or Mercedes-Benz, a Rolex watch, or a Mont Blanc pen. Persuaders frequently appeal to our need for achievement or success. Most military recruitment advertisements and slogans promise that by starting a career in the Army, Navy, Air Force, Marines, or Coast Guard you will be able to climb the ladder to success faster. If you read the *Wall Street Journal*, success and status will be yours. First impressions count, so be sure to "dress for success" by shopping at Nordstrom's, and don't wear pierced jewelry to the interview. Self-help books and programs will help you to be an achiever and will contribute to your success. The achievement and success value, like the cultural myths, seems to ebb and flow with time. Thus, self-improvement will continue to be marketed even when the values of achievement and success seem most dormant.

Change and Progress

The **change and progress** value is typified by the belief that change of almost any kind will lead to progress and that progress is inherently good for us. This is the appeal of any product that is "new" or "new and improved." It was the ever present theme of the 2008 political campaigns at all levels—national, state, and local. Product life-cycle theory, which you may have studied in a marketing class, almost dictates that change and progress in the form of improvement must recur repeatedly to delay a decline of brand sales, and the phrase "New and Improved" is the life preserver for many a brand.

From a legal point, the producer of a laundry product, for example, can claim that its product is "new and improved" merely by changing the color of the "beads of bleach" in it or by slightly altering the ratio of ingredients or offering a new pouring spout. General Electric once had as its slogan "At GE, Progress Is Our Most Important Product." The word new is one of the most powerful words in advertising, almost equaling the champion "Free!" in getting brand switching. Indeed, many changes across time obviously have been beneficial, such as the downsizing of the American automobile and the increase in its fuel efficiency. And few would disagree on the value of the new generations of home and business computers, or digital audio and video, or many new medical technologies. The Internet has made an enormous quantity of information on any and every topic available to almost everyone as well as making communication with people all over the globe instantaneous. Change is everywhere and blasting at us with breathtaking speed.

At the same time, certain products and brands intentionally have built-in obsolescence. While annual models make sense for automobiles where styling is the watchword, many other products bring in new models year after year when change isn't really called for and they tell the world about it in advertising that is probably also unnecessary. The new and improved Whirlpool dryer may just have a new coating on its tumbler or a new latch on its door but does that justify a major advertising effort? Yet every year manufacturers bring out new models of their product or brands that really aren't changed that much. Nonetheless, the value of change and progress continues to be a powerful first premise in many enthymemes we encounter. If you don't change and make progress, you are falling behind in life. It certainly isn't a very exciting claim that you're the same as the last guy or that your 2010 model is identical to your 2009 offer. Instead we are persuaded when we feel progress and change is in the mix.

Ethical Equality

The **ethical equality** value reflects the belief that all persons ought to be treated equally. They should

have an equal opportunity to get an education, to work and be paid a fair wage, to live where they choose, and to hold political office. But we all know that, although this value may be laudable, the reality is that not everyone is born equal, nor do they all have an equal opportunity for jobs, education, or decent housing. Nonetheless, since the nation's founding, through the abolition, women's suffrage, civil rights, and other movements, attempts to create a situation of equality have been a part of the American cultural landscape. The words from the Declaration of Independence, "All men are created equal," best illustrate the power of this value.

Effort and Optimism

The **effort and optimism** value expresses the belief that even the most unattainable goals can be reached if one just works hard enough and "keeps smilin'." The myths of the triumphant individual and the possibility of success are examples of these values in action. And in today's business world, it is important to be a "striver" or a "self-starter." Nuggets of folk wisdom such as "Every cloud must have a silver lining," "If at first you don't succeed, try, try again," "Keep on the sunny side," and "Lighten up" serve as cultural metaphors of the value we place on effort and optimism. And phrases such as "a hard worker" and "the eternal optimist" reflect how we much we believe in the value of effort and optimism. If you don't let the world get you down and keep plugging away, things will work out. This value motivates many of our life decisions. Our literature and popular culture emphasize this value repeatedly in our entertainment channels, our politics, and in the pep talks of corporations, religions, good causes, and the professions.

Efficiency, Practicality, and Pragmatism

The **efficiency, practicality, and pragmatism** value is based on our need for solutions. It is the sixth of our Seven Faces of Persuasion—Persuasion in a Results-Oriented world. What counts is what

---

B O X 9.3   Propaganda, Harp Seals, and Canadian vs. U.S. Cultural Values

 Most U.S. citizens are horrified by the Canadian harvest of baby Harp seals by clubbing them to death as the newborn seal pups climb onto the ice to unite with their mothers who are resting on the ice following giving birth. Recall that this was visualized in an anti-hunt ad back in Chapter 1. The average American is likely to ask "How can Canadian citizens possibly tolerate such a brutal and heartless slaughter?" The Canadian answer is "It's for their pelts" The U.S. questioners are likely to gasp in surprise at the mindset that could believe this after seeing pictures and videos of the harvest. Go to www.harpseals.org/poliics/index.html and link to the page entitled "Seal Hunting Politics, Propaganda, and Culture: Examining the Mindset that Accepts and Promotes the Annual Slaughter" which addresses both sides of the issue. Use the "Quick Links" in the right hand margin to trace the debate and explore the rest of the site. Keep in mind that while the site is discussing propaganda, it is itself a kind of propaganda based on the cultural differences between Canadians and Americans—groups one would assume to be very similar.

---

is most efficient and effective in getting to the final goal. The key question often asked of any piece of legislation is "Will it work?" whether it be a new set of tax revisions, a new cabinet office such as the Office of Homeland Security, or new immigration statutes. This value extends to other parts of our lives, too. Years ago, my family was among the first purchasers of a microwave oven, which cost $400 then. Before making the purchase, we wanted to know whether a microwave oven would be energy efficient, practical, and handy, and not merely another fad. And of course, we now know that they are energy efficient, handy, and practical; but now they are available for less than $100. And the same pattern occurred in technological innovation after innovation—the PC, DVDs, and the digital world. On another issue, we want to be certain that an advanced education will lead to a rewarding job. We are fascinated by questions of efficiency—fuel efficiency in our cars, energy efficiency in our appliances, and efficiency of movement on the production line. And we go for practical solutions, whether it is the most efficient way to lose weight, to get in good shape, or to be able to buy one's first home. In other words, we value what is quick, workable, and practical.

Even though these values were cataloged more than 40 years ago, they still have a great deal of relevance. We find them recurring in every national election and in advertising year after year. And the fact that they are held in high regard by liberals and conservatives speaks for their credibility and for the conviction that they are indeed "core" American values. Our culture is effective in instilling these values in nearly all its members; radicals, moderates, and reactionaries may believe in the same values, but they tend to apply them quite differently. The power of a social system or culture to train its members is immense—even though people do not often realize it, they react to the dictates deeply ingrained in them. Does this mean that values remain essentially static and cannot be changed? Not necessarily. It means only that they are so deeply ingrained in a culture that its members often forget how strong they are as shown in the different responses likely to be given to the Canadian harvest of Harp seal pups discussed in Box 9.3. They are probably processed in the peripheral channel of the ELM.

REVIEW AND CONCLUSION

By this time, you know that the world of the persuadee in a diverse and interactive, the media-saturated and multicultural information age is not a simple one. There are so many things to be aware of: the persuader's self-revelation in the language used and their style, the internal or process premises operating within each of us, and the interactive rules for content or logical premises. In addition, societal and cultural predispositions for persuasion can and do act as premises in persuasive arguments. Persuaders instinctively appeal to values that rely on the societal training in the target audience. On separate levels, this training has an effect on each of us—in the cultural myths, images, or parables to which we respond, in the sets of values we consciously articulate. And in an evermore diverse world, both persuaders and receivers need to be aware that the cultural premises of today may not be the only way to see the world.

KEY TERMS

After reading this chapter, you should be able to identify, explain, and give an example of the following key terms or concepts:

cultural patterns	the myth of the eternal return	image or charisma	achievement and success
cultural images and myths	mob at the gates	expertise	change and progress
the wisdom of the rustic	triumphant individual	trustworthiness	ethical equality
possibility of success	the benevolent community	dynamism	effort and optimism
coming of a messiah		charisma	efficiency, practicality, and pragmatism
presence of conspiracy	rot at the top	image	
paranoid style	man's man	Puritan and pioneer morality	
the value of challenge	woman's woman	value of the individual	

APPLICATION OF ETHICS

Dr. L. teaches a course in "Research Methods in Mass Communication," which is a difficult course for most communication majors, especially the quantitative topics like inferential statistics. A female student who is a member of a minority has been absent from classes frequently and has done poorly on all the tests. Dr. L. calls her in to discuss the problem and discovers that she is a single mother who is putting herself through school by holding down several part-time jobs. She is getting good grades in all of her other communication courses and expects to graduate at the end of the semester. Furthermore, she has been promised an excellent job as an anchor newsperson and in all likelihood will never need to know statistics or research methods in order to report on upcoming changes. The Affirmative Action Office has issued a memo stating that students who are members of a protected minority (including females) should be given special consideration and help. What should Dr. L. do? (1) Give the student a "D" grade so she can graduate. (2) Give the student an Incomplete to be made up when the semester is over. (3) Give the student a failing grade. (4) Offer to give the student private tutoring in statistics—something Dr. L has not done before and is not doing for other students in a similar situation.

QUESTIONS FOR FURTHER THOUGHT

1. What are the three types of culturally or socially learned predispositions for persuasion? Give examples of each from your own experience.

2. How does a culture or society train its members? Give examples from your own experience.

3. How do you rank the core values mentioned in this chapter? How do you put them into practice? Are there other values in your value system not mentioned here? What are they? Are they restatements of the core values? If so, how? If not, how do they differ?

4. Considering today's headlines, is there a mob at the gates presently? Explain.

5. To what degree can you identify a benevolent community in your life? Explain.

6. In the popular Harrison Ford film "Patriot Games," there clearly is rot at the top. At what critical moment does the "narrator" of the film discover the "rot"? What does he do about it?

7. Explain the ethos of the hosts of the various TV talk shows. How does each host's ethos differ from the others'—for example, does Jay Leno seem more or less sincere, expert, or dynamic than David Letterman?

8. How have the core values described by Steele and Redding operated on your campus? In your own life?

9. How have American values changed since September 11, 2001? What examples can you give?

10. The slogan "These Colors Don't Run" that appeared in many places following the events of 9/11 clearly articulate an American value. What is it?

11. How are the Seven Faces of Persuasion reflected in the cultural premises offered here?

✳

For online activities, go to the *Persuasion* book companion Web site at http://academic.cengage.com/communication/larson12.

10

✳

Nonverbal Messages
in Persuasion

LEARNING GOALS

After reading this chapter, you should be able to:

1. Differentiate and give examples of the various channels of nonverbal communication.

2. Explain what various tactics of nonverbal communication can indicate.

3. Recognize nonverbal messages in your everyday life (e.g., in interpersonal relations, advertising, entertainment, and other communication situations).

4. Alter your own nonverbal communication behaviors and determine the differences in meaning they cause (e.g., look puzzled when someone is trying to explain something to you, and see if that causes them to elaborate).

5. Identify and explain what various gestures communicate (e.g., Allstate's bowl gesture).

6. Discuss the ethical issues involved in manipulating nonverbal behavior.

7. Identify how and where nonverbal messages interact with the Seven Faces of Persuasion.

Videotapes of persons shopping in stores during a devastating earthquake in San Francisco show that the first thing people did to check the environment was to see whether objects fell from shelves, windows broke, and walls cracked. The next thing they did was to check out the nonverbal behavior of the people around them and in the same scene and circumstances. They looked for facial expressions, movement, and other cues of impending danger. During the Gulf War of the 1990s, Saddam Hussein tried to win worldwide public approval for his invasion of Kuwait by being photographed and filmed talking with young Western children who were being "detained" (or held hostage) in Iraq (see Figure 10.1—interestingly enough this image is no longer available for public publication). During his interviews, he touched the children in a parental way, prompting widespread criticism and even outrage, especially because armed guards stood at attention in the background and the children appeared frightened and looked past Saddam, perhaps at more armed guards behind him. This photo was part of our 24/7 world of mediated persuasion and was seen and processed by millions accurately or inaccurately thus changing world opinion about the dictator. What do you think it communicated about the dictator at that time? What about as it is viewed today? In another example of how revealing nonverbal premises can be, consider fictional hero Jason Bourne, in Robert Ludlum's best sellers and popular films. In *The Bourne Ultimatum*, Bourne is able to identify the disguised assassin and terrorist Carlos the Jackal by recognizing the Jackal's walk. Later books and films in the series revealed even more ways the hero used nonverbal communication to get him into and out of various crises. Can you name any? We also know that advertising researchers now can observe and record the dilation of the pupil of the eye as it travels the eye's path across a print advertisement. We know, for example, that it travels clockwise beginning at the upper left corner, pausing at the lower right slightly before it moves to 10 percent below the center of the page. This makes the lower right corner the most fertile or useful for ad messages, such as coupons, followed by the upper left corner. Guess where advertisers put their logos, slogans, pictures of the package and coupons? The fallow corners are the upper right and lower left. Guess where the tobacco companies put the surgeon general's warning against their use for health reasons.

FIGURE 10.1

What kinds of meaning do you derive from this photograph? How is the meaning communicated? Is the young boy looking at Saddam Hussein or past him? How does the presence of uniformed guards standing at attention in the background affect the kindly, concerned, and grandfatherly image that Saddam wanted to convey?

These are a few examples of nonverbal communication that occur every day, and which we process unconsciously. We process thousands of such nonverbal messages daily. In fact, researcher Albert Mehrabian (1971) estimated that nonverbal communication accounts for over 80 percent of the meaning transferred between people. Others agree with him (Burgoon, Bufler, & Woodall, 1996; Knapp & Hall, 2002; Guerrero, DeVito, & Hecht, 1999). Nonverbal messages also accompany most persuasive appeals we process. Do they help or do they hinder persuasion? Nonverbal premises in persuasion resemble cultural premises in that both are taught by our cultures and learned by us from infancy onward via processes of reinforcement. Remember that everything is some kind of reinforcement. When a baby smiles and gets cuddles, it is being reinforced in a positive manner just as a dog that jumps up on you is reinforced when you scratch it behind the ears or under the chin—the likelihood of future jumping up on people is reinforced. The baby's smile and the dog's jumping will recur more often as a result of the reinforcement. So, people smile when meeting both familiar persons and strangers. A difference between cultural and nonverbal premises is that nonverbal ones seldom are carefully analyzed while verbally expressed ones are more carefully considered. We may sense that a certain persuader seems dishonest, and that it has something to do with his or her shifty eyes. However, we rarely dissect the interaction to find out exactly what causes us to distrust the other person.

Another difference is that nonverbal premises usually occur at a very low level of awareness and so aren't readily apparent. We almost certainly process them in the peripheral route of the elaboration likelihood model (ELM). We need to sensitize ourselves to some of the nonverbal factors that enter into persuasion. This sensitization serves two purposes: (1) It increases the information on which we can base our decisions and (2) it can tip us off to persuaders' hidden agendas, favorite tactics, and ultimate goals.

Communication researcher Donald Orban (1999) points out the power of these nonverbal "tip-offs" when he wonders if, "When a person glares at you, forms a fist, invades your space, [or] uses a harsh and loud voice to accompany a verbal argument demanding that you do it his way instead of your way, are you intimidated? Are you more likely to be influenced by the manner of the argument behavior or the validity of the argument?" (Orban, n.p.) Most nonverbal communication occurs almost instinctively or automatically. It is hard to fake, and even then, the persuader intent seems to "leak" true meaning through his or her nonverbal channels. Eckman (1999) points out that some persons (such as law enforcement officers and psychologists) can detect liars from their nonverbal behaviors. These liars leak nonverbal cues that indicate that they are lying.

NONVERBAL CHANNELS

There are several channels through which we can communicate nonverbal meaning. Communication researchers J. K. Burgoon, N. E. Dunbar, and C. Segrin (2002) have identified three classes of nonverbal appeals: (1) appeals to attractiveness, similarity, intimacy, and trust; (2) dominance and power displays; and (3) expectancy signaling and expectancy violations. With regard to appeals to attraction and similarity, we have long been aware that physical attractiveness is strongly correlated with persuasiveness, regardless of the expertise, sincerity, or trustworthiness of the persuader. And we have also long known that the degree of similarity between persuader and persuadee is a powerful predictor of attractiveness and hence of persuasiveness. Remember that Heider's balance theory indicates that people like and believe in persons who hold opinions similar to their own and may find those individuals attractive for this reason. Since Heider's time, a variety of other persuasion theories have confirmed his predictions. For instance, cognitive va-

lence theory (CVT), proposed by P. A. Andersen (1999), predicts that the nonverbal immediacy of the persuader leads to what he calls arousal, which, in turn, leads to relational nearness or closeness between the two. Another theory, proposed by H. Giles, N. Coupland, and J. Coupland (1991), is called communication accommodation theory (CAT). It predicts that people respond more positively to persuaders whose nonverbal style is similar to their own. This is particularly true when their vocal qualities are similar (tone of voice, articulation, volume, etc.) although other nonverbal channels have influence as well. Both theories link similarity and attractiveness with persuasiveness because acting and thinking like a physically attractive source is seen as socially rewarding. This accounts for various fads in clothing and communicating that are patterned after a famous or attractive person. For example, until rock music stars and film idols began piercing body parts, few thought these nonverbal messages were of much value. It turns out that bodily piercing is a real turn-off in job interviews, so some nonverbal messages may boomerang on us. Both theories recognize the various channels or cues of attractiveness and similarity. They include physical movements, or **kinesics**; the use of interpersonal space, or **proxemics**; touch and texture, or **haptics**; the way one looks, or **physical appearance**; use of time, or **chronemics**; and the use of symbolic objects, or **artifactual communication**.

Communication researcher Dale G. Leathers (1986) identified seven **nonverbal channels**, including facial expression, eye behavior, bodily communication, proxemics, personal appearance, vocal factors, and haptics or the sense of touch. Communication researchers Mark Knapp and J. Hall (2002) identified eight channels: environment (including architecture and furniture), proxemics and territoriality, physical appearance and dress, physical behavior and movement, touching another person, facial expression, eye behavior, and vocal cues. Orban (1999) identified nine channels that affect argumentation. They are eye contact, facial expression, gesture, and bodily movement (of which there are five types: emblems, illustrators, regulators, affect displays, and adaptors). So you can see that even among the experts there are broad areas of agreement as to what nonverbal channels (and hence premises) are involved in any act of persuasion. Some researchers study nonverbal cues of deception and the nonverbal behavior of liars (Knapp & Comendena, 1985). And remember that in our 24/7, media-saturated and multicultural world, the multiple factors make nonverbal communication even more perplexing. We can't begin to examine all these, but we can focus on some of them, especially those that affect persuasion, beginning with Orban's and Leathers's categories.

Facial Expression and Eye Behavior

Leathers's (1986) first two nonverbal channels are **facial expression** (affect displays) and **eye behavior**. According to Leathers, the face is "the most important source of nonverbal information" (p. 19). Facial expression is familiar and readily noticed, and subtle nuances in facial expression can greatly alter perceived meaning. Orban (1999) defines eye contact as "visual interaction with the eyes of listeners" and facial expression as "variations of facial muscles that convey perceptual stimuli to listeners." He claims that these two channels can combine to "create emotional and credibility cues that can ignite or diffuse argument potential" (n. p.). Naturally, credibility is essential to persuasion, so persuaders can enhance their communication credibility via the nonverbal channel. We notice this not only in interpersonal interactions but in the interactions we observe in our media saturated world of advocacy/propaganda.

Knapp and Hall (2002) noted that people often use the face as a measure of personality, which frequently determines persuasiveness. Leathers also identified ten general classes or categories of facial expressiosn which include: disgust, happiness, interest, sadness, bewilderment, contempt, surprise, anger, determination, and fear. Among his more specific kinds of expressions, Leathers also included rage, amazement, terror, hate, arrogance, astonishment, stupidity, amusement, pensiveness, and belligerence. Any of these could help or hinder persuasion. Quite a list—I didn't know I was capable of them

all. Leathers (1986) also identified six functions that the eyes serve. One is the attention function indicated by mutual gazing. Some persons at parties or other social events continually look over your shoulder and past you as if they are looking for more interesting conversational possibilities. Would you believe persuasion coming from them? Other eye behavior serves a regulatory function by indicating when a conversation is to begin or stop. When speakers look back at a person or audience and drop their chins, this is a signal for listeners to take their turn. Naturally, being able to express one's opinion to the source would build that source's credibility and persuasiveness, especially in interpersonal settings. Eyes can serve a power function as well, as when a leader stares at an audience. Observers noted that this was the case with Adolf Hitler and cult leader Charles Manson. When you next see an image of either man, look at his eyes. Can you think of any other persons with such "gaze power?"

Eye behavior also serves an affective function by indicating positive and negative emotions. When your parents' eyes look like they are angry with you, do you listen to their persuasion? Further, eyes function in impression formation, as when persons first meet and communicate a winning image or high self-esteem. Finally, Leathers noted the persuasive function of eye behavior. We rate speakers who maintain eye contact as more credible, and we are suspicious of those whose gaze is continually shifting. If people avert their eyes when talking to us, we assume that they are either shy or hiding something. This may help explain some of the problems real estate representatives had when communicating with Asian or Indian prospects as discussed in Box 10.1. Orban (1999) puts it this way: "Through our eyes we reflect cognitive and emotional behavior. We project impressions of penetrating thought, confusion, and inattentiveness. We show our emotions of fear, anger, happiness, and sadness. We do not realize the hidden messages eye contact reveals" (n. p.).

Bodily Communication

Bodily communication has several dimensions, one of which is kinesics, or physical movements of

B O X 10.1 Interactive Media and Nonverbal Communication

Go to www.villagehero.com/nonverbal communication and explore topics such as reading female body language, nonverbal communication and intimacy, how to listen with your eyes, how to be a subject in national research on nonverbal communication, how nonverbal communication operates in real estate transactions involving Asian and buyers from India, and other research reports on the power of nonverbal communication in the process of persuasion. Other interesting sites where you can test your ability to "read" nonverbal messages are www.nonverbal.ucsc.edu, www.natcom.org/tronline/nonverb, and members.aol.com/nonverbal.

the body, such as how a person holds her or his body (tense or relaxed), and whether the person is moving about or gesturing with the shoulders, hands, or head. Persuaders indicate power by seeming to be physically or perceptually above their audiences. They demonstrate a relaxed but erect posture, not slouching, dynamic gestures, good eye contact, and variations in their speaking rate and inflection. Powerless persuaders, in contrast, behave more submissively and exhibit lots of body tension, little direct eye contact, closed postures with legs and arms crossed, and use few gestures.

Knapp and Hall (2002) identified several head movements that convey meaning, including cocking, tilting, nodding, and shaking the head, as well as thrusting out the jaw. And, of course, other bodily movements convey meaning, such as clenching a fist, putting hands on hips, and standing in an open stance with legs spread apart. These movements can indicate anger, intensity, and degree of commitment or dedication, all of which can help or hinder persuasion. In some cases, gestures and bodily movements are emblematic—they stand for a particular meaning. For example, in U.S. culture, stroking the index finger while pointing it at someone indicates "shame on you," crossed fingers indicate "good luck," and the hitchhiker's closed fist and extended thumb are emblematic of wanting a ride. Orban (1999) points out several others, including the A-OK sign, (but it conveys the same meaning as "flipping the bird" to Latin Americans, so persuaders need to consider who is in the audience before using that one). Some emblems perform a regulatory function (index finger on lips means "shush"); communicate positive, negative, or neutral values (thumbs up, thumbs down, or shoulder shrugging); or provide an evaluation (as in the thumbs up or the A-OK gesture in the United States). Most obscene gestures can quickly provoke anger and usually reduce the source's credibility, depending on the cultural background of the receiver, and in a multicultural society such as ours, pesuaders must always keep this in mind.

Proxemics

Proxemics, or the use of physical space, is the fourth nonverbal channel in Leathers's system. You have undoubtedly noticed, for example, how most people fall silent and don't look at one another when they are in crowded elevators or public restrooms. Try facing the passengers in an elevator and perhaps try to strike up a conversation. You'll be surprised at the results. Report them back to the class. Edward T. Hall identified several kinds of space in his best-selling book *The Silent Language* (1959), which have been confirmed by numerous researchers since then. They are:

Public distance. **Public distance** is often found in public speaking settings in which speakers are 15 to 25 feet or more from their audiences. Informal persuasion probably will not work in these circumstances, and persuaders who try to be informal in a formal situation don't usually meet success.

Social or formal distance. **Social or formal distance** is used in formal but nonpublic situations, such as job interviews or committee meetings. Persuaders in these situations are formal but not oratorical. Formal distance ranges from about 7 to 12 feet between persuader and persuadee. Persuaders never become chummy in this context, but they do not deliver a speech, either. You probably select this distance when you go to your professor's office for a conference and sit across the desk in the guest chair.

Personal or informal distance. Two colleagues might use **personal or informal distance** when discussing a matter of mutual concern—such as roommates discussing a problem they share. Here, communication is less structured, and both persuader and persuadee relax and interact with one another, bringing up and questioning evidence or asking for clarification. In U.S. culture, informal distance is about 3½ to 4 feet—the eye-to-eye distance when sitting at the corner of a teacher's desk as opposed to the formal distance created when you sit across the desk. You probably use informal distance when you sit around a banquet table or in an informal meeting.

Intimate distance. People use **intimate distance** when they whisper messages they do not want others to overhear or when they are involved in a conspiratorial, intimate, or other secret conversation. Persuasion may or may not occur in these instances. Usually, the message is one that will not be questioned by the receiver. He or she will nod in agreement, follow the suggestion given, or respond to the question asked. When two communicators are in this kind of close relationship, they probably have similar aims. The distance ranges from 6 to 18 inches and probably communicates as much to those observing the intimate pair as is communicated to the pair. When forced into intimate distance (e.g., sitting next to someone in a bus), we usually do not communicate face-to-face but instead lean away from the person while talking. In an elevator we create informal distance by speaking toward the door instead of to fellow passengers.

How do persuaders use these distance boundaries? Are we vulnerable to persuasion using proxemics? Actual examples of such persuasion often escape our notice because communication is transmitted at such a low level of awareness. Take automobile sales. When customers come into a showroom, imagine the results if the salesperson rushes over to them and, within personal or even intimate distance, asks something like, "What can I do for you folks today?" The customers will probably flee totally or at least distance themselves from the salesperson, saying something like, "Well, we're just looking around." Clever salespeople stay within public distance of customers until they perceive an indication of interest or a verbal or nonverbal signal that the customers want help, such as catching the salesperson's eyes, raised eyebrows, and so on. Only then will they move into formal or even informal distance. If they are overly personal, they may even move into intimate distance. What should persuadees do in such a case. Probably the best thing to do is to quickly signal disinterest or only faint interest as noted above and move back into formal distance, perhaps by moving around the car and putting it between you and the salesperson.

Look at the advertisements in any popular magazine, and you will notice the use of proxemics as a persuasive device (see Figure 10.2). The young adults who "go for it" in beer ads are having fun and enjoying one another in personal or intimate space. Recently, people in the real estate profession have become interested in the communicative power of the strategic use of space. Industry publications have discussed such questions as how close a real estate agent should be to prospective buyers during a tour of a home and whether the agent should lead or follow the buyers. In many other contexts—offices, hospitals, banks, prisons, and factories—serious consideration is given to the use of space as a communicative device or a communication facilitator. There are cultural differences in the use of space.

Try to be alert to the uses of space in your life. How have you arranged the furniture in your room or apartment? Does the arrangement facilitate or deter communication and persuasion? How do various people whom you know use space? Do persons from other cultures use space differently than you do? Observe how other people use space and discover how this nonverbal channel affects persuasion.

ENJOY

Savor a spectacular weekend at a sensational rate.

Hotel Inter-Continental Chicago invites you to enjoy the perfect weekend getaway at an enticing weekend rate, good any Thursday through Sunday . . . up to December 30. Ideally located at 505 North Michigan Avenue, this historic landmark presides right on the "Magnificent Mile." Surrounded by splendid shops, theaters, galleries and museums, the hotel is also home to The Boulevard Restaurant, Chicago's finest new dining establishment.

Hotel Inter-Continental Chicago . . . offering elegant accommodations, incomparable dining and impeccable service. Not to mention a spectacular weekend rate **$125*** on a luxurious single or double guest room, a refreshingly low . . .

For reservations contact your travel agent or call (312) 944-4100, toll-free 800-327-0200.

HOTEL INTER·CONTINENTAL CHICAGO

505 North Michigan Avenue • Chicago, Illinois 60611

* Single or double occupancy, per night. Stay must include a Friday or Saturday night. Subject to availability and advance reservations. Not to be used in conjunction with any other program. Local taxes and gratuities not included. Not available to groups.

FIGURE 10.2 Which of Hall's four types of communication distance seems to be operating in this ad? Why do you suppose this distance was chosen?

SOURCE: Reprinted by permission of Hotel Intercontinental, Chicago.

Physical Appearance

It's always easy to guess what's going on toward the middle of the spring semester when my students come to class dressed to kill. It is job interview time on campus, and everyone knows that appearance sends a message to interviewers. As noted above, pierced body parts are deadly. But physical appearance involves much more than simply good grooming and proper attire. Leathers (1986) claimed that larger-than-normal facial features (nose, ears, and lips) are generally considered unattractive. Knapp (2002) reports other findings regarding physical appearance. For instance, first-born females who are attractive are likely to sit toward the front of the class, make more comments during class, and get good grades. Attractive females are also more likely to persuade male audiences than are unattractive females. You may wonder what is meant by "attractive" in these cases. In one study, the same female subject appeared in both the attractive and unattractive conditions. In the unattractive condition, she wore loose-fitting clothes, wore no makeup, had messy hair, and was generally poorly groomed (p. 155). In the attractive condition she wore tailored clothes, used makeup, was coifed, and well groomed. The attractive condition resulted in more persuasion.

Another element in physical appearance is bodily attractiveness, according to Leathers (1986). Specifically, slenderness is considered attractive in females, whereas larger-waisted and hippier females are perceived as less attractive. A fashion trend called "heroin chic" features attractive but emaciated-appearing female models that look like they should be immediately taken to an all-you-can-eat buffet. They are neither attractive nor persuasive to the average audience member. For males, broad shoulders, a muscled body, and a tapering upper trunk result in high attractiveness ratings. Leathers found that self-image also has a lot to do with ratings of attractiveness. If you feel good about yourself, you will probably practice good grooming and keep in good physical condition. Clothing and adornments such as jewelry also contribute to people's physical appearance (see Figure 10.3). With regard to jewelry, think of the different evaluations you might make of a person wearing a Rolex as opposed to a Timex or the degree to which heavy gold jewelry attracts your attention. Or think about what one's "bling, bling" can communicate of being overdone or underdone. Yet, the evidence shows that regardless of what nature has given us, good grooming and taste and a sensitivity to the occasion can all add up to a more attractive and hence a more persuasive self.

✍Artifacts

Artifacts are physical objects that are used in construction, display, and decoration of oneself or of a setting.

Birds feather their nests with bits of string, straw, and lint. We humans feather our nests for highly symbolic and persuasive reasons. Look at your work area or at that of a roommate or friend. You will find that it is arranged not only for work but for other reasons as well, and is usually decorated with things that symbolize the owner's sense of self, such as posters, pictures, a favorite coffee mug, and so on. **Artifactual communication**, or the messages others get from the objects we choose to display, decorate, or wear, is also symbolic. Culture teaches us how to react to the artifacts of others and the way they are used. These patterns of response form premises for persuasion. A common type of artifactual communication is revealed in the objects surrounding a political persuader in a public speech—the banners, bunting, persons, ,and flags all contribute to the ultimate success or failure of the persuasive attempt. Clothing is another type of artifact. What people wear sends signals about what they are like and what they believe or represent (e.g., a clerical collar or a nurse's or army officer's uniform). During the 2008 presidential primary campaigns for the Democratic nomination, candidate Hillary Clinton almost always wore pantsuits. What did that communicate? In an earlier period female agents of the F.B.I. were permitted to wear pantsuits but not slacks and a blouse or sweater. What do you suppose that directive communicated? Another type of artifact is exemplified in the personal objects surrounding persuaders. Consider how you feel when you go into a doctor's or professor's office that only has diplomas on the walls—no art, no pictures of the family, one's pet, or of one's hobby. What kind of person is the doctor or professor likely to be? Will he or she be more or less persuasive? Compare that with the feeling you have when you enter the doctor's or prof's office that has posters, family photos, children's art, bowling trophies, and art reproductions. These artifacts cue the kind of persuasion you are likely to hear. In the "diplomas only" case, it will probably be concrete, formal, and prescriptive whereas in the posters and family photo office, it will be abstract and informal, and empathic.

Large objects like furniture also send signals. We expect a certain kind of persuasion when we are told to sit down at a table and the persuader sits on the

Put on a Highlight trouser suit and take over the company.

You can imagine them all in your power when you wear a success like this in **Courtelle**. Immaculate trouser suit, with separate toning shirt. A brilliant investment for washing and keeping in shape. Start at the top in big-deal colours of burgundy, purple, midnight, black, dark brown. The suit from about 12 gns., the shirt about £3.15.0.

Or how to succeed in business without trying at all.

RCG 17

Courtelle's got imagination.

COURTAULDS
Courtelle

Courtaulds Limited 22 Hanover Square London W1A 1BS

FIGURE 10.3 Clothing is used to communicate. What message is being communicated in this ad?

SOURCE: Image courtesy of The Advertising Archives.

opposite side. Persuaders who put a lectern between themselves and the audience will engage in formal communication. If they step out from behind the lectern or walk around while talking, they will come across as more informal. Which approach seems more persuasive? Types of furniture can also symbolize certain characteristics. What kinds of persuasion and persons do you associate with French provincial versus early American furniture? What kind of persuasion is likely to occur in a room with metal office furniture versus one with wooden desks and leather chairs? In many ad agencies, the creative floor differs dramatically in décor from the other floors of the agency. Instead of desks and cubicles, the creative floor has futons, pinball machines, video games, and conversation pits. What do these kinds of furnishings

F I G U R E 10.4 What message(s) are sent by altering one's hair color? What about piercing parts of one's body?

SOURCE: Reprinted by permission of Nick Jeffrey.

communicate about the activities likely to occur? Consider how artifactual communication is discussed by the characters in Figure 10.4. Artifactual messages vary among cultures and even subcultures. They make the difference between successful and unsuccessful persuasion. Try to identify the most effective kinds of artifacts for persuading you and for persuading others. Try to see what kinds persuade you.

Vocal Features

Each of us has had the experience of answering the phone and not being able to figure out who is calling. We are embarrassed and so we listen carefully and ask innocuous questions until something the person says triggers recognition of his or her **vocal features**. Then we breathe a sigh of relief, say to ourselves "Oh, so it's you! I should have known," and carry on as if we knew who was calling all along. Leathers (1986) notes that a semantics of sound—or the meanings we deduce from the sound of a voice or other sounds like hesitation or heavy breathing—can affect the way we respond to persuaders' messages. The factors in each voice include volume or loudness, pitch, rate, vocal quality, clarity of pronunciation, intonation pattern, breathiness, and the use of silence. They influence whether you are persuaded by a given source, and they frequently indicate a lot about persuaders and their emotions, goals, and sincerity. So in interpersonal persuasion, the recognition of a personality from their voice seems important.

Monotonic persuaders are boring and lose most of their persuasiveness. High-pitched voices can indicate excitement while low-pitched but tense voices indicate anger; and rate of speech can indicate nervousness or confidence. Vocal quality communicates a number of things. Breathy voices in females communicate a stereotype of simplemindedness and shallowness, whereas breathy voices in males may indicate that the speaker is effeminate. Screeching or tense voices indicate stress and concern, and nasality is often associated with arrogance. Persons who articulate poorly, mispronounce words, or have a speech impediment generally lose some of their credibility and effectiveness (see Figure 10.5).

Knapp (2002) reported on research indicating that people can fairly reliably identify certain stereotypes from vocal cues. These stereotypes include such characteristics as masculinity or femininity, age, enthusiasm or apathy, and activeness or laziness. Knapp also reported on research that identified the following correlations: (1) breathiness in males indicates youthfulness and an artistic nature; (2) a thin voice in females indicated social, physical, and emotional insecurity; (3) vocal flatness indicated sluggishness for both males and females; and (4) nasality was associated with snobbishness. Knapp noted that most listeners are sensitive to vocal cues in the communication coming from persuaders.

Tactile Communication and Haptics

Some of the more important nonverbal message carriers are the ways in which and the degree to which people touch one another or sense things communicated by the sense of touch. This is called **tactile communication**. We know that infants need to be touched and cuddled. We also know that this need doesn't diminish as the child matures. However, in

FIGURE 10.5 Here Malaprop Man demonstrates how mispronunciation can damage credibility and persuasive effectiveness.

SOURCE: *Frank and Ernest.* © United Feature Syndicate, Inc. Used with permission.

American culture the number, type, and duration of touches the growing child gets are greatly reduced as the child gets older. They may get more touching in other cultures and hence will behave differently in response to persuasion that involves touching. In fact, they may feel more or less comfortable with persuasive messages (e. g., ads or speeches) that involve heavy amounts of touching than in ones with less. Children (and others) may substitute other kinds of physical contact for the touches they received from their parents—they might sock or shove someone for instance, or use tickling a pal, holding hands, and so on. Leathers (1986) observes that we live in a non-contact society, with touch absent in public places, particularly between males. We probably would not accept the male vice president of the United States hugging and kissing the male president on his return from abroad, yet such behavior is perfectly acceptable in many cultures.

These Western norms for the use of touch, Leathers notes, usually relate to two general factors:

(1) the part of the body being touched; and (2) the demographic characteristics of the persons interacting, such as age, gender, social class, race, and status. The head, shoulders, and arms are the most frequently touched parts of the body, with other parts being more or less off limits to public touch. Touching is also more frequent among minorities, and persuaders who touch persuadees are the most successful (Kotulak, 1985). Persuaders who touch too much probably offend. Credibility can be drastically undermined if persuaders misread a relationship and touch or respond to touch inappropriately. Touch also conveys special kinds of emotional persuasion like empathy, warmth, and reassurance. Touching or hugging is frequent at wakes and weddings. Among firefighters, about the only acceptable touch off the job, from another male, is a handshake or backslap. However, firefighters on the job must sometimes calm frantic men, women, and children to save them, and they often use touch to facilitate that. So willingness

to touch varies depending on the situation and the persons involved. In some religions, the laying on of hands signifies ordination and is sometimes given credit for religious conversions or faith healing.

Touch can be extremely important in facilitating certain kinds of communication. Terminal cancer patients, for example, need more touch than less ill patients. Touch expresses sympathy for someone who has been fired or who failed in some other way. In another study, strangers were asked for information by a researcher posing as an ordinary citizen. In half the cases, the researcher lightly touched the stranger on the shoulder before saying, "Excuse me, but I'm sort of lost. Can you tell me where the nearest bus stop is located?" The researcher got much more information and even conversation when using the light touch than when not using it. How does touch affect you in communication associations? What if the touching person is from another culture? Would you feel more or less comfortable? Depending on the situation and culture involved, some touches are taboo, such as the touching of strangers for no reason. Other taboo touches include touching that inflicts pain (touching a wound); touching that interferes with another's activities or conversation; touching that moves others aside; playful touching that is too aggressive, as in mock wrestling, tickling, or pinching; and double-whammy touching used to emphasize a negative point, as in touching someone's belly when mentioning that they have put on weight (Kotulak, 1985). Receivers as well as persuaders need to become aware of the communicative impact of touching.

As you continue to improve your abilities as a receiver, one of the nonverbal channels of communication to observe closely is the use of touch, whether it occurs at a first meeting with a stranger, or punctuates the closing of a business deal, expresses empathic sensitivity toward another person, or provides the assurance to help move people out of dangerous situations. For example, firefighters often need to use touch to guide trapped persons in a fire to safety. Grief is often affected by touch, and touching someone during a wake is often therapeutic. Tactile communication says many things.

Haptics relates to touch, but not between persons. Instead it is what is communicated by the texture or the feel of objects or other things in the situation—temperature, humidity, and so on. And it usually communicates something to the receiver, either accidentally or intentionally. Velvet communicates different things than does silk; rough-hewn lumber walls communicate something different than plaster, which communicates something different than concrete.

Chronemics

Chronemics is the way we use time, such as being prompt, late, or long-winded. Indeed, the use and misuse of time can communicate many messages to others. It too is changing in our 24/7, multicultural world of persuasion. Different cultures have different chronemic behaviors, and now that we are media saturated everyday and all day, we no longer use or even think of time in the ways we used to use or think about it. The computer makes time practically disappear when we are involved with it. We may even become impatient when it operates too slowly. However, there are still some widely held chronemic patterns—like showing up for professional or formal appointments. For example, few of us anticipate being showed right in to the examination room when we show up on time for a doctor's appointment, but we don't mind being a few minutes late or even unannounced for an appointment with a professor, and we are okay with not getting right in.

Suppose you have set a time and reserved a place for the meeting of a work group. Because you set up the meeting, you show up ten minutes early to make sure things are in order. A few minutes before the meeting is to start, two members of the group arrive and begin to chat. Right on time, to the minute, in comes another group member. Now only two people are missing. You probably suggest waiting a few minutes. After five minutes, one of your missing members shows up, so you start the meeting. Nearly half an hour later, the final member arrives. What messages were sent by each member of the group? In U.S. culture, it is permissible to arrive at a meeting five minutes late, but arrive much later than that, and you'd better have a good excuse such as a flat tire, impossible traffic jam, a stalled elevator, or a speeding ticket. By coming late, you communicate to the others that you don't care about the appointment or that you are a thoughtless person and a *prima donna*. I always showed up a little early for my physical therapy appointments because I was aware that the office charged $75 for each 15 minute segment of the appointment, but I didn't mind arriving a little late for choir practice. However, if you are invited to a party, be sure to show up at least 15 minutes late if it is a dinner party and 45 minutes late if it is a college bash. If you arrive on time, the hosts might still be grooming themselves or putting the final touches on the place settings.

If you really want to put people in their place, make sure they have to wait to get to see you. This is a favorite trick of some police officers, corporate executives, and even some college professors who make you wait in the hall. However, in other cultures, students might feel honored if the professor saw them at all, thus demonstrating that there are important cultural factors related to chronemics. One of the most familiar of these is the way time is handled by African-Americans, which has come to be called "CPT," or colored people's time, even by African-Americans. In a scene in the 1999 play *OO BLA DEE*, the story of an all-black women's jazz band during the 1940s, the members of the band discuss CPT. One character traces the concept to the emancipation from slavery. Before that, she says, slaves had to work from "cain't" until "cain't" six days a week, or from when you "cain't" yet see the sunrise until you "cain't" see the sunset because it's already set. Free of this grueling schedule, she goes on to say, made flexibility of time use one of the prime features of the new-found freedom, and the idea carried on across generations. Begin to observe how time works in your culture or subculture, but don't be surprised if it doesn't operate the same way in other cultures. And don't forget that our 24/7 world has reset many person's time clocks. On an individual basis, time use may also reflect our results-oriented world. I, personally, cannot stand meetings where nothing is accomplished and have

to bite my tongue as one or two members of the committee carry on and on and on, thus "wasting" the time of the rest of us. Other cultures are more tolerant of long-winded consideration of issues.

GENDER DIFFERENCES IN NONVERBAL COMMUNICATION

Recently, researchers investigated **gender differences** in nonverbal communication. For example, in a 1989 study of attitudes toward the use of touch, researchers found that women are significantly more comfortable with touch than are men, have higher levels of touch comfort than men, and that the touches are signs of a greater level of socialization (Fromme et al., 1989). Communication scholar Brenda Major (1984) noted significant gender differences in the way individuals touch others and receive such touches. While men tend to initiate touching in cross-gender encounters, they are less likely to initiate touch in same-gender encounters. Women are more comfortable about touching other women and about touching in general. Although touch often expresses warmth and intimacy, especially among women, it can also communicate power or status relationships. Men touch more frequently if they perceive themselves to be superior to the person they touch. In terms of reactions to touch, Major noted that if the toucher is of the same status as the touchee, women react more positively and men more negatively, particularly if the toucher is a woman. Major concluded that, overall, women tend to react more positively to touch than do men and that this probably stems from the fact that girls are touched more frequently from birth on.

There are other gender-related differences in the use of touch as well. The average U.S. woman touches someone else about twelve times per day, but the average man touches someone only eight times a day (Kotulak, 1985). Touches by both males and females in the United States are more likely to involve a person of the opposite gender, which is the reverse of what occurs in some other cultures. In Western culture, touch between men generally is limited to shaking hands or backslapping with the occasional manly hug, especially in sporting events. In some cultures, it is not uncommon for males to walk down the street hand in hand.

Use of time also differs between the genders. Males tend to spend more time in leisure activities than do females who tend to interact in social activities and conversations not related to entertainment more than males (e.g., family, friends). Research also shows that family time tends to reduce the risk of substance abuse and sexual activity while peer time promotes such activities in both genders (Barnes et al., 2007). And among adolescents, females spend more time in interpersonal relationships than do males. Unless sports or business is involved (Smith, 1997). Scholars N. Porter and F. Geis (1984) wondered if gender and nonverbal communication were related to leadership in small groups. They found that, in both all-male and all-female groups, physical placement at the head of the table is the best predictor of who gets to be the leader. But in mixed-gender groups, males emerge as the leader if they sit in the leadership position, but women do not. Researchers S. Ellyson, J. Dovidio, and B. J. Fehr (1984) investigated dominance in men and women as it relates to visual behavior. They found that dominance is usually indicated by what they called "look/speak" rather than "look/listen" behavior. Look/speak attempts to indicate dominance by speaking rather than by listening when catching the eyes of others. If women use the look/speak strategy, they are just as likely to be evaluated as dominant as are men who use the same strategy. Communication scholar Judy Hall (1984) found that women have more expressive faces than men and smile and laugh more often than men, especially when they are in all-female groups. She speculated that smiling and laughing may be seen as unmasculine, which tends to discourage males from exhibiting these behaviors.

Regarding gaze and gaze holding, Hall found that women tend to gaze more at other persons than do men and that they are more uncomfortable than men when they cannot see the person to whom they are speaking. They also seem to be gazed at more frequently than men. Hall hinted that gaze differences between men and women exist because females are perceived as having more warmth than males. Also, males avoid the gazes of other males to avoid the potential sexual implications of such behavior.

Hall also observed that men maintain greater distances from others when in conversation and that women are approached more closely than men are. Women tend to face more directly toward the person with whom they are interacting. When given the choice of sitting adjacent to or across from others, men tend to occupy the across position, whereas women prefer the adjacent position. Finally, females are more approachable than males. She also found that women initiate touching more than men. Hall speculated that this may be due to women's appreciation for being touched more and that there may be gender-related differences for various kinds of touch, such as where on the body and how emphatic the touch happens to be.

Hall found little research on which to base generalizations regarding body movements and positions. However, it does appear that men are more relaxed and, more physically expansive—spreading their arms and legs and leaning back in chairs with their legs forward—and are more restless than women, fidgeting, playing with objects, and shifting their bodies in various ways. Another difference is that, while women tend to carry things in front of them, men carry things at their side. Hall also reported several gender-related differences in the use of the voice. Men are less fluent than women, make more verbal errors, and use more vocalized pauses such as "uh" or "um." Women's voices tend to have higher pitches even though their vocal mechanisms permit them to use lower ones. Women's voices have more variability in pitch, are more musical, and are more expressive than men's voices. Women's voices are also softer than men's and are judged to be more positive, pleasant, honest, meek, respectful, delicate, enthusiastic, and anxious and less confident, domineering, and awkward. Men's voices tend to be demanding, blunt, forceful, and militant (see Figure 10.6).

FIGURE 10.6

There are some verbal gender differences in this cartoon, but notice some of the nonverbal differences, including facial expressions or affect displays, the use of touch, and the use of proxemics.

SOURCE: Reprinted by permission of Todd Michaels.

So there are important gender differences in nonverbal communication beyond dress and vocalic features, and successful persuaders as well as skeptical persuadees are aware of these and use and respond to them when attempting to persuade or when being persuaded.

DIALECT

Dialect, or patterns and styles of pronunciation and usage, is also culture bound and often indicates an individual's socioeconomic or regional background. We learn dialect culturally. It communicates many things about us. Many of my students come from Chicago or its suburbs. South Siders cheer for the Sox but also get angry with me when I tell some of them to stop using factory talk. They do not hear themselves saying "dis" for "this" and "dat" for "that" and "dem" for "them." Yet they will be discriminated against if they keep their dialect. Students from the North Side cheer for the Cubs, and some have another dialect that may cause equal problems for them. They say "Dubbie" for "Debbie," "Shovie" for "Chevy," and "newahth" for "north."

And it would be easy to document the kind of discrimination that occurs when African-American or Latino dialects are used. Be aware of your responses to various dialects, and see whether people respond to your dialect in certain ways. I have a sing-songy Minnesota dialect and get certain responses because of my frequent use of "Yup," "Don't cha know?" and "You betcha." People look for hayseeds in my hair.

THE USE
OF NONVERBAL TACTICS

Nonverbal message carriers can be manipulated by persuaders in a process that scholar Ervin Goffman (1959) called "impression management." This means using powerful verbal and nonverbal signals to convince the audience that the source is a certain kind of person. One candidate for the presidential nomination wore red-and-black checked lumberjack shirts when he campaigned in New Hampshire and hip boots when his opponents began to engage in mudslinging. Bill Clinton managed our impressions of him by wearing jogging suits and other

BOX 10.2   Diversity and Nonverbal Communication

It is fascinating how members of diverse groups react differently to nonverbal messages. In low-context cultures like the United States, and Canada, there is less emphasis on the nonverbal aspects of communication than in high-context cultures like Japan or Colombia. The nonverbal messages are there for both contexts but are not paid attention to by persons in low-context cultures. Gender is another diversity factor in expressing nonverbal behavior like facial expression. In the United States it is acceptable for women to show fear in their facial expression but not anger. The opposite is true for males. North Americans need and occupy more space than persons in Europe, who occupy more space than persons in Japan or China. And while some facial expressions are consistent across cultures, such as enjoyment, anger, fear, sadness, disgust, and surprise, there are major differences between diverse groups as to when and where it is

appropriate to display such emotions. Laughter can communicate nervousness or fear in some cultures. Differences occur over how members of various cultures respond to the placement or movement of furniture. One German corporate executive working in the United States became so upset about visitors to his office moving the "guest chair" that he had it bolted down. Some mediators in conflict resolution meetings spend more time getting the furniture arrangement just right than they do in preparing for the agenda. To learn more about these examples and many others, go to www.beyondintract ability.org/m/cross_cultural_ communication and scroll down to the section on nonverbal communication. Be sure to visit some of the links there and learn how nonverbal communication works in such diverse groups as Jewish and Arab Israelis, Angolans, and blacks and whites and in Islamic cultures. Listen to participants in Beyond Intractibility experiments.

casual clothing in the White House. Or consider the use of timing discussed in Box 10.2 when used by the President to announce "victory" in Iraq. This mis-use of timing continued to be used as criticism of his handling of the war until the end of his term five years later. He wore a pilot's uniform and landed on an aircraft carrier announcing "Mission Accomplished!" in Iraq the day after the initial invasion in 2003, even though he was not a pilot, never landed the airplane and the mission was not close to being accomplished as the nest more than 1000 days of conflict and casualties demonstrated.

The use of artifacts of clothing to communicate nonverbally in impression management is a popular topic in the corporate world. In her book *The Power of Dress*, Jacqueline Murray (1989) provides a number of case studies to demonstrate the persuasive use of dress. For example, at Electronic Data Systems, everyone has a military look, with clean-shaven faces, shiny, black, plain-toed shoes, white shirts, dark suits, and army-style haircuts for men. Murray identifies

three categories of business dress: (1) "corporate dress," which is used by bankers, attorneys, and executives; (2) "communication dress," which is used by persons in sales, marketing, education, personnel, and high-tech industries; and (3) "creative dress," which is used by interior decorators, commercial artists, persons in advertising, boutique owners, and entrepreneurs. Corporate dress is simple in line, shape, and design, tends to be tailored, and features gray and blue colors for suits, and off-white or light blue for shirts and blouses. Corporate dress also uses fabrics such as silks, herringbones, tweeds, and flannels in suits or dresses, and plain cottons, wools, or linens in shirts and blouses. Communication dress features suits and dresses that are practical, relaxed, and semi-traditional, and includes blazers and sports coats. Communication dress includes a mix of colors for the blouses and shirts, featuring stripes or relaxed prints, and fabrics such as knits and loose or bulky weaves. Creative dress tends to be loose-fitting, with elongated lines and exaggerated design in both suits and dresses and blouses and shirts. The preferred colors in this category are striking, dramatic hues, as well as

BOX 10.3 Nonverbal Propaganda

When you think about the many kinds of things besides words than can convey meaning, you soon realize that the list is going to get quite long. For example, there's the old reliable propaganda poster. Then there are famous propaganda films like "Triumph of the Will" from the WW II era and more recently by films like "Fahrenheit 9/11" and "Sicko" both by Michael Moore or "An Inconvenient Truth" by Al Gore, all of which carry ideological messages. And many propaganda experts claim that even music, art, architecture, jewelry, dance, drama, perfume, automobiles (after all what did owning a Rolls Royce "mean" if not that being a capitalist was a good life model?) clothing, furniture, and even many simple crafts like cooking can be used for propaganda purposes—don't you think gourmet cooking promotes a certain lifestyle or that the vegan lifestyle has propaganda implications? Go to any search engine and enter the word "Propaganda" and any of the examples noted above (i.e., "music," "architecture," "cartoons," "perfume," etc.) and visit some of the sites you find there. For a real insight into the works of a modern propagandist, go to www.michaelmoore.com and explore the many links and sublinks that employ nonverbal messages or view a DVD of some of his films. Report back to the class what you find or perhaps even prepare a brief PowerPoint presentation that imports some of these nonverbal examples of propaganda to show how ubiquitous propaganda is and use it in place of a term paper.

understated taupes, peaches, and basics. Although some may question Murray's conclusions, few would argue with her premise that dress is important as a nonverbal channel of communication.

We rely on the visual medium for a large percentage of our impressions of others. In cyberspace, the research shows that people make impressions on how people look act without many visual cues, and these impressions often vary from offline reality (Jacobson, 1999). When you consider that fact with the multicultural aspect of our 24/7 world, you need to take virtual impressions come to without the visual medium with a grain of salt.

OTHER NONVERBAL MESSAGES

Eye movements and other movements of the head can also communicate. We are all aware of the negative impression we have of persons whose eyes are continuously darting about or who can't look us in the eye for more than a brief moment. Completely different meaning can come from what is called "gaze holding," or maintaining eye contact. Albert

Scheflen (1973) found that when a psychiatrist uses the "bowl gesture," patients often open up and reveal more about themselves and their problems. This gesture in used in persuasion and is the logo for the Allstate company. As Box 10.3 demonstrates, many things including music, art, and even cooking styles can have meanings—even propagandistic meanings.

People also use their bodies to invite or inhibit communication. This is termed **blocking behavior**. Notice the two configurations in Figure 10.7. In triad A, the body positions of the three persons would inhibit a fourth person from joining in the conversation, whereas in triad B, the body positions invite participation.

Another way to block or invite communication is using objects such as furniture or piles of books on a library table to block communication. Research shows that lifting or lowering the chin at the ends of sentences serves as a signal that the person intends to continue to speak or that he or she is finished speaking and someone else can join in. And, of course, we are all aware of the communicative power of head nodding, winking, and various obscene gestures, which vary in meaning from culture to culture. Orban (1999) and others

Top view

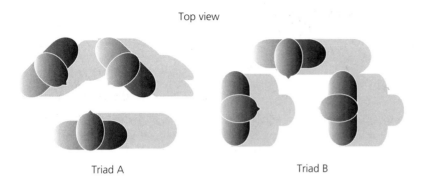

Triad A   Triad B

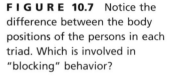

FIGURE 10.7 Notice the difference between the body positions of the persons in each triad. Which is involved in "blocking" behavior?

call these nonverbal indicators "regulators." Among the regulators are those that involve turn taking, turn requesting, and turn yielding or "back channeling," where the listener encourages the speaker to continue instead of taking his or her turn. Orban says back channeling indicates a listener's full attention and interest, which means back-channeled persuaders will advocate longer and with more enthusiasm. As you begin to observe the nonverbal messages occurring around you, you will discover an almost infinite number of potential nonverbal message carriers. Who reaches for the check at a restaurant first? What do nervous gestures or twitches, volume, tone, and pauses communicate? How do you interpret curious habits such as cracking one's knuckles or doodling, which could communicate subconscious tensions?

Even the sense of smell seems to be an important carrier of information. We are all aware, for example, of the person who uses too much perfume, cologne, or after-shave lotion or of the person with body odor. Apparently, we can detect more subtle odors as well. For instance, some persons claim to be able to smell hostility or tension in the air upon entering a room. Many homes have unique and characteristic odors caused by the kinds of food cooked in them, the kinds of cleaning solutions used, the presence of pets, or the kinds of wood used in their construction or furnishings. The fragrance of a new car is now available in aerosol cans to spray in used cars, thus making them seem newer and "fresher."

REVIEW AND CONCLUSION

By this time, you know that the world of the persuadee in an information age is not an easy one. You need to be aware of so many things including the persuader's self-revelation via language choices and the internal or process premises operating for each of us. The responsible receiver recognizes the variety of nonverbal channels, including facial expression, eye behavior, and bodily communication. You need to be aware of the ways in which gestures and posture, proxemics, physical appearance, and artifacts can communicate. You also need to realize that vocal communication, tactile communication, haptics, chronemics, and gender all send messages. These premises do not make receivers' tasks any easier, given that they operate at particularly low levels of awareness, and we often overlook them as we analyze persuasion. That's probably because they are processed in the peripheral channel of the ELM where we don't really do much analysis. You will have to train yourself to be more sensitive to nonverbal elements in the persuasive process, so you can skillfully use these channels in your own communication, but, more importantly, so you can accurately decode the real meaning of the messages aimed at you every day.

KEY TERMS

After reading this chapter, you should be able to identify, explain, and give an example of the following key terms or concepts:

kinesics

proxemics

haptics

physical appearance

chronemics

artifactual communication

nonverbal channels

facial expression

eye behavior

bodily communication

proxemics

public distance

social or formal distance

personal or informal distance

intimate distance

artifactual communication

vocal features

tactile communication

gender differences

dialect

blocking behavior

APPLICATION OF ETHICS

You are in charge of nurse/patient relations at a small-town hospital, and recently you have hired nurses from other cultures. You are just beginning to realize that there are great cultural differences in the way nurses view their work and interact with patients. For example, in the United States nurses value individualism and reliance, while 70 percent of the rest of the world's nurses value collectivism over individualism. This is exemplified by two contrary philosophies regarding health care: (1) to each person according to what is available in a free market; and (2) to each patient according to their need. Your hospital has limited resources and diverse patients, nurses, doctors, and staff working together, often on the same patients. How will you go about training the various diversities to cooperate, especially when their philosophies on health care are so different? Your options are (1) have an open free-for-all discussion of the issues; (2) conduct individual counseling with nurses, doctors, and staff who must work together but disagree about the two opposing philosophies; (3) hire a professional consulting group specializing in diversity and nursing to conduct a series of diversity seminars; or (4) handle the conflicts on a case-by-case basis.

QUESTIONS FOR FURTHER THOUGHT

1. What are some of the facial expressions you find easiest to identify? Which is most difficult?

2. What is kinesics? Give some examples, and explain how and what they communicate.

3. Which one of your friends uses gestures most effectively? What does he or she do that makes the gestures so effective?

4. What are some examples of how physical appearance sends messages in your world? What are some examples of the way physical appearance identifies a contemporary musical artist or group?

5. With what artifacts do you surround yourself? What do they mean to you? (Some students have reported that the first thing they do after unpacking for dormitory living is to purchase "conversation pieces" or artifacts that symbolize themselves.) What about your roommate? What artifacts does he or she use? What do they symbolize about him or

her? What about your family members'
artifacts?

6. How often do you touch others? Try to
increase the number of touches you use, and
observe the responses of others. Does the
increase have any effect? If so, what?

7. What are some examples of how chronemics
operates in your life—on campus, in the dorm,
in the classroom, and at home?

8. What are some of the gender differences in
nonverbal communication as they appear in
contemporary advertising?

9. What is the predominant dialect where you
live? Are there any other dialects that you can
identify in your community? What effects do
they have on people's attitudes and behaviors?

10. What is "blocking" behavior? Give examples
from your everyday life.

11. What are some ways you respond to texture or
haptics?

12. What are some cultural differences in
nonverbal communication?

13. Would it be ethical to manipulate your nonverbal
behavior to affect persuasive outcomes?

✳

 For online activities, go to the *Persuasion* book companion Web site at
http://academic.cengage.com/communication/larson12.

PART III

✳

Applications
of Persuasive Premises

P art III studies persuasion in a variety of contexts. We ask how our analyses of these contexts help us to make critical judgments about whether to buy, elect, join, quit, give, or believe. Chapter 11 explores a familiar application, the persuasive campaign or movement—a series of messages designed to lead receivers to specific ends. Chapter 12 focuses on how to become a persuader. In addition to helping you persuade others, what you learn will help you to become a more critical consumer of persuasive messages aimed at you. In Chapter 13 we explore mass media. Mass-mediated messages range from the brief but influential TV or radio commercial spot to more extensive magazine, newspaper, and direct mail advertisements, speeches, documentaries, and news reports. We will discover that the media of our time, especially the interactive media, may be the determining factor in deciding which problems our culture should concentrate on. Finally, Chapter 14 investigates print and electronic advertising and discusses how they have come to dominate contemporary American society. Once again, in all of these chapters we will find the Seven Faces of Persuasion and the ELM returning in a variety of ways—either as backdrops for our discussion or as direct parts of our commentary. Keep them in mind as you progress through this third and final part of your study of *Persuasion: Reception and Responsibility*.

11

The Persuasive Campaign
or Movement   P.336

Yes we can

LEARNING GOALS

After reading this chapter, you should be able to:

1. Compare and contrast campaigns and single-shot persuasion.

2. Explain why campaigns are communication systems.

3. Differentiate among the three types of campaigns and give examples of each.

4. Demonstrate how campaign goals, strategies, and tactics are used in campaigns.

5. Identify and explain the five stages of the Yale campaign model.

6. Explain the hierarchy of effects model.

7. Differentiate between social movements and other types of campaigns.

8. Discuss symbolic convergence and show how it is used in persuasive campaigns for products, persons, and ideas.

9. Identify and discuss various kinds of campaign communication including buzz marketing.

For many years, the study of persuasion focused mainly on the public speech and "single-shot" or "hypodermic needle" perspective on persuasive communication. This model placed a receiver at a certain position on an issue prior to an injection or "shot" of persuasion. Following the persuasion, the researcher either speculated about or tried to statistically measure any changes that might have occurred in the receiver. This approach makes for simple models for persuasion, but it hardly matches reality. After all, instances in which a single persuasive message changed the outcome of events are rare indeed. Most persuasion is incremental and cumulative instead, and this is especially true in a multicultural, 24/7, networked, and media-saturated world of advocacy/propaganda. For instance, if you were considering whether to buy a digital camcorder, vote for a candidate for office, give money to a charity, or join a cause, your decision would not be instantaneous. Rather, it would be the result of a series of messages. Some would be processed in the peripheral path of the elaboration likelihood model (ELM), such as the ads for the camcorder, the candidate's appearance, your history with the charity, or the stirring words of the leader of the movement or cause. Other elements in your persuasion would be processed via the central route. These might include what *Consumer Reports* says about the camcorder or what editorials say about the candidate or statistics donation administrative costs.

Until the 1990s, marketing, advertising, and public relations campaign planning were dominated by the single-shot approach. Ad and public relations campaigns were both seen as periods of time during which many messages were being sent, but it was still assumed that a single ad or news release could sell a product, candidate, or cause. Then a new term came into vogue—**integrated marketing communication** (IMC)—which refers to more carefully coordinated activities of marketing, advertising, public relations, sales promotion, packaging, personal selling, Web sites, branding, brand contacts, and event staging. Each element works with the others and leads to synergies that make the whole far greater than the sum of the parts. For a long time, political scientists also ignored the communication dimensions of political campaigns, with the possible exception of research on campaign financing and public opinion polling. They remained focused on the nature and structure of *government* and ignored the electoral process as "mere politics." Meanwhile, most of the research done on campaigns occurred in advertising or marketing departments and was proprietary, meaning that it belonged to the client, candidate, or cause leader who paid for it, and they seldom made it public. The fact that candidates used focus groups to determine their dress or hairstyle was the best kept secret in town. Remember the politician who changed her style of dress and mode of transportation when she shifted from a GOP women's luncheon audience to a college campus? No doubt her campaign committee wished the revelation hadn't become public.

Campaign and movement theory has come a long way, and this is appropriate, given that the persuasive campaign is probably the most prevalent form of persuasion today. In this chapter, we look at three general types of persuasive campaigns: **product-oriented**, **person- or candidate-oriented**, and **idea- or ideologically-oriented**. We shouldn't underestimate the impact of advancing technology and research on persuasion and especially on the strategy considerations of persuasive campaigns—multi-mediated, psychologically constructed, interactive and highly sophisticated messages that don't occur in an "all at onceness" but over time. They are targeted at specifically designated campaign or market "segments" and

LIKE A ROCK

lead the persuadee through a series of steps to the final campaign goal whether it be adoption of a new practice (such as recycling) a new product type (e.g., a pharmaceutical) or brand (Viagra) or a particular candidate or organization. The Internet, interactive media, digital audio, video, and graphics all can and do convey powerfully persuasive messages in such campaigns that interact with one another and with receivers for overall effect. In the future, the number and sophistication of persuasive campaigns will increase exponentially as we increase the use of the Internet, digital technologies such as Wii dual-digital, air wave broadcasting, computer/television interfaces and many others. Market segmentation will be much easier to accomplish. Experts predict that soon most campaigns will be aimed at a segment of one—you will be in one separate segment getting a tailored set of messages specifically designed with you in mind and everyone else each getting the same kind of individually tailored separate appeal—sort of in a "Big Brother is Watching You" approach. In a way it is too immense and frightening to consider—accounting for our uniform reactions, votes, purchases, and so forth for individually focused and strategically planned bits of persuasion layered to come together in the end with near identical behaviors.

CAMPAIGNS VERSUS SINGLE SHOT PERSUASIVE MESSAGES

As noted above, campaigns are not merely a series of messages sent to audiences, although they once were thought of that way. Political campaigns used to always start on Labor Day and end on the day of the election. Now they might begin years in advance and will surely encompass much more than just debates over specific issues, position

papers, attack and support television spots, and so on. Campaigns have and will continue to differ from single shots of persuasion or from collections of persuasive messages delivered over time in several ways.

1. Campaigns create "positions" in the audience's minds for the product, candidate, or idea. So, for instance, the "Mountain Grown Coffee" is the position occupied by Folgers (even though all coffees are grown in mountains), and Maxwell house occupies the "Reheatable" position.

2. Campaigns are intentionally designed to develop over time. They have stages for getting the audience's attention, preparing them to act, and, finally calling the audience to action.
   - Politicians announce their candidacy, then appoint their staff, then agree to debates, then begin to produce commercials, and so on with each step following the other like the acts and scenes in a drama.

3. Campaigns dramatize the product, candidate, idea, or ideology for the audience, inviting members to participate with the campaign and its goal(s) in real or symbolic ways. We want our brand to have a personality so Pepsi is a younger person's drink and "GetSoClean" detergent is engaged in continual warfare with germs and dirt—all cast in the dramatic mode.

4. Campaigns use sophisticated communication technologies to reach target prospects.

Starting in the late 1980s, computers began to store large amounts of information about potential voters, customers, donors, and joiners. These technological advances led to what is called "data-based marketing" where the persuader gathers information about prospective voters, customers, donors, or joiners to be used in future campaigns long before they are actually put to use.

Following movements or campaigns is like watching a TV series. Although the episodes can stand alone (each has its own beginning, middle, and end), together they form a collage of messages that meld together until an entire image, and overall beginning, middle, and end or the big picture of the campaign is perceived and stored. If it is well-designed, large segments of the population will have been exposed to enough "episodes" that most will come away with a similar image of the product, candidate, or idea.

SIMILARITIES AMONG THE TYPES OF CAMPAIGNS

The three campaign types (product, person, and idea or ideology) share some similarities. All of them occur over time. Most are targeted and use mass media to accomplish their goals. Several high profile individuals are usually present in person and idea and propaganda campaigns, but not necessarily in product-oriented campaigns. In the person-oriented political campaign, the focus is on an individual's name and the purpose associated with the name. For politicians this is always election to office or nomination to office. However, in other person-oriented campaigns the focus may be on donating to pay for an operation or save the person's home or to engage in action to further a cause such as in righting a wrong done to someone in the past, such as an unjust conviction. The slogan might feature a candidate's name—"Be Sure to Vote for John Countryman"— or it may feature a person needing financial support—"Dollars for Jimmy, Our County's Liver Transplant Candidate." In issue or cause-oriented campaigns the slogan or theme usually features the cause—"think Globally; Act Locally," "Stop Smoking Now," or "Stop Importation of Foreign Made Toys." Political campaigns might focus on a cause or issue such as stem cell research policy, terrorism, or school vouchers. There are also some differences among the three types of campaign, which we'll discuss later in this chapter. All campaigns, of course, use mass media to further their goals and strategies, and employ mass media-driven tactics in our media-saturated, 24/7 networked world.

GOALS, STRATEGIES, AND TACTICS IN CAMPAIGNS

Campaigns don't sell anything, but they do deliver a prospective consumer, voter, donor, or joiner to the point of sale, donation, voting, joining, or a Web site of the good cause where further persuasion occurs. The successful campaign must also educate and prepare the consumer, voter, or joiner to take action. To accomplish this task, campaigns must (1) zero in on well-defined goals, (2) create appropriate strategies to accomplish the goals, and then (3) use various tactics to put the strategy into action. This pattern of goals leading to strategies, which in turn lead to tactics, applies to all three types of campaigns.

A recent goal for a Claussen's pickles campaign was to increase sales in specified test markets by 10 percent. Claussen's differs from its competition because its pickles are much crispier and crunchier since they are refrigerated, not cooked and canned like other brands. Usually in product campaigns product/brand features are tied consumer benefits. In this campaign for Claussen, this kind of feature/benefit linkage was—refrigerated (the feature) means crunchier (the benefit). The campaign staff then works out a promising strategy to demonstrate the feature/benefit equation. For Claussen's, the strategy was to use TV spots to show the unique features and benefits of the brand. As noted, the product is refrigerated rather than cooked, so the pickles are crisper and crunchier than the competition. Previously, Claussen's had only used print ads, which can't show crispy and crunchy very well. To implement the TV strategy, Claussen's used the tactic of comparative advertising, matching Claussen's against Vlasic's in the TV spots. The tactic was to show Vlasic's cooked pickle being bent in half and not breaking, while Claussen's pickle was bent and snapped in two, giving off a spray of brine accompanied by a crunchy sound effect.

In a political example, the goal in primary election campaigns is to win the party's nomination from opposing candidates. Strategies for achieving this include ignoring the opposition, taking the high road on the issues, simply letting the candidates attack one another or again stressing the feature/benefit linkage. Such a linkage might be that the candidate had opposed the costly and foolish decision to go to war in Iraq. The benefit was obviously that he or she would make wise decisions in the future and thus avoid costly wars. A tactic for implementing the strategy might be to stage a debate against several empty chairs, each labeled with the name of one of the opponents who had voted to go to war. The campaign models highlighted in the following discussion demonstrate similarities and differences among campaign types. Your task is to use the models to help you make decisions about purchasing, voting, joining, or supporting causes.

DEVELOPMENTAL STAGES IN CAMPAIGNS

All three types of campaigns pass through a series of predictable stages as they grow, mature, and adapt to audience feedback along the way to the competition, the issues, and the demands of the persuasive situation. One campaign goal of a new product, candidate, or idea is to establish itself in the audience's consciousness. A variety of strategies can accomplish this identification. For instance, a company might give out free samples or hire a celebrity to be associated with the brand, a candidate might announce his or her candidacy, or a group might stage a dramatic protest against a policy in an idea oriented campaign. This initial message helps the campaigner learn about the audience. Perhaps prospects buy the brand because of its warranty and not its price. Maybe the voters don't favor increasing taxes on gasoline but do respond to the issue of deficit reduction. Animal rights supporters may respond to some issues but not others. So, in all three types of campaigns, strategies are tried and kept, altered, or dropped as the campaign develops, and based always on audience response to the persuasion beginning with its goals and moving to its strategies and tactics.

The Yale Five-Stage Developmental Model

Most campaigns include one or more of the stages of a model developed by researchers at Yale University (Binder, 1971). The **Yale five-stage developmental model** is highly applicable to product, person, and ideological campaigns and has been used to analyze hundreds of campaigns since it was first put forward by researchers at Yale. The five functional stages noted by the researchers are identification, legitimacy, participation, penetration, and distribution.

Identification. **Identification** is defined as establishing a position in the minds of consumers, voters, and potential converts. Many products and causes use logos to create audience identification. The well-established logo of the Goodyear Tire and Rubber Company, shown in Figure 11.1, has the winged foot of Mercury inserted between the two syllables of Goodyear, to suggest that the company's products are swift and safe. The lower case "e" used to identify the environmental movement was inserted inside the capital letter "C" to create the logo of the Commonwealth Edison electric company, suggesting that the company is environmentally conscientious—a good position for an energy monopoly. A series of arrows in a triangle with the point of each arrow bent to point at the base of the next arrow is the logo for any kind of recycling. The name associated with the product, candidate, or cause is also critical and closely related to the logo. The cold and flu medicine, Theraflu, is a good example because it suggests that it is a good therapy against the two sicknesses. It is a much better name than Smith's Brother's Cold and Flu Syrup.

The name *Newsweek* is a good example too. It suggests that it contains the news of the past week (much more descriptive than competitor *Time*). The name of Cadillac's "Escalade" SUV is meant to suggest good taste, classiness, and European distinction since the brand's name is similar to the French term for a walking path. Candidates for office may label themselves the "people's candidate" or "The Candidate for True Change" or a similar term to create identification. In the abortion controversy, anti-abortion advocates chose "pro-life"

FIGURE 11.1 Many devices are used to establish product, person, or idea identification in campaigns. Logos such as this are one kind of identification device. Why is the winged foot of Mercury used? What does it communicate? Why put it between "GOOD" and "YEAR"? Answers to these questions help explain how product image or identification develops. SOURCE: Getty Images

for their cause. It "framed" the issue by suggesting that advocates are in favor of life. Who would disagree? It also implies that opponents of the movement are either anti-life or pro–death. Upstaged by the "pro-life" framing label, abortion rights advocates had to settle for the far less effective "pro-choice." So choosing the best name for your idea or ideological campaign is also critical.

To demonstrate the potency of a good name, ask a sample of people to name three brands of turkey. Butterball will be on everyone's list while many competitors' names will not. Then ask what the key benefit of a Butterball turkey is, and they will tell you that it is the most moist brand. Why? Consider the name again and you will soon see why "Butterball" is a far better choice than Armour or Jenni-O. Figure 11.2 shows an ad for NameLab, a company that designs and tests various names to help organizations establish an identity for a product, political entity, or cause.

Another device that helps create identification is the use of consistent color coding and typefaces on all printed or televised promotional items for the brand, candidate, or cause. These things create what are called "brand contacts" in the advertising business. The campaigner picks a color code and uses it in packaging, advertising, letterheads, and perhaps uniforms. For instance, UPS carriers wear dark brown uniforms, and their trucks are painted dark brown. Political candidates usually select some combination of red, white, and blue. The successful Stop ERA movement to defeat the Equal Rights Amendment adopted the color red, used signs shaped like stop signs, and had movement supporters wear red and white clothes when they demonstrated. On my campus, the university accepted $8 million a year for its general scholarship fund in return for naming Pepsi products as its official soft drink company. Now all napkins, soft drink cups, and so on have the Pepsi name, colors, and typeface on them. This not only rivets the brand name into student's minds but builds brand loyalty in them.

Slogans can also promote identification, "Folgers—The Mountain Grown Coffee," "When You Care Enough to Send the Very Best," "You're in Good Hands with Allstate," and "Smart. Very Smart" are all successful examples of identification gaining tactics. Consider how coordinated and successful the campaign for State Farm Insurance Company has been over the years. The slogan and jingle "Like a Good Neighbor, State Farm Is There" is the central theme,

MAKING NAMES

A leading name development firm since 1981, NameLab has created brand and company names like Acura, Acuvue, Aeron, American Century, Compaq, CompUSA, Luxor, Olive Garden, Renova, simplehuman, Slice and Viactiv. We quote costs accurately in advance and complete most projects within 4 weeks.

San Francisco, CA
415-517-0803   www.namelab.com   info@namelab.com

FIGURE 11.2 The name of a product, political entity, or cause is part of the mix of factors that create identification for the brand.

SOURCE: Used by permission of NameLab.

as is the red and white color code and the unique type-face. Agents are urged to live in the community they serve, to join civic organizations there, and to be visible and active in their communities. All ads must include the slogan, colors, and the agents' pictures. Agents are advised to send congratulatory cards to customers and their families on important days. National advertising usually includes a feature on a specific agent who was there when needed. Finally, jingles, uniforms, salutes, and all sorts of campaign paraphernalia like balloons or buttons help establish name and purpose identification in all three types of campaigns. The State Farm and Allstate insurance slogans are good examples—most of you can name them.

Legitimacy.   The second stage in the Yale model is the establishment of **legitimacy**, which is defined as being considered a worthy, believable, and trustworthy brand, candidate, or cause. Candidates usually achieve legitimacy by gaining endorsements or by winning primaries. Legitimacy can also serve as a power base from which to get financial and other support. Candidates demonstrate their power by holding rallies, appearing with well-known supporters or celebrities, being photographed with symbols of legitimacy, such as the U.S. Capitol building, the Lincoln Memorial, or the White House, or having ads currently being seen on TV and having lots of visible signs, bumper stickers, buttons, and so on— all "brand contacts" in political propaganda. For incumbents, legitimacy also derives powerfully from holding office. In my congressional district the incumbent retired and a run-off for the remaining six

months of his term was held. Winning this campaign was almost more important than winning the true general election six months hence because of the legitimacy obtained from incumbency. This relates to the bottom line, efficiency and effective face of the 7 Faces. A favorite tactic for both incumbents and challengers is getting endorsed by local newspapers, politicians, and well-known and respected citizens. Another is to list experience in government or community groups, church affiliations, family accomplishments, and so on. Expertise, sincerity, and dynamism or charisma are also elements in establishing candidate legitimacy.

Product campaigns sometimes gain legitimacy by demonstrating the product in use—a favorite tactic in the television marketing of exercise machines and kitchen gadgets. Professional athletes wear Nikes to demonstrate the legitimacy of the shoes and may offer a testimonial for the product. Established endorsers like the Underwriter's Laboratory and Good Housekeeping seals of approval also create legitimacy. Brands also develop legitimacy by associating themselves with good causes, or by sponsoring sports events such as the Virginia Slims Tennis Tournament or by getting testimonials on their behalf by well-known celebrities such as athletes or movie stars. They might also use endorsements by experts. For example, Promise (who makes a margarine), spread claims that in a study of 326 cardiologist, 9 out of 10 endorsed the brand and even printed the words "Cardiologist Endorsed" on their packaging.

In ideological campaigns such as supporting the U.S. Olympic swim team, well known personages and products are often teamed for the purpose of giving legitimacy to the idea of supporting the team. As shown in Figure 11.3, this is the case in the ad featuring eight-time Olympic gold medal winner Michael Phelps and the Planet Ocean Chronograph by Omega—they legitimize one another. Newspaper ads with the names of known supporters who endorse the movement also help establish legitimacy—even in seemingly minor causes like adding on to the local library. Large numbers of angry citizens show up at council meetings, and these events turn up on the evening news. In one high school, students protested their school lunch program and showed their legitimacy using nonviolent protest tactics. One day, hundreds of students boycotted the hot lunch, leaving the school with tons of leftovers. The next day, all students bought the hot lunch, leaving the school short of supplies. The following day, everyone paid with a large bill, running the cashiers out of change. The next day, they paid in pennies, creating havoc in the checkout lines as cashiers had to count pennies. On the fifth day, the school met with students about improving the lunches.

Participation.   The legitimacy stage of campaigns usually blends so smoothly with the **participation** stage that it is almost impossible to tell when one ends and the next begins. The participation stage is defined as the recruitment and involvement of previously uncommitted persons. In the legitimacy stage, the participants are considered known supporters who are not actively involved in the campaign. In the participation stage, the leaders seek to show their clout by getting these inactive persons actively involved in real or symbolic ways. There are many techniques for doing this. Some require effort by potential participants, such as marching at a protest or standing in a candlelight vigil while others require minimal or only symbolic participation, such as signing a petition or wearing a button. Customer rebates are another form of participation in product oriented campaigns. The customer picks up, fills out, clips the UPC code and mails it and the rebate form to get money—all steps requiring effort. And of those who pick up the rebate form or clip it out, only a small percentage actually follow

through. But even the small act of participation of picking up the rebate form and clipping the UPC code gets the person involved. All these items encourage real and/or symbolic participation with the brand. Customers even advertise the brand by wearing clothing imprinted with the brand logo. Coupon offers are another way to promote participation—clipping the coupon is a behavioral intention and symbolic participation.

A movement may also urge participation in real or symbolic ways. People wear armbands or badges, yell slogans at rallies, put signs on their lawns or auto bumpers, or distribute leaflets. Candidates running for student body president may ask others to canvass dormitory floors or student groups. These kinds of activity get people involved in the campaign or movement and guarantee further active support. Sometimes new ad technologies are used to encourage participation. Examples of this kind of participation may include holograms and scratch-and-sniff perfume strips, or free music downloads as part of the ad. We see participation also in the uses of interactive media where prospective customers can "try out" the brand in virtual ways (see www.greenpeace.com) and thus become "pre-sold" on the ultimate purchase of the brand.

During the nominating process and primaries of the presidential campaign of 2004, Governor Howard Dean used the participative interactivity of the Internet to generate previously unheard amounts of donations to his candidacy. Following the election, though not nominated, he was named head of the Democratic Party largely because of his fund-raising success using interactive media. We can anticipate that both parties will be replicating his efforts for the 2008 campaign and that as head of the party he will be their guru and model. If you are taking this class during an election year, visit the Web sites of some of the candidates looking for new uses of interactivity to generate candidate support—financial or other kinds of help. All these participative devices are designed to get the audience involved with the product, candidate, or cause, and even symbolic behavior represents both commitment and participation. Participation fits nicely with the idea of persuasion as a process of

**WATER IS MICHAEL PHELPS' NATURAL ELEMENT,
PLANET OCEAN IS HIS CHRONOGRAPH.**

Ω
OMEGA

FIGURE 11.3 Legitimacy is built both for the product and for the U.S. Olympic swim team in this ad featuring the Omega Planet Ocean Chronograph and record-setting swimmer Michael Phelps.

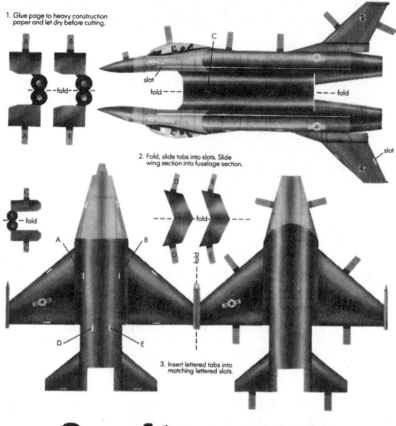

1. Glue page to heavy construction paper and let dry before cutting.

slot
fold
fold
slot

2. Fold, slide tabs into slots. Slide wing section into fuselage section.

fold

fold

fold

3. Insert lettered tabs into matching lettered slots.

One of two ways to get your hands on an F-16.

If you think you're too young to fly, cut it out.

Fold. Assemble. And prepare for take-off.

While your paper airplane may not quite reach the speed of sound, use it as a reminder of just how fast the Air National Guard can help you get your future off the ground.

And we're not just talking about a military career. Air Guard training can prepare you for a civilian career in over 200 fields of technical expertise. Every-

thing from meteorology to security. Tele-communications to computer technology.

We'll even pay part of your college tuition. What's more, you'll have the chance to take part in exciting adventures that can lead you around the world.

All you have to do is serve as little as two days a month and two weeks a year.

Want to learn more? Call your local recruiter. And find out if you're cut out for the Air National Guard.

 the Air National Guard.

Americans At Their Best.

88-501

FIGURE 11.4 This ad for the Air National Guard encourages real, not symbolic, participation by cutting out the model F-16 and gluing it together, or by joining the Air National Guard.

SOURCE: Courtesy Air National Guard.

co-creation, as discussed in Chapter 1 and elsewhere. As Figure 11.4 demonstrates, participation can include interacting with an advertisement. Box 11.1

demonstrates how one can interact with other commercial messages on media to the point where you can design your own automobile.

B O X 11.1   Interactive Media and Campaign Participation

 Mitsubishi recently launched an interactive Internet campaign in which an Eclipse drives from one Mitsubishi banner ad on the screen to another. Then the viewer can take over the car and drive it around the screen. Following the test drive, viewers are invited to play the "Thrill Ride Challenge" game and drive around one of four race courses. Depending on their score, they could win a Mitsubishi flat-screen TV or an Apple iPod. The company hopes to harvest 20,000 dealer leads from the campaign. Viewers are also directed to a link where they can build their own Eclipse—including options, color, and so forth—and get a price quote (Morrissey, 2005). To see how interactive media can be used to sell products go to www.modemmedia.co.uk.

Penetration.   The **penetration** stage can be defined as the point at which a person, product, or idea has earned a meaningful share of the market, electorate, or other constituency. Meaningful might be defined as enough to be noticed by the opposition brand, candidate, or cause. For products, gaining a significant market share is enough to achieve the penetration stage. Chrysler's various innovations, including front-wheel drive, the mini-van, and the 7-year/70,000-mile warranty enabled it to penetrate the auto market. The market share that these captured forced the competition to follow suit. That is a sure sign that a campaign has reached the penetration stage. The old idea that imitation is the most sincere kind of compliment one can get applies here. A successful penetration stage in campaigns for products usually prompts a response from the competition.

Early in the primary campaign season, candidates don't have to win the most delegates to establish penetration. Running third or even unexpectedly strong might be enough. Other indications of political penetration include higher ratings in opinion polls, increases in financial contributions, increases in the number of persons volunteering to help, and larger crowds showing up for campaign events. This was surely the case with Barack Obama in 2007 and 2008. Following his unexpected win in the Iowa caucuses (the "kick-off" to the traditional primary campaign season), the Hillary Clinton campaign sat up and took notice, and responded to him and his messages, and as his crowds continued to grow it became even more clear that he was a true contender until he finally exceeded Clintons delegate count. The Clinton campaign responded more and more negatively, even criticizing the remarks of his childhood minister to show Obama's weakness—clear proof that he had penetrated the primary electorate's consciousness. Communication scholar T. A. Borchers (2001, 2005) reports that one key to Jesse Ventura's becoming governor was his use of e-mail and his Web site to turn out large crowds on short notice—700 people in the small town of Willmar, Minnesota within an hour.

In ideology-oriented campaigns, penetration is achieved when those in power find that they are barraged by mail or have to repeatedly answer questions about the campaign topic. This reflects the power of the Results-Oriented Face of Persuasion more effectively that can be imagined. Other indicators of penetration in these campaigns include large rally crowds that inconvenience supporters of the status quo and increased financial and volunteer support.

Distribution.   The fifth and final stage of development, **distribution**, is defined as the campaign or movement's succeeding and rewarding supporters in some way. The candidates now live up to their promises. They signal their supporters that social change is going to occur. Patronage or government jobs are given to supporters to help distribute the rewards won by the campaign. In movement campaigns, persons on the campaign staff or in leadership are appointed to office or positions of power. One problem with ideological and political campaigns is that sometimes the persuaders don't live up to their promises, and this is often the case with propagandistic movements as was the case with Nazism and many of the militant and Jihadist propaganda campaigns like those conducted by Al Quaida. No one got any real rewards following the bombings, unless one considers the promise of life in paradise for the suicide bombers. The potential recruits or lower level supporters of the terror only got internal rewards such as feelings of revenge.

Distributors and users of products can also participate in the distribution stage by sharing some of the profits from the products, free supplies of the brands that they can turn around and sell, or some kind of symbolic acknowledgment like being named salesperson of the month. Stores are paid "slotting allowances" for devoting some of their shelf space for special offers for the brand. They can get extra discounts for pushing certain products. Dealers also are urged to participate in contests to win prizes and luxury vacation trips by increasing monthly sales. The retailers are given "dealer loaders" or free valuable display containers like wheelbarrows or garden carts in which to display the brand of garden glove and which are theirs to keep or offer as mini-sweepstake prizes for their local customer base. And both dealers and customers can earn prized items such as an NBA Championship warm-up jacket. Devices such as rebates, money-back coupons, and other purchase incentives act as kinds of distribution to customers.

Product-Focused Models

Some campaign models help to describe all three types of campaign, and other models focus on one type of campaign. Let's examine models that are appropriate for and focused on product-oriented campaigns.

The Hierarchy of Effects Model.   Advertising and marketing experts Robert Lavidge and Gary Steiner (1961) suggested a model that for many decades has set goals in marketing and advertising agencies. This model assumes that potential customers must pass through a series of stages beginning with initial lack of **brand awareness** and ending with ultimate purchase. The **hierarchy of effects model** remains as valid today as it was when first suggested (Schultz & Barnes, 1999).

The model has seven distinct stages and employs various communication, advertising, research, and promotional strategies and techniques at each stage. In the first stage, consumers are completely unaware of the product, brand, or service being promoted or of the promised benefits. So the persuader's first task is to identify current patterns of use of similar products, brands, or services using focus groups, surveys, and other research methods, and then to build prospect awareness of their own brand as a superior competitor. In a hypothetical example, suppose the makers of Oreo cookies want to add a new product to the Oreo and Double Stuffs line. They do research using focus groups and observing people eating the regular Oreos and the Double Stuffs. Most people start eating the cookies by splitting the cookie layers in two, licking off the filling, then eating the cookie portion—behavior that had originally inspired Double Stuffs (Fortini-Campbell, 1992). Consumers rate the filling as the best part of Oreos/Double Stuffs and say that a cookie stuffed with a different flavored filling would sell. So they introduce the Double Chocolate Stuff by Oreo. With a consumer-driven product like cookies, the hierarchy of effects model suggests creating consumer awareness of the product and then developing consumer knowledge about it. The brand gets a name, a slogan, and a jingle, and public relations sends invitations to the media for the premiere taste-testing press conference. Then "teaser ads" communicate that "Double Chocolate Stuffs are coming soon!" Various promotional devices are used, such as free samples, events, and coupons. As the awareness stage merges with the developing knowledge stage, the ads teach consumers about the brand, and researchers use tests to discover consumers' knowledge level using surveys, mall intercepts, and unaided and aided recall.

In the fourth and fifth steps—liking and preferring—the advertiser uses "image ads" that communicate that status and glamour are associated with the brand by using such tactics as celebrity testimonials. If the brand has competition, the advertiser might use comparative ads or contests with taste tests that demonstrate that Double Chocolate Stuffs are better than the competition's single lemon-filled cookies. Consumers are now aware of the brand and have reason to like and even prefer it. The only task remaining is to convince them to try it. A goal of many persuasive campaigns is to induce trial, and this occurs in the final two stages of the hierarchy or the conviction and purchase stages, where consumers are convinced that the brand deserves a try and then go out and purchase it. Lavidge and Steiner's hierarchy of effects model is but one model that helps us understand the **goals, strategies**, and **tactics** of product-oriented campaigns. Let's continue with some others.

The Positioning Model. In their best-selling books *Positioning: The Battle for Your Mind* (Trout & Ries, 1986) and *The New Positioning* (Trout, 1995), marketing experts Jack Trout and Al Ries offer their **positioning model** as a way to attract prospects. The definition of positioning is to get the brand, candidate, or idea/ideology into top of mind awareness (TOMA) among consumers, voters, or joiners. Having top of mind awareness is defined as being in the consumer's top 7 plus or minus 2 (or 5 to 9) identifiable brands, depending on the complexity of the product. Trout and Ries advise searching for unoccupied "niches" in the marketplace and then positioning the brand in that psychological space. These niches and appeals to them are almost always processed in the peripheral channel of the ELM. Here are some ways to position a brand in the marketplace.

Be the First. The first brand to appear in a product class has the natural advantage of being the pioneer in that product class. Lunchables by Oscar Mayer, now a 20-year success story, are such a brand and were initially positioned in the "first" niche in 1990 and continued to stress their "first" position throughout their introductory and subsequent campaigns. Other snack-pack brands followed, but none could claim pioneer status. Lunchables were subsequently able to offer line extensions, or new and improved versions of the product/brand such as Lunchables with a Dijon mustard packet and a chocolate mint dessert and later a pizza lunch and a "wrap" version of the brand.

Be the Best. Consumers shop for quality and are usually willing to pay a reasonable price for high-quality brands. This niche is filled by the brand that can claim to be the best in the product category. Swift's Butterball turkey, noted earlier, is one of the most expensive brands, and claims to be best because a full pound of butter is injected into each turkey, resulting in butter-basting during cooking, a feature which leads to the benefits of moistness and good taste. Research shows that Butterball consumers spend more time in the supermarket and buy more premium condiments and desserts, like cranberry relishes or bakery pies, than other brand consumers. As a result retailers are glad to more prominently advertise and display the brand to extend purchases like these, which usually have a higher profit ratio. Over the years, several imported car brands have tried to claim the best position. Once, Mercedes-Benz seemed to be the permanent "Number 1." Later, other brands such as Jaguar and BMW also claimed to be best, resulting in a more advertising by all three focused on various features and benefits.

Be the Least Expensive. Besides shopping for quality, consumers often shop for price, so being able to claim that one's brand is the least expensive is a definite advantage. A good example is the burger and cola wars which continued until everyone offered a 99 cent menu version of their brand. Another is Wal-Mart's "Every-Day Low Pricing" which eventually included eye examinations, bank services, and $4 prescriptions. Even with high-ticket items such as cars, computers, and camcorders, price wars proliferate. The Geo, Hyundai, and other brands compete to offer the best value. The airline industry goes through regular cycles of fare wars. Various banks and credit cards engage in price wars related to annual fees, low initial finance rates, and loyalty programs with "points." And the same is true for mortgage rates.

Be the Most Expensive. Status is always critical to some buyers and frequently important to others, and they demonstrate their status by buying the most expensive brand on the market. Coco Chanel, the renowned French clothing designer and perfumer, insisted on marketing only the most expensive brand. We see this trend in the worlds of fashion, jewelry, home decorating and even gourmet cooking.

Tell What You're Not. Another position for gaining TOMA is telling consumers what the brand is not, thus differentiating it from the competition. On the brink of bankruptcy, 7-Up was saved by claiming that the soft drink was the "Uncola." Dr. Pepper imitated this strategy and also captured a portion of the cola market. Given recent interest in various health issues, numerous brands claim to be fat free or to have no carbs. Pharmaceuticals sometimes advertise that they do not make you sleepy.

Position by Gender.   Many brands target only one gender by positioning themselves as the woman's brand or the man's brand. Virginia Slims and Eve cigarettes are examples. After learning that pro football players and many outdoor workers wear pantyhose in cold weather for warmth, one company considered marketing a male version of pantyhose. Among its strategies were naming the brand Mach-Hose, getting testimonials from outdoor construction workers and firemen, offering it in camouflage colors, and selling it in six packs. Calvin Klein's Obsession for Men and the magazine *Gentleman's Quarterly* are obviously positioned by gender, as is the ad for Lincoln Financing Company shown in Figure 11.5. Communication researcher A. N. Valdivia (1997) analyzed product advertising for women's lingerie and discovered that both gender and class positioning of competing brands. After looking at catalogs for Victoria's Secret and Frederick's of Hollywood, she concluded that Victoria's is targeted at the female upper middle class while Frederick's is targeted at the male and female lower middle class. Victoria's Secret sounds discreet and Victorian, whereas Frederick's of Hollywood sounds male dominated, voyeuristic, and glitzy. Victoria's address is "London" and a prerecorded English voice answers when you place a telephone order. Frederick's models are unknowns and usually are photographed against simple fabric backdrops. Victoria's models are well-known and usually are photographed in indoor and old-world settings suggesting elegance and class.

Position by Age.   Advertisers often target a given cohort as the most likely prospect for a product or brand. Cohorts can be defined either as those born in the same year or those born in a certain set of years, like Baby Boomers or Generation Xers. Targeting a specific set of potential consumers has many advantages because you can custom tailor all aspects of advertising and other appeals for that specific cohort. For example, one of the most targeted cohorts is the Baby Boom generation or persons born between 1946 and 1964 and subsequently their children or the "mini-boomers." The American Association of Retired Persons (AARP) chose a brilliant name to appeal to this cohort and marketed itself based on the benefits of features like lobbying efforts on behalf of retirees, discounts on certain products, group activities like low rates on travel, and information about topics like retirement planning, inexpensive health insurance, and exercise equipment. People are invited to join AARP at age 45 instead of 65, and they receive a subscription to *Modern Maturity* magazine (an aptly named publication). It has the largest circulation in the country, making it an ideal magazine for targeting this affluent and growing cohort. Imagine how the targeting of cohorts affects packaging, slogans, message strategies, and media buys. And in an age of advocacy and propaganda, it is nice to have someone working for you.

Politically Oriented Campaign Models

Although they share some characteristics with product-oriented campaigns, politically oriented campaigns differ in many ways from the marketing of products or brands. For example, there is only limited research data available to candidates, and politically oriented campaigns usually must communicate much more sophisticated information than product/brand campaigns, and they have a definite end day—the election—which doesn't happen to products or most idea oriented campaigns. Let us now turn to developmental models that help explain political campaigns.

The Communicative Functions Model.   Communication researchers Judith Trent and Robert Friedenberg (2000) describe four stages that a political campaign must achieve if it is to be successful. They call their approach the **communicative**

FIGURE 11.5 In this ad, Lincoln Financial promotes its product by appealing to the independent woman, thus positioning Lincoln's services by gender. Considering the increased number of women in the labor force and in various kinds of investment plans, the strategy seems to be a good one.

SOURCE: Used by permission of the Lincoln Financial Group.

functions model. In the first stage, the candidate makes a formal announcement of candidacy and lays some groundwork by mapping out the district, organizing financial committees, developing contacts in key areas of the district, and so on. This stage is called the "surfacing" stage. The main campaign themes are floated and focused, and the candidate's image is tested and promoted. Issues are addressed, position papers are issued, and, with luck, adequate funds are raised. In presidential politics, this process may begin as early as

the day after the most recent presidential election. In stage 2 of this model, the "winnowing" stage, the primary election campaigns serve to narrow or winnow the field of candidates and to focus issues. In 2008, the initial fields of candidates for both Democratic and Republican parties were crowded and support for each was thus spread out. But as more people get involved (as in the participation stage of the Yale model) some of these withdraw or are forced out because of lack of money or appeal. The newcomer supporters or shifters from other candidates may pass out leaflets, attend rallies, sponsor fund-raisers, or perform some activity that gets them involved and this puts pressure on the remaining candidates. In presidential politics, this stage is extremely expensive, even with the matching funds the government gives to candidates. As much as $50 million or more can be spent in pursuing a presidential nomination (National Public Radio, 1999). Of course, the costs are smaller with lower offices, but even senate primaries cost several million dollars. This is a dangerous stage for candidates because they might make promises that they later can't fulfill or they might reveal plans that come back to haunt them. They also might make mistakes, misstatements, or "gaffes" that undermine their legitimacy.

During stage 3, the "nomination" stage, the candidate is legitimized in the eyes of the media and potential voters, as are the party's platform and themes. The final stage, the "election stage," is that period between nomination and election day when candidates hectically go from state to state and crowd to crowd saying basically the same thing, over and over again. Here, the use of the press is critical in paid-for political promotions like billboards, signs, bumper stickers, buttons, TV ads, radio spots, or newspaper ads. Unpaid media coverage such as interview programs or short sound bites on the evening news can be critical. Candidates also use purchased media spots aimed at the right target audience at the right time, in the right way, and in a cost-efficient manner. In 2008, this stage occurred quite early (though informally) for candidate John McCain, and he was able to use the extra time to raise a huge war chest for the general election and could afford lots of media time, signs, travel, and so forth.

The advent of the Internet in national politics during the 1996 presidential primaries means that future candidates at all levels must use this method of communicating with their constituencies. This interactive and highly personal medium will only increase in importance in campaigns in the future. Both candidates for mayor of my small town (population 12,000) had Web pages with multiple links back in 2000. As we will see in Chapter 13, this use of media is sophisticated and complex. Political campaign mes-

sages are probably processed in both paths of information-processing of the ELM. Issue-oriented messages probably follow the central path and require rational thinking and preparation. Image-oriented messages, though they may be rationally thought out, are probably processed peripherally.

In the third edition of *Political Communication in America*, Robert Denton and Gary Woodward (1998) focus on the strategies and tactics used in political campaigns. They say that strategies are the various plans a campaigner forms in hopes of achieving the campaign goal or goals; tactics are the means used to implement the strategies or to put them into action. In political campaigns, of course, there is but one goal—to win election to office—but several strategies could be used to meet that goal, such as winning a primary, raising money, or getting favorable voters registered. Referring to R. Faucheux (1998), Denton and Woodward identify four strategy types that occur in any political campaign. The first is a "message sequence strategy" that addresses the order in which various campaign messages should be sent out. These could be messages about issues, the candidate or the opponent, qualifications for office, and personal beliefs. Second, a "timing and intensity strategy" suggests when messages should go out, and how much effort, money, and other resources should be dedicated to that phase of the campaign. Third, a "mobilization and persuasion strategy" focuses on reaching and convincing groups of voters who might be favorable to the candidate, such as first-time voters, homeowners, minority voters, and the party faithful. Finally, an "opportunity strategy" allows the campaign to respond to the unexpected events, opportunities, or threats that inevitably arise. Examples include revelation of the amount of spending and its source, negative advertising, a candidate's key misstatement, or a scandal involving the candidate or his or her opponent. Several message sequence strategies are possible. The "ignore the opposition" strategy usually means being positive in speeches, news releases, interviews, and comments from the beginning of the campaign until election day and rarely or never referring to the opponent. The "aggressive message sequence" strategy begins the campaign on a positive note but then quickly turns to negative campaigning focused on the opponent's shortcomings. In the final days of the campaign, this strategy is implemented by using a dual-track approach with both positive and negative or comparative appeals. With the "frontal attack strategy," the candidate begins with negative and comparative ads focusing on the opponent's shortcomings, turns positive in the middle portions of the campaign, and then closes using the same dual-track approach as in the "aggressive" strategy.

Several message timing and intensity strategies are available as well. With the "tortoise strategy," the candidate begins slowly, communicating and spending only modestly, and then builds momentum until election day, when a message and spending blitz happens. The "bookend strategy" uses a big, flashy, and expensive opening with a steady buildup and the same blitz strategy used to close the campaign the day before election day. With the "Pearl Harbor strategy," the candidate starts very slowly and is barely noticeable. This is intended to lull the opposition into underestimating the candidate's strength, which then allows him or her to sneak attack the opponent at an opportune moment.

Opportunity strategies might include "setting a trap," whereby the candidate attacks the opponent over a minor shortfall to set the opponent up to respond in such a way as to lead to much more criticism. For instance, the candidate might accuse the opponent of being financed by an enormously rich father who is trying to buy the election for his spoiled son or daughter. The opponent responds by saying that it is no sin to be successful and to spend money on what one truly believes. Then the candidate springs the trap by revealing that dear old Dad amassed his fortune by exploiting slave labor in China. The "technological advantage strategy" was used in the 1996 presidential campaign by numerous candidates who were aware of the newly emerging Internet and put up sophisticated Web pages, which surprised their uninformed opponents.

"Three's a crowd" is a strategy that takes advantage of a crowded field by financing a minor third or fourth opponent who will siphon off votes from the real opponent. The "lightning rod strategy" gets a controversial person to endorse the opponent or introduces a controversial issue to which the opponent can only respond in a negative, controversial, and highly visible way.

Persuasion and mobilization strategies relate to how the candidate deals with voter groups—the party faithful, undecided voters, and those favoring the opponent. Candidates identify their voter base and the undecided voters and then reinforce them with messages and turn them out to vote.

Idea/Ideological Campaigns

In the idea or ideological campaign, neither a product nor a person nor a candidate is promoted. Instead, the persuader wants the audience to engage in or change some behavior or to embrace some religion or other ideology. In the change of behavior option, campaigns might promote preventive measures that individuals might take to avoid contracting STDs. Other campaigns solicit donations to various not-for-profit churches, charities, or other good causes. Idea campaigns urge people to help the environment by recycling aluminum, glass, tin cans, and plastic containers or to practice factory safety or defensive driving. A protest campaign might persuade people to wear black armbands on a certain day to indicate their displeasure with a policy or law. In early 2003, the group Women Against Military Madness (WAMM) protested the saber-rattling rhetoric of various members of the second Bush administration directed toward Iraq. They held rallies, sold yard signs and bumper stickers reading "Say No! to War with Iraq," and used other tactics to implement their strategies for avoiding a U.S. invasion of Iraq, which we now know happened with disastrous results both economically and in terms of casualties despite their efforts. Any of the elements in the Yale model help explain the strategies of such campaigns, and some elements of the product/person campaign models can also apply. But other models specifically explain idea/ideological campaigns or social movements.

The Social Movements Model. Communication researchers Charles J. Stewart, Craig A. Smith, and Robert E. Denton, Jr. (2001) define and describe the **social movement model** of idea/ideological campaigns. They maintain that social movements have seven unique characteristics that set them apart from product- or person-oriented campaigns. First, social movements are organized groups of people, with leaders who usually act as spokespersons for the movement. Second, although they are organized, social movements are not institutionalized or recognized by those in power. Third, they attract large numbers of persons and are large in scope either geographically or historically. Thus, pro-lifers would qualify as a social movement, whereas promoting radon-free drinking water probably wouldn't because of its limited scope. Fourth, social movements either promote or oppose social change. There are three subtypes of groups promoting or opposing change. The "innovative movement" wants to totally replace existing social values and norms, and includes movements like gay liberation or radical feminism. The "revivalistic movement" seeks only partial change in society and a return to past values. The "resistance movement" seeks to block instead of favor change. For example, the pro-choice movement wants to keep Roe v. Wade in effect, and the NRA opposes limitations on the right to own handguns. Fifth, social movements are moralistic, preaching about good versus evil, right versus wrong, or patriotism versus opposition to the government policy. Sixth, social movements encounter opposition from those in power. The power may be held by formal groups such as the military, police, or a regulatory body. This opposition often leads to symbolic and then real violence, as has happened in a number of dramatic cases. For their part, those promoting change might begin by shouting slogans, then move to violence against property, and ultimately against people. Finally, persuasion is the essential tool for attracting new converts, changing people's minds, and ultimately motivating members to take action. The persuasion, verbal or nonverbal, may attempt to use mass media, and it usually includes a call to action on the part of the persuadee.

Social movements also have their own set of developmental stages. Stewart, Smith, and Denton's model of a social movement outlines five stages: "genesis," "social unrest," "enthusiastic mobilization," "maintenance," and "termination" stages. In the "genesis stage," ideologues preach about perceived shortcomings or injustices. These early prophets might go unheard for a long time, but finally, like-minded persons are drawn to these prophets, and the first stage creates a core of devoted supporters. Then, usually, a dramatic event catapults the issue into the public spotlight. In the "social unrest" stage, growing numbers of people identify with the movement and now are agitated by the identification of the devils and gods of the movement. This leads to the third stage of "enthusiastic mobilization" when the true believers begin to convert more and more people and continue to encounter opposition from those in power. These converts are now activists, not merely persons who identify with the movement. Fourth, in the "maintenance" stage the movement adopts a lower profile as the media attention turns to other events, and some success is perceived by converts. These successes dull enthusiasm for and drain energy from the movement, so it must bide its time until a significant event occurs to rekindle enthusiasm. In some cases, the movement achieves its goal(s), or it may merely wither and die in the "termination" stage. Perhaps supporters lose faith and patience, or the movement becomes outmoded, or its leaders are assimilated into the establishment, or it becomes irrelevant.

The Agitation and Control Model. In their book *The Rhetoric of Agitation and Control*, John Bowers, Donovan Ochs, and R. J. Jensen (1993) describe several stages in ideological movements that must occur before the movements ultimately fail or succeed. In the first stage, the "petition stage," agitators petition the sources of power such as the government, a corporation, or a school district, making demands or "requests" that slightly exceed what the power source will give up. The power source thus appears unreasonable. The agitators now initiate the "promulgation stage" or the marketing of the movement. Using handbills, leaflets, and rallies, the agitators develop their movement by informing outsiders of the unreasonableness of the power source. At this stage, the movement leaders hope to gain recruits and get publicity that will attract even more recruits, as was the case in 2005 when the American Civil Liberties Union and other free speech groups objected to illegal surveillance of American citizens by the Bush administration and a nationally publicized social movement was born. If promulgation succeeds, the movement moves into the "solidification stage." Now the newly recruited members are hyped up through rallies, marches, and protest songs like "We Shall Overcome" or "We Shall Not Be Moved." They may use salutes and symbols or uniforms. In the "polarization stage," the movement leaders target the uncommitted population. They do this by focusing on a flag issue or person. The reason they are called flag issues or persons is that they epitomize the ultimate enemy or are the most easily recognized symbol of what the movement or ideology objects to or hates. Past flag issues have been the aborting of fetuses, the use of napalm on civilians, the mistreatment of refugees, illegal surveillance of citizens, and the bombing of civilian targets. Flag persons personify the issue. Past flag persons have included President Lyndon Johnson, Saddam Hussein, and President George W. Bush. In local politics, flag persons might include mayors, councilpersons, senators, representatives, or others depicted as the root of the problem. The polarization stage forces the onlookers to choose between us and them.

In the fifth stage, the "nonviolent resistance stage," such tactics as name-calling or rent strikes are used. For instance, police call in sick with the "blue flu," or students occupy a building and claim that they have liberated it. These and other devices call attention to the movement and usually bring some sort of response from the power source, such as calling out the army or police. Usually, the media will cover the confrontation. Then agitators claim repression or Gestapo tactics. Usually, this leads to the "escalation stage," which increases tensions in the power source. Perhaps threats are made, such as rumors of planted bombs or public displays of weapons. Perhaps some

violent act occurs, such as a strike with brickbats and fistfights, a killing or kidnapping, or the bombing of an important building or landmark like the Twin Towers. If the power source represses the movement at this time, there usually is a split within the movement between those who favor violence and those who favor nonviolence. Bowers, Ochs, and Jensen call this the "Gandhi versus guerrilla stage." Usually, the nonviolent segment goes to the power source and argues that, unless they give in, the guerrillas will take over. Violence will escalate, as was the case in Operation Iraqi Freedom when the numbers of bombings by insurgents increased radically as the occupation wore on. Depending on the power source's response, the final stage may or may not emerge.

This last stage—the "revolution stage" rarely happens, but social movements using the rhetoric of agitation and control have led to revolutions in a variety of places in recent decades. With the world focused on global terrorism and the United States engaged in a costly war, we will very likely continue to see such agitation and control tactics used as objection to the actions of various governments increase. The ability of the agitation and control model to describe, explain, and even predict stages in movements across time testifies to both its validity and its reliability.

The Diffusion of Innovation Model. Some idea campaigns hope to induce people to adopt new practices or change their behaviors, such as following safer procedures in a factory, reducing their intake of red meats and fats, or conserving energy. Everett Rogers (1962) studied the stages through which people approach the adoption of any new technology such as computers, cell phones, e-mail, the Internet, or one's BlackBerry. The stages also occur with adopting new practices such as recycling or changing values such as favoring the hybrid automobile. Rogers' **diffusion of innovation model** also has some applicability to product and person-oriented campaigns. He outlined four stages on the way to adopting change. In the first stage—the "information/knowledge stage"—the potential adopter acquires or actively seeks information about the innovation. How does it work? What are its features

---

B O X 11.2   Cultural Diversity in Campaigns

In 2005, three media and advertising professional organizations sponsored the first National Expo of Ethnic Media to identify how best to target campaigns to the over 50 million ethnic Americans. Soon the number of ethnic consumers, voters, joiners, and donors will outnumber nonethnic ones, thus representing an enormously powerful market segment. Take just one part of this huge segment—Hispanics and/or Latinos. They presently represent an advertising expenditure of $3.5 billion per year, but they are changing. Why? Because by 2020, only 34 percent of Hispanics/Latinos in the United States will be from the first-born generation. The newer generations will be more acculturated, be better educated, will speak English, and probably will be more affluent, according to the Pew Hispanic Center. Today, 88 percent of Hispanics/Latinos under the age of 18 are foreign born. When you combine the Hispanic/Latino minorities with other culturally diverse groups, you get a "New American Mainstream," according to Guy Garcia (2005) in his best-selling book of the same title. What are the implications for politicians, advertisers, and idea/ideological persuaders? What do these numbers imply for other culturally diverse minorities?

---

and benefits? How much will it cost? How have other adopters rated it? When people first became aware of the practice of recycling, which was a time-consuming activity with little direct payoff, few persons rushed out and got containers for aluminum, glass, tin cans, newspaper, and mixed paper.

However, being made aware of recycling drew people's attention to various pieces of information like the life expectancy of local landfills and the effects of deforestation on the climate. In the second stage—the "persuasion stage"—the potential adopter processes information aimed at inducing him or her to actually try the new product or practice. Those advocating the change might use testimonials from well-known persons who have adopted the new product or practice. In the third stage—the "decision, adoption, and trial stage"—the potential adopters decide to try the new practice. They get the recycling containers, or they order prescriptions, groceries, books, or other items via the Internet. Then they use the new technology, product, or practice. Sometimes, marketers request that new users respond to the product/brand/practice by completing a rating survey. This technique moves potential adopters into the final state—the "confirmation and evaluation stage"—in which they reconsider the adoption and measure its performance against their expectations. They ask if it delivered what it promised, and was it worth the costs. If they continue us-

age, they then search for information that confirms the adoption.

The Rogers model is helpful in considering campaigns that offer new and innovative practices to consumers and can be especially helpful in persuading culturally diverse audiences as discussed in Box 11.2. With the rate of change accelerating in our information age, we will undoubtedly go through these stages repeatedly. Knowing what is happening in such situations helps put decisions to adopt new practices into a clearer perspective, resulting in wiser choices. Besides these developmental models of campaigns, several other theories help explain the success or failure of a given product-oriented, person-oriented, or idea/ideological campaign.

Symbolic Convergence Theory

Most of us like to affiliate with people with whom we agree and who are like us in Burke's "substantial" ways, and we seek to find communities of agreement or groups of people who share our basic values and lifestyles. This usually requires the merging of my meanings for events and values with your meanings for those same things. Having similar values and lifestyles identifies us as a particular audience to whom advertisers, politicians, and ideologues try to appeal. How do such "communities of agreement" develop?

The first clues to the power inherent in the social creation of meaning came from the work of Robert F. Bales (1970), a professor of sociology at Harvard. His initial interest was in identifying the kinds of verbal interactions in small, task-oriented groups. He noticed that in one category of interaction, group tension was released through the telling of stories. Bales called this category "dramatizes." He began to describe the way these stories or mini-dramas seemed to develop or, as he put it, "**chain outs**" in the group, resulting in what he called **fantasy themes**. At this point, Bales' work caught the attention of E. G. Bormann and his students and colleagues. They had also noticed fantasy sharing in task-oriented small groups and thought that the process of small-group building of reality had a wider application. This wider application of fantasy sharing was ultimately developed by Bormann (1985), his students, and other researchers, and it helps explain how shared meanings begin, develop, continue, and finally motivate us to action. The theory is known as "**symbolic convergence theory**," and its technique of analysis is called **fantasy theme analysis**. This theory was initially applied to small-group communication. After witnessing the power of the theory and methodology in the analysis and explanation of group communication, Bormann and his followers applied them to interpersonal, corporate, institutional, creative, and organizational communication. For our purposes as students of persuasion, the theory and methodology are ideal for doing audience analysis for product, idea, and political campaigns. When combined with focus group interviews and research techniques like surveys and Q-sort analysis, the theory and method have great power for analyzing the kinds of dramas to which specified groups of consumers and voters respond (Cragan & Shields, 1994, 1995).

A basic premise of symbolic convergence theory is that reality is socially based and symbolically constructed. That means that each of us perceives the world as a result of our interactions with others and our adoption of and addition to the meanings of these interactions using symbols. Second, many

of these interactions include stories or narratives, a pattern we have noted in earlier chapters. As we initially hear these stories or fantasies, we ignore them, embrace them, or participate in them. It is in the participative behavior that we create social reality and come together in symbolic convergence. That is, we share common symbols, meanings, and cues to them. A brief example might help here. At the halftime show of the 2005 Super Bowl, Janet Jackson, either intentionally or unintentionally exposed her naked breast. The incident got instant and widespread media coverage and triggered thousands of group discussions among the massive audience. One person says, "Well that family's been messed up since they were kids." Another person chimes in, "Right, just look at her bleached brother molesting kids." A third says, "His goofiness started with that moonwalk thing." The story or fantasy is beginning to chain out or become a shared version of reality. Media reports added to the fire, and when brother Michael was acquitted of ten molestation charges, another set of "reality links" and "**fantasy links**" probably chained out. The fantasy continued even into subsequent Super Bowl halftime shows with people wondered if the starring celebrity would try to stage some similar stunt. When aided by media coverage, enough of these group fantasies resemble one another and symbolic convergence has occurred.

Borman called these composite fantasies a **rhetorical vision**, which he maintained could become the national purpose of an entire country. Past rhetorical visions in our time include a worldwide terrorism conspiracy, exploitation of the little guy by big oil, and global warming. It doesn't matter what the truth or reality about the event is, it is what people participate in and come to believe that forms our social reality. While there were many who said global warming was just part of the natural cycle of things (including then-President Bush) the rhetorical vision became cemented into reality in an unusual way—the film/documentary, "An Inconvenient Truth" by former Vice President Al Gore, who won international recognition and an Oscar award. Because we share our inputs and interpretations with others in our social groups, we come to believe them even more devotedly than if we got them from a respected authority. People might ask one another if they have seen Gore's film. Others may discuss it at church choir, bowling league, or fraternity/sorority meetings. If the story becomes widely believed, we have a national rhetorical vision that can motivate nations to take drastic action. We saw this with Nazism, Communism, and terrorism.

In thousands of studies Bormann, his students, colleagues, and followers identified the operation of symbolic convergence in political and other campaigns including those using the techniques of propaganda as described in Box 11.3.

This pattern replicated itself in studies of purchasing and joining behavior. The technique was used to generate plot ideas for a popular prime time comedy series. In political campaigns fantasy types, favorite topics, themes, or images emerge. Reporters cover the campaigns and develop their own rhetorical vision in which they "dig out the real truth." (Bormann, 1985). One fantasy theme is that of the "frontrunner," or the candidate with the early legitimacy who is focused on by the media, which covers such issues as whether the candidate is showing signs

of stumbling, is hiding something, or is acting as a stalking horse for other candidates. Another political campaign fantasy theme is that of the baseball game, with the candidates being in the "early or final innings" or unable to "get to first base" with the electorate. Another theme makes use of boxing images, with candidates being "on the ropes" or "delivering knockout blows" to the opposition, who is just a "lightweight" and not a real "contender." In political and product-oriented advertising, the ad agency puts "spin" on the product by issuing press releases about it, by getting press coverage for giving the product away to some worthy group, or by emphasizing the product's astounding benefits. Bert Metter (1990), chairman of the J. Walter Thompson USA advertising agency, puts it this way:

> We are in the age of spin. The art and science of creating images is out of the closet.... As spin becomes more common...we've got to deliver more effectiveness.... The agencies with the answers will succeed. Others will have a lot of spinning to do (p. 36).

In product-related campaigns, Cragan and Shields (1995) found various types of individuals who have differing principles and beliefs. Their symbolic convergence tends to happen on one of three "planes" or philosophies. They are the "**pragmatic (or practical) plane**," "**the righteous (or highly principled) plane**," and the "**social (or interactive) plane**." Suppose you want to sell growth-enhancing ingredients to livestock growers, and you want to reach those growers on each plane. For the pragmatic cattle growers, you would stress the practical statistics on cost, effectiveness, and increased yield and profits. For the righteous cattle growers, you would stress that the enhancer is totally natural and does not violate any USDA regulations. For the social cattle growers, you would want to use testimonials from other cattle growers to the effect that just about everybody in the know is using the enhancer. Cragan and Shields have used this model to help sell products ranging from livestock estrogen and drugs, to increasing enrollment in private schools, and to training programs for firefighters. (If you are interested in which plane or philosophy you fit, go to our book companion Web site at http://academic.cengage.com/ communication/larson12 and the Web site for their book [Cragan & Shields, 1995]. Then briefly survey the kinds of activities and beliefs you like or hold dear and discover whether you are a pragmatic, righteous, or social type of consumer.) Cragan and Shields also related how such spin operated in idea or ideological campaigns. Symbolic convergence "spin" was used to convince the Iowa legislature to permit riverboat casinos, to recruit physicians to small towns, and to help train firefighter instructors.

We shouldn't forget that symbolic convergence is not limited to political campaigns. Following the train, bus, and subway bombings in London and Spain by various groups of terrorists, the public meaning of the word "terrorism" took on new dimensions. Terrorism was associated with a series of small cells of individuals around the world and not a worldwide organization, which meant no country was safe, not even neutral ones. Perhaps the cells were coordinated by Osama Bin Laden and the leadership of other "rogue nations" that formed an "axis of evil," which justified a "War on Terrorism." Those key words got picked up by the press and soon by the public also, and ultimately emerged into a global rhetorical vision.

REVIEW AND CONCLUSION

All persuasion involves self-persuasion. We must agree to be persuaded and then find good reasons for deciding. Many of these good reasons are already embedded in our conscious or subconscious memory. Clever persuaders identify ways to cue these memories and connect them to a product, candidate, or idea or ideology. Persuaders tune persuadees' ears to the kinds of messages that will be communicated in campaigns seeking new buyers, new voters, or new joiners. The formal and functional characteristics of campaigns that we have explored seem to persist over time, forming permanent patterns. The ever-shifting issues and increasingly sophisticated technologies of product testing, public opinion polling, media production, and direct marketing are a few of the elements of change.

Among the recurring aspects of campaigns is the establishment of formal goals, strategies, and tactics and the creation of a position or niche in the audience's mind all communicated not by single messages but by a series of messages. There are also stages through which most campaigns must pass, which usually involve a participatory dramatization of the product, candidate, or idea/ideology in which the audience is involved in real or symbolic ways. Then there are the kinds of appeals that unify and recruit zealots for the mass movement and the "chaining out" of rhetorical visions in campaigns/social movements that ultimately involve mass audiences.

You need to become a critical receiver who makes responsible decisions about which product to buy, which candidate to vote for, and which ideas or ideologies to endorse. These decisions are appropriate only after thorough analysis of the campaigns. Ask yourself how the campaign responds to feedback and what its objectives, strategies, and tactics are. Ask how the campaign positions the product, person, or idea and what developmental stages emerge during the campaign and in what kind of drama you are being invited to participate. When you have answered these questions, you will be ready to make a responsible decision.

KEY TERMS

After reading this chapter, you should be able to identify, explain, and give an example of the following key terms or concepts:

integrated marketing communication	Yale five-stage developmental model	positioning model	symbolic convergence theory
product-oriented	identification	communicative functions model	fantasy theme analysis
person- or candidate-oriented	legitimacy	social movement model	fantasy links
idea- or ideologically-oriented	participation	agitation and control model	rhetorical vision
goals	penetration	diffusion of innovation model	pragmatic (or practical) plane
strategies	distribution	chain outs	the righteous (or highly principled) plane
tactics	brand awareness	fantasy themes	social (or interactive) plane
	hierarchy of effects model		

APPLICATION OF ETHICS

A rapidly growing approach to campaign persuasion, whether for product, person, or idea/ideological campaigns is known as "stealth marketing" or "buzz marketing." It is based on the old adage that the best kind of advertising is word of mouth and is a response to increasing consumer, voter, and joiner skepticism about traditional advertising and to the increasing use of TiVo technology and remote controls to zap television ads. Buzz marketing hires people to engage in "word of mouth" advertising without informing the potential consumer that they (the sources or testifiers) are being paid for telling the consumer positive things about the product/brand, person, or cause being promoted (Ahuja, 2005). It has changed the whole landscape of the marketing and advertising industries. Take a look at examples at www.buzzmarketing.com (2008).

One of the most vulnerable market segments for this approach is teens, and the "buzz agents" being hired are usually between the ages of 13 and 19. In addition to promoting the brand or service, these agents also do consumer research by asking those they buzz about the competition, their preferences, and so on. Sometimes they give out free samples. Tremor Inc., which is a subsidiary of Proctor and Gamble, employs over 280,000 such agents. The parents are informed prior to recruitment that their lucky child has been selected to influence family and friends by joining the "Tremor Crew" and getting paid at the same time. This gets around the parental consent issue. Tremor Inc. has been very successful in marketing the Toyota Matrix, Coca Cola, Cover Girl makeup, and movies like "My Big Fat Greek Wedding." What are the ethical implications of this type of "honest deception" marketing (Ahuja, 2005)? What are some of the critical issues? Is the practice fair if the consumer doesn't know the word of mouth is paid for? If you were asked to become a part of a Tremor Crew, would you? Why or why not?

QUESTIONS FOR FURTHER THOUGHT

1. Choose a current campaign for a product, person, or idea/ideology. What appear to be its objectives, strategies, and tactics?

2. Define each of the Yale developmental terms. Can you identify examples of the first three stages in a magazine or newspaper campaign?

3. In the agitation/control model, what stage of a campaign or movement is represented when we vote for or against a particular candidate or proposition? Why?

4. What are some ways now being used to position products you use? Candidates running for office? Idea campaigns requesting your active or financial support? Mass movements seeking converts?

5. Identify a social movement that is either going on or seems to be developing. Use the social movements model and agitation/control model to trace its development. Which most accurately describes what is happening?

6. Using Bormann's symbolic convergence theory, explain the same social movement identified in question 5. Which of the methods seems most message-oriented? Which is most audience-related?

7. Which plane or philosophy fits with you—pragmatic, righteous, or social? How do you know?

8. Identify several fantasy types in a campaign for a product made popular in the previous decade. Are they similar to those for today's products?

9. Using the diffusion of innovation model, study the development of a new product in the marketplace.

10. Enter the words "buzz marketing" into a search engine and peruse the sites offered there. What do you think of this method. Would you be influenced by it? Why?

✳

 For online activities, go to the *Persuasion* book companion Web site at http://academic.cengage.com/communication/larson12.

12

✳

Becoming a Persuader

LEARNING GOALS

After reading this chapter, you should be able to:

1. Conduct an analysis of a hypothetical audience using demographics and identifying their needs.

2. Organize the same speech via the three formats of space, topic, and chronology.

3. Identify, explain, and give examples of stock issues used in considering a policy issue such as randomly assigned registration dates being debated on campus.

4. Give a speech using the motivated sequence format and exhibiting good delivery techniques and persuasive language.

5. Explain how you can improve your own credibility.

6. Identify various forms of proof statement in the mass media.

7. Explain the critical effects that the choice of channel can have on persuasion.

Thus far, we have focused on receiver skills: how to be a critical, responsible, and ethical consumer of persuasion as the title of this book implies. Aside from lawyers, teachers, politicians, ministers and a few other professions, few of us are regularly asked to deliver a speech, sermon, or lecture. However, sometimes, we must become persuaders. Luckily, we can apply the knowledge we gained in our role as persuadee to our occasional role as persuader. We can use tactics of intensification and/or downplaying; we can mold our persuasion using process, content, cultural, and nonverbal premises; and we can apply our knowledge of what is ethical in persuasion and what is not.

As a persuader, you'll take your first steps in preparing your message by learning about your audience and shaping your message. Remember that your audience is regularly confronting the Seven Faces of Persuasion and you are going to have to compete with a 24/7, networked, and ethically challenged world of advocacy and/or propaganda, so you must be well-prepared, interesting, and above all persuasive. Here, considerations such as patterns of organization, kinds of proof, and styling of messages will all be important. Also, you must choose how to go about delivering your message, which includes choosing the channel—face-to-face, radio, TV, Internet, e-mail, memo, etc., as well as thinking about your voice and posture, making eye contact

with your audience, gestures, and so on. Finally, you want to be aware of some common persuasive tactics and how they vary from culture to culture and audience to audience, which we will cover in this chapter. Throughout this entire process, you need to ask whether what you are doing is ethical in terms of the models presented by Richard Johannesen in Chapter 2.

Sometimes, you need to ask questions about the lasting, larger issues in life—not just how to make the next sale, convince the professor that your answer to the test item is justified, or persuade your friend to accompany you to some activity, and so on. One such question is, "Is what I am being persuasive about likely to have a more negative or more positive effect on my listener's lives? For that matter, will it make for a better or worse world?" Being an ethical persuader means being part of a community larger than yourself in which your persuasion has a potentially positive effect on relationships in that community.

✎ AUDIENCE ANALYSIS: KNOWING YOUR AUDIENCE

It is easy to assert that persuaders should always know as much as possible about their audience, but it is not always so easy to prescribe specific ways you can get to know them. One of the best ways is to listen to them when they persuade, because they will probably use tactics in their persuasion that would seem convincing to them in the persuasion they receive. For example, you may have noticed that I often use narratives and life examples in this book to get you to take my advice or at least pay attention to it. I rarely use statistics or charts and graphs. I am not a numbers person—in fact I have problems balancing my checkbook. Most communication majors are like that. If you want to persuade me, you should probably lace your message with narratives, anecdotes, and examples— not with numbers and charts. So listening to your audience when doing **audience analysis** is an essential idea. When doing audience analysis, I also look at my audience's patterns of processing information in terms of the elaboration likelihood model (ELM). I want to use the central information-processing route when that is appropriate (usually when detailed reasoning is called for), and I want to allow the audience to use the peripheral information-processing route when that is called for (when their responses are more likely to be emotionally prompted from their memory and don't need lots of thought elaboration).

In other words, you and I will need to do some audience analysis—which is defined as learning as much as possible about your projected audience and what is likely to motivate them. So we'll need to know some basic things like their ages, their majors, the gender split in the audience, their attitudes on the topic, and many other things. We will want to think about what their needs and wants are and what might most effectively move them to belief or action. Study your audience members, observe them, listen to them, and analyze what they say and how they say it. When your parents try to persuade, how do they go about it? What kinds of evidence do they use? What kind of reasoning—elaborate or peripheral? Some people, for example, are most easily persuaded when they think they are the ones who came up with the idea for change. It is best to give such persons several alternatives and let them make the choice—a tactic sometimes called "Putting It Up to You" or "Don't Ask If; Ask Which" by some theorists. In either case

the thing that makes this tactic really effective is that the audience feels as if it "owns" the idea or innovation and is therefore highly motivated to take action or change belief in accord with their "own" ideas. Others are most satisfied with a decision if they see that significant others (perhaps friends, authority figures or experts) have made or are making the same or similar decisions. Best-selling author Robert Cialdini (2001) calls this tool of influence "social proof," which means viewing a behavior or decision as correct "to the degree that we see others performing it" (p. 100). Knowing how your target audience—parents, teachers, your boss, friends, coworkers, and others are persuaded will give you a clue as to how to persuade them. This is pretty obvious when you think about it. After all, most people tend to desire to be like others and to go along with what others, maybe the majority of others, are doing. It's why fads catch on or why a candidate for political office gets what is called "momentum" on the road to victory and why some brands seem to be adopted by nearly everyone.

But is it ethical for the persuader to use such "social proof" to win the day? That depends on the issue, the costs to you and others, and the potential benefits for you and them for following the decisions, actions, or the benefits of the outcome. It is far more important for us as persuadees (sensing that a persuader is using social proof to convince us) to ask ourselves whether we should decide or act simply because others have acted in a certain way. The ancients called this tactic ad populum or appeal to the populace or the popular. Sometimes the masses are wrong, and we need to forge a different path. Thus, the ethical issue reverts back to where it should be— with receivers of persuasion. It is certainly true that persuaders ought to be ethical, but unfortunately that is not always the case. We need to be on guard for unethical persuaders and not be fooled by affinity appeals or social proof such that we follow the advice of persons who only seem to be like us but in reality are not. Recognizing ethical and unethical appeals aimed at us as persuadees also helps us to practice good ethical persuasion when we are in the persuader's role.

FIGURE 12.1 If you were preparing to speak in an informal situation such as this, how would you do your audience analysis?

SOURCE: Cengage Learning.

▼AUDIENCE DEMOGRAPHICS

When persuasion is aimed at large audiences—in the hundreds, thousands or more—professional persuaders like advertisers or politicians can use professionally gathered demographics to analyze the audience. In less formal situations like that described in Figure 12.1, one must do a more casual analysis. **Demographics** describes people in quantifiable terms of their shared attributes—their likes, dislikes, and habits, as well as age, gender, education, religious beliefs (if any), and income. If you subscribe to *Outdoor Life*, *Field and Stream*, and *Sports Illustrated*, you likely differ from the person who subscribes to *The Atlantic Monthly*, *Horticulture*, *Organic Gardening*, and *Bon Appétit*. Both of you would be good bets for catalogs featuring outdoor clothing. Probably neither of you is interested in rock music or MTV. Your affiliations (church, fraternal, or community groups) are another demographic index.

Some marketing firms specialize in doing such demographic research and it is sometimes readily available online or in a library.

Among the professional databases, census data, state government records such as driver's and fishing licenses, returned warranty cards, and many other sources, all of us have been identified demographically in great depth, and some of it easily available even though we are unaware of its existence as exemplified in Box 12.1. Most of us don't do this kind of in-depth and elaborate analysis of a potential audience, but we can do a lot even with limited time and resources as the online advice given above indicates. For example, suppose you plan to make a presentation to the athletic board of your college or university. You want the board to ban smoking in all areas of the football stadium during home games. It is already banned in indoor athletic facilities, but this is an outdoor facility. This will be a controversial proposal, and it could have unintended effects such as a campus-wide ban on smoking anywhere. In fact in my home state, an attempt was made in the legislature to ban smoking anywhere in the entire state, so be aware that total bans are not unheard of in this day and age. Try an Internet search with words like "smoking, bans, and stadiums." You will find that smoking has been banned at Arrowhead and Busch stadiums as well as many other professional sports venues. This will lead your athletic board to believe that such bans are realistic, especially since the professionals depend on the audience for their financial support far more than do college programs, so tell then in your speech about these

Try entering a word or two describing your audience (e.g., "demographics" and "my space") into any search engine and review the results that appear. You will discover that many users of "My Space" are between the ages of 16 and 34, are high school but not college graduates, and tend to be enlistees in the Armed Services rather than officers. There are lots of "My Space" users who have important interests in music and popular culture and are ideal customers for those products and brands. What other things do you find about them? Now try using the words that describe your audience and explore the results. What do you find about them?

examples. You also need to find out who the board members are, what they do for a living, and where they live. How have they voted or acted in the past on issues which restrict audience behaviors? What kinds of past funding have they used to enact such actions? What kinds of alternatives have they allowed? Why? What kinds of things do they tend to reject? Most of that kind of information will be a part of the public record and easily found in their minutes, quotes in the student newspaper, and so forth. Probably the most important source for this information is members of the board themselves so interview them if possible.

Not all demographic or psychological audience factors make a critical difference, and they will vary with the goal of your presentation so you need to look at them carefully. In regard to the smoking ban, average board members' ages may enter in. Age is important if you are discussing tax planning for retirement, but not if your topic is recycling. Also, there are more persons who have quit smoking among older populations than among younger folks. They are probably easier to convince than present smokers among your peers. Gender is also possibly important for the smoking ban (it certainly would be if your topic was the necessity of screening for cervical cancer) but it may not matter for a presentation about the smoking ban. Other factors such as level of income, political affiliations, and many other factors may be more or less relevant in some situations than others, so spend some time thinking these through. The board has both male and female students, faculty, athletes, administrators, and alumni on it; they will certainly vary in their backgrounds that need to be considered as

you craft your message, and don't forget that one of the members is the athletic director whose job may be affected by the decision. What issues, facts, examples, and so on will you want to present to your audience before urging them to enact the smoking ban in an open air stadium? Let's review a few of them.

Average age.   Will it matter how many are over 50 or under 18? Probably. The older ones may see the proposal as just another "do-gooder" idea. Younger ones could see it as another infringement.

Income.   Will it matter if they are well-to-do or struggling to get by? Probably not all of them smoke, but smoking has become an expensive habit. So income could have some impact. Also remember that older persons are among those who are most likely to have quit smoking, and that old saw about "reformed sinners" being the toughest to change usually holds true. Again, use the Internet to help you educate yourself before the presentation. Enter the words "age, smoking, quit" and you will find that older smokers quit for health reasons while younger ones tend to succeed or fail depending on such factors as financial reasons, because of obesity, ethnicity, past attempts to quit, and so on.

Gender.   The board is made up of both genders, so that may or may not be an important factor. Again, use the Internet and enter "gender, smoking, quit" and you will discover that females are more sensitive to the effects of nicotine and that it is harder for them to quit. But if they have health

BOX 12.2 YouTube and Interactive Audience Analysis

 We are all aware of the presence of e-mail spam. Why do you think some spammers pick on you and others don't? How do they know to what you might respond? To get an idea of how detailed audience analysis has become in the interactive age, type the words "audience analysis spam" into the search engine and peruse the many items which appear. Go to http://www.youtube.com/watch?v=UuXEZa6xpnw and view the 3-minute video there and find out how a group of recent college grads turned out as judged by the groups they fell into while in school. View some of the other videos available there. How might you use sites like these when you need to do audience analysis?

issues, they are more likely than similar males to be successful at quitting.

Religion. This factor is one you can probably ignore. However, if your proposal was to have board approval for pregnancy counseling, it clearly would be important.

Family size. Will it matter if your audience members have two or five children? Probably not, but it will depend on how many and which members of the family are smokers. Some large families are composed of only smokers. Most parents try to discourage their children from smoking, and again the Internet will inform you. Most families do urge their members who smoke to quit, but with mixed results.

Political party. In this case, political affiliation would have little bearing, unless the state has been aggressively pursuing no-smoking regulations, and even if that is the case party affiliation rarely is critical. However, cessation is less likely to happen in tobacco-producing states, so it may depend on where someone lives.

Occupation. Will the board members' occupations affect their willingness to consider the proposal? Research seems to support this. Outside workers smoke more than inside workers where smoking is already banned, so knowing the occupations of your audience may be critical. If the non-student board members are white-collar workers, they might know how smoking regulations are resented by some in the workplace, while blue collar workers are more willing to allow smoking in the workplace. Some

persons are well aware of the dangers of secondhand smoke, so knowing how many board members are nonsmokers will be important. How many of them smoke or smoked at one time? This will be a critical and key factor. Smokers usually resent being told when and where they can indulge. Former smokers usually know how repulsive the smell and mess caused by smokers are and usually object to someone smoking in their presence.

How will you find out which board members have smoked, are still smoking, or have quit? Perhaps you could distribute a questionnaire to board members designed to get other demographic information and include a question about their smoking and drinking habits. This will of course require that you allow enough time before the presentation for you to gather the data. Do you think the athletic director will be concerned about loss of ticket and concession income if smokers boycott the games? Ask a question related to that in your interview or questionnaire. Do any of the participants use interactive media as discussed in Box 12.2? If so you might suggest some insightful interactive sites on the trends in college sports in more "modern times." Townspeople may occupy the stadium seats and are more likely to be smokers, and they represent an important part of the revenue stream for the athletic department, so that might make a difference.

Once you know some of these key demographic factors for your group/topic/context, the next stage is to explore them in further detail. The public relations people at your school can provide information about where board members live, and this can cue you as to their income and age. For example, some students live in fraternity or sorority houses while others live in dorms or apartments, and many live at home and have families of their own and smoking habits will vary depending on living circumstances. Nonstudent members could live in town or commute from the suburbs. If the board has turned down past requests from students versus faculty versus administrators, you need to know why. Sometimes, merely talking to one or two typical members of a group before you attempt to persuade can be helpful in getting to know the audience. Any characteristics they share as a group can be useful in shaping your message for that audience. Would it be ethical for you to do demographic research for your presentation?

Determining Audience Needs

Some audience touchstones are emotional, some logical, some cultural, and some nonverbal. We can do some fairly sophisticated analysis of our target to determine **audience needs**. We might focus on the responsibility of the university to protect the health of students, faculty, and visitors to sell our idea. Or we could talk about the need of university decision-makers to constantly keep up to date with social and environmental issues. Most of the "hot buttons" that help persuade others can be traced back to emotions, memories, and experiences that are common to large percentages of the population.

All audiences have some sets of shared experiences—familiar chords. Everyone remembers taking their first test to get a driver's license (I failed the first time and was too embarrassed to tell anyone). Most of you remember your first visit to the campus where you now go to school and not knowing where the various buildings were located. Stored memories like these can be persuasive building blocks. What might be some of these stored experiences for the members of the governing board? Of course you will have to guess, but you can be pretty sure of some of your hunches. Those who smoke or have smoked will certainly remember their first cigarette—the rush was extraordinary and never quite as good again. Former smokers will remember how difficult it was to finally

quit—watching others inhale was pure torture. Some board members may remember not being particularly bothered by smoking when outdoors but finding it offensive in closed quarters. Others will recall even moving to a different seat to avoid smokers. After all, everyone moves away from the smoke when standing around a campfire, don't they? The next time you need to persuade someone, try to list the experiences he or she likely has had for yourself and see if any of them can be tied into your message.

Tony Schwartz (1973) identified what he called the "task-oriented" approach to persuading, which is also useful for audience analysis. He said that it was useless to tell your audience to do something if the circumstances didn't permit them to do it fairly easily. If you want them to communicate with their representative on the student government, make it easy for them and have a sample e-mail message ready for them to cut and paste. Ask yourself whether your goal fits with the athletic board's authority to enact your proposal. Try to find out the state of mind of your audience—the board, the sales force, or the job interviewer. What is their likely mood? Will they be relaxed? Will they have doubts? Take these things into account, and design your message accordingly. In other words, ask yourself "What job to I want this message to successfully complete?" and then sculpt your message to fit the job. In the smoking ban case, this may not be necessary since the board members will vote in open session.

Once you know something about your target group and how its members feel about your topic, you can shape the message. People are more likely to recall messages that are well organized, so you need to consider the various forms of organization available to you. These may not relate to the smoking ban issue, but they do apply to many cases in which you become the persuader.

FORMS OF ORGANIZATION

There are a number of ways to organize messages to make sure they are memorable and persuasive. We will look at five such formats here: (1) the **topic**

format, (2) the **space format**, (3) the **chronological format**, (4) the **stock–issues format**, and (5) the **motivated sequence format**. For the first three of these formats, we will use the following example: A student group on my campus wanted to bring back a highly successful filmmaker (a former student) as a guest speaker to discuss the challenges of film production as a potential job opportunity—how to get a job, what kind of pay to expect, etc. The speaker was even willing to donate his honorarium to the sponsoring student group to be used for field trips, travel to national conferences, and funding for a career day. The persuasive challenge was to convince the Student Association to budget several thousand dollars to pay for the expenses of the visit such as speaker's airfare, the honorarium (which was being donated to the student group as noted above), his housing and meals, receptions, and so forth. Below are several ways the student group considered for its presentation, which was both in public speaking and written formats.

Organization by Topic

Organizing by topic is most useful when the message you want to convey covers several topics or issues. Here is a list of topics the student group might present in the filmmaker alumni example:

1. His fame and success as a reason to bring him to campus
2. The kind of role model he would provide
3. The special opportunity to preview his latest film
4. The degree to which he is in demand on the speaking circuit
5. His generosity in donating his fee to the student group in the department
6. The other benefits to be derived from his presence on campus: publicity for the school, the added programming made possible by his donation, and the career counseling he might be able to give to aspiring student filmmakers.

By presenting these topics with supporting evidence, you give the student government a variety of good reasons to fund the speaker. The topic format is a good choice when presenting specific reasons for some suggested action.

Organization by Space

Organizing by space is a good choice when you want to compare your topic to some larger picture. In the filmmaker example, you might compare the relative cost of the desired speaker to that of speakers invited by other groups. The filmmaker's fee was less than half of that asked by another student group for a less well-known speaker. Further, his fee represented only 5 percent of the total guest speaker budget for the semester while majors in film programs in several departments represented a higher percent of the student population so the fee was a fair use of student fees. And the student group was only one of more than 20 similar groups in the university, so the fee was not out of line. In the spatial format, you might draw several pie graphs. In one, you could visually depict your speaker's fee as one-twentieth of the pie and label the remainder "Other Speaker Fees." Another graph might show your 5-percent share as only a fraction of the funds allocated to other student groups. Another might show share of speaker fees requested by major. In all these examples, you are using space as an organizing principle.

Organization by Chronology

Sometimes, the essential message in persuasive communication is best relayed by taking the audience through the issues in historical sequence or organizing by chronology so that it is sort of a narrative or story—both of which are very persuasive forms. You might relate the filmmaker's career as follows:

1. In 1975, he became a major in our department and took his first media classes there.
2. Two years later, he transferred to the USC film school, but he still values the basics of filmmaking he learned while he was with us.

3. He made his first picture as an independent writer/producer a year later.

4. It was released the next June, and as a minor summer hit, it recaptured the initial investment plus a small profit.

5. Later that year, the film got several "honorable mentions" at film festivals, and he then signed a contract to make pictures for one of the largest film studios.

6. In the next few years, he turned out several moneymakers and prize winners.

7. Then, in 1982, he made his first blockbuster, and went on to win the Oscar for writing and directing and has followed that up with several more prize-winningblockbusters.

8. He is now one of the best-known writer/ producers in Hollywood.

9. His family still lives in the area and his speaking visit might allow him to visit them and for them to attend the presentation, perhaps enlarging the audience with friends of his from his youth, neighborhood, etc.

As a result of these facts, the committee backed the proposal and provided funding.

✘ Organization by Stock Issues

The stock-issues organizational format is most useful for persuaders who are proposing a change in policy such as changing the present system of registering for classes to a random one. The name "**stock issues**" refers to the fact that there are three universal (stock) issues that must be addressed when major policy changes are considered. They are sort of like the stock characters in melodrama: the villain, the hero, the heroine, the hero's helper, and so on. Anytime there is a policy change under consideration the stock issues will be discussed. These stock issues are the **need for change**, a **plan to solve the need**, and your proof statements showing that the **plan meets the need** or removes the problem(s) you have raised and recognized. We frequently see stock issues used as content premises

in the world of politics and business, and in other policy-making forums as well.

As a persuader attempting to bring about a change in policy, you need to begin by demonstrating a strong need for altering the status quo. You have the **burden of proof**. (As a receiver, you should also be aware of the stock issues. Anytime you are the target of persuasion focused on policy change, identify which side of the debate is suggesting change. That will tell you who has the burden of proof.) In the case of the random method for class registration, the side promoting it has the burden of proof. They would need to establish the need for change by citing symptoms of the problem such as some transfer students getting no requested classes in their first semester. You should research specific instances that demonstrate to the audience that students are suffering something unfairly, are losing something, or are in danger of losing it. In terms of the FUD (Fear, Uncertainty, and Doubt) model mentioned in Chapter 4, you should create fear, uncertainty, and/or doubt in your audience's mind regarding the unfairness of present registration polity in order to establish a need for change. Tie the symptoms of the problem being considered to a cause that, if removed and replaced, will solve the problem. For instance, you might state that there is a need to ensure fairness for transfer students in order to encourage future transfers to select your school. Next, present a reasonable alternative or plan to the status quo—the plan or the new policy. You are suggesting a totally random basis for class registrations, but what will that do to those expecting to graduate on time. One way to do this is to show that the plan has been successful in other places. Perhaps a random registration policy has been adopted at a neighboring university with great success. Again use the Internet to help you find examples. This is called "arguing from precedent," and it is a powerful tool to the persuader. Still another way is to use expert testimony to the effect that the plan for change has a reasonable chance of succeeding and in fact increasing patronage or profit.

At each stage in the stock-issues organization, you can usually expect a rebuttal. In some cases, it will be openly stated, as in a policy debate within your student government. If you are giving a speech covering all three stock issues—need, plan, and plan meets need—anticipate such rebuttals and be ready to counter them in your own question and answer period. You might also short-circuit anticipated rebuttals by presenting a two-sided message in which you state the anticipated rebuttals and answer them then and there, prior to them even being brought up. This deprives the opposition of an opportunity to impress the audience with its rebuttal and shows you to be a fair persuader at the same time.

Organization by the Motivated Sequence

Another organizational pattern, one that resembles the stock-issues approach, is the **motivated sequence format**, suggested by communication scholars Alan Monroe, Douglas Ehninger, and Bruce Gronbeck (1982). This format uses five steps to get persuadees to attend to the message, to feel a need to follow the persuader's advice, and, most importantly, to take action related to the advice. The motivated sequence is an especially successful pattern when used in sales, recruitment, politics, and many other contexts where one needs audience members to take a specific action such as making purchases, joining, etc. The first step—the attention step—aims at capturing the attention of the audience. If you don't get your audience interested at the beginning, you'll never get them to pay attention to the rest of the message. You could begin your message with a question, a startling statistic, or a fear appeal. Or you could use a quotation, a joke, or an anecdote—a brief incident or cliché that makes the point. A good example of the anecdote relates to the umpire who was asked if he called strikes and balls the way he saw them or the way they were. He responded, "They ain't nothing until I calls 'em." That story could make a good beginning to many issues where the judgment of others (umpires of a sort) is critical.

Other approaches are to make an important announcement in the first few moments of the message, begin with a narrative or story, or use a visual aid. The audience may process the attention gaining emotionally or in the peripheral channel of the ELM, but you want listeners to process more of your claims centrally. In the second step of the motivated sequence, you try to convince the audience that they are losing something, are about to lose something, or could be gaining something but aren't This is the need step (as in the stock issues approach), and it can be tied to the attention-getter.

Steps 3 and 4 are the visualization and satisfaction steps. Here you give examples that tie directly to the audience and make them feel as if this issue will affect their lives. Here is a good place to use individual data testimony from persons like themselves, or some other form of proof to induce the audience to visualize what life will be like for them if they follow your advice. For instance, if they invest part of their student loan in inexpensive student housing such as a mobile home, they will be able to build up a nest egg for the future from the savings over a fraternal, dorm or apartment for their college days. Or you might take the opposite tack pointing out what life will be like if they don't invest in the mobile home and instead graduate with the burden of student loans at high rates of interest that may take years to repay. And they will graduate without the experience of having been in business for themselves, and, most importantly, without a nest egg to build their future on. Following this visualization step, you can then offer some way to satisfy the positive need or to avoid some negative consequences—for example, showing them how easy getting a student loan is, how little is needed for a down payment on mobile homes, and how little initial upkeep is needed.

Finally, the persuader needs to ask the audience to take a definite, specific, and realistic action step. It probably will do little to no good to ask audience members to alter their attitudes on the topic. They must show that they have changed their attitudes by doing something. Asking for change is different from providing good reasons for changing an attitude. And attitudes are fickle. It is hard to know whether an audience has really changed. It is far better to give the audience specific action type things to do, such as flossing to avoid tooth decay or saving energy by turning down the thermostat. Point out to them that making a wise real estate investment, and graduating with no debt and a handsome nest egg, is easy;

the first step is to apply for the student loan and consult a mobile home park about costs and their own eligibility for owning one. In one research study, people given a booklet with specific action steps to cut electricity consumption registered less use of electricity on their meters in the following two weeks than did those not given the specific action steps (Cantola, Syme, and Campbell, 1985). Again, if you want the audience to write to their elected representative, it is a good idea to have a petition on hand that members can sign or to announce the phone number and e-mail address of the legislator's local office and perhaps a sample e-mail or note. After all, phoning or e-mailing is much easier than writing a letter, especially if you have to start by finding an address.

A related model for making a persuasive appeal is called the **AIDA** approach—short for attention, interest, desire, action. In this model (as in the Motivated Sequence) the first step is to capture the audience's attention using any of the tactics cited earlier (i.e., startling examples or statistics, narratives, quotations, etc.). In the second step, the persuader's goal is to heighten the audience's interest in his or her topic or proposal. This might be done using a satisfaction or a visualization process, as in the motivated sequence. Or the persuader might tell how many persons have already tried the product or procedure and found it to be useful, or point out unforeseen problems with continuing the present practice, or note the increased revenues, votes, or other signs of success. Once attention and interest have been gained, the next task is to create a desire or need in persuadees to purchase the product or service, vote for the candidate, take the action, or follow the advice. In product-related persuasion, this usually is done by providing some product benefit or product promise. For example, Chrysler advertised built-in air bags for the front seat and side doors. The obvious benefit of this feature was that it could save lives in an accident. In its action step, Chrysler asked the customer to go to the nearest Chrysler dealer to learn more about the air bag and to take a test drive. Of course, the purpose of the visit and test drive was to expose the prospect to the product

and to let the salesperson try to make the ultimate sale (which usually follows a test drive).

Rank's Desire-Stimulating Model

Hugh Rank (1982) (whose intensify/downplay model was introduced in Chapter 1) has offered a simple four-part model for creating the kind of audience desire needed to cause the audience to take the requested action step that is part of all of the forms of organization noted above. His techniques are not a method of organizing a presentation. Instead, his techniques and examples relate to product promotion, but they can be easily adapted and used in other kinds of persuasion such as you might face in the future and as discussed in all of the forms of organization addressed in the preceding section. Rank says that persuaders can use four kinds of desire-stimulating tactics with this model (see Figure 12.2). First, they can promise the audience's security or protection by demonstrating that their advice will allow the audience to do one of two things: **keep a good** they already have but might be in danger of losing or the possibility of **getting a good**. Politicians frequently point out all the funding they have brought to their home districts (e.g., road funds, increased security programs) each of which is considered a "good" and then claim that their reelection will mean keeping this good flow of positive programs. The other approach to motivating persons via various kinds of "good" is to point out that, although they are not going to lose something they already have, they are not taking advantage of an available good. It might be an inexpensive online account for buying and selling stocks and mutual funds or something as simple as trying Jell-O's No-Bake Cheesecake—the ideal dessert to take along on a backpacking or wilderness canoe trip. If audience members have not tried the new good, then telling them about it might motivate them to acquire it.

A third desire-stimulating tactic relates to either **avoiding a bad** (or preventing an uncomfortable situation, problem, symptom, or feeling) or by following the persuader's advice on how to **get rid of a bad**, or experience relief from it. For example, you probably would consider reducing credit card debt a good thing to do, but at the same time it is good advice to never

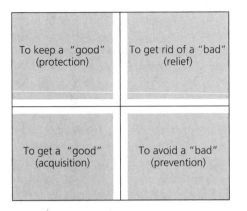

| To keep a "good" (protection) | To get rid of a "bad" (relief) |
| To get a "good" (acquisition) | To avoid a "bad" (prevention) |

FIGURE 12.2 Rank's model for ways to create desire in audiences.

get the credit card debt in the first place. Rank called these approaches the "prevention" and "relief" appeals. Advertisers often promise that their products will prevent the embarrassments of bad breath, body odor, or dandruff or will provide relief or help avoid headaches, heartburn, fly-away hair, acne, etc. Such "scare and sell" approaches can also be used in non-product persuasion. Recently, universities and school districts have had to reassure both students and parents that their campus including all school buildings and grounds are safe and secure because of the presence of security devices and increased security personnel on duty and in a variety of ways (e.g., bicycle patrols, metal detectors). The idea is that these precautions will prevent killings such as occurred on my campus on Valentines Day, 2008, and elsewhere in the nation's colleges, universities, and even in the public schools. These actions demonstrate that the school board or university trustees are responsible and credible and are genuinely concerned with student welfare. Therefore, that university or school is a good place to send one's kids. In other words, sending them there is a good way to "avoid a bad" that seems to be becoming ever more prevalent.

The other kind of advice is involved when we already have a problem and we want to get rid of it as in the case of reducing credit card debt. The persuader might advise converting all of one's credit card debt into a single card (watch for the zero balance offers and then pay at least the minimum but on time) and then cutting up all other cards and placing a reminder strip of duct

tape on the card to "tickle" your guilt at ever using the card. Or they might advise taking out a relatively low interest account from one's credit union (if you're not already a member, it's easy to join one) and using the loan to pay off credit cards while retaining only one for emergency and needed purchases. You can easily think of bad things that most persons would want to get rid of in most situations, occupations, and circumstances, and these can form excellent topics for persuasive speeches or presentations. Remember to do careful audience analysis and to organize your presentation in such a way as to prompt the desired action step

FORMS OF PROOF

People want good reasons for changing their attitudes, beliefs, decisions, and especially their behaviors or actions. The proofs required for taking action steps, even good ones, are always the most demanding and your audience will be no different. You must convince them that your suggestions or proposals make good sense and are at least worth considering. Let's look at the forms of proof available to persuaders like yourself and discuss how you can use them to prompt audiences to change attitudes or take action.

Statistical Evidence

Sometimes the most effective proof or support is convincing **statistical evidence**. For instance, an important goal of some potential car buyers is to get a model that gets good gas mileage. In this case, EPA data will probably help persuade them to choose a car model more effectively than will a salesperson's reassurances that the car is a real gas saver. Statistics also persuade best when they are simple and easy to understand. When you decide to use statistics, make them clear and provide a reference point for the numbers. For instance, if you are warning persuaders about the severity of the U.S. national debt, make it real to them. Don't just tell them how much the debt is. Tell them that interest on the debt amounts to $1,800 per year for every man, woman, and child in the country and that the average family has to pay taxes from January 1 until March 15 to work off its share of the interest on the debt. Or tell them that the debt has doubled or tripled since the last administration. In other words, make the statistics really mean something in relative terms. Give them some measure against which to compare or evaluate the impact of your statistics.

In recent years, there has been much concern about the proliferation of the use of plastic containers (especially for drinking water, which is readily available from fountains, and most of which simply comes from the public water supply). In fact, some cities have put a tax on such bottles to prevent them being discarded in landfills (reducing their life expectancies) or tossed away creating dangerous pollution—particularly in our oceans. If persuading on this topic using statistics, make them meaningful: "It will take a more than a two years to clear the Pacific Ocean of algae-gathering, aquatic life-destroying empty plastic water bottles that are being thrown away each year." or "We are falling ever more behind in cleaning our precious natural resources of these useless containers and we are fouling the future. After all, more than 90 percent of plastic water bottles contain nothing but tap water, so refill yours at the nearest water fountain!" and help save the planet.

Narratives and Anecdotes

Earlier, we noted the power of drama, stories, and jokes. **Narratives** make examples come alive and real and also make them easy to recall, relevant in personal terms, and easy to relate to. The story of a person rising from rags to riches probably persuades more people than any set of statistics of the percentages of successful start-ups or franchise operations ever could. A former professor of mine used to observe that an effective narrative can carry a lot of persuasive freight. In order to persuade my advertising students of the power of the one word "Free!" in advertising (and hence to keep it in mind when advising future advertising clients), I use a simple narrative. I tell about how the Cabela family and its widely distributed outdoors catalog

and several retail outlets became so successful by simply using the word "Free!" wisely. Mr. Cabela began in the 1950s by purchasing hand-tied trout flies from Japan at a fraction of a penny each. He advertised them in newspapers in trout country using an initial offer of "Five Hand-Tied Trout Flies—Only $.25!!! Free Shipping and Handling," and he got some orders. Notice that "Free" was offered for shipping and handling—things that no one can touch, feel, see, hear, or taste. But the venture didn't really take off until Mr. Cabela changed his ad to attach "Free!" to touchable things—the flies. The new ad read, "Five Hand-Tied Trout Flies—Absolutely Free!!! Shipping and Handling—Only $.25." The offer was really the same except for the way the word "free" was used. This narrative not only persuades my students but also persuaded several of my advertising clients to include the word "Free!" in their ads.

Testimony

We usually suspect people who attempt to persuade us using only their own feelings or opinions. They could easily be simply biased in one direction or another. This is why the **testimony** of another or secondary witness person (or more) is valuable. Of course expert testimony is the best kind, but even unqualified testimony, delivered sincerely, has powerful impacts on persuadees. As you plan your presentation, go back to your original audience analysis and try to determine what kind of testimony your audience will most appreciate and believe. Ask yourself who or what kind of persons would they most likely believe. In other words, since testimonials act as a kind of social proof (to use Cialdini's term), pick the kind of person whom the audience would most likely feel attracted to and would feel as if they were friends with or could become friends with. We tend to believe persons who are like us socially, intellectually, and in terms of lifestyle. Most ads that use testimonials use persons or celebrities whom they (the audience) would like to be friends with in real life. Choose your testimony with the same kind of things in mind—"birds of a feather, flock together" is a good rule of thumb.

Visual Evidence

Walk into any store where a salesperson or a videotape is demonstrating a food processor, a pasta
machine, or a recipe for using some unusual kind
of vegetable, and you will see the power of **visual
evidence**. The many television offers for various
cooking gadgets also testify to the power of the demonstration. Ron Popeil has made millions of dollars
using the technique, beginning with his Pocket
Fisherman and continuing with his Ronco glass and
bottle cutter and various other unlikely kitchen devices such as his current rotary oven. Much of the
information offered in the demonstration is processed
in the peripheral channel of the ELM "Seeing is believing" is the cliché that is proof of this fact.

Visual persuasion also can be used—and
misused—in political news coverage and all kinds
of advertising—especially where we see before/af-
ter formats (Simons, 2001). You can probably
come up with visual aid of your own (e.g., posters,
charts, graphs), and you may have presentational
skills that can use computerized visual aids like
Power Point. A critical thing to remember with
all visual aids that you use in persuasion is this—
the visual always draws attention from what you
are saying, so plan to reveal your visuals as you use
them and do not—repeat NOT—*repeat* NOT
show or distribute them prior to when you are
going to talk about them—do it during or afterward instead. If you do it before, you will lose
your audience immediately. I can't tell you how
many Power Point presentations I have seen where
the speaker reveals the point he or she is trying to
make prior to trying to make that point, and as a
result they lose the audience's attention. After all,
why pay much attention to what the speaker is saying if you have already read what he or she is going
to say? Instead reveal your visuals—graphs, pictures,
PowerPoint slides, or whatever, slightly *after* or *during* the point you want to make. That way you keep
the audience focused on you (where it should be
after all) and not on the visual evidence, which is
just to make things easier to remember or to take
notes on. The visual evidence then becomes reinforcement of what it is that you have just said.

Of course, actual demonstrations of products
are not always feasible, but persuaders can develop
various kinds of visual evidence (one student
brought a backpack and gear to demonstrate how
to pack for a canoe trip) to help the audience understand the problem. Visuals should be large enough that everyone can see them (e.g., a postage
stamp would be too little—ha, ha). They should
also be simple, because complex charts will only
confuse the audience. For example, a student successfully promoted a trip to Jamaica sponsored by
the student association by using simple travel posters, large pictures of local cuisine, easily seen cut-
outs of sandy beaches, and other images of tropical
life to motivate her audience.

Keep visual evidence simple or unobtrusive.
Don't let it overtake the audience as it did when
one student brought in his entire sets of camping,
canoeing, and fishing gear for a speech. It might be
better to use drawings or only a few examples of
the gear. Another student wanted to tell about how
to fend off an attacking dog. She actually brought
her dog to class and had it pretend to attack while
demonstrating how to fend it off, but the dog unfortunately had an "accident" during the speech,
thus ruining all of her careful preparation. As noted
above, if you plan to use graphs, charts, and/or
informational handouts in your presentation, be
sure to hold the handouts until the end or they
will get all of the audience's attention and you
will have none, thus destroying the effect of all of
your work.

Comparison and Contrast

Sometimes it is difficult to put problems in perspective. But we know that **comparison and contrast**
work from thousands of "before/after" ads and presentations we have seen or heard. People tend to
see issues from single viewpoints and then judge
them inaccurately. For instance, how big is the
problem of disposing of your old cell phone or
other small batteries in landfills? Most people simply
toss them into waste baskets or dumpsters. They
don't know how this small disposal compares with
the problem of the disposal of auto or flashlight

batteries? It is a little hard to know, so persuaders should provide something with which to compare or contrast their point about small battery disposal, like comparing the quantity of pollution from one discarded cell phone battery compared with one discarded flashlight battery, compared with a dry cell. As another example, it doesn't help the audience much to know that OPEC decided to increase crude oil production by 550,000 barrels per day. It will be more meaningful to mention that this is an increase of 20 percent over previous production level. Or tell your audience that the increased production will reduce the price of a gallon of gas by as much as 25¢—that will mean even more to them than the number of barrels of oil. Or compare the gas mileage of the new gasoline/electric-powered hybrids with that of other fuel-efficient car models.

BUILDING YOUR CREDIBILITY

All the evidence in the world, organized perfectly and delivered well, will not persuade if listeners do not trust the persuader. In matters such as persuading the boss to give us a raise, **credibility** is a key factor. What makes some people credible and others not? How can we build our own credibility before and during persuasion? In Chapter 1 and elsewhere, we discussed the idea of credibility using Aristotle's ideas about the reputation of the speaker, the speaker's delivery during the speech, and the audience's response to the speaker's image.

In more modern times, ethos or credibility has translated into several dimensions. We roughly equate reputation with the known expertise or knowledge level of the speaker. For example, when in research studies an identical speech is attributed to clearly labeled experts in some cases and to novices in others, the "expert's" speech is always rated as more persuasive than the "novice's." Effective delivery is related to sincerity, dynamism, and charisma and these dimensions of credibility rely on your delivery in large measure. We don't believe speakers who cannot maintain eye contact or those who are sloppily groomed, and tall speakers have more persuasive potential than do short ones. Further, speakers with an animated delivery persuade more effectively than do speakers who are frozen at the podium. Exciting language usually helps make the speech more credible, and a relaxed but firm posture is more credible than a stiff or sloppy one. Most of these points seem obvious, yet they are overlooked daily by sales reps, politicians, spouses, teachers, students, and parents. Here are some examples from everyday life in which the elements of credibility can be used.

Trust

We **trust** people for many reasons. We trust them because they have been trustworthy in the past, because they have made direct eye contact, and because they have a calm voice. We also try to give off trust cues. We look at our persuadees directly; we try to sound sincere; we remind our audience of our past record for trust; and we refer to times when it would have been easy to break that trust. You might, for example, remind your boss of the many times when she was out of town and you could have slacked off but didn't Or you might remind your parents of the many opportunities you had to party but studied instead. All these devices help build credibility. Take a minute and make a list of why the audience should believe you and then mention those reasons at the very outset of your presentation. Here is a simple example: "I have taken over a dozen classes in this major and had an internship at a prestigious ad agency over the summer; so I learned a lot about the ad industry that might be of interest to you."

Expertise

How do we know whether someone is a true expert on something? Generally, we look for **expertise** in past success at a task—at their record. If a person was a good treasurer for the fraternity or sorority, he or she will probably be a good treasurer for the student government. You can also signal expertise by being well-prepared and by demonstrating knowledge about the topic. Being willing to engage in question and answer sessions when you have finished speaking also communicates knowledge and expertise. Even if you do not have direct expertise on a given topic, you can "borrow" it by referring to known experts in your presentation. It is always useful and ethical to refer to your sources' background so receivers can judge the credibility of their testimony.

Dynamism

Dynamism is an elusive quality. It is sometimes related to physical appearance, in that attractive people tend to hold attention better than less attractive persons. Attractiveness or charisma probably cannot be developed much. However, many people who aren't particularly attractive are nonetheless persuasive and dynamic. Dynamic speakers seem to take up a lot of psychic space—they have stage presence. You can project a dynamic image in several ways. One is to speak with authority—project your voice, maintain appropriate volume, and choose words that indicate certainty. Try speaking a little more rapidly than you do in normal conversations—about 125 words per minute instead of 90—you'll be able to cover more information as well. Good posture and good grooming also signal dynamism, as do appropriate gestures, facial expressions, bodily movement instead of being riveted to one spot, and direct eye contact with various areas of the audience and not a point at the center back of the room just above their heads.

WORDING YOUR MESSAGE

Stylistic speeches and exciting language choices persuade better than dull speeches. How do persuaders develop style in their presentations? What kinds of factors make some speeches, advertisements, or other persuasion memorable while other presentations are quickly forgotten or even ignored? At the very leas,t use the thesaurus function on your computer and work at developing a varied and interesting vocabulary.

Varied Vocabulary

Most of us need to improve our vocabularies. You should try to rewrite your speeches using word variety to make them livelier, flashier, more dramatic, or more humorous. It helps to develop an interest in puns and other wordplay, as they can help you get the attention and earn the goodwill of your audience. Study the eloquence of great speakers from the past. Pay attention to the language used in government news releases, by politicians, and in advertisements. Try to learn a new word a day and, as noted above, use the thesaurus feature on your computer.

Figures of Speech, Alliteration, and Assonance

Enhance your style by using appropriate **figures of speech** at the right time. We discussed several in Chapters 5 and 6. Metaphors and similes help your audience visualize a point. The audience ties the information to the metaphorical structure and then remembers the information better as a result. Alliteration—the repetition of consonant sounds—and assonance—the repetition of vowel sounds—also enliven style. Both create a kind of internal rhythm in the message, which makes it more lively and memorable. We see both alliteration and assonance in "A portable phone system? Gee! No, GTE." Both devices help improve your style.

Vivid Language

Choose **vivid language** to catch your audience's interest. Although vividness can be overdone, it is more frequently overlooked in favor of dull and uninteresting language. Which of the following is more vivid?

> I'm offended by your representation of lutefisk. It is not rubbery!

> Lutefisk may be "a rubbery and repulsive ethnic dish" to the socially deprived, but to the properly initiated, it is the nearest thing to ambrosia this earth has ever produced. While this may not be the most

BOX 12.3   Vivid Language and Propaganda

 Go to http://wordwhirl.wordpress. com/ and learn about the many figures of speech, tropes, and other types of vivid language and how it has been used and is continuing to be used in various kinds of communication including propaganda, copy writing, and more. To learn how vivid terms like "shock and awe" were related to a poetry conference promoted by First Lady Laura Bush, and how the poets became a force of propaganda themselves go to http://www.common dreams.org/views06/0928-21.htm. Increasing your vocabulary of

vivid language will help make you a more convincing and interesting persuader. You don't need to become a propagandist—you can just be an effective advocate for worthy causes. Vivid and colorful language helps make a persuasive presentation memorable and effective. Developing your vocabulary arms you with more vivid and persuasive language. Familiarize yourself with famous quotations, which you can find by a subject search on any Internet search engine. Just enter the words "famous quotations" and you will find what you're looking for. There are also Web sites dedicated to listing quotations by category.

"vivid" language, Box 12.3 may lead you to Web sites that will help you discover vivid language to use in your persuasive efforts.

Concise Language

A good way to ensure that you are using compact and **concise language** in your presentation is to script it. Then go back over it and pretend you are paying 50 cents per word to send it by telegraph; see how much excess baggage you can cut. Don't try to memorize it and deliver it word for word, but try to boil it down and "tell" it rather than "read" it to your audience. You can come up with more concise language that way. Straightforward statements are usually most effective ones for your audience to absorb. Make your major point as a concise assertion or frame it in a provoking question. For example, "We need to put a tax on all plastic water bottles to encourage their proper recycling or reuse." Then follow up with elaboration: "Most plastic water bottles are discarded into landfills thus cutting the life of the facility and costing us all more now and in the future." If you try to say everything in the opening sentence, you will confuse your audience. The use of concise language also will help build your credibility and will improve the organization of your presentation.

Parallel Structure

Parallel structure uses similar or even identical wording or sentence structure to make a presentation memorable. For example, in a speech to the American Legion, former President Bill Clinton once said, "I am not the only American whose life has been made better by your continuing service here at home. From baseball to Boy Scouts; from keeping veterans hospitals open to keeping kids off drugs; from addressing homelessness to preventing child abuse to instilling a deep sense of patriotism into still another generation of Americans, a grateful nation owes you a debt of gratitude." His repeated use of the "from … to …" format provides parallel structure and symmetry in the speech. The idea behind parallel structure is to build audience expectations. For example Cicero once said, "Ask not what your country can do for you: rather ask what you can do for your country." President John Kennedy used almost exactly the same words in his inaugural speech in 1960.

Imagery

Imagery appeals to our senses. Perhaps you can't bring the smell, taste, touch, sight, or sound of something to the audience, but you can use words that conjure up sensuous memories. It might be of a "tall, cool glass of chilled beer dripping with beads of perspiration" or the "fragrant smell of Mom's pot roast, ready to fall apart, with its juices making a savory gravy that

B O X 12.4   Interactive Exercises for Language Improvement

Want to try fun and easy ways to improve your vocabulary? Once again the good old Internet is a tool of first choice. Initially, go to http://www.better-english.com/vocabulary.htm where you will find a wide variety of multiple choice exercises on the proper word(s) to use in various business situations. Even if you are planning on a nonbusiness occupation, working your way through exercises on word variety for emotions like "anger" or "happy" can help improve your language variety. They'll even put you on a weekly e-mail short course to help you improve further. For more advanced vocabulary building go to http://www.vocabulary.com/ where you will find a host of interactive word puzzles, learn Latin roots so you can decipher new words, and see numerous videos hosted by current television personalities.

B O X 12.5   Interactivity and Developing Humorous Examples

If you have been asked to or have volunteered to make a public speech or other kind of persuasive presentation and want to use a few humorous examples to liven up your presentation, go to any search engine and enter the word "humor" and the topic of your speech. Keep surfing until you find what you want. If you have difficulty, think of a synonym for your topic and enter it. I tried it with the topic "Bad Breath" and found a number of humorous lines (e.g., "It was the onion dip, wasn't it?") as well as visuals (e.g., two elephants fighting head to head with the caption "Hey Joe! Did you ever try mouthwash?"). Using the humor loosens your audience and gets your audience involved in your topic. It's memorable too.

starts your mouth watering." A famous salesman once said, "don't try to sell the steak; sell the sizzle." Think about the sensory experiences your audience has had that relate to your topic and that you can evoke. See Box 12.4 on using interactive sites to improve your sensory language. For example, "I'm sure that all of you have seen what a mess discarded plastic water bottles make. But you can't imagine the stink they create when simply left to stand partially filled in a landfill or floating and covered with slimy algae in our oceans." A good way to develop this skill is to take a given product and try to restate its appeals in terms of the various senses. For instance, Campbell's soups are "Mmm, Mmm, Good" (taste). How might they be described using the sense of sight? Of smell? Of the other senses?

Humor

The use of **humor** in persuasion is an obvious stylistic asset if handled properly, and it can build credibility as well. But a word of warning is necessary here: If a persuader uses humor that is inappropriate, in bad taste, or just plain not funny, it will likely backfire and actually destroy credibility and persuasiveness. If you are going to use humor in your persuasion, test it out with friends and relatives. How can you develop humorous examples, comparisons, anecdotes, and stories?

People who regularly engage in public speaking usually have a ready supply of humorous material with which to embellish their speeches (see Box 12.5). They develop the humorous aspects as they work up other materials for their speeches. Humor sometimes relies on the breaking of expectations as can be seen in Figure 12.3. If you can never remember a story or joke, keep a file of stories or jokes or just punch lines. When you need the material, the file will trigger your memory. Late night television can provide you with humorous examples, as can your daily newspaper, *Reader's Digest*, and friends who frequently tell jokes. Don't forget the Internet. Just enter your subject and the word "humor," and have some fun while building a successful and entertaining presentation. You can also use visual humor such as cartoons, perhaps by using PowerPoint.

FIGURE 12.3 The trapeze artists seen in the cartoon face broken expectation, which accounts for the humor in the cartoon, along with the surprised looks on their faces.

SOURCE: Used with permission of Doug Walker.

BOX 12.6 **Propaganda Speakers, Then and Now**

The oldest media for carrying propaganda are the public speech and the propaganda poster, of which we have seen several throughout this text. To see and listen to some of these propagandistic speeches and/or speakers go to http://www.weshow. com/us/videos/post/search?text=+Propaganda where you will see clips from examples ranging from WW II Nazi propaganda to Tom Cruise on behalf of Scientology, to Iraqi warlord speeches to 1935 anti-drug propaganda used to dramatic the classic "Reefer Madness" film with the speaker as the audio track to animated speakers.

DELIVERING YOUR MESSAGE

Usually, we think of delivery as relating just to the source or speaker. But other factors can affect the delivery of your message, including the channel and the means of audience involvement. Persuaders often overlook these. For example, consider the sample propagandistic referred to in the video clips noted in Box 12.6. In the following section, we will look at all these factors.

The Persuader

Among the factors that persuaders adjust before and during delivery are their posture, eye contact, body movement and gesture, articulation, dress, grooming, and vocal quality. Other factors under the speaker's control are the use of visual aids and other nonverbal cues. Some persuaders are so nervous that they cannot stop pacing back and forth. And when they do stop, they stand ramrod stiff, looking as if they might freeze into statues. Other speakers are so relaxed that they seem uninterested in their own messages. They slouch over the podium or slide down into their chairs during a meeting. What does the posture of the speaker in Figure 12.4 suggest?

Clearly, the persuader's posture can signal the audience that you are either nervous or too relaxed. Observe persuaders in differing contexts—interviews, speeches, arguments—and you will see that the effective ones avoid both extremes. The ideal posture lies somewhere in between. You should be alert and erect, and your shoulders should not tense or slump. Your posture should communicate confidence. You will be more believable if you maintain eye contact with your audience. You don't need to look at everyone individually (unless you are speaking to only one person). Instead, look at various areas in the room. Politicians look directly into the TV camera and so seem to make eye contact with each viewer. In meetings, establish eye contact with as many participants as possible. Body movement and gestures liven up a speech, as long as they don't distract. Using gestures during a speech keeps audience attention. However, it is a mistake to over-rehearse gestures, body movements, and facial expressions.

These nonverbal elements in delivery must appear natural, not staged, to have a positive effect. We all use

FIGURE 12.4 Posture is important in giving a persuasive message. Is this speaker's posture appropriate for the formal situation seen here?
SOURCE: Cengage Learning.

gestures every day without thinking about them. Let your natural impulses guide you in your use of gestures in formal and interpersonal exchanges. Nothing can add more to your message than a natural gesture, movement, or facial expression (Scheflen, 1964). But rehearsed gestures usually backfire so let them come naturally—do what feels right. Articulation and vocal quality also affect your delivery. Everyone has heard people who pronounce words incorrectly; as a result, the audience focuses on the error and not on the message. Successful persuaders work on articulation, pronunciation, and vocal quality. Listening to yourself on tape will help you pinpoint your mistakes and focus on your vocal quality. As Box 12.7 demonstrates, the successful persuader will also examine the speech in view of the ethnicity of the audience and the ethnicity issue in general. The mistake in using the word "oriental" (which refers to rugs or a type of cuisine as opposed to the ethnicity of a person or persons) is a classic example. Listening to yourself on tape will help you pinpoint your mistakes and focus on your vocal quality. Some persons, especially females, think that a breathy or "thin" voice makes them sound sexier, but just the opposite is true. If you are interested in persuading others, spend some time working on your voice and your articulation.

The Channel

Choosing the correct channel for sending your message is another key element in delivery. In one rural political campaign for the U.S. House of Representatives on which I worked, the candidates put most of their money into billboard space—which was rather surprising in this electronic media age. In this case, however, the candidate's district was large, stretching nearly half the length of the state, and no single TV network or cable channel reached all of it. Using TV would have meant having to pay a huge amount to get a single message across—the candidate's name and a brief statement of his goal. But because the district was so large, all residents had to drive to shop, do business, socialize, worship, and farm. Thus, the billboard was the one channel that could touch nearly all voters in the district.

Recent presidents have returned to using radio for regular Saturday persuasive talks, which are then responded to by representatives of the opposing party—sort of mini-debates. Why is radio such an appropriate channel for political persuasion? It is because we use much more radio than we imagine—almost as much as we use television. It is estimated that Americans listen to the radio an average of four hours a day, and more than half listen

BOX 12.7 Honoring Diversity in Public Speaking

 Lenora Billings-Harris is an internationally known public speaker working on diversity issues with Fortune 500 companies, and she offers the following advice for public speakers wanting to be diversity conscious. First, select your language carefully. One ill-chosen word can undo you in an instant. For example, saying "Hey guys …" in a mixed gender group can offend some. Pointing to your "flip chart" can offend any Filipinos in the audience—refer to your easel instead. Research your audience first—who will be there? Be careful about using humor even if it is self-deprecating. Whenever possible use people's names, especially during question and answer sessions, and don't refer to someone as "the tall guy in the back." If you do refer to ethnicity make sure that you've got the right word. Some Latinos resent being referred to as "Hispanic" since that term groups together persons from Cuba, Mexico, Latin and South America, and Puerto Rico. (The word was invented by the U.S. Census Bureau more than 35 years ago to categorize people who spoke only Spanish.) One way around this potential trap is to use the words "Americans of (blank) heritage." The same goes for the word "Oriental," which refers to rugs, a certain cuisine, and certain styles of furniture. When speaking of people, use the adjective "Asian." If a member of the audience uses a potentially insensitive word, don't call attention to it in public unless it is truly offensive; instead talk to the person privately after the presentation. If the word is truly offensive, point that out by saying something like, "Most persons consider that usage offensive and using it reduces your credibility." Billings-Harris notes some potentially offensive usages and offers acceptable alternatives. Use "outcasts" instead of "black sheep." Refer to occupations in non-gendered ways—"postal workers" not "postmen." Can you think of other examples of embracing diversity in your public speaking? For further study, explore the work of Billings-Harris at www.lenoraspeaks.com and the many other interesting links on public speaking.

---

at work, especially females (Russell & Lane, 1999). People also listen to the radio while they are doing something else—driving, reading, commuting, exercising, and so on. By choosing the relatively inexpensive medium of daytime radio, politicians can reach people they otherwise might not, and at a reasonable price.

On a more personal level, ask yourself what is the best way to inform your boss that you will look for another job if you don't get a raise or promotion. Perhaps tapping into the channel of the grapevine might be best (usually done by identifying the group's gossip and letting them know that they shouldn't "pass this along, but I have a job interview scheduled next week"), or maybe sending a straightforward memo, or asking her to be a reference so she will not get an out-of-the-blue inquiry about you from another firm. At the same time, you are letting her know that you are looking.

In general, start by listing all the potential channels that could be used to send your message. Then try to match them with your audience. If your audience uses a particular channel over others, then that is probably a good one to use. Sometimes the correct channel will give persuaders a chance to encourage audience participation, which in turn can increase audience energy, interest, motivation and activity. Get your audience involved by asking direct open-ended questions (ones that can't be answered by a simple "yes" or "no" but that need elaboration instead), and don't forget to address people by name if at all possible (if not possible, then by pointing and describing their dress or some other distinguishing characteristic such as if they have a briefcase or some other object). Or leave a sentence incomplete and let listeners finish it. One speaker got audience involvement right away by asking everyone to stand up before he even began his speech. He then asked them to become aware of the muscles they were using in their feet, ankles, calves, and thighs at that moment and tied this awareness to his topic—the need to develop communication awareness on the job. One word of caution: don't distribute any printed material until the end of the speech. Audiences start reading right away, and you will lose them.

COMMON TACTICS OF PERSUASION

We mentioned some persuasive tactics that are used frequently and even are emphasized in public speaking and sales short courses. Let's consider some of the more common ones.

The Foot in the Door or Door in the Face

Robert Cialdini (2001) describes several persuasive tactics, including the **foot-in-the-door** and the **door-in-the face** techniques. The foot-in-the-door technique relies on getting a potential customer, joiner, donor, or convert to make a small initial commitment that starts what will become a long-term relationship resulting in ever larger sales, contributions, and commitments. To illustrate, some time ago I signed a protest petition from the Citizens' Utility Board (CUB), which promised to use the petition to prevent price increases by Illinois utilities—Commonwealth Edison, Ameritech phone services, and the gas company, for example. Soon after, I received a newsletter explaining that CUB had stopped one of the utilities from instituting a 15 percent price increase. But the battle was not over, because the utility was appealing. Could I donate $50, $25, or even just $10 to help carry on the fight. I donated $10. Next, a letter from CUB informed me of another victory, but warned that the other utilities were suing CUB, and asked that I become a full-fledged, dues-paying member of the organization for only $25. My signature on the petition was merely a foot in the door, and I continue to receive requests for donations.

In the retail field, this technique might mean getting a prospective retailer to agree to carry one item in a product line. That commitment becomes the foot in the door to the retailer's finally agreeing to carry the entire product line. As Cialdini puts it, "You can use small commitments to manipulate a person's self-image; you can turn citizens into 'public servants,' prospects into 'customers,' prisoners into 'collaborators' " (p. 67). Cialdini relates how the same technique is used by the highly successful Amway

Corporation. Staff members are asked to set specific sales goals and then to write them down: "There is something magical about writing things down. So set a goal and write it down. When you reach that goal, set another and write that down. You'll be off and running" (p. 71). The written commitment somehow translates into motivation and action.

The door-in-the-face tactic is what a persuader uses when turned down on a request for a significant commitment, and then settles for an initial small commitment or engages in what Cialdini calls the **rejection-then-retreat** strategy. In other words, if a salesperson tries to get the prospect to go for the top-of-the-line or "loaded" version of the brand but is rejected, he or she can always retreat by offering a stripped-down version of the brand. Cialdini attributes the effectiveness of this strategy to feelings of responsibility and satisfaction on the part of customers, joiners, or donors. By agreeing to the lower commitment, they can feel as if they are in control of the situation and have "dictated" the deal. This satisfaction makes them happier with their decisions. So try to think of simple or partial commitments to your proposal that your audience can take and which can then be upgraded to more significant actions.

A related persuasive approach is to "sell up" after retreating to a position of concession. Thus, once you've signed the contract to buy the new car, a good salesperson will offer you the extras—the undercoating and soundproofing, the extended warranty, the upholstery fabric protection, and so on. Others have suggested similar tactics using somewhat different terms. The following are some tactics suggested by Drs. William Howell and Ernest Bormann (1988). They may overlap with some of the other techniques discussed previously. Examine your world of persuasion for examples of these tactics in action.

The Yes-Yes Technique

A common tactic in sales and other persuasive appeals is called **yes-yes**. The source attempts to get the target group or person to respond positively to several parts of the appeal, withholding the key request until last. Having agreed to most parts of the appeal, the persuadee is likely to say yes to the key and final request. For example, suppose you are trying to sell a lawn service. You might ask the homeowner, "You would like to have a beautiful lawn, wouldn't you?" The answer is going to be yes. Then you ask, "And you'd like to get rid of the weeds?" Another yes is likely. "And wouldn't it be nice if these things could be effort-free?" A yes answer is likely again. Now that the homeowner has accepted all your points in favor of the service, it is nearly impossible to respond with a "no" to "Then you'll want to sign up for our lawn service, won't you?" By accepting the yes pattern, the buyer accedes to your final request. At another university close to mine, the topic "Hate Speech Should Be Outlawed on Campus" is being debated by some classes. The "yes-yes" tactic could be incorporated here. For example, the pro advocate might begin by saying, "You'd like to avoid racial and ethnic confrontation on our campus, wouldn't you?" (the audience is most likely to agree—yes). The advocate could then go on by asking "And it would be good, wouldn't it, if this could be done by each of us simply trying not to use language that is offensive to various minorities?" (again, the audience is likely to agree). And the advocate could continue asking questions resulting in yes answers that led to the logical conclusion that outlawing hate speech was a good idea. The same technique is useful in a meeting in which a persuader gets the participants to agree to all but the final point in favor of, say, a change in work schedules. They agree that flexibility is good, that more free time for workers is good, that changing schedules would relieve boredom, and so on. They are then likely to agree that the change is a good one.

The Tactic of Asking Not "If" but "Which"

It is easier to make a choice between two alternatives than from among many. This is the strategy behind the "**don't ask if; ask which**" persuasive tactic. I learned as a parent of young children that the worst thing to ask on Saturday mornings was,

"What would you like Dad to make for breakfast today?" It was better to say, "Which would you like for breakfast today—Dad's blueberry pancakes or Dad's blueberry coffee-cake?" The same thing applies in persuasion. don't ask your audience to choose from too many options; ask them to choose from only a few or only two as in the following use of the technique by a car salesperson—"Would you rather have us undercoat your new car, or do you want to take it elsewhere?" Another employment example might be "Would you rather meet on your promotion this week or next?" It comes down to "Do you want guns or butter?" a favorite tactic of many propagandists. It was the basis for the initial approval for the war in Iraq. The real question posed by the Bush administration was "Do we attack them now and in their own country, or do we wait for them to attack us again—maybe in more terrible ways and here at home?" Although this tactic can be manipulative and is frequently used that way, and hence can be used unethically, it has the distinct advantage and value of forcing some decision or action when buyers, voters, or others are stubbornly trying to avoid it. You might use such a technique in a speech on stopping global warming by starting with questions that are going to be answered "yes" in the audiences' mind (e.g., "We all want to slow down global warming don't we?") and then adding others until you have a pattern of yes responses. Then you can ten ask for a key commitment (e.g., "So why not try changing all the lightbulbs in your home or apartment to the low-energy, fluorescent-coiled ones—you'll save money in the long run as well!").

A Question for a Question

A tactic some people in audiences use to throw others off guard is to ask an embarrassing or tough question. Asking someone a question in the first place puts the ball in their court. But if you find yourself in this situation, a good tactic is putting the ball back into their court by asking them a question in return instead of answering their original question. It buys you time to boot. For example, if asked, "Wouldn't you like to sign up for the

National Guard?" or " Would you like to pledge Tappa Kanna Bru tonight and join our pledge class?" you might say, "Why do you think I would want to do that?" or "What gave you that idea?" Responding with a question, or asking the person to repeat or even to elaborate on the question also gives you time to think.

Answering a question with a question puts the ball back in the other person's court. People who question you sometimes are trying to discredit or annoy you. Turn the tables—answer with another question. Suppose a prospect for advertising services asks, "Who else has used your services? Maybe I could check with them before deciding to go with your agency." A good response is, "I can bring you written testimonials about how successful we are in generating qualified leads" or "I can give you names and phone numbers for local businesses that might be slightly different than yours, and you can call. Or I can do both. Which would you prefer?" Now the other person has to make a commitment, which puts them somewhat in debt to you, even if only in a tiny way.

The Partial Commitment

The **partial commitment** tactic resembles the door-in-the-face or rejection-then-retreat strategy discussed above, but uses acts instead of words to lead the prospect to the final request. Once you are partially committed, you are a good prospect for full commitment. Evangelists often close their pitches by asking people in the tent or auditorium to bow their heads and close their eyes for prayer. This gets a partial commitment from the audience. The preacher then asks the Lord to enter the hearts of all and asks those who want God to come into their lives to raise their hands. The final request may then be, "Those of you with your hands up come to the front and be saved." We see this tactic elsewhere, too. Trying a sample of a product represents a partial commitment, as does clipping a coupon. The smart auto salesperson won't ask you to sign a sales agreement right off the bat. Instead, he or she will suggest that you look around and see whether you find anything that appeals to you and then suggests

that you take it for a test drive. Merely by looking around, you are partially committing to the sales pitch, and the test drive is usually the clincher.

Of course, other kinds of commitment are used to persuade. When a politician asks you to sign a petition to put his or her name on the ballot, your signature is a form of partial commitment to that politician, and research shows that you are more likely to vote for him or her when you get to the ballot box. A favorite way to generate "qualified leads" in the marketing of some products is to run a sweepstakes. Anyone who submits an entry for the free version of the product has already made a partial commitment to buy it and thus is a good sales lead to follow up. You can use this tactic in your presentations by asking for an almost insignificant action—raising one's hand, for example. Then having got agreement to your initial proposition—say buying a season ticket for athletic events—you can ask for more significant steps for supporting the school's athletic program such as joining the Huskie Club or buying a Huskie Club Hoodie and then pledging to go to as many games as possible.

Planting

Memory responds best, it seems, to messages that have sensory data as raw material. The tactic of **planting** uses one or more of the five senses to open a channel to the audience's memory of how they experienced the product, idea, or candidate. Recall that the five senses we have are smell, taste, touch, hearing, and seeing. Earlier we asked you to describe Campbell's soup using each of these senses and not the obvious one of taste—Mmm, Mmm Good. This kind of use of the sensual memory is almost certainly processed in the peripheral information-processing channel of the ELM. Restaurant ads often appeal to several senses at once, and not just the obvious sense of taste. They describe the "crisp and crunchy garden salad" to appeal to the sense of touch. They offer "'sizzling hot steaks seared on a grill" to appeal to the sense of hearing. They describe the "thick red tomato sauce" to appeal to the sense of vision and use the words "a steaming fragrance of garlic and spices" to appeal to the sense of smell.

In a classic case of invoking the sense of touch in an ad campaign, Charmin toilet paper was successfully marketed as an uncommonly soft bathroom tissue in TV ads because the grocer, a nerdy fellow named Mr. Whipple, was always caught squeezing the packages of the stuff when he thought no one was looking, and he was always getting caught and scolded for it. Of course the humor of the spots caught and maintained audience attention, but the squeeze he always gave the package was a sensual reminder that the brand was supposed to be unusually soft. No other of our five senses could have communicated that concept more successfully than touch or feel. An ad for a new automobile might have someone slam the door or trunk lid so audience members hears the solid "thunk" and mentally compares it with experiential memories of the sounds and rattles of their own five-year-old car when doors or trunk lids are slammed. No other of our senses could have communicated the aging of the owner's present car than that of sound (other than perhaps sight). Tie persuasion to the senses of sight, sound, touch, taste, and smell if at all possible using this technique of planting, and the audience will recall your message better and longer. In other words "Don't sell the steak; sell the sizzle."

The IOU

Sometimes called the reciprocity tactic**,** the **IOU technique** gets listeners to feel they owe you something. For instance, the insurance salesperson spends several hours doing a complex assets-and-debts analysis to prove to the prospect that he or she needs more insurance. The sales rep then spends several more hours explaining the figures to the spouse, perhaps taking the couple out to lunch or dinner. By the end of all the special treatment, the couple may feel that they really ought to buy something even though they may not need it or cannot afford it. They respond to the obligation—the IOU—that was created by the salesperson's effort. After observing how reciprocity works in various cultures, Cialdini (2001) notes that the need to reciprocate—the IOU—transcends "great cultural differences, long distances, acute famine, many years, and self interest" (p. 21). Persuaders find this tactic useful when it is hard to make a first contact with buyers, voters, or joiners. You can place your audience in your debt by giving them free samples or offers of help. As a listener, you may want to remember that "There's no such thing as a free lunch."

REVIEW AND CONCLUSION

We all have to persuade at some point. To be effective, we need to analyze the audience before planning how our format will affect the message. And to do that we need to remember that they, like us, are living and processing information in the same world. They too daily encounter the Seven Faces of Persuasion and respond to or become advocates and/or (hopefully not) propagandists. We must develop our forms of support and our use of language as we think about which will be most persuasive to persons facing those 7 Faces. We must also control factors in delivery. We need to use source factors, such as posture, eye contact, and dress all in a world of scams and deceptions. Start your planning by assuming that your audience will not believe you initially and then work to build your credibility through the various techniques we have discussed here.

Remember that even channel factors are subject to our control as well. And receiver factors can be used to get the target group involved in its own persuasion through techniques such as "Yes-Yes" or "Putting It Up to You" or "Don't Ask If; Ask Which" and others. As you are called on to persuade, use these skills in preparing. Rely on the audience analysis and demographics that the receiver-oriented approach teaches—listen to your audience. Get messages out of them, not into them.

KEY TERMS

After reading this chapter, you should be able to identify, explain, and give an example of the following key terms or concepts:

audience analysis

demographics

audience needs

topic format

space format

chronological format

stock-issues format

stock-issues

need for change

plan to solve the need

plan meets the need

burden of proof

motivated sequence format

AIDA

keep a good

getting a good

avoiding a bad

get rid of a bad

statistical evidence

narratives

testimony

visual evidence

comparison and contrast

credibility

trust

expertise

dynamism

figures of speech

vivid language

concise language

parallel structure

imagery

humor

foot-in-the-door

door-in-the-face

rejection-then-retreat

yes-yes

"don't ask if; ask which"

answering a question with a question

partial commitment

planting

IOU technique

APPLICATION OF ETHICS

A fellow student in your public speaking class gives a speech on the dangers to freedom of speech posed by renewing the Patriot Act. After listening to the speech, you realize that your classmate has made inaccurate claims based on inadequate research. Apparently the rest of your classmates are enthusiastic about her speech. You also know that she has stage fright and just getting through the speech has been a victory for her. There is a question and answer period where you could point out her inaccuracies. Should you remain silent, hoping that no harm will come to the class from hearing the speech? Or should you approach her privately and tell her that her claims are inaccurate and her research is inadequate? Or should you inform the instructor about the inaccuracies and research shortcomings?

QUESTIONS FOR FURTHER THOUGHT

1. What demographic clusters can you identify for the people in your class? In your dorm? In a club? Elsewhere? How might the Internet help you?

2. What is a task-oriented message? Give examples from ads in which persuaders used this technique effectively. Give other examples from ads in which they failed.

3. What are the forms of organization? How do they differ from the forms of support? What might be other ways to organize a message?

4. What is AIDA, and how does it differ from the motivated sequence?

5. What are Rank's desire-building tactics? How do they work?

6. What are the factors that make up a speaker's credibility? Give examples of people who have them. Find ads that rely on each factor.

7. Where does humor fit into the persuasion process? Give examples of sources that use humor. Does it relate to the audience? How? How might the Internet help you develop humor for a specific topic?

8. How can a persuader get his or her audience more involved? What are some examples you have seen or heard recently? What techniques mentioned here might help?

9. What is the difference between the forms of proof discussed here and those discussed in Chapter 8?

10. How does "planting" work? What about "getting an IOU"? What are the five senses? Can you restate a proposition using all of them?

 For online activities, go to the *Persuasion* book companion Web site at http://academic.cengage.com/communication/larson12.

13

✴

Modern Media and Persuasion

LEARNING GOALS

After reading this chapter, you should be able to:

1. Appreciate societal changes that followed the introduction of the spoken, written, printed, electronic, and interactive words.

2. Show how the interactive word has already begun to change global society.

3. Explain the resonance principle and how it relates to Schwartz's theory of evoked recall.

4. Explain and give examples of what Schwartz means by "experiential meaning."

5. Explain Marshall McLuhan's concepts of hot and cool media.

6. Explain and give examples of the various reasons people use media, as discussed in Uses and Gratifications Theory.

7. Explain and give examples of news manipulation and Agenda-Setting Theory.

8. Explain and give examples of Social Learning and Cultivation Theories.

9. Demonstrate familiarity with the wide variety of information available on the Internet.

10. Apply ethical standards to Internet communication.

Since the development of spoken language, other media of communication have developed and gradually each has superseded its predecessor in important ways; each of them has made communication and hence persuasion easier, more prevalent and enduring, and enormously more far-reaching and effective. Each of these media innovations has changed the scale and pace of human life in breathtaking ways that we can only vaguely imagine. What would it have been like to comprehend the impacts of writing when we only had speaking with which to communicate? It must have been breathtaking, and we had centuries to absorb its impact. The same must have been true for those first realizing the potentials of printing or the telegraph, telephones, and radio. And today we are being introduced to new and interactive media at what might be called "super-sonic" speed although that is too ancient of a word to accurately describe the changes we face. Let's set the stage by a brief examination of the history of five human communication innovations.

MEDIA INNOVATIONS

Each of the five major human communication innovations was tied to the development of a new medium or technology, and all have shaped and changed the world and the way we see it. These innovations or technologies are: (1) the spoken word, (2) the written word, (3) the printed word, (4) the electronic word, and (5) the interactive digital word. And it is in this fifth and final media innovation that we have most seen, experienced, and probably adopted and used in the past decade; and we will continue to see new developments in future decades, all relating to the remarkable changes facing us in the ways in which humans communicate with others and themselves and how technology affects them. These devices and activities will change forever the structure of human life as we know it, and we are already beginning to feel that great shift in human life with devices like iPods; cell phones that text, photograph, link to the Internet and are GPS devices; digital television and radio; and activities like texting, blogging, twittering; and a host of others yet to come. In a way we are expanding our roles as both sources and receivers of communication many, many fold.

The Spoken Word

The first communication innovation in human history was the ability to speak and to symbolize. As Lederer pointed out in Chapter 5, prior to language we were not truly human beings. We were just grunting, mating, killing, and consuming sorts of creatures. We sense the reverence for the **spoken word** in many avenues of human activity. In religion, for instance, the Judeo-Christian story of the creation in the book of *Genesis* indicates that each creative act was accomplished by God using the spoken word (e.g., "And God said 'Let there be light, and there was light—the first night and the first day'"). In our daily social life, this reverent attitude toward the spoken word continues even today. We must be sworn in to testify, or to speak to the court, and, except in unusual cases such as if the defendant is deaf, the judge must speak the sentence before the convicted person can be taken to prison. We rely "on a person's word," actions "speak for themselves," and we look for "the final word" on various issues. We swear in political officials with the spoken word, and we require new citizens to take a spoken oath of loyalty. The spoken word permitted humans to become social animals and to work together for the common good. It allowed one generation to pass down the history and knowledge of the tribe in myths, ballads, or legends, and thus progress could occur. The wheel didn't have to be reinvented each generation. Rules didn't have to be re-instituted (though they could be altered via the spoken word). And the spoken word led to the organization of information that could be shared by everyone—the tanning of hides, the preservation of meats and vegetables, birthing, death. In oral/aural cultures, information or knowledge is most fully held by the old; thus, age became and remained valued and honored until recently. For example, among the Lakota, every newly married couple was given an "Old One" to live in the couple's tepee for tending fires, comforting the babies, and giving advice. This helped the couple learn the lessons of parenting, marriage, and family as well, and the practice provided the Old One with a home and sustenance for life. There were no bag ladies among the Lakota nor any "nursing homes" in which to warehouse them. The spoken word still exists, of course, but not in the same way it did in an oral/aural world where it was the only means of communication (Ong, 1982). It was largely the province of the leaders—chiefs and medicine men. In the oral/aural world, and even after, the spoken word was experiential—an event that was felt and witnessed in real time—after which it disappeared. It also occupied time and not space and had to be thought over rather quickly before it was easily forgotten. It was ephemeral—the beginning of the word was gone before its end was uttered. Its only permanence was in the human mind, memory, and sometimes encapsulated in stories and legends, so people re-experienced it only by re-uttering it. One couldn't have real history with the spoken word—only a dramatic narrative of events that could be somewhat accurately recalled when the spoken event or the word was gone. It was a primitive world, but it produced many beautiful things and much wisdom and still does in some oral/aural cultures that still exist in some places in the world today.

The Written Word

The next major communication innovation was the development of the phonetic alphabet, which unlike the pictographs of the ancient Egyptian or Chinese languages, is tied to speech sounds. With this alphabet, people could collect knowledge and store it for long periods of time—far longer and more reliable than history in the old spoken word. Advances of various kinds could be based on these stored records of what others had tried to do and how. The **written word** allowed societies to develop complex sets of knowledge, legal systems (you could write down laws and not have to recall them from memory), behavior patterns and such to assign or deed land and other possessions and to declare behaviors illegal by common definition. Unlike knowledge stored in the spoken word, information in writing can be recalled very precisely—there is no reliance on the fallibility of memory for the information is truly palpable. For centuries, however, few people were literate, and thus only the rich and powerful could read and write (or afford scribes if they couldn't) so knowledge stored in writing was hoarded by the rich and powerful. Knowledge and information (and hence power) could be and was obtained and centralized by those who controlled the written word—kings, emperors, feudal lords, and church leaders. Information became individual property (scrolls, books, etc.) that could be owned and certainly not widely shared. The great ancient libraries, like the one at Alexandria, Egypt, were the repositories of society's knowledge and information, but they didn't loan out scrolls or "books" to just anyone. That would have to wait until Benjamin Franklin invented the remarkably generous concept of a lending library back in the mid 1700s. Therefore, not everyone had access to the gathered knowledge or information of the culture, and without it the average person remained ignorant and at the bottom of the social order, or peasants—it was the Dark Ages. Once writing made the ownership of knowledge possible in Europe, Asia, and elsewhere, the concept of ownership was applied to other property besides knowledge encapsulated in writing—things like land, cattle, horses, jewelry, and buildings could also be owned; whereas, in the oral/aural culture those things belonged to the tribe. It made sense that if you could own knowledge, you could own other things that symbolized, created, and ensured power. No such concept existed in the oral/aural cultures of Native North Americans, to whom the claims to land treaties, which they signed with a simple mark, were written down and kept by those in power to be used later to prove ownership of the land. To these oral/aural beings, the treaties were "worthless scraps of paper" that could be destroyed by tearing them up or casting them into a fire, but to the designers of the treaties (who kept copies) they were the law.

The written word in the treaties took up space, was not ephemeral, didn't disappear, and unlike spoken agreements, could be seen and touched time and again and lasted across generations (Ong, 1967). This permanence made people not only rely on written records for the "last word" on an issue but to respect written words. Indeed, the written word came to be thought of as far more trustworthy than the spoken word (even "holy" in a sense) as seen in the ways we preserve and honor written documents like our "Declaration of Independence." Even those who couldn't read insisted regularly on seeing the documents in writing before they would believe them and placed a high reverence in them. Even as recently as my mother's youth (about the time of WW I, people from her Scandinavian village would come to her uncle's house simply to see (not borrow and read) his single book (of course it was printed not handwritten, but the point remains). As Ong (1967) observed:

> Ancient Hebrews and Christians knew not only the spoken word but the alphabet as well .... But for them and all men of early times, the word, even when written, was much closer to the spoken word than it normally is for … technological man. Today we have often to labor to regain the awareness that the word is still always at root the spoken word. Early man had no such problem: he felt the word, even when written, as primarily an event in sound" (p. ix).

So with the written word, humans experienced an enormous change in life—especially in terms of knowledge, ownership, and power. No longer did the entire village or tribe own knowledge, but only an elite few did, and they were the ones who came to great power and ruled over the others whether in the church, in government, or throughout the rest of society. If they happened to already have power and wealth but couldn't read or write themselves, they hired scribes. So knowledge and information became and remains the equivalent of power, and even today with the advancements of print and electronic record keeping—information equals power. Imagine what would happen if all the electronic records or information of our society were wiped out in an instant (a military strategy related to the so-called "Star Wars" theory). No bank records, no laws, no permanence. Perhaps the "hard copies" of the past (writing and printing) are still critical to us today.

The Printed Word

The third communication innovation came with Johannes Gutenberg's moveable type and the printing press in the late 1400s. Of course it was just a way of duplicating its predecessor, the written word, but it could do this repeatedly and much cheaper. This made knowledge less expensive, more portable, and far more easily available to more persons. Hence print was an enormously liberating and democratic communication innovation even though it took centuries for its use to spread. The effects of spreading this power of the **printed word** to more and more "average" people were immense, beginning with more widespread literacy (of course that also took centuries and is still going on), the emergence of a middle class of merchants and tradesmen, and eventually making possible such intellectual revolutions in Europe as the Renaissance and the Reformation. Because information could be spread and shared fairly inexpensively, the "New Science" developed rapidly. Scientists could read about one another's work and experiments and build on what they had done and on the theories they proposed. Musical scores could be cheaply duplicated and sent to others, including composers who could learn and adapt the newly composed works. The same phenomenon occurred in other areas such as philosophy, commerce, and religion. People could read the writings of Martin Luther, and his objections to the Church, and they were printed and distributed widely. The notions of serfdom were superseded by the idea of individual ownership of land or a business. And governments weren't unaware of this diffusion of knowledge—such a thing could be dangerous! As a defensive measure, soon most of them set up censorship policies to help them control this potentially dangerous spread of information. Not until John Peter Zenger was tried for sedition for printing a tract criticizing a British colonial governor did the notion of freedom of the press come into being. Curiously, Zenger was tried not for writing the criticism but for printing it. The British government held all printers responsible for what they published, in effect making every printer an unofficial censor.

Like the power of the spoken and written words, the power of the printed word has diminished but still remains potent as any illiterate person trying to read a job application will tell you. Although the number of newspapers published in the United States has actually increased since the advent of television, readership of both newspapers and news is down—sometimes to as little as eight minutes a day, and the average age of newspaper readers is becoming older and older—few persons younger than 35 read one regularly, and only a small portion subscribe. Besides your student paper, what others do you read? Besides your assigned text and other readings, how many books do you read for general knowledge and entertainment?

Remember that more than 30 percent of the U.S. population is functionally illiterate today, meaning that they can't read such simple things as menus, directions for operating appliances, labels, and street signs. In the nineteenth century the literacy rate was nearly 90 percent for similar everyday purposes (Kaplan, Wingert, & Chideya, 1993). Some estimates indicate that even those who do read newspapers today devote their time to only special sections of interest to them and not to important "issue" pages like the editorial or business pages. The rate of book reading in the United States is less than one-third of a book per year per person, and that includes students like you.

Yes, the printed word brought about a veritable revolution in many areas of human accomplishment. Musical scores, scientific theories, and artistic images were readily exchanged among scientists, composers, and artists across national boundaries, and those who read or saw these items learned from one another's works. In terms of persuasion, the printed word ultimately gave us widespread literacy, and greatly influenced the way people formulated and shared their thoughts. Literacy in the Western world led to a new view of humans as unique individuals and led to great discoveries and inventions in Europe, America, and elsewhere. Literacy also resulted from shared knowledge via print. Interestingly enough, literacy perhaps made childhood necessary (and surely extended it) by making protracted formal education and literacy both possible and essential if one were to have a chance to succeed in business or civic life. Prior to the printed word, children were considered to be just like tiny adults and were sent to work in the coal mines, city streets, or farm fields just like the grownups. It took time, but eventually the emerging middle class realized that it was essential for their children to learn to read and write and so set aside a time of life for the kids to learn to do those things. That was the beginning of childhood. My emigrant parents did not go past sixth grade, but they were tremendously advantaged over other illiterate immigrants when it came to getting jobs, moving up in society, and training their children to achieve even more than they themselves had. And of course the many new immigrants we have today feel the same way and honor the printed word in similar ways.

The Electronic Word

The **electronic word** came into being in 1844 with the invention of the telegraph. Of course, it didn't supersede books for it couldn't rapidly transmit books or even lengthy messages; but it could transmit dots and dashes which, when decoded, communicated words and, thus, short messages with meaning. But more far-reaching and truly communicative inventions utilizing electricity were soon on the way in numerous forms of the electronic word. The successor to the telegraph—the "wireless" or radio, which also transformed dots and dashes, was ultimately to translate the electrical impulses into spoken words via electronically produced sound waves, and not long afterward was actually sending human speech through the airwaves to homes across the globe—to most it must have seemed remarkable. It is possible to get a glimmering of the effect these inventions had from a quaint example. While the Pony Express got a written message across the country in just 10 days, people could telegraph the message in minutes. In a sense, the electronic word wiped out not only space but time as well. People now could learn almost immediately about election results, sports events, catastrophes, stock and commodity prices, and joyous and sad family events.

In 1876, came the telephone, transforming the spoken word into electronic impulses that could be transmitted long distances via wires and could be understood as words and complete messages, thus almost eliminating space. The "distance" between New York and Boston could be measured in mi-

croseconds, not miles, as far as communication was concerned. Other channels of the electronic word—television, computers, video games, cell phones, VCRs, DVDs, CDs, and a host of others—are now bringing similarly remarkable changes to society as a whole, and as a result, we are undergoing similarly awesome changes in our individual lives. Some critics claim that this explosion of electronic media adversely affects us and may soon make us incapable of interacting with others on any truly face-to-face level, but only via a machine, thus creating a nation of isolates cocooned in front of computer screens. There may be some truth to that. For example, few of us ever writes a letter to another person anymore; we rely instead on e-mail. Imagine what kind of history can be recovered in the future from your e-mails versus the history retrieved from the extensive correspondences which persons exchanged in past times. In those days, many people set aside special times of the day and places from which to carry on these correspondences. People are also concerned about the amount of screen time being watched by the average U.S. child and the kinds of effects this is having on all kinds of human behavior including violent behavior, development of the brain, human relationships, and so on (Larson, 2009).

We live in a world in which electronic and print messages literally surround us—on billboards and in newsletters, magazines, catalogs, signs on shopping carts (some of which speak to you as you pass the shelves), Internet banners, unwanted spam and pop-ups, telemarketing, electronic kiosks in airport terminals, demonstration videos in supermarkets, ads in restrooms and more. Despite even newer technologies like TiVo or iPod that allow viewers to bypass ads, electronic mass media are still the most effective channels to persuade us to buy products, to vote for candidates, and to take up or join and donate to causes, sometimes without giving the actions much serious thought. One reason is that these electronic messages are inherently oral/aural in nature. That is, in the same way that spoken words are ephemeral or fleeting, electronic signals or images are also fleeting and ephemeral unless we choose to record them in some way.

We *experience* them more than we logically think them through, and we probably process them in the peripheral channel of the ELM and therefore fail to critically investigate them. In one way or another they reflect parts of our 24/7, networked and multicultural world of results-oriented advocacy and/or propaganda mentioned under the Seven Faces of Persuasion. And, of course, there is a multitude of other information one could bring up in regard to the quickly emerging and changing world of electronic media aimed at us as receivers. But, there is a new kind of electronic word impinging on our lives—the interactive word.

The Interactive Word

As I understand it, with the newest communication innovation of our times—interactive media—messages speed-up; have higher "definition" to use McLuhan's term, or greater fidelity in more colloquial terms' and as a result, become more numerous and ultimately less expensive to send and receive. Receivers can get much more into the act than with earlier electronic media. In a way we are reverting to an aural/oral world. but now it is with the experience and knowledge of print technology, literacy, and the electronic word. That is, we are rapidly becoming more able to be both source and receiver, even though we don't always use spoken words to do that. We are just beginning to deal with this new and highly dynamic communication channel, and we don't know quite what to make of it yet. It can be used in a variety of ways. Interaction via texting, for example, aids in cheating on tests and also bypasses most eavesdropping. Many persons today pay more attention to cell phones than they do to land lines or, of course, traffic; and Wii is becoming an important therapy in hospitals and nursing homes and assisted-living facilities instead of being considered a new kind of video game. The **interactive word** is more ephemeral than either the written or the spoken word even though we can retrieve it—at least out of the trash, the "C" drive, or some other device if needed.

To date, the electronic word has affected us mostly as receivers—we have been consuming more messages from these media than we have produced messages for them. Few of us produce broadcast television messages, and all of us consume them, but we can and do use interactive media to produce on-screen video that we can "narrowcast" to our friends and others. We can enter into chat groups and interact with persons we do not and never will "know" in the traditional sense. Advertising can invite us to "enter" it and "play" with it in ways the old advertising could never accommodate. And multiple other examples of various kinds of interactivity could be mentioned now or are soon on the way. So, while the audience is far smaller than in previous times, the interactive word has encouraged us to not only interact more often with others by geometric degrees, but it has also let us become skilled at producing effective persuasive messages to convince and challenge those audiences.

Yes, with newly emerging interactive media, we are becoming more and more both producers and consumers of messages. Consider just one of these interactive media—the at-one-time widely scoffed-at virtual reality technology, for example. At first, it was considered another sort of video war game that was entertaining because it had 360-degree surround sound and vision, but it was not considered of much true commercial use. But new and impressive uses have resulted from this technology of electronic interactivity. For example, surgeons now conduct virtual surgery for training purposes long before the actual highly technical and remote operation happens. Following enough "perfect" replications of the actual operation, the robotic laser scalpels are programmed, using the virtual operation, to perform the actual physical cutting and suturing. And most of the sorties flown in the 1990s was in Iraq and today's wars, there and elsewhere, were and are "rehearsed" in V.R. Many predict that virtual reality will soon replace the showroom floor or retail outlet in stores for "virtual shopping" and then what will we do with all those strip malls? Almost 20 years ago, Charles Madigan (1993) was criticized when he described a hypothetical virtual purchase this way:

B O X 13.1 Interactive Ralph Lauren

Madigan's prediction, now nearly 20 years old, seemed like a fantasy back then. To see how his imagination matches up with today's reality look at the similarity between what he described then and what is operating in our interactive world now by going to http://www.selfservice.org/article_1903_2.php. Read about his new kind of "window shopping" on Madison Avenue.

A customer in his or her own living room facing a bigger-than-life fully digitized television screen will say, "Shop Ralph Lauren." After a pause of only a few seconds, the image of Ralph Lauren will come, smiling to life on the screen.... Ralph will ask for some particulars.... Perhaps price will be discussed.... It won't really be Ralph Lauren.... More accurately, it will be virtual Ralph having a virtual conversation (p. 14).

Funny then but examine Box 13.1 for the near reality of his prediction.

Already you can try on items of clothing in "virtual reality" and on the screen alter the color schemes, accessories, sizes, and so on, and add or subtract what you wish. Other possible uses for virtual reality technology include such things as virtual golf lessons, perhaps taught by a virtual Tiger Woods using Wii. And imagine what the pornography industry might do with this new and disengaged interactive technology—one hesitates to imagine the possibilities—especially since there are already over 8 million pornographic Web sites available for the average voyeur. The military is particularly interested in this interactive media and how it can be used to measure the endurance of its troops under certain conditions (e.g., heat, humidity, freezing temps, carrying various weights of baggage). One only needs to stop and think of the possible applications of the interactive word to find that they too are breathtaking. This is one of the reasons we have included at least one interactive box in each chapter of this book—to remind you of the possibilities. Of course many of them are merely "fun," but then warfare on the interactive screen might be la-

beled "fun" by some persons as well. In a way, the interactive world involves the print, audio/video, and computer industries all at the same time.

According to Stewart Brand's (1987) description, these three industries realized over 20 years ago that phenomenal changes in communication technology were inevitable and that the ability to develop them effectively and prudently was far improved by pooling their resources. So the Media Lab at MIT was invented and funded, sought out the brightest and best media researchers, and asked them to literally "invent the future" in the various communications industries. The three industries were already beginning to converge before the Media Lab was instituted, as shown in Figure 13.1. Some examples of this convergence or overlapping of media include print that is computer typeset and enhanced visually by digital video technology, or computer-generated and produced video graphics, and electronic mail, faxes, and digital audio. Even some print ads, like birthday greeting cards, contain a chip that plays music like "Happy Birthday" when opened, and no one is surprised anymore. Some observers foresee a much broader convergence of the three technologies

Look at Brand's predicted new configuration, which he made years ago, and consider how the convergence has become even more unified in recent times as seen in Figure 13.2.

Already the predicted changes exceed by far Brand's wildest dreams of even a few decades ago, particularly when we consider the description of an interactive media department store as discussed in Box 13.2. A brief example demonstrates this point. Brand predicted, "Twenty years from now your TV set will probably have 50 megabytes of random access memory and run at 40 to 50 MIPS [millions

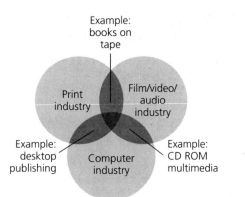

Example: books on tape

Print industry

Film/video/ audio industry

Example: desktop publishing

Computer industry

Example: CD ROM multimedia

FIGURE 13.1
The convergence of the print, film/video/audio, and computer industries and technology in the 1990s.

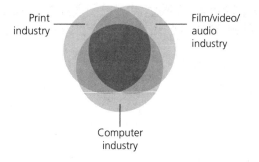

Print industry

Film/video/ audio industry

Computer industry

FIGURE 13.2
The convergence of the print, film/video/audio, and computer industries and technology today and in the future.

of information pieces per second]. It'll basically be a Cray computer" (Brand, 1987, pp. 77–78). While we're not there yet, we have come a long way and are closing in on Brand's predictions. In England, it is now possible to order goods and services directly over your television using an upgraded type pf remote control. Did all this change just suddenly appear or were there some who predicted that it would come and how it might be used to persuade us? Of course, the answer is "yes," and we will focus on the work of two of the most insightful of these innovative theorists who dared to imagine the future. They are both widely recognized as true pioneers in the study of media effects. One theorized more about the content of these amazing new media and how the messages sent via them would persuade; and the other theorized more about the media themselves and how the physics of their signals pattern our habits of being persuaded, both physiologically and psychologically, and how they ultimately shape our entire culture.

The work of these two important media theory pioneers—Tony Schwartz and Marshall McLuhan—can help us understand the experiential nature of the current electronic interactive technology and how and why it is so very effective in the process of persuasion so that we can begin to prepare for the nearly unbelievable developments we have been encountering in the recent

times and to get ready for the many more that we will have to encounter in the years ahead. Their theories can help us to become, accustomed to the changing world of the resulting persuasion and to use and be persuaded by those media. For both of them validity of their theories, like proof, is "in the pudding" or in the degree to which what they predicted early on in the electronic age has come true and persists in the persuasion each of us faces today.

SCHWARTZ'S PERSPECTIVES ON MEDIA USE

The ideas in Tony Schwartz's book *The Responsive Chord* (1973, 1983) have been used by sources ranging from presidential media staffs to business firms and ad agencies selling everything from baby powder to booze. Since its publication, Schwartz has consulted and still consults with politicians, industry, the mass media, and the government. In 2007, the Library of Congress decided to archive a complete compilation of his work from 1947 to 1999 as a resource for scholars wanting to study the growth of modern audio, television, and electronic communication technologies (Library of Congress, 2007). Schwartz's original interest was in radio (the understanding of which he believes is basic and essential for understanding all electronic

---

B O X 13.2   Interactive Media and "Department Store" Shopping

Most of us already shop for some things online, such as books and clothing, but what about an interactive site with a mega-menu that tops most major department stores? Go to www.shopping.com and surf through the multitude of options there, ranging from 11,000 baseball cards with price comparisons from over 20 sources or an online college degree in interactive media or interactive branding. Enter whatever you are shopping for at the top of the page and select from the categories in the next space. Click the "find" button and explore the interactive mega-market, which could run to thousands of options. What might sites like this do to traditional in-store, television, and catalog shopping? How might a political candidate use a similar site to compare positions on various issues, to solicit voter input, or to raise money? Check out http://technabob.com/blog/2007/01/23/spring-board-interactive-shopping-carts/ and see how the shopping cart in your local supermarket will be interacting with you to remind you of special offers, and so on. Or see how to get a custom-tailored suit in more than 1,000 styles and many more colors at http://www.idalot.com/shopping/recommendations.htm where your measurements are taken and clothing is custom-made electronically. Imagine how else this technology will impact our individual and personal lives in the future.

---

communication) and how radio was/is able to create emotional and highly involving effects in its listeners. Later he came to believe his theory also explained the effects of television—especially commercials—and other electronic communication technologies. One of his most famous commercials called "Daisy" is a classic in negative political campaigning. He has produced over 30,000 radio and TV spots for candidates, corporations, and not-for-profits. He has also demonstrated how citizens who feel neglected by the electronic media can use it in irregular and surprising ways, called "guerilla advertising" by some.

His theory compares two competing models for explaining the way radio and television media work to persuade us: (1) the **evoked recall** (or "resonance") model and (2) the transportation model, which is also called a "teaching" model. The outcome in the first approach is a highly emotional and motivating (almost physiological) recollection of past memories which move us to action, while the second relies on a belief that receivers are more logical and that they learn and believe in good reasons for why they should act as directed. Schwartz favors the first approach and offers reasons related to how we remember and learn at least some of the lessons of life. He has been called a "media guru," a "media muscleman," and a "media genius;" and the tobacco industry voluntarily agreed to stop their advertising on radio and television after viewing one of his anti-smoking commercials. (See http://www.tonyschwartz.org/ for many resources—audio and video—in which he explains or demonstrates his theory in action, and get insights to his theory at http://www.emusic.com/features/spotlight/293_200708-btn-tony-schwartz.html.)

Resonance and Experiential Meaning

As Kathleen Hall Jamieson, Dean of the Annenburg Scool of communication notes, Schwartz's theory closely resembles a concept put forth by Aristotle called "empathematic" communication, which means that the receiver becomes essential in creating meaning. This fits nicely with the communication of persuasion put forth in Chapter 1. Schwartz labeled his ideas the "evoked recall model" of communication, which rests on the "resonance principle," which is defined as using messages or message elements that almost unconsciously cue out meanings that receivers already have stored in their conscious or unconscious minds and which combine with the source's cues to create emotional and/or logical meaning. This recollection of past memories connects with present-day events and circumstances resulting in a harmony or a "resonance" between source, message, and receiver. The basic idea is that it is better to get "messages out of receivers" that will motivate them to action than to try to put, plant, or teach information into their memories, which they will then hopefully recall accurately when the time comes for action. In other words, the resonance principle relies on the sets of experiences and memories that people already have stored inside their heads. This set of past experiences can be cued to produce what Schwartz called "**experiential meaning**" via the resonance principle. It's as if the receiver says, "I've been there," after getting the message, and thus the source's reference to the stored experience resonates with the audience in the same way that notes of music resonate or harmonize with one another.

Using this approach, persuaders might address the problems people have, such as a stalled car, a stolen identity, a problematic child, or paying back a student loan. The potential buyer of a Triple A membership knows what a stalled auto is like, and the source can use that experience (or "experiential meaning" to use Schwartz's term) to build a persuasive message around those feelings that will convince you to join AAA even though you might never have given it any previous consideration. Actors in the ad might show frustration exactly like yours at having your car stall at just the most inconvenient time. Their verbal and nonverbal cues, coupled with the proper musical core, might signal the anxiety motorists have felt when they knew a stall would make them miss the commuter train, the important appointment, or meeting the critical person, and thus prevent them from accomplishing important things at work, in their personal lives and in other ways. As noted, technical effects like the music or score can heighten those fears using suspenseful sounds as the stall slowly becomes apparent to the motorist and perhaps stressful clanging as their appointment "emerges" in their mind's eye. The voice-over might then say soothingly, "When you've got to be there, Triple A gets you there." And we can then observe our now relaxed motorist cell phoning AAA accompanied by serene music as the driver starts to daydream about how successful his or her meeting will be. Schwartz observed that most experiential meanings such as those depicted in the ad are not usually cued with words in one's conscious memory because the experience and

feelings are not really stored in words. Instead, it is stored as a physiological feeling in the pit of our stomach or a sense of ease or uneasiness when problems disappear or emerge in our daily lives. We all know what it feels like to be embarrassed, and our recollection of that can be cued out of us in ways similar to the AAA ad described above.

The same is true for other emotions, such as those discussed in Chapter 7. And they are coming at us more and more dramatically in our 24/7, networked world of deceptive and dangerous persuasion for which we must be prepared. In all likelihood these cues are processed in the peripheral channel of the ELM. The surest way to cue such powerful and emotional feelings out of most receivers is via dramatic enactments (or the narrative), the importance of which we have discussed at length elsewhere. The source's message dramatizes the feeling in the receiver's unconscious memory through music, color, sound effects, the actors' facial expressions or tone of voice, the acoustics, or some other nonverbal and usually visual or auditory image or message—all communicated electronically. This experiential cue creates actual physical feelings in us, according to Schwartz, and results in the kind of cocreated meaning discussed in Chapter 1.

One of Schwartz's most famous and critical examples is the iconic and famous "Daisy" ad mentioned above. It was used in the 1964 Presidential campaign at a time when the country greatly feared nuclear war with the U.S.S.R. They had seen the destruction of Hiroshima and numerous televised nuclear tests. In the commercial the viewer processes the sounds and sights of a little girl counting the petals she pulls off a daisy which then merge with the countdown 10…9…8…7 and so on of a nuclear test—something with which viewers of that time would have been very familiar. This is finally accompanied by the mushroom cloud of a nuclear bomb, followed by a voice-over asking which candidate you want in charge. The images and sounds made viewers feel threatened and emotionally insecure—afraid in the pits of their stomachs—and the ad re-created those experiences and those feelings of fear and insecurity as the voice-over identified nuclear weapons with candidate Barry Goldwater who had previously suggested using nuclear weapons. We saw a Hillary Clinton commercial in the 2008 Presidential primaries which was quite similar. It featured a sleeping child and the visual of a ringing and flashing of the White House "nuclear hotline," after which the voice-over asked a similar question. It apparently did not have the same impact of the 1964 ad which many at the time thought had swung the entire election to LBJ. In terms of Schwartz's resonance theory, this makes perfect sense. Viewers in 2008 did not have the same experiential fears about nuclear war in their memories. They had never seen televised nuclear tests, demolished buildings, vaporized test dummies, and so on and had never been through a nuclear drill at school; not had they been unable to go to sleep for worrying over the possibility of such an attack. In other words, the ad had no "resonance" with the receivers.

Well, what are some stored experiences and emotions that are common to large numbers of people today and how can an electronic media interact with internal experiential memories in receivers to cue a recall of them? The job of persuaders is to try to catalog and use these experiential memories in their persuasive arsenals and be ready to pull them out when encountering a set of persuadees for whom these experiential meanings are stored, meaningful, and critical. Then the persuaders must design persuasion to tap those feelings and experiences. We've looked at the stalled car example already. Some others might include: (1) forgetting an important anniversary or event, (2) a plugged toilet or sink, (3) missing out on a great sale or important event, (4) losing one's wallet or car keys, and so on. Any event or situation—everyday or extraordinary—which you or I have experienced and to which people respond by saying something like "You're getting awfully close to home" probably is evoking experiential meaning in that/those receivers. Mass media persuaders, especially advertisers, cue out these resonating experiences using electronic and or interactive media in most cases. As you examine the media persuasion aimed at you in magazine ads, TV and radio spots, billboards, the Internet, or in interactive media, try to identify the common experiences being targeted in your experiential storehouse and the storehouses of others in the

greater audience. In all likelihood, we process such experiential meanings in the peripheral channel of the ELM without much intellectual evaluation or introspection. Instead, they simply "feel right," and we let them pass through the peripheral channel, taking them in at face value. In other words they are "resonating" in a **responsive chord** that "rings true" to us and leads to co-created persuasion that causes purchase, joining, or voting behavior—all of which are critical in the results oriented world of the Seven Faces of Persuasion. There are several "scripts" which can cue out these powerful meanings, especially now with virtual reality (e.g., the smell or olfactory script as in scratch-and-sniff ads or the use of various cues to the senses in 4-D movies now available at many theme parks) that can cue out these meanings, thus implementing Schwartz's resonance principle and resulting evoked recall.

We shall discuss three of them that are most familiar to the broader population. They are the verbal script, the visual script, and the auditory script. Depending on future technological developments, other scripts related to the physical senses will certainly emerge. Let us explore these three familiar scripts to discover how clever persuaders are using our experiential memories to convince us by strumming on our "responsive cords" and our experiential memory sets. Schwartz's suggestions seem to be even more true today than when he first wrote about them in those pioneer days of mass media research. You can think of the channels through which evoked recall can be prompted as the verbal, auditory, and visual "scripts" for, as media are being produced, their originators much look at all three.

The Verbal Script

Schwartz's ideas run counter to what many ad agencies practice in developing and testing commercials and to much persuasion theory, which emphasizes specificity, logic, and word choice in building and more importantly in testing the headlines and copy for most ads. Those ads and theories test such things as recall of specific statements, the logic of them, and the effects of the language of the copywriters, in prompting the desired behavior—purchase, donation, commitment, or other. In Schwartz's opposing view, the **verbal script** is the message in words that we see or hear, but more importantly this script is more than the mere information the words that are remembered. It includes the emotional feelings that they evoke in the receiver. When most ad agencies test their ads, they usually ask people to look at various ads and then to recall the words, images, statistics, and names in the ad. Rarely are respondents asked about their feelings or experiences, or about relating to the characters in the ads, which is what Schwartz does when he tests ads. For him, if the verbal script resonates and cues experiences from the audience, powerful results usually occur and remain long after the ephemeral words of the ad are gone. For example, a recent radio ad for a brokerage firm cued the experience of being trapped by an automated telephone answering system and its menu. The ad said, "If you want to check your balance, press 1 now. If you want to get a quote, press 2 now. If you want to talk to a real financial advisor, press 8 now and start over. Or try calling Financial Expertise at 1-800-MONEYAID." This message is probably processed in the peripheral channel of the ELM; because of its experiential nature, we all listen (and probably chuckle) to the ad because we've all had the experience of having to wait through similar irritating automated menus and despise them. That feeling is what makes the ad work, and it helps us remember the easily recalled phone number and how we despise the menu after menu of pre-recorded messages.

The Auditory Script

The typical TV spot also has an **auditory or sound script**, which are the things you hear that are not words. They are the "language" of sound—sizzles, pops, grinds, klunks, plops, and buzzes—that can often cue powerful, unconscious emotions like Schwartz describes and which he credits for the most powerful and persuasive message elements or "responsive cords" to which we are likely to respond. For instance, good feelings about parties could be cued by the sounds of beer being poured in mugs rather than by words that talk about the party. Of course the advertiser usually simply adds some words to reinforce the powerful feeling that the sounds have already called up: "We've got beer in a can that's as good as beer from a keg—Hamm's draft in the new aluminum can." This auditory script is then further reinforced by the positive musical score and more evocative sound effects such as laughing or beer-chugging sounds.

We have all had experiences cued out of our collective storehouses of auditory memories. For example, take a prize-winning classic ad for Diet Coke that was targeted at working women ages 18 to 34 a few years back. These women are the typical drinkers of diet cola but more importantly are in the age group when powerful brand loyalty is developed. We see and hear the murmurings of a group of attractive women starting to gather at the drinking fountain at break time, and we sense that something important is about to happen. They are laughing and joking with one another even though we don't hear their words. Soon they are all looking out the window, and one says something like, "Okay, it's time" (the only words spoken in the action portion of the ad or its verbal script). The camera cuts to a handsome muscular male construction worker across the street as he peels off his T-shirt revealing the body of a muscle builder (the visual script). The women sigh (again not words but sounds or the auditory script) as he pops open a Diet Coke and swigs it down. The words are practically nonexistent and irrelevant because it is the sounds of the women murmuring and sighing coupled with the sight of the male worker stripping off his shirt to reveal his physique that together made the ad work. These sounds and sights act as cues for the experience of voyeuristic lusting in the minds of the women in the ad, probably of the women watching it, and perhaps providing general viewers with at least a touch of humor watching the reality of female sexuality being dramatically revealed. There is nothing logical about the ad or in the responses it cues from viewers. There is little an advertising researcher could test regarding the actual copy used in the ad—it has only a few words. It works for reasons other than clever words—again, in Schwartz's terms, it "resonates" with the audience. The same kinds of experiences can be cued out of receivers in a variety of media contexts—an entertainment program, a radio spot ad, or a print ad containing a musical chip playing a "Jingle Bells" while advertising the ideal Christmas gift. They would all rely on stored experiential memories associated with a particular auditory cue like a sound effect or a musical score. Each (or taken together) would lead to a co-created or "empathematic" meaning.

The Sight or Visual Script

The **sight or visual script** also serves as an important source of experiential cues. Several cues happen in the Diet Coke ad—the male's muscles, his sweaty T-shirt being peeled off, and so on. In another example, we see (and hear) Liquid Plumber clearing an impossibly plugged kitchen sink as the yucky water whirlpools out of the plugged drain with a slurping sound. Another way the sight script cues feelings is by using various camera angles and movement as well as skillful visual editing—all things most beginning film students are taught. A low angle distorts size somewhat and says that this person is someone to be looked up to, is a cut above most people, and is probably a leader who is to be trusted and believed or a larger-than-life and fearful villain or monster. Quick-cut edits of new cars coming out of a tight S curve can convey a sense of action, power, and control. A snowmobile cuts through a huge snowdrift, suggesting action and excitement. The view then cuts quickly to downhill racers carving their way through a tough slalom course and bouncing through tough moguls, and then a final quick cut shows ice-boat racers zooming across a frozen lake and skidding around the iceboat race course skidding to a stoop at the finish line. Not until the end of the ad does the verbal script say, "Warm Up Winter This Year. Come to the Winter Wonderland of Lake Geneva." The ad then closes by showing an attractive couple snuggling in front of the fireplace in the ski lodge, and we all know that it's the end of a perfect day without a single word being spoken. An experiential feeling (e.g., the satisfaction we feel at the end of a taxing but remarkably enjoying day) is again cued out of receivers with only a few words being spoken if at all. The visual script does most of the work here. It builds the excitement and cues experiential meanings from the audience's subconscious. The verbal script tagged at the end of the spot merely tells viewers that Lake Geneva is where experiences like these happen and where memories can be brought to life.

Other aspects of the sight script include the set, costumes, props, and other visual things that continue the job of evoking experiential responses from us and thus resonating and resulting in co-created meaning. For example, many newscasts convey a "busy newsroom atmosphere" using a visual script that shows machines churning out copy for fast-breaking news stories while people rush around the set carrying pieces of paper meant to be news flashes; it looks like the anchorperson is engulfed in a functional and hectically busy newsroom. The actual anchors who read the news stories are in another room in front of a blue screen, which is simply superimposed on the staged newsroom that is meant to give the visual impression that they are in the middle of the hustle and bustle. Similarly, the background shots for political candidates can cue nuances of meaning. If candidates are standing in front of the Lincoln Memorial with the President, they must be devoted to issues of equality and justice. If they gather with a bunch of bowlers or drinkers at a local watering hole, they must be regular "guys." And though it's hackneyed for politicians to be shown kissing babies during parades, it also probably cues out experiential memories in many people. The visual script, especially when taken with the auditory script, may be far more powerful, persuasive, and memorable than the words that accompany the sights and sounds.

The titles of Schwartz's books, *The Responsive Chord* and *Media: The Second God*, both reflect the relationship between the audience and the message that is cued out by advertisements, the articles printed in magazines, banners on the Internet, or the programs we see on TV or the films we watch.

B O X 13.3   Resonance and Today's Propaganda

In a collection of quotations from propaganda experts, Kenneth Warren and John Guscott (2000) cite many examples of the resonance principle being used in propaganda. Go to http://www.lkwdpl.org/wildideas/propaganda.html and read a few examples and maybe report them back to the class. There is also an interesting discussion of how resonance worked in helping bring about the propaganda leading to the war in Iraq at http://bravenewfilms.org/ as well as video images and examples. To see how the resonance principle meshes with the work of Marshall McLuhan go to http://www.media-studies.ca/articles/echoland.htm.

Think of any of the familiar chase scenes in most thrillers—no words just sights and sounds—and we all end up on the edge of our seats, perhaps with adrenalin pumping through our veins. Schwartz also noted that the issue of truth is irrelevant in examining this kind of persuasion. In fact, that is what makes his principle and its accompanying scripts the raw material of contemporary propaganda as seen in Box 13.3.

Today, we see print ads with little or no copy that present a potentially dramatic script that could be brought to life on a television screen using the resonance principle and few words, relying instead on sights and sounds. You will see this principle being used by advertisers in the storyboard of an Acura Integra ad, shown in Figure 13.3. The ad aims at graying baby boomers who recall the experience of playing with a toy called "Hot Wheels" when they were kids. You may have played with a similar toy in your youth and could be a target for a similarly designed ad in the future. The script resonates with these experiences stored in the target's conscious or unconscious mind and uses the visual and auditory scripts to cue out experiential meanings shared by the intended receivers. Of course, the ad intends to use to experiential memories to prompt receivers to purchase the car. Persuaders identify such common experiences and then design print or electronic ads that prompt audiences to recall the experience while also mentioning the brand, candidate, or cause.

As it is used in contemporary advertising, Schwartz's resonance principle presents receivers of persuasion with several challenges. They need to identify common experiences that the persuasion aims to prompt out of them. They may need to analyze persuasive messages that plant such experiences to be triggered later at the point of purchase, voting, or donating. They also need to be aware of relationships between the verbal, auditory, and visual elements in any persuasion.

McLUHAN'S PERSPECTIVES ON MEDIA USE

The Modern Media Revolution

Marshall McLuhan (1963) has been called the "first father and leading prophet of the electronic age" and the "high priest of pop culture" (Kappelman, 2008). You may want to briefly learn who he was and why he is so important today as a pioneer of the electronic age like Schwartz was, If so, go to http://som1.csudh.edu/faculty/cis/lpress/articles/macl.htm (Press, 1995) where you will find a brief biography and some of his thoughts and slogans that seem extraordinarily current. He was the author of 36 widely acclaimed books on electronic media. Like Schwartz, he was also remarkably accurate in anticipating media effects and was thought of as a true media pioneer and perhaps a prophet of the future. As a result, his 40-year-old predictions, such as the **development of a "global village,"** the Internet, virtual reality, and other prophesies related to the media of modern times, have become far more than the simplistic messages that they carry. He also called

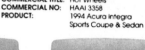

30 Second Television Commercial
COMMERCIAL TITLE: "Hot Wheels"
COMMERCIAL NO: HAAI 3358
PRODUCT: 1994 Acura Integra
                  Sports Coupe & Sedan

MUSIC AND SFX THROUGHOUT

Introducing the new 1994
Acura Integra.

Not since Hot Wheels®...

have cars been this much
fun.

Track sold separately.

© 1993 Acura Division of American Honda Motor Co. Inc. Acura and Integra are registered trademarks of
Honda Motor Co., Ltd. VTEC is a trademark of Honda Motor Co., Ltd. Make an intelligent decision. Buckle up.

FIGURE 13.3 This ad for the Acura Integra taps into the experience of having played with a Hot Wheels racetrack, thus resonating with the experiences of its target audience—male baby boomers and others who enjoyed the toy.

SOURCE: Reprinted by permission of American Honda Motor Co.

Tony Schwartz his "disciple" with 20 years of experience. The accuracy of his predictions can be partially realized by reading Box 13.4.

We might take the ubiquitous cell phone as an example of this global village. For example, not that many years ago you could only call Europe using a land line and sometimes only through an operator. As a child, I recall "booking" a call to my grand-parents in Sweden several weeks prior to Christmas for the annual phone call. Today you can make the same call from your car and for pennies compared to what is cost back then, thus fulfilling McLuhan's prediction of the global village and modern media's ability to "destroy space." On a proportional basis, very few truly essential messages are transmitted using cell phones, but who could live without

B O X 13.4   Interactivity with Marshall McLuhan

 If you want a quick and somewhat personal interaction with McLuhan and what he might have said about You Tube go to http://www.google.com/search?num=20 &hl=en&q=marshall+mcLuhan&btnG=Search where you will find video footage of him discussing media as extensions of our senses and bodies. Other short videos of him discussing such topics as cyberspace, the Internet, the "medium is the message," and other interesting parts of his theories are available. For a quick but excellent overview of his work go to http://www.leaderu.com/orgs/probe/docs/mcluhan.html.

one nowadays? Certainly none of my students can. Cell phones have become devices which I must outlaw being during exams (because answers to test items can be easily texted to one's friends in the class, and because the exams themselves can easily be photographed and quickly put into fraternity files).

The destruction of space and other of McLuhan's predictions are just now coming to pass. We saw the global village in action when nearly 100 countries around the world sent help to the victims of Hurricane Katrina in late 2005. A recent book by one of his critics is entitled *The Virtual McLuhan* (Theall, 2002), and his popularity is experiencing an enormous rebirth. Once again he is being labeled the "guru of new media," and most of his works are being reissued due to the relevance of his work. His work is being examined from the perspective of the new media, including interactive ones. As we said, he predicted virtual reality, cyberspace, the Internet, and that information would become the crucial commodity of the future—and all 40 years ago and long before any of the needed technology was even invented. See http://www.media-studies.ca/articles/echoland.htm for a quick overview.

McLuhan thought that most people were looking at the present through a "rearview mirror," viewing the past instead of the future and trying to use history as a guide to decisions and actions of the future. That's probably how we are looking at the mushrooming of terrorist organizations and their actions—we assume their past actions will be repeated and then we go about taking actions and enacting laws designed to prevent similar actions in the future. In reality, the past actions will probably not be repeated and new (and perhaps deadlier) tactics will be employed—Who would have predicted that someone would use a shoe for hiding an explosive device on airplanes? Yet you and I have to take off our shoes every time we want to get on a plane—I'm glad he didn't hide the explosives in his underwear. And who would have predicted that Wii technology would be used not so much as an entertaining video game but as a therapeutic technique in assisted-living facilities? Who would have predicted 40 years ago that we could shop online, and that information would become the prime product of our culture today with millions of Web sites from which to choose and glean it simply by entering a few key words into a search engine. And virtual reality is here for real—it's not just another video game, but the place where many things will be invented, designed, engineered, marketed, and accomplished in the future. Yes, McLuhan had much to tell us—especially about persuasion and being persuaded in an electronic and interactive age.

If you type the words "Marshall McLuhan" into any search engine, you will find that his work has taken on new relevancy in an interactive media age. Four years ago I found over 50,000 entries. Today I found 1,140,000. His relevancy is immediate, cogent, and still prophetic. McLuhan's most often quoted idea was that "The medium is the message" by which he meant that the effect any new medium has on culture is much greater than the actual messages it carries as we just noted. The invention of print is a good example as we noted above. The Renaissance was much more important than the books that were printed at the time. It became a whole new way of thinking, acting, and organizing. Television as a medium was much more important for its impact on modern life than any television programming has been. We were entertained by "I Love Lucy", but we were not really informed by the program. Instead, we were introduced to a new way of life. Your parents and grandparents had to learn a whole new way of family living and learning. We got live news on TV instead of yesterday's news in today's newspaper, and now we can get it 24/7. People used to wait impatiently for the delivery of the day's newspaper to get the latest stock reports, weather predictions, fast-breaking news stories, and more. Today fewer and fewer subscribe to a newspaper, especially if they are under age 35, and fewer yet read more than a few pages, which are usually in favorite sections like sports. Now, we can overdose on the news to the degree that it almost seems as if there is nothing that is really "new" news anymore—just the same re-runs of the 20-minute news cycle we hear on all news radio stations, and it doesn't matter if you watch FOX, CNN, MSNBC, or any of the 24/7 news sources. You will see petty much the same footage and hear the same interviews. Most students believe they are getting their political news from the monologues on late night television shows like David Letterman, their Facebook or MySpace site, or from blogs. The "real" news that you might see locally or read about in a news weekly magazine is much more in-depth of course; but it is much less dramatic, much less visually interesting, and much more work for you as a receiver. So television as a medium has also changed the nature of our news since the introduction of the 24/7 news networks. Of course, there isn't enough real news to fill all that time so "fillers" have had to be invented to fill all that excess "news" time. These have usually been in the form of talk television and radio or political humor shows—Bill O'Reilly, Rush Limbaugh, The Colbert Report, and others.

Another good example that demonstrates how the medium has become the message is pro-football. In order to work an extra timeout into each game (and thus squeeze in more money making commercials), some decades ago television in-

duced the leagues to insert a two-minute warning just before each half ended. This in turn led to the two-minute drill, which changed football from a running game to a short passing game with lots of quick plays being called in a short amount of time. This changed the game into one in which the great percentage of contests get decided by a few points scored in the last two minutes. So McLuhan's fans can argue that TV gave us an entirely new sport. Of course, while television gave us some good things, it also cost us others like long family talks at the evening dinner table and actual conversation in our leisure.

McLuhan's ideas resemble Schwartz's in many ways, and the two worked together at one time. McLuhan believed that we relate to media in two ways. First, he said that every medium is an extension of one of our senses or body parts. For example, print is an extension of our eyes—it allows us to see and absorb much more information than we could prior to its invention.

Speech speed is far slower than reading speed, so we can cover much more information than we ever could during the age of the spoken word. Radio and the telephone were an extension of our ears, so we could hear many more things from much farther away than we could without those media. Television is an extension of our eyes and our ears, so we can see and hear far more and from farther away than we ever could without it. And McLuhan predicted that the computer would become an extension of our brain, which is potentially frightening when you think of it. It allows us to think of much more than we could prior to its presence. What has that led to? Just think about all the new jobs, the new ways we do business, identity theft, blogging, the elimination of almost all written personal communication and correspondence (on which much of our written history has been based) other than via e-mail (which can be easily misunderstood, leading to various arguments and miscues).

Media also can change our way of thinking about our world. For example, when the telegraph gave people the ability to communicate quickly across great distances (thus "destroying" space) we began to think of our country as much smaller than we had before. We could now predict the future better. We could know the price of wheat at the Chicago markets in seconds, even way off in Kansas where it was grown. In fact, the power to predict may have led to what we now call the "futures market," in which we buy and sell wheat that hasn't yet been planted. TV also gave us new ways of organizing our lives around its programming, such as the six o'clock or ten o'clock news at night, "The Today Show" and its clones in the morning, and "Sesame Street" and other children's programming in the afternoon. In fact, most people schedule their lives to some degree around TV programming.

Television has surely altered our sense of community and belonging as well. Following the devastating submerging of New Orleans and other parts of the Gulf coast, millions of people altered their views about a variety of things like donating aid, and what it was like to be black and poor. Public opinion of the President took a nose dive after he did a "flyover" some days after the disaster. People also probably altered their viewing habits by watching 24/7 news channels and the Weather Channel during those days. And with TVs on more than seven hours a day in the average American home, there simply is not enough time for the socializing and family life that occurred prior to its existence. Imagine the possibilities that can emerge from the fact that 65 percent of children the age of eight or above have a television set in their bedrooms (and probably a computer as well, and possibly a cell phone) thus further fracturing family relations (Kaiser Family Foundation, 1999) and making child pornography and child stalking much easier in the new millennium than could ever have been imagined.

This media explosion has created what one critic labeled "the lonely crowd," in which people in neighborhoods and apartment complexes rarely know one another, and persons tend not to come to the aid of their neighbors like they used to do. Contrast that to some Third World countries where the only television set in the village is owned by the entire community and brings people together daily to interact and discuss things of which they were formerly unaware—world events, propaganda,

crops, visions of prosperity in other countries, and so on. And we must remember that television also has an easy **access code**, which means we don't have to learn to watch it in the same way we had to learn to read, calculate, or write, so the poorest peasant in the most wretched of circumstances can see how you and I live. Is it any wonder that others are jealous of America and that we have low ratings and are hated as a people by many across the world? As a result, living in contemporary times can be both positively and negatively affected by what we learn via TV, the Internet, and other media. MTV, for example, clearly altered American pop culture, and many believe it provided new and disturbing role models for the actions and emerging values of young people like yourselves—things like violence, sexual role models, and the denigration of women. What has TV and the computer taught us about the treatment of minorities, children, and women? MTV was so concerned about these possibilities that the network partnered with the American Psychological Association to develop a warning system that gave indications of the link. Prisoners at a minimal security facility in Minnesota used the Internet to access local small-town newspapers. There they harvested the names of young children whose parents or grandparents put birthday greetings into the newspaper along with a picture. The harvested pictures and names were then collected into a sort of "catalog" and sold presumably to at least some, if not most, persons who were pedophiles (Larson, 2008).

In a curious and unexpected surprise to most readers, McLuhan distinguished the difference between the **signal** used by a medium (sounds which activated the ear drum or visual dots on a television screen which triggered nerves in the eyes to send information to the central nervous system) and the messages that the signal conveyed via the radio or television program. The signal is what stimulates our information-processing receptors, so print stimulates our eyes, radio stimulates our ears, and television stimulates both, and the computer stimulates our brain waves via one or more of the senses according to McLuhan. The message is the meaning intended and conveyed by the signal. McLuhan felt that some signals come to us in what he called a

T A B L E 13.1   **Hot and Cool Media**

Medium	Source of Information	Definition	Participation	Type of Medium
Television	Lighted dots	Low	High	Cool
Books	Completed letters	High	Low	Hot
Cartoons	Dots on paper	Low	High	Cool
Photographs	Image on film	High	Low	Hot
Telephone	Low-fidelity sound wave	Low	High	Cool
Movies	Moving image on film	High	Low	Hot
Telegraph	Dots and dashes in sound	Low	High	Cool
Digital audio	High-fidelity sound wave	High	Low	Hot
Personal computer and Internet	Lighted dots	Low	High	Cool

complete (or high fidelity) form, while others come to us in an incomplete (or low fidelity) form. He further speculated that **high-fidelity forms**, such as radio with its complete words, sentences, and music, or film with its series of complete 35-mm visual pictures (interrupted by brief spaces of no light to give the illusion of movement) require little effort from our information-processing receptors like our eyes or ears. They only send high-definition signals that we are then intellectually assemble into complete messages that have meanings to us. **Low-fidelity forms**, on the other hand (e.g., the telegraph, whose electronic impulses or dots and dashes had to be translated into letters and then into words, cartoons, or television) require much more effort before meaning and be derived. These low-fidelity media signals may only consist of dots on a lighted screen (and even then far less than half of those possible), and they require us to stretch our senses to convert the incomplete signals into complete signals before assembling them in order to derive meaning. So, though its content may be insipid, televisions signal is complex. According to McLuhan, the same message content sent via the two forms—one high fidelity and the other low fidelity—would have different meanings to a greater or lesser degree. The high-fidelity forms, such as film, result in little physiological or **sensory involvement** in decoding the signal, and it doesn't take much *physiological* effort to process these completed signals into the meaningful message. The low-fidelity form is quite the opposite. It requires much more *physiological* participation in order to decode the signal and assemble its parts into meaningful elements. This results in high physiological or **sensory participation** according to McLuhan. He called the high-fidelity or complete message signals like film "hot" media and the low-fidelity or incomplete ones like the TV screen "cool" media (see Table 13.1).

Hot Media

Hot media rely on signals having high fidelity, completeness, or **definition** as McLuhan called it. Hot media include film (but not TV, which was cool since its only partially lighted pixels had to be completed by the central nervous system), digital music (but not analog music for the same reasons), photos (but not cartoons—ditto), and books (but not comic books—ditto again). McLuhan considered them hot because, unlike cool media such as television or the computer screen, they do not require much effort from our sensory receptors to communicate complete signals with which the central nervous system finally arrives at meaning. Hot media, conversely, have complete or fully defined and high-fidelity or "finished" signals. As noted earlier, films used to be made up of sequential photographs (usually 35-mm "slides" filling the whole screen) that are separated by a brief blackout to create the illusion of motion while television "pictures" are quite incomplete, in comparison, since not all pixels on any lines of resolution glow on the screen at any one instant and even then only half of the lines of resolution are lit at the same time. As a result, there is a far less complete signal being processed to the central nervous system where it must be assembled to yield meaning.

Cool Media

As noted, the signals we perceive and process in **cool media** have low fidelity, definition, or completeness, so we must work harder to *physiologically* process them, as just explained regarding the television versus the film signal. Cool media include television, the telephone, and the computer screen. Consider the telephone. It does not have a high-fidelity speaker in the earpiece. If you really want to know what the fidelity of its speaker is, just hold it away from your ear by a foot or two. That is why it is sometimes difficult to determine who is calling us. In fact, if we don't recognize who is speaking, we fake it until we pick up a cue that allows us to correctly identify who it is that is calling us. Similarly, we had to imagine a lot of sound quality with the old windup phonograph and even with the early electronic phonographs, though they had much greater "fidelity" in their sound. To be decoded, these cool media require far greater physiological and later psychological effort on our part in order to decode the signals and assemble the meaning of the messages they carry to us. For example, a cartoon's signal consists of simple line drawings that are far less complete than a photograph. Charlie Brown's head and face consist of a round ball with two dots, an upside down letter "u" line for a nose, a wiggle line for a mouth, and a squiggle of hair—almost nothing to put together. A photograph of the young boy who may have served as Charles Schultz's model for Charlie Brown would be far more complete—in fact, a near replica. So the cartoon is cool while the photo is hot.

What kinds of messages are best for cool media? McLuhan said that cool media breed cool messages. More than a decade early, he predicted that someday a cool person—perhaps a movie star—would be elected president, and 16 years later, that's what happened. Today, the politicians who catch on seem to be are easy-going and cool, like Bill Clinton, George W. Bush, and perhaps Barack Obama. They are informal, relaxed, personable, and sometimes even ambiguous in their style and messages. They might differ widely on policies, but they will be very similar in communication style. Likewise, we see more and more TV commercials relying less and less on specific and concrete words or scripts and more and more on the creation of a mood or feeling using Schwartz's visual and auditory scripts. Viewers add to or subtract from such commercials and arrive at their own final meanings. Think of the spots that create a sense of anticipation through the use of music, sets, or lighting. We hear the sounds of a love ballad. Then we see a well-dressed couple slowly walking down the stairs of the fancy restaurant. The man gives the valet the keys to get his car. Up drives a Volkswagen Passat. Only then does the voiceover tell us (and then only with a few words) that the "Passat is in good taste anytime, anywhere." The specific content of the message (the words spoken) is almost as incomplete as the signals used—the visual and auditory scripts—and so the message matches the cool quality of the TV signal.

It is interesting to apply some of McLuhan's ideas about hot and cool media to recent communication technologies that have become widespread only since his death. As cellular technology increases, for instance, we have processed more and more cool digital signals such as digital photographic and televised images. And you have probably experienced how cool these messages are—the photos need re-touching, the already cool signal from a cell phone breaks up, the flat screen television seems to have "lines" that divide it into quadrants, and so on. What we experience is the further cooling of signals sent by a cool medium. It may get so cool that both cell phone parties agree to hang up and try again later. And texters don't even use complete words. McLuhan also accurately predicted a great increase in the use of cool media, resulting in increased audience participation. And he predicted that when coupled with satellite transmission of TV, radio, telephone, and computer messages, these cool media would lead to his global village, in which everybody would be interested in everybody else's business. We are now beginning to experience just that in the form of the Internet, chat groups, blogs, twitter, and e-mail, all of which are highly participative and involving, as his theory predicted. However, the global village is not very peaceful because everyone's business is somehow impacting on everyone else's business, so conflict becomes more and more likely. Most of us have had the experience of being almost totally misunderstood when using e-mail and losing track of real-life cues when having an argument via cell phone. And taken together with Schwartz's idea of resonance, the involving and participatory trend, coupled with evoked emotional experiences that are prompted by mini-cues and allow people to add their own meanings, provides a powerful set of tools in the hands of creative and insightful persuaders.

In addition to the highly philosophical, predictive, and almost "rhetorical" theories of both Schwartz and McLuhan, the study of media and media effects on people and culture have been enriched by several other more "scientific" theories developed by social scientists versus philosophers and continue to be enriched by the development of other theories meant to explain human behavior in terms of the effects of the mass media of our times. Let us examine some of them now.

USES AND GRATIFICATION THEORY

Uses and gratification theory is another approach to studying the effects of mass media, and it focuses on how receivers use media to gratify or meet or satisfy their individual needs. It assumes that we all have differing primary, secondary, and even tertiary needs for various types of information in our complex and sometimes confusing world. In order to make sense of our lives, to help us make decisions about the various circumstances we meet in a 24/7, networked, potentially dangerous world of advocacy and propaganda, or just to learn and avoid boredom, it has become essential for us to use various media at different times and in different situations to get highly critical as well as inconsequential information (Blumler, 1979; Rubin, 2002). As we watch ourselves using media we can easily identify that there are four basic or primary needs and many secondary or even tertiary ones for which information is needed and for which we turn to mass media to gather that information.

The first need is **surveillance**, or the need to keep track of our daily physical and human environment—the events that can impinge on our lives like the price of gasoline, the likely candidates for political office, the economy, new brands, our favorite sports team, community events, and of course, the weather. There is too much happening for us to keep track of all the events and persons and things affecting our daily lives, so we usually turn to the media to keep up to date, and we use that information to decide which items to focus on and attend to in order to maintain order in our busy lives and to avoid chaos.

The second need is **curiosity**, or the need to discover and learn about previously unknown information that is not necessarily critical to our interests and daily lives but which could possibly be important someday and which also simply interests us. Topics about which we are curious might include the upcoming TV season, the latest celebrity gossip that might come up in conversation, new technologies that we might adopt, world events that could affect our lives, new developments in medicine, or the details of a direct mail or direct television sales offer. News tabloids have always traded on this curiosity need, and it is no surprise that the *National Enquirer* claims to be the "newspaper" with the largest circulation in the country. No one really believes in Elvis sightings, or 40-pound babies being born, but people continue to buy the tabloids that publicize these unlikely and unbelievable events out of curiosity. Our curiosity gets piqued by the sensationalist headlines (I even pick them up sometimes while waiting in the checkout line) and the paper regularly sells out. And, of course, there are far more intelligent and "true" sources that deal with topics that pique our curiosity. We view them on some television channels like A&E, the History Channel, public television, and news specials, or we read about them in specialized publications like news weeklies and special interest magazines (*Golf, Tennis, Family Circle, Architecture, National Geographic*).

The third need we experience and use media to gratify is **diversion**, or relief from boredom which is a problem for many if not most persons at one time or another. For example, we watch movies or sporting events on TV, read newspapers or magazines, play video games, attend films or watch DVDs of them, listen to the radio or our iPod while we drive, or read novels for pleasure. We use all these examples and many others in order to gratify our need to simply relax and to avoid being bored, according to Uses and Gratifications theory. Media are used in these cases to simply fill time in some cases but not really to gather information that we believe we must know or which will impact our daily lives.

The fourth need is for **personal identity**. We are all uncertain about our identities, our life goals, and the impact of certain events in an ever-changing and networked world, so we turn to media to help us discover who we are, what we stand for, what we should strive for, what will make us feel satisfied with ourselves, and how we are living out our lives. To fill this need we might read about places we have never visited, or simply watch "The Learning Channel," or learn what we believe regarding political issues and government policies by listening to or watching radio and television talk shows. We learn what we are not by watching "Trash TV" shows such as the Jerry Springer Show, "Judge Judy," or other programming, or by reading about current events, the lives of other persons whom we admire, or by paying attention to cultural issues. Interestingly enough, persons who are more self-assured and outgoing fill

personal identity needs by reading, whereas less self-assured and outgoing persons rely on television to fill this need. Other lesser or secondary needs (e.g., the need for mastery and control) are served in simple and complex ways by media. We want to feel competent at things so we reassure ourselves of our competence by watching or reading about carpentry, auto mechanics, gourmet cooking, home decorating, and a host of other secondary needs. There are even tertiary competence needs that we gratify by watching game shows to see if we know more than the contestants, playing video games and challenging others at them, listening to nostalgic music of the past, attending revivals of old Broadway hits like "South Pacific" or "Oklahoma" or by gambling online to see if we can beat the odds. Our primary, secondary, or tertiary social needs can be gratified by entering into and participating with others chat groups to compare accomplishments, discuss issues, learn about the latest fad, and others with and from our chat "partners."

All these primary needs, as well as some secondary and tertiary ones, frequently can serve as attention-getting devices in persuasion and even in some cases as first premises in enthymemes. They appeal to us to keep up with the world around us, not to miss out on the latest technology, and above all to avoid becoming just another bored loser. Knowing how people are using media to gratify needs can help us plan targeted persuasion. As receivers, we need to monitor our own uses of media and what are we turning to media for in hopes of gratifying our personal needs for persuaders—politicians, marketers, ideologues, etc.—often target and shape their messages at those needs and use various media to gratify them.

AGENDA SETTING

Another explanation of the ways mass media persuade us relates to their **agenda-setting** function (McCombs & Shaw, 1972). According to this theory, the public's agenda of what is important and needs our attention includes the kinds of issues people discuss, think, and worry about. Further, the theory holds that that this public agenda is powerfully shaped and directed by what the news media

BOX 13.5 Agenda Setting and Propaganda

 For a good review of the agenda setting research, go to http://www.firstmonday.org/ISSUES/issue10_12/del wiche/index.html. An important implication to the theory of agenda setting is how this characteristic of media can be used to create propaganda. We are all aware that the media focus on the topic of "weapons of mass destruction in Iraq" helped set the agenda for the U.S. invasion and the mammoth expenditures in lives and materials that resulted in that agenda-setting item and which may be preparing the United States for a war with Iran. (See http://bellaciao.org/en/spip.php?article16846 for a complete analysis of how this happened.) A very complete catalog of both print and video propaganda flowing out of agenda setting can be found at http://www.au.af.mil/info-ops/influence.htm#marketing.

choose to highlight and report on repeatedly as well as what they choose to downplay, dismiss, or ignore. This is especially important since the concentration of media ownership has increased with mega-media giants like Rupert Murdoch, Time Warner, Disney, General Electric, or ViaCom, all of whom own and control multiple information outlets and feed us much of what we read, see, hear, and "think" we know and ultimately believe. The main point about agenda setting is that mass media do not tell us what to think; but they do tell us *what to think about* and ultimately believe and act upon. How many persons would have stayed glued to their TVs during the O. J. Simpson trial if the media hadn't reported on it daily? Would we be thinking about the war on terrorism if the media hadn't run stories about various bombings around the world *after* September 11th? After all, few ever heard of Osama Bin Laden or Al Quaida prior to then. The decisions about what to focus on and, equally important, what not to focus on in reporting the day's events fall to a small number of persons.

Agenda-Setting theory calls such persons "gatekeepers" and they include people like reporters for the wire services, editors, news photographers, and others. They are called "gatekeepers" because they decide what gets covered in the news and what doesn't; which pictures of the crime scene are televised and which ones are not; which victim interviews get used and which get discarded. In other words, they decide what gets past the "gate" or the finite space and time used for print or electronic news. This agenda setting can be seen, particularly as it can convey propaganda in Box 13.5. The gatekeepers have access to more news than they can ever possibly report on and so they must choose what stories to run, which way to point their cameras, whom to interview, and what point of view to use in reporting the events of the day. How do they make program decisions, and by what criteria? Why, during the 2008 primary elections, did they focus on Barack Obama's former pastor and some of his inflammatory sermons but not on some other issue such as what he himself believed? Why didn't they give Hillary Clinton's pastor similar attention?

Not as much is exactly known about the process gatekeepers go through and what criteria goes into making such decisions, but there are some hints as to how and why the decisions are made. Media scholar J. Meyrowitz (1985) refers to one criterion called "least objectionable programming," which he defines as "... a program that is least likely to be turned off, rather than a program viewers will actively seek out" (p. 73). Some media critics note that, although media advertisements purportedly sell products to viewers, the real economic design of the mass media industry is to sell *audiences* to advertisers. With TV, for example, we think of programs as products for which we pay a price in that we have to watch ads from the programs' sponsors. In reality, *we are the products*, and *we are being sold to the advertisers*. That's why "Sweeps Week" is so critical. The amount a network can charge for a commercial during a program that gets high ratings during sweeps week is much higher with a high rating versus a low one, so it all comes down to what advertisers are willing to pay for the real product—you and me! Thus, according to Meyrowitz, the media's agenda-setting goal is to design programming that will capture, hold the attention, inform, educate, etc., the largest number of people, but they aim for the most likely segment of people who might purchase, vote, and/or join and whom advertisers and policymakers want to reach as a result (e.g., upscale spenders, gourmet cooks, sports fans, or college students willing to adopt a credit card).

One criterion for determining what news to present is the nature of the audience (sometimes called the "target" or the "prospect" by marketing experts). Persons who read *U.S. News & World Report* or who watch "The O'Reilly Factor" will be more conservative than those who read *Newsweek* and who watch "The Colbert Report" or public television news. Gatekeepers frequently select stories that put a conservative slant on an issue, thus setting a different agenda for the conservative viewers, listeners, or readers than for the liberal ones. Another criterion for deciding what as is to be broadcast or printed is whether it can be delivered as a 20- to 30-second sound "bite" on TV or told simply and quickly in a magazine story or a television news report to sufficiently answer the journalist's five key questions—who, what, when, where, and why. Communication scholars Hall Jamieson and Kohrs-Campbell (1996) define such reportage as a **news bite** or a piece of news "less than 35 seconds long, delivered by a credible source in an energetic way." If the first story in the broadcast is an unexciting news bite, then it hasn't been an important news day. However, if the first story is a fascinating news bite of a national or international tragedy like the cyclone that killed 100,000 or a breaking scandal to be followed up later in the broadcast, viewers know that an in-depth report will follow. Because they provide us with yesterday's news tomorrow, newspapers and news weeklies are practically compelled to run a version of the stories that TV news programmers ran the day before. In a sense, television sets the agenda for

print versions of the news, and together they set the public agenda of things that must be taken care of or attended to. Try to keep track of this progression—see what the top story on the television evening news is and see if that isn't tomorrow's headline or front page item in your newspaper and later in the week the focus of the news weeklies. Both the newspaper and the news weekly can do in-depth coverage of issues, but fewer and fewer people are reading them and for less and less time.

Another criterion used by gatekeepers to determine what gets reported and what does not is the expressiveness or dramatic quality of both the audio and video in the story (Meyrowitz, 1985). The old chestnut about "man bites dog!" being more interesting and newsworthy than if the dog bit the man applies here. Newsworthy stories include the instantaneous reactions of parents who just heard that their children have been killed in an auto accident. The camera zooms up to their faces, and the audience supposedly experiences how they must feel. Or if the lead story on the 10 o'clock television news is "Washington, D.C., Madam Commits Suicide in Trailer Park!" watch for a front page feature on her history. Another criterion that may or may not have important implications for the larger question of agenda setting is the degree to which today's citizenry is getting part or most of their daily news from Internet sources like YouTube, MySpace, FaceBook, various search engines, the blogosphere, and so on. A recent example may give us a hint. In Spring of 2008, actress, dancer, celebrity, and judge on "American Idol," Paula Abdul, made an on-air blunder by reading her critique of one of the contestants before the contestant had yet performed. It was fairly obvious she was reading her critique from a script (due perhaps to her being treated with a "pain patch" for a back ailment). Naturally, the mistake was noted by the usual news sources but it was the Number One topic on YouTube the next day, indicating that that's where the news was and is really happening! In fact, many college instructors no longer use e-mail addresses to send class notices to their students, but instead request their YouTube addresses since the students check them far more frequently than they check their e-mail. Perhaps we are seeing an entire revolution in the news industry—it is the receiver who is *really* reporting the news and not the standard news media sources.

How can ordinary receivers like you and me protect ourselves from these agenda-setting and gate-keeping functions of the standard media sources and get at least a sense of what is "really" important to pay attention to in today's 24/7, networked news world that is results-oriented, rapid fire, and emotionally driven? Critical receivers of persuasion need to diversify their reading of, listening to, and viewing of news and information to expose themselves to as many divergent sources as possible. Try listening to the news as reported on public television stations or National Public Radio. Watch several television news programs including your local one. Try to read at least one news magazine per week. Above all, don't let one medium so dominate your awareness of the world that you overlook other sources of news and information. Even if you watch as much television as others, vary your sources of information.

Agenda setting tells us what to think about in terms of the public agenda, but what about our private agendas? What kind of persons do we want to be? How should a good employee behave in the workplace? What is good parenting? The answers to these are questions used to be learned when people lived in nuclear families and in small communities by observing how persons they knew behaved. How do we learn these things now? Let us turn to two other media theories that may shed a little light on the potentially disturbing answers to these questions.

LEARNING FROM THE MEDIA AND PERSUASION

Since most of us no longer live in nuclear families containing three living generations, and rarely do we live in insular or very small communities, how to we learn the proper behavior for acceptable members of our societies? Further, in a constantly changing world of values and norms, what can we expect of various situations, occupations, personal

encounters, and situations that we will meet up with in the future? Remember such new and expected occasions and behaviors can occur wherever and whenever you live whether in cities, suburbs, gated communities, or "rurban" or rural/urban locales, and we need to learn what is okay and what is not. These questions are the focus of two theories about how and what we learn regarding events and behaviors from the media of our time and which relate to the process of being a responsible receiver—the goal of this book. These theories are called the Social Learning and Cultivation theories, and of course they are not the only other theories about media effects and persuasion. A good way to remember which is which is that **Social Learning theory** tells us what to think and do with ourselves and how to behave in given situations (Bandura, 1994). **Cultivation theory**, on the other hand, teaches us what to expect in future possible situations or, to think of it in another way, we learn what to prepare for in future situations from the media (Signorelli & Morgan, 1990).

It is the difference between how to enact violence or when to expect it and maybe how to respond to it in certain situations as well as the degree to which we can expect to experience violence in the future. For example, heavy watchers of television, especially violent programming, believe in a much more violent world out there and expect to encounter violence sometimes in their lives. This learning can greatly impact us in persuasive ways and can influence how we are persuaded by politicians, advertisers, propagandists, and others. A few examples might help here. You can learn from a television news show (or perhaps a fictional program) that it is possible to smuggle a gun into a classroom or a school in a backpack, or a guitar case, or whatever, and you can learn that you can use it to intimidate someone who is bullying you by threatening them with violence—it was done on my campus this year. In other words you can learn how to commit the crime known as "assault" (which means threatening someone with harm). That's one kind of social learning—you learn how to behave in unpleasant ways as well as pleasant ones. Of course, you can learn many other good things as well such as how to be polite, how to interview for a job, how to ask for a date, or how to behave when asking your professor about your grade. On the other hand, you can also learn from the same news or fictional programming just how likely this kind of event is to occur in your future, at your school, on your job, or at home. A more benign example might help here. Suppose you are a female school student who is regularly watching a daytime "soap opera" that features teenage moms as characters. Social Learning theory would tell you how such moms behave (e.g., how they dress, what they talk like, how they interact with others—both male and female, old or young, how they care for their children). For example, they might learn that such moms use profanity around their children all the time, that they frequently are antagonistic to authority figures like the school counselor or their parents and neighbors, and that belonging to a gang will help you.

Cultivation theory, on the other hand, resembles what we called the "Surveillance Need" in our discussion of Uses and Gratification theory. In other words, Cultivation theory tells us what is happening in the world around us and what kinds of things we can expect to happen, when, where, and how often. In other words, it "grows" or "cultivates" expectations about the world in which we live. It would tell the same viewers of the sitcom involving teenaged, single, moms about what kind of lives they could expect to live in the future. It might teach them that as a teenage single mom, they can expect lots of boyfriends, extensive wardrobes, exciting times, good jobs, and babies that never cry or are sick. In a very real sense, both theories *persuade* media users about how to behave and what to expect from life. Now those views or expectations might range from totally or partially accurate to totally or partially inaccurate, but nonetheless, the viewers tend to believe them and as a result to expect a certain lifestyle. In fact, the theory's developer, George Gerbner, felt that television watching dramatically affected viewer's beliefs about what the world outside of television was really like. Furthermore, he thought that these views developed slowly and with repeated viewings and that

they were cumulative. In other words, if you watched a lot of television, and particularly similar type of programming, your views of the world "out there" would "build up" until you came to sincerely believe—almost fervently—in their reality. These views of the world didn't necessarily tell you how to behave (as with Social Learning theory), but instead led you to develop a mindset or a worldview that affected your attitudes toward teen motherhood, or violence in the streets, or going to college rather than learning what to do or what behavior to display about those things.

Recall what we said back in Chapter 7 about the difference between attitudes and behavior. Attitudes are much easier to change than behaviors—they are fickle in a way. This is probably why Cultivation theory predicts changes only after *extended viewing* and even then over repeated times. The theory also holds that these worldviews aren't invented by those who articulate them or demonstrate them through television programming and other media. Rather, they lie dormant in the culture—such as the likelihood of violence happening to you—and are "cultivated" by media exposures to various forms of them. Further, the theory holds that media exposure only has a *tendency* to help them grow and then primarily with heavy viewers who are more likely to overestimate the amount of violence in our culture rather than light media viewers whose beliefs are more realistic (Gerbner et al., 1986). This worldview can also be magnified when the viewer actually does experience events that are similar to the media events but in the real world. Most students at my school who were in that lecture hall when the shooter opened fire, killing six and injuring dozens, dreaded ever going back to the room or any large lecture hall as a matter of fact. Actually, the room never again was used as a lecture hall and many wanted it totally destroyed. Most important, for our purposes here, is that both kinds of beliefs—those growing out of the "how to" school of Social Learning theory and the worldviews/mind sets growing out of Cultivation theory frequently serve as major premises in persuasion that is highly effective in persuading us (see Chapter 8).

Both theories really go back to the Surgeon General's Report on Violence of over 40 years ago (Baker & Ball, 1969). The report was commissioned back them to look at why the 1960s had been so violent, and why had violence increased particularly in terms of protest movements over civil rights and the war in Vietnam that ultimately spawned violent acts. The statistics of the times (and more recently) showed increasing violence in the streets, at home, in schools and elsewhere. Naturally, the interest and research into the media violence grew in the decades following. Most recently, this interest has heightened because of incidents like the shooting and killing of students in various levels of schools (e.g., Columbine High School, on our campus, at Virginia Tech in 2007–2008, and elsewhere). Later other major and minor incidents, such as bathroom graffiti, forced school officials at various levels to close schools and to institute severe security procedures (e.g., metal detectors at school entrances, strip searches, and armed security officers in schools) and caused officials and scholars to look to media messages as the underlying causes of this increase in violence. This interest persists but, as in the hypothetical example of teenage moms, the media effects on human behavior of all sorts have been scrutinized using these two "learning theories," which now are well-based in past research.

Critical receivers need to ask of themselves "What things have I learned, not from direct observation or experience, but from media sources ranging from television to video games, to the Internet?" "How have they implanted major premises in my conscious and unconscious mind that might be used in persuasive arguments to get me to engage in behaviors that I otherwise might have avoided?" Further, "What expectations do I have about the future world that I may have absorbed from seeing them via media and not from any reality or direct experience?" and "How might they be used as major premises of arguments to me about preparing for or avoiding such expected circumstances?" After all, in a 24/7, networked world that is inundated with media of various sorts that bombard us daily, no one should be surprised that

persuasion of various kinds—deceptive and accurate, advocacy and propaganda, and the bottom line—is occurring constantly and that receivers should be prepared for it or they risk being scammed, deceived, and misled. In past times we could usually rely on newspapers, magazines, radio news, and television news to keep us prepared for this onslaught of persuasion; with the growing monopolization and centralization of our news services, this is no longer necessarily the case. For example, Time Warner now owns CNN, HBO, Cinemax, the Cartoon Network, TBS, TNT, America Online, Mapquest, Movietone, Netscape, Warner Bros., and over 150 magazines like *Time, People,* and others. These many outlets also have implications for the possibility of propaganda being used against our citizenry by convincing them that just because we have more news media outlets reporting 24/7 they are necessarily getting the news we need.

NEWS MANIPULATION AND PERSUASION

The news industry is a business, a very centralized and profitable industry, as just mentioned; and the news media stand to profit from the success of their advertiser clients and customers. As a result, no one should be surprised to learn that they don't always print the whole truth and nothing but the whole truth, particularly when it involves their clients—the advertisers—and not us, the consumers of the news. Consider the discussion in Box 13.6 as you struggle as receivers to make decisions about everything ranging from which brand to buy, to which candidate to vote for, to what is the appropriate governmental policy to promote, we need to ask ourselves if the news we get is as truly unbiased as it claims to be. Do the media ever manipulate the news, as some critics suggest? If so, how often? By how much? In what ways? If we have reason to suspect unbiased news reporting, we ought to acquaint ourselves with the possible tactics that can make or unmake the news. This knowledge will allow us an extra safeguard against possible "hidden persuasion" in news programs that can affect us as receivers and as we try to make decisions that can affect us in major or minor ways.

Key News Sources and Conglomerates

Three major wire services (AP, UPI, and Reuters) used to supply most of the news we see, hear, and read. There was/is nothing wrong with that small number of sources, as long as the news is accurate and as long as the key news items get printed or broadcast. But today even with the numerous and continuous news networks like FOX, CNN, MSNBC, and other, the key items don't always get prominent coverage, and it can't all be blamed on the gatekeepers any longer. Even your local half-hour 10 p.m. TV news programs contain only 22 minutes of news or only about 3000 total words. The average 400-words-per-minute reader can cover that in only 7 to 8 minutes, and that, in fact, is about the average time spent per day by newspaper subscribers on reading their newspapers. So we miss a lot of important information if we rely on only one electronic media for news; and surfing between them doesn't always do much good either—they all seem to be reporting the same things at the same time and they even use much of the same footage—some of which, of course, is to be blamed on the old wire service system, but much more of which is related to the

massive media conglomerates we have mentioned. When you are trying to gain a certain segment of the market (which is what news broadcasts must do to earn profits for the corporate networks and their shareholders) the temptation is to manipulate the news to make it more dramatic, interesting, sexy, sensational, and/or entertaining, so that's why we get the most coverage of sensational or controversial topics. More recently this need for controversy and drama has led to programming that has a certain political bias with programs like "The O'Reilly Factor" and broadcast demagogues like Rush Limbaugh (Larson, 1997). As electronic news pioneer Edward R. Murrow put it: "One of the basic troubles with radio and television news is that both instruments have grown up as an incompatible combination of show business, advertising, and news. Each of the three is a rather bizarre and demanding profession, and when you get all three under one tent, the dust never settles" (Matusow, 1983, p. 304). The show-business aspects of today's news distort electronic news more than ever and can easily let us fall prey to some of the traps in the Seven Faces of Persuasion. What are some specific ways news can be manipulated that we should be watching out for as receivers?

Methods of Manipulation

Ignoring.   One way gatekeepers and media moguls who control news conglomerates can distort the news is by simply **ignoring** and not ever reporting it or by minimizing it by giving something else a larger portion of the news space and time than the topic really deserves (e.g., Paris Hilton) or by giving it a bad position in the newspaper, magazine, or television news time. For example, news media initially ignored the danger of global warming and not until former Vice President Al Gore produced a feature film "An Inconvenient Truth," which also won an Academy Award, did any news source really give the topic the space or time it deserved. Following the film and its awards, numerous specials on various aspects of the problem began appearing on the news media and on special programming on channels like A&E. Until a decade ago, few persons in the United States could say where Afghanistan was located, and fewer knew who Osama Bin Laden was and why he mattered to them in any way. And many important political issues are initially ignored because they don't seem interesting or sensational enough.

Favoring the Sponsor.   Because every commercial news program has several sponsors, news reporters and editors may soft-pedal any negative news about these sponsors (**favoring the sponsor**). In an old but classic example, it took years to pass a law forcing broadcasters to refuse advertising from cigarette manufacturers. But remember, it pays to "fight fire with fire" and only when our old friend, Tony Schwartz, crafted his devastating anti-smoking ad and the industry saw the damage it could suffer when taken on by a true expert did they voluntarily withdraw their ads. How much news time/space is devoted to the profits of the big oil companies even though we all know that the profits are obscene? It is always wise to ask who the sponsor is for a newscast, and getting our news from several sources helps us to avoid sponsor-favoring editing; this is getting even harder to do as news conglomerates continue to grow and slant the news their way. Sometimes, broadcasters have even previewed the news story for advertisers to make certain there is no objection. There is a practice in some television news of distancing advertisers' commercials from the place in the program that could result in negative publicity.

The Pseudoevent.   Although there is an overabundance of news each day, not all of it is interesting or entertaining, so news reporters are often drawn to highly dramatic or bizarre events. Historian Daniel Boorstin (1961) called these **pseudoevents** or "planned news." A more modern term is "hyperreality" which sounds like "virtual reality" (and indeed can use virtual reality) but is different. It is a supposedly newsworthy event or story that is carefully scripted and rehearsed. French philosopher and critic Jean Baudrillard defined it as "The simulation of something which never really existed." And Umberto Eco called it "the authentic fake." Basically, it is the reportage of an event that has been totally planned in advance and hence isn't really news at all. Such stories fall somewhere between public relations and soft news, such as reporting on a sports celebrity like Michael Jordan deciding to play minor league baseball or coming out of retirement to play basketball again. Various mass movements hold fully planned marches, rallies, or vigils or use violent tactics such as bomb scares to get media attention. A bomb scare is not a natural or ordinary event. It had to be planned and executed, hence the prefix "pseudo" in "pseudo-event" denoting an unreal event. Numerous pranksters are getting exams and even school canceled by leaving cryptic graffiti threatening bombs or shootings on restroom walls at the schools, thus forcing administrators to be overly cautious out of necessity.

Bias: Verbal and Nonverbal Cues.   A skillful interviewer can make an interviewee seem to be quite different from his or her real self. Politicians complain about being misrepresented by the news industry all the time. For example, during the 2008 Democratic primary contests, candidate Barack Obama appeared nervous when questioned about his Pastor Jeremiah Wright's comments during a sermon that Obama hadn't even attended or heard about. Wright had said "God Damn America!" during the sermon, thus raising the audience's emotions and anger and enraging elements of the viewing audience, especially among religious working class families—one of Obama's hoped for constituencies.

And Obama's nonverbal discomfort when questioned by the reporter was mentioned as part of the coverage of the news event on my local television evening news report. Naturally, the news reporter nearly "raised an eyebrow" as he commented on the item, and later Obama had to ultimately renounce his pastor, which of course again made a big news item on both local and national network and cable news programs for several days—due at least in part to nonverbal cues. News reporters can make a candidate seem controversial by dubbing an audio track of booing on a video track showing people cheering and then having the announcer say, with a frown on his or her face, that the candidate faces opposition from left and right. Or editors might superimpose two or more conflicting images such as angry housewives complaining about higher food prices and farmers and grain dealers trying to explain why ethanol production was causing higher food prices. The news sources select who is featured, choosing only pro or only con advocates or ones that can be expected to make emotional and exciting quotes. How can we protect ourselves from all these ways of manipulating what we are to believe?

You and I can't possibly look at and listen to all the print and electronic news available to combat this sort of bias, but we all can diversify our exposure to news and especially the sources from which we get it. Recognize that much of the news we see, hear, and read is at least somewhat emotional and biased and must be taken with a "grain of salt." Again, try reading at least part of a newspaper and news weekly magazine regularly. Listen to the news on a pubic radio station instead of one that relies on commercial sponsors. If you have to rely on cable all-news stations, try to vary the ones that you choose—don't just watch FOX or CNN or MSNBC—vary your selections. And above all, don't assume that all the news you are getting is the most important, the most accurate and reliable, or the most unbiased.

In reality, most of you don't regularly do any of the above. In fact, most of you are now relying on the MSN home page, FaceBook, MySpace, various blogs, and other Internet sources to find out what you will believe is happening in the world and which is *truly* important to you. But at least keep in mind that the news can be manipulated there as well, and its reliability is difficult to determine. As a critical receiver, gather all the information you have time to get, but judge all of it with a critical eye. Let us now turn briefly to the newest entrant in not only the news industry but more importantly the advertising and related persuasion industries—the Internet.

THE INTERNET AND PERSUASION

A recent editorial in the *Chicago Tribune* noted that early in its life (i.e., the 1980s), the Internet was unregulated and reliant upon the good will of its "Netizens," or citizens of the net. But there was a dark side. "Then came the hackers, the viruses, the worms, spyware, phishing and spam.... A handful of groups are now looking into whether the entire Internet needs an overhaul.... With more than a billion Internet users ... a structural overhaul is not an outlandish idea" (*Chicago Tribune*, July 4, 2005). Considering what is discussed in Box 13.7, do think such an "Overhaul" will ever happen?

At this stage, it is obvious that there will be no such structural overhaul, so we must deal with what we now have. With the bursting of the dot-com bubble and falling Internet advertising revenue, many dismissed the importance of the Internet as a persuasive channel, and some countries like China even forbid its citizens to log on to many sites. And while we can trace the number of hits a certain site gets, we don't yet really know yet very well whether people actually read what is there or whether they process it at all or in the central or peripheral routes of the ELM. Most importantly, we remain unsure that it actually persuades them, but the trend is beginning to emerge that this is so—the Internet not only engages people, it does indeed persuade them and in important ways. Those "in the know" point to the sweeping effects the Internet continues to

---

BOX 13.7   Diversity and the Media

The Freeman Institute (go to http://www.freemaninstitute.com/cultures.htm) is an educational resource that celebrates cultural diversity in a number of ways, such as providing training in dealing with diversity and books and videos on the topic and many other issues. Their slogan is "Dealing with People Who Drive You Crazy." Go to their Web page and explore the links that direct you to a number of diverse communities. Select from among the options that deal with the diversity groups and media and explore their content. For example, regarding Latinos, you might want to select the "Electric Mercado" link and discover how media are now advertising to the $331 billion global Latino retail markets and the $3.2 trillion business-to-business markets. Or you might want to try some of the Black, Native American, or Asian-American sites. Or watch "The Value of Mutual Respect" as well as many other interesting links.

---

have on such things as the global economy, world politics, international relations, and a host of other important issues. It is clear that the Internet is changing the structure of persuasion as perhaps no other medium has since television, and it will probably continue to change persuasion by much more than television ever did. It is a major technological revolution that is changing the structure of our communication practices, and it has democratized the voice of the individual and turned receivers into potential sources with yet-to-be-determined audiences. There are now new ways for persuasion to be delivered (e.g., the viral persuasion mentioned earlier at http://www.subservientchicken.com/ sponsored by Burger King to market its chicken offerings) and "Guerilla marketing" (see http://www.gmarketing.com/articles/ for hundreds of related articles, strategies, tactics and sites) in which students like yourselves and other persons are paid to spread what used to be called "word of mouth" advertising. The Internet is also changing the persuasive process by altering the power structure of its participants, which now includes a huge percentage of the U.S. population. Let's review how the Internet is changing the way we persuade and are persuaded.

Changes in the Information Power Structure

When we considered the massive changes resulting from the printed word earlier, we noted that the biggest change was the redistribution of information as it represented power. When information was difficult to obtain, people could easily be taken advantage of and scammed. But when this information became easier to obtain because of the printing press, a middle class of merchants and tradesmen emerged and soon began to accumulate various kinds of power—economic, political, and philosophical. Imagine that kind of change multiplied many, many fold—that's what the access to information via the Internet has meant. It isn't hyperbolic to say that the single most significant contributions of the Internet are the redistribution of the control of information and the democratizing of individual voices in the persuasion process. A tiny example might help. Automobile salespersons do not like the Internet because dealer costs for vehicles are available online to potential customers, who can then solicit competitive bids from various dealers knowing what they stand to make on the sale. In other words, the consumer access to that information allows them to bargain for the best price, interest rate, rebate offer, and so on. What a great tool for the persuadee! Or take travel agents who were previously the major source of information for long-distance trips, airfares, and reservations for accommodations (all of which used to pay the agents a commission—but no longer). Now, travel agencies are closing their doors in droves due to competition from the Internet. As you well know, reservations can be made without direct human assistance, and some carriers provide additional incentives for using the Internet, such as special fares online and preferred member programs. Southwest Airlines, the most profitable airline over the past decade, uses the Internet as its *primary source* of booking trips and no longer pays commissions to travel agents. Its new discount service called DING at www. southwest.com/ding might interest those of you interested in saving money on travel.

Companies such as Priceline.com and Travelocity.com also enable consumers to find bargain fares. So the Internet is changing the travel and lodging industries as well and that is just one small example in the great multitude of businesses now being affected by Internet commerce, not to mention the many new start-up businesses that have emerged as a result of the Internet and its ability to make information available to the masses. As noted above, the Internet is a democratizing technology as well. For example, it is a marvelous boon to small individually owned bed-and-breakfasts, enabling them to publicize their presence very inexpensively. Prior to Internet advertising, they had to rely on road signs, the Yellow Pages, or relatively expensive advertisements in their local town tourist magazine and elsewhere. Imagine the impact of http://www.inetgiant.com/ on local and even larger newspaper classified advertising—traditionally the "cash cow" for most dailys. The site now offers free classified ads, run in "thousands of free sites" and e-mail "blasted" to over 5 million "targeted" customers. How does any newspaper compete with that? The critical receiver will ask, "How many read them?" or "Does it work?" and "How do they make any money doing that?" Yes, the Internet democratizes small voices, but it can't guarantee an audience that pays attention.

The challenge for persuaders is to frame persuasion in ways that draws visitors to their sites and not those of their competitors, and then to draw the customers into reading (and that requires literacy), and more importantly, to ensure that the customers carefully consider what is being offered for what is being given. In other words, the consumer must ask what are the costs and benefits if he or she decides to read and process this information. And this is where critical reception comes in once again. Are there a significant number of audience members paying any attention to the millions of bloggers, chat groups, MySpace, and Facebook members out there aside from a handful of perhaps 250 "friends" (who perhaps are really just occasional readers or "acquaintances")? If not, then we are possibly facing an electronic "cage" where crowds of persons and/or businesses are communicating with an insignificant minority of possibly bored participants. We may be like a cage full of chimpanzees chirping at one another to no effect.

Of course, television had the same problem in its infancy when only 100,000 persons owned a set (programming sometimes consisted of a "test pattern" or simple puppet shows), and critics labeled it a temporary gimmick. Yet look how it changed our lives (although when you surf today's channel selections, the fare seems awfully watery). So the democratization of the individual may, in the end, not add up to as much as hoped for, even though it has made information readily available and the opinion of others is ubiquitous. On the other hand, it may prove to be more beneficial than was Guttenberg's printing press, and look what it brought.

Information on Demand

A major selling point of the Internet is its ability to deliver information (especially advertising and other persuasive messages) immediately to a 24/7, networked, potentially enormous global audience as we noted in our discussion of the Seven Faces of Persuasion. As one critic put it "the gold rush is on" for advertising revenues (see http://www. catalogs.com/info/gadgets/effective-internet-advertising.html for a few insights). Of course, while traditional businesses still struggle to find hours to accommodate customers across time zones in just our nation, the Internet has already "seen it overtake newspaper and magazine revenue with TV in its sights" (Walters, 2007). Naturally, the Internet provides and collects information worldwide regardless of the hour. And, of course, in complex situations that involves many issues, it's still preferable to deal with a person than a machine. However, many routine transactions are well suited to the Internet, just as automatic teller machines can handle most of our banking needs.

Whether we like it or not, the Internet does provide advertising information to consumers like you and me on this 24/7 basis so we must learn to respond to it. The task for persuaders promoting products and brands is how to attract potential customers to their site to harvest the information, and in terms of persons like yourselves—aged 18 to 34—keep in mind that advertising vendors didn't pay over $2 billion for YouTube and MySpace on a whim. They know that you receivers out there in the blogosphere are looking for all that free information/power that is so easily available. Know also that you are in your most impressionable years, just when you are developing your deepest brand loyalties (Walters, 2007) so be prepared to critically process and respond to the persuasion you are and will continue to face. We are only in the first stages of experimenting with the Internet advertising challenge. In the meantime, while the Internet allows persuadees to easily research available information on candidates, brands, donating to, or joining a particular organization, remember that Internet ads also create what are called "brand impressions" or instants when the name of the brand is processed by one of your senses into your central nervous system to be stored and recalled (as both Schwartz and McLuhan predicted) when making an important decision. Be ready to exercise your critical skills.

Direct-to-Consumer Markets Without Geographic Boundaries

Naturally, the Direct Marketing Industry has discovered the Internet very early on—no kidding? But even starting so early, at present over 30 percent of their revenues is being reaped from online consumers and this is in a time when most of them are basically niche marketers targeting very small audiences with specialized needs. In a way, that is very good. Consumers who previously were ignored by giant industries are now getting services they never had. The Internet also provides direct

market access to people around the globe, whereas earlier direct marketing was geographically limited. Direct marketers doing business online are also much more able to provide more and better customer service. But remember that they are also able to more carefully test variables—the price they ask, the extras they include, the subject line in the message, the signature, and so on—to get results almost immediately. This allows them to fine-tune and craft their messages and offers, again making the receiver more and more vulnerable to such appeals. So once again the receiver needs to hone critical skills. And the power of Internet information goes further than exploiting catalog customers; it can aid small businesses that were previously cut out of the marketplace. Small, independent organic coffee growers now possess the means to sell their crops internationally for better prices by cutting out the middleman—a process called disintermediation. And in the arts, many fine artists now use the Internet's direct-to-consumer capability to sell their art and avoid paying commissions. People can use eBay, Craigslist, and other networks to buy and sell across national boundaries and thus avoid taxes and regulations and re-sell merchandise to their own benefit. For persuadees, the Internet can make price, quality, quantity, and selection available before they have to make a purchase decision, as was the case with auto buyers armed with accurate information about the real costs. It seems highly probable that site evaluation or rating systems will soon emerge for each and every category of product, cause, candidate for office, religious philosophy, and a host more. The receivers will have to be aware of such developments in order to continue to be critical processors of the most important information available from among all the options.

Increased Access and Convenience

As shown in Figure 13.4, CDW-G is dedicated to improving the technological efficiency and capabilities of college campuses. That could translate to more time instructors can spend with students and less time being hampered by outmoded technology. Outside the working world, increased Internet ac-

We don't know much about
Molecular Biochemistry. But when it comes
to technology, we're quite educated.

College is supposed to be challenging, but your campus's technology shouldn't be. That's why CDW-G has everything
your institution needs to take advantage of the latest technology and move toward creating a 21st Century Campus.
We can help you attract new students and staff with everything from more interactive classrooms to creating a
wireless campus. Our technology can also help support your institution's broader goals like research, academic and
administrative computing. With account managers and technology specialists who understand the needs of higher
education, and a broad range of products and services, CDW-G has the resources and technology solutions for your
campus. Visit the21stcenturycampus.com today. It's an education all its own.

The 21ˢᵗ Century Campus™

the21stcenturycampus.com | 800.767.4239

The Right Technology. Right Away.™

©2008 CDW Government, Inc.

FIGURE 13.4 CDW
Government, Inc., in addition
to offering its regular products,
are now working to share technology with college campuses.
It should increase student access
and convenience to Internet
resources.

SOURCE: Courtesy of CDW. All Rights
Reserved. Visit www.cdwg.com.

cess and technological innovations offer instructors
and students (and all consumers) the opportunity to
spend more time with their families and friends,
more time on commitments, and more time to enjoy activities and pursue other interests.

Consumers may now choose online purchase
opportunities such as http://www.peapod.com/
and can consider many more choices than are generally available locally to save time, travel costs, and
other troubles having to do with real-time shopping.
This option is changing the retail industry in favor of

persuadees as is niche marketing via the Internet, and
this can accrue advantages and convenience for consumers with special needs. For example, people with
very narrow or very wide feet have more shoe options
via the Internet than at the shoe store in the mall. This
tactic, with the help of the Internet will result in many
more new and successful start-up home businesses.
Persuaders who wish to focus on niche or specialty
markets can now do so far more easily than ever before. But an old-fashioned word of consumer caution
is needed—"Let the Buyer Beware."

Ethical Behavior on the Internet

To this point, ethical use of the Internet has mainly focused on using the Internet for research, but many newer and more critical issues are emerging daily, and codes of Internet ethics are emerging covering many different issues like student use of e-mail, health care, pornography, privacy issues, financial issues, Internet counseling, legal issues, and a host more. (I find over 177,000 Web sites on this topic right now.) The Internet's potentially unseemly underbelly brings opportunities to exploit others, and critical receivers again need to be prepared for these and how they can affect our communities and our quality of life. As with mail-order houses, consumers must always question whether a persuader is trustworthy. A key issue for persuaders on the Internet involves establishing their credibility, and for persuadees, their task is to search out credible sources. Again, rating systems may help. Many merchants and persons doing business on the Internet are forming associations that provide some level of assurance of trustworthiness. The best advice we can give to Internet users—whether senders or receivers—is to give careful thought to what might or might not be ethical regarding the issue, brand, candidate, or other commodity you are dealing with, and ironically, you can get advice simply by entering the words "internet" "ethics" and a word or words describing the topic or issue about which you are unsure.

REVIEW AND CONCLUSION

The average college freshman has watched tens of thousands of hours of television and hundreds of thousands of commercials by the time he or she comes to school. And TV is just one media channel being used for persuasion. Billboards, films, magazines, and newspapers affect most of us. Labels, bumper stickers, T-shirts, and other paraphernalia persuade us. And most recently we opened the potential "Pandora's Box" of the Internet. Positive and negative things beyond our imaginations will come from it. All in all, we live in a highly persuasive, media-rich environment, and we need to be aware of how media affect us, especially in regard to persuasion.

New media have effected great changes in how we were persuaded in the past and how we are being persuaded in the present. We have looked at the major communication innovations over time and how they changed persuasion and society forever after their introduction. We need to be persuaded about some things, and media persuasion is sometimes the best way to get information about alternatives. You can protect yourself from unscrupulous persuasive attempts made by various media by looking beneath the surface. Look for the responsive chords being plucked via the verbal, visual, and auditory scripts, and whether the messages that elicit them are hot or cool. Examine how the introduction of a new medium extends one of your senses or body parts. Consider whether "the medium is the message" and what the implications of that concept are as you are targeted by persuaders. In public affairs, look for the agendas being set by the media, what you are being forced to think about, and how that can affect you as a persuadee.

You also need to examine your own patterns of behavior in media use. Why do you turn to media, and to which media do you turn? What needs do they meet for you? What do you learn from them? Also consider the immense changes we are facing because of the development of new communications media (Gumpert & Drucker, 2002; Larson, 2002; Postman, 1996; Zettl, 1996). Establishing trustworthiness remains important across all of these media innovations, but it is particularly important with regard to the Internet. To restate previous advice—"Let the Receiver Beware."

KEY TERMS

After reading this chapter, you should be able to identify, explain, and give an example of the following key terms or concepts:

spoken word

written word

printed word

electronic word

interactive word

evoked recall

experiential meaning

responsive chord

verbal script

auditory or sound script

sight or visual script

development of a "global village"

access code

signal

high-fidelity forms

low-fidelity forms

sensory involvement

sensory participation

hot media

definition

cool media

uses and gratification theory

surveillance

curiosity

diversion

personal identity

agenda-setting

social learning theory

cultivation theory

news bite

ignoring

favoring the sponsor

pseudoevents

bias: verbal and nonverbal

APPLICATION OF ETHICS

On April 2, 2004, editors at two newspapers decided to publish a controversial front-page picture of the dismembered and charred remains of four American civilian contractors with their body parts hanging from a bridge. A crowd of Iraqis were cheering the sight in the foreground. The editors had to consider a number of ethical issues before deciding to publish the photo. Here are a few of those issues to consider. Should the picture have been published at all? From the "Letters to the Editor" in the days following, publication opinion ran from "outlandish" to "necessary for the public to see" to one suggesting the papers get a Pulitzer Prize for poor taste. What if the bodies were of soldiers? What if the bodies were Iraqi? What if they hadn't been dismembered or charred? What if they had been of women and/or children? Could running the photo affect public opinion about the war? Would you run the picture on the front page? Inside? Would you warn readers of the graphic nature of the photos? Why or why not? It also ran on various television news reports. Would it be ethical to display the event on an Internet site?

QUESTIONS FOR FURTHER THOUGHT

1. What are some similarities between primitive oral/aural cultures and the electronic culture in which we now live?

2. Why is information associated with power? Give examples.

3. How was the concept of ownership associated with the development of writing? Print? Television and radio? The Internet?

4. What changes in literacy resulted from the development of print?

5. How did literacy both free us and enslave us?

6. What are some of the developments at the Media Lab at MIT? How will they affect us in the future?

7. Which media type—hot or cool—dominates our times?

8. What are some examples of the criteria gatekeepers may be using to determine what to put on the evening news?

9. What are the implications of an unregulated Internet? What are we doing about it?

10. What should the ethics of Internet communication include?

11. What are the implications of the exploding presence of interactive media?

12. How does cultural diversity affect the many media of our times?

13. What are the implications of the many potentially propagandistic appeals being made on the Internet?

14. How can receivers possibly navigate the many options on the Internet when choosing to shop, vote, join, donate, and so on?

 For online activities, go to the *Persuasion* book companion Web site at http://academic.cengage.com/communication/larson12.

14

✳

The Use of Persuasive Premises in Advertising and IMC

LEARNING GOALS

After reading this chapter, you should be able to:

1. Describe, explain, and give examples of the various tasks that advertising can accomplish and the tactics that are used to achieve them.

2. Explain the difference between advertising and integrated marketing communication (IMC).

3. Differentiate among the various elements of IMC, such as consumer advertising, sales promotion, P.R., event planning, and others.

4. Explain the functions of demographic, sociographic, psychographic, and ethnographic advertising research.

5. Identify and explain various techniques for positioning a brand and name some of those positions, and discuss repositioning a brand.

6. Explain the VALS model's major and minor categories of consumers.

7. Recognize weasel words used in advertising, explain and give examples of them.

8. Apply Rank's 30-second-spot quiz to several television spots.

9. Differentiate between obvious, sophisticated, and subliminal sexual appeals in advertising.

We have referred to many examples of advertising that effectively persuade receivers in our 24/7, media-saturated and diverse world of advocacy and propaganda. Of course advertising is rooted in a results-oriented perspective that will improve the "bottom line" of the company or organization and yield "profit" to someone or some group in the forms of purchases, votes, donations, and so on. In this chapter we will examine this form of persuasion—the almost constant, insistent, and sometimes annoying world of commercial advertising on behalf of brands, persons, or ideas. We will look in-depth at the several jobs it can do or tasks it can accomplish, as well as what tactics it uses to do those jobs or tasks. We will also examine how it works with other forms of marketing persuasion, and how ad researchers analyze and target the audiences most likely to purchase. This will include how they position or reposition their brands against the competition, how ad agents develop persuasive advertising strategies, tactics, and especially how they use language in the ads—sometimes accurately but sometimes deceptively as well. We will also explore the many recent changes in advertising and their implications for the future. Additionally, we will explore the increasingly controversial topic of sexual appeals in advertising and the possibility of subliminal persuasion in advertising.

Advertising is a fascinating kind of persuasion to study, especially in a rapidly changing culture such as ours. Just mention the word "advertising" in almost any group and a lively conversation will follow—everyone has an opinion on it. Since the inception of modern brand advertising in the late 1900s, it has had dramatic impact on our purchasing, voting, donating, joining, and other decisions since at least the time of widely distributed newspapers and magazines, if not earlier. It affects our identification with brands, our forming of attitudes toward them, our evaluations and adoption or rejection of them, and even our choosing of a preferred lifestyle that promises us certain amenities associated with the brand. In previous chapters, we discussed various approaches to direct and interactive marketing, Internet ads, market segmentation, and other examples of what is sometimes called the "marketing mix." A more recent term for this varied array of persuasive techniques is called **integrated marketing communication**, or **IMC**, and it is a new and unique way to promote brands, persons, and ideas using more than the traditional consumer advertising and promotional forms of persuasion on behalf of brands used in the past. A major goal of IMC is to build a one-to-one dialogue or a unified and personalized "relationship" between brands and consumers using various kinds of persuasion. It uses advertising as its major component most of the time, but IMC also includes direct marketing, public relations, event planning, sales promotion, packaging, personal

selling tactics, and interactive and Internet communication of various kinds to name a few. All of these operate together to create a unified message with unique appeal about most brands. Using highly sophisticated research data, these ads are "customized" for certain "slices" or segments of the consumer market. In the case of IMC, this customization results in the whole being greater than the sum of its parts. This means that the advertising is reinforced by the public relations, which in turn strengthens the brand's use of direct marketing, sales promotion, public relations, and so on. As a result, each tactic of persuasion makes every other tactic stronger and more effective than it would have been alone, and so the whole package becomes highly persuasive.

This chapter focuses particularly on consumer advertising as the key (but not the only) element in successful IMC. Other elements in IMC are important as well, but not generally part of this chapter. Additionally, there are various new emerging trends in advertising like the need to respond to the increasing diversity in our society, new technologies that are being adapted to advertising, and so on that will come to play and be noted as a part in our considerations. For example, take advertising targeted at Latinos in the United States whose portion of the economy continues to grow. At 13 percent of the U.S. population, they are the largest ethnic minority. In fact, McDonald's devotes 10 percent of its general-market ads to Spanish-language spots (Wentz & Cuneo, 2002). At the same time, the fastest growing and most affluent ethnic group in the country is Asians from a variety of countries, while the fastest growing market segment is consumers who are aged 50+ years and who are also usually affluent. The diversity of the marketplace is increasing, thus presenting the ad industry with many challenges in getting brand acceptance, use, and ultimately brand loyalty. And these segmentations are only part of the ever changing industry.

At this point let's distinguish between a "brand" and a "product" since many people use those terms interchangeably as in "Downey is the best *product* for softening clothes," when they mean it is the best *brand* in their opinion. There are many brands in each product category, and the role of advertising is to distinguish among them (often they are near clones of one another) and then to get as many consumers as possible to favor and purchase one particular brand from among the many others. To do this they use the elements of IMC and especially advertising to accomplish one or more of the several "tasks" or jobs necessary in order to move the brand off the shelves, into the shopping baskets, and ultimately to their homes or places of business. Let us now briefly examine some of those tasks and the persuasive tactics they use.

THE TASKS OF ADVERTISING AND THEIR TACTICS

It is obvious that the underlying task of all advertising is to increase sales and profits—to increase or "lift" sales of the brand—but there are many ways that advertising can help do this. One basic model that we discussed back in Chapter 11 is the "Hierarchy of Effects" model which sets out several sequential stages of persuasion (in this case advertising) that occur on the way to the purchase of a brand, a vote for a candidate, a donation to the good cause, or the adoption of an ideology or a practice such as recycling. Most consumers, voters, donors, and so on begin by being totally unaware of the brand, candidate, or idea that is being promoted, so the first task of advertising is to create:

Stage 1. *Awareness*, which then needs to be led to

Stage 2. *Increased Knowledge* about the brand before

Stage 3. *Preference* will develop. Once the brand is known, this preference for the brand is usually based on its advertising or word of mouth from friends. If it is disliked, of course, the persuasion and the brand fail. But if it is liked, based on its ads and/or word of mouth, advertising may even lead to the consumers becoming

Stage 4. *Convinced* of its superiority. Of course, they will never know if this is true unless they can be induced to try it, so another task of advertising is to lead to

Stage 5. *Prompting of Trial* of the brand. If the trial goes well, they will ultimately

Stage 6. *Evaluate* the brand positively and finally move to the hoped for

Stage 7. *Development of Brand Loyalty* and will thus repurchase it many times over. At least that is the hope of the brand and its advertiser. In fact, marketing experts often refer to this brand loyalty as "The Lifetime Value of the Customer" which, as you can imagine can be enormous.

And now with the Internet and interactive advertising increasing, the job of the copywriter in achieving any of these tasks is more challenging. A few tips that will help can be discovered by following up on suggestions given in Box 14.1.

We will discuss this concept in more depth later. In any case, moving consumers through those stages is the prime task of all advertising. Now, what advertising strategies and appropriate tactics might be used to get consumers moving into and through those stages? Let's look at a few.

Promote Brand Features and Benefits

Every successful brand has some *perceived benefit* in the consumer's mind. That particular benefit makes them choose the brand time after time. Usually, the benefit comes from some *feature of the brand*. For example, independent wheel suspension in autos is a feature that yields the benefits of a smoother rides and better and safer handling, so the advertising needs to not only mention the feature but also

---

BOX 14.1   Interactive Short Course on Ad Copy

For an informative and fun short course on developing ad copy go to http://search engineland.com/070904-150912.php where you will find a discussion of five search questions a copywriter should ask when trying to develop copy for an ad—captivating headlines, features, benefits, unique selling propositions, and calls to action. For a few chuckles go to the link at http://searchengineland .com/070904-141959.php where you will find mock ads for cereals with humorous names like "Larryos, Raisin Brin, Porn Flakes, and Other Google Cereals." Follow some of the other links there for some good laughs.

---

to stress its personal benefits to the consumer. For example, Cheerios, traditionally a children's brand but losing market share to sugared cereals, responded to concerns older Americans have about the amount of fiber in their diets, Cheerios now advertises that the brand contains 100 percent oat bran as a feature, as opposed to being a "fun" cereal. Now it always did have bran or whole oats in it, but children weren't concerned about that, so it had no appeal for them and it gave them no reason to ask their parents to buy it. Naturally, the perceived benefit of 100 percent oats for older folks is that bran has lots of fiber so it results in a healthier and fiber-full diet.

A common feature of electronically operated devices (whose benefit is obviously the saving of time) is to advertise "Batteries Included" when selling these battery-powered toys or appliances. "Open 24 Hours" is another feature, and of course it yields a convenience benefit for the consumer. Another good way to show benefits is to actually demonstrate them to consumers, and TV is an excellent medium for demonstrations, which is why we see so many TV ads that use the tactic (the Bow Flex or other exercise machine, or various gourmet cooking devices like the revolving oven or special knives and food processors). Promoting a brand's features and the resulting benefits is one task that advertising can achieve using several tactics of persuasion—testimonials, statistics, examples, demonstrations, and others.

Generate Traffic

In order for consumers to make most purchases, they have to be in the retail store, reading the cata-

log or direct mail offer, watching the right TV channel at the right time, listening to the radio ad while they have a cell phone handy to place the order, or go to the correct Web site to order. Therefore, another task of advertising is to get them there or to create traffic at the Point of Purchase, also known in the industry as the POP. You are probably most familiar with how this is done in grocery ads. They usually do this by offering some familiar and even staple goods like milk or eggs at below cost. These items are called "loss leaders" because they lead consumers to the store by taking a loss. These special prices draw consumers to the store or POP where they make many other purchases. In fact, some estimates say that as many as 60 percent of the items in the shopping cart at the checkout counter are purchased on impulse, even if the customer brings a shopping list with them to the store.

Another time-proven tactic for generating store traffic is a "Free" offer. Consumers come in for the free item(s) and stay to purchase other things. Sweepstakes work this way also. Folks come in to try the key they got in the mail to see if it opens the new SUV, and if it does, they win it. Naturally if their key doesn't fit, they can look around at other models. Money off on the first purchase from a catalog also works as does "Pay per Click" (in which the Internet advertiser pays search engines for placing them early in the log of relevant sites. Yet another tactic for generating traffic is to offer some service or advice for "Free" if the consumer comes in—checking the battery in your watch, for example. Internet free offers include things like "Install a Free Screensaver on Your Laptop!" or "Free Music Downloads Now!" and all of them have worked in the past. As we noted several times, "Free" is probably the most powerful word in the ad master's vocabulary.

Another way to get traffic is to have some special attraction or event happening. The event might be a celebrity who is signing autographs at the store, attention-getting giant balloons or blimps flying over the store, sweepstakes where the customer must come in to enter, or having a "kiddie carnival" in the store's parking lot; all have been used to generate store traffic. More recently, creating traffic for Web sites has become a major issue and the use of ad or e-mail "Blasting" and using advertising on eBay and Craigslist have also been successfully used to generate traffic and thus increase sales. Of course, more are being invented all the time. Go to http://www.kewego.com/search/?q=generate+traffic+for+free for a tour of how extreme videos have been used to create traffic and have some fun at the same time.

Make Brand Comparisons

To be truly successful, all brands need to be perceived of as superior to the competition in the minds of consumers. Comparative advertising is one way to convince them that Brand X is superior to the others. Comparative advertising is defined as advertising in which there is mention of a *specific competing brand* (not just "the competition" or "other brands") and some sort of comparison that must be stated or implied to show why the competitor is inferior. Consider a Duracell ad in which a "bunny" operating on a Duracell outlasts a "bunny" running on a no-brand black battery. The end of the ad makes the claim that cheaper batteries wear out faster, and the implication is that since Eveready batteries are cheaper, they won't last as long as Duracells. Naturally, the competition is likely to cry "foul," so the FTC has had to establish a number of regulations (e.g., full disclosure, complete substantiation, improper disparagement) regulating comparative advertising. That's why the vague "other brands" is so frequently used to avoid noncompliance with the FTC regulations. Advertisers want consumers to believe that their brand or candidate is better than the opposition especially in regard to price, quality, and performance. These kinds of comparison ads are especially good ways to do this and, of course, guarantees, warranties, and demonstrations are also excellent ways to make comparisons so again TV is frequently used, but according to the FTC, the demonstrations may not be deceptive in any way. Comparison lists of statistics, specifications, or ingredients are also good ways to show superiority using such things as different mileage or interest rates, costs, standards, performance, quotations from users or rating services, and so on. Usually the basis of most ad comparisons relates to the way features produce consumer benefits. Taste tests are also a tactic to make comparisons using actual consumers to do the comparing. The consumer tastes both Pepsi and Coke and then rates them; and if the advertiser's brand wins, the results are ballyhooed far and wide. The tactic has been used to compare numerous products including pet foods, organically grown vegetables and fruits, garden plants, and "healthy" snacks for teenagers. One potential drawback to comparison advertising is that there is always the danger that simply mentioning the competition's name will increase and reinforce that competing brand's memorability at the POP. The old advice of making sure the persuader is not comparing "apples to oranges" is always good advice for receivers when comparisons are being made in ads or when confronting demonstrations of competing brands.

Induce Trial

One of the most difficult stages to get one's prospects to reach is actually trying the brand or idea, and this is especially true if the brand is a new introduction on the market, expensive, or complex to use. The task is made more difficult because many brands are nearly identical in contents, features, and benefits. A good example is "Sure" versus "Secret" deodorants. Their list of ingredients is identical as are their sizes and recommended price, so how does the advertiser get consumers to try one of them over the other? Free samples are a favorite tactic to persuade consumers to try the brand, but another way is to come up with an ad slogan and copy that tells the brand story. Secret's long-lasting winner is "Strong Enough for a

Man. But Made for a Woman," which, according to research, targets the key audience—insecure females, aged 12 to 24 with uncertainty about gender identity (see http://www.killianadvertising.com/wp16.html for a more detailed analysis). The slogan sounds kind of daring as well. A more familiar example of the free sample being used to induce trial is seen in supermarkets all the time—especially on Saturdays when one can "graze" through the store on free samples. The free sample is usually accompanied by a coupon for the brand, thus giving the consumer two reasons to make the purchase—the free taste and the monetary savings.

A favorite way that car dealers have used for many decades to induce trial is to urge the prospect to "Take 'er out for a test drive." And the prospect usually notices the difference between the demonstrator and their existing car, which often helps make the sale. Using an ingenious tactic, one auto company sold many of its models at greatly reduced prices to auto rental companies, convinced that if only the potential customers drove the vehicles, they would like, prefer, and hopefully, finally buy the brand. In this way, renting one of the models induced trial, and it worked to lift sales. Of course, discounts such as coupons and rebates can also induce trial. In the final analysis, however, the product must perform as promised or even in a superior way.

Generate Qualified Leads

Some product types (especially high-priced and complex ones) are difficult to sell using traditional methods (e.g., energy efficient furnaces, home theatre systems). They are hard to demonstrate, even on television, and are expensive to demonstrate in a home for a single trial purpose (given the salesperson's time and wages plus the risk of damaging the system during set-up and take-down). While the trial works well in finally getting the sale, (and is sometimes possible onsite), advertisers want their sales personnel to spend time and resources on only those prospects who are most likely to ultimately buy the product type. These good prospects usually already like the product type and are shopping for the best brand; with the proper sales technique, they will buy the demonstrator's brand. What the advertiser wants to do is to identify those persons who most likely want or need the product category and then to promote their brand of that product in one way or another. One of the ways to do this is to focus on the knowledge stage of the hierarchy of effects. In other words, the advertiser needs to educate the potential buyer not only about the product category (which they already want to purchase) but also about their brand and its strengths (and especially against the competition and its flaws). As noted, it's hard to do a demonstration of a furnace or a complete home theatre system on a short 30-second or even longer television commercial or to stage a live demonstration in the home. Therefore, many advertisers rely on television, direct mail, or another medium to offer further free information about the product type and the brand in the form of booklets, DVDs, extended free trials, or trips to the factory, as tactics to induce the prospect to become educated about the product type and the brand.

Sometimes interactive advertising can do the trick. If a consumer is researching something like a furnace, he or she might use the Internet as a resource, and "pay per click" advertising may be the most economical way to get users involved, particularly if a clever "hook" is used to get the prospect to make the click to go into the brand's Web site and see an extended video demonstration of the brand. In some cases, prospective consumers can request to see an even longer and more detailed video. This technique is called "Permission Advertising." Casinos frequently get potential customers to try the games of chance by giving then an initial "stake" or free spins of the wheel, and even children's versions of some gaming to get them "hooked" early, thus assuring a greater "Lifetime Value of the Customer."

Prompt Purchase.   Most salespersons will tell you that the hardest part of a sale is "closing" or "asking for the order" as it is sometimes called. Most advertisers want consumers to make "on the spot" purchase decisions, but there is a lot of customer resistance to making the decision too quickly. While all consumers make some impulse purchases, most need to be motivated in some way to finally get out their wallets and make the ultimate purchase. The usual strategy is for the advertiser to create some sense of *urgency* or the need to take prompt action, warning that they will lose the opportunity by waiting to decide. There are several tactics for doing this. For example, urgency can be communicated by setting a time limit that the consumer must meet in order to get the special promoted price, so expiration dates work well on some devices (e.g., coupons, rebates) as do phrases like "13 Hour Sale!" or "Only a Few Left at This Price!" "Supplies Limited!" or the old reliable "Act Now!" all of which usually work well at creating this need for prompt action.

Promising quick action for a service is also a good way to trigger the purchases of the service such as plumbing. "We'll Be There in Fifteen Minutes or You Can Reduce the Price 25%!" is a clever promise, especially since the consumer doesn't know what the price was initially. When the issue is prompt payment of bills, the offer of a reduction if paid within 10 days or less often works. Offering a bonus or even a "surprise bonus" is another tactic. We often see this on direct television pitches. The original offer is made, but if you call the 1-800 number in the next 15 minutes, they'll send you not one, not two, but three of the kitchen food processors, and then there is usually another tagged on "Plus, if you act now…" to get you to make the call, place the order, and get the added bonus blade sharpener. Prompt ordering is always increased by making it easy for the consumer to respond. That's why the "inbound" 1-800 telephone numbers and plastic credit have both been boons to these advertisers, and they regularly succeed. Besides, they offer the well-trained operator/salespersons who answer your call to "up-sell" and get you to buy the two pair of wool socks to go with the hunting boots that were all you really intended to purchase.

Building the Brand

Of course "Building the Brand" has been a major task of advertising since the inception of branded goods back in the late nineteenth century, and it is a even more of a byword in today's ad industry. At first, most consumer goods were basically generic. You bought unbranded soda crackers from a barrel by the bagful at the general store, and they varied in quality and freshness. Then in the late 1890s, the National Biscuit Company branded and advertised its version of soda crackers as "U-Needa Biscuit" and packaged them in a protective and well-sealed package, thus reducing breakage and avoiding staleness. Furthermore, the package itself was useful for storing things like nuts and bolts when the crackers were gone. So advertising and packaging began to help "Build the Brand" and the rest is history for Nabisco and its many "line extensions" (e.g., Ritz Crackers, Barnum's Animal Crackers, Oreos, and more).

There are many strategies and tactics used to build brands, but none is more familiar than simple repetition done through a combination of advertising, packaging, logos, jingles, slogans, brand names, and the use of multiple media types to assure that the brand name is repeatedly picked up by one or more of the consumer's physical senses (see "Planting" in Chapter 12). One kind of brand-building ad tactic is the testimonial given by a satisfied user who seems trustworthy and gives you the details from his or her point of view. Weight loss and special diet products frequently use this combined with before and after pictures—both Don Shula and his wife lost noticeable pounds on Nutri-System. Another brand-building device is the use of powerful images, music, and words in the advertising and packaging, examples of which we all can recall (e.g., "Wheaties—the Breakfast of Champions" accompanied by pictures of a famous athlete on the package). Another way is to make the advertising of the brand entertaining and memorable—Tony the Tiger is but one enduring example, as is Geico's caveman. Some advertisers choose to tell the "story" of the brand. Others may target new market segments like minorities and gays, or by using a gender focus. Still others make their brand into a symbol of a lifestyle that target individuals want to emulate (e.g., Rolex, Victoria's Secret).

Advertisers may associate the brand with certain experiences like world travel, whitewater rafting, or kayaking. Some suggest new uses or recipes for the brand so that consumers try the new applications and thus increase use and repurchase. Avon's "Skin So Soft" claims to have over 80 uses, including use as an insect repellant. Interestingly enough, coupons associated with recipes succeed better than the coupon alone, and coupons with a dotted border work even better. If there is a tiny scissors on the dotted line, redemption rates will increase even more. In a way, clipping a coupon is a behavioral intention (see Chapter 7). When we clip a coupon, we intend to purchase the brand, wherein lies its selling power. There are many other tactics for building the brand (e.g., contests where entrants must write a slogan for the brand, sweepstakes, free prizes, clothing with the brand name imprinted on it) but regardless of which ones are used, the basic goal is to create brand awareness, preference, and ultimately brand loyalty because it is the repeat purchase or the number of sales that really counts—the focus is on the "lifetime value of the customer." Building the brand involves IMC and all of its dimensions, repeated exposures over long periods of time, and clever advertising copy and design coordinated with memorable packaging and tempting sales promotion.

Adapting to Change

The advertising industry like many others is constantly changing with many new forces—especially technology—coming into play. If the most powerful word in advertising is "Free!" certainly the word "New" must rank nearly as high. We are a culture that is fascinated by the new, the entertaining, and the different; and this is reflected in advertising as well. So advertisers and their receivers must be constantly aware that new and innovative ways are always being tried on consumers to "get the sale." No change has affected advertising in the last decades more than the Internet and digital technologies. MSN sponsored an extended study entitled "The Consumer in Control" whose results indicate that power in advertising today has shifted from the various media to the consumers who now have many more options for purchasing goods, much more convenience in doing so, and are becoming more and more empowered and savvy in their me-

dia use decisions. As a result, "future advertising needs to be more engaging, interactive, and relevant if it is to succeed." says Joanne Oates of Brand Republic. The report notes that the days of the 30-second television commercial are over. In large measure, these changes are due to digital technology plus the extraordinary fragmentation in the number and type of media choices available, the fragmentation of the audiences into ever more discreet segments, and the proliferation of brands within all product categories. The future promises to bring the consumer the opportunity to be rewarded for watching or reading advertisements through free music downloads, interactive games, things like airships with 30′ by 70′ interactive "billboards" overhead, new techniques by Neilson ratings to measure audiences, new applications for search engines, advertisements on siwickis, a change in how advertisers buy ad time during the "upfront" season (due in part to a writer's strike that crippled "Sweeps Week"), and a host of others yet to be introduced. Some ad experts have characterized our contemporary era as a "sea change" in the world of advertising with the main problem for advertisers being that of trying to anticipate where that change is most likely going to occur—via the Internet, interactive advertising, stealth advertising, viral advertising, or other new techniques, all of which have come into being only recently. A great example was the degree to which the "Ball Girl" video clip (see www.Break.com and YouTube. Hughlett & Benderdorf, 2008) The video of a ball girl making an unbelievable catch of a foul ball that the pro left fielder didn't even attempt to catch got 1.5 to 2 million views on YouTube and was the most shared video on Break.com, another video-sharing Web site. The video clip of her catch then followed her back to the ball girl's seat where a partially finished bottle of Gatorade was standing. That's all the advertising it took to spur Gatorade's image. As receivers, we need to attend carefully to these changes as they catch on and hone our critical skills to be ready to meet the new ad challenges facing us. And well we should—look at how advertising dominates the culture of our modern times. And as Box 14.2 demonstrates how it will continue to dominate our culture even more in the future.

Many of the changes that we can't yet even foresee in the world of advertising are anticipated for us at http://www.youtube.com/watch?v=K-eF4getQy0&feature=related in a three-part half-hour video series (three 10 to 11 minute segments that can be viewed one at a time) produced by PBS. Follow some of the links there and learn about various topics like how to get your video on YouTube, how mass culture will persevere in spite of dire predictions, and what to expect (at least in part) from the future of advertising.

A few simple statistics tell the story. While we excel at many things, we Americans produce more popular culture than all of the rest of the world taken together. Americans are also the world's biggest and best producers, as well as consumers, of the kind of pop culture known as advertising. Consider the following surprising statistics:

- The average per capita expenditure on advertising in the United States is now well over $1,000/year.

- The average American sees or hears between 2,000 to 5,000 or perhaps more advertisements per day according to various estimates. No wonder there is what the industry calls "clutter."

Compare those numbers with what the rest of the world spends on advertising, including the Western democracies such as the United Kingdom, Canada, the rest of "old" Europe, Japan, and increasingly India and China. They spend less than $100/year per person. No wonder the many newcomers to the United States cannot believe that anyone can process all that advertising—radio, television, papers, magazines, billboards, signs, T-shirts, spaces to print on, buses, airports, the Internet, and on and on. The fact is: No one can begin to process even a small part of what we are exposed to each day, so advertisers need to be extraordinarily creative in "breaking through the clutter," Nonetheless, the rate of U.S. spending on ads is increasing annually and is predicted to do so for the foreseeable future. And that's reason enough for persuadees to learn about this form of highly persuasive communication (Larson, 2007).

Some advertising ranks as pop art and is creative and entertaining, and some of it is simply junk. Our goal in this chapter, however, is not to evaluate the creative side of the industry (take an advertising design class for that) but to learn how advertising affects human society and behavior, how it persuades, and where it is likely to go in the future (here and throughout the emerging global economy), and especially how it persuades us. We need to discover whether those effects are bad or good for us in particular and for humanity in general, as well as how understanding advertising can help us understand ourselves as consumers. Marxist critics see advertising as a tool of the upper classes used to exploit the lower classes because it creates wants for unneeded goods and thus tempts people to waste their "wage slave" earnings on them. Advertising executives see ads as a way to beat the competition while making big bucks. And consumers see them as either just so much clutter or as a silly kind of entertainment. Often advertisements intend not only to persuade but also to inform us, and that is one of the values put forward by ad executives for the industry in addition to the claim that by creating competition there will ultimately be a reduction in prices. They will stress that competition brings new product types to market—some of which are actually beneficial. We need product, political, and idea/ideological information to make purchase, voting, donating, and joining decisions; sometimes that information comes from advertising.

Consider how the introduction of the Internet has changed our lives and how it has changed our purchasing and voting behavior. The Internet is also changing the face of advertising enormously, and it will play a major role in the future by all predictions (Cuneo, 2002). "All Things Considered" reported early in 2006 that more and more traditional advertising efforts (e.g., television spots, print ads) are being replaced with Internet ads and banners (N.P.R., January 3, 2006). As noted above, the Internet is also being used for what is called "permission advertising" where the consumer actually asks to receive an extended ad on behalf of the brand—perhaps as much as 20 minutes of informative material to help them make decisions about a variety of brands, candidates, and other issues. ("All Things Considered," January 3, 2006). That's remarkable if you think of it—consumers actually *requesting* advertising! Research shows that 92 percent of the large audience of mainly affluent teens are online and seeing advertising all the while. Don't you think that advertising works? And don't you wonder if they are going to change our over-advertised culture for better or worse? Hoping to tap into this teen market, Frito-Lay devotes 9 percent of its marketing budget to Internet ads (Thompson, 2002). A Frito-Lay promotion with Microsoft's Xbox prompted 700,000 new customer registrations at http://Doritos.com, where you can also get a form to enter a sweepstakes. The world of advertising is in flux like everything else, and persuadees need to be ready for its new forms, strategies, and tactics.

ADVERTISING, SALES PROMOTION, AND POSITIONING

As we just noted in our discussion of the tasks of advertising and the advertisers' tactics, we all are targets of this form of persuasion in multiple ways that perhaps we never consciously thought of, or considered in detail. We ought to be aware of the kinds of appeals targeted at us in order to make wise purchasing, voting, joining, and donating decisions. With increasing exposure to advocacy and propaganda (Box 14.3), making sensible decisions is becoming more difficult. This is especially true in regard to various national policies—even more critical for receivers to consider.

There are multiple factors that go into the advertising that we see, hear, read, and feel so let's begin with some basic principles of modern advertising. Some have been with us for a long time and will probably persist a lot longer, while some are of more modern vintage and may change the market in major ways; all can be used in modern propaganda to further political, economic, and ideological agendas. Let's explore some of these.

Branding, Brand Names, Slogans, Jingles, and Logos

As noted in reference to Nabisco crackers, contemporary advertising grew out of the development of packaged goods in the late nineteenth and the early twentieth centuries. Producers needed to differentiate their version of a product type from the competition to promote brand recognition, purchase decisions, and brand loyalty in consumers' eyes. Earlier consumers bought generic and unbranded products from barrels, sacks, countertop jars, and other containers at a general store. One way to differentiate your kind of coffee was to give it a name or brand—Folgers, for example. It's probably never wise to name your brand after yourself as this one did—it communicates little about the brand, its features, benefits, or comparisons with the competition. Yet that's how many brand names came into being in those early days—Maytag, Hamm's, Pillsbury, Disney, Sears, and McDonald's are a few examples. More recent brand names usually try to use some benefit or words that describe the brand—Taster's Choice or Lunchables are examples.

A definition of the term "brand" might read as follows: **Brands** are the names given to a certain manufacturer's version of a product type. Different brands of coffees compete with one another, but they also compete with teas, cocoa, and spiced ciders in the "hot drink" product category and with soft drinks, juice, bottled water, and others in the "beverage" category, so brands compete not only within but across product categories. Advertising slogans and especially jingles really became part of the popular culture and branding with the advent of radio and radio advertising in the 1920s and 1930s. Advertisers wanted to remind consumers of their

BOX 14.3   Persuasion, Manipulation, Advertising, and Propaganda

"All propaganda must be so popular and on such an intellectual level that even the most stupid of those to whom it is directed will understand it" (Adolf Hitler from *Mein Kampf*, Chapter IV).

While the propaganda that Hitler used was so heavy handed and obvious that today's sophisticated audiences nearly laugh it off the page, and while the word "propaganda" had such a disagreeable connotation to persons after the fall of the Soviet Union that an entire chapter on the topic was removed from following editions, propaganda is still with us and is becoming more sophisticated than ever. This is particularly true as it appears in popular culture—in things like advertising. For a good tour of the history of modern propaganda and how it has manipulated us through advertising and other means of persuasion, go to http://doggo.tripod.com/doggmanip.html where you will find print and video examples of propaganda old and new. These examples deal with propaganda as it occurs in political advertising as well as propaganda as it has occurred and continues to do so in popular advertising and how it influences such topics as the war in Iraq, the fast food industry, toxic chemical waste, media ownership, obesity, brainwashing, and others. This is a good site to use for beginning a term paper on propaganda. To get a sense of advertising as propaganda used in nations emerging from third-world status go to http://findarticles.com/p/articles/mi_m1510/is_1987_Spring/ai_4793270.

brand in short, easy to remember, and interesting ways. **Slogans** are defined as catch phrases that express a brand name, its benefits, and its "personality." Gatorade has a different personality than Gulp, which is different from Snapple or Blast. **Jingles** are usually a musical version of the slogan combined with lyrics that tell the "story" of the brand. Television emerged in the 1950s and permitted advertisers to not only talk and write about the brand, but also to demonstrate it using print, visuals, special effects, animation, mood music, sound effects, and various other audio and video techniques. Several strategies to market the brand and to make it stand out more effectively emerged in those early years of modern advertising. For instance, the name of the brand made a big difference in the way it was perceived and embedded in consumers' minds. LifeSavers was a good early brand name because it described how the brand looked, and since it was the first hard candy to be branded, it needed to look different from generic hard candies in a jar. One of the earliest facial soaps to be marketed was called "Palmolive," suggesting that the product contained a combination of coconut and olive oils.

Another way to differentiate a brand from the competition is to make an attractive offer. Consider Cracker Jacks, which came up with a novel offer in the 1880s to differentiate itself from other popcorn snacks.

Each package offered consumers a "Free Prize" inside. And in 120 years, there has probably never been a worthwhile prize, yet consumers go for the prize before they go for the caramel corn and nuts. Netflix differentiates itself from the competition by offering a free trial period in addition to no late fees.

Packaging is another way to differentiate a brand. Coors and Coors Light now come in unbreakable 16-ounce plastic bottles rather than glass ones or aluminum cans, making them useful on backpacking, canoeing, and other outdoor trips where breakage is more likely. Some brands come in a reusable container that is hard to throw away. Consider other brand names to see whether they differentiate the brand from the competition and if so, in what ways. In the frozen turkey market, one brand excels as we observed earlier. Ask people to name a brand of frozen turkey, and few if any will say Armour or Jennie-O. Most will say "Butterball," the brand with the greatest name recognition. The name is memorable and says something about the brand's attributes and benefits. Butterball turkeys have the reputation of being the moistest brand because they are supposedly pre-basted with a pound of butter before being packaged. Furthermore, Butterball purchasers stay in the store longer and buy more and more expensive condiments for their Thanksgiving dinner. That kind of statistic will convince the grocer to devote more shelf or freezer space and more advertising to the brand (Dollas, 1986). Consider a few other brand names that demonstrate their benefits, such as Sears DieHard batteries, Easy Off oven cleaner, No Pest Strip insect repellant, Jiffy Lube oil changes, Taster's Choice instant coffee, Fruitopia fruit drinks, and many more.

A good brand name describes product benefits, fits with company image, and is memorable. It should also be easy to pronounce and promote, suited to the product packaging, contemporary, and persuasive. Naturally, there will be exceptions like Snapple, which describes nothing about the brand and may be why it took so long for it to gain market share. Research on shopping lists shows that consumers often list brands and not product types on their shopping reminder lists (Rothschild, 1987). Closely related to the brand name are the brand's slogan and **logo** or its corporate emblem. You all probably know which brand of coffee is "good to the last drop" by its slogan and logo. Maxwell House wins with its "last drop" slogan and its unique logo of a coffee cup with the last drop about to fall out of the cup. Starbuck's name is an anomaly since it doesn't communicate much about the brand or its benefits, but it has an identity as an upscale young person's coffee house specialty brand, probably gained from word of mouth advertising, which is also very effective. Consumer advertising aims at getting Word of Mouth, which is a "too clever" way of saying many persons respond by giving word of mouth testimony. As a result of the advertising. And of course as noted, Folger's is the "Mountain Grown" coffee even though that's where all coffees are grown. So one of the multiple factors that goes into promoting a brand is its use of easy and fun to recall names, slogans, and later musical jingles that may incorporate the slogan. The idea is to imprint the slogan and brand name on the consumer's unconscious mind so that it is evoked in a recall when he or she is ready to make a purchase, voting, or joining decision, just as Tony Schwartz predicted in his "resonance theory" discussed in Chapter 13.

Packaging

Packaging is defined as the container or wrapping that protects and identifies the product, reinforces the brand name, and builds **brand equity** (or easy brand recognition), and it can have value as a promotional device—it's cute, contemporary, can be a toy, and so forth. By law, packaging must provide information about the brand's contents in the order of their proportion in the brand and should inform consumers about its functions, features, benefits, and methods of use. From an advertising perspective, the package should also make the brand attractive, recognizable, and easy to see and stock on store shelves and displays.

Showing the package in ads helps consumers recall the product's advertised characteristics and benefits at the **point of purchase**. This is usually in the retail store, but as noted there are other ways to purchase goods nowadays, such as by phone, from a catalog, or online where a picture of a well-designed and distinctive package can also increase sales just as it does on store shelves. The package can also carry a sales promotion, such as a coupon or a travel size of the brand, and it can seem valuable in and of itself as was the Nabisco package mentioned earlier. Another example is the Grolsch beer bottle, which has a ceramic stopper and can be used to store other liquids once the beer is gone; and the name even sounds German, The L'Eggs plastic "egg" containers were famous for being used for storage, crafts, and containers for jelly beans in Easter baskets, as well as serving as the package for hosiery. L'Eggs was also the first hosiery to be sold in supermarkets (thus also occupying a "Being First" niche or position in the market). Packages make a brand impression, especially when used in the strategy of package/brand placement in movies and television programming. There, characters make conspicuous use of familiar brands like Coke, Sweet Success Foods, Toyota, Proctor and Gamble, and GM, to name a few. But is it effective in leading to sales increases? Communication scholar T. Borchers (2002) reports that sales of Red Stripe beer jumped 50 percent after Tom Cruise sipped from a can of the brew in the popular film "Top Gun." As a critical consumer, try to identify the effects of branding, packaging, and labeling and how they interact with brand advertising (e.g., look at the packaging of Mrs. Butterworth's and Log Cabin syrups). We consumers tend to disregard the effects package design have on our brand perceptions.

Sales Promotion

Sales promotion is defined as temporary inducements used to encourage immediate purchase. This marketing tactic has grown greatly in the past two decades due to the overbuilding of retail strip malls, catalogs, telemarketing, and online shopping, all of which make for greater competition for the consumer's discretionary income. Every marketer wants to induce the consumer to spend this discretionary money in their store, on their brand, in their catalog, and they use gimmicks to prompt purchase—some of them are aimed at consumers and some are aimed at the trade (i.e., wholesalers and retailers) to get them to "push" the brand onto store shelves. Consumer-targeted sales promotions include special sale pricing like "two for the price of one" and short-term price reductions like "special six hour sales." Basically, they are designed to get the goods off the shelves and into consumer's hands. Other more familiar sales promotion tactics include coupons, rebates, extra product in the package, travel sizes that go with the main package, contests, premiums, sweepstakes, recipes, and bonus packs.

These advertising tactics have the same goal—all sales promotional offers are designed to increase demand. They try to "pull" the brand through the supply pipeline using artificially pumped-up consumer demand for the brand by using techniques such as temporary price reductions or contest possibilities as the carrot, and short-term exclusions such as expiration dates or limited supplies as the stick to prompt quick purchase. As far as the trade is concerned, sales promotions can motivate sales staff through "bonuses" such as winning a free trip to Alaska for topping the previous sales records for the period. Sales promotions also alert retailers to upcoming increases in demand and the need to stock up. If wholesalers know coupons or rebates are coming out and that they going to be accompanied by a large advertising campaign, they will advise their retail customers that the demand is soon going to increase sufficiently so the retail man-

agers order extra supplies and thus has been "pulled" into moving the brand onto store shelves, The manages, in turn, will probably use "push" tactics like special pricing, discounts, and store displays as well as the nationally advertised coupons or rebates to move the brand off store shelves. All these sales promotions work hand-in-hand with brand advertising, brand naming, packaging, P.R., and other sales promotion practices to form the IMC that persuades us to buy certain brands right now before it's too late.

TOMA and Positioning

We live in a world filled with too many of almost everything—too many television channels, too many product categories, too many media options, and too many brands in most categories to ever remember, yet alone to purchase. Research shows that we can only recall a finite number of brands in each product category, depending on the product category complexity. Actually the number seems to be 7 plus or minus 2 or somewhere between 5 and 9 brands. Some theorists speculate that this "top of mind awareness," or **TOMA** as it is called, is limited to categories other than products or brands. That's probably why your car radio has only about 5 or 6 buttons to set for favorite radio stations—after all, that's probably about the number that you regularly tune into. And TOMA applies to favorite TV channels, recipes, car brands, and so forth. For complex product categories such as computers or cell phones, most consumers usually can recall only about 5 brands, whereas they recall as many as 9 brands in less complex categories such as beer or breakfast foods. As a result, a brand needs to stand out so it will be remembered at the point of purchase when TOMA most significantly affects purchase behavior.

TOMA is most likely created through information processed in the peripheral channel of the ELM—through repeated things like slogans, jingles, mood music, logos, and packaging. Most contemporary professionals in the field agree that advertising as a tool of marketing has changed the whole structure of bringing products to market. In other words, companies don't usually come up with a product and then try to sell it to consumers using advertising messages any more. That strategy is known as an "outside-in" strategy, which means beginning with the product type or brand approach. Instead, today's most successful marketer begins with the minds of consumers, and tries to identify their potentially unmet or unsolved needs or problems. Then the R & D department designs a brand or redefines an existing brand to fill the consumer's perceived needs or to solve their perceived problems. That is an "inside-out" strategy. This approach of beginning with consumers was made popular by Al Ries and Jack Trout. In their bestselling books *Positioning: The Battle for Your Mind* (Ries & Trout, 1986), *The New Positioning* (Trout, 1995), and *Focus: The Future of Your Company Depends on It* (Reis, 1996), they deal with the concepts of positioning and repositioning, which are strategies for finding an empty niche in the consumer's minds—a perceived need or problem—that a given brand might fill and then targeting that niche with advertising that stresses the need-meeting or problem-solving features and benefits of the brand. For example, the designers of a new snack chip food asked consumers to open bags of potato chips, pour them into serving dishes, eat a few, and discuss what each of their five senses processed. Customers in these "focus groups" then were asked to comment on the chips and tell what they liked and disliked about them, and how they would use them in entertaining. They said the chips were hard to store, and sometimes they were burned or had parts of the green peel on them—can't serve those to guests. They also smelled and felt greasy and broke easily, leaving small pieces that no one wanted to serve or take—they were the discards left at the end of the party. In response, the company designed an alternative—which was, of course, Pringles. They were easy to store, were never burned, weren't greasy because they were baked, not fried, were all the same size and shape, and rarely broke because of their protective packaging. Pringles were positioned as the easiest (and classiest) chip to store and serve.

Once a position has been established for a product, advertising prepares customers for trial, ul-timate purchase, and hopefully repeat purchases. Advertising lays the groundwork for sales by increasing brand awareness using repeated slogans, jingles, memorable packaging, and by communicating and improving the brand's attributes, features, and benefits. And this is done especially with interactive advertising as seen in Box 14.4. What is needed is advertising that makes an attractive offer that will move consumers to the point of purchase. Once consumers are at the POP, sales promotion and personal selling take over to "close the deal." What a change from early branding attempts!

PROBLEMS OF AN OVERCOMMUNICATED SOCIETY

One of Ries and Trout's (1986), Trout (1995), and Reis (1996) main points is that we live in an **overcommunicated society**. There is simply too much communication for the average person to even hope to process. They claim that, in response, the average consumer develops an oversimplified mind, which largely ignores or tries to forget most of the information to which it is exposed. This oversimplification leads to the "positions" in the average person's TOMA. People select the brands they think are good and then stick with those preferences because it makes shopping easier. We call these preferences brand loyalty. **Brand loyalty** makes it easier to live in an overcommunicated society because you never have to change your mind, and you can easily ignore all the ads for competing brands. Furthermore, you can rely on those brands no matter where in the country you happen to reside. Interestingly, brand loyalty is most strongly developed in consumers like yourselves who are between the ages of 18 and 24. Brands are portable. You can take them with you wherever you go—it's like taking part of home with you when you move, and in a mobile society like ours, you will move many times. Research shows that most college grads move a dozen or so times in the first decade after graduation. Nationally, 20 percent of the population is on the move every year,

---

B O X   14.4   Interactive Media and Consumers—Mainly Kids

Over 16 million children had Internet access in 2000, and the number increases every year. Most of the time parents don't monitor their children's online activity except to block pornographic sites using the V-chip. A proposal is now under consideration to turn the V-chip into an A-chip that would block interactive advertising as well as pornographic Web sites. In its Spring 2005 issue, *ChildrenNow* raised a number of questions regarding interactive advertising and how it might be used in the coming digital age. It said that soon the Internet will be accessible from your digital television set, and kids will be able to make purchases using a remote control and a parent's credit card. The most advertised product types aimed at children today are breakfast cereals, soda pop, and fast foods. Critics attribute the 300 percent increase in childhood obesity in part to advertising these product categories. Some predict an average shortening of the life expectancy of today's children of about five years as a result of such ads.

Many companies also create Web sites (and soon TV sites) that attract children into them by making video games available for free and then promoting the brand via the game. Examples include the Kool-Aid Mad Scientists "Mix it Up" game, Kraft's "TooMuchFun.com" and "Chips Ahoy! Cookie Guys' Housewarming Party" on the http://NabiscoWorld.com Web site. This strategy of offering free games laced with advertising for the brand is called "advergaming" and is a part of "T-commerce," or television commerce, and defined as the ability to purchase goods using your digital television and its remote control. It is now in operation in the United Kingdom, and Domino's Pizza is using it very successfully there to take orders (Espejo & Romano, 2005). To explore the implications of these innovations, go to http://www.watercoolergames.org/archives/000005.shtml and then go to http://www.kff.org/entmedia/upload/7536.pdf to see how the technique is being used to market food to children.

You can also go to http://www.micropersuasion.com/advergaming/ to learn more about how companies are advertising to adults and children via interactive media in sophisticated games like "Second Life" and others. Do these tactics seem ethical? Why or why not?

---

which averages out to a move every five years. It's why most retailers, professionals like dentists and doctors, and others must continually seek to add to their customer base to replace those who are moving away. Also, brand loyalty helps consumers predict quality and value from place to place. This is appealing to those in the early years of their careers, and those who face frequent job or location changes.

Advertising agencies often face the criticism that they sell people unnecessary products or brands that might even be harmful, like tobacco, alcohol, and foods high in sodium or fat. As Michael Schudson notes (1984), they defend themselves by claiming that their aim is "not to change people's product choices but to change their brand choices. Advertising ... is a competitive war against commercial rivals for a share of a market" (p. 54). To break through the cluttered media landscape and get into oversimplified minds, advertisers must find something that is already in the audience's mind and then tie it to their brand. This is similar to Schwartz's evoked recall model, which identifies critical experiential information in consu-

mer's minds and then gets messages out of audiences, not into them. Ries and Trout (1986), Trout (1995), and Reis (1996) suggest that the best way to do so is to use an oversimplified message. They report the results of a name recognition survey in which only 44 percent of persons recognized a photo of the then-Vice President of the United States, while 93 percent of them quickly recognized Mr. Clean—he was a much simpler message. The over-communication problem is also exacerbated by what Ries and Trout call the "media explosion" that we looked at in Chapter 13. In the near future it includes potential doubling of TV, cable, satellite, and radio options due to digital programming. We are also likely to witness an increase in newspapers, news weeklies, magazines, catalogs, direct mail, billboards, and other kinds of "out-of-home" ads, bus signs, interactive media, and signage in public restrooms. And that doesn't even take into account the ever increasing use of the Internet for advertising purposes. There are other message carriers at work as well (see Figure 14.1). Not only do we have too many messages coming at us, but now they are everywhere.

FIGURE 14.1 One of the major problems for advertisers today is what Ries and Trout call the "advertising explosion," by which they mean not only the increased volume of advertising but also the new advertising vehicles, surfaces, or places where advertising can appear.

SOURCE: Used with permission of Al Ochsner.

Even the human body carries trademarks like Calvin Klein, Gucci, Benetton, and Guess. Retailers like McDonald's and Subway insist that their staff members become branded by wearing the brand logo on their uniforms, adding on buttons for the latest special offers, and more.

Ries and Trout also call attention to the "product explosion." For example, there are mega-supermarkets (mainly in Europe and the United States) that contain more than 60,000 items from which to choose, compared to the 12,000 to 20,000 we find in the usual supermarket. Each year 25,000 new trademarks are registered at the U.S. Patent Office, with "hundreds of thousands of products and brands being sold without trademarks" (Ries & Trout, 1986, p. 14; Trout, 1995; Reis, 1996). Not only is there an increase in the volume of brand advertising, but unlike in the past, ads are now used to promote professionals and non-profits like lawyers, doctors, universities, pharmaceutical companies, and hospitals—institutions that rarely if ever used to feel the need to advertise to potential clients. As a result, brands must seek to gain a unique position or niche in the consumer's mind. We have discussed Ries and Trout's traditional forms of positioning earlier (see Chapter 11) and once again, its need seems due to too much competition. No wonder brand loyalty develops early and persists for many

years—how else are we to choose from among the many alternatives? Positioning became one way to break through all the brand, media, and advertising proliferation and resulting advertising clutter. Let's take a closer look.

Positioning, Repositioning, and Breaking Through the Clutter

How do advertisers overcome the triple whammy of burgeoning media, products, and advertisements? In other words, how do they break through all of this clutter? The technique known as "**positioning**" provides one way to do so. We encountered some of these tactics back in Chapter 11, which covered market segmentation in persuasive campaigns. Here are some of them again. "Being first" among the alternatives in a product category helped many products to be recalled by the consumer—products such as Jell-O, Kleenex, and Xerox copiers didn't have to break the clutter because initially, there was none. They were the only show in town and being exclusive, they were permanently implanted in consumers' minds right away. These brand names and more recent "first" additions like Lunchables are now virtually generic terms for the product category and are therefore known as **master**

brands in the ad industry. Not only was the Apple Personal Computer the first in the PC market, but it was also the first user-friendly PC. This let Apple get the jump on IBM, which had deferred going into the consumer computer market, preferring to focus on business computers costing millions. Later, when IBM and other brands entered the consumer market, Apple lost its competitive edge to these other brands that offered new, better, and more universally adopted, user-friendly, software such as "Windows" by Microsoft. Being first doesn't always guarantee that you will remain in that position or that you will become a master brand someday.

For brands not first in the market, positioning becomes even more important and complex. They don't want to be "me too" brands by saying that they were "grown in the mountains too" or that they were good to the "next to the last drop." In earlier advertising eras (the brand benefit or the "unique selling proposition") and in the "brand image" era, the competition wasn't nearly as fierce as it is today; there wasn't as much competing "clutter" to overcome or break through. With more and more "me too" versions on the market including things like house brands and generics, neither product benefits nor image ads work as well as they used to work. Brands have to be unique in the marketplace alright, and they should be perceived as having a high-quality image (e.g., like Bayer aspirin used to and may still be perceived), but this is no longer enough. Now price, selection, and equivalence, plus simple but distinctive ad copy are all needed to make a brand break through and communicate their similarities to the more expensive high-image brands; and those brands have to face the advantages of the less expensive but nearly equivalent options for the consumer. The "poetry of product benefits" can still work as can be seen by the many enduring brands that have been around for 75 years or more. Folger's "Mountain Grown" and Maxwell's "Good to the Last Drop" still have brand loyalty and are readily recalled by consumers, but they are the exception and not the rule.

Circumstances can also change for a brand. Take the example of Ivory Soap whose slogan "99 and 44/100% Pure—It Floats" was among the earliest product benefit ads; its slogan is still often

recalled. Interestingly enough, the "It Floats" benefit was the result of a factory worker who accidentally pumped too much air into the soap, making it buoyant. Not long after that, consumers asked for the floating version of Ivory because it was easier to find in the bathtub. It has now dropped from being the leader in the bar soap product category down to being the number six selling soap. Why? Not because of poor advertising, but because circumstances changed—more people now take showers and finding the bar of soap isn't a major problem anymore (Parente, 2004). Other examples of positioning to breaking through the clutter include convincing ad benefit copy such as "At Ford, Quality Is Job #1," "Introducing the Smell of Luxury," and "Dermatologist Recommended." We still encounter colorful poetic ad copy, as Figure 14.2 demonstrates.

A variety of techniques can make a product seem to be the only, the sexiest, the most exciting one on the market. A relatively new position is the "Environmentalist" niche or positioning oneself as the "greenest" brand in the product category, which convinces consumers of the brand with a certain desirable and socially responsible benefit. Other niches we have discussed earlier include Positioning by Age (AARP) Positioning by Gender (Virginia Slims) Being Best (Mercedes), Being the Most Expensive (Rolex) Being the Least Expensive (Hyundai), and "User Friendly" (Microsoft Windows). There aren't many new niches or "positions" in a given product category, so if competitors are firmly entrenched in the audience's mind as "first" or as a "master brand" for example, what can be done? One possibility is to go up against one of them with comparative advertising, which we discussed in-depth earlier. Ries and Trout give an example of this approach in the Avis Rent-a-Car campaign, whose slogan was, "Avis is Number 2 in Rent-a-Cars, so We Try Harder." What was the result of this comparison? After 13 years of losing money, Avis made $1.2 million the first year after it admitted to being second. The strategy netted $2.6 million in profits for the second year, and $5 million the third year. Then ITT, their parent company, decided to ditch the "We're Number Two, So We Try Harder" idea and promptly began to lose money. Interestingly enough, the "We Try

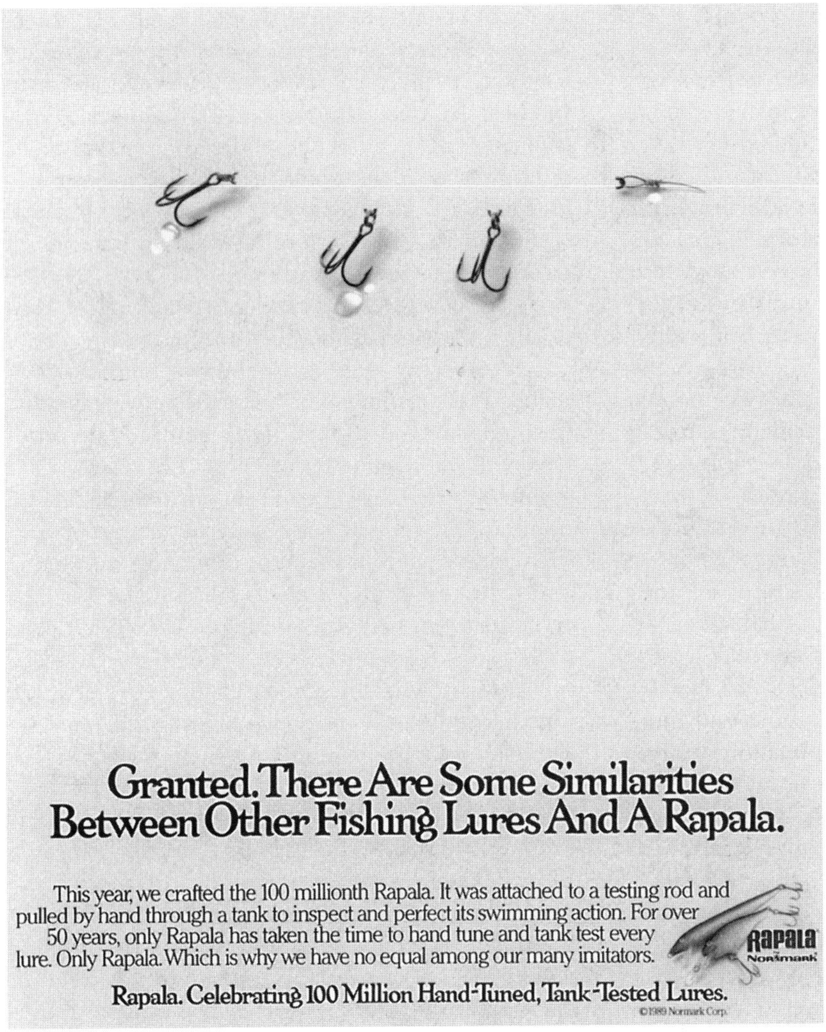

FIGURE 14.2 How did this hard-hitting product ad by Rapala break through the clutter?

SOURCE: Reprinted by permission of Normark Corp.

Harder" ads didn't really hurt the market leader, Hertz. Instead, the campaign took business away from other brands in the market like National and Budget. Consumers must have perceived that Avis tried harder than them but not that much harder than Hertz, or simple brand loyalty to Hertz may be the explanation.

Another way a brand can break through clutter is to reposition itself (Trout, 1995) by telling consumers "What We're Not." Seven-Up was near bankruptcy when its advertising agency came up with one of the most successful "What We're Not" brand turnarounds in advertising history with the invention of the word "Un-cola," which they then used in very creative ways. For example, the brand advertised itself was being delivered by the "Man from Uncola," which was a take-off on the title of a popular television series of the time—a spy thriller called "The Man from U.N.C.L.E." Other humorous ads were also part of the campaign, so the humor acted as a tactic to put the "What We're Not" strategy to work. The campaign not only saved the company from bankruptcy, but it ultimately positioned Seven-Up as third in the soft drink category, right behind Coke and Pepsi. Later, Dr. Pepper used a similar tactic by claiming not to be like a cola either, which also moved it up in market share.

Another approach to positioning a brand is to take advantage of an existing brand image or reputation, and build on it by bringing new product categories on the market, which also carry the original brand name. For example, Arm & Hammer has always produced its well-known baking soda, but more recently it began to make and sell the stuff in bulk to cattle farms to aid in digestion and the resulting increases in weight gain. Arm & Hammer also positioned its added categories to its product line by carrying the parent company name; we now have Arm & Hammer laundry detergent, carpet cleaner, toothpaste, and so on. This practice of bringing new brand products to market under the parent company's name is called **line extension** and relies on one's reputation or brand equity to break through the clutter. Inventing *new uses* for a brand also helps to reposition it. Again, Arm & Hammer's traditional baking soda provides a great example of this tactic. The brand has an unaided recognition of 97 percent and can be found in almost 100 percent of kitchen cupboards, so there was no need to increase brand awareness. It just wasn't being used very much. It only takes a small amount for a batch of chocolate chip cookies or to pour on an acid covered battery connection, and few persons use it in their baths or as a substitute for toothpaste. In 1972, the company decided to advertise a previously mentioned but not heavily promoted alternate use for the brand. They repositioned it as a "deodorant" for your refrigerator. The baking soda had always been used to clean refrigerators (which most of us don't do often enough). The usual result is gross discoveries and disgusting smells which the consumer feels ashamed of—for being so lazy. Clever ads used embarrassing visuals and gross odors coming out of the refrigerator, which were then "absorbed" by the box of Arm & Hammer baking soda put there for exactly that purpose. Sales increased 72 percent in less than two years (Honomichl, 1984). Analysts attributed the increase to consumers who felt "refrigerator guilt" because they weren't as diligent at cleaning as their mothers, who used to clean the fridge once a month. But they could relieve their guilt by putting a box of baking soda into the refrigerator to absorb the smells. Later sales increases were accomplished by hitch-hiking on this idea and urging consumers to put a box in the freezer compartment, in the refrigerator of their camper, and so on. The ultimate pitch warned consumers that the odor-absorbing quality of the soda got weaker in a few months but could still be of use if you put it down the garbage grinder, getting rid of bad odors there too. This assured the company of ongoing demand for its "new use" for the Arm & Hammer product.

Another strategy used by many "me too" brands is the claim to be better than old standbys in some way and thus to break clutter. The problem is that it's hard to convince consumers that a brand is better than an old favorite. Sometimes a minor improvement such as a new ingredient—beads of bleach—or making the brand available in a new form—"Now in the handy spray bottle!"—can reposition the brand. Price can be another clutter breaker. A product can find a low-priced niche, such as that filled by the Hyundai or Focus, or it can find a high-priced niche like Jaguars and BMWs (see Figure 14.3).

Other clutter breakers noted above and also in Chapter 11 are "positioning by gender or age." One product occupying the age niche in a major way is *Modern Maturity* magazine, which has the leading magazine circulation in the country and is aimed at persons aged 45 years or older who have joined AARP. Naturally, brands such as high-fiber or low-sodium foods, cholesterol and arthritis remedies, supplemental health care, erectile dysfunction medications, and retirement planning advertise there. Consider the marketing of such products and services as iPods, Zappos, the BlackBerry, Nads hair remover, or resumé writing companies, all of which position by age to reach the younger consumer who is looking for new technologies, a better appearance or job opportunities in these cases.

Distribution and packaging can also break clutter. We have already mentioned L'Eggs as using egg-shaped packaging to increase sales, but it was also the first hosiery to be distributed in supermarkets—a new position "Available in Supermarkets" that really worked. That fact *and* its packaging gave

Take me to your husband.

Tell him you want him to test-drive me. The BMW 2000. Let him take the wheel. And watch him fall.

I was made for a man like yours — I respond to his slightest command. I am fast. In fact, I can cruise at 108 mph. Hour after hour with ease. Which is great for those continental holidays. But in a tight situation, it's good to have an engine that delivers so much power.

And my BMW suspension. Independent on all four wheels. I'm proud of how it enables me to hold the road no matter how fast I run.

You'll notice that I am elegantly styled.

I'm roomy. I have reclining seats. With space for five adults and plenty of luggage. But the best thing about me: I'm fun to drive for the man who enjoys driving.

So, go ahead and take me to your husband. What if he *does* fall in love? It's better than having him fall for another woman.

2000 brief specification — 4 cylinder 1990 c.c. overhead camshaft. 113 bhp (SAE) at 5,800 rpm. Price: £2,199. Price shown is recommended retail price incl. P.T.

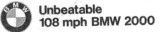 Unbeatable
108 mph BMW 2000

For the man who can please himself

Other models include : 106 mph BMW 1600 £1648. – 113 mph BMW 2002 £1874. – 106 mph BMW 1800 £1796-97. 121 mph BMW 2500 £2999. – 125 mph BMW 2800 £3499. – 130 mph BMW 2800 CS £4996-98.

BMW Concessionaires GB Ltd., BMW House, Chiswick High Road, London W.4. Telephone: 01-995 4051 · London Showroom, N.A.T.O. Diplomatic and Export Office : 56 Park Lane, London W.1. Tel : 01-499 6881.

29

FIGURE 14.3 This clever ad plays on the husband/wife/automobile triad and makes the point that the BMW is the vehicle for the upscale consumer who wants to please his wife as well as himself (though the entire high-priced niche transaction is engineered by the wife and the vehicle).

SOURCE: Image courtesy of The Advertising Archives.

it a unique position in the hosiery market and raised its market share incredibly while saving the manufacturer packaging costs (Ries & Trout,

1986). In contrast to ordinary envelope hosiery packaging that needs to be folded and packed by hand, the L'Eggs hosiery could simply be stuffed into the container by machine, thus eliminating labor costs and reducing price, both positioning the brand as a unique one. The egg-shaped container was also used by consumers to make craft items or for storage as we noted above (Dollas, 1986). Advertisers can also break through the clutter by **repositioning** an existing brand, as was the earlier case with Seven-Up. A more recent repositioning is the changing of Cheerios from a children's brand to an adult one by stressing its high-fiber content (see Trout, 1995). The brand always had high fiber, but ads never mentioned that until recently, probably because Cheerios was losing its children's market segment to sweetened brands like Fruit Loops or Pebbles. Choosing the right name for a brand not only cuts through the clutter but can also create a position for the brand. A powerful bathroom cleaner named itself "The Works," which fits with the idea of trying the ultimate—consumers were urged to "Give It The Works!" All these clutter-breaking techniques grow out of various ad research on ways to get into consumers' heads and create ads that will "resonate," to use Schwartz's term (1973). The major way advertiser's get into consumer's experiential and other memories is via one of four kinds of research, which allows them to target specific markets by studying consumer behavior.

GETTING INTO THE CONSUMER'S HEAD: ADVERTISING RESEARCH

Four kinds of advertising or integrated marketing research can be used to get consumer data that reveals much about how and why consumers purchase. They are (1) demographics, (2) psychographics, (3) **geographics** or socio-graphics, and (4) ethnography (O'Guinn, Allen, & Semenik, 2006). Sometimes one, two, three, or all four kinds are used. Specific ways of conducting these kinds of research include gathering information that comes from pubic archives like census data, conducting surveys among users and non-users, questionnaires used to ask shoppers in malls and elsewhere, warranty cards that require the giving of purchase information, state and local government archives such as hunting and fishing licenses, the department of motor vehicles and state and local tax records, focus group interviews where typical users discuss the brand and its ads, the pupilometer (which tracks the eye as it scans a printed ad), the tachistoscope (which measures how quickly the human eye can read the words on a sign or a page), and many others. All attempt to identify Feig's (1997) consumer "hot buttons" and "cold buttons" with the idea being to design ads that press those buttons and thus help to break through the cluttered marketplace of brands, ads, and media.

Demographics

Demographics identify specific market segments on the basis of data—usually numerical—like annual family income, religious affiliation, political preferences, age, family size, gender, purchase patterns, or any combination of such factors (O'Guinn, Allen, & Semenik, 2009). Most of such data is available from the U.S. census, state and local governments, warranty cards, and other sources. Based on these data, advertisers design ads that feature certain kinds of characters and spokespersons or that have certain settings, props, and so on. One demographic pattern involves the growing number of DINKs (or folks with Double-Incomes and No Kids). DINKs actually comprise two separate subgroups: (1) those who intentionally have no children, are largely self-indulgent, and usually have lots of discretionary income to spend on the extras; and (2) those whose children have left home and are now independent, and who finally have some discretionary income. The first group tends to be younger and love spending their discretionary income on things like travel, club memberships, fashion, upscale autos, and other items for themselves. The second group is the now-aging front edge of the baby boom, who are retiring in increasing numbers, and who spend their discretionary income in different ways—on travel, grandchildren, health, retirement savings, and so forth.

Aging boomers are increasing at the rate of more than 2 million new consumers a year. Advertisers need to appeal to these subgroups in very different ways, and demographic data helps advertisers know a lot about these folks. For example, there are about 157 women for every 102 men in this age group, and their rate of divorce is three times the national rate. They tend to get up earlier in the day and retire earlier at night. They spend lots on grandchildren, recreation, medications, organically grown foods, and travel to name a few. Now, you play advertising executive with these data and tell when, where, and how you would appeal to this market segment and for what kinds of brands. Your product is a nationwide network of health clubs that can be used anywhere in the country while traveling. Would you advertise in *Modern Maturity*, with the world's largest subscription base with lots of **reach**, (defined as the number of persons who see or hear the ad) but not much **frequency** (defined as how often they see the ad)? Or would you make your appeal during local evening news shows that most of them do watch on a regular basis—mainly for the weather forecast and local interest? These programs have a much smaller reach but greater frequency and are far less expensive? How about using the History Channel, which also shows a higher age demographic? Would you use direct mail to persons over the age of 60 in the states where many older citizens retire such as Florida, Arizona, or Nevada? Whom would you pick to be your spokesperson—Angela Lansbury, Burt Reynolds, Mike Ditka, Tina Turner, or someone under the age of 30? As you can see, demographics help target segments, and can also help design effective ad copy and make wise choices about which media to use, suitable spokespersons, and even the time of day to run the ads. What about another similar cluster known in the Chicago area as DITKAS, which stands for "Double Incomes with Two Kids Away at School"? How would you target them? Whom would you choose for a spokesperson?

Psychographics

Psychographics is the study of consumers' lifestyles, attitudes, and interests as well as how they feel about a product or brand—that is, what happens to them emotionally when they hear the name of a brand (Amft, 2004). Again Schwartz's theory

comes into play because what psychographics really aims to find out is how a brand "resonates" with audiences. This information can then be used to customize ads. Psychographics also provides data about how consumers spend their time and money, what activities they engage in, what interests them, what their opinions and attitudes are on various brand-related issues (O'Guinn, Allen, & Semenik, 2009). Frequently, this research method measures such things by cataloging people's values, attitudes, and their preferred lifestyles using a variety of research techniques—attitude polls, mall intercepts, in-depth or focus group interviews, telephone surveys, analysis of leisure time, and so on.

Activities, Interests, and Opinions. These three terms form the central focus of a nationally established market segmentation system called VALS, standing for "Values, Attitudes, and Lifestyles." Examples of activities are work, social events, vacations, hobbies, entertainment, club memberships, church, sports, and community activities. The subcategory of "good-life activities" includes cultural events, gourmet cooking, investing, travel, wine tasting, and collections. Advertisers could look at outdoor activities like skeet shooting, fly fishing, RVing, or motorcycling. In each of these subcategories, consumer advertising needs to be tailored to fit the way target groups spend at least some of their time. The golfer interested in gourmet cooking, skeet shooting, and digital photography is different from the bowler who is focused on the same things. Each needs to receive personalized advertising messages for maximum effect, and that is the ultimate goal of consumer research—to customize advertising messages to fit every individual having similar (but not identical) activities. This is known as "one-to-one" segmentation.

Attitudes were discussed in Chapter 7, but to review a bit, they are "predispositions to behave" or propensities to support or disapprove of certain positions and issues such as global warming, living the vegan life, becoming a day-trader, and Individual Retirement Accounts in Social Security. Examples of an individual's interests include the family and home, church, achievements, health issues, investing,

BOX 14.5 Hidden Propaganda—the New Camouflage

Ever since 9/11, we have seen increasing amounts of governmental propaganda characterizing enemies such as terrorists, Jihadists, and others. But what about more subtle and disguised forms of propaganda that remains invisible at first glance? Many critics are concerned by such camouflaged propagandistic appeals that address social and political values? Take the "Letters to the Editor" portion of a daily newspaper. It is assumed that these opinions are coming from everyday citizens just like yourselves or your neighbors. Go to http://www.washingtonpost .com/wp-dyn/articles/A22539-2004Aug21.html to learn how both the John Kerry and George W. Bush

presidential campaigns of 2004 used this seemingly harmless form to create hundreds of "false" letters to the editor by using simple "cut and paste" technology to pepper the letters section of daily papers with bogus letters. In a more surprising example, learn how Warner Brothers' holiday dancing-penguins film "Happy Feet" was interpreted by critics as propaganda espousing ecological issues like pollution, human over-consumption, and environmental exploitation in the film at http://blogs .usatoday.com/oped/2006/11/preschoolers_an.html. Other critics were carrying the propaganda idea a bit too far when they reasoned that because the penguins danced with one another, that the film was propaganda for the gay lifestyle.

recreation, fashion, technology, food, and media use patterns. You can easily imagine the differences between a person interested in family, fashion, and technology who reads *Cosmopolitan* and *Elle* and watches Oprah will differ from someone interested in achievements, health, orchids, and gourmet cooking and who reads *Organic Gardening, Gourmet,* and *Southwest Living,* and who watches the Food and Home and Garden cable channels. They are obviously different and would respond positively to customized ad messages that included references to their personal interests. Using consumers' interests can also help advertisers pick spokespersons and appropriate media when making their targeting decisions, just as other elements in ad research can.

Opinions relate to oneself; international, social, and political issues (e.g., global terrorism, energy alternatives, global warming); business and economics (e.g., the rate of inflation, the home mortgage or credit crisis); religion and culture; education; film; and the future (e.g., interactive television, virtual reality). Remember, as we said in Chapter 7, opinions are weaker than attitudes and can easily change almost overnight. You often see this fickle nature pf opinion in the public opinion polls about politicians and candidates. However, they aren't particularly strong predictors of actual behavior. You could profile two very different persons with differing opinions and make

appropriate advertising decisions for each of them. This would be especially true with issues like politics and propaganda as seen in Box 14.5.

As you can imagine from the invented profiles of "typical" individuals noted above, taken together attitudes, activities, interests, and opinions can spawn an almost infinite number of such profiles and an equally huge number and complicated mix of media decisions and advertising appeals. Obviously, such a goal is out of our reach at present, but with emerging technologies and the means of measuring the elements in psychographics, advertisers are coming closer and closer every day to the goal of a single-person market—segments with individually customized ads that are aimed at each of our individual prejudices, quirks, activities, opinions, and interests.

Psychographics also ask people to respond to questions about their activities, attitudes, interests, and opinions but in a different way. They ask about these things, but in relation to specific brands. Advertisers then infer the respondents' lifestyles and how they are likely to respond to a brand and its advertising package. Claussen's pickles are a good example. The brand is not cooked like its competitors' brands and therefore must be refrigerated, and the pickles are significantly more expensive than the competition. They are also much crunchier and "gourmet" tasting, and you won't find them on the canned goods shelves but in the refrigerator case. They are the kind of pickle you "used to" find in barrels. They are associated with upscale consumers who don't shop for price and who want to be perceived of as persons of good taste. Knowing these things allows the advertiser to tell how well a particular brand or ad for that brand will "fit" that particular kind of consumer and about how this information can be used to promote the brand to similar-minded individuals with the proper spokesperson, setting, script, music, and so on. Initially, Claussen's were sold in a plastic quart jar, but that packaging decision proved to be a poor one. Think about it. When you reach for a jar of some product category in the refrigerator case, you want it to feel cold. Plastic doesn't transfer temperature nearly as well as glass, and it somehow seems "chintzy" and downscale. As a result the company switched to packaging the brand in glass jars. Consumers wanted to not only taste how expensive their chosen brand was, but they wanted to physically feel its refrigerated quality.

In another example, a study determined what type of consumer would be likely to bring a malpractice suit against their doctor (perhaps useful information for the doctor, his malpractice insurance programs, and even our government). Items in the survey included some like these:

1. I have a great deal of confidence in my own doctor.
2. Many physicians are out of date.
3. Physicians are overpaid.
4. Malpractice is hard to prove.
5. You are your own best doctor.
6. Various other statements.

Responses ranged from "strongly agree" to "strongly disagree." Trends in responses were then correlated to persons actually bringing malpractice suits, and conclusions were drawn about what kind of malpractice insurance the doctor should buy, and given what they know about their own patient base, which individuals should be referred to another doctor or specialist in order to reduce the likelihood of having a suit brought.

In another example, persons strongly agreeing with the following items are highly likely to use Listerine mouthwash rather than Listermint mouthwash:

1. I do not feel clean without a daily bath.
2. Everyone should use a deodorant.
3. A house should be dusted three times a week.
4. Odors in the house embarrass me.
5. The kind of dirt you can't see is worse than the kind you can see.
6. I am a very neat person.
7. Dirty dishes should be washed after every meal.
8. It is very important for people to wash their hands before eating each meal.
9. I use one or more household disinfectants.
10. Various other statements.

Effective ads based on this data and the resulting trends included appeals to the germ-killing and antiseptic qualities in Listerine ads, such as "Clean Doesn't Mean 'Good Tasting' in Mouthwashes—Use Listerine Today!"

Interestingly enough, Listerine was not initially marketed as a mouthwash but as an antiseptic cleaner to be used in sterilized operating room floors. Only when mouth freshness emerged as a consumer need did the company go into the mouthwash category. Of course the above psychographic information would be useful for brands in other product categories—household floor cleaners, bathroom cleansers, and so forth, so psychographics is a powerful way to get into the consumer's head and can be applied in ads promoting various brands and product categories.

Socio-graphics

Socio-graphics refers to and individual's social grouping, where they live (i.e., what kinds of neighborhoods with what characteristics) and other sociological factors such as their life stage (e.g., single, married without kids, married with kids, divorced) ethnicity, affiliations, and so on. If one were to define it in one sentence it would be "Birds of a feather flock together." This makes sense. We choose to buy or rent in neighborhoods that house persons like ourselves, or who are in a similar life stage. We like to belong to groups that reflect ourselves and our ideals, attitudes, and values. For example, many people prefer to live in "gated" communities, but others would hate living there. If we're single, we'd like to live in an apartment complex with persons our age, one that has a party room and health facility and neighbors who are interested in the things that interest us. If we have children, we'd prefer to live in a community that has lots of families with kids—especially children near the age of our kids. If our children have grown, we'd probably prefer not to live in a neighborhood with lots of pre-school kids or lots of teens. As a result we tend to gravitate to neighborhoods that reflect our Values, Attitudes and Lifestyles or our VALS, which is the acronym or initialized name of the socio-graphic model most widely used in advertising and marketing and which is used by many advertising and IMC agencies. It can be studied in more detail than we can do here if you are interested by going to http://www.sric-bi.com/VALS/ for a fuller description and explanation from its originator and vendor, the Stanford Research Institute.

VALS can be used in many ways. For example, if you were in the HVAC business and could identify the kind of neighborhood that was 30 or years older, you could infer that most of the homes are inhabited by older persons, have energy inefficient furnaces, and that a direct mail or telemarketing campaign there would be successful. The system describes three general lifestyles and then breaks them down into subcategories giving typical things which characterize their attitudes toward a variety of things, their lifestyles or how and where they tend to live, the purchasing habits of persons in each segment, and the approximate portion of the population that the segment represents (Borchers, 2004). The general categories are (1) persons who are need-driven, (2) persons who are outer-directed, and (3) persons who are inner-directed (see Table 14.1). Notice that under each of the three major segments are several subsegments and percentages of the population represented by that segment, their values and lifestyles, their demographics, and their buying patterns—powerful tools in the hands of ad and IMC agencies.

Need-Driven Consumers. These consumers live in the midst of poverty. They represent only 11 percent of the population and have little, if any, discretionary income. Advertisers simply ignore them in most cases except in subsistence-type product categories such as oatmeal. They are forced to use most if not all of their income to buy the essentials. Most merchants do not cater to their needs or incomes. They are usually without much access to convenient transportation, and thus are not likely to get to major food outlets. The essentials that they do buy are usually higher priced than they would be in a chain store. There are two subcategories of Need-Drivens: Survivors (4 percent of the population) and Sustainers (7 percent).

Survivors struggle to buy the daily necessities, they tend to mistrust most people and brands, and they are usually social misfits. They live in slums, have limited education, major or minor criminal records, and meager incomes, and most likely are from a minority group. Most advertising for brands is irrelevant to them—they ignore it because it is basically means nothing to them.

Sustainers' buying patterns are slightly different and are dominated by price and daily needs. They are a little better off, are very concerned with security and safety; they really want to get ahead, and believe they can because they are street wise. They have limited educations, low incomes, and aren't necessarily from a minority. Price is important to them, but they also are cautious and want warranties and other guarantees. They want to get ahead and are targets for get-rich-quick schemes such as multilevel marketing, the lottery, or dealing drugs.

Outer-Directed Consumers. They make up a total of 67 percent of the marketplace and are crucial targets for all advertisers and all brands. These persons are also interested in various brands—especially new ones—and can spend a good part of their discretionary incomes on preferred brands.

T A B L E 14.1   VALS Segmentation

Percentage of Population (age 18 & over)	Consumer Type	Values and Lifestyles	Demographics	Buying Patterns
NEED-DRIVEN CONSUMERS				
4%	Survivors	Struggle for survival Distrustful Social misfits Ruled by appetites	Poverty-level income Little education Many minority members Many live in city slums	Price dominant Focused on basics Buying for immediate needs Few amenities Crime
7%	Sustainers	Concern with safety, security Insecure, compulsive Dependent, following Streetwise, determined to get ahead	Low income Low education Much unemployment May live in country as well as cities	Price important Want warranty Cautious buyers Willing to take risks
OUTER-DIRECTED CONSUMERS				
35%	Belongers	Conforming, conventional Not experimental Traditional, formal Nostalgic	Low to middle income Low to average education Blue-collar jobs Tend toward noncity living: rural, suburban, or rurban	Family Home Fads Middle and lower income mass market Price and warranties are important
10%	Emulators	Ambitious, show-offs Status conscious Upwardly mobile Macho Highly competitive	Good to excellent income Youngish Highly urban Traditionally male, but changing	Conspicuous consumption "In" items Imitative Popular fashion and activities are important
22%	Achievers	Achievement, success, fame Materialism Leadership, efficiency Comfort	Excellent income Leaders in business, politics, etc. Suburban and city living	Give evidence of success Purchase "top of the line" Luxury and gift markets are focus "New and improved" products appeal

T A B L E 14.1   **(Continued)**

Percentage of Population (age 18 & over)	Consumer Type	Values and Lifestyles	Demographics	Buying Patterns
INNER-DIRECTED CONSUMERS				
5%	I-am-me	Fiercely-individualistic Dramatic, impulsive Experimental Volatile	Young Many are single students or just starting jobs Affluent background	Display one's taste Experimental fads Source of far-out fads Clique buying
7%	Experiential	Drive to experience direct daring activities Active participant Person-centered Artistic	Bimodal income Most under 40 Many young families Good education	Prefer process over product Vigorous outdoor sports "Making" home pursuits Crafts and Introspection
8%	Socially conscious	Emphasis on societal responsibility Simple living Smallness of scale Inner growth	Bimodal low and high incomes Excellent education Diverse ages and places of residence Largely white	Conservation emphasis Simplicity Frugality Have high environmental concerns Belong to environmental groups
2%	Integrated	Psychological maturity Sense of fitting-in Tolerant, self-actualizing Have a global perspective	Good to excellent incomes Bimodal in age Excellent education Diverse jobs and residential patterns	Varied self-expression Esthetically oriented Ecologically aware Prefer one-of-a-kind items

SOURCE: Reprinted with permission of Macmillan Publishing Company from Arnold Mitchell, Nine American Lifestyles: Who We Are and Where We Are Going (New York: Macmillan, 1983). Copyright © 1983 by Arnold Mitchell.

They tend to develop and maintain brand loyalties early in their lives. Outer-Directeds include three subcategories—belongers, emulators, and achievers.

Belongers, who make up 35 percent of this segment, are conventional, traditional, rarely experiment with new products or services, and tend to be blue-collar workers with low to middle levels of education. They are family oriented, like products with domestic appeals, are nostalgic, buy U.S.A., and are good targets for direct-response television ads such as those for "Great Music of the 80s," and they are frequently affected by fads.

Emulators, who make up 10 percent of the segment, are upwardly mobile, ambitious, status conscious, and competitive. They compare themselves and their lifestyles with others who have achieved more than they have. They have good incomes, tend to be young, and live in urban areas. Emulators are into conspicuous consumption, especially compared with those they seek to emulate, they tend to purchase "in" products or brands regardless of costs, and they are good targets for the newest, most expensive styles in clothing, automobiles, and upscale leisure time activities.

Achievers, who comprise 22 percent of the category, have "made it" in their occupations and are interested in efficiency, leadership, achievement, success, fame, comfort, and conspicuous consumption. They have high incomes and levels of education, and live in upscale suburbs, gated communities populated by McMansions, and in trendy parts of large cities if they are single or childless. They tend to be leaders in politics, business, and community activities, buy top-of-the-line brands and new products, are interested in the arts, and are good targets for luxury items.

Inner-Directed Consumers.   Inner-directed consumers, who are 22 percent of the overall market, are divided into four subcategories—"I am Me," Experientials, the Socially Conscious, and Integrated consumers. They tend to be highly individualistic and somewhat unpredictable.

"I am me" consumers, who are 5 percent of this category, are individualistic, experimental, impulsive, dramatic, and volatile, come from affluent backgrounds, reject traditional possessions or ways, but may not have much discretionary income. They are students or are just starting on the occupational ladder and want to experiment with their lifestyle.

Comprising 7 percent of this segment, *Experientials* want to have many and varied experiences and participate in many athletic activities. They are introspective, frequently artistic, and have high or low incomes depending on their life choices. They have good educations, support the arts, are likely to have families, and tend to be under 40 years old. Experientials' buying habits focus on vigorous outdoor sports like mountain climbing, kayaking, back-packing. They are also into do-it-yourself projects related to the home, and they are good targets for products from L. L. Bean or Eddie Bauer.

Socially Conscious consumers, or about 8 percent of the inner directed segment, want simple living and are concerned with the environment, pollution, global warming, and recycling. They have a sense of societal responsibility and may join the Sierra Club, Greenpeace, the Nuclear Freeze Movement, or the Green Party. They seek smallness of scale and inner growth. They are mainly white and have excellent educations but bimodal incomes. These consumers live in large cities, small towns, "rurban" communities, or on farms. They have a conservation orientation and focus on simplicity and frugality. They are good targets for energy-saving devices, good gas mileage hybrids, organic gardening, self-improvement, wine making, and living off the land.

Integrated consumer, the smallest subsegment with just 2 percent of the category, feel good about themselves, are tolerant, and have a sense of psychological and social maturity. They self-actualize and take a broad view of the world, are concerned over issues like acid rain and products that pollute. But they have good-to-excellent incomes, vary in age, work in diverse occupations, and are good targets for products that allow for self-expression, such as restoring historic homes or collecting unique things. They are good targets for art, music, or drama.

Advertisers use these patterns to design brands, the ads for promoting them, and targeting offers that appeal to the values, lifestyles, and purchase patterns of each group or segment. It is a powerful analytic system and has resulted in many marketing successes. As noted, the basic assumption of sociographics is that "Birds of a feather flock together." Generally, this means they live in identical or adjacent zip codes or in similar and usually nearby geographic areas. People choose to live with or near persons similar to themselves. Socio-graphics or geographics is a combination of the places people live, their demographics (the clusterings of variables associated with them), and their psychographics (O'Guinn, Allen, and Semenik, 2006). Research on all of these data is done by sampling persons from a zip code area or areas that resemble the kind of neighborhood the advertiser believes will be attracted to the brand. Then the researchers invite residents to participate in focus groups and answer a survey about the brand and its competitors. Researchers look for patterns in the survey responses and words used repeatedly in focus group commentary. Then the ad agency's creative staff designs messages around the consumer-generated copy points. Socio-graphics also show media-use patterns and program preferences for persons in these "typical" zip codes as well as a wealth of other data related to them (e.g., most recent financial transactions).

A related system is PRIZM, which is marketed by the Claritas Corporation. The system has identified 62 distinct psychographic and socio-graphic neighborhood types or what it calls "clusters." It uses catchy names that suggest what the neighborhood is like. For example, one is called "two more rungs," for the young emulators on their way up. "shotguns and pickups" are high-school-educated or non-grads, blue-collar belonger-workers who live in mobile homes, have a flat screen TV, a dusty pickup, and drink generic brands of sugared soft drinks. They are frequently overweight and usually go to fast food or all-you-can-eat buffet restaurants. Claritas knows an amazing amount about "Town and Gown," or typical college towns like the one where my university is located or where you might be going to school. The "Town and Gown" zip codes are populated largely by white singles who are college students or recent grads. They tend to vote Republican and jog. They use ATM machines, bounce checks frequently, and are unlikely to have a van, a toy-sized dog, mutual funds, or burglar alarm systems. However, they do have personal loans, like to water and snow ski, and read *Modern Bride* or *Gentleman's Quarterly*. They tend to drive Subaru DL4s, Toyota Tercels, Hyundai Excels, or Volkswagen Passats. They like David Letterman and Jay Leno but hate Sunday morning interview programs like "Meet the Press." One can easily imagine how a variety of product types and brands thereof can be marketed to persons like you by using data such as these.

Ethnographics

A research technique called **ethnographics** depends on the researcher going out into the field and observing how consumers select and use brands. Then they interview users and probe for details. For example, they might watch shoppers in the bread department of a supermarket and see if and how many shoppers examine the expiration date on the packages. If they are interested in how consumers use and consume food, they might go to the consumers' homes and receive permission to see and photograph their refrigerator, freezer, pantry, and cookbooks. Then they ask questions about which ingredients are used most frequently, how long things have been in the freezer, and what the homemaker's favorite recipes are.

Based on the results, the researchers go to their R & D department and either develop a new brand or reposition an old one (e.g., Cheerios) to fit the consumers' reported habits and needs.

A good recent example was the development of Gillette's Sensor 3 disposable razor. It is specifically designed for women (Parente, 2004) and was based on the differences between the ways men and women shave. For example, researchers noted that when men cut themselves while shaving, they blamed the shaver. When women cut themselves when shaving their legs, they blame themselves. When interviewed, men said they wanted a sharper razor, whereas women wanted a duller one. After asking more probing questions, researchers found that women used a razor with the handle pointing up while men shaved with the handle pointing down. This makes sense since men usually shave their face while standing at a sink, while women usually shave their legs by bending over while showering. The women got upset when they dropped the razor, which meant bending down farther to pick it up and thus getting water and soap or shampoo in their eyes. Women reported that a thicker, non-slippery handle would be preferred. Armed with this research, designers created the Sensor 3 for women with three spring-loaded blades, protective microfins, and an ergonomically styled, thicker, rubber-coated handle with grip-holding ridges. The men's Sensor had two razor blades with a similar handle but with a smaller head to shave hard-to-reach places around the nose and mouth. Both razors got high marks, and Gillette launched a successful nationwide rollout in 2002. Taken together with demographic, psychographic, and socio-graphic research, ethnographics assure that marketers are well-prepared to design products and brands as well as ads that speak in a very personal way to consumers like yourself.

FROM RESEARCH TO COPY: THE LANGUAGES OF ADVERTISING

Research results next go to the agency's creative staff for conversion into attention-getting and memorable ad and P.R. copy. It must be believable but should also sell the brand amidst the clutter. John O'Toole (1985), the former CEO of a major ad agency and past president of the American Association of Advertising Agencies, made some interesting observations about reaching the audience. He believes the consumer should be at the center of the process, and that the only kind of language—verbal and/or nonverbal—that effectively persuades targets the consumer as an individual. The first task with a new brand is to develop a personal profile of the consumer and then to custom design personal language and copy, especially using the word "you," which makes the message feel personalized, such as, "Aren't you glad you use Dial? Don't you wish everybody did?" or the Sears DieHard battery ad copy that follows a demonstration of the battery in action and has copy targeting the individual: "The DieHard. Starts Your Car When Most Other Batteries Won't." Consumers recognize their experiences in the words and visuals of the ad. We could cite many other examples, but consumers and critical receivers need to be ready for a set of usually misleading language that one ad executive, Carl Wrighter, calls "Weasel Words." Let's examine some of his examples of words that "weasel" or sneak their way out of the brand's promised features and benefits and which can deceive the consumer.

WEASEL WORDS
IN ADVERTISING

We need to examine how clever persuaders use words in ads to mislead us. Carl Wrighter's classic book, *I Can Sell You Anything* (1972), focuses on some of the key words used to deceive us. He calls them **weasel words** because they allow persuaders to seem to say something without really saying anything. Wikipedia defines a weasel word as "deliberately misleading or ambiguous elements of language used to avoid making a straightforward statement while simultaneously generating the illusion that a direct, clear form of language is being used." These "bogus" words allow sources to neatly slide

their way out of the brand's seemed promises. Politicians facing some sort of political blunder often say "Mistakes were made" and in doing so, they seem to be taking the blame, but look more carefully—mistakes made by whom? When? What kinds of mistakes? With what intent? These are the critical types of queries that responsible receivers need to raise in such situations. Otherwise the comment is just so much "spin." The use of the term "weasel" goes back at least to Teddy Roosevelt, who warned receivers to strip them away and thus discover nothing of substance. For you, they are key tip-offs to the kind of pitch to guard against. Though Wrighter identified them for us years ago, you will discover that they are still frequently used in today's advertisements and how up-to-date his predictions are. Let's investigate a few of them, and if you find them interesting, enter "weasel words" into any search engine and you will find that we have barely touched the surface in this discussion.

Helps

The word "helps" seems to offer aid, relief, or perhaps even a solution to a consumer's problem but in reality promises nothing very concrete. For example, take the slogan "Listerine mouthwash helps prevent colds." What is the promise here? Can you expect that you will feel better in a few days if you use Listerine? If you did, was your improvement from the help Listerine gave or was it because you drank lots of fluids and got lots of rest? When you really think about it, drinking lots of liquids and getting enough rest is what really helps. So the word "helps" has lots of "wiggle room" and lets the brand escape from being held to its supposed promise.

Like

Another weasel is the word "like." A tennis star says, "Driving a Nissan Maxima is like driving an expensive European model." The house brand is "just like" the expensive name brands. You can easily see the deception with a word that has as many loopholes as "like." It only means that something seems to resemble something else that is supposedly superior—and even that resemblance may be a stretch. Cindy Crawford is supposed to be *like* women all over the world. A prepared food tastes just *like* homemade. A jug wine tastes *like* the expensive French brands. Fruitopia will make you feel *like* you are an athletic champion—ha, ha. When you encounter the word "like" ask yourself if there are any ways that the advertised brand *differs* from the supposedly superior one and if those ways are beneficial or detrimental to you.

Virtually

The weasel word "virtually" resembles "like," except that it seems to make an even more genuine and concrete promise. The new cotton chamois shirts are "virtually indestructible." Leatherette feels "virtually" like hand-buffed cowhide. Cascade leaves your dishes and glassware "virtually spotless." The promises seem so specific, yet there is only a tiny loophole—does one or two spots on a glass qualify as "virtually spotless? What about three or five? That tiny loophole widens depending on the circumstances. When the customer says that the leatherette wore out after several months or finds spots on the dishes just washed with Cascade, has it "virtually" done the job? If the product truly did the job it promises to do, the word "virtually" would be irrelevant. So when you run into the weasel word "virtually" don't expect 100 percent fulfillment of the benefit promised in the advertisement. You may get only an approximation of that benefit, and even then it might miss the mark by a lot.

Faster or Better

Some products need to be fast acting, such as over-the-counter medication for intense physical symptoms or products related to personal safety and promising to give you a faster response time to dangerous events. The brands in this product category frequently use the weasel word "faster" to sell the brand. Goodyear tires stop faster. Faster than what? Another brand? Than a donut? They give no basis for comparison. When you encounter the weasel words "**faster**" or "better," start making comparisons with the competition and make

sure the conditions under which the faster or better response happens are really the same. Are the advertisers comparing the incomparable; are they simply comparing apples to oranges?

As Much As

This weasel word seems to offer high performance but only to up to a point. If your doctor tells you to get more exercise by joining a health club, some clubs promise that it's possible that "You can save as much as 50 percent with a Good Health Club Prescription Membership." Unless you really know the initial offering price and not just a bogus figure, you really can't tell if it's a true bargain or not. You may save nothing, a little, or maybe 50 percent, but there are no guarantees on the supposed 50 percent savings. When you see the words "**as much as**" or "up to," try to find out the regular everyday price; then make the true comparison.

In addition to these few examples given to raise your consciousness, there are many more offshoots of weasel words. For instance, "more" is a promise that doesn't answer the question "More than what?" "Better" or "quieter" and many others words are used to compare the brand with its competitors. These weasels are simply "implied comparisons" that really promise little in any concrete way. Also watch out for words like "unique," "only," or made-up names like "Polyglas," which is just a synonym for the generic fiberglass. Some critics refer to these made-up words as simply advertising "gobbedly-gook," which is probably pretty close to the truth. Again, the receiver needs to be alert to the many weasel words that populate modern advertisements.

DECEPTIVE CLAIMS IN ADVERTISING

Wrighter also identified another kind of deception in ads, in addition to the widespread use of weasel words. These deceivers are housed in the claims that brands often make about themselves. Clever promoters use deceptive claims or promises to attract our attention and to prompt us to buy, to vote for candidates, or to adopt certain practices, but they promise little in actuality. Let us look at several kinds of such claims identified by Wrighter (1972).

The Irrelevant Claim

Some ads make claims that sound impressive but are irrelevant if you really look at them closely. The basic tactic is to make a truthful claim that has little to do with the benefits of the brand. Then the claim is dramatized in such a way as to link the claim with the product, candidate, or movement and to expound on its superiority. For example, J & B scotch claims to be "rare" and "natural." That sounds good, doesn't it? Faced with claims like this one, receivers need to probe and ask questions like "Are other scotch whiskeys unnatural?" If you can't find an answer to your question, you have identified an irrelevant claim. Wrigley's new "Green Apple Extra" chewing gum has a scratch-and-sniff feature, but that's also irrelevant. You chew gum, not scratch it. And you usually buy it for its flavor, and its not the aroma. The Ford Escape is "built for the road." Well, so are all brands and models. The old Ivory claim about being able to float is probably 99 and 44/00 percent irrelevant now that few folks take sitdown baths. Shell Oil recently ran an ad with the claim that they "Don't Throw Anything Away—There Is No Away" and went on to claim that they were a "pro-environmental" corporation because they were concerned with recycling. The picture in the ad showed oil refineries exuding flowers from their smokestacks instead of fumes. What do the claim and the smokestacks actually have to do with Shell's environmentalist claim? Very little in all probability. "Bio-degradable" is another such green term and is meant to suggest that the brand is the only one which is biodegradable, but that's not true—all detergents have to be biodegradable today. The "pro-green" image is just a new "position" within which a company can place itself, but "green" is a clever position claim that receivers need to watch for in ads today. Most such claims are simply irrelevant when looked at carefully.

Receivers need to examine how the claim really fits or doesn't fit the true situation.

The Question Claim

Wrighter also noted a kind of claim that asks a question. By asking a question, the advertiser puts the ball in the receiver's court and often there is no answer, leaving the consumer wondering. For example, take the question claim of Prestone antifreeze. "If you can't trust Prestone, who can you trust?" Well I'd trust my friends who maybe recommended another brand or my parents who always used a different one. But beginning the ad with a question usually puts the receivers on the defensive—feeling like they need to come up with an answer. Consider these question claims for example: "Why not buy the original?" "Would a bunch of guys really go at it this hard just for a Michelob?" and "Why not catch a lunker—with Stren monofilament?" How can receivers answer them? All examples of the question claim can have differing answers without there being any quibbles or real difference. Sure, I'd like to catch a lunker and I'd love it with any brand of line—just so long as it's a lunker; and I know other brands can catch and land them too. Some guys I know go at it even harder, and they do it for a cheaper brand like Old Milwaukee. And so on. Notice that the product advantage is only implied. Trusting one's antifreeze is okay, but the question implies that dependability is to be found *only* in Prestone. Why buy the overpriced original? Maybe the Michelob is just an afterthought to the hard workout and not the *only* reason for playing hard. Will using Stren guarantee that you'll get a big one? Not likely. When receivers see a question mark, they should ask for details and guarantees.

The Advantage Claim

Wrighter noted some claims that seem to offer a unique advantage for the brand. For example, Mother's Noodles claim to be made with 100 percent semolina wheat, which seems to be a unique advantage to the brand, but so are all the other brands of noodles, including the generics. Compare the levels of vitamins in several types of breakfast cereal. You will discover that they are all about the same, and most of the protein that is promised comes from the milk you add. These are advantages that aren't advantages at all. Most generics have the same or similar advantages or additives. Politicians often claim to have humble origins; this is supposed to be an advantage, but it may in fact be a real disadvantage. People who had humble beginnings might be very insecure and even greedy. They might also have limited educations, weak social skills, and an inability to communicate with leaders who come from a higher social strata. So the claim to an advantage might be a disadvantage in reality, and receivers need to probe deeper when they hear a brand, politician, or idea claim to have some sort of advantage. Whenever you are faced with a person, product, or idea that claims some significant advantage, ask if it is real and if it is exclusive to that brand, candidate, or cause.

The Hazy Claim

The hazy claim is designed to confuse the buyer, voter, donor, or joiner. While the claim seems to be related to the evidence presented and the logic involved, closer examination usually reveals that this is not so. Early ads for Dannon Yogurt used examples of persons from Soviet Georgia who ate yogurt regularly and lived to be over a hundred years old. The ads then went on to recommend that everyone should eat yogurt because "It couldn't hurt!" That is among the haziest claims I have ever read. In fact, the evidence presented and the logic involved may not even be vaguely related. Hazy claims are also widely used in the world of politics. For example, a politician says that she supports both global economic policies and tariffs. Those two things could be mutually exclusive or even diametrically opposed.

The Mysterious
or Magic Ingredient Claim

Wrighter says that some claims refer to a magical or mysterious ingredient that supposedly makes their brand better. Noxzema sells a brand called Acne 12, which they say contains a secret ingredient dermatologists prescribe most—it may be one that all creams contain, such as alcohol or lanolin. Oxy-Clean contains "a powerful yet gentle medication no ordinary cleanser has." What is this powerful and gentle stuff, anyway? And let's not forget that Zantrex-3 claims to have a highly scientific sounding and confusing ingredient—bifurcated compounds—that can increase weight loss by 546 percent when compared to pills having ephedrine—Huh? That mysterious or magic ingredient claim would be difficult to track down, let alone truly test. Chlorets succeeded wildly when it was introduced by claiming that each tablet had a magic drop of "retsyn" in it, which accounted for the brand's superiority. Retsyn is an invented word for salad oil, which was used as a binder in the manufacture of Chlorets. Early on many breath fresheners claimed to prevent "halitosis," another word invented in 1875. You will discover many other kinds of claims made through mass media advertisements. In the Presidential campaign of 1968 over 35 years ago, Richard Nixon claimed to have a secret plan to end the war in Vietnam, but it was a plan that he could not reveal until elected president. Once elected he revealed his plan, which was nothing more than to gradually withdraw U.S. troops from Vietnam and then to let the Vietnamese do the fighting—about the same thing as the Bush administrations plan to "Draw Down" our troops in Iraq and let the Iraqis do the security work. The important thing for receivers is to maintain a critical attitude toward all claims made for brands, candidates, and organizations claiming to have magical or secret ingredients or ideas.

Rank's 30-Second-Spot Quiz

Hugh Rank, whom we first met in Chapter 1, outlined an easy-to-apply set of key questions to ask about advertising appeals that appear in television spots, and they are still useful for critical receivers today. His system, the 30-second-spot quiz, is in his book *The Pitch* (1991). Rank began by pointing out that any advertisements, but especially TV spots, are a synthesis of complex variables like research, scripts, settings, camera angles, acting, props, costumes, colors, and so on. Responsible consumers need to look at the spots in a sequential way. Rank suggested listing the shots or visual frames that make up a TV spot in the sequence in which they appear or are seen and heard by receivers. There might be up to 40 quick-cut edited shots in a 30-second spot, and most have an "establishing shot" (or opening shots that set the scene) which prepares the viewer for the ad or even the campaign. For example, various versions of a spot for a new brand of beer used establishing shots that were images of familiar sights in the famous cities in which the advertising was tested. So, in the San Francisco version viewers saw the Golden Gate Bridge, the New York City shot used the Statue of Liberty, the Chicago version used the Sears Tower, and in other cities the same type of establishing shot was used. The overall and implied message of the campaign was that, across the entire country, the new brand was pleasing discriminating beer drinkers. And then the spot used other shots (e.g., close-ups of guys guzzling the stuff from a German stein or a frosted mug) to tell that story. By listing the elements in the ad in order, the receiver can trace the persuasive flow of the ad.

For example, a spot begins with a medium shot showing a couple from the waist up involved in an argument tells us that conflict is central to the story. Then the audio comes up, and we discover that they are arguing about whether to buy an American or a foreign-made automobile and we hear a few arguments for each side with visuals of both types of automobiles and factory workers putting them together. The camera moves in for a close-up shot of the man's face, and we hear musical tension increasing as we see and hear the tension in his face and voice when he says he will only "Buy American!" brands. Then the close-up shot shifts to the woman's face, and we hear her say, "You know, you're cute when you're serious like this." Then we hear a giggle and see them nuzzle with one another as they look at their new Hyundai. The shots and the details tell the story. Your job as a receiver is to list the shots, audio, music, colors, and so on in order until the ad is completely described. Then try to identify the underlying structure of the spot. For example, the underlying structure

of the ad just described is conflict resolution, but a surface variation could have used two males for the argument. This would have altered the dialogue, tension, drama, and meaning of the ad.

Rank also suggests recognizing the audience's involvement in the spot. In other words, does the spot demonstrate features of the brand or the benefits that flow to the brand itself or does it speak to what is actually being promised to the consumer of the brand? For example, the Ford Escort initially advertised that it had aerodynamic styling, independent wheel suspension, and rack and pinion steering. These are features of the Escort, not benefits to the consumer. They don't tell the consumer how he or she will personally gain anything from purchasing the brand. Features should offer some personal benefit to the consumer. For instance, aerodynamic styling offers better handling, less wind resistance, better gas mileage, a sexier appearance, and a quieter interior. Once these preparatory steps of listing shots and audio are taken, Rank suggests asking five basic analytical questions:

1. What attention-getting techniques are being used? Most ads appeal to one or more of the five senses (see Figure 14.4). Most also appeal to consumers' emotions and use the unexpected, the interesting, and the noticeable to capture consumer attention and often keep the consumer wondering until the end what brand the ad is trying to sell.

2. What confidence-building techniques are being used to convince consumers that they can trust the brand? Authority figures, repetition, references to the number of years the brand has been successful, guarantees, and appeals to trust and sincerity all inspire trust. The use of expert testimony from a doctor or lawyer, demonstrations, and warranties all build consumer trust and confidence as do mentions of such things as 100,000 mile warranties. Zero percent financing, or ratings by testing agencies all are confidence building techniques.

3. What desire-stimulating techniques are being used to motivate consumers to try the brand? Rank said identifying the benefits is a good

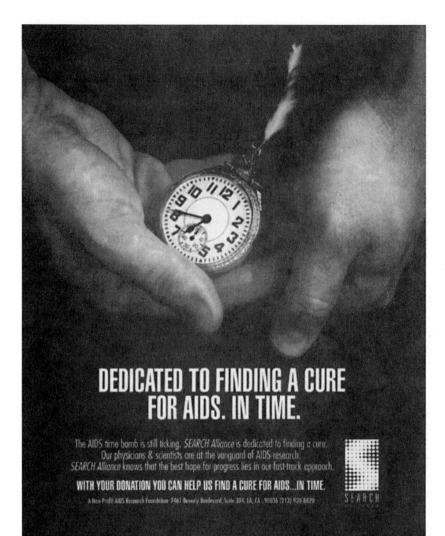

DEDICATED TO FINDING A CURE FOR AIDS. IN TIME.

The AIDS time bomb is still ticking. *SEARCH Alliance* is dedicated to finding a cure. Our physicians & scientists are at the vanguard of AIDS research. *SEARCH Alliance* knows that the best hope for progress lies in our fast-track approach.

WITH YOUR DONATION YOU CAN HELP US FIND A CURE FOR AIDS...IN TIME.

A Non-Profit AIDS Research Foundation 7461 Beverly Boulevard, Suite 304, LA, CA .90036 (213) 930 8820

SEARCH

F I G U R E 14.4 Using Rank's 30-second-spot quiz, explain how this ad gets consumer attention.

SOURCE: By permission of AIDS Search Alliance. For information on AIDS research and what is being done to find a cure, go to the organization's Web site at www.aidsresearch.org.

way to discover these techniques. He noted that most ads offer one or more of the following as desire-stimulating reasons to try the brand: Preventing or avoiding some bad thing (discomfort or embarrassment), protecting or keeping some good thing (status, appearance, or wealth), gaining relief or getting rid of some bad thing (dandruff or financial worry), and acquiring or getting some good thing (a new economical car that gets great mileage or a good interest rate on a home loan).

4. What urgency-stressing techniques are being used to get consumers to "act now"? Examples include expiration dates or language warning that the price is only good "while supplies last."

5. What response-seeking techniques are being used to tell consumers what kind of action is

being sought? Examples include "try" the brand, "purchase it," "join," or "call" the 1-800 number.

CHANGES IN OUR WORLD: IMPLICATIONS FOR ADVERTISING

Recall the trends noted at the beginning of this chapter. Markets are becoming more global, fragmented, and diverse. More families than ever now rely on two or more incomes per household and are often strapped for time. These types of families are the prime targets of ads promising convenience and the saving of time, but the receiver also needs to ask who is the actual beneficiary. Working spouses? Widows and widowers? Single persons? Divorced persons? Workers earning overtime? Or the company making extra profit? To some extent all of these benefit, because busy two-income families and kids who have increased activities aren't the only ones who need convenience and time-saving brands. But some of these persons can't afford to pay for the convenience or the savings in time, and in some cases all of these types of persons can benefit from convenience and time savings. Meals are no longer the traditional family around the dinner table. Families and singles are both dining out, bringing home meals, or having home delivery of dinner. Americans now eat more than half of their meals out, including breakfast, so convenience and time saving may mean a drive-up window to some persons.

Another change has been the emphasis on another kind of convenience for these same consumers. Since the introduction of 1-800 dialing, it is easier to purchase anything from clothing to baseball tickets. Time is a commodity for most two-income families and should be spent carefully, so mail-order and online purchasing not only save time but allows you to avoid the inconvenience of finding a parking spot, walking to the store, and waiting in line to check out. The marketing

of convenience and the saving of time are also new changes in the marketplace. The direct marketing industry, which concentrates on convenience and saving of time, now accounts for about 20 percent of all advertising dollars spent in the United States. In fact, many strip malls and even mega-malls have "space for lease" because we now face a very competitive marketplace, especially given the amount of income spent using catalogs, the Internet, shopping channels, and other direct-marketed outlets; nobody wants to take the time to drive to the mall, park and wait. As a result, another change in today's marketplace is the rush to get to the consumer's discretionary dollars before the competition can grab it. Today we see pre-Christmas sales right after Halloween as well as the traditional post-Christmas sales. We start selling back-to-school stuff right after the Fourth of July. Retailers want to get a jump on the competition. Large discount chains have increased as well, so advertising had to increase to beat the competition. In the years to come, there will be still more clutter for us to try to sift through, and we are only on the front edge of interactive and Internet advertising.

Creating Interest, Desire, and Conviction

Advertising consultants Vestergaard and Schroeder advise getting attention for an ad by asking a question that consumers cannot answer. This provokes curiosity and leads the audience to interact with the ad. Other examples include scratch-and-sniff ads, recipes in ads that use the brand as an ingredient, and ads including a true/false quiz for the reader to answer. An ad by General Motors asks, "Do you know where your next fender is coming from?" Then they satisfy the reader's curiosity by answering, "America's body shops are being flooded with imitation parts. Look-alike doors. Copycat hoods. Imitation bumpers, grills, fenders, and more.... Insist on genuine GM parts." This ad copy not only answers the attention-getting question in the headline, but it also creates interest, desire, and conviction in the consumer via product benefits and at the same time creates fears that they might not get the genuine article. Notice the frequent use of sentence fragments in the ad—"Look-alike doors." and "Copycat Hoods." These give the advertiser extra shots at the reader in less time and space.

Advertisers also need to avoid looking like "me too" imitations of the original. All dog food looks pretty much the same—either like gravel if it is dry or like glop if it is canned. But look at what Gaines Burger did. In the first place, the name sounds like and the product looks like hamburger—the all-American food. Of course, its redness is not natural. It's just iron oxide, and it won't hurt your dog, but it will cause your mind to make a link with human hamburgers on the grill. Another tactic used to create interest, desire, and conviction for a "me too" brand is to stress its high quality. For example, a face powder named Solar Power SPF-20 is marketed by a company named Physicians Formula. Now if a physician formulated the powder, it must be good. But the name may not describe who actually formulated the brand. Its slogan is "Your eyes won't believe your face." If they claim that the brand has the best quality for the price, they are not likely to be asked to prove the claim. Another approach is to appeal to anything scientific by including some scientific-sounding ingredient such as got2b, DZM-21, or Aididas' "aluminum free deodorant with cotton TECH that absorbs wetness." An advertiser can also make a scientific claim like "Contains the pain reliever recommended most by doctors and hospitals." Of course that ingredient is aspirin. Or someone wearing a white lab smock tells us about the features and benefits of the brand.

Getting Action

As we have noted several times, the hardest thing to do in sales is to "close the sale" or to "ask for the order" or, in other words, prompt or get action. Vestergaard and Schroeder also speak to this goal. They note that while "Buy now!" would seem to be the most direct call to action, there are other ways to say "buy" without using the word "buy," which can turn many prospects off. For example, "act now," "phone now," and "send now" say the same thing but avoid the potentially negative word "buy." Other urgency-stressing words stress Cialdini's scarcity principle to **prompt action**, as in "offer good until," "24-hour sale," or "only a few left at this price." Of the many ads studied by Vestergaard and Schroeder, 32 percent used this kind of directive language. Directive language falls into one of several categories.

1. The imperative clause, which gives an order. "Get one today" is one example. Another example is in an ad for a fishing lure supposedly in short supply—the Shadrap. The ad copy for it implied that the company was only able to send a limited quantity to the United States and then added, "That's enough for every serious fisherman…as long as they take only one—if you see one, grab it!" Interestingly, the company publicized that they were only available to rent and then for a limited time in Ely, Minnesota.

2. Other less directive and more suggestive language encouraging purchase, or asking questions like "Isn't it time you tried Dial?" or "Why not try Dial?" or "Dial is Worth a Try."

3. Directive language invites the reader/viewer to send for details, use the trial sample, or remember the product. These appeals might get a sale, but more often, they create what are called "qualified leads" that can be followed up on later. For example, if consumers send in for a free pamphlet on energy saving, they are probably good prospects for storm windows, aluminum siding, insulation, energy efficient furnaces and air conditioners, or solar panels. Vestergaard and Schroeder recommend seventeen verbs than can be used instead of the word "Buy." They are "try," "ask for," "take," "send for," "call," "make," "come on," "hurry," "come," "see," "give," "remember," "discover," "serve," "introduce," "choose," and "look for."

BOX 14.6 Cultural Diversity and Advertising

The fastest growing and most fascinating segments of the ad industry are the multicultural and diversity markets. A variety of agencies specializing in diverse and multicultural advertising have mushroomed in the past decade. A prime example is the Associated Content Corporation located online at http://www.associated content.com/article/286866/advertising_cultural_diversity_ the.html. Just consider a few of the services it offers for advertisers to target various cultures and ethnic segments: public relations, media planning, direct marketing, media design and placement, event planning, Web design, multimedia productions, mailing lists, ethnic radio and television, and translation. Visit its Web site, and you will be amazed at the depth and breath of the kinds of skills and services now emerging to address the advertising needs of our increasingly diverse and multicultural country and world.

SEXUAL APPEALS AND SUBLIMINAL PERSUASION IN ADVERTISING

The use of sexual appeals (and for some subliminal persuasion) in advertising is not new and has always been credited with success, but it is sometimes very controversial in today's changing marketplace. For example, feminists are concerned about the use of sexual images in advertising's as being an exploitation of the female body. Others, like parents, school officials, and physicians are concerned about increases in STDs in today's youth and as possible causes of increased teenage pregnancy and wonder if all the sexual appeals in advertising might be the cause. They question very much the ethics of subliminal appeals—sexual or otherwise. And the gay market has objections as well, which is where cultural diversity becomes an issue as one of the Seven Faces of Persuasion and is reflected in Box 14.6. Sexual appeals in ads range from the blatant ones promising sexual success and satisfaction with use of the brand (e.g., Viagra or Cialis) to more sophisticated and symbolic appeals that only *suggest* sexual success if the brand is used (e.g., Victoria's Secret). There are also possibly subliminal ads that suggest sexual success but that target the unconscious or subliminal level.

Freud maintained that the sexual and procreative urges are among the most powerful motivators of human motivation and behavior, even if not overtly apparent. They frequently lead to some symbolic behaviors such as fathers passing out cigars on the birth of a new child and other examples of symbolic sexual activities which abound. These symbolic actions often give sexual meanings to objects and actions. Freud saw cylindrical or rod-like objects such as pens, cigarettes, and guns as symbols of male genitalia and round or open objects such as goblets or open windows and doors as symbols of female genitalia. To him all sorts of ordinary everyday activities such as smoking a cigarette, cupping the hands, or fiddling with one's pen unconsciously symbolized various kinds of sexual activities. His work was ridiculed by many, but it was and is still taken very seriously by many people in the field of advertising. Whatever the case, simple observation makes it clear that sexual appeals abound in ads, and you won't have to look very long to identify objects that exemplify Freud's phallic and vaginal symbols. Let's examine some *obvious* and overt uses of sex in ads; some *more sophisticated* and not so obvious ones; and some *possibly subliminal* uses of sexual appeals in print and electronic ads. It is quite certain that three of these kinds of appeals are probably processed in the peripheral channel of the ELM without much conscious thought or evaluation.

In a very revealing analysis, researcher A. N. Valdivia (1997) deconstructed two very different kinds of sexual appeals in lingerie catalogs. The merchandise was priced almost the same, but the quality was very different, and the ad appeals for the two different brands were not nearly equivalent. For example, the name of one company, Victoria's Secret, connotes an old-world class that seems almost prudish. On the other hand, the other catalog, Frederick's of Hollywood, connotes a kind of leering glitziness. The settings in Victoria's Secret ads connote wealth, leisure, class, and an English country house atmosphere—a gentile lifestyle. In Frederick's of Hollywood, the photos are mostly shot against fabric backdrops, and the only items of furniture in them are beds, couches, and poolside lounge chairs—implying quite a different lifestyle. Victoria's Secret models appear demure and look away from the camera. Frederick's of Hollywood models leer at the camera, hands on hips, eyes closed, and jaws clenched. The Victoria's Secret catalog is published every month and costs $3 (although no one really pays for it), the company's home address is in London, their telephone operators speak with an English accent, and the catalog is mailed from England. So the range from sophisticated sexual appeals to more blatant and obvious appeals is clear in the difference between these two lingerie catalogs.

Blatant Sexual Appeals

Blatant sexual appeals usually *overtly promise* sexual success or satisfaction to the user in both the verbal and the nonverbal channels. Ads for any of the male brands designed to "cure" or aid in reducing ED or erectile dysfunction abound on television and elsewhere and use macho spokespersons like pro-football stars and coaches in ads for these types of products and brands. They are relatively new in the field of advertising. They are not exactly blatant, but they do fit the definition of promising sexual satisfaction to the user and are usually accompanied by a nude couple nuzzling or lying in twin bathtubs gazing at a sunset with wine glasses in hand. In the Pomegreat ad (Figure 14.5), blatant sexual appeals are being used. First and most obvious is the naked woman and the bed ready for lovemaking. Second is the use of the words "Sex kittens," which suggests the

type of women depicted. The words get your juices flowing—an obvious reference to sexual intercourse. Note that she doesn't drink milk like most kittens but prefers Pomegreat Liquor. Additionally, she is surrounded by pomegranates which initially resemble the apples that Eve used to seduce Adam, and many have bites already taken out of them, suggesting that she is experienced at seduction and many times over. The reader would have to be awfully slow not to get the meaning here.

More Sophisticated Sexual Appeals

More **sophisticated sexual appeals** only *hint* at sexual satisfaction if a consumer uses the brand—no promises here. Such appeals contain subtle cues (some perhaps "Freudian") to indicate sexual prowess and satisfaction. For example, in an ad by Tiffany for a sterling silver flask that can be worn as a Pendant (also the name of the piece of jewelry) is shown in a close-up photo showing the Pendant flask, dripping wet, and resting in the cleavage of a well-endowed and apparently nude woman. The long stem of an orchid is inserted into the flask on which a praying mantis is perched. The ad contains the brand name but no words or promise of sexual success, prowess, or satisfaction, but what would Freud make of it? The ad clearly uses a sexual appeal via the nudity, and he would probably note the symbolism of the phallic orchid stem inserted into the vaginally shaped flask, and the abundance of water as symbolic of completed intercourse. But why the praying mantis? How does it mate?

Subliminal Appeals

Subliminal appeals are a highly controversial topic (Phillips & Goodkin, 1983). In fact, many people doubt their very existence while others swear that not only does subliminal appeal exist, but it works to prompt sales and votes. For example, in a nationally distributed campaign of TV ads during the 2000 Presidential race, the letters R A T S

FIGURE 14.5 Blatant uses of sexual appeals promise sexual success to the user of the product.

SOURCE: Image courtesy of The Advertising Archives.

in the word DEMOCRATS were repeatedly highlighted and flashed on the screen and may have persuaded voters to reject the Democratic candidate—Al Gore, though that was repeatedly denied by the George W. Bush campaign offices. Why should this topic stir up so much controversy? It does so because it runs counter to the idea that human beings are by nature logical, not emotional, especially in making political decisions. And it would be highly unethical if they were motivated by subliminal appeals. So subliminal appeals are not limited to sexual ones. Then, too, **subliminal persuasion** smacks of sensationalism beginning with its first reportage ages ago in the 1950s when it was claimed that during a movie, the word "popcorn" was flashed instantaneously on the screen several times resulting in a huge reported increase in sales. Most dismissed the report as mere fantasy. Let us examine the arguments of those who claim that subliminal messages do indeed exist and the controversy over whether the technique actually works. Box 14.7 should inform you fully of the controversy.

BOX 14.7   Subliminal Sexual Appeals

 As noted, this topic has always been controversial with one side claiming to see or hear subliminal appeals, "embedded" sexually suggestive words, images, actions, and so on practically everywhere in print and video advertising, and the other side claiming that those folks must be some sort of perverts who only think about sex and therefore interpret everything as sexually suggestive. For an excellent analysis of the topic (and some fascinating examples—both visual and verbal) go to http://www.poleshift.org/sublim/ where you will find an in-depth discussion of the topic including controversial titles, references, books, and examples on the topic ranging from scientific reports on subliminal perception to pop sellers like *Subliminal Seduction* by Wilson Bryan Key who created a big media stir over the topic in the 70s. This background is followed by a tour of the "easy to identify" examples (those that we are calling "blatant") to the "harder to notice" examples (those that we are calling "more sophisticated") to those that are "hardest to identify" examples (those that we call "subliminal" appeals). The site also discusses and gives examples of non-sexual but still subliminal appeals or claims. A 7-minute video discussion of the topic by Derren Brown and two employees of an English ad agency with videos of subliminal ads on behalf of brands ranging from McDonald's to The Food Network can be found at http://www.youtube.com/watch?v=ZyQjr1YL0zg. Enter the words "subliminal advertising" into any search engine if you want to explore both sides of the controversy further. This also provides an interesting topic for a term paper.

Support for the Existence of Subliminal Messages.   The basic premise underlying subliminal persuasion rests on the notion of the unconscious mind and that its impulses are so powerful that they must be enacted in conscious life, even if in only symbolic ways. Freud believed that the unconscious mind is constantly at work processing information that the conscious mind simply ignores. Those who believe in the existence of subliminal appeals maintain that such appeals are sometimes so short-lived and disguised that the conscious mind ignores them, yet at the subconscious level, they are extremely powerful and highly motivating. As noted, the technique was dismissed when first publicized in the 1950s, but it was and still is barred from use in the electronic media by the FCC because of fears that the report might be accurate. However, their ruling did not cover the print, film, and video media, and we know that blatant pornography is readily available in those media. But from a non-porn perspective, we also know that over a dozen commercial research firms in Chicago and New York still offer services in producing subliminal messages for advertisers. So there remains concern that subliminal persuasion, particularly using sexual appeals, is "secretly" being used

in advertising, and that possibility is disturbing to some. The issue re-emerged in the presidential campaign of 2000 when the aforementioned negative television "R A T S" ad was commissioned by the Republican National Committee to criticize Al Gore's prescription drug proposal, and some at the time credited the ad with Gore's defeat. At the same time, there were many other irregularities over the election which finally had to be determined by the U.S. Supreme Court leaving the RATS episode unresolved. Also, it is known that the CIA has an ongoing interest in subliminal persuasion in intelligence work, espionage, and counterespionage, which tends to give one pause as to the presence and effectiveness of subliminal cues in persuasion—especially in advertising (Goodkin & Phillips, 1983). Researcher and professor of advertising,

Wilson Bryan Key (noted in Box 14.6) popularized and sensationalized the issue of subliminal sexual appeals in his books *Subliminal Seduction* (1973), *Media Sexploitation* (1977), and *Clambake Orgy* (1980). All the books claimed that subliminal and erotic cues were "embedded" or airbrushed into magazine ads that were appealing to subconscious and repressed sex drives. These **embeds** were faintly airbrushed into many liquor ads in the final stages of production Key claimed, and they were supposedly then subconsciously remembered later when cued by a store display to buy the brand. Key was originally struck by the need to retouch photos in most liquor ads by airbrushing in images of ice cubes in the glasses—real ice cubes melted under the hot lights needed for magazine-quality photos. Since the persuaders were airbrushing in the ice cubes, he reasoned that they might consider airbrushing in a subtle message such as the words "sex," "buy," or "good" in the cubes. Key showed 1,000 persons such an ad and asked them to describe the feelings they had while looking at them when the word "sex" was embedded in the ice cube. Although 38 percent didn't respond, 62 percent reported that the ad made them feel sensual, aroused, romantic, sexy, and even horny. Key says that he replicated the test with several different ads and other audiences with similar results.

More recently, Kevin Hogan (2005) observed that subliminal perception has been back on the front burner since 1990. His research and that of others show that while subliminal *audio* messages do not work—with the exception of "priming" and "stealth marketing." The story is much different with visual or video subliminal messages. Hogan contends that the visual cortex does not respond to stimuli in conscious awareness and instead, takes unseen or unperceived information and shares it with other parts of the brain, causing actions to be taken. He reports an experiment on paying for drinking water conducted by Piotr Winkleman, a psychology professor at the University of California at San Diego in 2004. Testing undergraduate students there, Winkelman used thirst, amount of consumption, and the price that a person was willing to pay for a glass of water as dependent or outcome variables. Subjects would be offered a glass of water in two conditions—one after seeing a happy face and the other after seeing an angry face. Thirsty subjects drank twice as much after being exposed to the happy face versus an angry one and were willing to pay $0.38 versus only $0.10 after the angry face. At present the whole subliminal issue is unclear and may or may not be just so much overly active imagining. Let's look at several ads which use sexual appeals and try to determine where the line between simply sexually oriented advertising and subliminally sexually oriented advertising may or may not exist.

Some Possible Subliminal Ads. Let's explore some definitions of advertisements that indeed use subliminal or near-subliminal persuasion. "Near subliminal" is used here because in these ads, someone usually has to point out the subliminal stimuli to the casual observer. This is similar to the picture puzzles where someone points out both the old woman and the young woman in the visual puzzles which we all have seen. It's a case where one's perception of a visual stimuli shifts (sometimes called a "gestalt shift"), and the viewer can see two very different images when they are pointed out. In all example ads used here, the advertising appeals seem to promise sexual prowess, success, and satisfaction, and one can only infer if their use is subliminal or not. If the cues must be pointed out to the observer, then they come close to being labeled subliminal. If they are even fairly obvious and don't require such help, they are not.

Consider the two perfume ads in Figures 14.6 and 14.7. The first ad is called "The Promise Made," and the second is called "The Promise Kept." The difference in titles immediately and quite obviously suggests that some sort of change has occurred, especially since on first glance, the ads appear to be nearly identical except for their headlines. They were run side by side or on consecutive pages. Their sponsor, Lanvin Parfums Inc. admitted to your author by telephone that the changes were intentional and was quite surprised that anyone would question them. Observe what has changed between "The Promise Made" and "The Promise Kept." For instance, in "The Promise Kept," the champagne bottle is empty, the phone is off the hook, the fire has died down, the woman's shoes and perfume atomizer are now on the dais, the flowers on the left seem to have "blossomed" and "opened" in the heat, and the woman's earrings are off, as is her stole. Now that these changes have been called to your attention, you will naturally infer the answers to what has happened in the time period between the two ads. You might also

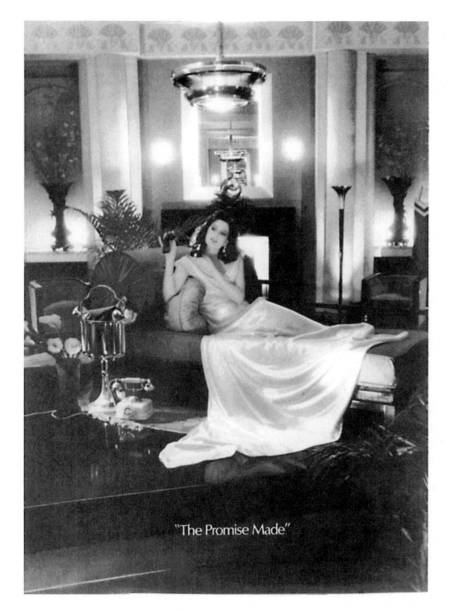

"The Promise Made"

FIGURE 14.6 What kind of promise is being made?

notice other changes that are far more subtle and likely to be overlooked. For example, what subtle sexual messages do you find in the nonverbal differences between the two ads? (See Chapter 10 on nonverbal communication.) For example, consider the expression on the woman's face. In which ad does she smile more? In which does her body language seem more tense or relaxed? In which ad is more of her body revealed? In which ad does her hair seem more or less coiffed? In which ad do the lights seem brightest? What about the fire? What has happened to the pillow on the couch? And so on. Do these changes and the headlines imply any dual meanings?

Arpège
Promises

"The Promise Kept"

Arpège Parfum

FIGURE 14.7 What differences imply that the promise was kept?

Are Subliminals Effective? If subliminal messages such as those apparently visible above are intentionally used in an ad, the next question to be asked is if they are effective in persuasion? In other words, do they sell the brand or are they just amusing tomfoolery? Most information from the brands and the ad agencies for all advertising is called "proprietary information," which means that they are held in confidence and can't be released unless both parties agree to reveal these data. As a result, no direct message/purchase linkages are possible to quote or otherwise demonstrate, so we must

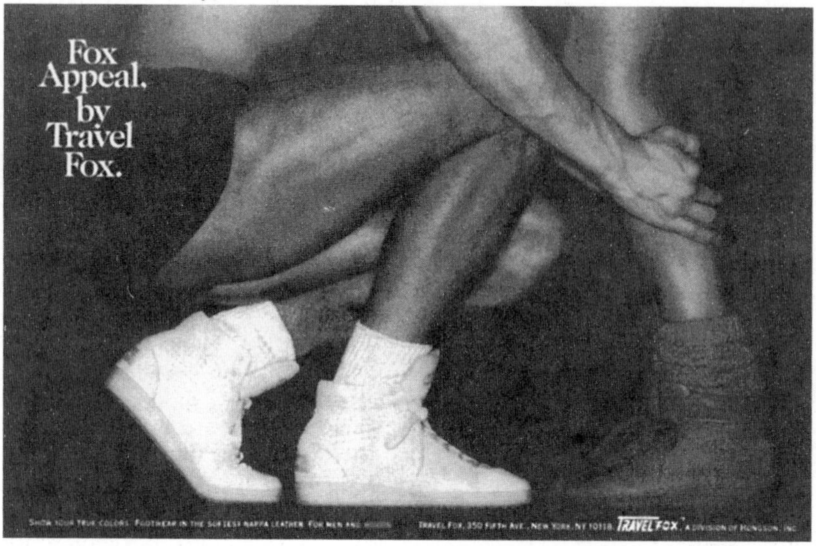

Subconscious

FIGURE 14.8 In this ad for Travel Fox sneakers, the words "Fox" and "appeal" tell you what is going on as we see a man and woman obviously in a sexual position.

SOURCE: Used by permission of Hall & Cederquist Advertising, Inc.

operate on inference, admittedly a weak form of reasoning. Also, another question that arises is "Are the embeds intentional or merely accidental?" Are they caused perhaps by the melting of the ice cubes or a slip of the airbrusher's hands? Key notes that when such photos are taken in a studio lit with hot lights, the ice cubes do melt and very quickly which is why, he says, they have to be airbrushed in after the photo shoot is completed, and wouldn't the clever artist dream up the idea of brushing words and images into the cubes? The ad agencies reply that they would never think of using such a sullied and unethical technique just to sell the brand, but would they admit to doing it even if that was their purpose? Here's what the past president of the American Psychology Association's Division of Consumer Psychology says about the existence of subliminal cues in ads, "Absolutely.... The controversy has always been over changing people's attitudes. That you can't do. What you can do is trigger a prior attitude or predisposition" (Lander, 1981, p. 45). So perhaps the embeds act as unconscious "triggers" for purchase behavior. That statement reflects what we have been talking about all along—the most effective persuasion taps information that receivers already possess—such as images of sexual satisfaction, and similar fantasies such as conflict or violence could be embedded as Key claimed. As we have repeatedly observed, effective persuaders get messages out of their audiences, not into them, so while the ad people deny using the technique as noted, there's room for doubt as to the veracity of their denials. We do know that subliminal self-help tapes have become a multibillion-dollar business to which their creators openly admit, and many users of the tapes are true believers in the methods and testify to their usefulness in learning languages, quitting smoking, and so on. Of course, certain ads that use sex aren't at all subliminal about their messages. The Calvin Klein ads promoting Obsession for Men are good examples. Others border on the subliminal. Their message is hazy but clear enough to give you a linkage between the brand and the "imagined" or "subliminal" and "embedded" images the advertiser wants you to perceive and process. A good example is the campaign to promote Travel Fox sneakers using ads that contained little to no ad copy. The visuals used in the entire campaign showed various permutations of a man and a woman wearing the shoes and posing in a highly suggestive position that would be unnatural one for both partners unless oral sex were involved, as shown in Figure 14.8. Did it work? Sales in the New York market tripled in the year following publication of this and partner campaign ads.

REVIEW AND CONCLUSION

As noted earlier, we live in a world exploding with new products, brands, and media that are even more cluttered with ads for those products and brands. This trend is sure to continue with more and more surfaces being used to imprint with ad messages—carpeting in a store, "free" T-shirts, the giant digital TV screens now being used on the sides of balloons and blimps flown over high attendance events, the backs of doors in public bathroom stalls, interactive Web sites, and a host of others. Advertisers want to capture our attention and try to educate us about their brands' features, benefits, and advantages. They use clever cues and sales promotions to prompt us to buy at the point of purchase.

These ads and sales promotions are but two elements in what is now termed IMC, which integrates several elements with advertising to make "brand impressions" or "brand contacts" on or with consumers. These elements include public relations, packaging, imprinted items (such as clothing, napkins, wrapping paper, and soft drink cups), and special events that feature the brand (such as the Pepsi Challenge or the Virginia Slims Tennis Tournament), consumer trade sales promotions like coupons, sweepstakes, rebates and many others; and increasingly the direct marketing industry is becoming more and more sophisticated not only in creating motivating offers and ad packages but at developing highly sophisticated data bases to target only their most promising prospects in ever smaller and highly defined segments. IMC specialists use sophisticated kinds of research, including demographics, socio-graphics, psychographics, and ethnographics to target narrower and narrower seg-

ments of the general audience. Based on this research, they develop products (e.g., Pringles and the Sensor 3 disposable razors), ad copy, layouts, music, and scripts to appeal to various needs and desires.

Ads often use misleading and even deceptive weasel words and misleading claims. And advertisers sometimes use blatant, sophisticated, and subliminal sexual appeals to hype their brands. As consumers, we need to be on guard, for there is an ethical dimension to advertising, and ads can easily be detrimental instead of being informative.

According to John Chaffee (1998), the positive side of advertising is that it provides consumers with valuable information about brand benefits in important areas like safety, health, nutrition, and cleanliness, as well as about more mundane issues like being attractive, sexy, and successful. He also argues that advertising as a tool of competition inevitably leads to lower prices, which is inherently advantageous for consumers. At the same time, author Russ Baker (1997) points to more questionable practices such as brand manufacturers trying to manipulate the editorial content of the media in which their advertising appears. They warn media executives that they intend to withhold advertising if editorial content is critical of the brand or even of the product category. They have been successful in censoring programming and articles to their benefit, and in some cases, they have managed to spike certain programs or articles. Recently, the Bush White House was discovered paying supposedly neutral news media personalities to slant news stories in favor of the President's words and actions. You might want to take a look at advocates on both sides of the issues in A. Alexander and J. Hanson's (2003) provocative book Taking *Sides: Clashing Views on Controversial Issues in Mass Media and Society*. In any case, whether you as a consumer are encountering advertising, public relations, special events, sales promotions, brand contacts, and so on you need to be vigilant and critical of what you choose to reject and what you choose to process and evaluate before making purchase, voting, donating, or joining decisions.

KEY TERMS

After reading this chapter, you should be able to identify, explain, and give an example of the following key terms or concepts:

integrated marketing communication (IMC)	TOMA	frequency	weasel words
brands	positioning	psychographics	faster
slogans	repositioning	need-driven consumers	as much as
jingles	overcommunicated society	outer-directed consumers	prompt action
logo	brand loyalty	inner-directed consumers	blatant sexual appeals
packaging	master brands	socio-graphics	sophisticated sexual appeals
brand equity	line extension	geographics	subliminal appeals
point of purchase	demographics	ethnographics	subliminal persuasion
sales promotion	reach		embeds

APPLICATION OF ETHICS

You work for East/West Medical Corporation, which performs medical testing. It has purchased ad time on television news programs to announce that consumers can get a "free" test kit for melanoma screening at the local Kroger supermarket. The ads masquerade as informational news items using the same anchorperson as the news program uses. A question concerning the ads has been raised. Critics ask, "Is it ethical to make an ad appear to be a news item?" The screening kit is free, and the consumer simply sends it in to East/West and gets results back in a week or so for a small processing fee. The fee is mentioned in the directions for use of the kit but not in the ad. Some say that if it saves lives, it can not be unethical. Others say that society relies on news journalists to present the truth, the whole truth, and nothing but the truth, and the "ad as news" violates the social contract between viewers and journalists. There are several options open to East/West. They could label the TV commercial as an advertisement at the outset of the spot, thus alerting the viewer. They could label it at the end of the ad after it has been processed by viewers. They could change their appeal by not emphasizing the "free" aspect of the offer and telling the viewer that there will be a processing charge. They could stop using the news program as an envelope for the ad. Which option would you choose and why?

QUESTIONS FOR FURTHER THOUGHT

1. How much money is spent for advertising in the United States per person compared with that spent in other countries?

2. How might advertising reflect the values and norms of a culture?

3. What might a Marxist critic say about the purpose of advertising?

4. What is "positioning," and how does it relate to the term "niche"?

5. What product features can serve as niches?

6. What are some of the problems of an "over-communicated society"?

7. What is the "product explosion," and how does it affect us?

8. What does "breaking through the clutter" mean?

9. Why is "American-made" an example of positioning?

10. What are the differences between demographics, socio-graphics, and psychographics?

11. What is a DINK?

12. What is VALS, and how does it work?

13. What are focus groups, and what is their purpose?

14. What are some of the languages of advertising? Give examples.

15. How does advertising research lead to advertising copy? Give examples.

16. What are weasel words? Give examples.

17. What are some deceptive claims? Give examples.

18. What is meant when we say that a product has become semanticized? Give examples.

19. What differentiates blatant sexual appeals in advertising from sophisticated ones? Give examples.

20. How are subliminals used in advertising? How effective do you think they are?

For online activities, go to the *Persuasion* book companion Web site at http://academic.cengage.com/communication/larson12.

Epilogue

One recurring phenomenon that I have noted while revising *Persuasion: Reception and Responsibility* is the continually increasing rate of change. Not only have we seen the rise of terrorist networks across the globe, but many of them seek to destroy the American economy and our sense of security. After the events of 9/11, no one can travel by air with the same sense of confidence that this is the safest mode of transport. New technologies emerge practically weekly. Another ongoing change involves the "boomer" effect. The baby boomer generation that opposed the Vietnam War as "hippies" and "yippies" have moved beyond their trend-setting (and frequently greedy) years as "yuppies" (young urban professionals). Some are now past their highest-earning years as "muppies" (mature urban professionals) and well into their "ruppie" (retired urban professionals) stage of life. They continue to impact our society enormously. Since the last edition of this book, we have seen the dot-com bubble burst and the economy go from boom to bust, and now we are running an enormous budget deficit with no end in sight. And following the corporate scandals and bankruptcies of the late 1990s and early millennium years, our faith in the integrity of CEOs of major corporations and large accounting firms is shot. We have become an incredibly diverse nation as compared to just a few years ago, and this diversity will have sweeping effects in the new millennium.

Technology continues to affect us in unexpected ways. For example, the wreckage of the space shuttle *Columbia* recovered by mountain hunters and fishermen using inexpensive but sophisticated global positioning system (GPS) devices. They simply recorded the coordinates of the wreckage and reported that to the authorities. And, of course, use of the Internet, email, e-commerce, and so on, has grown exponentially. When I revised the ninth edition of this book, the Internet contained about 10,000 pornographic sites; it now carries millions. And there are other technologies and sophisticated techniques of persuasion yet to be introduced. As all of these and other changes unfold, the number and sophistication of persuasive messages continues to mushroom. The increase in persuasion is almost becoming exponential. Thus, it's more important than ever for us to become critical receivers of persuasion. My feelings are reinforced by Rod Hart (1999), a noted communication researcher and professor of communication at the University of Texas at Austin. He describes the dramatic appeal he makes to his students each term:

> On the first day of class, I observe to my students that all persuaders ask is to borrow just a bit of their minds just for a little while.... I tell my students that my course will return their minds to them. I tell them that the cups-full of themselves they willingly loan out to teachers and preachers and cheerleaders in the bleachers can lead to an empty cupboard. I tell them that if they keep giving portions of themselves away that there will be nothing left when they need themselves most—when confused, when frightened, when pressed for a decision. I tell them that persuasion is a science that moves in increments, that it happens most powerfully when it least seems to happen at all.... I try to instill a kind of arrogant humility in my students, a mindset that gives them the courage to disassemble rhetoric but also the wisdom never to underestimate it.... The persuasion course is the most important course they will take in college (n. p.).

As you conclude this course, I hope you will not cease practicing the critical reception skills discussed here. I hope you will try to expand your efforts, skills, and abilities to critically disassemble rhetoric. I hope you will continue to recognize the complexities of the world in which we live and the many persuasive messages we receive. I trust in your instinctive suspicion of persuasive appeals. Together with Professor Hart, I "trust, mostly, in the critical mind's wondrous capacity to call a spade a spade and a rhetoric a rhetoric, to depuff puffery and to make mortals of gods and to maintain a tenacious resolve that we shall not all fall, lemming-like into the sea."

References

Chapter 1

All Things Considered, April 11, 2005.

Alter, J. (2002). "The Body": So Jesse's act is suddenly very old. We've learned that wrestlers can govern until government has to wrestle with something truly important. *Newsweek*, July 1, p. 37.

Beckett, J. (1989). "Ad pitches popping up in unusual places". *San Francisco Examiner*, July 17.

Berger, A. A. (2000). *Ads, fads, and consumer culture: Advertising's impact on American character and culture.* Oxford: Rowan & Littlefield.

Berkowitz, L. (Ed.). *Advances in experimental social psychology* (Vol. 19, pp. 123–205). Orlando, FL: Academic Press.

Brembeck, W., & Howell, W. S. (1952). *Persuasion: A means of social control.* Englewood Cliffs, NJ: Prentice-Hall.

Brembeck, W., & Howell, W. S. (1976). *Persuasion: A means of social control* (2nd ed.). Englewood Cliffs, NJ: Prentice-Hall.

Burke, K. (1970). *A grammar of motives.* Berkeley: University of California Press.

Burke, K. (1970). *A rhetoric of motives.* Berkeley: University of California Press.

Callahan, D. (2004). *The cheating culture.* New York, Harcourt.

Campbell, J. (1991). *Transformations of myth through time.* New York: Harper and Row.

Campbell, J. (1972). *The hero with a thousand faces.* Princeton: Princeton University Press.

Cook, P. (1996). *The winner take all society.* New York, Martin Kessler Books.

Cialdini, R.B. (2001). *Influence: Science and practice.* Boston: Allyn and Bacon.

Donaldson. D. and Wamberg, S. (2001). *Pinocchio nation: Embracing truth in a culture of lies.* Colorado Springs, Pinion Press.

Fishbein, M. and Azjen, I. (1980). *Understanding attitudes and predicting social behavior.* Englewood Cliffs, N. J.: Prentice Hall Inc.

Fishbein, M. & Azjen, J. (1991). "The theory of planned behavior," *Organizational behavior and human decision processes.* (Vol. 50, pp. 179–211).

Fisher, W. F. (1987). *Human communication as narration: Toward a philosophy of reason, value and action.* Columbia: University of South Carolina Press.

Fotheringham, W. (1966). *Perspectives on persuasion.* Boston: Allyn & Bacon.

Gearhart, S. M. (1979). The womanization of rhetoric. *Women's Studies International Quarterly*, 2, 195–201.

Hall Jamieson, K. (1992). *Dirty politics: Deception, distraction and democracy.* New York: Oxford University Press.

Ithaca, J.S. (2007). *Time.* October 8 2007, p.65.

Kies, R. (2004). *The post-truth era: Dishonesty and deception in contemporary life.* New York: St. Martin's Press.

Klein, J. (2007) *Newsweek*. October 8, 2007. "Inflating a little man." P. 30.

Larson, C. U. (2007). *Persuasion: Reception and responsibility*. Belmont, Thomson.

Levy, S. (2007). *Newsweek*. October 8, 2007. "The technologist." P. 20.

Levy, S. (2007). *Newsweek*. November 26, 2007. "The future of reading. Pp. 56–64.

Marwell, G., & Schmitt, D. R. (1990). An introduction. In J. P. Dillard (Ed.), *Seeking compliance: The production of interpersonal influence messages* (pp. 3–5). Scottsdale, AZ: Gorsuch Scarisbrick.

McLuhan, M. (1964). *Understanding media: The extensions of man*. New York: Signet.

News Record, Gillette, Wyoming, May 10, 2005.

Obama, B. (2007). *Dreams from my father: A story or race and harmony*. New York: Crown Publishers.

Obama, B. (2006). *The audacity of hope: Thoughts on reclaiming the American dream*. New York: Crown Publishers.

Petty, R. E., & Cacioppo, J. T. (1986). The elaboration likelihood model of persuasion. In L. Berkowitz (Ed.), *Advances in experimental social psychology* (Vol. 19, pp. 123–205).

Postman, N. (1981). Interview. *U.S. News & World Report*, Jan. 19, p. 43.

Postman, N. (1985). *Amusing ourselves to death: Public discourse in the age of show business*. New York: Penguin Books.

Rank, H. (1976). Teaching about public persuasion. In D. Dieterich (Ed.), *Teaching and doublespeak*. Urbana, IL: National Council of Teachers of English.

Roberts, R. (1924). *The works of Aristotle*. Oxford: Clarendon.

Rosen, R. (2003). *The San Francisco Chronicle*. "Bush doublespeak." July 14, 2003. P. 23.

Shannon, C. E., & Weaver, W. (1949). *The mathematical theory of communication*. Urbana: University of Illinois Press.

Simons, H. W. (1986). *Persuasion: Understanding, practice, and analysis*. Reading, New York: Random House.

Simons, H. W. (2001). *Persuasion in Society*. Thousand Oaks, Sage, Inc.

Sullivan, P. A. (1993). Signification and Afro-American rhetoric: A case study of Jesse Jackson's "Common ground and common sense" speech. *Communication Quarterly, 41,* 1–15.

Chapter 2

Adam, A. (2005). *Gender, ethics, and information technology*. New York: Palgrave Macmillan.

Bailey, R. W. (1984). George Orwell and the English language. In E. J. Jensen (Ed.), *The future of nineteen eighty-four* (pp. 23–46). Ann Arbor: University of Michigan Press.

Baker, S., & Martinson, D. L. (2001). The TARES test: Five principles for ethical persuasion. *Journal of Mass Media Ethics,* 16, 148–175.

Bate, B. (1992). *Communication and the sexes*. (Reissue). Prospect Heights, IL: Waveland Press.

Berkman, R. I., & Shumway, C. A. (2003). *Digital dilemmas: Ethical issues for online media professionals*. Ames, IA: Blackwell Publishing.

Bennett, M. J. (1979). Overcoming the golden rule: Sympathy and empathy. In D. Nimmo (Ed.), *Communication yearbook 3* (pp. 407–422). New Brunswick, NJ: Transaction Books.

Blood, R. (2002). *The weblog handbook*. Cambridge, MA: Perseus.

Booth, W. C. (2004). *The rhetoric of RHETORIC: The quest for effective communication*. Malden, MA: Blackwell Publishing.

Bosmajian, H. (1983). *The language of oppression* (rpt. ed.). Lanham, MD: University Press of America.

Bovee, W. G. (1991). The end can justify the means —but rarely. *Journal of Mass Media Ethics,* 6, 135–145

Buursma, B. (1987). Do-or-die deadline rallies Roberts' flock. *Chicago Tribune*, Jan. 17, pp. 1, 10.

Callahan, D. (2004). *The cheating culture: Why more Americans are doing wrong to get ahead*. New York: Harcourt.

Cavalier, R. J. (Ed.). (2005). *The impact of the Internet on our moral lives*. Albany: State University of New York Press.

Cooper, M. (2002). Covering tragedy: Media ethics and TWA flight 800. In R. L. Johannesen (Ed.), *Ethics in human communication* (5th ed.) (pp. 319–331). Prospect Heights, IL: Waveland Press.

Corn, D. (2003). *The lies of George W. Bush: Mastering the politics of deception*. New York: Crown.

Cunningham, S. B. (2002). *The idea of propaganda.* Westport, CT: Praeger.

DeGeorge, R. (1999). *Business ethics* (5th ed.). New York: Prentice-Hall.

Ermann, D. M., Williams, M. B., & Shauf, M. S. (1997). *Computers, ethics, and society* (2nd ed.). New York: Oxford University Press.

Foss, S. K., & Griffin, C. (1995). Beyond persuasion: A proposal for an invitational rhetoric. *Communication Monographs, 62,* 2–18.

Freund, L. (1960). Responsibility: Definitions, distinctions, and applications. In J. Friedrich (Ed.), *Nomos III: Responsibility* (pp. 28–42). New York: Liberal Arts Press.

Froman, L. A. (1966). A realistic approach to campaign strategies and tactics. In M. K. Jennings & L. H. Ziegler (Eds.), *The electoral process.* Englewood Cliffs, NJ: Prentice-Hall.

Gorsevski, E. W. (2004). *Peaceful persuasion: The geopolitics of nonviolent rhetoric.* Albany: The State University of New York Press.

Green, M., & MacColl, G. (1987). *There he goes again: Ronald Reagan's reign of error* (rev. ed.). New York: Pantheon Books.

Griffin, E. A. (1976). *The mind changers: The art of Christian persuasion.* Wheaton, IL: Tyndale House.

Gunkel, D. J. (2001). *Hacking cyberspace.* Boulder, CO: Westview.

Hamelink, C. J. (2000). *The ethics of cyberspace.* London: Sage.

Hatzfeld, J. (2005). *Machete season: The killers in Rwanda speak.* Trans. Linda Coverdale. New York: Farrar, Straus, and Giroux.

Hauerwas, S. (1977). *Truthfulness and tragedy.* Notre Dame, IN: University of Notre Dame Press.

Horsey. (2007). The speech Mitt Romney *should* give. *Chicago Tribune,* December 10, sec. 1, p. 20.

Hsing, Y. (1998). *Being good: Buddhist ethics for everyday life.* New York: Weatherhill.

Johannesen, R. L. (1971). The emerging concept of communication as dialogue. *Quarterly Journal of Speech, 57,* 373–382.

Johannesen, R. L. (1985). An ethical assessment of the Reagan rhetoric: 1981–1982. In K. R. Sanders, L. L. Kaid, & D. Nimmo (Eds.), *Political communication yearbook 1984* (pp. 226–241). Carbondale: Southern Illinois University Press.

Johannesen, R. L. (1991). Virtue ethics, character, and political communication. In R. E. Denton, Jr. (Ed.), *Ethical dimensions of political communication* (pp. 69–90). New York: Praeger.

Johannesen, R. L. (1997). Diversity, freedom, and responsibility. In J. Makau & R. C. Arnett (Eds.), *Communication ethics in an age of diversity* (pp. 155–186). Champaign: University of Illinois Press.

Johannesen, R. L. (2000). Nel Noddings' uses of Martin Buber's philosophy of dialogue. *Southern Communication Journal, 65,* 151–160.

Johannesen, R. L., Valde, K. S., & Whedbee, K. E. (2008). *Ethics in human communication.* (6th ed.). Long Grove, IL: Waveland Press.

Johnson, D. G. (2001). *Computer ethics* (3rd ed.). Upper Saddle River, NJ: Prentice-Hall.

Kane, R. (1994). *Through the moral maze: Searching for absolute values in a pluralistic world.* New York: Paragon.

Kessler, R. (2004). *A matter of character.* New York: Sentinel/Penguin Group.

Klaidman, S., & Beauchamp, T. L. (1987). *The virtuous journalist.* New York: Oxford University Press.

Kramer, J., & Kramerae, C. (1997). Gendered ethics on the Internet. In J. M. Makau and R. C. Arnett (Eds.), *Communication in an age of diversity* (pp. 226–243). Urbana: University of Illinois Press.

Lebacqz, K. (1985). *Professional ethics.* Nashville, TN: Abingdon.

Lesher, S. (1972). The new image of George Wallace. *Chicago Tribune,* January 2, sec. 1A, p.1.

Lester, P. M. (1991). *Photojournalism: An ethical approach.* Hillsdale, NJ: Erlbaum.

Lester, P. M. (2003). *Visual communication* (3rd ed.). Belmont, CA: Wadsworth.

Ludwig, A. (1965). *The importance of lying.* Springfield, IL: Thomas.

McCammond, D. B. (2004). Critical incidents: The practical side of ethics. In D. Lattimore et al., *Public relations: The profession and the practice* (5th ed.) (pp. 84–85). New York: McGraw Hill.

Meiklejohn, A. (1948; 1960). *Political freedom.* NewYork: Harper and Brothers.

Miller, C., & Swift, K. (1981). *The handbook of nonsexist writing.* New York: Barnes & Noble.

Niebuhr, H. R. (1963). *The responsible self.* New York: Harper & Row.

Opotow, S. (1990). Moral exclusion and injustice: An introduction. *Journal of Social Issues, 46*, 1–20.

Pennock, J. R. (1960). The problem of responsibility. In C. J. Friedrich (Ed.), *Nomos III: Responsibility* (pp. 3–27). New York: Liberal Arts Press.

Pincoffs, E. L. (1975). On being responsible for what one says. Paper presented at Speech Communication Association convention, Houston, TX, Dec. 1975.

Primer: Blogs and blogging. (2005). *Media Ethics* (Spring), 16, pp. 14–16.

Samovar, L. A., Porter, R. E., & Stefani, L. A. (1998). *Communication between cultures* (3rd ed.). Belmont, CA: Wadsworth.

Schwartz, T. (1974). *The responsive chord.* Garden City, NY: Anchor.

Sellers, M. (2004). Ideals of public discourse. In C. T. Sistare (Ed.), *Civility and its discontents* (Ch. 1). Lawrence: University Press of Kansas.

Singer, J. B. (2002). The unforgiving truth in the unforgivable photo. *Media Ethics, 13*, 30–31.

Singer, M. G. (1963). The golden rule. *Philosophy, 38*, 293–314.

Singer, M. G. (1967). The golden rule. In P. Edwards (Ed.), *Encyclopedia of philosophy*, Vol. 3 (pp. 365–366). New York: MacMillan.

Singer, P. (2004). *The president of good and evil: The ethics of George W. Bush.* New York: Dutton/Penguin Group.

Spence, E. H., & Van Heekeren, B. (2005). *Advertising ethics.* Upper Saddle River, NJ: Pearson/ PrenticeHall.

Stewart, J., & Zediker, K. (2000). Dialogue as tensional, ethical practice. *Southern Communication Journal, 65*, 224–242.

Toulmin, S. (1950). *An examination of the place of reason in ethics.* Cambridge: Cambridge University Press.

Wheeler, T. H. (2002). *Phototruth or photofiction? Ethics and media imagery in the digital age.* Mahwah, NJ: Erlbaum.

Williams, H. M. (1974). What do we do now, boss? Marketing and advertising. *Vital Speeches of the Day, 40*, 285–288.

Wolf, M. J. P. (Ed.). (2003). *Virtual morality: Morals, ethics, and the new media.* New York: Peter Lang.

Wood, J. T. (1994). *Gendered lives: Communication, gender, and culture.* Belmont, CA: Wadsworth.

Chapter 3

Andrews, J. (1980). History and theory in the study of the rhetoric of social movements. *Central States Speech Journal*, 31, 274–281.

Aristotle. (1984). *Rhetoric.* (W. R. Roberts, Trans.). New York: Modern Library.

Bowers, J. W., & Ochs, D. J. (1971). *The rhetoric of agitation and control.* Reading, MA: Addison-Wesley.

Burke, K. (1969). A rhetoric of motives. Berkely: University of California Press (originally published in 1950).

Burns, S. (1990). *Social movements of the 1960s: Searching for democracy.* Boston: Twayne.

Campbell, K. K. (1998). Inventing women: From Amaterasu to Virginia Woolf. *Women's Studies in Communication, 21,* 111–126.

Fairhurst, G. T., & Sarr, R. A. (1996). *The art of framing: Managing the language of leadership.* San Francisco: Jossey-Bass.

Fisher, W. R. (1978). Toward a logic of good reasons. *Quarterly Journal of Speech, 64*, 376–384.

Fisher, W. R. (1984). Narration as a human communication paradigm: The case of public moral argument. *Communication Monographs, 51*, 1–22.

Fisher, W. R. (1987). *Human communication as narration: Toward a philosophy of reason, value, and action.* Columbia: University of South Carolina Press.

Foss, K. A., Foss, S. K., & Griffin, C. L. (1999). *Feminist rhetorical theories.* Thousand Oaks, CA: Sage.

Foss, S. K., & Griffin, C. L. (1995). Beyond persuasion: A proposal for an invitational rhetoric. *Communication Monographs, 62*, 2–18.

Foss, S. K. (1996). *Rhetorical criticism: Exploration and practice* (2nd ed.). Prospect Heights, IL: Waveland Press.

Kansas Baptist church intends to picket Heath Ledger's funeral because he played gay character. (January, 2008). Retrieved March 1, 2008 from http://www.foxnews.com/story/0,2933,324966,00.html.

Kilbourne, J. (1979). *Killing us softly.* Cambridge, MA: Cambridge Documentary Films.

Kilbourne, J. (2001). *Deadly persuasion: Why women and girls must fight the addictive power of advertising.* New York: Free Press.

McGee, M. C. (1980). The ideograph: A link between rhetoric and ideology. *Quarterly Journal of Speech, 66,* 1–16.

Measuring the 'decoy effect' in political races (April, 2007). Retrieved March 1, 2008 from National Public Radio Web site: http://www.npr.org/templates/story/story.php?storyId=9585221.

Nichols, M. H. (1952). Kenneth Burke and the 'New Rhetoric.' *Quarterly Journal of Speech, 38,* 133–144.

Plato. (1937). *The dialogues of Plato* (Vol. 1). (B. Jowett, Trans.). New York: Random House.

Rowland, R. C. (1989). On limiting the narrative paradigm: Three case studies. *Communication Monographs, 56,* 39–54.

Scott, R. L. (1993). Rhetoric is epistemic: What difference does that make? In T. Enos & S. C. Brown (Eds.), *Defining the new rhetoric* (pp. 120–136). Mahwah, NJ: Erlbaum.

Warnick, Barbara (1987). The narrative paradigm: Another story. *Quarterly Journal of Speech, 73,* 172–182.

Chapter 4

Ajzen, I. (1991). The theory of planned behavior. *Organizational Behavior and Human Decision Processes, 50,* 179–211.

Ajzen, I. (2001). Nature and operation of attitudes. *Annual Review of Psychology, 52,* 27–58.

Allen, M. (1998). Comparing the persuasive effectiveness of one and two-sided messages. In M. Allen & R. W. Preiss (Eds.), *Persuasion: Advances through meta-analysis* (pp. 87–98). Cresskill, NJ: Hampton Press.

Allen, M., & Stiff, J. (1998). The sleeper effect. In M. Allen & R. W. Preiss (Eds.), *Persuasion: Advances through meta-analysis* (pp. 175–188). Cresskill, NJ: Hampton Press.

Armitage, C. J., & Christian, J. (2003). From attitudes to behavior: Basic and applied research on the theory of planned behavior. *Current Psychology, 22,* 187–195.

Bless, H., & Schwarz, N. (1999). Sufficient and necessary conditions in dual-process models. In S. Chaiken & Y. Trope (Eds.), *Dual-process theories in social psychology* (pp. 423–440). New York: Guilford Press.

Bornstein, R. F. (1989). Exposure and affect: Overview and meta-analysis of research, 1968–1987. *Psychological Bulletin, 106,* 265–289.

Brown, K. M., Morris-Villagran, M., & Villagran, P. D. (2001). The effects of anger, sadness, and happiness on persuasive message processing: A test of the negative state relief model. Communication Monographs, 68, 347–359.

Chaiken, S., Giner-Sorolla, R., & Chen, S. (1996). Beyond accuracy: Defense and impression motives in heuristic and systematic information processing. In P. M. Gollwitzer & J. A. Bargh (Eds.), *The psychology of action: Linking cognitions and motivation to behavior* (pp. 553–578). New York: Guilford Press.

Chaiken, S., & Trope, Y. (Eds.). (1999). *Dual process theories in social psychology.* New York: Guilford Press.

Cody, M. J., Canary, D., & Smith, S. (1987). Compliance-gaining strategy selection: Episodes and goals. In J. Daly & J. Wiemann (Eds.), *Communicating strategically.* Hillsdale, NJ: Erlbaum.

Dahl, D. W., Frankenberger, K. D., & Manchanda, R. V. (2003). Does it pay to shock? Reactions to shocking and nonshocking advertising content among university students. *Journal of Advertising Research, 43,* 268–280.

DeSteno, D., Petty, R. E., Rucker, D. D., Wegener, D. T., & Braverman, J. (2004). Discrete emotions and persuasion: The role of emotion-induced expectancies. *Journal of Personality and Social Psychology, 86,* 43–56.

Dillard, J. P. (Ed.). (1990). *Seeking compliance: The production of interpersonal influence messages.* Scottsdale, AZ: Gorsuch Scarisbrick.

Fazio, R. H. (1989). On the power and functionality of attitudes: The role of attitude accessibility. In A. R. Pratkanis, S. J. Breckler, & A. G. Greenwald (Eds.), Attitude structure and function (pp. 153–179). Hillsdale, NJ: Erlbaum.

Fishbein, M., & Ajzen, I. (1975). Belief, attitude, intention, and behavior. Reading, MA: Addison-Wesley.

Fishbein, M., & Ajzen, I. (1981). Acceptance, yielding and impact: Cognitive processes in persuasion. In R. E. Petty, T. M. Ostrom, & T. C. Brock (Eds.), *Cognitive responses in persuasion* (pp. 339–359). Hillsdale, NJ: Erlbaum.

Frey, K. P., & Eagly, A. (1993). Vividness can undermine the persuasiveness of messages. *Journal of Personality & Social Psychology, 65*, 32–44.

FUD-Counter. (2001). How does FUD relate to Linux? Nov. 1. Accessed Dec. 17, 2002, at http://fud-counter.nl.linux.org/rationale.html.

Griffin, L. M. (1952). The rhetoric of historical movements. The Quarterly Journal of Speech, 38, 184–188.

Grush, J. E., McKeough, K. L., & Ahlering, R. F. (1978). Extrapolating laboratory exposure research to actual political elections. *Journal of Personality and Social Psychology, 36*, 257–270.

Hovland, C. I. (1957). *The order of presentation in persuasion.* New Haven, CT: Yale University Press.

Hovland, C. I., Janis, I. L., & Kelley, H. H. (1953). *Communication and persuasion.* New Haven, CT: Yale University Press.

Janis, I. L. (1967). Effects of fear arousal on attitude change: Recent developments in theory and experimental research. In L. Berkowitz (Ed.), *Advances in experimental social psychology* (Vol. 3, pp. 166-224). New York: Academic Press.

Janis, I. R., & Feshbach, S. (1953). Effects of fear arousing communications. *Journal of Abnormal Social Psychology, 48*, 78–92.

Kellermann, K. (2004). A goal-directed approach to gaining compliance. *Communication Research, 31*, 397–446.

Kellermann, K., & Cole, T. (1994). Classifying compliance-gaining messages: Taxonomic disorder and strategic confusion. *Communication Theory, 4*, 3–60.

Kipnis, D., Schmidt, S. M., & Wilkinson, I. (1980). Intraorganizational influence tactics: Explorations in getting one's way. *Journal of Applied Psychology, 65*, 440–452.

Kumkale, G. T., & Albarracin, D. (2004). The sleeper effect in persuasion: A meta-analytic review. *Psychological Bulletin, 130*, 143–171.

Lavine, H., Thomsen, C. J., Zanna, M. P., & Borgida, E. (1998). On the primacy of affect in the determination of attitudes and behavior: The moderating role of affective-cognitive ambivalence. *Journal of Experimental Social Psychology, 34*, 398–421.

Leventhal, H. (1970). Findings and theory in the study of fear communications. In L. Berkowitz (Ed.), *Advances in experimental social psychology* (Vol. 5, pp. 119–186). New York: Academic Press.

Lund, F. H. (1925). The psychology of belief, IV: The law of primacy in persuasion. *Journal of Abnormal Social Psychology, 20*, 183–191.

Mackie, D. L., & Worth, L. T. (1989). Cognitive deficits and the mediation of positive affect in persuasion. *Journal of Personality and Social Psychology, 57*, 27–40.

Martin, P. Y., Laing, J., Martin, R., & Mitchell, M. (2005). Caffeine, cognition, and persuasion: Evidence for caffeine increasing the systematic process of persuasive messages. *Journal of Applied Social Psychology, 35*, 160–183.

Marwell, G., & Schmitt, D. R. (1967). Dimensions of compliance-gaining behavior: An empirical analysis. *Sociometry, 30*, 350–364.

Miller, G. R., Boster, F. J., Roloff, M. E., & Seibold, D. R. (1977). Compliance-gaining message strategies: A typology and some findings concerning effects of situational differences. *Communication Monographs, 44*, 37–51.

Mitchell, M. M. (2000). Able but not motivated? The relative effects of happy and sad mood on persuasive message processing. *Communication Monographs, 67*, 215–226.

Mongeau, P. A. (1998). Another look at fear arousing persuasive appeals. In M. Allen & R. W. Preiss (Eds.), *Persuasion: Advances through meta-analysis* (pp. 53–68). Cresskill, NJ: Hampton Press.

Nabi, R. L. (1998). The effect of disgust-eliciting visuals on attitudes toward animal experimentation. *Communication Quarterly, 46*, 472–484.

Nabi, R. L. (2002). Anger, fear, uncertainty, and attitudes: A test of the cognitive-functional model. *Communication Monographs, 69*, 204–216.

Petty, R. E., & Cacioppo, J. T. (1979). Effects of forewarning of persuasive intent and involvement on cognitive responses and persuasion. *Journal of Personality and Social Psychology, 37*, 1915–1926.

Petty, R. E., & Cacioppo, J. T. (1986). *Communication and persuasion: Central and peripheral routes to attitude change.* New York: Springer-Verlag.

Petty, R. E., Wegener, D. T., & Fabrigar, L. R. (1997). Attitudes and attitude change. *Annual Review of Psychology, 48*, 609–647.

Petty, R. E., & Wegener, D .T. (1999). The elaboration likelihood model: Current status and controversies. In S. Chaiken & Y. Trope (Eds.), *Dual-process theories in social psychology* (pp. 41–72). New York: Guilford Press.

Pfau, M., Szabo, E. A., Anderson, J., Norrill, J., Zubric, J. C., & Wan, H. (2001). The role and impact of affect in the process of resistance to persuasion. *Human Communication Research, 27,* 216–252.

Pornpitakpan, C. (2004). The persuasiveness of source credibility: A critical review of five decades' evidence. *Journal of Applied Social Psychology, 34,* 243–281.

Rogers, R. W. (1975). A protection motivation theory of fear appeals and attitude change. *Journal of Psychology, 91,* 93–114.

Roskos-Ewoldsen, D. R. (2004). Fear appeal messages affect accessibility of attitudes toward the threat and adaptive behaviors. *Communication Monographs, 71,* 49–69.

Rule, B. G., Bisanz, G. L., & Kohn, M. (1985). Anatomy of a persuasion schema: Targets, goals, and strategies. *Journal of Personality and Social Psychology, 48,* 1127–1140.

Sherif, M., & Hovland, C. I. (1961). *Social judgment: Assimilation and contrast effects in communication and attitude change.* New Haven, CT: Yale University Press.

Smith, S. M., & Petty, R. E. (1996). Message framing and persuasion: A message processing analysis. *Personality and Social Psychology Bulletin, 22,* 257–268.

Stone, J., Wiegand, A.W., Cooper, J., & Aronson, E. (1997). When exemplification fails: Hypocrisy and the motive for self-integrity. *Journal of Personality and Social Psychology, 72,* 54–65.

Wegener, D. T., Petty, R. E., & Smith, S. M. (1995). Positive mood can increase or decrease message scrutiny: The hedonic contingency view of mood and message processing. *Journal of Personality and Social Psychology, 69,* 5–15.

Wilson, S. R. (2002). *Seeking and resisting compliance: Why people say what they do when trying to influence others.* Thousand Oaks, CA: Sage.

Wiseman, R. L., & Schenk-Hamlin, W. (1981). A multidimensional scaling validation of an inductively-derived set of compliance-gaining strategies. *Communication Monographs, 48,* 251–270.

Witte, K. (1992). Putting the fear back into fear appeals: The extended parallel process model. *Communication Monographs, 59,* 329–349.

Witte, K., & Allen, M. (2000). A meta-analysis of fear appeals: Implications for effective public health campaigns. *Health Education & Behavior, 27,* 591–615.

Zajonc, R. B. (1968). Attitudinal effects of mere exposure. *Journal of Personality and Social Psychology, 9,* 1–27.

Chapter 5

American Heritage Dictionary (1985). Boston: Houghton Mifflin.

The American Heritage Dictionary Second College Edition, (2005). Boston: Houghton Mifflin.

Berger, A. A. (1989). *Signs in contemporary society: An introduction to semiotics.* Salem, WI: Sheffield.

Burke, K. (1970) *A grammar of motives.* Berkeley: University of California Press.

Burke, K. (1970). *A rhetoric of motives.* Berkeley: University of California Press.

Burke, K. (1966). *Language as symbolic action: Essays on life, literature, and method.* Berkeley: University of California Press.

Burke, K. (1986). *Language as symbolic action.* Berkeley: University of California Press.

Deeds Done in Words: Presidential Rhetoric and the Genres of Governance, University of Chicago Press. Chicago, Illinois, 1990.

Feig, B. (1997). *Marketing straight to the heart: From product to positioning to advertising.* Chicago: American Management Association.

Hahn, D. (1998). *Political communication: Rhetoric, government and citizens.* State College, PA: Strata.

Korzybski, A. (1947). *Science and sanity.* Lakeville, CT: Non-Aristotelian Library.

Langer, S. K. (1951). *Philosophy in a new key.* New York: New American Library.

Langer, S. K. *Philosophy in a New Key* (1957) New York, New American Library.

Lederer, R. (1991). *The miracle of language.* New York: Pocket Books.

National Public Radio. (1999). *Morning Edition,* Feb. 3.

O'Harrow, R. (2005). No Place to Hide. New York: Simon & Schuster.

Osborne, M. (1967). Archetypal metaphors in rhetoric: the light dark family. *Quarterly Journal of Speech.* April, 1967. Pp. 216–226.

Postman, N. (1992). *Technopoly: The surrender of culture to technology.* New York: Vintage Books.

Solove, D. (2005). *The Digital Person: Technology and Privacy in the Information Age.* New York: NYU Press.

Sopory, P., & Dillard, J. (2002). Figurative language and persuasion. In Dillard and Pfau (Eds.), *The persuasion handbook: Developments in theory and practice.* Thousand Oaks, CA: Sage.

Suplee, K. (1987). Semiotics: In search of more perfect persuasion. *Washington Post,* Jan. 18, Outposts sec., pp. 1–3.

Chapter 6

American Heritage Dictionary. (1985). Boston: Houghton Mifflin.

Andrews, L. A. (1984). Exhibit A: Language. *Psychology Today,* Feb., p. 30.

Barol, B. (1988). The 80s are over. *Newsweek,* Jan. 4, pp. 40–48.

Benoit, W. L. (2006). Image repair in President Bush's Aoril, 2004 news conference. *Public relations review.* June, 2006. Pp. 137–143.

Berger, A. (1984). *Signs in contemporary culture.* New York: Longman.

Black Elk. (1971). *Touch the earth.* New York: Outerbridge & Dienstfrey.

Broder, D. (1984). The great American values test. *Psychology Today,* Nov., p. 41.

Buissac, P. (1976). *Circus and culture: A semiotic approach.* Bloomington: Indiana University Press.

Burke, K. (1960). *A grammar of motives.* Berkeley: University of California Press.

Chicago Daily News. November 24, 1972. "Fed up? It may lead to an ulcer."

Cialdini, R. (2001). *Influence: Science and practice.* Boston: Allyn & Bacon.

Democracy Project (1999). www.ipa.udel.edu/democracy.

Dillard, J. P., & Pfau, M. (2002). *The persuasion handbook: Developments in theory and practice.* Thousand Oaks, CA: Sage.

Domzal, T., & Kernan, J. (1993). Mirror, mirror: Some postmodern reflections on global marketing. *Journal of Advertising,* Dec., p. 20.

Eco, U. (1979). *The role of the reader.* Bloomington: Indiana University Press.

Eco, U. (1984). *Semiotics and the philosophy of language.* London: Macmillan.

Eisenberg, E. M. (1984). Ambiguity as a strategy in organizational communication.f *Communication monographs, 51,* 227–242.

Farrell, W. (1974). *The liberated male.* New York: Random House.

Hahn, D. (1998). *Political communication: Rhetoric, government and citizens.* State College, PA: Strata.

Hosman, L. H. (2002). Language and persuasion. In J. P. Dillard & M. Pfau (Eds.), *The persuasion handbook: Developments in theory and practice.* Thousand Oaks, CA: Sage.

Kallend, J. S. (2002). Skydiving responsibility lies solely with jumper. *Chicago Tribune,* Aug. 11, sec. 2, p 8.

Kittredge, W. (1996). The war for Montana's soul. *Newsweek,* April 15, p. 43.

Koenig, P. (1972). Death doth defer. *Psychology Today,* Nov., p. 83.

Larson, C. U. (1982). Media metaphors: Two models for rhetorically criticizing the political spot advertisement. *Central States Speech Journal.* (Winter, 1982). Pp. 533–546.

Lederer, R. (1991). *The miracle of language.* New York: Pocket Books.

Lewis, C. (1999). The athletes are the games. *Newsweek,* Feb. 15, p. 56.

Lewis, H., & Lewis, M. (1972). *Psychosomatics: How your emotions can damage your health.* New York: Viking Press.

Marshall, D. (1999). An Olympic-size problem. *Newsweek,* Feb. 15, p. 20.

Messner, M. R. (1998). *Politics and masculinity: Men in movements.* Thousand Oaks, CA: Sage.

Nimmo, D., & Combs, J. (1984). *Mediated political realities.* New York: Longman.

Osborn, M. (1967). Archetypal metaphors in rhetoric: The light-dark family. *Quarterly Journal of Speech,* April, 1967. Pp. 115–126.

Seigel, B. (1989). *The healing power of communicating with your body.* New York: Weider.

Swanson, S. L. (1981). Sensory language in the courtroom. *Trial Diplomacy Journal,* Winter, pp. 37–43.

Tannen, D. (1990). *You just don't understand: Men and women in conversation.* New York: Morrow.

Weaver, R. (1953). *The ethics of rhetoric.* Chicago: Regnery.

Yates, S. J. (2001). Gender, language and CMC for education. *Learning and instruction, 11,* 23–34.

Zhang, J. (2007). Beyond anti-terrorism: Metaphors as message strategy of post-September 11-U.S. Public diplomacy. *Public relations review,* March, 2007. Pp. 31–39.

Chapter 7

Austin, N. (2002). The power of the pyramid: The foundation of human psychology, and thereby motivation; Maslow's hierarchy is one powerful pyramid. *Incentive,* July, p. 10.

Bellah, R. N., Madsen, R., Sullivan, W. M., Swoder, A., & Tipton, S. M. (1985). *Habits of the heart: Individualism and commitment in American life.* New York: Harper & Row.

Booth, E. (1999). Getting inside a shopper's mind: Direct marketers are working out how and why consumers arrive at decisions, in order to satisfy their needs. *Marketing,* June 3, p. 32.

Booth-Butterfield, S., & Welbourne, J. (2002). The elaboration likelihood model: Its impact on persuasion theory and research. In J. P. Dillard & M. Pfau (Eds.), *The persuasion handbook: Developments in theory and practice* (pp. 155–173). Thousand Oaks, CA: Sage.

Borchers, T. A. (2005). *Persuasion in the media age.* (2nd ed.). Boston: McGraw-Hill.

Burke, K. (1961). *The rhetoric of religion: Studies in logology.* Boston: Beacon Press.

Carnegie, D. (1952). *How to win friends and influence people.* New York: Simon & Schuster.

Colley, R. H. (1961). *Defining advertising goals for measured attitude results.* New York: Association of National Advertisers.

De Bono, K. G., & Harnish, R. (1988). Source expertise, source attractiveness, and the processing of persuasive information. *Journal of Personality and Social Psychology, 55,* 541–546.

Egley, A. H., & Chaiken, S. (1993). *The psychology of attitudes.* New York: Harcourt Brace Jovanovich.

Eiser, R. J. (1987). *The expression of attitude.* New York: Springer-Verlag.

Feig, B. (1997). *Marketing straight to the heart: From product to positioning to advertising-how smart companies use the power of emotion to win loyal customers.* New York: American Marketing Association.

Festinger, L. (1962). *A theory of cognitive dissonance.* Stanford, CA: Stanford University Press.

Fishbein, M., & Ajzen, I. (1975). *Belief, attitude, intention, and behavior: An introduction to theory and research.* Reading, MA: Addison-Wesley.

Fonda, J. (2005). *My life so far.* New York: Random House.

Frankl, V. (1962). *Man's search for meaning: An introduction to logotherapy.* New York: Washington Square.

Freedman, D. H. (1988). Why you watch some commercials—whether you want to or not. *TV Guide,* Feb. 20.

Friedman, J. L., & Dagnoli, J. (1988). Brand name spreading: Line extensions are marketers' lifeline. *Advertising Age,* Feb. 22.

Hoveland, C.I. and others (1953). *Communication and persuasion: Psychological studies of opinion change.* New Haven: Yale University Press.

Lafavore, R. (1995). From here to eternity: Men's desire for immortality. *Men's Health,* Nov., p. 74.

Lane, W. R., King, K. W., & Russell, J. T. (2005), *Kleppner's advertising procedure* (16th ed.). Upper Saddle River, NJ: Pearson Education.

Larson, C. U., & Sanders, R. (1975). Faith, mystery, and data: An analysis of "scientific" studies of persuasion. *Quarterly Journal of Speech,* 61, 178–194.

Lears, T. J. J. (1983). From salvation to self realization: Advertising and the therapeutic roots of the consumer culture. In *The culture of consumption: Critical essays in American culture, 1880–1980.* New York: Pantheon Books.

Levitt, S., & Dubner, S. (2005). *Freakonomics: A rogue economist explores the hidden side of everything.* New York: Harper Collins.

Maslow, A. (1954). *Motivation and personality.* New York: Harper & Row.

Nabi, R.L. (2002). Discrete emotions and persuasion. In J. P. Dillard & M. Pfau (Eds.), *The persuasion handbook: Developments in theory and practice.* (pp. 289–309). Thousand Oaks, CA: Sage.

National Public Radio. (2002). *All things considered,* Aug. 30.

Naughton, R. (2002). More headwind for Martha: As investigators run out of patience, the diva of domesticity may be ordered to testify in Washington. *Newsweek,* Sept. 2, p. 45.

Nelson, R. (2001). On the shape of verbal networks in organizations. *Organization Studies*, Sept.–Oct., 797.

Osgood, C. E., & Tannenbaum, P. H. (1955). The principle of congruity in the prediction of attitude change. *Psychological Review, 62*, 43.

Packard, V. (1964). *The hidden persuaders*. New York: Pocket Books.

Petty, R., & Cacioppo, J. (1986). *Communication and persuasion*. New York: Springer-Verlag.

Petty, R. E., & Wegener, D. T. (1998). Attitude change: Multiple roles for persuasion variables. In D. T. Gilbert, S. T. Fiske, & G. Lindsay (Eds.), *Handbook of social psychology*. Boston: McGraw-Hill.

Pinsky, M. S. (2002). Houston minister views Gospel according to the Sopranos. *Orlando Sentinel*, Sept. 4, 2000.

Porter, R., & Samovar, L. (1998). *Intercultural communication: A reader*. Belmont, CA: Wadsworth Publishing Co.

Putnam, R. (1995). Bowling alone: America's declining social capital. *Journal of Democracy, 6*, 65–68.

Putnam, R. D. (2000). *Bowling alone: The collapse and revival of American community*. New York: Simon & Schuster.

Rokeach, M. (1968). *Beliefs, attitudes, and values: A theory of organization and change*. San Francisco: Jossey-Bass.

Rowan, J. (1998). Maslow amended. *The Journal of Humanistic Psychology*, Winter, 84.

Rowell, R. (2002). Martha's taste, not her ethics lures fans. Knight Rider/*Business News*, Oct. 2.

Schiffman, L., & Kanuk, L. (1997). *Consumer behavior*. Upper Saddle River, NJ: Prentice Hall.

Schrader, D. C. (1999). Goal complexity and the perceived competence of interpersonal influence messages. *Communication Studies*, Fall, 188.

Shavitt, S. (1990). The role of attitude objects in attitude functions. *Journal of Experimental Psychology, 26*, 124–148.

Sibley, K. (1997). The e-mail dilemma: To spy or not to spy. *Computing Canada*, March 31, p. 14.

Staal, S. (2001). Warning: living together may ruin your relationship. *Cosmopolitan*, Sept., p. 286.

Williams, M.A. (2001). *The ten lenses: Your guide to living and working in a multicultural world*. Herndon, VA: Capitol Books.

Wood, W. (2000). Attitude change: Persuasion and social influence. *Annual Review of Psychology*, 539.

Zemke, R. (1998). Maslow for a new millennium. *Training*, Dec., 54.

Zimbardo, P. G., Ebbesen, E. E., & Maslach, C. (1976). *Influencing attitudes and changing behavior*. Reading, MA: Addison-Wesley.

Zimbardo, P. G., & Leippe, M. R. (1991). *The psychology of attitude change and social influence*. New York: McGraw-Hill.

Chapter 8

American Heritage Dictionary (1985). Boston: Houghton Mifflin.

Burke, K. (1985). Dramatism and logology. *Communication Quarterly, 33*, 89–93.

Butler, L. D., Koopman, C., & Zimbardo, P. (1995). The psychological impact of watching the film JFK: Emotions, beliefs and political intensions. *Political Psychology, 16*, 237–257.

Clark, H. H. (1969). Linguistic processes in deductive reasoning. *Psychological Review, 76*, 387–404.

Consider the facts. (2002). *Pine County Courier*, July 25, p. 10.

Dahl, S. (2000) *Communications and cultural transformation: Cultural diversity, globalization, and cultural convergence*. London: E.C.E.

Deardorf, J., & Finan, E. (1999). Barton wins $29.6 million. *Chicago Tribune*, March 2, p. 1.

Fishbein, M., & Ajzen, I. (1975). *Beliefs, attitude, intention and behavior: An introduction to theory and research*. Reading, MA: Addison-Wesley.

Fishbein, M., & Ajzen, I. (1980). Predicting and understanding consumer behavior: Attitude behavior correspondence. In I. Ajzen & M. Fishbein (Eds.), *Understanding attitudes and predicting social behavior*. Englewood Cliffs, NJ: Prentice-Hall.

Fisher, W. R. (1987). *Human communication as narration: Toward a philosophy of reason, value, and action*. Columbia: University of South Carolina Press.

Garfield, B. (1988). Ad review: Good commercials finally outnumber the bad ones on TV. *Advertising Age*, March 14, p. 86.

Guttmacher, A. (1993). Social science and the citizen. *Society*, July–Aug., p. 2.

Huglen, M, & Clark, N. (2004). *Argument strategies from Aristotle*. Belmont: Thomson Learning.

Jensen, J. V. (1981). *Argumentation: Reasoning in communication.* New York: Van Nostrand.

Kahane, H. (1992). *Logic and contemporary rhetoric: The use of reason in everyday life.* Belmont, CA: Wadsworth.

Loftus, E. F. (1980). *Eyewitness testimony.* Cambridge, MA: Harvard University Press.

Loftus, E. F. (1984). Eyewitness testimony. *Psychology Today,* Feb., p. 25.

Lunsford, A., & Ruszkiewicz, J. (2004). *Everything's an argument.* Boston: Bedford/St. Martins Press.

Moore, C. (1909). *A short life of Abraham Lincoln.* Chicago: Houghton Mifflin.

The payoffs for preschooling. 1984, *Chicago Tribune,* Dec. 25, p. 25.

Peck, M. S. (1983). *People of the lie: The hope for healing human evil.* New York: Simon & Schuster.

Reinard, J. C. (1988). The empirical study of evidence: The status after fifty years of research. *Human Communication Research,* Fall, pp. 25–36.

Reynolds, R., & Burgoon, M. (1983). Belief processing, reasoning and evidence. *Communication Yearbook,* 7, 83–104.

Reynolds, R., & Reynolds, J. L. (2002). Evidence. In J. P. Dillard & M. Pfau (Eds.), *The persuasion handbook: Developments in theory and practice* (pp. 427-444). Thousand Oaks, CA: Sage.

Santos, M. (1961). *These were the Sioux.* New York: Dell books, p. 148.

Scott, B. (1989). *Rockford Register Star,* Nov. 8, editorial page.

Sutton, S. (1998). *The Persuasion Handbook: Developments in Theory and Practice.* Eds. James Dillard and Michael Pfau, Sage Publications, Thousand Oaks, Calif. P. 264.

Thompson, W. N. (1971). *Modern argumentation and debate: Principles and practices.* New York: Harper & Row.

Toulmin, S. (1964). *The uses of argument.* Cambridge: Cambridge University Press.

Zorn, E. (2002). Season to kill enriches some, repulses many. *Chicago Tribune,* Nov. 11, sec. 2.

Chapter 9

American Heritage Dictionary (1985). Boston: Houghton Mifflin.

America's abortion dilemma. (1985). *Newsweek,* Jan. 14, pp. 20–23.

Baudhin, S., & Davis, M. (1972). Scales for the measurement of ethos: Another attempt. *Speech Monographs,* 39, 296–301.

Beane, W. C., & Doty, W. G. (1975). *Myths, rites, and symbols: A Mercia Eliade reader.* New York: Harper Colophon.

Bellah, R. N., Madsen, R., Sullivan, W. M., Swidler, A., & Tipton, S. M. (1985). *Habits of the heart: Individualism and commitment in American life.* New York: Harper & Row.

Berlo, D., Lemmert, J., & Davis, M. (1969). Dimensions for evaluating the acceptability of message sources. *Public Opinion Quarterly,* 33, 563–576.

Cialdini, R. (2001). *Influence: Science and practice* (4th ed.). Needham Heights, MA: Allyn & Bacon.

Edelman, M. (1967). Myths, metaphors and political conformity. *Psychiatry,* 30, 217–228.

Eliade, M. (1971). *The myth of the eternal return: Of cosmos and history.* Princeton, NJ: Princeton University Press.

Hahn, D. (1998). *Political communication: Rhetoric, government, and citizens.* State College, PA: Strata.

Hofstadter, R. (1963). *Anti-intellectualism in America.* New York: Knopf.

Hofstadter, R. (1967). *The paranoid style in American politics and other essays.* New York: Vintage Books.

Hovland, C., Janis, I., & Kelley, H. (1953). *Communication and persuasion.* New Haven, CT: Yale University Press.

Kelman, H., & Hovland, C. (1953). Reinstatement of the communicator: Delayed measurement of opinion changes. *Journal of Abnormal and Social Psychology,* 48, 327–335.

Kosicki, G. M. (2002). The media priming effect: News media and considerations affecting political judgments. In J. P. Dillard & M. Pfau (Eds.), *The persuasion handbook: Developments in theory and practice* (pp. 63–82). Thousand Oaks, CA: Sage.

Parenti, M. (1994). *Land of idols: Political mythology in America.* New York: St. Martin's Press.

Reich, R. (1987). *Tales of a new America.* New York: Times Books.

Santos, M. (1961). *These were the Sioux.* New York: Dell.

Steele, E. D., & Redding, W. C. (1962). The American value system: Premises for persuasion. *Western Speech,* 26, 83–91.

Tocqueville, A. de (1965). *Democracy in America.* New York: Mentor.

Chapter 10

Andersen, P. A. (1985). Nonverbal immediacy in interpersonal communication. In A. W. Seligman & S. Feldstein (Eds.), *Multichannel integrations of nonverbal behavior* (pp. 1–6). Hillsdale NJ: Erlbaum.

Andersen, P. A. (1999). *Nonverbal communication: Forms and functions.* Mountain View, CA: Mayfield.

Barnes, G. et al. (2007). Adolescents time use: Effects on substance use, delinquency, and sexual activity. *Journal of Youth and Adolescence.* Vol. 36. July, 2007.

Burgoon, J., Bufler, D., & Woodall, W. (1996). *Nonverbal communication: The unspoken dialog* (2nd ed.). New York: McGraw Hill.

Burgoon, J. K., Dunbar, N. E., & Segrin, C. (2002). Nonverbal influences. In J. P. Dillard & M. Pfau (Eds.) *The persuasion handbook: Developments in theory and practice* (pp. 445–473). Thousand Oaks, CA: Sage.

Ekman, P. (1999). A few can catch a liar. *Psychological Science,* 10, 3.

Ekman, P. (2004). *Emotions revealed.* New York: Times Books.

Ekman, P., & Friesen, W. V. (1975). *Unmasking the face: A guide to recognizing emotions from facial expression.* Englewood Cliffs, NJ: Prentice-Hall.

Ellyson, S., Dovidio, J., & Fehr, B. J. (1984). Visual behavior and dominance in men and women. In C. Mayo & N. Henley (Eds.), *Gender and nonverbal behavior.* New York: Springer-Verlag.

Fornoff, S. (2005). Money talks, so builders listen to the experts. *The San Francisco Chronicle.* June 4, 2005.

Fromme, D., Jaynes, W., Taylor, D., Hanhold, E., Daniell, J., Rountree, R., & Fromme, M. (1989). Nonverbal behavior and attitude toward touch. *Journal of Nonverbal Behavior,* 13, 3–13.

Giles, H., Coupland, N., & Coupland, J. (1991). Accommodation theory: Communication, context, and consequence. In H. Giles, J. Coupland, & N. Coupland (Eds.), *Contexts of accommodation: Developments in applied sociolinguistics* (pp. 1–68). Cambridge: Cambridge University Press.

Goffman, E. (1959). *The presentation of self in everyday life.* New York: Doubleday.

Guerrero, L., DeVito, J., & Hecht, M. (1999). *The nonverbal communication reader: Classic and contemporary readings.* Mt. Prospect, IL: Waveland Press.

Hall, E. T. (1959). *The silent language.* Garden City, NY: Doubleday.

Hall, J. A. (1984). *Nonverbal sexual differences: Communication accuracy and expressive style.* Baltimore, MD: Johns Hopkins University Press.

Jacobson, D. (1999). Impression formation in cyberspace: Online expectations and offline experiences in text-based virtual communities. *Journal of Computer-mediated Communication.* September, 1999.

Knapp, M. and Hall, J. (2002). *Nonverbal communication in human behavior.* 5th edition. Belmont CA: Wadsworth/Thomson Publishing Company.

Knapp, M. L., & Comendena, M. E. (1985). Telling it like it isn't: A review of theory and research on deceptive communication. *Human Communication Research,* 5, 270–285.

Knapp, M. L., & Hall, J. (2002). *Nonverbal communication in human interaction* (5th ed.). Belmont, CA: Wadsworth.

Kotulak, R. (1985). Researchers decipher a powerful "language." *Chicago Tribune,* April 7, sec. 6. Leathers, D. (1986). *Successful nonverbal communication: Principles and applications.* New York: Macmillan.

Major, B. (1984). Gender patterns in touching behavior. In C. Mayo & N. Henley (Eds.), *Gender and nonverbal behavior.* New York: Springer-Verlag.

Mehrabian, A. (1971). *Silent messages.* Belmont, CA: Wadsworth.

Murray, J. (1989). *The power of dress.* Minneapolis, MN: Semiotics.

Orban, D. K. (1999). The integrative nature of argument and non-verbal communication in different communication contexts. Unpublished paper delivered to Midwest Basic Course Directors Conference, Feb., 4–6.

Packard, V. (1964). *The hidden persuaders.* New York: Pocket Books.

Porter, N., & Geis, F. (1984). Women and nonverbal leadership cues: When seeing is not believing. In C. Mayo & N. Henley (Eds.), *Gender and nonverbal behavior.* New York: SpringerVerlag.

Scheflen, A. (1973). *Communicational structure: Analysis of a psychotherapy session.* Bloomington: Indiana University Press.

Siennicki, J. (2000). Gender Differences in Nonverbal Communication. www.colostate.edu/Depts/Speech/recs/theory20.

Smith. T. (1997). Adolescent gender differences in time alone and time devoted to conversation. *Adolescence.* Vol. 32. 1997.

Umiker-Sebeok, J. (1984). The seven ages of women: A view from American magazine advertisements. In C. Mayo & N. Henley (Eds.), *Gender and nonverbal behavior.* New York: Springer-Verlag.

Chapter 11

Ahuja, B. (2005). *Buzz marketing: Honest deception.* www.commercialfreechildhood.org/articles/4thsummit/ahuja.

Bales, R. F. (1970). *Personality and interpersonal behavior.* New York: Holt, Rinehart & Winston.

Binder, L. (1971). *Crisis and sequence in political development.* Princeton, NJ: Princeton University Press.

Borchers, T. A. (2005). *Persuasion in the media age* (2nd ed.). Boston: McGraw-Hill.

Bormann, E. G. (1985). *The force of fantasy.* Carbondale and Edwardsville: Southern Illinois University Press.

Bowers, J. W., Ochs, D. J., & Jensen, R. J. (1993). *The rhetoric of agitation and control.* Prospect Heights, IL: Waveland Press.

Cragan, J. F., & Shields, D. C. (1994). *Applied communication research: A dramatistic approach.* Annandale, VA: Speech Communication Association and Creskill, NJ: Hampton Press.

Cragan, J. F., & Shields, D. C. (1995). *Symbolic theories in applied communication research: Bormann, Burke, and Fisher.* Cresskill, NJ: Hampton Press.

Denton, R., & Woodward, D. (1998). *Political communication in America* (3rd ed.). Westport, CT: Praeger.

Faucheux, R. (1998). Strategies that win! *Campaigns and Elections,* Jan., pp. 24–32.

Fortini-Campbell, K. (1992). *The consumer insight book.* Chicago: Copy Workshop.

Garcia, G. (2005). *American mainstream: How the multicultural consumer is transforming American business.* New York: Harper Collins/Rayo.

Hughlett, M., & Benderoff, E. (2008) "Ball Girl' scores buzz for Gatorade." *The Chicago Tribune,* June 26, 2008. Section 3 p. 2.

Larson, M. (2009). *Watch it: What parents need to know to raise media smart kids.* Highland City, FL: Rainbow Books Inc.

Lavidge, R. J., & Steiner, G. A. (1961). A model for predictive measurements of advertising effectiveness. *Journal of Marketing, 24,* 59–62.

Metter, B. (1990). Advertising in the age of spin. *Advertising Age,* Sept. 17, p. 36.

Morrissey, B. (2005). Mitsubishi issues web "Thrill ride challenge." *Adweek,* June 8, 2005.

National Public Radio. (1999). *All things considered,* April 2.

Rogers, E. (1962). *The diffusion of innovation.* New York: Free Press.

Schultz, D. E., & Barnes, B. (1999). *Strategic advertising campaigns* (4th ed.). Lincolnwood, IL: N.T.C. Business Books.

Schwartz, T. (1973). *The responsive chord.* New York: Anchor/Doubleday.

Stewart, C. J., Smith, C. A., & Denton, R. E., Jr. (2001). *Persuasion and social movements* (4th ed.). Prospect Heights, IL: Waveland Press.

Trent, J. S., & Friedenberg, R. V. (2000). *Political campaign communication* (4th ed.). New York and London: Praeger.

Trout, J. (1995). *The new positioning: The latest on the world's # 1 business strategy.* New York: McGraw Hill.

Trout, J. & Ries, A. (1986). *Positioning: The battle for your mind.* New York: Harper & Row.

Valdivia, A. N. (1997). The secret of my desire: Gender, class, and sexuality in lingerie catalogs. In K. T. Frith (Ed.), *Undressing the ad: Reading culture in advertising.* New York: Peter Lang.

Warren, K., & Guscott, J. (2000). Wild ideas Lecture Series *The battle for your mind: Proaganda, PR, and Psyops.* http://www.lkwdpl.org/wildideas/propaganda.html.

Chapter 12

Cantola, S. J., Syme, G. I., & Campbell, N. A. (1985). Creating conflict to conserve energy. *Psychology Today,* Feb., p. 14.

Carnegie, D. (1952). *How to win friends and influence people.* New York: Simon & Schuster.

Cialdini, R. (2001). *Influence: Science and practice.* Boston: Allyn & Bacon.

German, K. Gronbeck, B, Ehninger, D., & Monroe, A. (2004). *Principles of public speaking.* New York: Allyn & Bacon.

Howell, W. S., & Bormann, E. G. (1988). *The process of presentational speaking*. New York: Harper & Row.

Molloy, J. T. (1977). *The dress for success book*. Chicago: Reardon & Walsh.

Monroe, A., Ehninger, D., & Gronbeck, B. (1982). *Principles and types of speech communication*. Chicago: Scott, Foresman.

Rank, H. (1982). *The pitch*. Park Forest, IL: Counter Propaganda Press.

Russell, J. T., & Lane, W. R. (2005). *Kleppner's advertising procedure* (16th ed.). Upper Saddle River, NJ: Prentice-Hall.

Scheflen, A. E. (1964). The significance of posture in communication systems. *Psychiatry, 27*, 316–331.

Schwartz, T. (1973). *The responsive chord*. Garden City, NY: Anchor.

Selby, P. (1902). *Lincoln's life story and speeches*. Chicago: Thompson & Thomas.

Simons, H. (2001). *Persuasion in society*. Thousand Oaks, CA: Sage.

Woods, M. (1993). Toothbrush tips for wellness. *Chicago Tribune*, Sept. 12, sec. 5, p. 3.

Chapter 13

Bandura, A. (1994). Social cognitive theory of mass communication" In J. Bryant and D. Zillman, eds. *Media effects: Advances in Theory and Research*. Hillsdale N.J. Erlbaum.

Baker, R. K., & Ball, S. K. (1969). *Violence and the media: A staff report to the national commission on the causes and prevention of violence*. Volume 9a. Washington, U.S. Government.

Blumler, J. (1979). The role of theory in uses and gratifications studies. *Communication Studies*, 6, pp. 9–34.

Boorstin, D. (1961). *The image: A guide to pseudo-events in America*. New York: Harper & Row.

Brand, S. (1987). *The media lab: Inventing the future at M.I.T.* New York: Viking Penguin Books.

Chicago Tribune. (2005). Time to explode the Internet? July 4, 2005, editorial page.

Cirino, R. (1971). *Don't blame the people*. Los Angeles: Diversity.

Gerbner, G., Gross, L., Morgan, M., & Signorelli, N. (1986). Living with television: The dynamics of the cultivation

process. In J. Bryant & D. Zillman, (Eds.), *Perspectives on media effects*. Hilsdale, N.J. Erlbaum.

Gumpert, G., & Drucker, S. J. (2002). From locomotion to telecommunication, or paths of safety, streets of gore. In L. Strate, R. Jacobson, & S. J. Gibson (Eds.), *Communication in cyberspace: Social interaction in an electronic environment* (2nd ed.). Cresskill, NJ: Hampton Press.

Hall Jamieson, K., & Kohrs-Campbell, K. (1996). *The interplay of influence* (4th ed.). Belmont, CA: Wadsworth.

Kaiser Family Foundation. (1999). *Kids and media at the new millennium*. Menlo Park, CA: Author.

Kaplan, D., Wingert, P., & Chideya, F. (1993). Dumber than we thought. *Newsweek*, Sept. 20, pp. 44–45.

Larson, C. U. (2002). Dramatism and virtual reality: Implications and predictions. In S. Gibson, R. Jacobson, & K, Strate (Eds.), *Communication and Cyberspace*. N.Y. Fordham University Press.

Larson, M. S. (2009). *Watch it: What parents need to know to raise media literate kids*. Highland City, FL: Rainbow Press.

Jacobson, & S. J. Gibson (Eds.), *Communication and cyberspace: Social interaction in an electronic environment* (2nd ed.). Cresskill, NJ: Hampton Press.

Kappelman, T. (2008). Marshall McLuhan: "The medium is the message" http://www.leaderu.com/orgs/probe/docs/mcluhan.html

Larson, M. (1997). Rush Limbaugh: Broadcast demagogue. *Journal of Radio Studies, IV*, 1997.

Lederer, R. (1991). *The miracle of language*. New York: Pocket Books.

Levin, D. (1998). *Remote control childhood?* Washington, DC: National Association for the Education of Young Children.

Library of Congress (2007). Library of Congress acquires media pioneer's collection. *News from the Library of Congress*, (News Release, August 2, 2007) Washington, D.C.

Madigan, C. M. (1993). Going with the flow. *Chicago Tribune Magazine*, May 2, pp. 14–26.

Matusow, B. (1983). *The evening stars: The making of a network news anchor*. New York: Ballantine Books.

McCombs, M., & Shaw, D. (1972). The agenda setting function of the media. *Public Opinion Quarterly, 36*, 176–187.

McLuhan, M. (1963). *Understanding media: The extensions of man*. New York: Signet.

Meyrowitz, J. (1985). *No sense of place: The impact of electronic media on social behavior.* New York: Oxford University Press.

Ong, W. S. (1967). *The presence of the word.* New Haven, CT: Yale University Press.

Ong, W. S. (1977). *Interfaces of the word.* Ithaca, NY: Cornell University Press.

Ong, W. S. (1982). *Orality and literacy: The technologizing of the word.* London: Metheun.

Postman, N. (1996). Cyberspace, schmyberspace. In L. Strate, R. Jacobson, & S. J. Gibson (Eds.), *Communication and cyberspace: Social interaction in an electronic environment.* Cresskill, NJ: Hampton Press.

Powers, R. (1978). *The newscasters: The news business as show business.* New York: St. Martin's Press.

Press, L. (1995). McLuhan meets the net. *Communications of the ACM.* July, 1995.

Ramhoff, R. (1990). Bart's not as bad as he seems: Simpsons as positive as other family. *Rockford Register Star,* Oct. 18, sec. 2, p. 1.

Rubin, A. (2002). The uses and gratifications perspective of media effects. In J. Bryant & D. Zillman (Eds.), *Media effects: Advances in theory and research.* Mahwah, NJ: Erlbaum.

Schwartz, T. (1973). *The responsive chord.* Garden City, NY: Anchor/Doubleday.

Schwartz, T. (1983). *Media: The Second God.* New York: Anchor Books.

Signorelli, N., & Morgan, M. (1990). *Cultivation analysis: New directions in media research.* Newbury Park, CA: Sage.

Theall, D. (2002). *The Virtual McLuhan.* Toronto: McGill–Queens University Press.

Victory, V. B. (1988). Pocket veto. *Advertising Age,* April 25, p. 20.

Walters, R. (2007). Effective internet advertising. http://www.catalogs.com/info/gadgets/effective-internet-advertising.html

Zettl, H. (1996). Back to Plato's cave: Virtual reality. In L. Strate, R. Jacobson, & S. J. Gibson (Eds.), *Communication and cyberspace: Social interaction in an electronic environment.* Cresskill, NJ: Hampton Press.

Chapter 14

Ajmone, T. (2004). *The Age of Subliminal Communication.* www.subliminal-message.info/age_of_subliminal_communication/html.

Alexander, A., & Hanson, J. (2003). *Taking sides: Clashing views on controversial issues in mass media and society.* Burr Ridge, IL: McGraw-Hill/Dushkin.

Amft, J. (2004). Psychographics: A Primer. www.psychographics.net.

Baker, R. (1997). The squeeze. *Columbia Journalism Review,* Sept.–Oct.

Becker, H., & Glanzer, N. (1978). *Subliminal communication: Advances in audiovisual engineering applications. Proceedings of the 1978 Institute of Electronical and Electronics Engineers: Region 3.* Atlanta: Institute of Electronical and Electronics Engineers.

Berger, A. (2000). *Ads, fads, and consumer culture: Advertising's impact on American character and society.* Lanham, MD: Rowan & Littlefield.

Borchers, T. (2002). *Persuasion in the media age.* Burr Ridge, IL: McGraw-Hill.

Borchers, T. (2005). *Persuasion in the media age.* New York: McGraw-Hill.

Chaffee, J. (1998). How advertising informs to our benefit. *Consumers' Research,* April.

Chicago Tribune (2005). Time to explode the Internet? July 12, p. 12.

Cuneo, A. (2002). Creative execs stress the importance of the Internet. Accessed Nov. 13, 2002, at www.adage.com using QuickFind Id: AAO20F.

Diamond, E., & Bates, S. (1984). *The spot: The rise of political advertising on television.* Cambridge, MA: M.I.T. Press.

Dollas, C. (1986). Butterball turkeys: An examination of advertising theory and practice. Unpublished starred paper, Department of Journalism, Northern Illinois University, De Kalb.

Engel, J., Blackwell, D., & Miniard, P. (1993). *Consumer behavior.* Chicago: Dryden.

Espejo, E., & Romano, C. (2005). Children and media policy brief. *Children Now,* Spring, pp. 1–8.

Feig, B. (1997). *Marketing straight to the heart: From product to positioning to advertising—how smart companies use the power of emotion to win loyal customers.* Chicago: American Management Association.

Gallonoy, T. (1970). *Down the tube: Or making television commercials is such a dog-eat-dog business, it's no wonder they're called spots.* Chicago: Regenery.

Global marketers spend $71 billion. (2002). *Advertising Age,* Nov. 11, pp. 1–18.

Goodkin, O., & Phillips, M. (1983). The subconscious taken captive. *Southern California Law Review,* 54, 1077–1140.

Happy 65th birthday to 5,500 Americans—daily. (1988). *Chicago Tribune,* April 20, sec. 8, p. 10.

Hogan, K. (2005) Covert subliminal persuasion: 7 facts that will change the way you influence forever. *The Science of Influence Library.* Eagan, MN: Network 3000 Publishing, Forthcoming.

Honomichl, J. (1984). *Marketing research people: Their behind-the-scenes-stories.* Chicago: Crain Books.

Key, W. B. (1973). *Subliminal seduction: Ad media's manipulation of a not so innocent America.* New York: Signet.

Key, W. B. (1977). *Media sexploitation.* Englewood Cliffs, NJ: Prentice-Hall.

Key, W. B. (1980). *The clam-plate orgy and other subliminals the media use to manipulate your behavior.* New York: Signet.

Lander, A. (1981). In through the out door. *OMNI,* Feb., p. 45.

Larson, C. (2007). *Persuasion: Reception and responsibility* (11th ed.). Belmont, CA: Wadsworth Publishing Company.

Mitchell, A. (1983). *Nine American lifestyles: Who we are and where we are going.* New York: Macmillan.

National Public Radio. (2006). *All things considered.* January 3.

Oates, J. (2006). MSN launches study on changes in advertising. *Brand Republic,* July 5, 2006. p. 1.

O' Guinn, T., Allen, C., & Semenik, R. (2009). *Advertising and integrated brand promotion.* Mason, OH: Thomson-Southwestern.

O'Toole, J. (1985). *The trouble with advertising.* New York: Times Books/Random House.

Parente, M. (2004). *Advertising Campaign Strategy* (4th ed.). Mason, OH: Thomson-Southwestern.

Phillips, M., & Goodkin, O. (1983). The subconscious taken captive: A social, ethical, and legal analysis of subliminal communication technology. *Southern California Law Review,* 54, 1077–1140.

Postman, N. (1987). *Amusing ourselves to death: Public discourse in the age of show business.* New York: Penguin Books.

Rank, H. (1991). *The pitch.* Park Forest, IL: Counter Propaganda Press.

Reis, A. (1996). *Focus: The future of your company depends on it.* New York: Harper Collins.

Ries, A., & Trout, J. (1986). *Positioning: The battle for your mind.* New York: McGraw-Hill.

Rogers, S. (1992). How a publicity blitz created the myth of subliminal advertising. *Public Relations Quarterly,* Winter, pp. 12–18.

Rothschild, M. (1987). *Advertising: From fundamentals to strategies.* Lexington, MA: Health.

Schudson, M. (1984). *Advertising, the uneasy persuasion: Its dubious impact on American society.* New York: Basic Books.

Schwartz, T. (1973). *The responsive chord.* New York: Anchor Doubleday.

Segmentation and targeting. (2004). At www.kellog.northwestern.edu/sterntha/htm/module2/1. Evanston, IL: Kellog School of Business.

Storch, C. (1988). Humble grocery cart now a video ad vehicle. *Chicago Tribune,* May 1, Tempo sec., pp. 1, 5.

Subliminals used to fight smoking. (1987). *De Kalb Daily Chronicle,* Nov. 18.

Thompson, S. (2002). Frito-Lay reports Doritos online ad success. Accessed Nov. 18, 2002, at www.adage.com using QuickFind Id: AAO21A.

Trout, J. (1995). *The new positioning: The latest on the world's # 1 business strategy.* New York: McGraw Hill.

Valdivia, A. H. (1997). The secret of my desire: Gender, class, and sexuality in lingerie catalogs. In K. T. Frith (Ed.), *Undressing the ad: Reading culture in advertising.* New York: Peter Lang.

Vestergaard, T., & Schroeder, K. (1985). *The language of advertising.* London: Basil Blackwell.

Weiss, M. J. (1989). *The clustering of America: A vivid portrait of the nation's 40 neighborhood types—Their values, lifestyles, and eccentricities.* New York: Harper & Row.

Wentz, L., & Cuneo, A. (2002). Double-digit Hispanic ad growth continues. Accessed Sept. 16, 2002, at www.adage.com using QuickFind Id: AAN95S.

Williamson, J. (1977). *Decoding advertising: Meaning and ideology in advertising.* London: Marion Boyers.

Winkelman, P. (2004). *Emotion and consciousness.* Eagan, MN: Network 3000 Publishing, Forthcoming.

Wrighter, C. (1972). *I can sell you anything.* New York: Ballantine Books.

Index